MAGICIAN
OF THE
MODERN

A. Everett Austin, Jr., 1936. Photograph by George Platt Lynes

MAGICIAN OF THE MODERN

CHICK AUSTIN

AND THE TRANSFORMATION

OF THE ARTS IN AMERICA

EUGENE R. GADDIS

ALFRED A. KNOPF   New York   2000

THIS IS A BORZOI BOOK
PUBLISHED BY ALFRED A. KNOPF

Published in the United States by Alfred A. Knopf, a division of Random House,
Inc., New York, and simultaneously in Canada by Random House of Canada
Limited, Toronto. Distributed by Random House, Inc., New York.

www.aaknopf.com

Portions of this work were originally published in *Ballet Review*.

Knopf, Borzoi Books, and the colophon are registered trademarks of
Random House, Inc.

Library of Congress Cataloging-in-Publication Data
Gaddis, Eugene R.
Magician of the modern : Chick Austin and the transformation
of the arts in America /
by Eugene R. Gaddis.—1st ed.
p.   cm.
Includes index.
ISBN 0-394-58777-4
1. Austin, Arthur Everett, 1900–1957.   2. Art museum directors—United
States—Biography.   3. Wadsworth Atheneum Museum of Art.   I. Title.
N576.H3 .G33 2000
700'.92—dc21
[B]   00-034905

Manufactured in the United States of America
First Edition

For Sally

and Nellie

Chick was a whole cultural movement in one man.

—*Virgil Thomson*

CONTENTS

An insert of full-color reproductions follows page 146.

The quotations in this book, particularly from personal correspondence, have been printed for the most part exactly as they were written, without the use of the term *"sic."* (Chick Austin, for instance, regularly omitted the apostrophe from contractions.) In a few cases, however, such as where a proper name was misspelled, *sic* has been used. Obvious typographical errors in newspaper articles and other periodicals generally have been corrected.

Some anecdotes, especially those from Austin's children, Sally and David Austin, were told to me in passing, or in different versions, or before this book was contemplated. Wherever this is the case, I have cited an approximate year instead of an exact date in the footnote.

MAGICIAN
OF THE
MODERN

The Navel of the World

On the night of February 7, 1934, two hundred and forty people in evening dress descended into the Art Deco lobby of a subterranean theater, its curved walls of West African bubinga wood newly installed and still faintly pungent. Above them was the sleek white court of the most advanced museum building in America. It had just opened to the public with the country's first comprehensive Picasso show, hung in third-floor galleries against walls that might have been lifted from the Bauhaus. Standing on the gleaming black marble floor of the lobby, amid the clicks and flashes of cameras, the audience milled noisily around, anticipating the climax of the evening. With an eye on the photographers, women in gowns designed for the occasion made discreet exits up one of the lobby's two staircases and conspicuous reappearances down the other.[1] Gradually, the audience moved into the theater.

This celebration of the modern had drawn a glittering assemblage. They had come by private railway car, airplane, and Rolls-Royce; even, as one observer suggested, by jeweled pogo stick: Alexander Calder and Isamu Noguchi; Carl Van Vechten and Lucius Beebe; Buckminster Fuller and Clare Boothe; *New Yorker* cover artist Constantine Alajalov; Paul Rosenberg, Picasso's dealer, from Paris; and Abby Aldrich Rockefeller. Having looked at nearly one hundred and fifty Picassos upstairs, they settled down to witness the first performance of an opera by Gertrude Stein and Virgil Thomson called *Four Saints in Three Acts*. It was directed by John Houseman—his first directing assignment—and choreographed by Frederick Ashton, making his American professional debut.

Twenty minutes behind schedule, the curtains opened on a set made of colored cellophane, designed by the reclusive New York painter Florine Stettheimer. The singers and dancers, dressed in velvets, satins, silks, and lace, were African-American—the first all-black cast in an opera. With its cubist language, its unexpectedly tuneful music, and its playfully voluptuous dancing, the performance created a sensation. Cheering erupted at the final curtain and did not stop for half an hour. A week later, *Four Saints in Three Acts* headed for a history-making run on Broadway.

The few who attended the opera's premiere, and the many who later imagined they did, would remember it as an exquisite, delightfully incomprehensible novelty. But a handful of sophisticates in the audience would look back to the twin heralds of the century's artistic upheaval—the New York Armory show and the Paris premiere of Stravinsky's *Rite of Spring*, both in 1913—to describe its impact.

Improbably, the museum and the theater were not in a great cosmopolitan city, but in Hartford, Connecticut. For a moment, the insurance capital of the world had become the greatest risk taker in the country. The museum was the venerable Wadsworth Atheneum, America's oldest public art museum, the steward of the J. Pierpont Morgan collection of ancient Egyptian, Greek, and Roman bronzes, and Meissen and Sèvres porcelains; the Wallace Nutting collection of Pilgrim furniture and household utensils; and pictures by a reassuringly familiar pantheon of American painters—John Singleton Copley, John Trumbull, Thomas Cole, and the Hudson River School. Only lately had it been transformed, as if by some mischievous spell, into a spearhead of the avant-garde.

The impresario of the evening, propelled to the stage at the insistence of the crowd, was the glamorous young director of the Atheneum, A. Everett Austin, Jr., known to nearly everyone as "Chick." The slim, graceful figure taking a bow, with his playful blue eyes and brilliantined hair, a gardenia in the lapel of his dinner jacket, was handsome enough to have stepped from the silver screen or out of a Noël Coward play. Yet his achievements at thirty-three were more substantial than might have been guessed from his boyish good looks. By 1934 he had already produced America's first great Italian baroque paintings exhibition, as well as its first surrealist show, in which Salvador Dalí's *Persistence of Memory* was seen for the first time in the United States. He and his friend Lincoln Kirstein, under the auspices of the Atheneum, had already engineered choreographer George Balanchine's immigration to America. Before the year was out, he would present, in this same theater, the first public performances of Balanchine's company, the forerunner of the New York City Ballet. And it was he who had fought and badgered his architects into designing the interiors of the Atheneum's new building, the Avery Memorial, to his modernist specifications. He would prove himself such a trailblazer in the arts that in 1935 the French architect Le Corbusier, after visiting what became known as "Chick's museum," would call Hartford "a spiritual center of America."[2]

Chick Austin embodied the cultural revolution that swept the United States between the two wars. He also helped make it happen. Seeing all art as alive in the present moment, he could look with equal keenness back to the seventeenth century, its sensual splendors still on the verge of rediscovery, and forward to the very edge of artistic experimentation. His eye for quality, and his courage to promote the unfamiliar, were not surpassed in his time.

In the rarefied world of old-master connoisseurs and crusaders for the avant-garde, such moving spirits have not often been known to the public whose tastes they have shaped. But to the tiny elite that directed the flow of art in the momentous years of the 1930s, Chick Austin became almost a legend. He was the spark, the most incandescent tastemaker of them all. Painter, teacher, tailor, superlative cook, actor, magician, creator of costumes and sets—he seemed prodigally gifted. In 1944, when Austin's Hartford career came to an end, a dismayed Alfred Barr, the founding director of the Museum of Modern Art, would tell him: "But you did things sooner and more brilliantly than anyone."[3]

The opening of the Avery Memorial was immediately recognized by Austin's peers as a pivotal moment in the history of modernism. It marked the confluence of European and American streams of modernity—in painting, architecture, and the performing arts—all brought together by an American museum director. That it happened in a provincial capital foretold the transformation of American culture, spreading radical new definitions of art, and new modes of living, from the metropolitan art centers to the quietest corners of the nation. The Machine Age was propelling society into a streamlined world of speed, unceasing change, unprecedented excitements, and, in the end, terrible uncertainty. Yet on that winter night in 1934, when Chick Austin acknowledged the applause, modernism in America was still in its adolescence. To him, the possibilities for artistic exploration seemed unlimited and the risks exhilarating.

Standing on the same stage fifty years after the event, architect Philip Johnson recalled, for another audience, the opening of *Four Saints* and the particular genius of Chick Austin. "He was the center around which things revolved," Johnson said, squinting past the bright television lights, scanning the first few rows of seats in the theater. "And it all culminated on that night—that one night when I sat either *there* or *there*. And I had the feeling—and I still have the feeling—that I was in the center of absolutely everything. You remember what the Greeks called Delphi—the *omphalos,* the navel of the world. That night, I was sitting at the *omphalos* of the culture of the West."[4]

CHAPTER ONE

"Boy Dear"

"I heard father and mother," he explained in a low voice,
"talking about what I was to be when I became a man."
He was extraordinarily agitated now. "I want always to
be a little boy and to have fun."

—J. M. Barrie, *Peter Pan*

When Chick Austin first saw the palace of Gustav III, near Stockholm, he was so enchanted that he said he must have been conceived in Sweden. It was not surprising that Drottningholm, the baroque residence of the eighteenth century's most captivating king—who fostered the arts at his court, performed on his own stage, and was murdered at a masked ball—made him feel at home. Chick was in his element in any palace fitted out with gilded rococo rooms, formal gardens, fountains, pools, and the private theaters of princes. He reveled in the settings, props, and costumes of Europe's most ornamental era.[1]

Yet he embraced the twentieth century as it unfolded. Fast cars and cocktails, cigarettes, the Ballets Russes, Picasso, Stravinsky, Erik Satie, movies, mobiles, and modern dance, Bauhaus buildings, machines for living, Balanchine, Dalí, and Gertrude Stein—if it was new, if it had quality and style, it was for Chick, first to experience and enjoy, then to share with the widest possible audience.

His arrival, coinciding almost exactly with that of the new century, occurred on December 18, 1900, in Brookline, Massachusetts. Coming into the world seven days before Christmas had a definite effect. As a child, he thought that evergreens and tinsel were hung up to celebrate his birth—a belief he never entirely outgrew.

He was christened Arthur Everett Austin, Jr. To his family he was known as Everett, but throughout his life, his mother, Laura Etnier Austin, addressed him, more often than not, as "Boy Dear." He was her only child, the center of her universe. Just before he was born, she made a will, leaving the bulk of her large estate to him and his descendants, naming her brother as guardian and her late uncle's business partner as sole executor, though the other contributor to his conception, Dr. Arthur Everett Austin—surgeon, professor of medicine, and expert on poisons—was in good health and living with her at the same address.

Laura Austin was an independent and inventive woman. As she charted Everett's future, she magnified their mutual past. Obsessively, and for decades, she delved into her ancestry, discovering in triumph that her mother's forebears, the Morrisons, could be traced to Scottish chieftains and Norse kings, and that the Etniers, on her father's side, were descended from at least one errant pope and several royal lines of France. But one of Laura's brothers, constructing a rival version of the family tree, reached a different conclusion based on overwhelming evidence: the Morrisons were solid Scottish immigrants, and the Etniers came from honest German peasant stock.

Johannes Eideneier, patriarch of the family in America, arrived in Philadelphia from one of the Protestant German states in 1751, and by 1785 a branch of the family, spelling the name "Etnier," had moved north to the fertile wilderness of Pennsylvania and put down roots in Germany Valley, along the Juniata River. Laura's father, David Etnier, was born on his family's farm outside Mount Union, Pennsylvania, in 1835. After working as a schoolteacher and bookkeeper, he helped establish a company in Mount Union that shipped grain down the Pennsylvania Canal to Baltimore and Philadelphia, and in the early 1870s, he bought a sawmill and a flour mill. He was tall, handsome, and commanding, his dark hair swept back above a reverse widow's peak, his eyes penetrating under graceful brows. Long after his death, beside his photograph in a family album, Laura mounted a picture of her son. The resemblance between the two, even to the hairline, was uncanny, as though Everett had descended exclusively from his mother's line.

In 1862 David Etnier married Hannah Jane (Jennie) Morrison, the daughter of John Morrison, a prominent Pennsylvania state legislator. Like the Etniers, the Morrisons were among the original settlers of Mount Union, having come from Virginia in the eighteenth century. They were well-to-do landowners, and Jennie's father bought the couple a new brick house in Mount Union. There Laura Ann, the second of their seven children, was born on March 14, 1864. Her only sister, Virginia Catharine (Virgie), ten years younger, was the last.

Although stern and self-righteous Methodism defined the Etnier men, they were not immune to the lure of gain. In 1849 Laura's grandfather, Oliver Etnier, left his wife and seven children to look for gold in California, but he returned empty-handed. Twenty-eight years later, when gold was found in California

*David Etnier, c. 1865, and A. Everett Austin, Jr., 1927, from a family
photograph album of Laura Etnier Austin*

again, David Etnier left his own wife and seven children to go off on a similarly
unprofitable quest. Laura may have inherited her powerful wanderlust from
them.

In 1878, when Jennie Etnier died unexpectedly, still in her forties, the
Morrisons swooped down on the children, persuading their father that life for
the young Etniers would be better with them. Laura, then fourteen, and the four
younger children were taken in by Jennie's unmarried sister, Mary Morrison,
who owned a large house in Mount Union. Their rich bachelor uncle, John Morrison, founder of the Roaring Spring Paper Mill, became their legal guardian.
Laura and Virgie eventually went to live with Uncle John in Tyrone, Pennsylvania, and they adored him. Unlike David Etnier, he was jovial and tolerant of
everything but what he called "professional Christians."[2] He encouraged the
girls to broaden their view of the world, sending them off on holidays at the New
Jersey shore. Having paid for Laura's education at Dickinson Seminary in
Williamsport, he sent Virgie to Wellesley Academy in Philadelphia. When he
died at fifty-two in 1890, he left his two sisters and his twelve nieces and
nephews the considerable sum of $10,000 each. Shrewdly invested for them by
his lawyer, these legacies rapidly grew.

Laura and Virgie, now financially independent, remained in Tyrone. Their
brothers had moved on to careers that would scatter most of them far from
Pennsylvania. As Virgie was only sixteen, Uncle John had appointed a close

business associate, rather than David Etnier, to succeed him as her guardian. The girls had little to do with their father, who still lived in their childhood home. They did not make the twenty-five-mile trip from Tyrone to Mount Union to see him at Christmas in 1891, nor did they come to nurse him when he contracted pneumonia and died early the next year.

Laura, at twenty-eight, was almost on the verge of spinsterhood, but she had grown into a gregarious, determined woman with a sense of humor. Her soft, girlish face and luxuriant dark red hair made her look younger than her age. A *carte de visite* taken at the time shows her perched on the arm of a wicker bench in the studio of a fancy Philadelphia photographer. In her frothy white summer frock, she seems the picture of innocence, but her keen gaze and the hint of a wry smile suggest a certain calculation. She began to call herself an "heiress" and had little use for her old Mount Union friends.[3] She had had enough of small-town life.

She and Virgie traveled, first in the United States and then, beginning in August 1895, to Europe. Their year-long trip took them throughout the Continent and to North Africa. Box camera in hand, Laura recorded palaces, parks, gardens, cathedrals, and cemeteries from Amsterdam to Potsdam, Munich to Milan. Her well-composed snapshots documented picturesque "types"—street urchins, well-starched nannies, and any members of European royalty who happened to come within range. She aimed her lens at Kaiser Wilhelm II in Berlin and at Princess Victoria Louise in Postdam. In Corfu, she snapped the huge steam yacht of the Austrian emperor, Franz Joseph II.

The Etnier sisters spent the winter of 1895–96 in Berlin, making excursions to Dresden, Nuremberg, and Munich. Among the Americans living in the German capital was Arthur Everett Austin, a thirty-four-year-old physician, a widower, on leave from the faculty of Tufts Medical School in Boston and now teaching at the University of Berlin. A man of solid build, reserved and unassuming, he had a handsome square face and a dark mustache that drooped at the corners very much like Uncle John's.

Laura, Virgie, and Arthur Austin struck up a friendship and traveled together that spring to Athens to attend the first Olympic Games since ancient times. On April 6, 1896, they were among the fifty thousand spectators who watched King George I of Greece open the games. When the unofficial American team won nine out of the twelve track-and-field events, Laura managed to round up three of the gold-medal winners for another snapshot. After the games, she and Virgie continued on their tour, arriving back in Tyrone by the end of August. Arthur returned to his medical work in Berlin and obtained permission from Tufts to extend his leave for a year. Laura kept in touch. As a doctor and a professor of medicine in Boston, Arthur was decidedly a cut above her Pennsylvania relatives and looked promising as the father of a child.

Laura Etnier, c. 1895

Like Laura, Arthur had risen from a modest rural background. The Austins had come to America from England, migrating from New Hampshire to Belgrade, Maine, by the end of the eighteenth century. Arthur's father, David Farnum Austin, moved to Boston in 1840 at twenty-one, and married Mary Josephine Weaver in 1859. Arthur Everett, the first of their six children, was born on April 11, 1861. Eight years later, David Austin moved his family from Boston to Readfield, Maine, near his childhood home, where he became one of the region's most prosperous farmers, living to a vigorous ninety-three.

Arthur attended high school in Augusta and in 1883 graduated from Bowdoin College in Brunswick, where he was an exceptional student and a track-and-field champion. After a year as principal of Somerset Academy in Athens, Maine, he entered Harvard Medical School, earned his M.D. in 1887, took an advanced degree at the University of Berlin, and then had further training in Heidelberg and Vienna. In 1891, soon after returning to Boston, he married Louise Bunker of New Bedford. But less than two years later, Louise died of kidney disease, and Arthur buried himself in his teaching and research. He joined the original faculty of the new Tufts Medical School in 1893, published a spate of articles on subjects ranging from renal failure to intestinal obstruction and anencephalic monsters, and spent his few free hours at athletic and political clubs.

Arthur Austin was plainspoken, self-assured, and as independent as Laura. In 1896, when Harvard reminded him that he had never received a diploma because he had not paid the graduation fee, he testily replied that he had a certificate from the university verifying his completion of the requirements for the degree and that "if Harvard declines to honor one of its certifi-

Arthur Everett Austin,
M.D., c. 1912

cates, it is a matter of utter indifference to me."[4]

As he moved into his late thirties, he found the thought of marrying again appealing. Laura, at thirty-five, had lost her slim figure and the freshness of youth, but she still had her beautiful red hair, her pleasing features, and her enthusiasm. And Laura knew what she wanted. She and Arthur were married on June 6, 1899, at the Holland House hotel in New York City. Her brother Oliver gave her away, and Virgie, then twenty-five, came along to live with the Austins in a house at 93 Perry Street in Brookline on the edge of Boston.

Within a year, Laura was pregnant. In the fall of 1900, determined to anchor her assets to her unborn child, she returned to Mount Union and asked Uncle John's attorney, who managed her investments, to draw up her will. Following the precedent established at her own mother's death, Laura directed that her brother Oliver, not her husband, be guardian of her children should she die. Her grandchildren were to receive the principal on her children's death, but if there were no grandchildren, half the assets would go to Virgie, the other half in equal shares to Laura's brothers. She named an old business partner of Uncle John's as executor of the will. As these arrangements were contrary to the statutes governing inheritance in Massachusetts, Arthur Austin had to agree to waive all his rights.[5] He had his own income, lived simply, and had no need of Laura's money. But his deference to her in relinquishing guardianship of his child if Laura should die foretold the pattern of their family life.

On December 18, in the house on Perry Street, Laura gave birth to a healthy baby boy weighing nine and a half pounds. She noted that among the gifts Everett received were "silver spoons, sweaters and sacque from Papa's grateful patients."[6] So began Laura's compulsively thorough record of her boy. Her light blue clothbound album, with "Baby Days" spelled out in gold letters

*Laura Austin and Everett in his
christening gown, June 1901*

on the cover, eventually bulged with mementos of Everett's progress through
life—tiny envelopes with baby teeth and locks of light chestnut hair; records of
his playmates, pets, houses, and schools; passenger lists from ocean liners,
documenting his crossings; his acceptance to college; and newspaper clippings
of his appointment as director of the Wadsworth Atheneum. There were photographs of him in costumes, from American Indian buckskins and feathered
headdresses to German lederhosen and Scottish kilts. Framed copies of these
pictures covered Laura's walls.

Early in June 1901, Laura took her six-month-old son to York, Pennsylvania, to visit her brother Carey and his new bride, Susan Smith, an old friend of
Virgie's. On June 24 Everett was baptized in the Mount Union Methodist Episcopal Church, and then whisked off to Atlantic City, Laura's favorite summer
resort. After being photographed in seaside attire against a studio backdrop,
"Baby" was weighed on a boardwalk machine, the paper slip annotated and

preserved. In mid-October Laura noted that Baby had eight teeth and liked to entertain his parents. He would blow a horn, vanish under a table, and magically reappear from the other side.[7]

That same year, before Everett had reached his first birthday, Laura and Arthur, like other comfortable New Englanders at the turn of the century, decided to build a summer cottage on the coast of Maine. They chose three and a half acres on a point of land along Ash Cove on Harpswell, a peninsula in Casco Bay. Their lot was a dozen miles down the road from Bowdoin College, Arthur's alma mater. In September, Laura bought the land with her own money and in her own name. She liked to intimate that she was the architect as well, and later, her son, who enjoyed dramatizing his mother's exploits, told friends that at the end of their summer holiday, she had sketched the design on a paper bag, handed it to a local contractor, and said, "That's what I want when I come back."[8]

In reality, the cottage was designed by a Boston architectural firm. It was a substantial two-story Dutch colonial house built of cedar and spruce, with five bedrooms upstairs and a generous veranda on the front, facing south down the bay to the open sea. Because it stood on the edge of a forest of birches, maples, beeches, and pines, Laura named it Wildwood.

Wildwood, South Harpswell, Maine, c. 1910

The Austins and their maid would take a steamer from Boston to Portland, where they would transfer to a steamboat in the Casco Bay Line and be met at the Harpswell dock by their caretaker in a motorboat. Pastimes were simple. Occasionally, Laura would host a quilting party, and there were amateur the-atricals at the local recreation hall. Laura's brother Carey and his wife, Susan, were soon drawn to Harpswell and built their own summer cottage on the other side of Ash Cove. Their son Stephen, who became a well-known painter in the region, was one of Everett's closest boyhood playmates.

In 1903 the Austins moved from Brookline to a larger house at 163 Suffolk Road in nearby Chestnut Hill. Not long after they had settled in, however, Arthur took another leave from Tufts to teach in Vienna for a semester, if not at Laura's urging, then certainly with her approval. On February 27, 1904, he, Laura, Virgie, Everett, and a nursemaid sailed from Boston on the *Romanic*.

This was three-year-old Everett's introduction to Europe. Laura had him photographed in Vienna, squealing with delight in a sailor suit, an outfit to which she was so attached that she put him in identical versions of it for the next six years. While Arthur worked in the Austrian capital, Laura and Virgie toured the Continent from Budapest to Venice, much as they had eight years earlier, but this time with their darling boy. Everett contracted chicken pox in Vienna in March and scarlet fever in Dresden in May, which sent him to a hospital for weeks. Laura thereupon decided that he had a delicate constitution and, throughout his early life, continually urged him to rest, insisting that exer-

*Everett at age three in
Vienna, 1904*

cise would damage his health. The Austins returned home to Chestnut Hill in the fall of 1904.

The following summer Arthur launched a new sloop, built on Harpswell, which he named *The Flying Dutchman*. It was a wedding present for Virgie, who married a young man from Tennessee named Hazen House at the family cottage in September 1905. To Everett, at the age of four, the departure of Aunt Virgin, as he called her, was a great loss. She felt the separation, too, as it became clear that her life would be centered in Knoxville. The next year, on the Fourth of July, she wrote to her little nephew, giving him *The Flying Dutchman:* "now since you are the Captain, you must always act like one—you must always *behave well—not cry not fuss* and *always* be *brave*."[9]

With Aunt Virgin gone, Laura became the center of Everett's affections. His earliest surviving letter, written in 1906, was to her, then on one of her jaunts to Atlantic City:

> DEAR MOTHER
> I AM A GOOD BOY. I LOVE YOU SO MUCH. I WILL NOT
> EAT ANY CANDY SO BRING ME SOMETHING NICE
> WITH LOVE AND KISS E.   EVERETT[10]

The bonds between mother and son grew stronger, and as Laura molded her boy into an extension of herself, Arthur receded further into the background, directing his energies toward his profession. He seemed more like a slightly bemused acquaintance than her mate. This was hardly surprising in light of the fact that from the time Everett was born until he was eleven years old, he, not Arthur, shared Laura's bed at night. It was a habit that did not die easily, and even after Everett was married, if he happened to be visiting, he climbed into bed with his mother on Sunday morning and discussed the week's events.

Early in 1907, Arthur accepted a position as a visiting professor of physiological chemistry at the University of Virginia, and the family moved to Charlottesville for a semester. Although the Austins returned to Chestnut Hill in the fall, the dislocations continued a year later when Arthur formally resigned from Tufts Medical School to become a professor of chemistry and toxicology at the University of Texas in Galveston.[11] For a man who found the scholarly atmosphere of German universities congenial, the University of Texas was not wholly satisfying. In the summer of 1909, having taught for two semesters, Arthur packed up his family and headed for Europe again, this time to Dresden.

On the way, the Austins stopped in Ireland, where they were photographed riding horseback through the Gap of Dunloe in County Kerry—Laura riding sidesaddle, swathed in a voluminous dark dress and wearing a huge hat secured under her chin; eight-year-old Everett in a well-tailored dark coat and

*Everett in his Morrison plaid,
in front of his Marlborough Street
home, 1910*

Scottish cap; and Arthur, a pipe clenched in his teeth. It was the only image of the three of them together that Laura kept.

They crossed from Ireland to Scotland so that Laura could see the homeland of her Morrison ancestors and delve into local histories. She wrote that she did not find the Scottish landscape "more beautiful than along the 'Blue Juniata' " of her childhood, but was delighted to discover that the Morrisons could trace their ancestry back to "Makurich, the son of a Norwegian King."[12] In Aberdeen, she bought Everett a custom-tailored Scottish costume, complete with kilt, sash, stockings, and cap in the Morrison plaid.

When the family arrived in Dresden, Everett was enrolled in a local school and quickly learned to speak and write German. Many years later, he told a reporter that it was in Dresden—known for more than a century as "Florence on the Elbe"—that he first began to paint. Perhaps inspired by a production at the Dresden Opera House, he also made miniature sets in a toy theater for Wagner's *Flying Dutchman* and presented his own rendition of the opera to his school friends.

In April 1910, the Austins left Dresden for Paris, where Everett attended a French school on the rue de la Grande Armée and began to learn his third language. One of the highlights of his stay was witnessing a famous circus act, Bostock's Jungle, at the Jardin Zoologique. On the back of a postcard of lions and tigers in performance, he inscribed, as though documenting an important historic occasion, "Everett Austin has seen this in Paris, 28 April 1910."[13] By this time, the nine-year-old boy, having developed a taste for performing himself, had begun to dabble in illusion and sleight of hand. Calling himself Professor Marvel, he presented a magic show to his French schoolmates.

On May 24, 1910, after nearly a year in Europe, Everett and his parents sailed on the Cunard Royal Mail Steamship *Ivernia* from Liverpool to Boston. They moved directly into a tall brick town house at 110 Marlborough Street, a fashionable address in Boston's Back Bay, where Arthur opened a private practice. This would be the Austins' official residence for the next twenty-eight years. The imposing four-story house was built in 1868. A wide staircase ran up a central hall to the top story, with railings around each floor. The kitchen was located beneath the ground floor, which contained the dining room and Dr. Austin's waiting room and office. It was a dark house, with heavy draperies and Victorian furniture, almost too spacious for a family of three. Laura joined Trinity Episcopal Church in nearby Copley Square, an ediface of Byzantine grandeur designed by H. H. Richardson. According to her address and place of worship, at least, Laura had joined the Boston elite.

In September 1910, Everett entered Noble and Greenough School in the class of 1917. Nobles was one of Boston's finest day schools, located in a mansion on Beacon Street within walking distance of the Austins' house. Its faculty was rigorous and progressive, and a high number of its graduates went on to Harvard College.

Everett had grown to be a handsome and beguiling child, and Laura put him in the most elegant clothes. Classmates, even at that age, thought of him as glamorous, and teachers singled him out as special.[14] He and his friends came up with nicknames for one another early in their school careers. Whether it was because he was slightly smaller than his classmates, or more spritelike, the name bestowed on Everett was "Chick."[15] Laura, however, made certain that his formal name was drummed into his head. Once a year, beginning when he was seven, she had him inscribe "A. Everett Austin, Jr." on the same page of the baby book. For most of his life, he would automatically introduce himself as his mother had taught him, including the "A." and the "Jr.," and then say, "But call me Chick—all my friends do."

He was eleven when he embarked on his third trip to Europe, on June 11, 1912, on the Cunard steamship *Franconia*. He spent most of the summer in Switzerland, where he was enrolled in the Institut de Jeunes Gens at Ouchy, near Lausanne, while Laura toured the Continent and Arthur studied medicine. Chick practiced his French and took up painting pictures again.

On August 30, 1912, Virginia Etnier House, not quite thirty-eight, died in Knoxville, and Laura set out alone for Tennessee from Boulogne-sur-Mer on September 21. After returning to Boston with his father, Chick wrote to Laura frequently while she was away:

I had such a good time at school and have just got home from Dexters we have two new teachers. The Latin is quite hard. We are going to the Electric Show to night "Little Boy Blue" the opera is coming I wish you

Chick Austin, Noble and
Greenough, 1915

would let me go. I hope you
slept well last night. I drank my
milk for you this morning give
my love to Uncle Carey won't
you? Vickery (who is in long
pants) told me that Pfaelzer had
already gone to Groton so I
wrote there. May I ask Leland
or Vickery to dinner. With Love
and kisses Everett.

As a postscript he added, "We are
going to have a telephone on the
third floor which room shall we put
it?"[16] The next day he wrote again,
reporting that "the Electric Show was pretty good I have been playing football
out at Dexters all afternoon would you let me go to the swimming tank with
Greenwood?"[17]

She issued orders from afar even though Arthur was on the spot. When she
forbade Everett to go on a boat ride, he wrote to her in Knoxville on October 10,
meekly asking her to explain: "please tell me why you dont want me to go in the
motor boat? there is no danger but I wont go if you dont want me to[.] come
home soon I am lonely."[18]

Much as he missed his mother, her absence gave him an opportunity to
entertain his friends. The eleven-year-old Chick Austin organized a party without first clearing it with her. "I am afraid I have done something bad," he confessed disarmingly. "I have invited four boys to dinner on Holloween but I dont
think you will mind once in the year I am so lonely here without you so come
home soon. Yours Everett" [in the margin: "Red Sox 3 Giants 2 HURAH"].[19]

Presumably, she let the invitation stand. Chick learned early that when
he wanted to carry out some novel, and therefore suspect, scheme, it was easier
to get it launched and then use his powers of persuasion to see it past the
authorities.

By twelve, Chick was developing a facility with language, using drama and
hyperbole to entertain his audience. In a school essay inspired by the loss of
the *Titanic* in April 1912, he imagined himself on the world's largest steamer,
the *Emperor Napoleon*, crossing from New York to Europe in the distant summer of 1998. One day out, at two in the morning, the ship struck something and

began going down. "Alas! the ship would sink in a very few minutes[.] I jumped and swam around a little while[.] there were awful groans and shrieks around me as men[,] women and children were drowned[.] I clung to a piece of wood and fainted. The next thing I knew I was flying through the air."

An airplane had saved him at the last minute. "It was the worst wreck in history except the Titanic away back in 1912."[20]

Chick relied on personality more than scholarship to carry him through school. He finished his third year at Noble and Greenough with an erratic report card: A's in Reading, Spelling, and French, B's in English and Algebra, a C in Latin, and a D in History. He worked hard in subjects that interested him and let the others go.

The next year, Chick's writing became more polished, as could be seen in a paragraph describing his father, whom he called "Our Doctor":

> He is fifty two years old and six feet tall, a gruff and outspoken man. His clothes are pressed carefully and have a look of freshness about them. His shoes are always shined and his necktie pulled closely up to his collar. His twinkling gray eyes look smilingly out at you from their setting of long lashes and a pair of gold-rimmed glasses are perched jauntily on his long straight nose. His mouth is small, and an even row of pure white teeth, scrupulously brushed, peep out from their frame of red lips when he smiles. A dimple in his chin completes an altogether jovial face. The top of his head is crowned with silvery white hair, precisely parted, which shows unmistakable signs of approaching baldness. A frock coat and tall hat complete the appearance of this very lovable and extraordinary man.[21]

But Laura made it difficult for him to love his father, constantly reminding Everett that he was only "half a Yankee" and steering him toward her own interests. As the years went on, the distance between his parents developed into an unhappy tension. "I never really knew my father very well," Chick told a friend. "He shut himself up in his office and I would not see him for days."[22] Chick was caught between a father who was emotionally absent and a mother who smothered him with affection. Irrepressible as his creativity was, his toy theater, his magic, and his painting provided an escape into a happier world.

In the summer of 1913, Laura took steps to find a special place for herself and her boy. The cottage on the Maine coast, the address in Boston's Back Bay, and Chick's enrollment at Noble and Greenough were all outward signs of the Austins' increasing social status. Now Laura wanted to join the landed gentry.

"Never had I seen the beautiful hills and mountains or lakes of New Hampshire until [1913]," she wrote in a rhapsodic memoir of her search for an estate,

Laura and "Boy Dear,"
South Harpswell, 1913

"when I decided to buy a farm in the country, where my boy could have a taste of country life, which I think is the inheritance of every boy, rather than a city street." As usual, she had definite requirements in mind. "The house must be absolutely Colonial, facing south. . . . It must be located on a high hill . . . and there must be water for the boy for skating, boating and to swim." It had to be close enough to Marlborough Street so that she and Everett could "run up any holiday or over Sunday, as other New England boys go to see their grandfathers, their uncles and aunts, but as my boy could not do."[23]

She heard of a piece of property on Range Road in Windham, New Hampshire, a tiny town about fifty miles from Boston. Comprising eighty acres of woods and fields, which Laura eventually enlarged to a hundred, it ran along the crest of a hill and included a farmhouse, two barns, and the colonial house of her imaginings, already furnished with antiques. The land went down to the edge of Cobbett's Pond, a picturesque body of water about four miles long and less than a mile wide. The main house looked out across forested hills to Mount Monadnock, sixty miles away.

Laura bought the property immediately and christened the house Uncle John's, in tribute to John Morrison, whose legacy paid for it. (Later she turned the barn next door into a Pennsylvania Dutch–style house, which she called Barn Manor.) With a decisive speed that would be characteristic of her son, she moved in less than a week later, accompanied by a party of ten, including three great-nephews and one great-niece of Uncle John, to celebrate the acquisition.

Looking over the deed, she discovered that an early owner of the house was a Morrison. She had been certain that "I had not a drop of 'Yankee' blood in my

"Uncle John's" house, Windham, New Hampshire, c. 1940

veins," she wrote, "and was only a 'Yankee' by marriage."[24] But now she conceived the notion that she was actually related to the Morrisons who had come to this New Hampshire town. Poring through historic records and collecting family lore—and soon progressing beyond rational thought—she began constructing an ancestral legend at least as grand as anything her Back Bay neighbors could produce.

Before long she was convinced that old porcelain held the key to her past. The scene painted on a blue and white dish from her grandfather became Robert the Bruce slaying the Moors, assisted by the Morrisons; a picture on a pink china platter, reputedly brought by her family to America, illustrated the expulsion of the Morrisons from Scotland after the uprising of 1715; a sugar bowl she found in the caretaker's room at Uncle John's documented their settlement in New Hampshire. And when the pattern of a cream pitcher she "repossessed" from the cottage of an old woman in Windham almost matched that of her soup tureen, Laura *knew* that the Morrisons of Pennsylvania and the Morrisons of New Hampshire were one and the same. "Now, to me," she recorded excitedly, "china seemed to be not only a useful bit of pottery for one's sugar and tea, but a book bearing messages from the great beyond."[25]

Befitting this rediscovered lineage, Laura had bookplates and stationery engraved for Everett and herself with the Morrison family crest, bearing three Moors' heads surmounted by a double-headed Moor and the motto *Praetio Pru-*

dentia Praestat (Wisdom is better than wealth). And for the little finger of Everett's right hand, she ordered a signet ring in platinum, which he wore for life. She wore an identical version in gold.

Chick's imagination took him elsewhere. As he entered his teenage years, he returned to his career as prestidigitator. In the summer of 1914, Professor Marvel entertained an appreciative crowd with his magic tricks at the Congregational Church in Windham for the benefit of the Junior Christian Endeavor Society. The program included a vocalist and a pianist, and ice cream was served at the end. The local press, prompted by Laura, was impressed: "Prof. Marvel, who is none other than Everett Austin, 13 year old son of Dr. and Mrs. A. E. Austin[,] . . . certainly is gifted in his line. He has performed in Paris and other places abroad as well as in this country and always draws a large audience."[26] Chick also took his show to Harpswell. He gave performances at the Auburn Colony Recreation Hall and turned a boathouse next to the family cottage into a miniature theater. His cousin Stephen Etnier remembered that "he was what we called a sissy at the time. Boys didn't go around having little theaters in their boathouses, the way he did. He wasn't much interested in sailing or sports of any kind."[27]

Chick graduated from Noble and Greenough in June 1917, one of twenty-one students. Though he took the college entrance examination in eight subjects, the results were apparently disappointing. (Laura cut off the scores on the bottom of the report when she pasted it into "Baby Days.") As he was still only sixteen, Chick was sent to Phillips Academy in Andover, Massachusetts, for a second senior year.

At Andover, as at Nobles, classmates found him fascinating. "He was a very handsome and attractive male," said one, "and he also had a vivacity that made a great impression. . . . He was someone you noticed." At the same time, he made light of his accomplishments. He tended to leave his homework until the last minute, but he impressed his friends by being able to dash off a page of Greek in twenty minutes on his way to doing something more entertaining. Chick also showed an appreciation for modern design. To a fellow student he declared, "I don't want to drive a Rolls-Royce, and I don't want to own a Rolls-Royce. I'd just like to have one to park outside the house because they're so beautiful."[28]

Laura was never far away. Chick often recounted the tale of one of her unexpected descents on the school. Although she had informed the administration that he was not to have any exercise, the physical education department wanted him to have some kind of outdoor activity. One day, Laura arrived to find him running around the track. "Everett, Everett," she shouted, "take those clothes off immediately! You're *never* to do any physical exercise, and you're to get your regular pants on!" Chick told the story to entertain, but there were clearly times when Laura was deeply embarrassing to the adolescent boy. Remembering his frustrations with Laura, he would tell his own children, "I loved my mother very much, but she was a very stupid woman."[29] Yet he spent most of his life pleasing her, placating her, circumventing her, and at some level enjoying her eccentricities.[30]

By the time Chick had arrived at Andover in September 1917, American troops were fighting in Europe in the World War. His father, a captain in the Reserve Officers Medical Corps, was promoted to major by the end of the year, and for much of 1918, he was the debarkation medical officer for the port of Boston.

Laura and Chick decided to make their own contribution to the war effort: they organized a party. In July 1918, for the benefit of the Red Cross, they recreated an old-fashioned market and fair on the grounds of what the local paper called "the Austin estate" in Windham. The news story recorded that they offered "fruits and vegetables, hot dogs, sandwiches, tea, tonics, cakes, ices and pink lemonade, also a punch and judy show, fish ponds, grabs and side shows for the kiddies," along with a balloon ascension and a barn dance. Huge crowds came from neighboring towns, and the profits reached nearly $300. The paper gave full credit to the two organizers, "Mrs. A. E. Austin and son, Everett Austin, who worked untiringly to make it successful."[31]

The Windham extravaganza, with mother and son unleashing their combined talents, was in a sense the perfect climax to Chick's childhood. He had graduated from Andover the previous month and, having made a respectable showing on his second attempt at the college entrance examinations, seemed poised to live up to Laura's expectations. He was going to Harvard.

CHAPTER TWO

Trouble with the Dean: Harvard, Egypt, and the Sudan

Even more than in the year before, Amory neglected his work, not deliberately but lazily and through a multitude of other interests. . . . Mostly there were parties. . . . They all cut more classes than were allowed, which meant an additional course the following year, but spring was too rare to let anything interfere with their colorful ramblings.

—F. Scott Fitzgerald, *This Side of Paradise*

On September 23, 1918, Chick Austin arrived at Harvard College as a freshman in the class of 1922. He had come alone from the farm in New Hampshire to start his independent life in Cambridge, but the Harvard he found was not the haven of ivy, tradition, and under-graduate exuberance that it had been even a year earlier. The War Department was taking over the school. Uniformed officers strode across campus, making preparations to induct all boys over eighteen into the hastily formed Students' Army Training Corps. Dormitories were converted into mess halls and barracks for the army, naval, and marine units of the corps. Military science had entered the curriculum, and the college administration was in disarray. Chick managed to register for classes, but when he reached his assigned room in Thayer Hall, it was already occupied. He turned around and went home to Marlborough Street.

Except for a caretaker, Chick was alone in the house. His mother was still at Uncle John's, and his father, now Major Austin, was at his post across town, working around the clock.[1] As Boston's debarkation medical officer, Arthur had far more to contend with than getting men onto ships. The worldwide influenza epidemic, which would claim more than twenty million lives before it ended the next year, had struck the city early in September. It reached its height throughout Boston a week after Chick entered Harvard.[2] With the death rate in local hospitals approaching 50 percent, Laura summoned her son back to New Hampshire, and there he stayed for more than a month, until the epidemic began to subside.

By the time Chick returned to college, Harvard had completed its transformation into an army post.[3] The Students' Army Training Corps, nearly fifteen hundred strong, drilled for two hours in the morning. Daily, at Soldiers Field, they rehearsed the proper use of bayonets; on Saturdays, they hiked to imitation trenches at Fresh Pond.[4] Even the few freshmen still too young to be inducted were marched to classes in anticipation of the time when they might march through the Argonne Forest. Chick was thoroughly out of place. Protected and coddled by Laura, he was barely ready to face the challenge of a college curriculum, let alone trench warfare.

With little faculty guidance, Chick chose courses unusual for a freshman. He bypassed the French and German requirements, promising he could fulfill them with an oral exam. He deferred first-year English and took two courses in the fine arts, along with an upper-level mechanical drawing class. Not able to escape science and mathematics, he tried astronomy and trigonometry. But by the time he actually showed up for classes, it was six weeks into the semester, and the hard work necessary to catch up was beyond him.

Then, on November 11, the Armistice was signed, the war was suddenly over, and the military machine that had rolled into Harvard immediately reversed itself. By December 21, three days after Chick's eighteenth birthday, the last student had been discharged from the training corps. In the euphoria and confusion of the postwar months, Chick, like many of his classmates, paid scant attention to the academic side of Harvard. He concentrated instead on what he did best—having fun.

The freedom of college life, even for a boy living at home, was a stimulant more exciting than any Chick had known. He plunged into all the enticing diversions that Boston and Cambridge offered—moving-picture shows, musicals, vaudeville, restaurants, and bars—and there were plenty of Harvard fellows ready to join him for a night on the town. With his looks, his well-tailored clothes, his mellifluous voice, his rapidly developing wit, and a joie de vivre tempered by a slightly mysterious reserve, he was extremely popular. He also had a generous allowance and a mother who could be cajoled into covering minor extravagances. He quickly mastered the art of drinking cocktails and smoking cigarettes. He danced, flirted, and filled his calendar with dinner parties and debutante balls.

Writing later, as a sage upperclassman, in an English composition called "The Undergraduate Library," Chick chronicled the stages of life at Harvard, and was, inevitably, autobiographical. Of the "typical" freshmen, he declared: "Serious reading is not in their category; so called 'parties' and Boston and red-paint seem far more to the point. . . . Classes are cut right and left; work is neglected, nay abandoned; all is forgotten in this unquenchable thirst for hitherto denied pleasure. . . . Required work is regarded at first by some as something which should be done but won't be done, in all cases a hellish insult devised by the faculty."

From personal experience, Chick noted the consequence of this devil-may-care attitude: "After the first grades go in . . . drawn faces wait their turn at the dean's doorway."[5] In April of his freshman year, he was placed on probation by the Administrative Board for poor grades and absenteeism. Assistant Dean Kenneth Murdock warned him that unless he earned at least three C's and a D, he could be "severed."[6] But his final report card was dismal.[7] Despite "gentleman's C's" in his two fine-arts courses, he had a D in astronomy and had failed both mathematics and mechanical drawing. In July, the dean informed Arthur Austin that Everett's ties with Harvard College had officially ceased.[8]

Later, in a disjointed defense of her son to Chester Greenough, dean of Harvard College, Laura tried to take some of the blame. It was she who had forced Everett to miss the beginning of his freshman year, she said, and he had not known how to make up his lost time. Skipping over the missed classes and poor performance throughout the year, she claimed that his precarious health had ruined the end of his second semester: "Then his final exams came in that intense heat . . . he came home very ill for several days two physicians could not decide whether or not it was ptomaine poisoning, typhoid or appendicitis— but of course he missed his other exams."[9]

Dean Murdock told Chick that if he had any hope of petitioning for reinstatement in the fall of 1919, summer studies were obligatory. Thus chastened, he set to work at home to make up the reading in his courses and spent some time auditing summer classes at the college. The dean's office gave him permission to take four makeup examinations in September. Chick then boarded a train with his mother and escaped to southern California to visit his uncle Clarence Etnier. From Long Beach, on August 28, having waited until the last possible moment, he petitioned the faculty for readmittance as a freshman. "I feel that I have not had a fair chance to show what I can really do," he wrote, "especially as I was forced to reside at home. This, I think is a great disadvantage."[10]

The deans were sympathetic, and Chick was provisionally readmitted as a freshman, though he was fined for having failed to hand in his study plan at the end of the first year. He moved into a popular rooming house at 5 Linden Street, half a block from Harvard Yard.

During this extra freshman year, hoping that the talent he had demonstrated for art would keep him afloat, Chick took two more fine-arts courses, a history of medieval, Renaissance, and "modern" art, and advanced drawing and painting, both taught by Arthur Pope, who had met Chick through his introductory studio course the previous year. Pope was the first professor to see promise in him, and though he felt Chick deserved no more than a C in drawing and painting, he gave him a B in the art history course. The rest of Chick's record, however, was so poor that he was placed back on probation in March. He had C's in geology and paleontology, squeaked through psychology with a D, was excluded from Spanish for doing no work, and received no credit in a survey of European history for failing to appear at the final exam. His transcript was covered with rubber-stamped notations about cutting classes and neglecting his studies.

Arthur Pope spoke up on Chick's behalf. To the dean's office he wrote: "He is inclined to be independent about the time he takes for his work in this course, which consists of laboratory work in painting, but he is intelligent, and I think will do all right, if I can keep after him closely enough."[11] The Administrative Board voted to pass Chick on as a sophomore, but again on probation.

As the summer of 1920 approached, Laura had to face two unpleasant realities—her son's failure and her own mortality. Although she wrote the dean that she had advised Everett to find a supervisor for summer studies, she acknowledged the fact that he might be leaving the college for good. She could "only hope for the best," she said, adding that "one never knows in this world what is really for the best—and [being] sent from Harvard may be the best for him."[12] (Arthur Austin had apparently already made it clear within the family that he did not think Chick would ever finish college.) Laura was more certain about what was best for herself. She was suffering from gallstones and knew she might require an operation. Rather than consulting Arthur or his colleagues in Boston, she went off to a Philadelphia hospital and proceeded with surgery. "You certainly sprang a surprise party on us in having your operation without our knowledge," Arthur wrote to her on June 2, "but Dr. Dorset telegraphed me that you came through all right for which many thanks. . . . I shall be much interested to learn how much medical practice or rather surgical practice in the city of Brotherly Love surpasses that in Bean Town." It was a friendly letter, but he signed himself with an impersonal "Yours A E Austin."[13]

Laura recovered quickly enough to spend the summer in Harpswell, where she continued to impose her will on Chick. When he invited an Andover classmate to spend a weekend sailing on *The Flying Dutchman*, Laura insisted that they drive her to a distant antiques fair instead. Chick's friend remembered Laura as a disheveled and demanding little woman whose flat Pennsylvania accent was embellished with aristocratic vowels in all the wrong places. (By this time, she had taken to wearing a red wig, generally askew, and her clothes were years out of date.) He got the impression that Chick found her exasperating.[14] But though Chick could shake his head at Laura's oddities, the ties between mother and son were far too close to allow him even to think of openly rebelling.

In September 1920, the start of his third year at Harvard, Chick concentrated formally on the fine arts. He made his way through another advanced course in drawing and painting, as well as ancient and medieval architecture, and a history of French painting taught by Paul Sachs, assistant director of Harvard's Fogg Art Museum. Though Sachs gave him only a C in his course, he took a strong liking to Chick. He earned C's in his other classes—English, anthropology (ominously titled "Criminal Anthropology & Race Mixture"), and philosophy.

Chick grew frustrated with the way some studio art courses were being taught that year. "It appalled me," he told a newspaper reporter a decade later. "I got fearfully tired of painting from photographs taken from magazines, and from pretty-colored ads. Taste was not encouraged, and all my interest in painting was destroyed during the next few years by the mechanical processes to which we were subjected."[15] Nevertheless, he took Arthur Pope's course in advanced drawing and painting (which could be repeated each year) three times as an undergraduate. His grades in fine arts amounted to a B, two C's, and a D in the drawing and painting course (probably because Pope was not teaching it that semester). It was hardly a stellar record, but there had been no disciplinary action, and he was never to be placed on probation again.

The real turning point in his college life came in the fall of 1921, when America's greatest living Egyptologist, George Andrew Reisner, returned to Harvard after an absence of nine years. Reisner had already advanced the technique of meticulously recorded excavation well beyond what the pioneering British archaeologist Sir William Matthew Flinders Petrie had accomplished in the previous century.[16] For more than two decades, he had been uncovering and documenting the royal cemeteries of Egypt and the Sudan. Since 1910, Reisner had held three positions simultaneously: professor of Egyptology at Harvard, curator of Egyptology at the Boston Museum of Fine Arts, and director of the Harvard University–Boston Museum of Fine Arts Egyptian Expedition, the longest-running and most productive of American excavations up to that time. He was in Boston to help the Museum of Fine Arts install the antiquities he had most recently discovered and to teach two half courses at Harvard in the fall semester—the history of Egypt and a survey of Egyptian art—before returning to the land of the pharaohs.

With the increase in archaeological expeditions from Europe and America in the early part of the century, tales of ancient Egypt and Egyptian magic were popular. Bram Stoker, already famous for *Dracula*, published a best-selling mummy novel in 1904 called *The Jewel of Seven Stars*, and Sax Rohmer, who invented the evil Fu Manchu, produced novels and short stories centering around mummies and curses, including *Tales of Secret Egypt* in 1919 and *The Green Eyes of Bast* in 1920. Moving-picture studios also brought horrifying tales of ancient Egypt to the public. There were three films called *The Mummy* in 1911 alone, and Ernst Lubitsch's *Eyes of the Mummy* of 1918, with Pola Negri and Emil Jannings, was so popular that he followed it three years later with *The Loves of Pharaoh*.[17] In 1921, Rudolph Valentino appeared in *The Sheik* and created a worldwide sensation. Responding to popular culture and to an obviously rare opportunity, Chick signed up for both of Reisner's courses.

In Reisner, Chick found a teacher who bore a distinct physical resemblance to Arthur Austin. He was solid and stocky, with a gruff and demanding exterior. He wore a closely cropped mustache and was invariably seen with a pipe clenched between his teeth. Ironically, Chick would find Reisner more approachable and encouraging than the father he resembled.

Indiana-born, Reisner was an undergraduate at Harvard in the class of 1889. He earned his doctorate from Harvard in Semitics and pursued further studies in Berlin. In 1912, having excavated at Giza and in Upper Egypt in the Aswan area for two years, Reisner had moved south and begun excavations in the Sudan. Most recently, he had been digging at Meroë, once a capital of Ethiopia. In this desolate region he had concentrated on the pyramids of the Ethiopian royal family, which had ruled the land during the first and second centuries B.C.

To Chick and the other Harvard undergraduates who took Reisner's courses, hearing firsthand reports of the latest discoveries was riveting. Chick applied himself with unprecedented effort. Reisner was impressed and gave him the first two of the three A's he would earn in college.

Chick found himself at a critical juncture. He knew he would not graduate with his class in the spring of 1922 because he still lacked several courses for the completion of his degree. He was not even sure that he wanted to continue his formal education. George Reisner now offered him a thrilling alternative. Before he returned to his expedition in January, he invited Chick to be his assistant for a season in Egypt and the Sudan during the winter of 1922–23. Reisner was not one to extend charity to a wayward undergraduate. He plainly saw talent in a young man who had excelled in his courses. Chick made a private arrangement to work for him, not as a student, but as a member of his team.

Years later, when Chick recounted his momentous departure for Egypt, he would dramatize it to the hilt, poking fun as usual at his mother. Glossing over his poor grades, he would tell his listeners that Harvard thought he should be doing something more serious and that he should get away from his mother's influence. He claimed that she prepared all of his trunks and saw him off on the boat. Soon after putting out to sea, he unpacked his things and went to look around the ship. He noticed that the door to the next stateroom

Laura Etnier Austin about to depart for Egypt
and the Sudan, passport photograph, 1922

was open and looked in. There was Laura with a pile of her own trunks, filled with clothes and equipment of every description, ready for a year in the Egyptian desert.[18]

In reality, Laura had been preparing for the trip for months. She had no intention of allowing her precious son to get away from her supervision in a distant land; and she seized an excuse to escape from what she had come to see as the dreary atmosphere of Boston, where, for all her efforts to join the Yankee upper crust, she had never felt entirely at home.

Though she wrongly assumed that Everett had seen the last of Harvard, Laura thought the experience would give him a chance to steady himself and perhaps find his life's work. In the spring of 1922 she wrote verses celebrating the upcoming trip—and thumbing her nose at Arthur:

> *We are sailing too*
> *To Egypts desert land*
> *Where Everett has a job*
> *With Reisners jolly band—*

> *Digging dried-up mummies*
> *   For Harvard and the Mus—*
> *With Mother as a Chaperone*
> *   To keep away the blues—*
>
> *Now my job is finished*
> *   And I take a well earned rest*
> *From Boston's cold roast beef*
> *   And seek a warmer nest*
>
> *I'll sit all day at Shephards*
> *   And watch the passing throng*
> *And forget about old Boston*
> *   And the days when we were young*
>
> *For the kid has finished Harvard*
> *   And its almost finished me—*
> *But we have the laugh on Father*
> *   As he said it could not be . . .*[19]

Laura and Chick went to the passport office in Boston together on August 8, and packed their trunks following recommendations in the latest edition of *Cook's Handbook for Egypt and the Sudan.* For "gentlemen," these requirements included multiple suits in flannel and tweed, riding breeches, gaiters, and a catalogue of coverings to keep off the sun: "straw and felt hats, cloth caps, white umbrella lined with green, cork sun helmet," and a *kafiyyah,* made of turban cloth, which was to be worn over the hat and tied to protect the neck and face.[20]

They sailed on one of Cunard's newest liners, the *Sythia,* on September 1, 1922, arriving at Liverpool eight days later. After a brief stay in London, they traveled through France, revisiting and photographing the museums, chateaux, and cathedrals that Chick had last seen when he was eleven. Having studied art history with the outstanding faculty at the Fogg, he looked at European art and architecture through very different eyes. He and Laura had five weeks to bask in these civilized surroundings before joining Reisner's expedition. In Paris, on October 2, they obtained visas for Egypt and Palestine.

On the seventh, they sailed from Toulon, stopping in Italy for a week, long enough to visit the Pitti Palace in Florence and see the largest exhibition of Italian baroque paintings ever held, *Pittura Italiana del Seicento e del Settecento,* before it closed at the end of the month. Chick had been attracted to the style through Chandler Post's course at Harvard, "Art and Culture of Spain." The Fogg had just acquired its first baroque masterpiece, *St. Jerome,* by Jusepe de Ribera, and Post used it to illustrate the technical brilliance of seventeenth-century painting.[21] The Pitti Palace show gave Chick a chance to see more than a thousand pictures from the seventeenth and eighteenth centuries. In this vast display, the art of the baroque, with its drama and illusionism, captivated him. It spoke to his love of magic and the theater.

Not until he was on the ship leaving Italy did Chick finally get around to writing Dean Edward Gay back at Harvard, letting him know his whereabouts and announcing that he wanted a break from academic work:

> I have decided to stay abroad for a year or so, working with Dr. Reisner in Egypt. I think that you will agree with me that this is a splendid opportunity for me; but perhaps you will also remember, that I still lack a whole course, I think, of the required number for my degree. I understand that I have five years in which to finish this work.
>
> Is this true? And do I need the formality of a leave of absence? Also I would like to know if I could possibly get any credits for this work abroad.[22]

Chick and Laura disembarked at Port Said, at the entrance to the Suez Canal, on October 18. From there they proceeded by train to Cairo, where Chick stepped into an atmosphere more foreign than anything he had ever experienced.

Egypt's capital was a city of nearly 800,000, with large populations of Christians and Jews as well as Moslems. Between November and April, when the weather was its mildest, European tourists swarmed to the city to escape colder climates, shop in the bazaars, and explore the ancient ruins. Conditions in Cairo had been improving dramatically since 1914, when the khedive was deposed and Egypt was declared a British protectorate. More than half the streets had been macadamized, the sidewalks had been paved, and the alleys of the bazaars asphalted. Where oil and gas lamps once hung, new electric arc and incandescent lamps had been installed; the streets had finally been named, and the chaotic traffic was now regulated by the police.

Chick and his mother checked into the grandest hostelry in Cairo, Shepheard's Hotel, in the heart of the European quarter, near the Sultanic Opera House and the Ezbakiyah Gardens. Surrounded by palms and exotic plantings, Shepheard's offered its guests every amenity, including daily concerts, weekly formal dances, and a French restaurant that was advertised in Chick's guidebook as providing the best cuisine in Egypt.[23]

After a few days in Cairo, Chick went out to join Reisner at Harvard Camp at Giza, literally in the shadow of the Great Pyramid of Cheops, eight miles southwest of the city. Consisting of low mud-brick buildings arranged into a four-sided compound, the camp sat on a broad sandy terrace, facing east across an ancient royal cemetery of small white limestone monuments called mastabas, lined up along streets like a miniature city, toward the three famous pyramids. Throughout the day, Chick could watch these massive structures change color and character as the light changed—gray and solemn as the sun rose, blindingly white at noon, intensely pink at sunset, black and serenely gigantic by moonlight. Chick took pictures of the pyramids and the nearby Sphinx in every light, hand-tinting the prints and giving them romantic captions in his photograph album: "Shadows on the Pyramid Road," "Time," "Clouds," "The Moon Rises at Gizeh."

His room, which he dubbed "The Salon," was furnished simply with a narrow bed covered by a brightly colored rug, pushed up against bare cracked walls. He soon got to know Reisner's wife and daughter, Mary, and the principal members of his team: Dows Dunham, Reisner's chief assistant, and Mrs. Dunham; Amory Goddard, a young Bostonian; and Mrs. Travers Symonds, Reisner's secretary, an Englishwoman who had just left her post as an editor of *The Egyptian Gazette,* the country's leading newspaper.

Reisner put Chick to work making plans of tombs and drawings of artifacts for several scholarly projects: an article about his latest discoveries at Meroë, a paper on the Meroitic chronology, and a book on Mycerinus (Menkaure), who built the third pyramid at Giza. For the first time in his life, Chick was no longer a student who would be graded, but a member of a team that would be depending on his consistent, meticulous effort for the success of its enterprise.

There were long, concentrated stretches of work, but there was time for excursions by camel and horseback to other ruins, like the necropolis of Sakkara, and trips to Cairo, where Chick's mother remained, occupying herself with writing sentimental poems about "little 'Gyppie' babies" and stringing necklaces of beads and reproductions of ancient scarabs. Reisner and Dunham chipped in on a Ford that fall—"in case of an emergency," Reisner explained to the Boston Museum, "a camel would be a bit slow"—and laid out a primitive road to town. Mrs. Reisner and Mary organized evening parties that included members of the team and, sometimes, a reluctant Reisner himself.[24]

Chick had his own forms of entertainment as well. He had brought along a windup gramophone and a few records, and played excerpts from Rimsky-Korsakov's *Scheherezade* continuously to heighten his enjoyment of the desert evenings.[25] Once, on a bet with a member of the expedition, he spent the night curled up beside the Great Pyramid, and he posed for a sequence of progressively undressed snapshots with the pyramids as backdrop. During other breaks in his schedule, he set out with his paint box and easel and produced watercolors of palm trees along the Nile, the pyramids, and the Sphinx. But mostly he was working.

At the end of November, the world was staggered to learn that the British archaeologist Howard Carter and his sponsor, Lord Carnarvon, working in the Valley of the Kings at Luxor, had discovered the antechamber to the tomb of a pharaoh named Tutankhamen, who had ruled Egypt twenty centuries before Christ. Stories of the golden treasures Carter was bringing to light made headlines around the globe.

Reisner was loudly disdainful of Carter's methods and what he called his "scandalous publicity campaign." To his visiting committee at the Boston Museum, he wrote that Carter was not a "scientific" archaeologist and had "a financial interest in booming the find." He characterized all those directing the digs in the Valley of the Kings as "amateurs or worse" and railed against Lord Carnarvon for buying antiquities outright for vast sums—money "which has of course gone into the pockets of thieves and illicit excavators and has caused the destruction of an unknown amount of historical material." He added that "this tomb will probably cause no end of trouble for all concerned. That trouble marks the beginning of the end of scientific excavation in Egypt proper."[26] It was no acci-

Chick posing at Giza, 1922. The first of the series

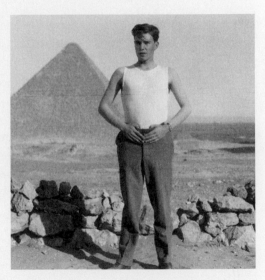

. . . the last of the series

dent that Reisner was not among the first to be invited to see what the world was soon calling King Tut's tomb, or that in December, Carter pointedly refused Dows Dunham a look when Dunham passed through the Valley of the Kings on his way back to Reisner's dig in the Sudan. But the discovery was tantalizing to anyone in the field, and as 1923 began, Chick could look forward to the next phase of his work with quickened excitement.

On February 5, he and the Reisners began the long journey southward to the site at Meroë. Laura Austin came along. They traveled by train to Luxor, 420 miles upriver from Cairo, then transferred to a smaller-gauge railway for the 130-mile journey from Luxor to Aswan. The rail line ended at Shellal, where the party boarded a Nile tourist steamer for the trip to Wadi Halfa at the second cataract, more than 200 miles away. This was the most pleasant part of the route, for first-class steamers were appointed with private baths, electricity, and hot and cold running water. Concerts and dances were offered by the ship's orchestra. As the desert drifted by, Chick snapped pictures of the landscape, mostly desolate except for a few palm trees at the river's edge and the occasional sight of a felucca with its tall triangle of sail. Among the stops was Abu Simbel, where Chick could see another of the great wonders of Egypt, the Temple of Ramses II (known to the Greeks—and the poet Shelley—as Ozymandias), its entrance guarded by four identical statues of the seated pharaoh, each over sixty feet high and carved out of the grit-stone cliff. At Wadi Halfa, the party boarded a train that cut through the uninhabited Nubian desert to Abu Ahmed and then down through the Sudan. On February 10, Chick, Laura, the Reisners, and the others in the party finally reached the station at the village of Begarawiyah, a fifteen-minute walk from the ruins at Meroë.

Reisner joined Dunham at the site, but allowed Chick—accompanied by Laura, Mrs. Travers Symonds, and Amory Goddard—to proceed another hundred miles south on the rail line to see Khartoum, at the confluence of the Blue Nile and the White Nile, where General Charles "Chinese" Gordon had been killed in 1885 by forces of the dervish leader known as the "mad Mahdi." There Laura bought Chick two exotic souvenirs—a leopard skin and a dagger.

On February 13, the party returned to the very spartan conditions of Reisner's dig at Meroë. When Chick saw the city in the winter of 1923, it was little more than a bleak and crumbling suggestion of its former glory. The wind and sand had worn away nearly everything but the foundations of temples and tombs. Large stone blocks lay scattered about the site, and only clusters of low broken step-pyramids, and a few pepper trees, interrupted the flat horizon. The most impressive site, whose exposed foundation was 450 feet long, was the temple of Amon, "the hidden one," the supreme god of Egypt. There were also the royal baths, somewhat more intact, with remnants of staircases and aqueducts, and walls decorated with frescoes, tiles, statues, and sculptures.

This ruin was once the rich and powerful capital of Kush, a kingdom mentioned in Genesis and known in the *Iliad* as the land of the gods. It was finally destroyed by the Abyssinians around 350 A.D., and Meroë fell into ruin and near oblivion. In the early 1820s, the French explorer Caillaud rediscovered

the city, as well as the older capital of Napata. The first serious excavations had
been carried out by an English team in the decade before the World War.

Reisner had worked on both Napata and Meroë for seven years and had
pieced together much of what was known of the kingdom's history.[27] In the fall
of 1920, he had begun a systematic excavation of the royal cemeteries at
Meroë. Now he had finished work on the northern and southern groups of pyramids in the hills and would be completing the excavation of the final section,
the Western Cemetery, in the plain. Begun in the eighth century B.C. as the
burying ground of minor members of the royal family of Meroë, this cemetery
was used for at least five centuries. Of more than eight hundred tombs excavated in this cemetery, the oldest proved to have been less disturbed by ancient
robbers than those at the other two sites.

The expedition was based at two camps. Chick, his mother, and the Reisners stayed in large round tents at the original campsite in the Northern Cemetery, while Dunham and his party had pitched their tents closer to the recent
excavations in the Western Cemetery and had built an excavating house,
roughly constructed of fieldstone with palm logs for a roof. Beyond the camps
and the ruins, the desert stretched to the horizon in every direction.

Chick was soon following a rigorous routine. The method of scientific excavation Reisner had developed would eventually become standard procedure for
all serious archaeological expeditions, but it was rare in its day. Chick told a
reporter five years later that at Meroë he "did a little bit of everything"[28]—
which meant digging, measuring and mapping the sites, minutely sifting
through the sand as the graves were uncovered, and helping to compile the
object register, which was kept in duplicate. The register listed every single
object or fragment that was unearthed. Among them were amulets and beads of
faience, lapis lazuli, and silver; a necklace of gold ring beads with a blue stone
pendant; gold figures of the goddess Isis suckling Horus; ornaments in the form
of birds, cats, lions, and apes; a vessel shaped like a gazelle, bound for slaugh-
ter. There were over five hundred scarabs alone, bearing names that Reisner
could identify as those of kings and high priestesses from several centuries.
Each was entered into the register, numbered, described, and drawn with precise measurements, along with the date and place of finding. In addition, every
object, no matter how minor, was photographed. Then, in the evening, Reisner
or Dows Dunham wrote the official diary, giving an exact account of every activity of the day with commentary on the meaning and importance of the work.[29]

Aside from the painstaking accuracy, the work was dirty, and the heat was
so intense that the metal parts of the expedition's camera would scorch the photographer's hands. Sometimes up to fifty sites were worked on in one day. Much
of the labor involved clearing stairs and chambers and measuring tombs that
had been plundered in ancient times. Many of the graves Chick and the diggers

uncovered on the western knoll of the Western Cemetery contained the skeletons of children.

On March 23, after weeks of this meticulous toil, the team came upon a treasure—the undisturbed tomb of a royal lady. Still partly encased in two or three wooden coffins, coated in gold, the mummy wore a silver mask. A silver hawk with outstretched wings surmounted the head. Traces of gilding could be seen on other silver ornaments covering the body. A row of blue faience shawabti figures stood in attendance along one wall. This was Chick's one chance to participate in a discovery of the kind that gave archaeology its romantic appeal.

Apart from this find, there was little else to enliven the workday. Occasionally, local British authorities and their wives visited the camp. The governor of Berber, the chief inspector of Berber Province, and the director of education at Khartoum all came to call, and the Reisners entertained them at dinner, lunch, or afternoon tea. And at the end of the day, a favorite relaxation was riding the few available animals—an overactive horse who liked to gallop, a plodding donkey, and a recalcitrant camel.[30]

For conversation, Chick found Mrs. Symonds especially congenial. As a former newspaper editor, she was an intelligent woman with literary interests and had brought copies of English periodicals. One day in March, she lent him an issue of *The New Statesman*, which he wanted to peruse for articles on art. Chick's mother discovered the journal among his things, and it was opened to an article that she found objectionable. The next morning Laura confronted the culprit. As Mrs. Symonds immediately reported to Reisner, "Mrs. Austin came up to me and in a very loud voice told me that she considers I am not fit etc to have anything to do with young men, meaning her son. . . . Instead of coming to me quietly and speaking to me alone, Mrs. Austin after *thinking about it all night* shouts out what she thinks before the whole camp and calls it speaking as 'woman to woman'!" She was so appalled by Laura's behavior that she packed her bags and informed Reisner that "either you kindly let me go to the other camp or let me return to Cairo, or if necessary, I resign my post."[31]

What Chick, at twenty-two, thought of his mother inspecting his reading material and publicly insulting a member of the staff is not recorded, but it was not the first example he had seen of her high-handedness, nor the first time she had shown herself to be oblivious to anyone's feelings but her own. Laura's outburst notwithstanding, Reisner made peace in the land, and Mrs. Symonds remained with the expedition.

Not long afterward, with the approach of April and the hottest weather, the excavating season came to an end. On March 30, the pottery and other objects that Reisner judged as less than museum quality were stored in the last tomb examined in the Northern Cemetery. Inside one of the chambers, Reisner placed a bottle containing a dated note describing the excavations that year and listing the members of the expedition. Then the tomb was sealed with sandstone masonry. The next day, a British official arrived from Khartoum to make the division of objects between the Americans and the Egyptians, and on April 1, after some last-minute work on eight sites and the refilling of a staircase, the expedition at Meroë was officially concluded.

Chick stayed for ten days to help pack the objects assigned to the Boston Museum before departing with his mother back across the Nubian Desert to Abu Ahmed and west along the Nile to see the ancient sites Reisner had previously excavated. Continuing north by train and steamer, they stopped at Luxor and nearby Karnak and Thebes. There they saw the most extensive and best-preserved ruins in Egypt: the Colossi of Memnon; the obelisks of Ramses II; and the great temples of Luxor, Karnak, Ramses III, and Queen Hatshepsut. In the Valley of the Kings, Chick could only take pictures of the entrance to Tutankhamen's tomb, which had been sealed until the next season. He bought souvenir photographs of Carter's workers carrying treasures out into the sunshine after three thousand years in the dark. After an excursion to Palestine, where they spent most of May exploring Jerusalem and the outlying holy places, Laura and Chick sailed from Alexandria for Marseilles on the first of June. By the tenth, they were back in Paris.

Paris that summer vibrated with the very latest in fashion and the arts. Chick met up with Paul Sachs, now associate director of the Fogg Art Museum, whom he had known since taking the French paintings course three years earlier. Sachs invited him to attend a performance of Serge Diaghilev's Ballets Russes at the Gaîeté-Lyrique Theater. In one evening, he saw two of Igor Stravinsky's greatest works: *Pulcinella* of 1920, with choreography by Leonide Massine and costumes and a set—a haunting Cubist vision of Naples and its bay in moonlight—by Picasso; and *Les Noces,* choreographed by Bronislava Nijinska and designed in shades of blue, brown, and white by Nathalie Gontcharova, which had just had its premiere on June 13. This new ballet caused leading French critics to rail against Stravinsky's strident modernism.[32] For Chick, the experience was a revelation. From that moment, as he later wrote, "through those summers when every year I went to London for two or three weeks of ballet, every season brought to me the joy of experiencing new artistic forms." There were no superlatives too great to describe the impact Diaghilev's artistic vision had on him. "To me, his Russian Ballet, with its music by modern composers, its scenery by contemporary painters and its choreography by such great and rare masters as Fokine, Nikinsky, Massine, Nijinska and Balanchine, has been the most intense emotional experience of my life."[33] That first night at the Ballets Russes started him on the path to becoming a champion of modern art in all its forms. Equally important, it gave

him a vision of the brilliant achievements that were possible through the collaboration of artists in the theater.

It was also in Paris that month that Chick was introduced, undoubtedly by
Sachs, to the director of the Fogg, Edward Waldo Forbes. Forbes, a grandson of
Ralph Waldo Emerson, had been in Europe for nearly a year, preparing an
expanded version of the single course he taught at Harvard each spring. This
was an introduction to connoisseurship through a study of the precise techniques by which early Renaissance pictures were painted. His advanced teaching method, requiring students to practice those techniques themselves, was
unrivaled in the United States. Paul Sachs had just begun offering graduate
students an equally pioneering course that explored every aspect of museum
work.

Fresh from George Reisner's most recent dig in the Sudan, Chick had a
certain luster, and Forbes and Sachs invited him to dine with them and a three-
man committee from Harvard that was considering a possible excavation at
Carthage to be sponsored by the Fogg. Seeing Forbes and Sachs socially, far
from their classrooms, gave Chick personal connections that would prove
immensely beneficial to him sooner than he realized.

He and his mother left Paris on July 1 and traveled throughout Europe,
from Switzerland to Austria, Czechoslovakia, and Germany. Chick looked tirelessly at pictures and architecture, finding time for his own painting as well. On
September 9, they returned to England. From London, a more mature Chick
Austin wrote to Dean Gay at Harvard: "I am now planning to return to college
in February 1924—which will give me a half-year to take the courses I still
require for my degree. Then if all goes well, I shall enter the architectural
school in the fall."[34]

He had decided not to pursue archaeology. He later claimed that the food
and the climate had not agreed with his stomach, but the truth was that the
cloistered life of the dig and the constant reminders of mortality were not for
him. More than ever, he was vividly aware that life was short and should be
seized and savored. Art and architecture could transcend death. Seeing the
greatest Egyptian monuments and tombs had turned his thoughts to becoming a
builder for his own time. He had also begun to lay the foundation for his future
connoisseurship. In the course of his work, Chick had handled, measured, and
recorded so many ornaments and artifacts that they had lost their mystique.
They were no longer precious and rare specimens, but objects of varying quality that could both teach and give pleasure. And he had developed a different
sense of time. He and Reisner's team had been among the first to see things that
had been hidden for thousands of years but, in a sense, were just as new as they
had been on the day they were sealed up by the Meroitic priests. Chick began
to catch glimmers of the insight he would later promote unceasingly—that all

art becomes alive, contemporary, in fact—each time it is looked at with an open and engaged mind.

In his letter to the dean at Harvard, Chick added that he did not want to ask for credit for his work with Reisner because "it would make my status in Egypt seem too much that of a student."[35] His demanding activities, he felt, had put him well above that level. It seemed far more than a year since he had left Boston.

Chick and his mother resumed their frenetic schedule for the rest of the year. They were back in Paris at the end of September, returned to England in October, crossed the Channel again at the end of the month, visited Antwerp, Belgium, for which Laura developed a particular fondness, and in November wandered through France, Switzerland, and Italy. On December 5, Chick embarked from Cherbourg for home.

Laura decided not to go with him. The year away had been a watershed for her as well as Chick. She was not ready to return to Arthur and resume her former life in Boston. She had money of her own, her son was nearly grown up, and she was enjoying the freedom of going wherever her interests, or her whims, might take her. By now she was addicted to visiting museums and art dealers, and she began buying up inexpensive seventeenth- and eighteenth-century paintings, mostly portraits that would cover the walls at 110 Marlborough Street. These purchases helped satisfy her craving for distinguished ancestors; she was more interested in the sitters than the art and took lengthy notes on their lives and lineage.

In the spring of 1924, the proprietor of a bookstore in Nice noticed Laura's maiden name and convinced her that it was derived from the French surname "Etienne." This started her on a fifteen-year odyssey, tracing the line back to both French and British royalty. She was related not only to Saint Stephen, she found, but to William the Conqueror, and a French cardinal who, upon arriving in America, fell in love with an English baroness and became a Huguenot in order to marry her.[36]

Oliver Etnier told his sister that the notion of their French origin was "a lot of bunk" and, infected with the genealogical virus himself, sent her voluminous and, to anyone but Laura, irrefutable evidence of their German peasant past.[37] Her brother Carey likewise found her conclusions dubious. "I think your father thinks I have gone a little mad," Laura told Carey's son Stephen, "but, I assure you, there is no lineage in this country that quite comes up to this."[38] At last, through the Etniers, Laura could boast a pedigree nobler than any mere American aristocrat. As she had done with the Morrisons, she contrived to prove it with another painted piece of family china, this time a washbasin.[39]

While his mother moved through France pursuing genealogical flights of fancy, Chick settled into the comparative reality of the Harvard curriculum. To finish his degree in fine arts before continuing on with architecture, he signed up for a final semester with Arthur Pope in drawing and painting, a history of Greek sculpture, and "Primitive Sociology." He also chose "Methods and Processes of Italian Painting," the course taught by Edward Forbes. This kindly, soft-spoken, rumpled, absentminded, and profoundly curious man of fifty understood how the art he loved was created, and he knew how to make it understood to others. He could fathom, as well, the talents and temperaments of his students, and could, as one of his successors said, "inspire the young and feckless to focus their gifts for at least one moment of significant creativity."[40] That spring Forbes transformed Chick's enjoyment of the fine arts into a vocation.

Forbes had a clear mission for his students. Soon after Chick took his course, Forbes wrote:

> The purpose of a university Fine Arts Department is not the creation of artists. It is in the first place to give to a large number of men a familiarity with the art heritage of our civilization and to arouse or create in them that love of the arts which is theirs by inherent right, and to make it an integral, vital part of their lives. In the second place it should give to a limited number of men the training and experience necessary to enable them to serve as curators and directors of museums, or connoisseurs, critics, and teachers of the arts.[41]

This was the first semester that the Methods course was devoted almost exclusively to the techniques of painting. Forbes lectured two days a week at the Fogg Art Museum; on Saturday mornings his students came to Gerry's Landing, the red brick Federal Revival house he had built above Mount Auburn Street in Cambridge for his growing family. There the students carried out their laboratory work in a large room on the third floor, which the Forbeses called "the gymnasium."[42] One of those students, Chick's friend Agnes Mongan, the preeminent master drawings connoisseur, who followed him in Forbes's class by only a few years and later became director of the Fogg, described the impact of what was affectionately known as "The Egg and Plaster Course":

> Those students who, year after year, became happily involved in its unfolding discoveries will never forget their excitement as they prepared the satin-smooth gesso surfaces of their wooden panels, then applied the brick-red "bollo," burnished their carefully laid gold leaf, and mixed their egg yolks with tempera. Nor will they forget working their rough plaster, then when all was ready, applying earth colors to a section of a wet wall, or, later in the year, discovering the magic of

Venetian glazes. Always present and sharing their excitement was their gentle mentor.[43]

Chick became completely absorbed in his classwork for Forbes. By meticulously imitating the painting techniques used during the Italian Renaissance, he began to see old master paintings, like the artifacts from Egypt, as objects to be judged rather than icons to be revered.

Forbes watched his awakening and, as George Reisner had done, rewarded him with more than an A on his transcript. He was so impressed with Chick's eye for quality, his manual dexterity, and his lively mind that he offered him a position as his sole assistant in the Methods course for the spring of 1925. To prepare, Forbes suggested that Chick go to Italy in the fall to study with some of that country's greatest restorers and copyists, promising to supply him with letters of introduction to leading curators and collectors, dealers and connoisseurs, among them his close friend Bernard Berenson, the most famous living authority on Italian painting. Chick's thoughts of a career in architecture receded.

Meanwhile, Laura Austin had crossed the Atlantic in time to witness, on June 18, 1924, the conferring of a bachelor's degree from Harvard College on her son, "as of the Class of 1922."

Hearing about the opportunity at the Fogg, Laura swung into action. She summoned Forbes to Marlborough Street, and the two of them discussed Everett's future. In a note thanking Forbes for his visit, she expressed her deepest maternal wish: "I am hoping that this year he will decide what he really wants to do."[44] Unable to resist the urge to continue promoting her son, she enclosed a selection of what she thought were Everett's better undergraduate writings. But Laura's influence was fading; Chick was moving into another sphere.

CHAPTER THREE

Darling of the Fogg

In a sense, the works of art themselves are the only
materials of the student of the history of art. All that
remains of an event in general history is the account of it
in document or tradition; but in art, the work of art itself
is the event.

—Bernard Berenson, "Rudiments of Connoisseurship"

In the third week of September 1924, just before embarking for Europe,
Chick stopped at the Fogg to pick up a large envelope left for him by
Edward Forbes. It bulged with the promised letters of introduction, a stack
of Forbes's calling cards, a check for $150 for museum expenses, and
detailed advice about approaching the men in Italy who could teach him
secrets of how old masters were painted, restored, and bought and sold—how
authenticity was determined and imitation detected. It was his passport to a
world inaccessible to all but a few students of art history.

Forbes trusted Chick to immerse himself in that world, to look intently at
the objects and images from the early Renaissance that could be found by the
thousands in churches, museums, and dealers' storerooms throughout central
Italy. Whenever possible, he should touch them, turn them in the light, teach
his fingers to remember weight and texture, train his eye to see the subtle variations of color, composition, and line, to look through the layers of varnish and
paint and sense the artistry within. Then, if he had the gift that Forbes suspected, Chick would come to know the almost instinctive feeling that could
instantly discern—without regard to artists' names or reputations—quality.

Forbes counted, too, on having Chick's help to advance the Methods course,
for this was a continuously evolving exploration, as much a measure of Forbes's
own curiosity as his mission to educate. He wanted Chick to make drawings and
buy photographs of certain key paintings, to acquire inexpensive samples of
early works, and to procure the special ingredients for fresco-making that could

be found only in Europe. Most especially, Chick was to hone his promising technical skills by practicing over the winter; then he would be well prepared to take on the next phase of his education as both apprentice and teacher at the Fogg.

To shepherd Chick around Italy during his first weeks, Forbes had enlisted his most recent assistant in the Methods course, Dan Thompson. Though two years younger than Chick, Thompson was an honors graduate of Chick's class of 1922. He was an amateur painter and musician and was fast becoming an authority on the chemistry of painting—what he later called the "cookery" of fine arts.[1] During the previous two summers, he had traveled and studied in Europe with Forbes and his family and was now back on the Continent on a university fellowship for more study before going off to examine endangered wall paintings in India and China.

Chick sailed for Liverpool on the *Sythia*, as he had two years earlier, arriving at the beginning of October. Once again, Laura had decided to make the crossing with him, though by now even she understood that Everett had outgrown the need for a chaperone. Besides, she had her ancestral quest to continue, and the two parted company soon after reaching London.

Chick went on to Rome via Paris, joining Thompson at the Hotel Ingleterre, and together they made a quick survey of early pictures, mosaics, and frescoes throughout the city. Thompson, who was suffering from a violent reaction to a smallpox vaccination, found Chick's uninhibited enthusiasm exhausting. "I am afraid my tendency to get tired in Museums and Churches," he told Forbes, "rather 'cramped Austin's style.' "[2]

Arriving in Florence on October 11, they began making arrangements to see the many experts, from professors to simple plasterers, whom Forbes had described in his written instructions to Chick. High on the agenda was the Russian copyist and restorer Nicholas Lochoff, a brilliant perfectionist, working at the Uffizi Gallery. While Forbes was preparing the revision of the Methods course the previous summer, he and Thompson had both studied with Lochoff. Forbes suggested that Chick ask the Russian to give him lessons in copying and restoration, compensating him with dinners at fine restaurants and gifts of little luxuries, as he was too proud to take money.

Forbes also advised Chick to see several American expatriates in Florence. In return for free food and lodging, the art critic F. Mason Perkins, who acted on commission as a private picture dealer for museums and collectors, would happily escort Chick through Tuscany and Umbria, which he knew intimately. Two other men, both Harvard graduates, were worth meeting: Charles Hotel, a well-connected collector and dilettante; and Philip Gentner, former director of the Worcester Museum, who also knew the local dealers and collectors. As Gentner was reclusive, Forbes advised Chick to go to a certain tea room, lie in wait for him, "and present my card." Forbes's name opened all doors.

Then, of course, there was Berenson. A member of Harvard's class of 1887, eight years ahead of Forbes, Bernard Berenson was by far the greatest connoisseur America had produced. Traveling through Europe immediately after his graduation, he had made an exhaustive study of Renaissance painting by visiting every museum, church, and private collection in Italy he could find, no matter how obscure. Inspired by the preeminent nineteenth-century Italian connoisseur Giovanni Morelli, he had developed a formal method of judging the quality and attribution of pictures, in which details in the work itself, rather than its history or even subject matter, became the central focus of study. This was a decisive advance over the personal and subjective approach to art that had been followed for centuries. His way of looking at pictures had begun to dominate art criticism and had permeated the courses Chick had taken at Harvard. Forbes's letter of introduction guaranteed Chick a warm reception at I Tatti, Berenson's villa at Settignano in the hills above Florence. With the proceeds from his books and the commissions from his pronouncements to collectors and dealers on the merit and authenticity of old master paintings, Berenson had filled I Tatti with splendid Renaissance pictures and was creating one of the greatest private art libraries in Italy.

Forbes urged Chick to use these men to expand his knowledge and gain further access to experts and collections. But he warned of the shoals Chick would have to negotiate: "Remember that in Florence there are apt to be jealousies and rivalries and you can never tell whether Perkins and Hotel and Berenson are on speaking terms or not. Once in a while they quarrel with each other, so it is well to put on the soft pedal about speaking of your relations with the other ones."[3] In the education of what Forbes liked to call "the Museum Man," diplomacy was sometimes to be considered one of the fine arts.

After Florence, Chick was scheduled to go to Siena, the mecca of pre-Renaissance art and architecture, and set up a course of study with Federigo Ioni, a well-known, if not notorious, restorer. Ioni was in fact spoken of openly in Siena as "the king of forgers." His income from masterly restorations of authentic paintings was supplemented by the fabrication of pictures and elaborately tooled book bindings, which he passed off as fifteenth-century originals. Dan Thompson had taken lessons from Ioni a year earlier and hoped to join Chick in further study. As soon as he had heard of Chick's travel plans, Thompson had written to Ioni, asking him to teach them both the art of fresco-making, how to work with gesso and tempera, how to prepare and apply gilt, and, most difficult of all, how to transfer frescoes so they could be moved to the safety of museums.[4] Thompson planned to take Chick to Siena at the end of October.

For anyone expecting to understand Italian art on a professional level, learning the language was essential, and Thompson had been tutoring Chick since his arrival.[5] Chick's knowledge of Latin and several modern European languages enabled him to become fluent quickly, though he was always best at the German and French he had learned as a child.

By the end of their first week, they had seen Lochoff and the painting by Simone Martini he was working on; they had visited Mason Perkins, who spent hours telling them about the subtleties of forgeries; and they had gone to I Tatti. Though the great man was out of town, they had been welcomed by Mrs. Berenson and had looked at the collection.

Bent on seeing as wide a range of quality as possible, Chick and Thompson sifted through the offerings of the Florentine dealers. At twenty-three, Chick alternated between presenting himself as a sophisticated connoisseur and a tentative novice: "I found yesterday some rather amusing forgeries in a small shop and bought one for myself for about ten dollars," he wrote Forbes. This was a tempera panel of a Madonna and angels, with a gold background which Chick found "not unattractively stamped" and over the entire surface "a most amusing crackly, which is neither scratched nor of the egg variety." (A genuine cracked surface came from the natural aging of wood panels.) "They have other more ambitious ones in the shop, seemingly by the same hand, but of a more costly price. One especially, Dan says, is most awfully good but, at a hundred dollars, seems hardly desirable.

"We have had a great time looking through the collections of small dealers and I find this practice of great help in training the eye, though of course I dare venture an opinion only to myself as yet."[6]

Before he and Thompson had a chance to move on to Siena, word came from Harvard that civil war had delayed the China expedition but that Thompson should proceed immediately to India. After little more than two weeks with his experienced companion, Chick was on his own—more completely independent than he had ever been. He decided to postpone his visit to Ioni and, following Berenson's example, traveled around central Italy, practicing the language and looking at as much early art as he could.

He explored the hill towns, starting in Perugia at the gallery of Umbrian art in the Palazzo Pubblico, with its frescoes, altarpieces, and panels by early fifteenth-century artists. The Madonnas and baby Jesuses, the saints, the annunciations, adorations, visitations, crucifixions, resurrections—these images of love and death and redemption, endlessly repeated, while mind-numbing to the average museum-goer, only increased Chick's exhilaration as he felt his eyes opening, his knowledge deepening. For what he saw were no longer pictures. They were decisions about color and design and meaning. They were mirrors of the era in which they were created, bringing the past to the present and the present to the past. Here again was the broad insight that had begun to take shape for Chick in Egypt—that all art was contemporary art. Throughout this trip, it was as though he were experiencing, firsthand, the tumultuous energy of the late medieval world as it spun toward the Renaissance and the emergence of modern man.

From Perugia he went on to Assisi, to explore a place of pilgrimage to all serious students of European art: the monastery and double church of Saint Francis, erected as two buildings, one above the other against the hillside. The Lower Church was famous for frescoes by Giotto, but rather than being attracted to the works of that great father of Renaissance painting, Chick was "hypnotized," he told Forbes, by the Simone Martini frescoes in the chapel of Saint Martin. In the dim light, under the vaulted ceiling, on walls, in lunettes and arches, a crowd of fourteenth-century faces, in the guise of characters from the life of the saint, looked out from the dark opulence of golden halos and golden grounds. Bold and varied textures—impossible to discern in reproduction—revealed the arduous labor of the master and his assistants. For Chick, the works vibrated with immediacy, and in these spaces, though five centuries had passed, he could conjure up Simone himself, bending toward the wall, his hand deftly applying pigment to plaster before it dried. Chick was careful not to sound like the naive art student at a popular shrine when describing the visit to Forbes. He wrote that he found many of the attributions of works in the church so doubtful that "I have attempted aesthetic rather than critical enjoyment."

After dashing back down to Rome to revisit the principal churches and galleries, Chick reached Siena in mid-November, and he first tried lodging at a modest pensione. There he was subjected to "no heat, no hot water, and bad food," he told Forbes. He soon departed for the costlier comforts of the Grand Hotel, where "I am enjoying a roaring fire in my room night and morning and very good food."[7] Chick could afford to indulge himself not because of any stipend from the Fogg, but because his mother continued to pay him an allowance, a subsidy that in one form or another he would count on for the rest of Laura's life.

With its medieval color, its intimate variety of maze and vista, and the warmth of its people, Siena was much more appealing to Chick than Florence. Not long after his arrival, he called on Ioni, who for a fee of two thousand lire agreed to initiate him into the mysteries of copying early pictures with authentic techniques, beginning with tempera applied to gesso on a wood panel. Chick reported to Forbes that Ioni

suggested first that I start to work copying a picture in the Belli Arti, but the photos I brought to him of possibilities, on the next day, didnt appear to please him, and, after a great deal of beating about, he finally said that a friend of his had a Lippo Memmi Madonna which could be borrowed for the occasion. He showed me a photo of this and I was very pleased, and armed with it, went to the carpenters to have the panel made. This will be ready tomorrow and I am to start in work then.

Chick added that while exploring the stock of Sienese dealers, he came upon the very picture he was about to copy:

> I went into an antiquity shop on the Via Rossi simply filled with junk, (four floors of it); But finally I was led into a smaller room and the first thing I saw was the same Memmi Madonna! It is a beauty and seems genuine enough and in fine state. I kept discreetly silent but asked the price, which was a hundred and sixty thousand lire. In addition thre was a St. Catherine called Neroccio which seemed real but repainted (I realize my judgments in these matters are immature and thoroughly unreliable) and a panel painted on both sides which, (so I thought), was a splendid forgery, the best I have seen so far. The actual painting was tremendously good but the crackle seemed to be of the scratched variety. I am keeping my ears open and mouth shut: I am fascinated by the forgery game.[8]

He had found a letter from Forbes waiting for him when he arrived in Siena, suggesting that "it might interest and amuse" him to undertake some business for the Fogg. He should meet with the executor of the estate of an American woman who had lived in a villa outside Florence and had offered the Fogg its choice of paintings in her collection. The prospect was complicated by the fact that her will also indicated that the pictures might be sold for the benefit of institutions other than Harvard. Like all museum directors, Forbes was concerned, he told Chick, with the perennial problem of "how we can get them without buying them." Chick was to look at this collection and report on its quality.

Forbes also asked him to help clarify a basic technical question that was still unanswered in the 1920s: When during the Renaissance did the method of painting on wet plaster (*buon fresco*) supplant the application of pigment to dry plaster (*fresco secco*)? And did Giotto ever paint in *buon fresco*? Chick should scrutinize Giotto's frescos at the Church of Santa Croce in Florence and at other sites in Assisi and Padua. He should examine the frescoes by Masaccio and Filippino Lippi at the Brancacci Chapel in the Church of Santa Maria del Carmine in Florence—and any other frescoes painted during the first half of the fourteenth century. He should look for the telltale joints on the surfaces of these paintings, revealing the end of a day's work, which could be seen from certain angles in paintings done in *buon fresco*. Forbes asked Chick to get photographs of these works and mark them in pencil with lines corresponding to each section.[9]

Chick was grateful for the assignments. "I have felt very much the need of something definite to do," he responded, "after my month of merely 'absorbing,' so to speak."

Chick's copy of the Memmi Madonna, Siena, 1924

Nevertheless, throughout the weeks he worked with Ioni, Chick continued "absorbing" in Siena's great public collections—the Pinacoteca in the Palazzo Buonsignori, where he could study works by Siena's greatest masters; the Palazzo Pubblico, with its famous allegorical frescoes by Ambrogio Lorenzetti; and the Duomo, the finest Gothic cathedral in Tuscany. He also haunted the dealers, acquiring cheap examples of early works that revealed their underpinnings, both for the course and for himself. He reported to Forbes that he had bought a Sienese Madonna of wood and gesso, a panel fragment showing a saint dressed in a robe of an unusual violet color that appealed to him, and, for an investment of five dollars, "a very ruined madonna on wood to which the gesso is hanging by its eyelashes, but the under painting and drawing is still discernible."[10]

Chick settled into a routine, working closely with Ioni, learning the lesser-known ways of tempera on panel and the more subtle techniques of fresco. But some secrets were not revealed. The door to one room in Ioni's house was always closed. Whenever Chick ventured down the hall toward that door, he was diverted by Ioni or one of his assistants. It was obvious that the forbidden room contained imitations in progress, which would eventually find their way into great houses and even museums. In Forbes's circle, it was often said that many of Ioni's paintings were in American collections—but under different names.[11]

Ioni's reticence was out of character. As early as 1903, one writer noted in an Italian art journal that often when Ioni was shown a forgery and asked whether it was his work, he would "indignantly complain that the imitation is not good enough to have been suspected as his."[12] For Chick, fascinated as he was by "the forgery game," Ioni was an entertaining blend of the eccentric charlatan and master craftsman.[13]

Chick experienced a more familiar brand of eccentricity when Laura Austin, who had been following her genealogical obsession in England, Scotland, and France, turned up in Siena. Taking a short break from his studies, Chick drove his mother to Assisi so that he could examine the frescoes there more critically, as Forbes had suggested. Laura had started expanding her own familiarity with old masters. She was not shy about asking for appointments with leading figures in the art world; her tiny leather notebooks were filling up with the names and addresses of dealers and museum officials, including the director of the Louvre. She was now aiming for very famous names and faces for her collection. Among her acquisitions in 1924 were a portrait of Robert Burns and a supposed masterpiece by Peter Paul Rubens, *The Holy Family*. Dealers were quick to provide exceptional "finds" when she marched into their shops, and unlike her son, she was no match for them. (In his memoirs, Ioni noted that the best customers were *nouveaux riches* and ignorant Americans.[14])

After checking on Chick, Laura departed again on her travels. She would spend the next several years wandering the Continent, making only occasional visits to Boston and Arthur, who quietly continued his medical work, resigned to his solitary life. In 1928 Laura would buy a seventeenth-century house in Antwerp, which she used as a base for extended trips and to house her growing collection of pictures and furniture.

Chick finished up his work with Ioni in January 1925 and prepared to return to the United States. As Forbes had foreseen, the months in Italy had given Chick intimate knowledge of the foundations of European painting, as well as increased technical facility with the materials of art. He also now knew firsthand about the operations of the old-master market and had an easy fluency in Italian. He came back to Cambridge more self-assured than ever.

His luggage was filled with material for the Fogg, including hundreds of sheets of *colla tontin,* a glue impossible to find in America, which was used for fixing paint onto surfaces.[15] He also had the finished copy of the Memmi Madonna that Ioni had supervised, an astonishingly convincing recreation of the picture. Forbes was so impressed with Chick's skill that he used the picture for years as a teaching device, alongside genuine works from the period, and eventually placed it in the Fogg's permanent collection.

Returning to Cambridge early in 1925, Chick was now a part-time staff member of the greatest training ground for the fine arts in the United States. He had arrived near the beginning of its most fertile era.

Fifty years earlier, in 1875, Harvard had become the first university in America to create a professorship in art history when its farsighted president, Charles Eliot, appointed his cousin, Charles Eliot Norton, to the position. For a quarter century, Norton lectured on Western culture, from antiquity through the Renaissance. He left an indelible mark on the undergraduates who took his course, Forbes and Berenson among them. Norton awakened his students to the realization that art was not a peripheral ornament to life but one of the most profound and revealing of all human expressions.[16] His survey was for many years the most popular course at Harvard.

Even so, in 1895 when the William Hayes Fogg Art Museum—built through a bequest from a Baltimore widow with no connections to the college—opened its doors on the edge of Harvard Yard, it was hardly a magnet for connoisseurs. Its collection consisted of little more than some Hudson River School landscapes, prints on deposit from Boston's Museum of Fine Arts, a small group of photographs, and a few plaster casts. Students could choose from only four fine arts courses. Despite Norton's popularity, the Harvard community as a whole was indifferent to art. Three decades later, by the time Chick became Forbes's assistant, the department had been completely transformed. Over forty courses were offered in the fine arts, and the Fogg had amassed the best teaching collection in any American university.[17]

This phenomenal growth would not have happened without the foresight and the zeal of two men who had already taken a personal interest in Chick—Edward Forbes and Paul Sachs.

It would be hard to imagine two people more different in appearance and temperament, and yet more united in purpose. Forbes was stately but unkempt, reserved, modest, and sometimes apparently lost in a daydream. Sachs was memorably short—just under five feet tall—round, well tailored, ebullient, and very punctual. Forbes was soft-spoken and kind; Sachs was prone to occasional but terrifying outbursts of rage. (Two oriental beasts were once installed in the courtyard of the Fogg, one smiling and the other growling, and instantly they were dubbed Edward and Paul.[18]) But Forbes and Sachs were devoted to each other and to their students, and formed one of the most influential partnerships in the history of American education. Sachs brought excitement, intensity, connoisseurship, and brilliant organizational skills to the Fogg program, but it was Forbes who provided the original conception.

Edward Forbes was born in 1873 on Naushon, the island in Buzzard's Bay off the coast of Massachusetts, collectively owned by the Forbes family. His father, William Hatheway Forbes, had organized the Bell Telephone Company with Alexander Graham Bell; and his mother, Edith Emerson Forbes, was the daughter of Ralph Waldo Emerson. The Forbeses were among the small group of distinguished old families, intertwined through long threads of kinship, education, and wealth, that were popularly known as "Boston Brahmins." Forbes was so well connected that once, when he tore his pants while visiting New York, he simply appeared at the Pierpont Morgan Library and asked its librarian, Belle Greene, for the loan of another pair from the closet of J. P. Morgan, Jr., who lived next door. Forbes also displayed the eccentricity of the Yankee aristocrat. In 1907, when he married the beautiful Margaret Laighton, a light-house keeper's daughter, the wedding took place in Manila at the mansion of his older brother William, the first civilian governor general of the Philippines. Forbes insisted on wearing tennis shoes to the ceremony and was persuaded only at the last minute that he should at least purchase a new pair of tennis shoes.[19]

He possessed the multiple accomplishments of the Boston gentleman of his generation. He sailed, he swam, he rode, and he hiked; he painted, wrote poetry, and played and composed music. But at first he was uncertain about where his interests might lead him. After earning his A.B. from Harvard in 1895, he pursued postgraduate studies in literature, history, and music, but found that Norton's compelling pronouncements on art stayed with him. In 1899, during an extended tour of Europe, he took up painting and bought his first Italian picture, a work attributed to Tintoretto, the sixteenth-century Venetian master. Because Forbes had no permanent home at the time, Norton's son Richard, then teaching in Rome, convinced him that he should loan or donate his growing collection of Renaissance art to the Fogg Art Museum.

Forbes returned to Cambridge in 1903. His expertise in art history, to say nothing of his family credentials, soon led to an invitation from the Boston Museum of Fine Arts to join its board of trustees, a position he would hold for more than sixty years. In 1904, not to be outdone, the Fogg invited him to join its visiting committee.

Like his grandfather Emerson, Forbes was a true visionary, but his particular vision went beyond Emersonian faith that human improvement could come through individual initiative and a closer study of nature. Forbes looked forward to an American civilization enriched and ennobled through a deeper knowledge of art. And he believed that Harvard could blaze that trail in the new century. With understated but irresistible force, he steered the Fogg's visiting committee toward making the museum a prominent component of the university. He steadily enlarged the collection with works of art that he, his family, and what became his vast network of collectors, most of them rich alumni, lent or gave to the museum. In 1909 Forbes was appointed director of the Fogg.

The collection became the touchstone of Forbes's mission, even though he was not happy with the museum that housed it. Later he described the Fogg as "a building with a lecture hall in which you could not hear, a gallery in which you could not see, working rooms in which you could not work, and a roof that leaked like a sieve."[20] But for the moment, these limitations were overshadowed by the growing number of masterpieces from many periods that he brought to the museum: Greek marbles and Oriental pictures, porcelains and prints, drawings, watercolors, and above all, European paintings, particularly Italian pictures from the thirteenth century to the Renaissance. By 1912 the

Fogg's holdings had grown so much that a renovation of the first two floors to increase exhibition space was necessary.

Meanwhile, Forbes became one of the world's pioneers in looking at the "inside" of paintings through the newly developed magic of the X ray. He developed into an expert in the detection of layers of restoration work, masterpieces hidden under later painted images, and outright forgeries. But it was his own eye and intuition that helped him as much as any machine.[21]

Such explorations reflected Forbes's concept of the Fogg as the "working laboratory" of the fine arts department. In an article written at the time Chick joined him, Forbes reiterated his unvarying theme:

> Those in charge of the policy of the Fogg Museum believe that students should come into actual contact with the works of art themselves. Book learning can be achieved by means of books. A certain amount of appreciation of art in visual terms can be gained by the study of photographs, but it is inspiration that breeds inspiration. When a student sees the actual work of art itself, if that work of art is explained in a stimulating way and is studied as a vital object in the chain of real experiences of real people, then art becomes living and the student can understand it as one of the great forms of the expression of human emotions.

"Living art" would be the credo of twentieth-century museums and, in a few short years, Chick Austin's personal rallying cry.

The Fogg's philosophy reflected the idealism of those who, in the aftermath of the horrors of the World War, envisioned a more civilized world guided by enlightened leaders, both political and intellectual. Forbes concluded his 1925 article by stating confidently that

> the Harvard Department of the Fine Arts, and its laboratory, the Fogg Art Museum, will be able to carry on their work in some measure to accord with their hopes and aspirations, and help to give to the Fine Arts their natural place in life; to make them a source of joy and inspiration—an element in a life of every nation which shall work for saneness and harmony, for "It is the love of the Beautiful that brings to order the world of the Gods."[22]

Like Berenson, Forbes never lost sight of one simple truth—that the reward of experiencing a work of art was the enhancement of life.

Paul Sachs soon became Forbes's equal partner in the effort to make the Fogg a leading disseminator of culture in America. A member of Harvard's

Paul Sachs and Edward Forbes with a bust of Victor Hugo
by Auguste Rodin, 1944

class of 1900, Sachs had developed a well-focused passion for the fine arts while studying at the Fogg. But for him, art was expected to be an avocation. He was the eldest of financier Samuel Sachs's three sons, and after graduation he dutifully joined the family's international investment banking firm in New York, Goldman Sachs. High finance had its advantages for an art lover. After closing a deal, he would treat himself to a new picture. His collecting of old masters became rigorous and obsessive, and he developed into a great connoisseur, but, unlike Forbes, Sachs had a taste for the new artists in the School of Paris. Invited to join the Fogg's visiting committee in 1911, he was soon one of the museum's most generous patrons, giving and lending large numbers of European paintings, prints, and drawings to the museum. In 1915, when Forbes asked him when he was going to join Harvard's fine arts department, Sachs did not hesitate. At the age of thirty-six, he moved to Cambridge with his wife and three daughters.

After teaching art history for a year at Wellesley College, Sachs was appointed assistant professor of fine arts at Harvard in 1917, then associate professor in 1922. His courses ranged from master drawings and prints to the history of French painting in the nineteenth century. In the spring of 1923, he began offering a course called "Museum Work and Problems," perhaps the first of its kind in the world.

Sachs shared Forbes's optimism about the place of the arts in American life, declaring in 1927 that "the growing enthusiasm for art, whether in collecting, or establishing museums, or encouraging the growth of fine arts departments in colleges, is one of the most hopeful features of our civilization." [23] Like Forbes, he foresaw a new role for the American art museum itself, declaring that "in the twentieth century in America a museum should be not only a treasure house, but also an educational institution."[24] This emphasis on public education, though not unique to Forbes and Sachs, was instilled in Chick and his contemporaries at the Fogg with powerful results for the country.

By the time Chick took Forbes's course in 1924, Forbes and Sachs had so expanded the Fogg collections and its ambitious teaching program that the university authorities finally recognized the inadequacy of the building. Harvard that year approved a two-million-dollar drive to build an entirely new Fogg Art Museum with modern facilities, based on the requirements specified by Forbes and Sachs themselves. In 1924 and 1925 they were preoccupied with fundraising activities, which required constant travel. Forbes and Sachs so often worked in tandem, both inside and outside their development efforts, that they became known by a series of nicknames—"the Heavenly Twins" (from the title of a best-selling novel published earlier in the century), "the Happy Beggars" (attributed to Bishop William Lawrence, the prominent Episcopal clergyman), or, as Harvard's President Lowell once called them publicly, "the Exuberant Mendicants."[25]

Watching Forbes and Sachs raise money from patrons and friends, and seeing a new museum take shape from the ground up, would be as valuable to Chick as any classroom experience. Nevertheless, in early 1925 he was learning the practical workings of the "Methods and Processes of Italian Painting" course, which Forbes described that spring as "designed especially for museum men and collectors who need an understanding of how pictures were painted in order to take proper care of them—for it is a well-known fact that many paintings of unsurpassable beauty are going to pieces in our modern museums and houses due to lack of knowledge as to how to care for them under the conditions of to-day."[26] Chick, at twenty-four, was in effect helping to prepare his own generation to be stewards of the masterpieces in American collections.

For the next three years, Chick was a fascinating and cosmopolitan presence at the Fogg. Coupled with his dashing appearance was the knowledge that he had been in some remote part of the Sudan, digging in the desert with the illustrious Reisner, that he knew the great museums of Europe intimately, and had worked with famous copyists and forgers in Italy.

He often gave demonstrations of fresco-making to undergraduates in classes taught by other art history professors. Julien Levy, soon one of Chick's best friends and a few years later the foremost surrealist dealer in America, saw him in action during that first semester of teaching. Levy was then a seventeen-year-old freshman, a student in Arthur Pope's course, "The Historical Techniques of Painting." Chick showed the class how to slake lime in fresco-making. As he shoveled plaster energetically into a tray of water, wet compound splashed and a fine powder billowed up around him. Many years later, Levy wrote: "I remember him vividly: all in white, with white spattered on his hair and on his face, with an ambiguous smile, almost melancholy, as he faced his students. This was the origin of my vision of A. Everett Austin as the clown 'Gilles,' painted by Watteau."[27]

The gaiety of Gilles, the mysterious figure of the commedia dell'arte, was far more visible in Chick than the melancholy. John McAndrew—later an assistant in Levy's New York gallery, a curator at the Museum of Modern Art, and a professor of art and architectural history at Vassar and Wellesley—met Chick in 1924 when they both took Forbes's course. As a postgraduate student at Harvard, he observed Chick's gift for extracting hilarity from the moment: "He'd tell you he went around the corner to buy a package of cigarettes, and it was the best story you heard all week."[28]

Chick was forming close ties with many of those who would be part of his inner circle. Henry-Russell Hitchcock, later America's most distinguished architectural historian, met Chick as early as 1924 while studying art and architecture at the Fogg. With his red beard hiding a bad skin condition, Hitchcock was a tall, heavyset, slovenly, long-winded, but somehow endearing young man who spoke rather formally in a booming voice. Chick prized his intellect, forgave his awkwardness, and enjoyed his sense of humor. From Hitchcock's point of view, Chick was a delightful companion, clever and discerning, someone who appreciated his considerable erudition and entertained him at the same time. Hitchcock was something of a burden to his friends in those years and so was doubly pleased that a man as attractive and stylish as Chick liked him. "He had that quality that great actors have," Hitchcock remembered long after. "He was conventionally a handsome man, but that's not really the point. He had charisma. He was quite witty and what seemed at the time slightly outrageous, but by present-day standards not outrageous at all."[29]

It was Hitchcock who, later in the 1920s, arranged a luncheon at Boston's Copley Plaza to bring Chick and future architect Philip Johnson together. Looking at Chick from the perspective of a Harvard undergraduate, Johnson thought he "knew everything, like a sort of a god."[30]

Chick was also introduced to a young composer named Virgil Thomson, who had taken his degree from Harvard in 1923 after serving in the war, and

Glamour at the Fogg: Chick Austin shortly before getting a job in "the 'all-time' line," 1927

had studied music in Paris with Nadia Boulanger. By the time Chick met him, Thomson already knew Picasso, Cocteau, and the contemporary French composers, including Arthur Honegger, Darius Milhaud, and Francis Poulenc. After a season in New York, he was back in Cambridge in 1925 as a teaching assistant, writing music and playing the organ on weekends at a church near Worcester. Thomson was to return that September to Paris, where he would live until the fall of France in 1940, but he frequently sailed back and forth between Europe and America. He had a knack for positioning himself at the intersection of art, music, theater, and dance in the transatlantic culture of the 1930s. Short, fair, balding, and baby-faced, with a high but commanding voice, he possessed a searing intelligence and an acerbic wit. He was strongly attracted to what he later called "the especial flamboyance in both intellect and character of the art history group that centered around Chick Austin." Thomson, who usually disdained superlatives, had no doubt that, of the gifted people based at Harvard's fine arts department in that era, Chick was the "most spectacular of all."[31] He was, Thomson said, "a sheer delight for wholeness as a man. He had talent, taste, energy, good looks and pride in them. Passion, too, and affection and warmth and loyalty."[32]

The bright young men at Harvard with whom Chick was developing relationships were all independent thinkers who reflected the explorations and experiments of their consciously modern generation. They were inventing the new American artistic milieu, and they were inventing themselves. They cared little for convention. Daring in their artistic and intellectual pursuits, many were unfettered in their love affairs and liaisons, whether heterosexual or homosexual. Beyond their natural preferences and predilections, sexual freedom was part of their revolt against the constraints of what they considered a bourgeois society.

Those who found fulfillment with members of their own sex generally accepted society's dictum that they be discreet. Not only was it good manners to refrain from discussing one's private life in company, but open homosexuality could be dangerous socially and professionally. At the same time, of course, the homosexual community was a brotherhood, a secret society with its own loyalties and bonds that greatly helped its members throughout their careers.

Chick appealed strongly to men and to women, and he was attracted to both sexes. "You'd fall in love with him the minute you'd meet him," Philip Johnson remarked. "All ages and sexes and colors."[33] Unlike some of his contemporaries, Chick was cheerfully uninhibited about his bisexuality, and could turn his love life into one more source of entertainment for his intimates. A story he loved to tell on himself as an undergraduate was about an old Irish chambermaid who opened the door to his room one morning, discovered him in bed with a young man, one of his classmates, and quickly departed. Seeing her later in the day, Chick said, "Oh, Mrs. Riley, you must think I'm awfully spoiled." She stoutly retorted, "You can't spoil a rotten egg, Mr. Austin."[34]

But despite his almost limitless capacity for fun, no one worked harder than Chick when he found something that interested him. In the "laboratory" of art at the Fogg, with his eye for quality, his intelligence, his enthusiasm, and his ability to inspire, Chick more than fulfilled Forbes's expectations. Forbes invited him to assist again with the Methods course in the spring of 1926.

In September 1925, with a semester's break before resuming work for Forbes, Chick revisited the idea that architecture might be his true calling. He entered the Harvard School of Architecture with a full five-course load. After only a few weeks, however, he disappeared from the classrooms, having taken a job with the painter Barry Faulkner. Faulkner had been commissioned to paint scenes on canvas wall coverings in the entrance hall of Kingsley Porter's Cambridge home, Elmwood, an eighteenth-century house in which the poet James Russell Lowell had spent his life. Painting the murals, which depicted the exterior of the house and its gardens, turned out to be more fun than sitting in a lecture hall; and with the self-absorption of the mercurial child, Chick paid no attention to his truancy. It was not until November that he finally wrote to George Edgell, dean of the school, lamely explaining his absence: "As I have already lost so much time in working for Mr. Faulkner in his decorations and will need much more time in my work for Mr. Forbes the second half year than I had supposed—I think it would be best for me to resign from the Architectural school for the rest of the year and to begin anew in the fall."[35]

Thinking practically of Chick's future, Forbes tried to persuade him not to abandon his architectural studies,[36] but soon after it was clear that Chick had made up his mind, Forbes heard of a job teaching painting at a girls' school in Cambridge and suggested that he would benefit from the experience. Chick expressed interest, Forbes recommended him for the job, but then, blithely wielding his paintbrush at Elmwood, Chick never followed through. By late November, even the kindly Forbes was irked at his lack of consideration. "Where have you been all this time?" he wrote. "I have been waiting all these weeks for you, and have been embarrassed at not giving Miss Childs a definite answer."[37]

But Forbes never stopped believing in Chick. He was the one person who always encouraged him, defended him, and stepped in with decisive help throughout his career. In Forbes, Chick had found a father figure.

Forbes soon asked him to help with another project. That fall the Carnegie Institution in Washington, D.C., had asked Forbes to go to Mexico early in 1926 to study the conservation problems of wall and ceiling paintings at the Mayan ruins of Chichén Itzá in the northern Yucatán. The site had been a religious and political center from the seventh through the twelfth centuries, and its extensive ruins were among the best-preserved examples of Classic Mayan and Postclassic Toltec architecture in Mexico. Intense sunlight and tropical downpours threatened to destroy newly uncovered wall paintings, and the painted ceiling of a chapel had recently fallen down in large blocks. The expedition had naturally turned to Forbes as one of the few people in America who had made a career of studying the problems of wall paintings. Forbes asked Chick to accompany him.

Plans changed in early January when Forbes's sister entered the last stages of a fatal illness. Entrusting Chick with sole responsibility for the trip, Forbes wrote detailed instructions about the procedures to be tried on the wall paintings, adding some practical advice: "Be sure to take quinine with you; also mosquito netting that you can tie up with tape over your bed. Never drink water that is not boiled. Take a bottle of oil of citronella to keep mosquitos away."

Chick had a great deal to accomplish in the month he was allotted for the work. He was to test glues and fixatives on unimportant sections of the wall paintings; then he was to try transferring some of the best examples onto canvas and bring them back to the Fogg. He promised to stay in close touch by telegraph.[38]

Arriving at the Mexican coastal city of Progresso on January 22, Chick was met by Dr. Sylvanus Morley, the distinguished archaeologist in charge of the excavation. Together they drove to Chichén Itzá. There Chick began work on the wall paintings amid the extraordinary remnants of Mayan civilization—the temples of the Warriors and the Jaguars, the Platform of the Tigers and Eagles—all vividly depicted in reds, greens, yellows, and blues, with images of priests and fighting men, exotic plants and wild beasts, and the god Quetzalcatl in the form of a feathered serpent. Chick treated the painted surfaces, but his attempts to transfer the frescoes failed because of the unending dampness, and he and Forbes did not take up the project the next year. Yet, just as on the Egypt trip, the unfamiliar atmosphere inspired Chick to open his paint box, and he produced handsome sketches and watercolors of the ruins. Forbes found these so appealing that, for years, three of them decorated the walls of his office at the Fogg.

Chick returned to Cambridge in time to help Forbes with the remainder of the Methods course. He also studied painting with Denman Ross in the fine arts department. Toward the end of the semester, Forbes arranged for Chick to accompany Harold Woodbury Parsons, the "European representative" of the Cleveland Museum of Art, on his annual summer trip to Europe. Parsons, who had attended Harvard briefly years earlier, was in effect a private dealer, a go-between for American museums and collectors in the European market. They were to meet up with William Milliken, then curator of paintings and decorative arts at the Cleveland museum and later its preeminent director, and Theodore Sizer, another curator at Cleveland.

Parsons wrote Sachs, who was finishing a year abroad, about the forthcoming trip, not realizing that Sachs had known Chick since his undergraduate days. "They say he is talented, but needs to work & study, and might work into Western Museum work. So he is to tag onto Milliken and me this summer. I have seen him only twice; but he seems very alert and intelligent."[39] Sachs replied that Chick was "indeed alert and intelligent and has the capacity, I am sure, for real and distinguished growth."[40]

Chick sailed with Parsons on the *Rotterdam* on June 5, and they joined Sachs in Paris at the end of the month. Then Chick went off on his own to England to attend performances of Diaghilev's Ballets Russes, where he could again experience the most imaginative expressions of contemporary art. He promised to rendezvous with his assigned mentors in Italy later in July. In fact, he and Harold Parsons were not compatible. Chick found Parsons insufferably pretentious, and Parsons thought the younger man frivolous, an impression Chick may have encouraged for the pleasure of annoying him. Parsons reported to Sachs in August that Chick had gone his own way in Paris, that he had seen Chick briefly in Venice, but that "he was surrounded by a gang, consequently I don't know his plans or purposes or whether he has either." He felt that Chick's salvation would be to return to Egyptology. "What Chick needs is hard and constant work and a strong hand on his neck. He is an extremely likeable fellow and has no end of natural talent." However, Parsons concluded, "museum work is the last thing he could manage, and, consequently, I can do nothing for him."[41]

A month later Parsons continued his finger-wagging to Sachs:

By the way, in Venice I ran into Chick Austin again, but it was hard to see him aside from his gang. However, I did finally have a good talk with him. He tells me that he cannot go back to Egypt again on account of some intestinal illness he had there. I cannot convince myself that he will ever make a museum man, because he is not a student by nature nor has he any steadfast purpose. His summer has been quite unprofitable, I should think and, apparently, he is returning to his dilettante life in Boston. If you could find him a whole-time job I think you would be doing him the greatest kindness in the world. As an interior decorator I think he would be a success, but not as a museum man nor as a creative artist.[42]

Austin had already confided to Forbes that he had little respect for Parsons. From the Grand Hotel Luna in Venice, on August 17, he wrote: "By this time, you have, I suppose—learned that the Partnership of Parsons and Co was dissolved about July 1st. I wrote you of it—but decided not to send you the letter—as it seemed a bit too much. I am afraid that P.s interest in art is chiefly social—conversational and financial."[43]

Chick was bound to break away from Parsons's supervision. He was no longer the fledgling who had studied Italian art in 1924. On this trip he had the expertise and confidence to expand his knowledge as he chose, and if Parsons encountered him only in social settings after they had separated, it was because Chick allowed himself time to sample the seductive diversions of the great European cities. From Paris to Berlin, from Vienna to Venice, Europe in the midtwenties was at its most tantalizing and unconventional. It had become the playground of the very rich and those fortunate expatriates of more modest means who could take advantage of the superior buying power of the English pound sterling or the American dollar. New bars, nightclubs, and cabarets offered every imaginable entertainment to a sophisticated clientele in an atmosphere of jazz, cigarette smoke, abundant alcohol, and sexual license.

But Chick was not neglecting art history. As he wrote to Forbes, "I have since been doing my best going over old fields and searching out a few new ones."[44] Agnes Rindge, who was to create an advanced fine arts department at Vassar and served briefly as a vice director of the Museum of Modern Art, was also doing postgraduate work at the Fogg in those years. One of Chick's closest confidantes, she remembered that she and Chick and others from the Fogg spent many days ferreting out undiscovered works in Europe. They dragged batteries connected to automobile headlights into obscure churches to examine pictures in dark corners, and they took photographs of their finds to bring back to Cambridge. They were encouraged by the Harvard faculty to cast away their timidity. Kingsley Porter would tell his students that if they wanted to get a photograph of an object in a country church, they should politely ask permission and, whether or not it was granted, "Just climb right up on the altar and take it!" Rindge described the extraordinary excitement they felt in their discoveries. "It was *uncharted*. Everything was a new horizon—things were still happening. That's why it was so exhilarating." They were continuously refining their perception of quality. "You didn't get it from books," she said, echoing Forbes and Sachs. "You got it off the wall."[45]

Although Parsons implied that Chick's "gang" was made up of young sybarites, students in art history ran into one another constantly in Europe during the summer, forming and reforming groups. "One misses none of the familiar Fogg faces!" Chick wrote Forbes from Venice, where he painted views of the city and visited churches and palazzi with Hitchcock.[46] The chance to tour Venice with someone like Hitchcock, who had already developed an encyclopedic knowledge of European architecture, was a precious opportunity.

The gaudy façades of Venice would never lose their appeal for Chick. "The architecture," as Virgil Thomson put it, "is a masked ball, a costume ball, and everything goes together. Chick liked that. Everybody likes the 'anything goes' atmosphere in Venice. Venice is a big caravansary."[47]

From Venice, Chick planned to visit Ravenna, Bologna, and Verona, looking at art and painting watercolors, and then return to Cambridge by October first. Uppermost in his mind, however, was beginning a career. Though he had agreed that, when he returned in the fall, he would copy a picture at the Fogg by the fifteenth-century Venetian painter Carlo Crivelli, he was now twenty-five and eager to find a full-time museum position, apparently with no concern about being far from Boston. "Are there any 'jobs' in sight?" he asked Forbes. "What do I hear about San Diego and Fort Wayne? Of course I want to do the Crivelli first; but I must get something in the 'all time' line—and (fortunately) not with WP's [Harold W. Parsons] stamp of approval on the recommendation." A few pages later, he returned to his underlying concern: "If you hear anything of a way to make me useful—would you mind awfully writing to me about it? Yrs. Chick."[48]

Forbes replied somewhat cryptically that he had no knowledge of needs in "Western" museums, but promised to let Chick know if something turned up.[49]

Now certain that he wanted to make a career of museum work, Chick took Paul Sachs's museum course in the fall of 1926. It met at Sachs's house, Shady Hill, the former home of Charles Eliot Norton, where Forbes had lived briefly. Chick was joined in the long library by an extraordinary group of future leaders of the arts: Russell Hitchcock; James Rorimer, later director of the Metropolitan Museum of Art; Alfred H. Barr, Jr., soon to be the founding director of the Museum of Modern Art; Jere Abbott, who worked with Barr at the beginning of the Modern and later directed the Smith College Museum of Art; and Kirk

Askew, one of Chick's close friends, who would head the New York branch of Durlacher Brothers, the noted London old-master dealer.

The Museum course was so thorough in laying out for its hand-picked post-graduate students the techniques of running a museum—cajoling trustees, courting donors, matching wits with dealers, organizing exhibitions, and completing the transformation of relatively static repositories of pictures and objects into vibrant centers of public education—that some of its most august veterans were known to keep their class notes in desk drawers, ready for immediate consultation.

At Shady Hill, Sachs would report on his most recent encounters in the art world, which were then discussed and analyzed, but he also took Chick and the other students on field trips to the homes of the greatest collectors in Boston, New York, and Philadelphia. In addition to first-class meals, the students were given tours of the collections and encouraged to scrutinize and discuss the objects. Sachs also got them into the vaults of museums and the back rooms of major international art dealers in New York—Duveen, Durlacher, Knoedler, Seligmann, Wildenstein—where they were introduced to the managers and owners.

He steered them toward contemporary art as well. "It seemed to me important," he wrote later, "to have the Fogg, as a living museum, offer students contact with the artistic production of our time—the world of actuality."[50] He himself collected pictures by Picasso and Matisse, and he emphasized to students that the intellectual processes for evaluating modern art were the same as those required for older works. Before the end of the decade, Sachs would be the adviser to the student-led Harvard Society for Contemporary Art and a central figure in the creation of the Museum of Modern Art in New York.

Sachs was an overwhelming presence: "He was filled with vigor and enthusiasm and occasionally rage and excitement," said Agnes Mongan. "You could come in the front of this building [the Fogg] and you'd know by the way the building was vibrating whether Uncle Paul was inside or not." He was not a typical professor of art history, composed, conservative, and aloof. He was incapable of restraining his intense response to beauty. Once, while reading his lecture to a class of undergraduates about the wonders of a picture by Cézanne, he glanced at the slide projected beside him, turned back to the class and exploded: "My God, just look at it!"[51] At the same time, he had no patience for the second-rate. One future museum director remembered that at the gallery of a leading New York dealer, "he picked up a recently acquired drawing attributed to Watteau and said, 'You call that Watteau? I call it impudence!' And he was out the door with his twenty students."[52] Sachs by his very nature demonstrated that professional expertise could, and should, go hand in hand with passion.

Throughout the second semester of Sachs's course, Chick assisted Edward Forbes for a third time. This was the last year the Methods course would be taught at Gerry's Landing. The new Fogg building was nearing completion during that spring of 1927. It was a large, symmetrical red brick Federal Revival structure, with an inner court in the Renaissance style rising four stories to a large skylight. It offered greatly expanded gallery space, offices, a large art library, proper lecture rooms, and an up-to-date studio for the "Egg and Plaster" course.

Chick was invited to write an article about the facilities for the course in *The Arts* magazine, to appear in the July 1927 issue. After describing the techniques practiced in the course, he noted that "the primary importance of this performance lies not so much in the production of a work of art, as in the training of the student to a better understanding and judgment of a given work, through a closer knowledge of the way in which it was or should have been produced." He emphasized the effect the course would have on the students' future: "These studies will prove of extreme importance to the man or woman who is contemplating either painting, museum work or even the making of a collection as a career."[53] Chick was now speaking as a voice of the Fogg, a true disciple of Forbes and Sachs. For their part, they had both come to see him as one of the most gifted young men ever to emerge from the program they had created.

The new Fogg was scheduled to open in June of 1927, but Chick did not expect to be working there. After nine years in the cradle and the crucible of Harvard, he knew it was time to find something in what he had described to Forbes the previous summer as "the 'all time' line." Perhaps a curatorship in European paintings at one of the newer museums would be available for the fall. But in the second week of May, Forbes came to him with startling news.

CHAPTER FOUR

From Harvard to the Land
of Steady Habits

These descendants of Ozias were not distinguished by
the more enterprising qualities of the pioneer type.
Once they had made the great effort of crossing the
Atlantic in the "Lion," the family had apparently had
enough of pioneering for a period of three hundred
years, because most of the direct descendants of this
branch have remained within a radius of a few miles of
the town of Hartford, Connecticut, during all that
time. . . . Now they seem faced with radical changes in
their habits.

—Philip L. Goodwin, *Rooftrees*

For his favored students, Edward Forbes was an astute career counselor.
Like a kindly god sitting on the Olympus of Harvard, he quietly manip-
ulated New England's old-boy network, the web of families, fortunes,
and scholastic ties that had spun out the fate of generations of America's intellectual elite. He pulled the strings and placed his band of protégés in
positions where they could help shape the country's artistic future. For Chick,
he had found a post of tantalizing promise.

When Forbes spoke to him on that spring day in 1927, Chick discovered
that, nine months earlier, almost at the moment that he was vacationing in
Venice, painting watercolors, Forbes had been sailing off Cataumet, Massachusetts. There he had seen Charles Goodwin, a scion of Connecticut's colonial
aristocracy. Forbes and Goodwin were contemporaries, acquainted through
Harvard connections and their mutual love of boats. Recently elected president
of Hartford's Wadsworth Atheneum, the oldest public art museum in the United
States, Goodwin had asked Forbes for advice in modernizing his institution.

Charles Archibald Goodwin was a great yachtsman, but he was no connoisseur of the fine arts. "His idea of how to go through a museum," his daughter Dorothy recalled, "was to walk in the front door, close both eyes tight, and run as fast as he could to the back door, and out, and then he'd done the museum."[1] He had, however, welcomed command of the Wadsworth Atheneum. More than a civic duty, it was a family inheritance. His father, the Reverend Francis Goodwin, had been the insurance capital's leading benefactor. He had led a crusade to rejuvenate a faltering Atheneum in the 1890s and was rewarded with the presidency of the board, which he held on to for twenty-nine years. Charles Goodwin's grandfather, Major James Goodwin, a rich merchant and businessman, had been a founder of the Atheneum in 1841 when the Hartford philanthropist and art patron Daniel Wadsworth proposed giving the city his Main Street property and part of his fortune for the establishment of a gallery of fine arts—this, three decades before either the Metropolitan or Boston's Museum of Fine Arts was begun. Ten generations back, Goodwin's ancestors, headed by Ozias Goodwin, had made the trek in 1636 from New Towne (later Cambridge), Massachusetts, to the west bank of the Connecticut River, where they founded Hartford and Connecticut itself. The very ground the Atheneum stood upon, before it came into Wadsworth's family in the eighteenth century, was originally Goodwin land, purchased from Sequasson, chief of the Saukiogs. Three centuries later, the Goodwins still dominated Hartford and regarded the management of the Wadsworth Atheneum as reserved exclusively for them and their social equals.

Charles Goodwin looked like a board president. Just fifty in 1926, he was courtly and condescending. Tall, heavyset, graying, with a handsome, rubicund face, he dressed with understated formality and rarely found it necessary to raise his resonant voice. One of the best-known lawyers in the state, he was a product of New England's upper-class educational system—St. Paul's, Yale (class of 1898), and Harvard Law School. He had founded the firm of Shipman & Goodwin in 1919 with his mentor, Arthur Leffingwell Shipman, Sr., a member of the circle that ruled the museum and the town. Goodwin had been executive secretary to two Connecticut governors, a Republican candidate for that office himself, and a director of banks, insurance companies, and charitable institutions. His most lasting achievement was as the founder of Hartford's Metropolitan District Commission, an innovative system of reservoirs and sewage treatment plants that assured the area a supply of pure water in perpetuity. Elected to the Atheneum's board in 1907, when his father was still at the helm, he was made treasurer in 1921 and president in April 1926. He was determined to improve the operations of the Atheneum, as his father had done before him.

At Cataumet, Goodwin told Forbes that the museum was on the brink of a transformation. Major gifts in the last twenty years had tilted a nineteenth-century atheneum—a cultural hodge-podge of an art gallery, two libraries, a natural history collection, and a historical society—irreversibly toward a fine arts museum. In 1905 Elizabeth Hart Jarvis Colt, widow of the Hartford firearms magnate Sam Colt and a patron of the arts, had bequeathed the museum her art collection and funds for a new wing to house it. Two years later, Hartford-born J. Pierpont Morgan had given another, far grander building in memory of his father, Junius, a founder of the Atheneum. First cousin of the Reverend Francis Goodwin, the financier was then president of the Metropolitan Museum of Art and the greatest art collector alive. In 1917, four years after his death, more than a thousand objects from his estate were bestowed on the museum, instantly lifting it out of its provincial niche. Most recently, in 1926, Charles Goodwin and his brother William had convinced J. P. Morgan, Jr. (Cousin Jack), to buy Wallace Nutting's highly coveted collection of "Pilgrim Century" New England furniture and decorative arts—the finest in the United States—for the Atheneum.

Now two other benefactions promised further changes. In 1918 Samuel Putnam Avery, Jr., a New York art dealer and philanthropist who had retired to Hartford, gave the museum a quarter of a million dollars for a third new building. The Avery Fund had more than doubled in the succeeding nine years, and the trustees were beginning to talk of launching another building program. Equally momentous was the will of Frank Sumner, the rags-to-riches head of the Hartford-Connecticut Trust Company, who had died in 1924. It declared that on the death of his widow (now in failing health), his estate of over a million dollars would come to the Atheneum as an endowment fund solely for the purchase of "choice paintings." Very few American museums had such a fund in those years. Given the many opportunities in the art market and the buying power of the dollar, Goodwin foresaw a great future for the Atheneum as an art museum.

To make way for the changes, he had moved swiftly, reorganizing the Atheneum corporation, streamlining the museum's administration, creating an executive committee for the first time, and reducing the number of other trustee committees. He had also strengthened the power of the president and did not relinquish the purse strings. For twenty of his twenty-eight years as president, he would continue to serve as treasurer—the only instance of such dual control in the museum's history, one that later would be considered an unacceptable conflict of interest in the museum world.

Next he had turned to rejuvenating the staff. The director, a short, dapper, bespectacled librarian of nearly seventy named Frank Gay, had worked at the institution since the American centennial. It was obviously time for him to step aside and devote himself to the Atheneum's rare book division, the Watkinson Library, which he had headed for thirty years. Goodwin wanted a young man with the finest modern museum training to chart the Atheneum's course. Before the year was out, Goodwin deftly fulfilled Frank Gay's fondest dream by getting him elected to the board in return for a promise that his resignation as director "could be had at any time."[2]

Goodwin asked Edward Forbes to propose a new director. After visiting Hartford early in 1927, Forbes sent Goodwin a long letter, listing six men he regarded as good candidates for the job, explaining that he had been influenced by Paul Sachs in the order of the names: "Professor Sachs has given a course at Harvard, training men for Museum work and he is a very good judge of men." The first choice was Theodore Sizer, curator of prints and drawings and oriental art at the Cleveland Museum of Art, where he seemed likely to remain. Forbes therefore suggested that "you will probably have to make up your mind to take a young man and give him a chance to develop, and then if he does not develop well, get rid of him and get a new man because there is not a great supply of mature men like Sizer."

The second name on the list was Chick's. Forbes described him with the perception of the experienced teacher, expressing faith in his potential without hiding his faults:

> Mr. A. E. Austin, Jr. received his degree from Harvard in 1924, but he is somewhat older than his year of graduation would indicate, for when in College he had some difficulties with the College Office because he was a little independent and would only work on the courses which interested him. His family decided to send him to Egypt to work with Professor Reisner of the Harvard-Museum of Fine Arts Expedition. Professor Reisner, as you may know, is one of the two or three most distinguished Egyptologists living. Austin became interested in the work there and waked up and did very well and Reisner thought highly of him.

Forbes enthusiastically traced Chick's success at the Fogg, mentioning his studies in Italy and his work on the preservation of Mayan ruins in Mexico: "He is an attractive man with brains and good taste," he concluded, "and I think he has the making of a very good Museum man. He has a very distinct gift for painting in addition. He has not as yet proved himself, however, and his tendency is to be a little bit flighty and irresponsible, but I am sure that he is the sort of man who would instantly settle down and make good if he had responsibility."

Chick's competitors merited less comment. The only other serious contender was Henry S. Francis, then an assistant in the department of prints at Boston's Museum of Fine Arts and soon to be Sizer's replacement in Cleveland.

Forbes found two other young men noteworthy, Henry-Russell Hitchcock and Alfred Barr, but judged them unsuitable for Hartford. Hitchcock, he said, was "a rather erratic person with a brilliant min[d] . . . an excellent scholar, but I am not sure how much I should trust his judgment at the present time in the selection of works of art." As for Barr, Forbes confessed, "I suggest his name with a little more hesitation than most of the others because I think he is rather egotistical and some people like him while others do not. He certainly has brains and capacity. We gave him an opportunity to lecture at the Fogg Museum on Modern Art the other day. I am sorry to say that the lecture was rather a disappointment."

Having thus disposed of the future dean of American architectural historians and the future founding director of the Museum of Modern Art, Forbes offered to have a luncheon in Cambridge so that Goodwin could meet Chick Austin and Henry Francis.[3] Instead, wanting nothing but the best for Hartford—and used to getting his way—Goodwin wrote in February to the top man on the list, Theodore Sizer, then in Florence. He hoped to persuade him to leave Cleveland, only to discover that he had just accepted a job at Yale as professor of art history and curator of paintings and sculpture. Goodwin was disappointed, but true to his alma mater. "No good Yale man," he told Sizer, "could be sorry to feel that you are connected with the Art Museum there."[4]

In April, Forbes again offered to set up a luncheon with Austin and Francis, but as Forbes had ranked Austin highest among the available men, Goodwin replied that trustees would offer him the job, "simply wishing before we close with him an opportunity to meet and talk with him."[5] In May, at Sachs's suggestion, he invited Forbes to become the "Honorary General Curator or Director" to give Austin and the Atheneum the benefit of his judgment and experience. Goodwin explained that there were only three trustees' meetings a year, but that "Mr. Austin could always run up and talk with you at Cambridge."[6] Forbes answered that he might accept the offer "experimentally" for a year. Goodwin understandably felt more comfortable hiring an untried man of twenty-six, knowing that Forbes would be watching over him.

Chick, of course, was the last to know. "I have not spoken to Mr. Austin about this matter at all yet," Forbes reminded Goodwin, "and I also feel it might be better, if you decide to offer him the position after you see him, to try him for one year, for he is young and still has his spurs to win."[7]

Forbes then told Chick about the opportunity awaiting him and, wasting no time, invited Goodwin and other Atheneum trustees to meet the two of them at the Fogg a few days later, on May 26. Goodwin was accompanied by George Gay, a wealthy Hartford dry-goods merchant and a leading American print collector who was chairman of the art committee, and Archibald Welch, president of the Phoenix Mutual Life Insurance Company and chairman of the house committee. A tour of the Fogg was followed by a luncheon at Forbes's house.[8]

Chick impressed the Hartford delegation with his intelligence, good looks, and patrician manner. He seemed cut from the same cloth as they. He was, after all, the son of a prominent Boston physician. He had been educated at the proper schools in America and Europe. His intimate knowledge of European culture from childhood and his fluency in four languages made him doubly attractive. And if he told them about his early summers spent sailing *The Flying Dutchman* at Harpswell, he would have warmed their nautical hearts. They invited him to visit the Atheneum for what was certainly the first time, as it was never on the itinerary of students at the Fogg.

When he came to Hartford on June 8, Chick found an art museum that jostled for space with three other institutions living incestuously under the Atheneum's jurisdiction: the Connecticut Historical Society, the Watkinson Library, and the Hartford Public Library. These expanding entities were housed in four connected buildings, each two stories high, covering a city block on Main Street.

The Atheneum was a lexicon of architectural styles. On the left, at the corner of Main Street and Atheneum Square North, stood the original Gothic Revival structure of tawny granite, begun in 1842—a square building with six castellated towers, battlements, and a portico of three pointed arches—a temple to Athena that looked like a cross between a fortress and a church. Extending to the rear was the Watkinson Library, a gloomy post–Civil War edifice of dark red brick, topped with brownstone battlements and a long peaked roof. To the right of the old Wadsworth building was the Colt Memorial wing of 1910, built of gray granite in the Tudor Revival style, its oversize bay window ornamented with a marble frieze glorifying the instruments of war. Finally, adjoining the Colt building was the massive Morgan Memorial, a Beaux-Arts mausoleum in pink marble, finished in 1915.

Two relics of Daniel Wadsworth stood a few steps from the Watkinson Library: the brick house his father built him in 1796, now called the Atheneum Annex, where small exhibitions were held; and his wooden barn of 1827, its façade reminiscent of a Palladian villa, which rested incongruously at the base of the Travelers Insurance Company's skyscraper of thirty-four stories, built in 1919, the tallest structure between Boston and New York.

Although once shown in a sepulchral gallery in the Wadsworth building, the Atheneum's art collection now filled the Colt and Morgan Memorials. The public entered the museum through the Morgan wing, passing through a tall curved marble portal flanked by elaborate wrought-iron gates, into an imposing front lobby featuring nine varieties of marble, a double staircase, and a stained-glass skylight. This opened into Tapestry Hall, a barrel-vaulted space lined with sculpture, American furniture, and eighteenth-century French tapestries on loan from the Morgan family. Along each side were three doors, framed in marble, leading to smaller galleries. The second floor contained spacious

The Wadsworth Atheneum, Hartford, c. 1920

paintings galleries at either end, joined by a series of rooms that ran along the outside walls of the great hall.

Here in the Morgan building, Chick saw works from the three original sources of the Atheneum's collection. There was Daniel Wadsworth's personal collection of landscapes by Thomas Cole, father of the Hudson River School. From the estate of painter John Trumbull (Wadsworth's uncle by marriage), the museum founders had bought five half-life-size copies of his Revolutionary War scenes, including *The Battle of Bunker's Hill* and *The Declaration of Independence,* famous from the earlier (and much superior) versions in the Capitol rotunda in Washington. And there were fifty pictures from the American Academy of the Fine Arts in New York, the earliest school of its kind in the United States, which had conveniently folded while the Atheneum was being built. These ranged from Sir Thomas Lawrence's full-length portrait of Benjamin West, the patriarch of American artists, to a Rembrandt Peale candlelight self-portrait and John Vanderlyn's gruesome *Death of Jane McCrea,* depicting the scalping of a white woman. There were other well-known works by Benjamin West, John Singleton Copley, Ralph Earl, Frederic Church, Albert Bierstadt, and George Inness. Although these were the foundation for a major American collection, they did not stir Austin's imagination. For those like him, trained at the Fogg Art Museum, American art took a backseat to European art.

Other rooms displayed the objects from Pierpont Morgan: bronze Egyptian gods, warriors, and cats; life-size Greek stone lions, two thousand years old; a red porphyry bathtub from ancient Rome; seventeenth-century German silver-gilt lions, ostriches, and nautilus shell cups; Sèvres porcelains; and the largest array of eighteenth-century Meissen figures in America.

In basement rooms under Tapestry Hall, Chick saw the Nutting Collection, an embodiment of the Colonial Revival that swept America at the end of the nineteenth century, settling permanently in Hartford. Consisting of over three hundred pieces of furniture and six hundred household items, the collection had drawn huge crowds when it went on view two years earlier. William B. Goodwin, the president's brother, who was honorary curator of colonial arts and a trustee, had written in the museum bulletin at the time that the assorted Hadley chests, chairs, cradles, and kitchen utensils represented "the evidence of the worthiness in the art and culture of our ancestors."[9] Chick found this collection of hallowed artifacts a bore.

In other galleries in the Morgan wing, Chick came upon grim remnants of the old Atheneum—a room lined with cabinets of minerals, racks of medals and military decorations, trays of coins and stamps; a gallery with acres of colonial pewter in cases taller than a man; a butterfly collection; and a bird room with eggs and skins and bird calls.

Moving into the Colt wing, with its carved oak staircases, doors, and paneling, Chick entered a dark library transplanted from Armsmear, the Colts' Italianate villa of 1857, half a mile from the museum. Here the galleries were crowded with Elizabeth Colt's collection of American paintings, along with cases of her glass, ceramics, jewelry, and sculpture, and Sam Colt's rare gun collection.

Chick knew that the Wadsworth Atheneum was not the Boston Museum of Fine Arts or the Fogg, and there were a few chambers of horrors, but its potential was obvious. There would be money to spend on pictures every year and a whole new museum building to design. Hartford was well situated. It was only two hours from Boston and not much farther from the dealers, collections, and pleasures of New York. Within a small radius were educational institutions that were developing strong art history departments—Yale, Wesleyan, Connecticut College, Vassar, Smith, and Wellesley—to say nothing of Hartford's own Trinity College. With Forbes likely to accept an honorary position at the museum, Chick could ease into his first job with an immensely influential ally to support him. Taken as a whole, Hartford offered him an extraordinary chance at the very beginning of his professional career to test his connoisseurship and to create the kind of modern museum program promoted by the Fogg.

Not that Chick was certain he wanted to spend his life as a museum director—he might be a teacher, a painter, or a designer for the stage—but whatever he did, he needed to be on his own in a new city away from Boston, something his mother, possessive as she was, understood. Later in the year, reflecting her own chronic restlessness, Laura agreed with him that Boston "was no place for you at this time, few people can live in Boston, and not sooner or later have an inferiority complex—it is in the air."[10]

On the morning of June 9, 1927, Goodwin offered Chick the position of acting director of the Wadsworth Atheneum at an annual salary of $3,500, to begin on October 15, and he accepted it.

A few hours later, Goodwin wrote to Forbes with the news, noting that the trustees "were favorably impressed with the brief opportunity they had to meet Mr. Austin. Personally I have become greatly taken with him and feel that he has the temperament and knowledge to carry him far." In a flourish of paternal optimism, he concluded, "This is about all you and I can do for him and after that it must be his own good sword and about the outcome I have not the shadow of a doubt."[11]

Forbes answered that he was delighted that Chick had been given the chance to prove himself, reiterating that, in terms of artistic judgment, he was "an exceedingly rare and valuable man." He himself accepted the position of honorary director for one year, a title he would retain, astoundingly, until his death forty-two years later.[12]

Chick immediately set out on his usual European summer travels, moving from Budapest to Vienna, Venice to Barcelona, Madrid, Toledo, and Salamanca, and painting watercolors along the way. He also spent time in London, where once again he eagerly attended performances of Diaghilev's Ballets Russes.

On June 29, the Hartford press announced Frank Gay's retirement and the appointment of his successor. Of the new director, the *Courant* observed that Austin was not only qualified "to judge art objects, both modern and ancient" and had "studied art extensively in foreign lands," but that he was also an artist in his own right.[13]

At the Atheneum, until Chick took up his duties, it was business as usual. In July, the museum mounted an exhibition of chintz, which included a commemorative print in honor of Charles Lindbergh's flight to Paris two months earlier. It was timed to coincide with the aviator's visit to Hartford. On July 20, he landed *The Spirit of St. Louis* at the city's Brainard Field, and over sixty thousand people mobbed the streets to welcome him. In retrospect, it would seem prophetic that the young hero who most symbolized America's growing internationalism and the new possibilities of the Machine Age had made Hartford the first stop after New York on his nationwide tour.

On August 11, Mary Louise Catlin Sumner died after two years of ill health, and five days later, Frank Gay wrote excitedly to Forbes that "the Frank Sumner estate now comes to us."[14] As expected, it amounted to just over a million dollars. Conservatively invested by the finance committee, the fund would give Chick more than $60,000 to spend on paintings during his first year.[15]

Chick had known the Sumner money would soon be available and had been looking for a splendid work for his first purchase. In London, at Durlacher Brothers, he found a picture attributed to the famous Venetian master Tintoretto. Painted about 1570, it depicted the deadly struggle between Hercules and the giant Antaeus; and it could be had for about $30,000. Chick ordered photographs, so that he could discuss it with Forbes and the Atheneum's trustees.[16] In September, Goodwin told Forbes that he was delighted by the idea of the Atheneum's acquiring an authentic Renaissance masterpiece.[17] It was an auspicious beginning.

On Monday, October 17, soon after he returned from Europe, Chick left Boston for Hartford. He arrived in time for the opening of the museum's new exhibition, *Wood Gravures* by Macowin Tuttle, an elderly American engraver, who lectured on his art that afternoon. The other loan shows on view at the Atheneum Annex were *Hand-Wrought Silver by Arthur J. Stone, Master Craftsman* and paintings by two conventional American artists, William Emerson and Robert Jackson. Chick was scheduled to meet the trustees at a luncheon with Forbes the following Tuesday. In the meantime, he had a chance to talk with his small staff and get a closer look at Hartford.

Frank Gay was only too happy to smooth the way for his successor, to whom he would always refer, in an amused Connecticut twang, as "the young directah." Chick's immediate challenge was to make friends with the formidable general curator, Florence Paull Berger. The first professionally trained staff member, she had arrived at the Atheneum in 1918, after the Morgan treasures were acquired, and remained on the payroll for forty years. Before coming to Hartford, she had worked at the Museum of Fine Arts in Boston (where she had known George Reisner) for two decades, eventually heading the department of Western Art. She had helped develop a system of registering objects that was adopted nationally, and in Hartford, she had organized the Atheneum's collection with single-minded diligence. Long before he gave up the title of director, Frank Gay had handed over the day-to-day running of the museum to her.

Fifty-five years old when Chick came to Hartford, terse and formal, her hair in a bun, Mrs. Berger (said with the French pronunciation) could reduce erring secretaries to tears, much to her apologetic surprise. Predictably, she was reluctant to relinquish power to the boyish new director. "She was Queen of the Atheneum," recalled Florence Berkman, one of Chick's first volunteers, who later became the art critic at the *Hartford Times*. Virtually all of the arrangements of works of art and period rooms in the museum had been installed under her eye. She was especially fond of mounting shows of textiles, silver, pewter, Early American furniture, and handicrafts, which Chick found less than riveting. One of the first things he did was to ask for the removal of Mrs. Berger's textile cases from the large galleries in the Morgan Memorial to the basement. The next morning he discovered them back in the galleries. The cases made several trips up and downstairs before Chick won the battle.[18] Nevertheless, she was soon devoted to him, and he came to look on her as an efficient aunt who complemented his haphazard spontaneity. Behind her back, he would affectionately refer to her as "Berge," perhaps the only person ever to dare use such a nickname.

Chick rented an apartment at 379 Farmington Avenue in the Mark Twain Apartments, a new group of four three-story brick buildings named for their proximity to the celebrated author's flamboyant Victorian mansion. He had a view of the Park River ("the Hog River" to the locals), a pastoral stream that meandered through town before emptying into the Connecticut River. The tenants at that time were a decidedly mixed group, from recent college graduates, just starting out in law or insurance, to the mistresses of Hartford businessmen.[19]

Chick had moved to one of the richest and most attractive cities in New England. Its system of public parks, all six created through the initiative of the Reverend Francis Goodwin (three designed by Frederick Law Olmsted), had helped make Hartford's reputation as a garden spot of the Northeast. Its boulevards were lined with mansions predominately in the Federal and Greek Revival style, their lawns and plantings carefully cultivated. The grandest of all, on Woodland Street, was a granite mansion in the English Tudor Revival style, designed by the Reverend Francis Goodwin for his father in the 1870s and owned at this time by Charles Goodwin's aunt, Mrs. James Junius Goodwin.

It was a city of literary traditions, famous for its Nook Farm section, where, fifty years earlier, Samuel Clemens had written many of his greatest works, including *Huckleberry Finn*, and where he, Charles Dudley Warner (Clemens's collaborator on *The Gilded Age*), Calvin and Harriet Beecher Stowe, and Francis Gillette (the senator, abolitionist, and father of actor William Gillette) had built houses and lived as intimate friends, entertaining international celebrities, and each other, with lavish hospitality.

Hartford was small but enterprising. Its population of 160,000—a large, mostly untapped, audience for the Atheneum—had doubled since 1900. Its fortunes were built on manufacturing and insurance. The Colt gun factory was still assembling thousands of new weapons for a world market; the Cheney Brothers silk mills in nearby Manchester were reputedly the most productive in America. Pratt & Whitney, famous for machine tools, had just opened its aircraft engine division. In 1926 Vulcan Radiator produced America's first baseboard radiators. Ensign-Bickford supplied detonating fuses, and the Capewell Horsenail Company claimed to be the largest producer of horseshoe nails on earth.

Above all, of course, Hartford was the insurance capital of the world. The home offices of Travelers, Aetna Life and Casualty, Phoenix Mutual, Connecticut Mutual, Connecticut General, the Hartford Steam Boiler Inspection and Insurance Company, and the Hartford Fire Insurance Company were all within a few blocks of the museum. Their officers and chief executives—along with the multitude of lawyers and bankers that business and industry required— were the reigning princes of the city, wealthy, self-confident, and, like Charles Goodwin, serious about fulfilling their civic duties. For them, exercising prudence, practicing fiscal responsibility, and minimizing risk constituted a way of life. They helped maintain Connecticut's long-standing reputation as "the land of steady habits."

The state had in fact been so straightlaced that the legislature had banned the theater entirely from 1800 to 1852, but in 1927 its capital city offered a surprising range of popular entertainment—theater, vaudeville, burlesque, movies, concerts, and lectures. A block north of the museum was the Parsons Theater, which often presented plays before they opened in New York and had brought to Hartford such stars as John Barrymore, Eva Le Gallienne, George Arliss, and Geraldine Farrar, along with the Moscow Art Theater, and once even Diaghilev's Ballets Russes. Within weeks of his arrival, Chick could have seen Walter Huston in *The Barker*, Ethel Barrymore in *The Constant Wife*, and a New York production of George Gershwin's recent musical *Oh Kay!* That same month, Poli's Capitol Theatre, across the street from the Morgan Memorial, offered vaudeville, as well as violinist Fritz Kreisler and the Boston Symphony. For further amusement, Capitol Park, not far from the museum, clattered with fun-filled rides and boasted the largest swimming pool in New England. "When we say good-bye," its motto promised, "we leave them laughing."[20]

Among the social elite like the Goodwins, however, entertainment was something one did in one's home. During his first months in Hartford, Chick was invited often to spend time with Charles Goodwin's family. Their Tudor-Revival house stood on the east side of Scarborough Street, an elegant boulevard recently laid out on land owned by the Goodwins, three miles from the museum. There Chick met Goodwin's beautiful but imposing wife, Ruth Cheney Goodwin, of the Cheney silk fortune; Goodwin's brothers, William and Spencer; and his sister-in-law, Fanny Goodwin, widow of the Reverend James Goodwin, whose children, Helen, Mary, Lucy, and Francis were Chick's contemporaries. The younger generation was thrilled to meet anyone who might bring some excitement to Hartford. They had been to too many parties whose high point was the singing of Yale songs.

More congenial to Chick among the older generation were his near neighbors, the last private owners of Mark Twain's house, Richard Bissell, president of the Hartford Fire Insurance Company, and his wife, Marie. The Bissells would soon move to nearby Farmington, but while Chick was in his apartment, he frequently visited Marie Bissell, who served a full English tea every afternoon. A midwesterner who found Hartford society stuffy, she was the liveliest hostess in the city. Even during Prohibition, champagne flowed liberally at her soirées, and on the morning after at least one party, a grand piano was spotted on her front lawn.[21]

Eventually, Laura Austin, staying at the Savoy Hotel in Paris, heard about her son's first days in Hartford—she told him that his sporadic correspondence seemed like "a long time between drinks"—and expressed her usual concern about his health with good humor, saying that the previous summer "you looked anything but fit when you landed in Marseilles and [I] think [the] only thing that cured you, was Carcasonne and Castor oil." Evidently he had reassured her about his well-being, reporting that his father had given him a physical before he left for Hartford. Laura then launched into a mother's pep talk: "Now go ahead and forget everything, and *particularly yourself,* and go in for a good year's work and make a real record for yourself and the cause."[22]

Soon afterward, when Chick sent her a newspaper clipping about his appointment, she was ecstatic: "As Lady Astor's nurse said when she rec'd her English honors: 'That time you sure did *out do* yourself.' " Her dreams for Everett were coming true: "Do you know, I have always felt you would become [some]thing *some day* and it would come out in the papers." Referring to Chick's relief at getting out of Boston, she wrote, "I know you will meet more congenial people, who are interested in you and your work[.] Somehow I cannot but feel everything is alright—that you have chosen the right work, and you will be happy in that work."[23] She was keen to spread the word about his success among the Etniers and instructed him to send copies of the clipping to relatives. When Aunt Sue Etnier read the article, she promised Chick that "you will always be the same Everett to me no matter how many laurels you win and I shall always love to see you whether I know what you are talking about or not."[24]

As Chick got his bearings, the museum schedule previously set by Mrs. Berger rolled on. A week after he arrived, the Atheneum presented a talk on the collections of the National Gallery of London by Stewart Dick, an English lecturer who informed his audience that "Modern Art is mediocre" and that "our present day artists are absolutely unable to produce art as beautiful and fine as did the painters and sculptors of centuries ago."[25] Such pronouncements would have met with pious approval from nearly everyone in the audience. They foretold the sentiments that much of the Hartford public and most of Chick's board would express during his tenure as director. A few days later, the *Hartford Courant* cited another Englishman, Sir Frank Dicksee, president of the Royal Academy, to the effect that "Futurist painters are mentally diseased contortionists and not artists" who were "a danger to art."[26] This was followed by an article about Hartford artist Robert Fulton Logan, who declared that "modernism is bolshevism in the ateliers."[27] Chick would not wait long to introduce the public to a different view.

Privately, he made no secret of his low opinion of the museum's existing collection. When Charles Goodwin's nephew, Francis Goodwin, the insurance agent for the museum, dropped by Chick's office to introduce himself, he noted conversationally that the Atheneum had "a pretty good plant." "Yes," Chick replied, "it's a pretty good plant. The only thing we need to do now is find something to put in it."[28]

CHAPTER FIVE

Setting Fires in Hartford

Many factors have contributed to the growth and prosperity of Hartford, the Capital City of Connecticut. We
recognize, and are proud of, the industry and progres-
siveness of her citizens, and we are glad to know that our
manufactured products and our services carry the name
of Hartford all over this country and to many corners of
the world.

—*Hartford*, 1927

On Tuesday, October 25, Chick was formally introduced to a dozen
trustees at a luncheon at the Hartford Club, a male bastion near
the Atheneum. Greeting him with cordial reserve were representatives of the social and financial power of Hartford. Most were at
least twice his age. They were gray-haired, dressed in dark business suits,
some sporting old-fashioned stiff collars, their faces glinting with pince-nez on
ribbons and horn- or wire-rimmed glasses. A few had been making decisions
for the museum since the turn of the century.

Charles Goodwin presided, as he would until his retirement in 1954. With
him was his close friend and permanent vice president, Charles F. T. Seaverns,
soon to head Hartford's Bushnell Memorial, a vast new public auditorium for
the performing arts built with his wife's money. Also present were the two other
Goodwins on the board: the president's brother, William, the colonial arts curator, an antiquarian, amateur archaeologist, and interpreter of Viking runes; and
his first cousin, Walter, a partner of Real Estate, Inc., the family company that
managed the Goodwin property—a man fonder of polo than art. Then there
were Charles Goodwin's senior law partner, Arthur L. Shipman, Sr., and attorney Charles Welles Gross, whose father had preceded Goodwin as president of
the Atheneum. The rest constituted a roll call of corporate Hartford—men who
sat in various combinations on the boards of each other's banks and insurance
companies. The Atheneum was the equivalent of their private club.[1]

In facing this seeming monolith for the first time, Chick was in the enviable position of having his Harvard mentor by his side to lay out the artistic program himself. Taking charge of the meeting, Edward Forbes told the trustees that the Atheneum should not *follow* public taste, but *lead* it. It should buy works of the highest quality, encourage private collecting, and educate the public through outstanding loan exhibitions. It should make Hartford "a place of pilgrimage" for art lovers.[2]

Clearing the way for his protégé, he said that one man should have full authority to choose works of art rather than leaving the selection to a committee.[3] The trustees promptly voted to empower Forbes, not Chick, to make acquisitions, though they gave the two of them the right to approve all purchases during the coming year. But a new policy had been established, and Forbes made it clear to Chick that he would have a free hand in choosing pictures. In December, Forbes offered to join him on a visit to the New York dealers, but added with his usual kindliness, "if you want to do it all by yourself, go ahead. I just want you to know that I will be there in case I can be of any service to you."[4]

Poised to follow the course Forbes had mapped out, Chick soon submitted to the trustees the Tintoretto he had found in London that fall, *Hercules and Antaeus.* Though he and Forbes felt confident that it was an authentic work by the master, they turned to Bernard Berenson for an unassailable stamp of approval. The sage of I Tatti replied with opaque brevity: "As in the photo I see nothing that speaks against its being an autograph Jacopo Tintoretto, as on the contrary a great deal speaks for it, I am cabling 'Tintoretto all right.' "[5]

In mid-December, the trustees agreed to buy the painting for $29,250, more than the museum had ever spent on a single picture. It was a striking image. Almost filling the canvas were the two protagonists, nude and muscular, locked in combat. The bearded Hercules, his back to the viewer, lifts the Libyan giant Antaeus, son of Terra and Neptune, whose arms are outstretched as if he were about to fly. Separated from his mother earth, the source of his strength, Antaeus is being crushed to death in the other man's arms. A languorous crowd of gods above, and a livelier group of demigods or mortals below, witness the mighty combat.

Eager to impress his new employers, Chick produced a virtuoso essay for the Atheneum bulletin, written on a level of expertise not seen in those pages since Mrs. Berger started the publication five years earlier. In the best Fogg Museum manner, he explored every aspect of the painting—the subject, the quality of the drawing, the use of color, the composition ("the diagonal, the pyramid and the diamond lozenge within a rectangle"), the artist's technical method, and the work's physical condition. He compared it minutely with eleven other works by Tintoretto in collections in Venice, Rome, Munich, and Berlin. With supreme confidence, he wrote: "In the rapidly executed drawing

Tintoretto, Hercules and Antaeus, *c. 1570. Oil
on canvas, 60¼ × 40⅜ inches, purchased 1927*

of the little subordinate figures we feel a masterly facility which is always sincere, always a means to an end—never a stupid satisfaction in its own accomplishment and very characteristically Tintoretto."[6]

Chick decided to make the picture the centerpiece of his first exhibition.
For the citizens of Hartford, he would conjure up a collection of dazzling quality, ranging throughout art history. He wanted to amaze them with how the galleries in their museum could look. In December, he announced that the
exhibition would open in a month's time.

This was Chick's first step toward realizing his ambitions for Hartford. He
told the press:

It is our object to bring to this city from time to time important art
objects of every sort, and men and women prominent in the world of

art. . . . In time we hope that the Wadsworth Atheneum will attract these people to Hartford as the art center of New England—for it should be within our scope to rank with Boston in that respect.

By gradually building up the collections at the Atheneum, as we plan to do, visiting European scholars and connoisseurs will desire, will find it necessary to come to Hartford, and so the reputation of Hartford's artistic vitality will spread even to the foreign cultural centers.[7]

To pull the exhibition together, he relied heavily on the major New York dealers, telling them that his show was meant to "stimulate private buying here."[8] He asked Forbes to write the celebrated dealer Sir Joseph Duveen for the loan of at least one major Renaissance painting, adding that he would like to have "any odds and ends at the Fogg that you would be willing to lend."[9] Two weeks later, Chick told Forbes that he was gathering up pictures thick and fast:

I saw Wildenstein in New York this week and accepted with great pleasure a David portrait and a late Renoir. . . . I have been on the trail of a Greco and have found a fairly nice one at Mrs. Sterner's. . . . I am still hoping for a Rembrandt from Duveen and a Goya from some place or other. . . . Durlacher's have most generously lent us a Burgundian Madonna and also the Autun Madonna which I like very much in addition to many small pictures, an ivory, enamel and other objects of that sort.[10]

Chick convinced the imperious Theodate Pope Riddle, Philip Johnson's cousin and the wife of John Wallace Riddle (the last American ambassador to tsarist Russia), to lend nine impressionist paintings from the cloistered collection at Hill-Stead, her Colonial Revival house, designed in part by Stanford White, in Farmington—the first time the Hartford public would see these pictures.

In just over four weeks, Austin and Forbes assembled seventy-five works spanning nearly three thousand years—sculpture from ancient Egypt, Greece, and Rome, from Persia and Thailand, from medieval and Renaissance Europe; illuminated manuscripts; paintings from the thirteenth to the twentieth century by such artists as Bellini, Velázquez, Tintoretto, El Greco, Rembrandt, Rubens, van Dyck, Hals, Tiepolo, Fragonard, David, Renoir, Degas, and Sargent; etchings by Dürer and Rembrandt; and American watercolors by Homer, Sargent, Prendergast, and Demuth.

With scarcely disguised disparagement of the museum's previous collecting program, Chick informed a correspondent in January that "the new policy of the Atheneum will be that of acquiring distinguished works of art rather than pictures of historical and decorative interest."[11] To emphasize his point, he called his exhibition simply *Distinguished Works of Art*.

Most of the objects arrived a week before the opening, some traveling to Hartford in specially reserved Pullman-car drawing rooms. Chick draped the walls of the Morgan Memorial's two upper galleries in two hundred yards of green silk which he had found in New York. A third gallery, for modern works, was covered in a lighter fabric. With his excess of ideas and a staff that was too small for his ambitions, Chick did most of the work himself and barely finished hanging the exhibition before the doors opened on January 18. Forbes genially reported to Sachs that Chick "made the same mistake that I used to make before you came and set me right, namely, the mistake of not allowing time enough to get ready for his show. The result was that he for several days had been going without meals and without sleep, working like a demon to get ready." Forbes added that he himself had pitched in on the day of the opening and "worked like fury all afternoon," and Chick was so pressed for time that he missed the dinner party in his honor attended by the cream of Hartford ssociety.[12]

That evening more than a thousand Atheneum members and their guests climbed up to the second floor of the museum for the opening reception (for which Chick had recruited no fewer than sixty patronesses). Just after nine o'clock, Charles Goodwin introduced Forbes, who noted that some of the pictures were for sale and might find their way into the museum through a few generous donors. Then he motioned to a section of the gallery wall covered by curtains, which Chick drew back dramatically to reveal the Tintoretto.[13]

The show put the Atheneum in the national spotlight. A photograph of the Tintoretto dominated the first page of *Art News*, and *The Christian Science Monitor* praised Austin for the quality of the exhibition and its installation.[14] The local press outdid itself with superlatives, and as proof of the show's significance for this capital of corporate underwriters, the *Hartford Times* reported that the objects were valued at over three million dollars and that six policeman would be guarding them twenty-four hours a day.[15]

More than four thousand people crowded into the museum on the first Sunday after the show opened, breaking all exhibition attendance records. It was clear that something had changed in Hartford. Even as cursory a museum-goer as Charles Goodwin visited the exhibition more than once. One evening, he told his family how touched he was to see a group of Italian immigrants standing in front of the Tintoretto, obviously proud that such a masterpiece had come to their adopted American city.[16]

Chick was already looking ahead to a systematic exhibition program that would educate the public over a period of many years. "This group of objects," he told a reporter, "will stand as a primer" for future exhibitions in which he would explore individual periods or schools of art. It was plain, he said, that his first show was "truly arousing and stimulating interest in the minds of all the people of Hartford," and, looking ahead, he declared that "the exposition of objects of supreme beauty will fill a long felt need in the hearts of many."

Yet there were complaints about the few modern pictures. Chick acknowledged that several of the contemporary American watercolors—undoubtedly the Prendergasts and the Demuths, with their mildly fauvist overtones—had aroused animosity, but he was not about to apologize for them: "It is the duty of a museum to show, by means of loan exhibitions, the manifestations of the art which is living, and which is being produced around us, the very moment almost, that we are observing it. So also it is the duty, nay, the passionate interest of the intellectual mind to observe all these manifestations. Whether to like them or dislike them is another matter, but to see them is all important." This was Chick's first public declaration of a mission he shared with a whole generation of American modernists.[17]

He urged the public to come to the show more than once. "One can get an idea of a picture, perhaps, by seeing it only once, but one can never judge it unless it has been seen many, many times." The response was everything he could have wished. When the exhibition closed after its two-week run, more than thirty-five thousand people had seen it.[18]

As for the picture that had inspired the show—for all the scrutiny of Forbes and Berenson, it was attributed many years later to Tintoretto's workshop rather than to the master himself.[19] The reattribution would not have bothered Chick. Working in territory still mostly uncharted, he knew that pictures were regularly reassigned to other artists.

Following the Fogg philosophy that a museum was both a treasure-house and a center of learning, Chick launched an education program with the exhibition and naturally called on Forbes to be his first lecturer. Showing lantern slides to an overflow audience in the Morgan Memorial, Forbes described his pioneering use of X rays in detecting spurious paintings and in illuminating the construction of masterpieces. Chick also enlisted Russell Hitchcock, then an assistant professor at Vassar, to lecture on Tintoretto and the Venetian Renaissance, a talk so popular that the crowd hovered in the hall outside the lecture room, hoping to catch some of his remarks.[20] This was the first of many appearances by Hitchcock, who came to Connecticut a year later to start up the fine arts department at Wesleyan University, in Middletown.

The serious study of the fine arts in American colleges and universities was just beginning to take hold, and Chick was part of the movement. He had already decided to combine his museum work with a teaching career. In mid-December, he arranged with the president of Trinity College, Remsen Ogilby, to offer an art history course for the undergraduates. He called it simply "An Introduction to the History of Art," a title he found "slightly less pompous" than "A History of Art," he explained.[21]

Writing to ask Forbes for permission to borrow the Fogg's lantern slides for the course, Chick noted that his mission was financial as well as pedagogical: "I am sure that by stressing the educational program of the Museum in this way, we will get a great deal of support from people who would rather give for educational purposes than for purely art reasons. It is the educational side of the Fogg Museum that appeals so strongly to so many outsiders and I hope to be able to stimulate the same sort of feeling in Hartford."[22] Chick taught his first course three days a week in the museum's lecture room, but moved it to the Trinity campus in 1929. He soon offered courses in the history of sculpture, architecture, and, after some coaxing of the college's faculty, modern art. He became, in effect, the founder of the college's fine arts department.

Teaching and lecturing brought out two of Chick's great strengths—the connoisseur and the entertainer. When he spoke about a work of art, it was transformed from a picture hanging on a wall, or projected onto a screen, into a living thing. Chick transmitted his knowledge of art history and his perception of quality with a flair far beyond what most of his listeners had ever experienced.

The young men in Chick's Trinity class were captivated by his sheer physical presence—his good looks, the peaked lapels on his custom-made English suits, the silk handkerchief spilling out of his breast pocket, his Italian suede shoes, and his unlimited energy. One moment he would be sitting on the corner of a desk, swinging his feet; the next, he would be walking back and forth in front of a pair of large black-and-white lantern slides projected by a favored student—speaking nonstop in his musical voice with its cultivated accent, gesticulating, chain-smoking his fashionable Fatima cigarettes, entertaining with irreverent asides, alluding to his sophisticated social life, and leaving a circle of cigarette butts in his wake. For his students, this was wonderful theater.[23]

A particularly dramatic moment occurred early in his teaching career. Chick's eight o'clock class met in an English-style basement room at Trinity that featured tall casement windows opening onto a short grassy bank sloping down from the street. One morning he failed to appear at the scheduled hour, and after waiting the six- or seven-minute leeway usually given to professors, his students prepared to depart. Suddenly there was a squeal of brakes and a grinding of gravel as a yellow cab skidded to a stop on the street above the classroom. Chick jumped out, ran down the bank, threw open a casement window, leaped into the room, and immediately began his lecture. What left his students pop-eyed was the fact that he was dressed in white tie, tails, and an evening cape, having just arrived by train from New York after a very late night on the town. Fifty years later, one member of the class exclaimed, "It was just the greatest stage appearance that ever happened."[24]

In contrast to the seemingly aloof professors at Trinity, Chick took his students into his confidence, often beginning his class with a report on his last twenty-four hours, especially if he had been to a particularly exciting party, which added to his aura of glamour. "He would tell us about that party and how it went," said a former student, "or the difficulties he was having in mounting a show, or how the trustees down at the museum didn't understand him at all and were all such old fuddy-duddies that he just couldn't endure it another minute. . . . We just felt that he was one of us."[25]

Following the practice of Forbes and Sachs, Chick took selected students to New York to give them a taste of the art market. They would pile into his car and make the trip to the city in a terrifyingly short time. ("He drove like an absolute fiend," one student recalled.) When they arrived at a gallery such as Knoedler's, they would be ushered into a back room where pictures were leaning against the walls in stacks. Chick would thumb through them as if they were prints. Then everyone would troop into a viewing room and sit down. Two porters in eighteenth-century livery would carry in a large painting, its back to the group, and flip it around with a flourish. The dealer would begin his sales pitch, and the students would see Chick in his greatest role—totally concentrated, discussing details of the painting, asking quick, incisive questions—the consummate museum professional.

It was obvious to his students that Chick moved in an entirely different sphere from the rest of the faculty, with whom he had very little contact, since he never attended faculty meetings. Though the other professors valued him for his reputation and popularity among the students, they looked on him as a Bohemian outsider. The only other member of the art department was an extremely conventional retired architect named Howard Greenley, who found Chick much too modern and therefore suspect.[26]

Chick usually spoke extemporaneously from his slide list on which he had jotted down a few dates and place names. For his opening lecture in his first course on the history of art, however, he wrote out the introductory pages. He began by explaining what he saw as the basis of connoisseurship. Great art, he told the students, "appeals entirely to the aesthetic sense, resulting in an emotional and intellectual reaction and enjoyment in the mind of the spectator. A work of art is the bridge over which the highly sensitized emotions of the artist must be transferred to the mind of the beholder."

Then, after outlining the requirements of the course, he raised the curtain on the origins of Western art with a sense of drama that had more in common with the cinema than the classroom: "From the top of the great pyramid," he began, speaking from his own vivid memories, "we look out on long horizontals,

as far as the eye can reach; a narrow valley through which meanders a glistening river, with a narrow fringe of green fields and palm groves, bordered on
either side by low barren cliffs from which extend vast undulating deserts; a
glorious sun in a cloudless sky—this is Egypt."[27]

Chick's college courses, which he taught continuously almost to end of his
tenure as director, constituted only one part of his speaking engagements. He
became the one-man education department of the museum and seemed to
appear everywhere. In addition to teaching Trinity and Wesleyan students that
spring, he gave public lectures three times a week in the museum. He spoke at
high schools and junior high schools, in front of civic groups, at garden clubs,
mental hospitals—anywhere he was invited—always carrying the message of
looking at art with critical eyes. At an opening of an exhibition of East Side
New York artists at the Hartford Y.M. and Y.W.H.A. one evening, he invited the
audience to "strip the work of its sentimentality, and judge its basic beauty.
Just because a landscape happens to remind a young lady of the place where
she used to stroll with her fiance, that does not give her the right to assume that
the picture is a work of art."[28] A few days later, *Hartford Courant* readers could
compare Chick's admonitions with President Calvin Coolidge's pronouncement
that "if we could surround ourselves with forms of beauty, the evil things of life
would tend to disappear and our moral standards would be raised."[29] Elevating
moral standards never appealed to Chick; he wanted to raise standards of taste,
and liberate imaginations from convention and mediocrity.

To tantalize the public further, he announced three more Atheneum shows
on the day that *Distinguished Works of Art* closed, all to be produced before the
summer. In April, there would be a survey of master drawings from Paul Sachs's
famous collection, ranging from Mantegna to Picasso, followed by a large group
of modern painters, beginning with Cézanne. In May, he would present an exhibition of modern American watercolors.[30]

But the project that would occupy most of his attention that spring was a
pure expression of his love of spectacle and fantasy. Carrying the theme of Tintoretto and the Venetian Renaissance into the eighteenth century, he told the
press in March that the Morgan wing would be the scene of a "Venetian Fete"
on April 20. Tapestry Hall would be lined with fancifully painted boxes to be
sold for $100 to $150 apiece. Beyond each of the six doors in the Hall would be
painted stage flats showing views of Venice—the Church of Santa Maria della
Salute, the Bridge of Sighs, the Grand Canal, winding streets, palaces, and gondolas. These backdrops would all be painted by Chick himself and would be
illuminated by theatrical lights. The whole extravaganza reflected Chick's irrepressible desire to bring theater into the museum setting. In describing the city
he wished to evoke, Chick suggested that party-goers should be prepared to
throw away their inhibitions:

The gayety of eighteenth-century Venice has perhaps never been surpassed, and this special quality of that irresponsible city was reflected in the costumes of the day. It was Venice in its decadence, Venice at the end of its period of supremacy; downfall was near, the people regarded it with composure, as something inevitable, and were out to have a whooping good time, come what may, while they had the chance.

To attach a more elevated purpose to the ball, he explained to the press that entertaining though the Fete would be, its underlying aim was to benefit the museum; he noted that the operating budget left "only a pittance for lectures and public exhibitions, which from the great attendance at the recent loan show of art masterpieces, the Hartford public apparently wants and appreciates."[31] For this first ball ever held in the Atheneum, he recruited the wife of its president, Ruth Goodwin, and his new friend Marie Bissell, as his two social chairmen.

Preparations for the ball occupied Chick, and those planning to attend, for weeks. J. P. Morgan, Jr., lent tapestries to decorate the walls. Costumes were brought from New York by local merchants. Longhi paintings from Mrs. Bissell's collection and books and prints depicting Venetian revels were put on display at the museum to guide guests in choosing or making their costumes. A Sunday rotogravure section in the *Hartford Courant* provided previews of Hartford luminaries posing in their elaborate finery. An enterprising hairdresser advertised that her beauty parlor could supply colonial wigs suitable for the Fete, "all sterilized and sanitary."[32] And Umberto, a large hippopotamus with mechanical parts, was constructed by an inventor in Farmington to lead to procession. Tickets sold rapidly, even at $5 apiece, and many of the boxes for six at $100 each were taken by Atheneum trustees. Laura Austin bought one of the larger boxes for eight at $150. She had been in Europe for a year and found the separation from Everett hard. In March she wrote from Antwerp: "Boy dearest I will be so glad to see you, and hear about everything. I have missed you so much, but am so happy in your work and success—and think of you constantly, but somehow I cannot locate you in Hartford—once I have seen you there it will be so different, but somehow I feel you are alright and doing good work, and in the right place—and among friends."[33]

On Thursday, April 19, the day before the ball, frenetic activity filled the museum. Electricians struggled to install high-power cables for Chick's lighting scheme and for the lamps of a cinematographer who was to record the event. Charles Goodwin wrote to the chief of police, politely but imperially instructing him to have the section of Main Street in front of the Morgan Memorial kept clear for the automobiles of arriving guests.[34]

*Chick chats with Mrs. Charles Goodwin, left, and Mrs. Richard Bissell, right,
at "The Venetian Fete," 1928.*

The next day, Chick and a small crew worked quickly to complete the
hanging of the modern French pictures on the second floor of the Morgan
Memorial. True to form, they finished just before the doors opened.

At nine o'clock on Friday evening, as the first of nearly a thousand party-
goers walked through canopied entrances at each end of the Morgan building's
Tapestry Hall, a twenty-six-piece orchestra launched into an hour's concert of
classical music, from Boccherini's *Minuet* to Stravinsky's *Pulcinella* and short
pieces by Mozart, Schubert, Liszt, and Wagner. Blue lightbulbs strung outside
the hall's upper windows created the mysterious atmosphere of a moonlit night,
while rows of Venetian lanterns on red-and-white-striped poles beside the
boxes gave off glowing orange light. Chick's painted Venetian scenes beyond
the six side gallery doors were illuminated dimly by other colored lights hidden
from view. As more and more merrymakers arrived, the museum became a luxurious fantasy world. Nothing like it had been seen in Hartford. Tapestry Hall
was a swirl of fabrics—cloth of gold and satins, silks, velvets, and heavy brocades of every imaginable color. There were silver wigs, gold-fringed tricorn
hats, masks, lace veils, feathers, furs, long cloaks, bizarre shoes—all inter-

spersed with the glint of jewels.[35] In this last year of prosperity before the Great Depression, even ordinarily restrained New Englanders were capable of going on a spending spree to dress themselves for such an event.

Guests included Hartford's elite—the Goodwins, the Cheneys, the Lyman Brainerds and the Morgan Brainards, the Morgan Bulkeleys and the Dexter Coffins, whose names would be better known later as streets and bridges— along with visitors from Boston, New York, Philadelphia, Baltimore, Chicago, and Santa Barbara. And ensconced in a gaily painted box with Mrs. Frank Gay and her daughter, Constance, was Mrs. A. Everett Austin, Sr., who had arrived alone. Swathed in yellow satin, she basked in the enchanted night conjured up by her son, already making, as she had urged, "a real record" for himself.

Eventually, the guests found their way up to the second-floor galleries for the preview of modern French masters, the first exhibition of its kind in Hartford. The dreamy atmosphere and make-believe attire prepared the viewers for pictures that were exceedingly strange to eyes used to scenes from the American Revolution, the landscapes of Thomas Cole, or even the old masters of Austin's first show. Now they were confronted by pictures like Rousseau's *Jungle,* Gauguin's *Native Woman,* Picasso's *Maternity,* Seurat's *Seated Woman,* nudes by Matisse and Maillol, a brooding van Gogh self-portrait, and dozens of other works by the classic moderns: Degas, Cézanne, Utrillo, Derain, Braque, Dufy, Redon, Vlaminck, Laurencin. It was supremely clever of Chick to choose this moment to introduce his board and Hartford society to the outskirts of modernism. To shake them loose from their comfortable conventions, he had, in effect, stripped them of their business suits, dressed them up in fantastic clothes, drenched them in moonlight, and brought them face-to-face with the reality of the new.

At ten-thirty, trumpeters strode through the galleries on both floors, blasting fanfares to announce that the grand march of revelers was about to begin. A procession of two hundred and fifty costumed guests was led by a gypsy Columbine astride the grinning Umberto, his red lips stretched over large white teeth, a garland of exotic blooms around his neck, a bunch of violets tied to his tail, and a little boy in blackface marching before him, beating a tom-tom. Clapping, shouting, and laughter filled the strangely lit museum, as one whimsical group followed another. There were characters from Carlo Goldoni's plays, Pietro Longhi's paintings, and the commedia dell'arte; dancers and strolling players, glass figurines, and a group depicting the marriage of Venice to the Adriatic. The procession wound through the upper floor, down the double marble staircase, and into Tapestry Hall, past hundreds of more reticent party-goers dressed in traditional evening clothes.[36]

The final entrée, "Ladies and Gentlemen of the Ducal Palace," featured Charles Goodwin as Doge Marco Foscarini, looking masterful in the heavy bro-

Charles A. Goodwin as the Doge of Venice, Hartford Times, *April 18, 1928*

caded robes of installation, a large volume of statutes cradled in his arm and a peaked skullcap on his head. The Dogaressa Isabella (also known as Ruth Cheney Goodwin) was equally stately in a maroon velvet jacket over a voluminous brocaded silk dress, ornamented with long strings of pearls.[37] No roles could have been more congenial to the president and his wife. And it was true to life, as well, that drifting in and out of the crowd, apparently not attached to any particular group, was the figure of Gilles from Watteau's *Fêtes galantes,* dressed in white satin from head to toe, a long black velvet cloak lined in ivory silk over his shoulders, a round white felt hat arching over his head, and a cigarette in his right hand. It was Chick, of course, who had stepped into the part that Julien Levy had imagined when he first caught sight of him at Harvard. Chick posed for a few seconds for the film that was made that night, flanked by Ruth Goodwin and Marie Bissell. Looking like a precocious eighteen-year-old, he chatted amiably, casting quick glances at the camera, the simplicity of his clothes contrasting with the excess of the others and giving him a slightly detached aura, as befitted the paradoxical Gilles.

At eleven, guests descended to the museum's darkened basement, which Chick had turned into the prison cells of the Ducal Palace, where they sat at small café tables and dined on bouillon, salad, ices, and coffee. After dinner, the crowd whirled around the floor of the great hall hour after hour as the orchestra played the latest jazz numbers and Broadway show tunes. Just before four in the morning, the last revelers reluctantly staggered home.[38]

The Fete was front-page news on Saturday, and the film of the ball was shown that night at the Capitol Theater for lesser mortals who had missed it. A few days later, Charles Goodwin asked the board for a resolution praising Chick and his committee for making the Fete a profitable venture (the net gain amounted to $3,013.74). The props and decorations remained on view for a week and then were sold for the museum's benefit. Chick was very proud of himself and sent photographs of the decor to Paul Sachs and reported to Forbes that "everyone agreed that it was a very brilliant affair and that it should be repeated every year."[39]

Chick won accolades from the press for his exhibition of "modernist art." The *Hartford Courant*'s critic, T. H. Parker (who, by coincidence, graduated from Harvard on the same day Chick took his degree), declared that it was "unthinkable" that Hartford had not previously been given the chance to see such pictures and that Chick's achievement "entitles him to hosannas."[40] Chick told the press that if people would look at the works with an open mind and try to find the idea behind the image, "the pictures will not seem so curiously out of place" and would eventually bring enjoyment.[41]

Though modern French paintings had been shown frequently in the United States since the New York Armory Show of 1913, most Americans had never seen them on view in their hometown. In 1918 Duncan Phillips had opened the Phillips Memorial Gallery in Washington, D.C., which he called an "experimental museum of modern art and its more or less remote sources."[42] The Pennsylvania Academy of Fine Arts had shown paintings from the School of Paris in Philadelphia as early as 1920. In the same year, Marcel Duchamp, Man Ray, and Katherine Dreier had founded the Société Anonyme, which regularly exhibited its traveling collection of advanced art in galleries in New York City and museums in the northeast, from Buffalo, New York, to Worcester, Massachusetts. In March 1921, the Brooklyn Museum had presented a provocative show of Impressionists and Post-Impressionists, followed a few months later by a similar exhibition at the Metropolitan, causing even more outrage in Manhattan than it had across the East River. The Arts Club of Chicago had exhibited very advanced works for nearly a decade, and there had been a large exhibition of contemporary French art in Baltimore in 1925. In December 1927, A. E. Gallatin had opened the Gallery of Living Art at New York University. Throughout the country, however, modern art was still regarded with suspicion, if not outright fury.

Chick's show was extended a few days because of healthy attendance, but the quiet criticism that had surfaced after his first exhibition became more vocal. Early in May, when the art critic Walter Pach spoke at the Atheneum on "Classic Elements in Modern Art," asserting that the modern artist "expresses the especial pulse or thrill of his life or time," some members of the audience were disgusted.[43] The *Courant* printed a letter from a local construction engineer and amateur artist, Nicholas Ballerini, who voiced the archetypal response to nonrepresentational works of art. He scoffed at the notion that modern art could possibly be representative of life in the twentieth century. "Modern art," he said, "with its deformity is utterly ridiculous and an insult to the public." Instead, contemporary artists should look for their inspiration to such objects as the Venus de Milo—"the most perfectly formed woman known in all ages." And he warned that "those who have deviated from the classic can only expect oblivion."[44]

This was the first criticism in print of any Atheneum program that advocated contemporary art. Such resistance to the new was no surprise to Chick, any more than it was to the organizers of the New York Armory Show fifteen years earlier or to Alfred Barr eighteen months later, when the Museum of Modern Art opened its first exhibition, also based on classics of French modernism.[45] Chick saw controversy as a necessary part of his educational goals. As he wrote to Rue Winterbotham Carpenter, the guiding spirit of the forward-looking Arts Club of Chicago, who had lent her important Rousseau to the show: "The pictures caused a great deal of comment as it was Hartford's first glimpse of a so-called 'Modern Show' and I am sure that we accomplished a good deal by having it now."[46]

He sensed resistance among his trustees, as well, to certain modern works that he wanted to buy for the museum. A watercolor by John Marin, *Green Head, Stonington, Maine,* had caught his eye at the Weyhe Gallery in New York. Chick knew that Marin's advanced style, with its slashing lines and intense colors, as well as the $650 price tag, would not be instantly enticing to his trustees, so he tried to win them over by stealth, a strategy he would often use. In May, he installed a watercolor show that included the picture he wanted, along with six Marins borrowed from the Fogg and from Charles Goodwin's first cousin, New York architect Philip Goodwin. To these he added eight works by Charles Demuth. "I am hoping that in this way," he confided to his friend Paul Vanderbilt at the Weyhe Gallery, "I shall be able to get the picture by the Board. It looks rather difficult at the moment."[47] The trustees were lukewarm about the loan show, and Chick did not present the Marin to them. But he could not bring himself to return it to the gallery. The picture remained in the Atheneum's basement for more than a year until repeated inquiries and a bill came to Mrs. Berger's attention while he was traveling in Europe.[48] Chick hated to give up works of art he liked, but on the other hand, things set aside were quickly eclipsed by the next object of desire.

In May, Edward Forbes urged Chick to spend the summer in Europe to survey the art market. Forbes had been making the rounds of European dealers since the spring and had seen appealing pictures in Rome, Florence, and Venice,[49] and Chick was eager to join him. "Everything seems to be very quiet," he told Forbes in June, referring to the New York dealers, "what with the general exodus for Europe and the closing up of the shops."[50] Hartford, too, was shutting down for the season as the Goodwins and other Hartford families began their exodus to summer homes and sailboats.[51]

On June 27, Chick sailed for England on Cunard's liner *Berengaria*, spending a few days in London visiting dealers, private collectors, and museums, as well as attending performances of Diaghilev's Ballets Russes. He found drawings by Tiepolo, Ingres, Goya, and Greuze to put on his list of possible acquisitions. Then he went on to Paris to see Forbes about other prospects.

Forbes had a list of thirty or forty works that he recommended for purchase, but reminded Chick that he was advising several museums and that there was a pecking order. The Fogg Museum had the first choice of the pictures, followed by the Boston Museum, then the Wadsworth Atheneum.[52] Chick, however, was keen to make his own survey. He went off on a lightning tour of Antwerp (where his mother had bought a seventeenth-century house that July), Venice, Rome, Munich, Dresden, Berlin, Vienna, and Budapest. He later told the Hartford press that he was struck by the growing scarcity of fine pictures in Europe as the great private collections were bought up by American and European museums. He predicted that the entrance of wealthy Japanese collectors into the market for the first time in history would make competition much keener.[53]

Chick had been tempted by only one picture, an El Greco in Munich, but when he returned to Paris and walked into René Gimpel's gallery on the rue Spontini, he saw the head of an angel, attributed to the Florentine artist Fra Angelico. It was a little gem, less than seven by six inches of tempera on a wood panel, a fragment of a larger picture—a Madonna and Child, Chick surmised—painted about 1440. Dressed in a blue mantle flecked with gold, her head and shoulders visible, the angel raises her left arm as if pulling aside a red, black, and gold curtain to reveal the unseen Madonna. The delicate half-turned head—framed with short, flowing blond hair, a small red flame rising just above the forehead, encircled with a golden halo—was placed against the gold-leaf background that medieval eyes recognized as eternity. "The head, of an extremely fragile and mystic beauty," Chick wrote later, "appearing as though lost in the contemplation of timeless and spaceless existence, is painted with that matchless and unbelievable technical mastery which reveals the author at once. The garment of ultrae marine blue over-laid in the shadows with terra verde, lends an exquisite enamel-like quality to the color scheme, with its tones here and there of rose madder and vermilion."[54] The artist's subtle modeling of the face and the individual personality he gave it made the image a harbinger of the Renaissance. Chick wanted it for the collection he imagined creating in Hartford and placed an option on it, pending approval from Forbes and Sachs, who were by now in different corners of Europe.

Nearby, at Paul Rosenberg's gallery on the rue de la Boetie, Chick discovered an entirely different masterpiece, *Les Saltimbanques Changing Place*, by Honoré Daumier. At first glance, it was almost a sketch, a stark monochromatic commingling of watercolor, gouache, ink, sanguine, charcoal, and pencil, painted about 1865. Trudging toward the viewer, a destitute family of street performers—a woman with a tambourine, a downcast man in a tired clown's costume, and a child with the emaciated body and hollow eyes of an old man—carry their few possessions from one section of Paris to another. For Chick, the image was as restrained in its emotion as it was forthright in its social commentary: "Solitude and suffering were not for Daumier sentimental nor yet completely ugly," he wrote, but in fact "heroic." Chick called the drawing "infinitely powerful," pointing out that "the tremendous luminosity of both light and dark passages" showed Daumier's artistic descent from Rembrandt. The "sheer vigor, energy and sculptural quality" of Daumier's best work, said Chick, "has rarely been excelled."[55]

These two works went to the top of his list. Unable to contact Forbes or Sachs, he returned to America at the end of August without buying either of them. His option on the Fra Angelico was set to expire on September first, and he waited for approval with some desperation. "WHAT SHALL I DO?" he cabled Sachs in Paris, warning of the deadline.[56] As with the first Austin acquisition, there was an attempt to get Berenson to ratify the purchase, but the effort was abandoned for lack of time.[57] At the end of August, Forbes cabled Chick to get two of the drawings he had seen in London—Goya's *Majo and Maja* and Greuze's *Seated Woman*—if the Daumier and the Angelico could also be secured. Chick in turn asked Forbes to buy the drawings for him and confirmed the purchase of the Daumier with Rosenberg for $16,000, a high price for a nineteenth-century watercolor. René Gimpel agreed to bring the Fra Angelico on approval to America. In September, Sachs finally cabled Forbes about the two works with his usual ebullience: "CONGRATULATE AUSTIN COURAGEOUS SUPERB PURCHASE DAUMIDER [sic] STOP TELL HIM I ENTHUSIASTIC GEMLIKE ANGELICO FRAGMENT. . . ."[58]

The Daumier became the second great work bought with the Sumner Fund. Chick organized a small exhibition of drawings around it in October for its first showing—including the Goya and the Greuze, along with recent additions to the Sachs collection and a few works on paper owned by Hartford collectors. The *Hartford Times,* probably coached by Chick, crowed that this latest acquisition was not only "one of the best Daumiers in the country," but "far and away better than the two indefinite paintings by this artist in the Metropolitan."[59]

A month later, Gimpel arrived in Hartford with the Fra Angelico angel so the trustees could appreciate its ethereal quality with their own eyes. Forbes gave his blessing,[60] and just before Christmas, the board agreed to purchase it for $24,000. It was precisely the kind of picture to delight a museum board.

Chick dealt differently with the oldest part of the Atheneum's collection. In surveying storage rooms, he had examined the pictures bought in 1841 from the American Academy of the Fine Arts by Daniel Wadsworth and a small group of

Honoré Daumier, The Saltimbanques Changing Place,
c. 1865. Charcoal and watercolor on paper,
14¼ × 11 inches, purchased 1928

other subscribers. He decided that at least eight of these, along with several
pictures bequeathed to the museum by Wadsworth, were either poor copies of
European paintings or in such bad condition that they were not worth keeping.
He consigned them to the museum's furnace on October 15, 1928. That this
unfortunate destruction of the museum's past occurred on his first anniversary
as director was more symbolic than anyone recognized at the time.

At the end of November, Chick presented an exhibition of Edward Hopper
watercolors, aimed at giving the public a look at the highest level of contemporary achievement in this medium by an accessible artist. Hopper had had his
first one-man show at the Whitney Studio Club in New York in 1920, but this
was his first solo museum exhibition. As a watercolorist himself, Chick had a
particular appreciation for Hopper's mastery of composition and his delineation of form through the use of light and shadow. The slightly eerie atmo-

sphere that infused many of the pictures made them even more appealing to Chick. The twelve works on view, nine from Hopper's dealer Frank K. M. Rehn, represented the maximum yearly output of this painstaking artist, whose pictures were difficult to obtain. Earlier in the year, Chick had bought Hopper's *Captain Strout's House,* an outstanding watercolor, and before the show closed he acquired a second example for the collection, *Rockport Harbor.* One of the trustees, Robert Huntington, himself an amateur artist, bought another work from the exhibition, *Customs House, Portland,* which he eventually gave to the museum.[61] Chick felt encouraged, at least temporarily, that he was beginning to stimulate local collecting.

Adding a new dimension to his artistic agenda, Chick announced that he would present a concert of twentieth-century music in December. He could neither play nor read music, but he had loved it since childhood and was particularly anxious to promote contemporary works. With a few Hartford friends, he organized a musical subscription society, christening it "The Friends and Enemies of Modern Music," a name chosen, he later told a concert audience, "so that the members would not be too frightened at the seriousness of our purpose." Chick coyly began letters to members with "Dear Friend or Enemy."

The Friends and Enemies of Modern Music was one more sign of Chick's determination to make the museum a place where horizons would be widened through experiencing the art of the present. Ten years later, he explained to a Hartford audience that he had come to enjoy the work of contemporary composers through his "constant attendance" at Diaghilev's ballets:

> Thus although not a musician, equipped with no musical vocabulary, not able to tell a tuba from a French horn, and having, as many people will tell you, no musical taste whatsoever, in listening to modern music, the music of my time, I at least did not feel like one of the three little pigs in the presence of the big bad wolf.
>
> I believed in the importance of the contemporary composer and felt more or less with him the sad plight of all modern creative spirits who have, alas, so limited an audience. I wanted to find him a small but sympathetic and intelligent audience in Hartford.[62]

Hartford people were used to sponsoring private chamber concerts in their homes. Trustee Archibald Welch, president of the Hartford School of Music, had concerts every Sunday evening in his house on Woodland Street.[63] Familiar piano pieces by Schumann and Brahms were among the favorite selections at such gatherings. Listening to works by modern composers was not even contemplated.[64]

Nevertheless, Chick persuaded the Charles Goodwins to host the first concert of the Friends and Enemies of Modern Music at their home on Scarborough

Edward Hopper, Captain Strout's House, Portland Head, *1927.*
Watercolor on paper, 14 × 20 inches, purchased 1928

Street. He invited a junior at Harvard, Elliott Carter, to play a two-piano program with his teacher, Clifton Furness. Recommended by Charles Ives for
admission to Harvard, Carter (who later won two Pulitzer Prizes) was in the
class of 1930. As Carter found that there was little interest in contemporary
music in the Harvard Music Department, he and his friends formed a modern
music society and played new works for each other.[65] Chick heard Carter perform at these private concerts and immediately recruited him to inaugurate his
own music society. Chick had a sixth sense about talent, which his peers
repeatedly mentioned. "He was so quick," said Philip Johnson. "Chick saw
what I could give, what everybody could give. He'd pick things up almost faster
than I could say them. . . . 'Firebrand'—that's not a bad word for him, because
he set fires everywhere."[66] Chick scheduled the Hartford concert for Wednesday, December 12, two days before Carter's twentieth birthday.

    Carter and Furness chose a sophisticated program, introducing Austin's
audience to a wide range of advanced—and sometimes conflicting—techniques
of composition, both European and American. The evening began arrestingly
with Stravinsky's *Sacre du printemps,* followed by other works which became
classics of twentieth-century music: Milhaud's *Le Boeuf sur le toit,* Schoenberg's
Six Piano Pieces, Poulenc's *Sonate à quatre mains,* Ives's "Thoreau" from his
sonata *Concord, 1840–1860,* and George Antheil's *Ballet mécanique,* played

with a piano roll on a mechanical piano. Furness predicted to Chick that Antheil's piece, so pointedly a reflection of the Machine Age, would be "the tour de force of the evening."[67] The program included other Stravinsky works, *Parade* by Erik Satie (one of Chick's favorite composers), and Paul Hindemith's *Nusch-Nuschi Dances.* It is likely that the small audience had a mixed reaction to the long concert, and undoubtedly Ruth and Charles Goodwin approached it as a novelty that quickly became tedious. But for many, there was pleasure in being *au courant.* Some members were uncertain about which camp they belonged to, but they did not want to be left out. An insurance vice president wrote Chick that he was "most interested in what you are trying to do and while I cannot detect whether I am a friend or enemy, I am enclosing my check."[68]

It was typical of Chick's manic energy that only a few hours before the first concert of the Friends and Enemies, he opened an exhibition of modern furnishings and decorative arts in his own apartment on Farmington Avenue. The idea came from a visit the previous March to Lord & Taylor's Fifth Avenue store for their *Exposition of Modern French Decorative Art,* the largest show of its kind in the country up to that time. The American marketplace was responding to the famous *Exposition Internationale des Arts Décoratifs et Industriels Modernes* (hence the later nickname "Art Deco") held in Paris in 1925, which had been seen the next year in an abbreviated version at major American museums. The modern French furniture, paintings, sculpture, ceramics, glassware, metalwork, rugs, and textiles were displayed in glamorous ensembles at Lord & Taylor—and in other shows at Macy's, Wanamaker's, Altman's, and Saks Fifth Avenue. These displays created a huge demand among fashionable New Yorkers for both the expensive originals and the copies that leading American department stores shamelessly commissioned.

Chick had been so taken with the Lord & Taylor show that he had approached the store's president about organizing a smaller version for the Atheneum.[69] Then, while he was traveling in Europe in the summer of 1928, Chick was impressed by the rapid progress of modern design in Germany. (The French had excluded German artists and firms from the Paris exposition.) He found modern German wallpaper, lighting fixtures, metalwork, and furniture "more robust and virile than that of the French." Chick liked both the Art Deco and the newer, more functional style in Germany. He told a Hartford reporter that

> the Germans realize that old-fashioned workmanship no longer exists in the new art and therefore seek to let the surface, planes, metal, wood and glass used in homes and buildings in that country reveal their own beauty. They make shape and simplicity count for everything. The rooms, too, are shaped in modern design with ceilings in some cases

fashioned in planes. I was in Germany four years ago and was surprised to discover that since that time a complete new art has sprung
up there. Even the advertisements, signs on buildings, printing and the
trolley cars assume the modern shape and design.[70]

In the fall, Chick returned to Lord & Taylor and made arrangements to purchase or borrow some of the choicest items from their spring show for an exhibition, not in the Atheneum but in a second apartment he added to his living
quarters on Farmington Avenue. He was about to install a series of earlier
period rooms in the museum, but it would have been difficult to convince the
board to buy modern furnishings. Besides, by this time he coveted them for
himself. They were luxurious and superbly crafted. Having them would put him
on the forward edge of his time, just where he liked to be. From the point of
view of his mission to educate the public, what better way to demonstrate the
beauty and utility of the new designs than to live with them? And Chick always
wanted to share his own excitement about something new.

In decorating the apartment, Chick combined advanced German accessories with furniture from Lord & Taylor. To strengthen the ensembles, he also
borrowed contemporary paintings and drawings by Elsie Driggs, Marie Laurencin, Juan Gris, John Marin, Yasuo Kuniyoshi, and others from New York
dealers and a Hartford collector.

The rooms were open to the public through the end of December, and the
city was agog. It was the first modern apartment in America ever put on view by
a museum.[71] The *Hartford Courant* ran a double-page rotogravure spread of the
spaces, interspersed with pictures from the earlier Lord & Taylor exhibition. A
Hartford Times reporter who previewed the rooms was wildly enthusiastic about
what she saw and about this museum director who had brought such a bold
manifestation of the modern to Hartford. "Think of the moral courage and
strength of will it must require to have a room painted with two walls gray and
two black! Consider the nice balance of neutrality attained by blending gray,
black and brown. . . . You will marvel at the ability of this young man, who is an
artist in his own right." Chick's decor captured "the spirit of the machine age
and the art represented by the modern skyscraper."[72] Such praise of Chick was
not uncommon in the *Times* and the *Courant*. The fact was that by 1928 most of
the local newspaper critics had fallen in love with him; they could not have
asked for a more stimulating antidote to conventional Hartford.

Visitors approached the four rooms—a living room, bathroom, study, and
sun porch—through Chick's original apartment of 1927, which he had decorated with antique French and Venetian furniture in muted colors. Stepping
from this traditional space into the connecting apartment was breathtaking. In
the first modern room, Chick had installed black wall-to-wall carpeting and

had painted the woodwork battleship gray and the ceiling silver. The windows were framed with straight drapes of oyster-white celanese, and the walls were covered with hand-blocked French paper by Andre Grult. This was printed in shades of black and gray on white with a design depicting little plump women amid exotic foliage and odd-looking birds. German lighting fixtures, flush against the walls and ceiling, were made of flat planes of frosted glass, silver, pewter, and iron. There was a desk of amboyna wood and ivory by Jules Leleu and a couch by Emile-Jacques Ruhlmann in taupe velour, accented with triangular cushions of ivory and hyacinth blue. A coffee set in silver and rosewood by Jean Puiforcat was displayed on a coffee table, and there were decorative objects by René Lalique and the Wiener Werkstätte placed around the room.

In the hall, against a wallpaper of citron-green and lemon stripes, there were pictures by Marin and Kuniyoshi (showing an artichoke in a wine glass). Chick had painted the woodwork lime green. Off the hall was a bathroom vibrating with orange, green, and yellow wallpaper from Germany, its window and shower curtains made of rough silk in a glaring shade of chartreuse.

Most memorable of all was the study, with a bed by Pierre Chareau, suspended from the ceiling by four wrought-iron tubes and decorated with palisander wood and heavy tan and ivory rayon hangings designed by Helene Henry. A recent watercolor of a female nude by Russian artist Ossip Zadkine was displayed against the hangings. In addition to a desk by Chareau, the study featured a Wassily chair designed by Marcel Breuer of the Bauhaus. More advanced than any of the Art Deco pieces, it was too daunting for the local reviewer: "I was not be lured into the modern German chair in this room—a contraption of steel tubing and gray canvas which has altogether too much suggestion of what one is perched upon in a doctor's office."[73]

Beyond the study was a sun porch with a dark eggplant carpet, Rodier curtains under coral draperies, walls covered in a subtle checkerboard of blond wood veneer, a chair in turquoise and silver, a sofa in violet and rose, and as a final, decisive note, a skyscraper bookstand painted in black and Chinese red.

The stir the apartment made remained vivid to visitors decades later. One remembered it as "bizarre. For that day and age, it was an absolute shot between the eyes. People had never seen anything like it, it was so extreme."[74]

In the *Courant,* Chick acknowledged the implications of the new style. It reflected "an age in which the craftsman has been supplanted by the machine. Ours is not a pretty moment, nor yet a graceful moment. It is a moment of the stern and somewhat cruel realization of the power of steam, of steel and electricity."[75] These rooms were only a prelude to the coming of the Machine Age to Hartford.

Chick invited his Trinity students to a party in the apartment so they could appreciate the new styles at close range. "There might have been a dozen of us

The sun porch in Chick's apartment, 1928

because Trinity classes were small," one of them remembered. "As we came in, he was ushering a young lady out the other door, and I remember as she went out, he gave her a pat on the fanny." It was only later that any of them realized that the woman making her escape was Helen Goodwin, niece of the president of the Atheneum.[76]

"Dearest Cunning"

For you, sir, are so clever
So obviously "the top."
I wish you'd go on forever,
I wish even more you'd stop.

For it's bad for me, it's bad for me,
This knowledge that you're going mad for me. . . .
It's so good for me, so new for me
To see someone in such a stew for me,
And when you say you'd do all you could for me
It's so good for me, it's bad for me. . . .

—Cole Porter, "It's Bad for Me"

H elen and Chick called each other "Cunning," an adjective most often
bestowed by the Goodwins on children, puppies, and anything else
they found adorable. Even late in Chick's life, when he was away
from Helen for long stretches of time, no letter went out from him to
her without the familiar salutation: "Dearest Cunning."

That they found a single name to describe each other was telling, for they
gave the impression of being two halves of a whole. "They were very, very different," said Russell Hitchcock, "but there was a very happy balance between
them. I think they both appreciated particularly what was most different about
the other."[1] It might also be said that if Chick Austin was a whirlwind, Helen
Goodwin became the eye of the storm. She seemed to be everything his irrepressible nature needed: the steady calm, the safe haven, the sympathetic
heart. And just as he knew quality in an undiscovered work of art, or promise in
an untried talent, he sensed instinctively what she could be to him.

He saw her first against a backdrop of drawing rooms in the stately homes
of Hartford, soon after he arrived. He was the prize dinner guest of the season,

the boy wonder of the Atheneum, and at every party—which amounted to the same party in different houses because this was a small town—among dignified museum officials, society matrons and the "right sort" of young people, Helen stood out.

At twenty-nine, two years older than he, she was the picture of an English beauty—slim, fair, and blue-eyed, with perfect manners and a gentle, soft-spoken reserve that had already attracted many eligible young men. Her aristo-cratic features radiated serenity, but a sardonic wit and a gift for mimicry (she could put on a convincing Down-East drawl) made her unexpectedly enter-taining.

They quickly discovered shared enthusiasms. Like Chick, Helen was just back from a summer in Europe on her own. During her one week in London, she had attended two performances of Diaghilev's Ballets Russes. Music meant as much to her as it did to him (unlike Chick, she could read a score and play the piano), and at the Paris Opera that summer she had seen both *Faust* and *Der Rosenkavalier*.[2] Her love of art was immense as well. In Venice, Florence, and Siena she had spent days exploring galleries, churches, and historic sites. Chick, of course, knew these cities intimately. They were kindred spirits.

Helen's knowledge of art was well grounded. Like most wellborn females of her generation, she learned to draw as a young girl, and at Miss Porter's School in Farmington, she had taken every art history course available. After graduat-ing in 1918, she had continued her studies at the Art Students League in New York, at life-drawing classes in Paris, and at the Hartford Art School, one of the oldest academies of its kind in the United States. Her aunt Ruth Goodwin presided over it just as her uncle Charlie presided over the Atheneum. Ruth Goodwin had recruited Helen as a trustee early on, and by the time Chick met her, she was the school's treasurer. As a Goodwin, Helen had a sense of fiscal responsibility bred into her, and she had thoroughly modernized the school's finances.[3]

Until Chick arrived, the Wadsworth Atheneum had never attracted Helen as a place where art could be enjoyed. She had known the museum as long as she could remember, but she shared her brother Francis's view that it was "a kind of a dingy place,"[4] and visited it only on state occasions like the opening of the Morgan Memorial wing in 1910, when J. Pierpont Morgan came to town in his private railroad car. (What had impressed the eleven-year-old Helen most that day was not the new building, but her cousin Pierpont's grotesquely disfigured nose.)

By the time her uncle Charlie was elected president, however, she knew enough about the revolutionary changes in the art world to urge him to bring the Atheneum up to date. It should show contemporary paintings. Though he had absolutely no taste for modern art, Goodwin made an effort to please her. The word came down to Mrs. Berger, who duly produced a loan exhibition in January 1927 from the Grand Central Galleries in New York, one of the more mundane sources of recent pictures by eminently forgettable artists. At the opening, obviously pleased with himself, Goodwin asked Helen how she liked the "modern" show. She informed him that it was not very interesting.[5] Chick Austin's appearance in Hartford nine months later transformed Helen's whole view of the Atheneum. Suddenly it was alive, full of possibilities, and he was someone who knew everything about the kind of art that she admired.

Everyone in Helen's immediate family—her mother, Mrs. James Goodwin; her brother, Francis, and his wife, Jane; her sister Mary and her husband, Wilton Graff; and her youngest sister, Lucy—quickly became Chick's adherents. On the surface, Helen's background was the same as that of most members of Hartford society whom Chick got to know. She had a privileged New England childhood. Her father, who died ten years before Chick met her, was the Reverend Dr. James Goodwin, the oldest of the Reverend Francis Goodwin's eight children. Rector of Hartford's Christ Church Cathedral, he had been a man of great erudition. After obtaining his degree from the General Theological Seminary in New York, he had pursued advanced studies at Oxford and the University of Paris and had traveled widely in Europe and Palestine. At the same time, he had liked nothing so much as sailing out of Castine, Maine, where he had a summer parish. Helen's mother, Frances Whittlesey Brown Goodwin, also came from an old Connecticut family. Fanny Goodwin was in her sixties when Chick met her, a stout, warm-hearted, and somewhat demanding widow, happy that her eldest daughter was still at home.

James's income from Christ Church was modest, and his children referred to themselves as the "poor Goodwins," but the family was subsidized by the Reverend Francis, whose fortune came by inheritance from insurance and railroad stocks and large tracts of Hartford real estate. He paid for James's domestic staff, handed down his Cadillac or Brewster when he bought a new automobile, and paid for his grandchildren's education. After his death in 1923, his descendants were the beneficiaries of what Helen's generation called "the Grandfather Trust."

Helen grew up in two successive rectories in downtown Hartford, a short walk from the cathedral. The household was typically late-Victorian, a period that did not die out in Hartford until considerably after the death of the Queen. The children were taught to be frugal, clean, and tidy. If they were disobedient, Nurse would invoke the name of their scariest Goodwin relative: "I'll tell Uncle Charlie," she would warn. When they were young, they took most of their meals in the nursery, except for breakfasts and Sunday dinners.

Helen's childhood was unusually happy, secure in the regular rhythms of going to school and church, calling on her numerous Hartford relations, listening to her mother read aloud in the evenings while she and her sisters drew or made paper dolls, and returning every summer to Castine.

But this tranquil life ended when James Goodwin developed leukemia and died in January 1917.[6] His death was a devastating blow to the children. Francis was a junior at Yale; Helen and Mary were students at Miss Porter's; and Lucy was four days from her tenth birthday.

James had been his father's pride, the scholar and full-time minister he never was, and for the remaining six years of his life, the Reverend Francis took care of his son's widow and children. When the family moved out of the rectory, he gave them the Goodwin farmhouse on Woodland Street and had his nephew, architect Philip Goodwin, remodel it for them.

It was Philip Goodwin's mother, Mrs. James Junius Goodwin, who broadened Helen's education after her father's death. Indeed, for her great-aunt Sallie, the former Josephine Sarah Lippincott of Philadelphia, widowed since 1915 and the mother of three sons, Helen became almost an adopted daughter. Aunt Sallie divided her time between a New York house on East Fifty-fourth Street and "Goodwin Castle" on Woodland Street in Hartford. Helen stayed with her in New York often in the early 1920s, filling the days with trips to museums and galleries; Aunt Sallie treated Helen to clothes at Bergdorf Goodman and performances at the Metropolitan Opera, and she saw that Helen was invited to the fashionable Beaux-Arts Ball. Above all, she encouraged Helen's study of art. She had a small collection of her own, including a van Gogh self-portrait. Twelve years before Chick came to Hartford, she gave the Atheneum $50,000 in memory of her husband—one of the museum's first endowment funds for the purchase of art.

Aunt Sallie took Helen first to San Francisco in 1920,[7] and then to Europe with her son Philip in the spring of 1921. They motored through France for a month. In Monte Carlo, Helen played her first game of roulette and in Nice, she went to a matinee of Diaghilev's Ballets Russes. For another month, they toured England from Oxford and Bath to Tintagel, and in London they saw the first Trooping of the Colour since the World War.[8]

In November 1923, after her grandfather's death, Helen returned to Europe with her sister Mary, then twenty-two. They boarded in small hotels in Paris for four months, studying French, attending life-drawing classes, going to the opera, making excursions into the countryside, and dancing until dawn with men they had met on the boat.[9]

Three years later, in the summer of 1927, feeling hemmed in by Hartford, Helen went off to Europe alone. As the Canadian Pacific's *Empress of France* set sail for England, Helen was entirely on her own for the first time. She enjoyed being a little daring. Like most passengers, she shed the constraints of Prohibition after getting under way, reporting to Mary that she drank "far too many" cocktails "for my good health" in one of the officer's cabins and in the "smoking." She also confessed that she had befriended "a cunning little British Colonel" on the ship and later met him for lunch at his London club. She spent time with another Englishman onboard and dined with him after they arrived as well, happily ignoring the fact that he was a married man: "He is another one who has a wife at home—," Helen wrote Mary, "she doesn't cramp his style in the least, however."[10]

Her love of adventure led her to make the trip from London to Paris by plane. Air travel was an experience few other people in Hartford—or anywhere else, for that matter—had yet attempted. Helen spared her family the anxiety of knowing about it in advance, but described the two-hour-and-ten-minute flight in detail after she had landed safely, obviously elated that she had done something even her mother might have found out of character: "Oh Mother!" she wrote. "It was a wonderful experience! I have wanted to go up in an aeroplane for so long—that it was terribly exciting to do it at last."[11]

Then, fresh from travels that opened her eyes to living more freely, she met Chick Austin. Helen eagerly took part in all his museum activities. She and her sister-in-law, Jane Goodwin, hosted a large dinner party before the Venetian Fete; and, dressed in a satin gown and tricorn hat, Helen led the procession of the Marriage of Venice to the Adriatic. After the ball, when the museum offered Chick's painted Venetian scenes for sale, she bought them all.[12] She and her mother hosted an early concert of the Friends and Enemies of Modern Music at their house. When Chick put his modern apartment on view, Helen was the only person in Hartford who lent a work of art to the exhibition—Kuniyoshi's offbeat watercolor of an artichoke in a wineglass. During his first year as director, Chick was seen with Helen often—at Goodwin family gatherings, dinners around town, restaurants and theaters, and intimate suppers in his own apartment, usually with Francis and Jane.

He was already a deft party-giver and a superb cook. For that era, his attitude toward cooking was more European than American in that he considered it a form of art. He preferred dishes that could be whipped up quickly and given an elegant presentation. Guests remembered oxtail soup, melon with prosciutto, and glazed apple tarts. His sauces were imaginative, and he was especially fond of cayenne. "I put it in everything," he told a friend. "It makes everything taste better."[13] And he always made his own mayonnaise. Magician that he was, he loved to produce soufflés, those delicate creations with the element of surprise at the end. He also happily demonstrated that his back-to-back apartments allowed him to leave the dishes unwashed in the first kitchen and move to the second kitchen for his next party, where he would pile up more dirty dishes. Only after the second dinner would he finally wash them all.[14] It was a practice he learned from his mother.

The better Chick knew her, the more Helen became the ideal mate of his dreams. But he who exuded such confidence was afraid of failing to win her. He kept the intensity of his love a secret from her for a year and lived instead "passionately in my imagination," he later confessed. By the end of 1928 it was apparent to many that Chick had what they called "a crush" on Helen.[15] But he could not bring himself to speak to anyone, including her, about it. His aunt Sue could see it when he visited her in Pennsylvania at Christmas. "I was quite sure he was in love," she later wrote to Helen, "but I couldn't make him tell me anything save that her name was Helen and that she was very charming and altogether wonderful."[16]

In January 1929, Chick could wait no longer. He told Helen he loved her and then, a little offhandedly, masking his nervousness, asked her to marry him. She responded with mixed emotions. First she demurred and called him "presumptuous." But she did not entirely discourage him. She said that she did not believe he loved her enough for marriage. She intimated that Chick saw marrying her simply as a convenient way to settle comfortably in Hartford. At the same time, she confessed to feelings of inferiority—a worry that haunted her all her life, though she was highly skilled at concealing it.[17] She knew she could never approach Chick's knowledge of art; she could never match his wit and inventiveness. Perhaps she would bore him in the end. And there was good reason for Helen to be cautious. Chick was very different from the stable lawyers and insurance executives most of her friends had married. A few of her Goodwin relatives urged her to think twice about being permanently attached to him.[18] Even for a museum director, Chick was a bit too "artistic" for some of them. Helen knew that he was impulsive, and she could see that marrying him would pull her into his world of speed and dazzle. Much as she loved parties, it might be disastrous to be married to someone for whom life was one continuous party. "Chick was flamboyant, and she was a little terrified of that," said Virgil Thomson.[19]

She may have been a little afraid of marriage itself. Though she was thirty years old, an age when many unmarried women were likely to jump at any reasonable offer, a part of her was still very young. She was used to a regular string of beaux and society parties and dances. The family icebox seemed always to be full of orchids for Helen from admirers whom she enjoyed but kept at a subtle distance. Her sister Lucy observed, "I don't think she wanted to be married. I think she wanted to be a sort of wonderfully popular girl forever. . . . Helen appealed to [certain men] because she was like something almost perfect. You felt warmth with Helen in conversation—she could be a pal, she was bright and witty—but she wasn't exactly what you would call a sexy kind of girl. . . . Maybe that's why all these men had such difficulty with her."[20]

Virgil Thomson also emphasized Helen's comparative reserve: "Chick was warm, hospitable, and lots of fun. Helen was not so warm. Helen was Stiff Little

Miss Hartford. You know those Goodwins: they all think they're God's direct descendants. Helen was redeemed and became a wonderful woman sheerly out of her love for Chick. The rest of those Goodwins are stiff as pokers."[21] In fact, years later, it would be clear that if anyone did any redeeming, it was Helen.

Thomson did not want to dwell on the amorous side of Chick's marriage, perhaps because he felt a twinge of jealousy. He was genuinely fond of Helen, but once described her physical appearance with marked exaggeration: "She wasn't beautiful at all. Oh no, skinny little thing, tight mouth and flat-chested, and she had red spots all over her face. She was nice as could be, but Helen was no beauty."[22] This was one instance in which the eye of the beholder was all-important.

For Chick, Helen was "altogether wonderful," and he wanted to marry her because he loved her more than he had ever loved anyone. Writing late in January, after being with her again, he kept his tone subdued, taking care not to scare her off; but he came to the heart of what he felt the relationship would bring him. "What with presumption urging me on and tact trying to restrain me, I find that I have little that I can say, except that my seeing you made me very very happy. With you I experience a peace which before I have never dared hope could be mine."[23]

What Helen did not know was that, with her, he had discovered something that he had not found in his relationships with men. He may have felt that his attachment to her would satisfy him completely. Up until now, the few women his age in the museum world who shared his love of the arts were close friends and colleagues, but they did not inspire romance. In Helen, he had found a woman who adored the arts and was his social and intellectual equal (though she never would have believed it), and who, though she had the backbone of a New England aristocrat, was gentle, sensitive, and fun.

Helen took her time to answer. She retreated to Aunt Sallie's house in New York. Early in February, she sent word that she was sick with the mumps. He was desperate to see her. He invited her to come to his mother's farm in Windham with Francis and Jane and her aunt Ruth Goodwin, presumably as a chaperone. "You must come. I want to talk with you for hours, and hours, alone," he wrote. "We have always been so hedged in by other people and other people's ideas—which is ridiculous as this whole business is our concern and no one elses, really."

He addressed Helen's worries directly and finally exposed the depth of his feelings:

I suppose that [you] dont really believe for a moment that I care for you—which is the natural result of your feelings of inferiority and my inability to show my <u>honest</u> emotions—for fear of being thought insincere, which is the result of living so passionately in my imagination (which is my closest approach to reality) that translation into actuality of my thoughts, I am afraid will sound hollow, particularly if you persist in keeping your little cage between us. . . .

My affection and love for you is built on the solid rock of great admiration for you, supreme delight in being with you and a feeling of entire mental and emotional accord, which is very apparent between us—and you cant deny it![24]

Echoing one of Helen's fears, Virgil Thomson suggested that Chick's motives in wooing Helen were not entirely inspired by love, a suspicion often repeated by people who did not know them well, but surprising coming from an old friend: "The next thing he did was marry into the best family. He didn't marry necessarily for money, because Chick's mother and father were both quite well-to-do. He didn't need money, but social position, or family placement, so to speak, in a town like Hartford was very important to him."[25] Though family ties did mean a great deal to Chick, his desires were more complicated and emotional than Thomson chose to see.

Chick was certainly aware of the advantages of marrying into the local aristocracy, but social status counted for little with him. Perhaps he half-believed his mother's fantasies about royal blood; or perhaps he saw what a fairy-tale muddle she had created, and dismissed the whole notion. And however strategic the marriage appeared, he often complained later about feeling hemmed in by family ties to the museum's most powerful trustees: "The outside world assumed that things were easier for Chick because the dominant members of the board were relatives of his wife," said Russell Hitchcock. "But he was inclined to feel it the other way around."[26]

Chick himself told Helen emphatically that he was not contemplating a "convenient" marriage; in fact, he loved the independent spirit that he saw under her decorous façade:

If you have any idea that I am simply thinking it will be a good plan for me to marry in Hartford and settle down, you are mistaken. I never want to [do] that and I certainly dont want you to do it. I want you have the freedom you need as much as I do, to really breathe and be happy. I should be very hurt if I thought you could think that I could ever want to include you, of all people, in a scheme which seems to me rather cold-blooded—and surely you must know me well enough to realize I am not that.

He was clearly not.

I need you terribly—you are all I ever dared hope to find in a person but thought I could never find. I've wanted so many times desperately to hold you very close and protect you from all those little hurts which the world gives people of our sensitive natures, hurts which are really so insignificant in themselves but which appear so monumental at moments. But I've been always so afraid that you would misunderstand. . . . Cant you realize that my respect for you has made me at times quite cowardly. I am always terrified that I may do something or say something which will make you dislike me. Its silly I suppose, but there you have one of my little difficulties.

And if one of yours is to refuse to believe that you are to me so far beyond any human being in this world, then you'd better start getting over it, and help me retrieve my mistake of not daring to tell it to you yet wanting to tell everyone else. . . .

Please forgive me for saying all this if it annoys you and especially for realizing the direction in which lies my happiness and fighting for it, and, as my happiness will always depend on yours, fighting for yours too. I shant read this over—I can never send letters if I do.

Please come to the farm—otherwise I shall have to move to New York.

All my love always—
(even if you wont believe it!!)
Chick[27]

Helen hesitated. But Chick would not be put off. Six days later, he wrote again: "Still no word from you—but I really dont want you to write—I know you dislike it—and I've put you in a difficult position, I suppose—but then you've put me in one too so we're quits—as far as that goes!" He had heard from Jane Goodwin that Helen had recovered and was going to Atlantic City the following Tuesday. He informed her that he would meet her there on Friday and that Francis would come on Saturday. "So you see," he teased, "even an invalid hasnt a chance in the world of escape and seclusion." He was not to be dissuaded: "Please dont be angry—we will all have such a lark, and anyway I cant possibly wait any longer without seeing you."

He pleaded with her to believe in his sincerity:

Oh, Helen my dearest, please dont say that my dream of sometime being near to you always is an impudence on my part. Think of it as anything else if you like, even an impossibility, but believe that the part you have played in my imagination for the past year is a supremely noble one, and that knowing you has given me the courage to go on in

Hartford. . . . I long so to see you . . . and if I dont, and very soon, the atheneum will either explode or be blown away as I cant keep my mind on it any longer![28]

In the face of his ardent sincerity, the doubts Helen had expressed melted away. Besides, she loved him. Their engagement was announced on March 23, 1929.

Helen and Chick were so openly affectionate that Hitchcock told mutual friends he "had never seen a couple that loved being together as much as Helen and Chick. They would sit holding hands in the evening like young lovers at the movies."[29]

Helen's family wished her well, concentrating on her superior qualities. "I am going to trust that he is good enough for you," wrote Aunt Sallie.[30] "He is very fortunate indeed," Cousin Philip Goodwin told Helen,[31] a point he reiterated to Chick, urging him on to greater professional heights: "If anything could convince me that you were qualified to fill the shoes of, say, Mr. Robinson of the Metropolitan Museum, it would be that your choice in a wife seems such discrimination that you must be unusually gifted. Ho then for the altar and the Metropolitan."[32]

With her usual insight, Chick's aunt Sue Etnier congratulated Helen and said that she had felt for some time that Chick "wouldn't be the man he might become until he had found a girl who would help him round out his life."[33]

And Trinity College's President Ogilby quaintly rhapsodized to Chick about the news, comparing him to the Prince in *Sleeping Beauty:* "And now here you are in Hartford, come like a fairy prince to awaken a sleeping city to a sense of beauty, breaking the spell that binds us as you win the Princess for your bride!"[34]

Helen and Chick decided to be married that summer in Paris. There they could escape what they saw as the fuss of a large Hartford wedding with the requisite summoning of the Goodwins, the Austins, and the Etniers. Besides, they reasoned, Chick needed to be in Europe on his usual scouting mission for the museum. They could stay in his mother's house in Antwerp for part of their wedding trip. And there was no livelier place for Americans abroad than Paris in 1929. Years later, Helen explained their decision simply: "We thought it would be fun."[35]

Meanwhile, the engagement had taken Chick's mother completely by surprise. She was in Belgium on another extended European stay and was not pleased to have had no warning. Knowing how possessive his mother was, Chick surely wanted to avoid discussing the matter until it was a fait accompli. He made light of her disgruntled reaction, however, and told Helen that "she forgives all provided we write to her." Laura agreed to investigate the legal requirements for marriage in France.[36]

Helen's sister Lucy, who had been studying art at Fontainebleau, was recruited to make arrangements for the wedding. The ceremony was to take place on July 11 at the American Cathedral of the Holy Trinity on the Avenue Georges V, the Episcopal church Helen had first visited with Aunt Sallie in 1921. She had worshiped there regularly during her winter in Paris two years later. Lucy reserved rooms for her mother and Helen nearby at the Hotel Georges V. She next booked part of the dining room at the Plaza Athénée for the reception. "We were used to being big fish in the small pond of Hartford," said Lucy. "So we thought, 'Why not in Paris, too?' " Costly surprises were in store for Mrs. Goodwin.[37]

Chick's mother's questions about the arrangements were so persistent that he finally apologized for annoying her, which resulted in her blunt denial of his concerns: "As to my being annoyed as to your wedding plans it is all imagination, forget it." She sent Helen an antique chest as an engagement present and wrote them separately that her wedding gift would be a country house—next door to hers at the farm in Windham. "Hope you will both love it—it will be a change for you to run up there sometimes for a week end, I am sure I already love Helen and hope she will love me." Again she praised Chick for his achievements at the museum: "I am so glad you are making such a success in your work, and know you must love it or you could not possibly accomplish so much."[38] As the impending change in her son's life approached, Laura felt a growing sense of loss. For all her independence, she still considered Everett the center of her world. "Boy dearest," she wrote in early June, "I am thinking of you, and wondering when I will see you—I hope I may have a little visit with you before you leave me entirely." Not that she hoped to keep him single. The Etnier and Morrison family tree was too precious to her not to want to perpetuate it. And, in the end, so was his happiness. But in case his thoughts were too full of his bride-to-be, she reminded him: "Do not forget I am too waiting for you."[39]

Chick embarked for Europe on the *Paris* on Tuesday, June 25, to meet Laura and accompany her to Paris. His father sailed alone the following Monday on the *France*.

Helen and her mother had arrived in Paris earlier in the month. Appalled at the rates at the Hotel Georges V, Mrs. Goodwin would not spend a single night there and moved the family to cheaper lodgings immediately. Lucy's other arrangements, however, prevailed. And she and Helen were allowed to book a table for the rehearsal dinner at the Café des Ambassadeurs, the fashionable nightclub on the Champs Elysées. The sisters also went together to choose a wedding dress. Helen felt that at thirty-one she was too old to be married in white, which in any case would have been too conventional for her. She and Lucy bought one of couturier Lucien Lelong's newest creations off the rack—an unusual gray-blue silk tulle dress with horizontal bands of satin above a split-level hemline, a style that anticipated the 1930s. A satin turban of the same color completed the very up-to-date ensemble.

The wedding party was small. Besides Mrs. Goodwin, her four children, two accompanied by their spouses, and Arthur and Laura Austin, there were a few people whom Helen's sister Mary and her husband, Wilton Graff, picked up on the boat; a handful of Hartford friends, including Chick's secretary, Peggy Parsons, who was one of Helen's childhood friends; and Edward Forbes, in Europe for his usual summer circuit to museums and dealers. At the last minute the Paris art dealer, René Gimpel, who had sold Chick the Fra Angelico, was invited to join the company.

On the evening before the ceremony, after a rehearsal at the cathedral, the wedding party and most of the guests attended a lavish dinner at the Ambassadeurs. The party occupied one long table, which the waiters kept well supplied with bottles. Attentively, they refilled glasses as soon as they were empty. Mrs. Goodwin, sitting at the head of the table, was not used to drinking. Suddenly she said quietly, "I've got to go," and rose unsteadily to her feet.[40] At that moment the head waiter materialized with an enormous bill, and, much to her embarrassment, Helen's mother found herself short of cash, a terrible predicament for a Goodwin. Overhearing the conversation, a none too sober middle-aged Hartford woman said, "Oh, do you want money?" and pulled up her dress, revealing a money bag hanging from her waist.[41] Helen's brother, Francis, took charge, gave the headwaiter a deposit out of his own pocket with only enough left for his taxi, and promised that his mother would pay the bill if it could be brought to her hotel the next day. This was acceptable, and Mrs. Goodwin was escorted away. The headwaiter appeared at her hotel at eight o'clock on the morning of the wedding to collect his money.[42]

By four in the afternoon of July 11, the small band of family and guests had arrived at the American Cathedral and assembled in the choir stalls just in front of the altar. Helen, holding a shower bouquet of white orchids, entered with her mother from a side door and mounted the few steps to the altar, where her mother gave her away. After photographs on the church steps in the bright sunlight, the party went to the Plaza Athénée for a champagne supper, where toasts were given to the bride, groom, and the "Two Mothers."

Among the guests caught by the wedding photographer was Arthur Austin, beaming as he strode out of the church. He was very likely rejoicing that his son was getting out from under Laura's wing and had found an attractive and personable woman with whom to share his life. Laura did not appear in Chick and Helen's wedding album, but she was vividly remembered. To Lucy Goodwin, "she seemed like a bossy woman—who wasn't quite sure of herself—and crazy about Chick. She had the charm of eccentricity and boldness. She was a force, you could see."[43]

Helen and Chick, newly married in Paris, July 11, 1929

Helen and Chick left immediately for Antwerp to spend the first part of their wedding trip alone in Laura's house. From Belgium they traveled back through France to Italy. By September, they were in Venice, where they found the inspiration for the house that they were already planning to build on Goodwin property in Hartford. The Reverend Francis Goodwin had amassed land in the nineteenth century, and his children and grandchildren were able to buy parcels on Scarborough Street for token sums. His son Charles had been the first to build a house on the street in 1911, and Helen's uncles William and Spencer and her brother, Francis, had followed his example. Helen and Chick acquired a lot next to Francis and Jane on the east side of the street. The Park River flowed along the rear of the property, dividing it from a wooded hillside. With three Goodwin uncles and his brother-in-law on the same block, Chick would be living deep inside Goodwin territory. His mother, with her weakness for acquiring houses, agreed to pay the building costs.

Chick and Helen had been uncertain about the design of the house until they spotted the Villa Ferretti on the Brenta River at the town of Dolo, not far from Venice. It was a classically simple country house, built in 1596 by Vincenzo Scamozzi, a student and rival of Andrea Palladio, the Renaissance master architect. Following no surviving Hartford precedents—except, strangely enough, Daniel Wadsworth's Palladian barn across the street from the Atheneum—they decided that this little-known villa would be the perfect model for their new home. The understated lines of its long white stucco façade could be translated into the painted wood of a New England house. They took snapshots to give their architect.

At the same time, Chick introduced Helen to one of his favorite dealers, Adolf Loewi, who also served as the German consul in Venice until the Nazis came to power four years later. Loewi specialized in baroque and rococo furnishings—the graceful chairs, gilded and elaborately carved console tables, mirrors, and woodwork that strongly appealed to Chick.

At Loewi's gallery, Chick and Helen found a large Bavarian wooden alcove, once a bed-niche, from the early eighteenth century, carved with leaves, flowers, and cherubs, its worn surface still showing traces of gilt, blue-green, and copper finishes. This rococo "boisserie" would form one wall of their dining room. Several months later they ordered yards of eighteenth-century Italian blue-green silk brocatelle from Loewi for $3,400, with which they covered the interior of the niche and the other three dining room walls.[44]

For the living room, they chose a French Louis XV mantelpiece of painted stone, surmounted by an eight-paned mirror in a rococo frame. Loewi also sold them eight large tempera panels, painted in Turin in the early eighteenth century, depicting fanciful voyages, rustic maidens, buccaneers, and a classical harbor scene after a work by Claude Lorrain that hung in the Louvre. These panels were to cover the living room walls.

From other dealers, Helen and Chick purchased a giant set of rococo doors from a French armoire, baroque sconces and doorway arches, a Venetian door that had been converted into a mirror, and two seventeenth-century polychromed wooden sculptures—one of a hollow-eyed St. Luke holding his gospel, the other of St. George killing a diminutive dragon. Chick already owned several Venetian Louis XV chairs, which he and Helen would combine with early nineteenth-century English and American pieces belonging to their families.

The charges from Loewi alone came to over $15,000, nearly four times Chick's salary. Chick assumed he would be able to pass them along to his mother as part of the building costs. He asked Loewi to bill him for the purchases, promising to pay as soon as he returned to the United States.[45] He continued to spend lavishly throughout the trip. At the end of September, shortly before they embarked for America, he and Helen were again in Paris. One afternoon, while Helen napped in the hotel room, Chick went out and, with most of their remaining cash, bought a magnificent Art Deco silver coffee service by Puiforcat.[46] They were then so strapped for money that they had to return third-class, much to Helen's annoyance.[47]

Chick's spending habits on his honeymoon gave Helen a foretaste of his extravagance. A few days after arriving back in Hartford and settling into the Farmington Avenue apartment, she opened a closet and found piles of unpaid bills. Then she discovered that none of the local grocers would give her credit because Chick was in debt to them all. This came as a shock; Helen had always kept meticulous accounts and paid her bills before they were due. Chick generally paid his bills only after he had exhausted every means of delay. For him, money existed to be spent and overspent, and he had a lifelong compulsion to acquire beautiful and expensive objects. Chick would buy things that he admired and then, not knowing what to do with them, would give them away. Early in the marriage, Helen repeatedly confided to her mother that Chick's cavalier attitude toward money worried her.[48]

Overspending had become ingrained in him in part because it was the most effective method of extracting money from his mother, who held a tight rein on her considerable income. Calling Laura "a miser type," Russell Hitchcock sympathized with Chick's complaints about his mother's parsimony when he wanted something: "She was rather cantankerous, and she had all the money, and she doled it out grudgingly to Chick. That was why he was always in debt. It was only by going into debt that he could get his mother to bail him out."[49] This of course would have been an easy way to keep her boy dependent, but Laura also knew that no matter how much she gave him, Chick would spend it at the first sight of a stylish wristwatch or a rococo tureen.

Money from his mother to pay Loewi's bills was not as readily forthcoming as Chick had anticipated. A month after he and Helen returned from Europe, the stock market crashed, ushering in the Great Depression. Though the Depression did not have a devastating effect on Laura's finances, it inevitably curtailed her income. Chick's communications from Loewi fell into an all too familiar pattern, as months turned into years: "BANK NOT RECEIVED PAYMENT AM ASTONISHED FURTHER DELAY HAVING BASED OWN ENGAGEMENTS ON YOUR PROMISE PLEASE PAY IMMEDIATELY."[50] This telegram was only the preamble to a long string of dunning letters from the dealer. Austin sent a few large checks to Loewi, but the only concrete explanation that he offered for his tardiness came in March 1932 when he claimed, not very convincingly, that he was in dire circumstances: "My financial difficulties have been such that we may yet be forced to sell our house at a great loss. However I think that, as we are not going abroad this summer, I shall be able to send you some money then."[51] The debt was finally settled after four years. In the interim, Russell Hitchcock's remarks to the contrary, Laura established a trust fund for Chick that generated a few thousand dollars a year, to give him a little security and room for his inevitable indulgences.

Financial considerations did not stop Helen and Chick from hiring the fashionable New York architect Leigh H. French, Jr., a friend of Philip Goodwin, to design the Scarborough Street house. Construction began in January 1930 and continued through the end of the summer. Chick was insistent about so many details that friction developed between him and the architect. Halfway through the job, French was fired, and Chick supervised the Hartford contractor himself. The final cost for construction was $43,000. With the furnishings, the total easily exceeded $60,000, a very large sum for those days.

As its Palladian façade rose up, the house attracted enormous publicity— the *Hartford Times* published an elevation and floor plan—and by the time it was finished, there was such widespread curiosity that the Austins opened it to Atheneum members for twelve hours on December 16, two days before Chick's thirtieth birthday. Over four hundred people inspected the premises, guided by Helen, Chick, and museum staff members. What they saw was a pristinely white miniature villa, eighty-six feet wide and only eighteen feet deep, set far back from the street on two and a half acres of recently graded land. The two-story house was dominated by a central bay, topped by a triangular pediment, and fronted with four shallow pilasters, each one capped by a modernized ionic scroll. The bays flanking the center each contained eight tall windows. At first glance, it seemed a perfectly symmetrical house, but two windows in each wing were false—window frames enclosed blank boards—and these false windows were not symmetrically placed. Chick seemed to be playing some kind of architectural joke on Palladio, and the effect was vaguely disturbing to some Hartford observers.

Indeed, the novelty of a Palladian villa in the midst of respectable Neo-Colonial and Tudor Revival houses did not sit well with many of the neighbors. "Odd" was the word most commonly used to describe the house, though the attorney who lived directly across the street called it "an excrescence."[52] A few Atheneum trustees found it both pretentious and frivolous; they dubbed it "the paste-board palace."[53] Others called it "the stage-set house," which Chick found appropriate. He told a friend that it looked like a painted theatrical set because he had a two-dimensional eye.[54] Later, when Chick and Helen painted the flat surfaces on the exterior a neutral gray, leaving the architectural details white, the house took on a truly surreal quality, and passersby began to believe that it was not even a house at all.[55]

It became the setting for the theater of Chick's life. In it he combined his two passions—the baroque and the modern. The first floor was a Venetian fantasy world. The curved central hall, with a graceful circular staircase, rose two

130 Scarborough Street, December 1930

stories up to a lighted dome. Its travertine floor authentically evoked an Italian villa, with a subtle nod to the modernists who favored the material as well. Moving down a short hall to the right of the entrance, visitors came to an intimate music room, extending from the front to the rear of the house, decorated with four framed eighteenth-century Venetian silk panels, painted with chinoiserie designs. As Chick had one panel left over, he simply affixed it to the ceiling. He painted the walls a golden beige with woodwork of a deeper gold, streaked with Chinese red to echo the frames of the panels. From there, guests walked through huge baroque double doors and down two steps into the living room. The ceiling was eleven feet high, giving the effect of great space, though the room was only the depth of the house. The tempera panels, the French mantel-piece, and the eighteenth-century furniture were set off by a dusty rose wall-to-wall carpet and lighter rose taffeta curtains. For these walls, Chick used a subtle dark green with undertones of blue and gray, a color Chick drew from the stormy skies in the painted panels. Decorative objects—Meissen figurines, silver bowls, small decorative boxes—were placed on the mantel and tables. (Chick was always a little cavalier about his furnishings. One winter afternoon, as a fire burned in the fireplace, a group of teachers came to tea. A large woman sat down heavily on a gilded chair, which collapsed into several pieces on the floor. After helping his mortified guest to her feet, Chick said cheerfully,

Living room, Austin House, 1930

Dining room, the "Venetian Lagoon," Austin House, 1930

"Think nothing of it. These eighteenth-century chairs make the best firewood," and tossed the pieces into the fire.)[56]

The dining room, reached by a rear passage or back through the entrance hall, was also two steps below the level of the central part of the house. This room was the most luxurious of all, with the Italian blue-green silk brocatelle shimmering from ceiling to floor complemented by a wall-to-wall carpet of a rich copper color. It was a stunning setting for the rococo boiserie. Chick framed this elaborate niche with a crown molding of antique white, which reinforced the fact that it had been taken from another place and time and incorporated into a twentieth-century house. The furnishings included a Louis XVI dining table and eighteenth-century Italian chairs. For years, guests would talk about dining in the "Venetian lagoon" or "the fishbowl."

Moving upstairs, visitors left the elegance of the eighteenth century and entered the arresting world of the modern. Helen's dressing room, adjoining the master bedroom, was modeled on that of Walter Gropius, designed in collaboration with Marcel Breuer, at the Bauhaus in Dessau, Germany. Here surfaces were flat, immaculate. One wall was a gray-blue, one cream, one beige, and one a deep cocoa; all the surfaces facing the same direction, including the interiors of cabinets and closets, were painted the same color. As Chick told the *Hartford Times,* "the difference in color is very restful as it follows the natural values of light. Thus the wall opposite the principal windows is finished in a light color, while the first wall, naturally in the shadow, is done in a dark color or black."[57] The floor was jet-black linoleum, polished to a high gloss, and the lighting fixtures were sleek chromium tubes from Germany. A chair and a chaise longue designed by Le Corbusier in chrome and canvas (the only examples of his furniture in America, Chick told the press) were lent to the Austins by Chick's friend Cary Ross at the Museum of Modern Art.[58] A chrome tubular stool and a circular glass-and-chrome table, both by Breuer, completed the streamlined furnishings. Chick's dressing room, reached through another door in the master bedroom, was decorated in a similar vein, its angled walls covered in a wallpaper with horizontal stripes of varying thicknesses and colors. Beyond that was his bathroom, with a freestanding stainless steel washstand, modern German lighting fixtures, a jet-black floor, a black tub with a stainless steel side, and walls of pale pink, intense blue, and cocoa. As in the other spaces, Chick mixed all the colors himself, imbuing the architecture of the Bauhaus with his own personality.

These dressing rooms were among the very earliest examples in an American private home of what would soon be christened the International Style. Architect Richard Neutra's Lovell house in Los Angeles, the first in this country to be entirely in that mode, was built only the previous year, in 1929; and Philip Johnson's unprecedented New York apartment, designed in the new style by Mies van der Rohe, was furnished at exactly the same time as the Austin house.[59] The Austins' dressing rooms were companion pieces to a Bauhaus-inspired office that Chick had installed for himself at the museum earlier in the year.

It was later assumed that Chick was instructed in his architectural pioneering by Russell Hitchcock and Philip Johnson, both good friends. But both denied it. Asked if he had been a "sounding board" for the house, Hitchcock replied, "I don't think so, particularly. It's true that [Chick] used many of his friends and acquaintances as experts on this and that, but he always knew what he wanted. We used to say that Chick picked up things by osmosis. I mean, he seemed always to know what was going on in the world."[60]

In the two years since his apartment exhibition, Chick had moved to the "purest" form of modernism, but the Art Deco he had promoted earlier was by no means neglected. A second-floor guest room contained furniture designed by German architect Bruno Paul in pale green and silver, set against green, yellow, and silver wallpaper. The basement bar successfully combined Art Deco with the Bauhaus style. The walls, like the dressing rooms, were painted different colors, and the fixtures were advanced, but the Chareau hanging bed was the centerpiece of the bar, and legions of the Austins' overnight guests made

Helen Austin's Bauhaus dressing room, 1930

good use of it. It was an eclectic room that serious adherents of each style would have found outrageous. "There are no two sides on an art subject today that are so opposed as the Art Deco and the modern were in those days," Philip Johnson remembered decades later, "but Chick knew where the streams were going. He knew better than the people who were in them."[61]

From the perspective of half a century, friends of Chick and Helen saw the house as a precursor. Lincoln Kirstein, remembering it as "a jewel-box" that combined "splendor and intimacy," suggested that its simplified Palladianism was "the first example of Post-Modernism, *avant la lettre,*—in fact before 'modernism' had even triumphed."[62] Philip Johnson agreed, claiming with sly humor that the pure modernists of that time (a rarefied handful, actually) were dismayed by the exterior. "Of course none of us could stand his house. We wouldn't do a copy of a Palladian house, heavens no. The least we could do was copy Gropius. Today every architect that I know under forty-five wouldn't think of building a house without going through his books of Palladio first. And there it sits on Scarborough—a postmodern house, if you please, fifty years ago."[63]

For most of Chick's contemporaries it was a place of odd enchantments, of strange harmonies where past opulence and romantic decay came face-to-face with the spare and gleaming reality of the new.

Chick had put down roots in Hartford. In marrying Helen Goodwin, he had mingled his fate with the city's oldest and most prominent family and had built, on their ancestral land, an extension of his personality—a house where he and Helen would celebrate his adventures in the arts.

One summer in the early thirties, while staying in Harpswell, Chick met a childhood friend, who asked him what his new house was like. His reply encompassed the disapproval of his stuffier neighbors, the skepticism of Hartford conservatives about his glamorous persona, and even, perhaps, his own secret insecurities: "The house is just like me—all façade."[64]

CHAPTER SEVEN

Innovator and Connoisseur

The Baroque epoch was, in truth, an age of experiment; and if for that reason alone, the present generation should find in those new stirrings much of interest and sympathy.

—Osbert Sitwell, "Pictures: Introduction," *Italian Art of the Seventeenth Century*

G entlemen: I have the honor to present the following report of the activities of the past year," Chick began reading at the Wadsworth Atheneum's annual meeting on a Saturday afternoon in January 1929, "which has been remarkable for the unusual number of lectures and exhibitions." With understated formality, he described the blitz on Hartford's sensibilities during his first full year as director. In twelve months, he had dangled five thousand years of art history before the public's unaccustomed eyes; he had cast Hartford society in his personal version of *A Night in Venice*, then led them into the world of Post-Impressionism and on to Matisse, Derain, Braque, and Picasso; he had carried the sounds of the twentieth century—Stravinsky and Satie, Schoenberg and Ives—into a stronghold of "old Hartford," Charles Goodwin's house. He had made himself conspicuously at home with the newest, most provocative European decor, inviting ordinary people to come in and see how it felt to be modern. And the public had responded. Chick told the board that attendance had increased by nearly forty thousand— a 30 percent jump in visitation, almost unmatched by other major American museums that year.[1]

Came the voice of a senior trustee: "Mr. Austin, do you think it *wise* to have the general public rampaging through *our* museum?"

"I saw the handwriting on the wall," Chick told friends years later, laughing at the memory.[2] Parochialism wedded to pomposity always amused him; but under the surface, it infuriated and depressed him as well. The following month, he would tell Helen Goodwin that only she had given him "the courage to go on in Hartford."[3] But whatever reactionary rumblings Chick heard that day, his achievements were recognized. The board appointed him full director and elected Edward Forbes, who remained honorary director, a trustee.

Launching into his second year, poised to sweep Helen off her feet, Chick turned his energies toward presenting his favorite epochs in art history and promoting every art form that interested him. His only criteria would be quality, innovation, and the challenge of outshining whatever had been done before.

On January 23, 1929, Chick inaugurated his promised series of annual shows with a sumptuous two-week exhibition, *French Art of the Eighteenth Century*. Here the public could discover what Chick liked to call the "delicate licentiousness"[4] of the reigns of Louis XV and Louis XVI—a time, he said, "of great artistic vitality, of enormous wealth and a spirit of pleasure and gaiety which has never been equalled."[5] No matter that he had said much the same thing about eighteenth-century Venice a year earlier.

He told the press that he would attract Bostonians and New Yorkers to Hartford because "no similar exhibition has ever been accomplished in this country."[6] In fact, audiences at the Arts Club of Chicago in 1925 and at the Detroit Institute of Arts in 1926 had already been introduced to eighteenth-century France, whose style contrasted so markedly with both the heavy Victorian opulence of their parents' generation and the comparative simplicity of the more recent American colonial revival.[7]

Nevertheless, during the one month he gave himself to prepare the show, Chick went beyond previous exhibitions by gathering examples of every art form he could lay his hands on. Relying heavily on Felix Wildenstein (who had supplied the Arts Club show), he rounded up outstanding pictures by such artists as Watteau, Fragonard, Boucher, Chardin, Greuze, and David. To complement the paintings, he persuaded Paul Sachs to lend some of his most prized drawings by the same masters.[8]

Chick intermingled the pictures with exquisite objects by the great French cabinetmakers—painted and gilded console tables, commodes, and chairs—two of them Louis XV side chairs from his own apartment. To the furniture he added sculpture from Duveen, a pair of Royal Beauvais tapestries (for sale at $65,000 each), and "porcelains and garnishings"—vases, clocks, fans, snuff boxes, music boxes—from the Morgan collection.[9] In case this display was not enough to give his audience a clear picture of the era brought down by the French Revolution, Chick assembled an entire Louis XVI paneled boudoir on the first floor. Complete with a marble mantelpiece, a bed-niche, richly upholstered furniture, luxurious drapes, gilded sconces, and shelves of eighteenth-century books, it was a lustrous confection. Chick claimed that it was the only room of its kind in America—something of an exaggeration, as Boston's

Museum of Fine Arts had recently installed three French rooms—but exhibiting period interiors was a relatively new practice in American museums.[10]

Deciding that no ordinary space would do for the unveiling of other recent acquisitions at the same time he opened the French show, he had the museum's carpenter build a miniature chapel in a side gallery. Here he installed the Fra Angelico angel, a French primitive called *Descent from the Cross*, also purchased from René Gimpel, and (somewhat profanely, for a chapel) a version of Hercules wrestling with Antaeus by Lucas Cranach the Elder, borrowed from Durlacher. Most impressive of all, however, was an early Goya of a quality rarely found outside the Prado, *Gossiping Women*, which he had just bought from Durlacher for more than $38,000, another record price for the Atheneum. An intimate view of two women in a landscape, one reclining on the grass and leaning toward the other, the work combined the eighteenth-century elegance of a Tiepolo with intimations of the darker Goya.

With Chick's encouragement, the local press trumpeted the value and rarity of the paintings in the show. It was reported that Watteau's *Les Comediens français*, loaned by New York financier Jules S. Bache, was insured for over a quarter of a million dollars. The picture aroused particular excitement, as it had descended to Kaiser Wilhelm II from Frederick the Great and had never been shown publicly in America. This and another equally valuable painting from Bache, Fragonard's *Le Billet-doux*, were seen as the most important works on view. But a version of Chardin's *Les Bulles de Savon* was a sensation. It showed a youth leaning out of a window, blowing a large soap bubble, and was available from Wildenstein for $40,000. "Only in the Louvre can one see a figure piece of Chardin so excellent," exclaimed the *Courant*.[11]

The day after the exhibition opened, Charles Goodwin wrote to Chick: "I enjoyed your show better than any one that you have ever put up and I feel a little as if it were your own show and not influenced by Mr. Forbes or Mr. Sachs. It was a beautiful presentation of a period and a very appealing one."[12] Forbes told Goodwin that Chick had succeeded "definitively and conspicuously" and offered to give up the title of honorary director. But Goodwin would not hear of it, and Chick kept his most valuable advocate in the museum's counsels.[13]

The show received national attention through *Art News*, but it was the *Courant* that stressed the level of artistic achievement in Connecticut's capital: "We know of no other city in Hartford's class which is privileged to attend exhibitions of art comparable to those which were held in the Morgan Memorial last year or to that which is being held there now."[14] Chick had the article transcribed with multiple carbon copies. To a Wall Street broker who had lent two paintings to the show, he wrote: "Hartford is just beginning to wake up artistically."[15]

One of Chick's fondest hopes was that his exhibitions would inspire the collecting of important pictures among his local audience. As early as his second month in Hartford, he had taken the chairman of his art committee, Archibald Welch, to New York to see the paintings for sale at Wildenstein. "I was very pleased with Mr. Welch's reactions," Chick told the dealer.[16] But as Welch was nearing eighty, he was not tempted to start collecting old masters. Chick spent a day escorting a wealthy West Hartford woman around the principal New York galleries. He was sure that he had persuaded her to take the plunge, only to discover that her husband felt that paintings were not worth buying.[17] In his frustration, Chick wrote boldly in the museum's bulletin for January 1929 that "it is to be deplored that Hartford, a city of wealth and culture, has so few important private collectors," a situation he hoped would be remedied "under continued stimulation by the Museum."[18] His constant harping on the dearth of collectors would begin to grate on older trustees who had assembled some of the country's finest collections of colonial furniture. Chick paid no attention to them, however, and many bequeathed their heirlooms to the Connecticut Historical Society rather than the Atheneum.

A month after the French exhibition, hearing that the museum's vice president, Charles Seaverns, and his wife wanted a picture for their dining room, Chick steered them to Kirk Askew at Durlacher. They liked an expensive work by the Italian baroque painter Alessandro Magnasco, who had become fashionable in the London market, and Kirk encouraged Chick to push them over the edge—which he did.[19] Chick seized on the Seavernses' purchase to demonstrate how the Atheneum could recognize local collectors. He featured the Magnasco on the cover of the July bulletin, displayed it in the museum for the summer, and included it in his next two winter exhibitions. But the Magnasco was one of his few successes among the trustees.

Other aspects of Chick's educational mission could sometimes take on a novel twist. One day in April, he hosted a visit by three Navajos from a New Mexico reservation. He installed them in a gallery, where, in full regalia, they spent hours weaving blankets, making sand paintings, and forging jewelry from silver coins they melted over a charcoal fire on the museum's marble floor, as six hundred visitors filed past.[20] Chick was delighted. "Friday was a mad day," he wrote to Helen in New York, "what with the three Navajos, their trainer, Mrs. Berger, Aunt Ruth and innumerable others all wanting different things at the same time! But I think it was a good plan to have them, the Navajos, I mean, as the children were beside themselves with excitement and crowds came into the museum."[21]

But Chick's most forward-looking activity that spring brought an entirely new medium into the museum. Inspired by a series of articles in the magazine *The Arts* on the most advanced European and American silent movies, he presented a six-week program, "The Art of the Motion Picture."[22] He gave a talk before each screening and played records of modern music on a Victrola during the films. In showing silents just when Hartford movie theaters were switching over to sound, Chick wanted to emphasize the artistic and psychological power of the cinema in its purely visual mode.

At Harvard, Chandler Post had urged Chick's generation of art history students to see the motion picture as an art form as well as a popular diversion, taking them to the latest movies and leading them in whistling at Gloria Swanson and laughing at Buster Keaton.[23] Chick naturally embraced the medium for its modernity and its play with illusion and reality.

Motion pictures were not entirely new to American museums. As early as 1911, the Brooklyn Museum had shown "Colored Moving Pictures" at the Academy of Music, and in 1922 the projected Denver Art Museum announced plans to put the cinema in its regular program, a goal that poet Vachel Lindsay applauded in a revised edition of his classic 1915 book *The Art of the Moving Picture:* "In the art museums should be set the final standards of civic life, rather than in any musty libraries or routine classrooms. And the great weapon of the art museums of all the land should be the hieroglyphic of the future, the truly artistic photoplay."[24] Denver's new museum building could not be funded, however, and the cinema project never materialized. Later in 1929, Alfred Barr included the establishment of a film department in his prospectus for the Museum of Modern Art, but movies were not shown there until 1936. It was Chick who developed one of the first significant museum film programs in the United States.[25]

Approaching this new enterprise with his usual self-assurance, he stepped into a quagmire for which his Harvard education had not prepared him. He found a bewildering and jealous network of New York distributors whose business practices and level of civility contrasted sharply with the art dealers he knew.[26] They would promise one film and substitute another; they would give him one price verbally and send a bill for a higher price. The principal features generally cost the museum one hundred dollars each, and to help cover expenses Chick charged a small admission fee. This caused agents to threaten to increase their fees, which would put the films out of his reach, as the Hartford Fire Commissioner would allow no more than 225 people in Tapestry Hall for each showing.[27] Each week he would be preoccupied with telephone calls and telegrams to New York, and it was only by switching from one agent to another that he would succeed.

The first program of the series, on April 16, presented Fritz Lang's *Metropolis* of 1927, already famous as one of the greatest "utopian" films of the Machine Age, along with *The Fall of the House of Usher* by J. Sibley Watson, coeditor of *The Dial*. Chick explained that this film was best appreciated as "a series of pictures and designs," but one Hartford critic complained that "the story is lost in the confusion of cubistic walls, moving staircases, falling hammers and other bewildering devices."[28]

For the next five weeks, Chick brought to Hartford films unlike anything his audience had seen. There were the modernist classics—Walter Ruttman's *Berlin: The Symphony of a City;* Man Ray's *Of What Are the Young Films Dreaming;* Fernand Léger's *Ballet mécanique,* accompanied by a player piano with George Antheil's music; and, most popular of all, Robert Wiene's *The Cabinet of Dr. Caligari,* starring Werner Krauss and Conrad Veidt. This was regarded as the first great German expressionist film, though few in America had actually seen it. The crush of people trying to get tickets at the door was so great that Chick repeated the program the next night. And there were novel documentaries. From UFA came two films showing battles between a mongoose and a cobra, and an octopus and a lobster. Members of Chick's audience found a third offering, *The Parasol Ant,* either so fascinating or so laughable that they exploded into applause when, after tremendous effort, one mighty Amazon ant succeeded in tearing off part of a leaf. More soothing was Ralph Steiner's beautiful *H2O;* viewers could settle back and watch water in motion—running off roofs, rushing from drain spouts, dropping on the surfaces of pools.[29] To lighten the fare, Chick added popular items to the mix—a melodrama such as *Nerves of Steel,* with Helen Holmes, or Charlie Chaplin's vintage comedy *Sunnyside.*

One of the most significant films in the series was the most difficult to obtain—Carl Dreyer's *The Passion of Joan of Arc,* a cinematic landmark starring Maria Falconetti and produced by the Société Générale de Films. Chick spent two months cajoling and relentlessly pursuing the distributor to extract the film for two days. It had been banned by the censor in Britain for its depiction of Saint Joan's brutal treatment by the English soldiers, and Chick's presentation was its first showing in America outside New York City. While he acknowledged that this slow-paced film would "inevitably seem dull to many who will not realize what they are seeing," he called it "one of the most beautiful motion pictures ever produced," with "a scope and dignity which is almost unbelievable."[30] *Joan of Arc* was one of the first films to be shot almost entirely in close-ups, and the actors wore no makeup. Conservatives grumbled about the film, and it had the poorest attendance of any in the series, but Chick was not surprised. His response was that some people "are irritated by anything of an artistic nature which they do not understand."[31] But the series as a whole was so popular that in May, Hartford's Grand Theater initiated a regular program of foreign and artistic films, starting with Sergei Eisentein's *Ten Days That Shook the World.*

Soon afterward, Chick left for his wedding in Paris and his travels through Europe. When he and Helen returned to Hartford in October, he prepared to make an unequivocal endorsement of modern art. Having introduced the city to the opulence of France during the ancien régime, Chick turned to the opposite and most challenging end of the spectrum with a show he called *Selected Con-*

temporary French Paintings. It was, in a sense, his salute to the Museum of Modern Art. It opened on November 22, two weeks after the New York museum was launched with an exhibition of four classic French moderns—Cézanne, Gauguin, Seurat, and van Gogh.

Chick brought together about forty pictures by Picasso, Braque, Matisse, Derain, Dufy, Chagall, Modigliani, and others. Thanks to Alfred Barr, he was able to borrow three paintings by Giorgio de Chirico from Lizzie Bliss, one of MOMA's founders.[32] There were also works by three young artists recently discovered in Paris by a few of Chick's friends: Christian Bérard, Eugène Berman, and Kristians Tonny. Known as Neo-Romantics, they painted in a lyrical style that seemed the antithesis of "modern art." They were so new to Chick that Kirk Askew had to telegraph Bérard's first name to him while the catalogue was being printed.[33]

Knowing his show would be even more controversial than his exhibition of French paintings a year earlier, Chick produced, in an article for the *Hartford Times,* his earliest comprehensive defense of contemporary art. He insisted, as with his first exhibition, that it was the duty of every inhabitant of Hartford to visit the museum and see

> examples of significant living art. Whether in this particular instance you like the paintings and derive pleasure from them, is not the question. The styles of the various painters should be intelligently distinguished and the names remembered. It must not be forgotten that the battle over modern art was won in Europe many years ago. The ideas expressed in the paintings are not new—they only appear new to us because we have had so little opportunity to become acquainted with them and because of the unfortunate newspaper publicity which has accompanied the exposures of such pictures as the "Nude Descending the Staircase" and the much more recent hanging of a picture upside down. We are very inclined to make fun of the things that we do not understand or are not familiar with, as part of what psychologists term a protective mechanism. . . .
>
> One of the most stimulating things about art is that intelligently studied it helps people in thinking for themselves and in developing their powers of selection. In a civilization such as we live in, which does everything in its power to dull personal esthetic judgments by means of the radio, motion pictures, book clubs, and other like instruments, a stimulation of such powers becomes artistically necessary. But unfortunately, significant art, which mirrors for all time the essence of the culture which produced it, is often cast aside for the trivial, the pretty, and the insignificant.[34]

Chick had dramatically broadened his scope during the two years since he arrived from the Fogg Museum. He was unfurling his modernist flag.

After the exhibition closed on December 6, a handful of the works were shown at the neighboring New Britain Institute (later the New Britain Museum of American Art). A small tempest arose when the art director of the local school system, Dewey Van Cott, who had once studied at the Académie Julian in Paris, wrote a scathing indictment of the show in the *New Britain Herald,* deploring "the fact that any public educational institution should allow folks to get the idea that such trash is really art" and, having heard Chick speak on the exhibition at the New Britain museum, asserted that no one was "fooled by the brilliant dissertation upon it last night by the many syllabled young man from Harvard, more lately from Hartford and the Wadsworth Atheneum."[35]

An editorial in the same paper a few days later applauded Van Cott:

All art nowadays inclines too much to the bizarre and the ridiculous. It is idle for the career-men in modernistic buffoonery to claim that to appreciate their style of vapid slapstick comedy one must be educated up to it. The education required is downwards, not upward. In the wild scramble to be "original" and to mistreat their canvasses, in a way never done before, a large school of light-headed near-and-far artists splotch hideous monstrosities and call it something absolutely new. It may be new, but it's no good.[36]

Russell Hitchcock published a rebuttal in the *Herald,* informing readers that Matisse and Dufy came out of a tradition "far older and far wider spread than the strange nineteenth-century hybrid of New-Classicism and Romanticism which passes for tradition with our academic painters and in certain of those respected academies from which New Britain's distinguished art critic holds degrees." He asserted that "a showing of the great European masters of the fourteenth and fifteenth centuries would have been quite as bewildering as was that of our own century."[37]

Art News gave the story national play, calling Van Cott's criticism of the show "reactionary peevishness."[38] Chick told Lizzie Bliss that he found the controversy "highly diverting" and sent her copies of the newspaper articles to read and pass along to Alfred Barr.[39]

For his third big winter exhibition, Chick turned his spotlight back to the old masters, but to a period and style that was still largely unfamiliar to most viewers—the baroque. In 1930 the term encompassed the art of both the seventeenth century and a good part of the eighteenth century, and Chick called the show *Italian Painting of the Sei- and Settecento.* It was the first comprehensive Italian baroque exhibition in America.

Chick naturally embraced the baroque. The revolutionary style that had emerged at the end of the sixteenth century in the aftermath of the Counter-Reformation was dark, sensual, and theatrical, becoming more extravagant as it approached the rococo of the eighteenth century. It displayed a dazzling technical virtuosity. And it had the attraction of being on the verge of rediscovery.

His enthusiasm reflected a radical change in taste. As far back as the mid-nineteenth century, baroque art had been shunned by the foremost critics and academicians. Except for the work of Dutch and Flemish artists like Rubens, Rembrandt, van Dyck and Vermeer, and Italians like Salvator Rosa (whose wild landscapes and dramatic portraits had been loved by the Romantics), seventeenth-century painting was looked on as false, grandiloquent, and even immoral. John Ruskin had done his best to quash whatever interest the mid-Victorians might have had in the style with his frequent castigations of baroque art—calling, for example, the period in landscape painting between the death of Titian in 1576 and the rise of Turner in the early nineteenth century "a great gap, full of nonentities and abortions; a gulph of foolishness, into which you may throw Claude [Lorrain] and Salvator [Rosa], neither of them deserving to give a name to anything."[40]

This dismissal was carried into the twentieth century by Bernard Berenson. "B.B. hated the seventeenth century," Agnes Mongan explained simply, decades after the battle had been won. "And he had influenced a whole generation not to bother paying any attention to the seventeenth-century Italians."[41] In the very year of Austin's baroque show, Berenson published *The Italian Painters of the Renaissance*, which he concluded with a chapter called "The Decline of Art." There he asserted that "although in the last three and a half centuries [Italy] has brought forth thousands of clever and even delightful painters, she has failed to produce a single great artist."[42] Even the 1926 edition of the textbook Chick used in his Trinity courses, *Art Through the Ages* by Helen Gardner (then teaching at the art school of the Art Institute of Chicago), made no mention of the baroque, cutting off its treatment of Italian painting and sculpture in 1600.

A great shift away from this point of view, however, had begun in 1922 with the monumental exhibition at the Pitti Palace in Florence, *La Mostra della Pittura Italiana dei Seicento e del Settecento*. With over thirteen hundred paintings on view for six months, it awakened the international art world—including Chick, on his way to Egypt—to the depth and quality of Italian baroque painting.

In England, the young "dandy-aesthetes" centered around Oxford immediately adopted the style as one of their passions, along with Diaghilev's Ballets Russes, and the commedia dell'arte. Undergraduate Harold Acton made the Pitti Palace show the centerpiece of the second number of his literary magazine, *Oxford Broom,* which lavishly praised Magnasco in particular. Osbert and Sacheverell Sitwell, who, along with their sister Edith, personified modernism for the British, founded the Magnasco Society in London "to cultivate a baroque taste, in literature, music, everything," according to a later critic.[43] In 1924 Sacheverell published *Southern Baroque Art,* the first of his volumes that followed the style as it spread outward from Italy. Sitwell's work had the quality of a travel book, but it planted the baroque and rococo in the consciousness of a new generation. Chick later told Osbert Sitwell that his brother's books were the foundation of his aesthetic taste.[44] A year after Sitwell's first volume appeared, the Burlington Arts Club mounted an exhibition of seventeenth-century Italian art in London.

In 1928 Chick's Harvard colleague Arthur McComb gave a groundbreaking lecture series on the baroque at the Fogg, which was followed early in 1929 by a modest exhibition of Italian paintings and drawings from the seventeenth and eighteenth centuries.[45]

At the time of the large Hartford show, American museums in Detroit, Chicago, New York, Cleveland, and Worcester had just started collecting pictures from the period with some enthusiasm.[46] "The current bulletins of at least six American museums," noted the influential English publication *Burlington Magazine* in 1929, "bear on their covers illustrations of recently acquired seventeenth-century paintings." And it was no secret among the cognoscenti that the baroque was a bargain. *Burlington* explained that "the price of a Piazzetta, for example, is negligible compared with that of an Italian primitive, an English portrait, or an American chair. In these fields the American museum cannot compete with the private collector. It naturally turns to periods which are less in vogue."[47]

Chick had begun buying in the field at the end of 1929, acquiring a small night scene with rustic figures attributed to Salvator Rosa, and a monumental pair of richly decorative pictures (each more than seven by six feet) by Luca Giordano, *The Rape of Europa* and *The Rape of Helen.* He would soon increase the quality and quantity of his baroque purchases considerably.

In November, Chick wrote to friends, dealers, and museum directors for the names of collectors who might make loans to a major baroque exhibition. To circus magnate John Ringling, the greatest American collector in the field, Chick explained that he was planning to have "as large a loan exhibition of Italian Baroque art as I can get together with the momentarily somewhat meagre material that can be found in this country." He declared that he wanted "to do all I can to change the under-estimation in which it has been held for so many years."[48] Ringling had just installed his paintings in the John and Mable Ringling Museum of Art, his private Italian Renaissance palace in Sarasota, Florida, and was one of the few who did not respond; but by the opening of the

Hartford show on January 22, Chick had persuaded more than thirty others to lend over sixty paintings and eighty drawings to the exhibition. These works represented nearly all the principal baroque artists, beginning with Michelangelo Merisi da Caravaggio, the leader of the baroque revolution, the master of light and shadow whose genius for evoking texture, volume, and psychological depth gave birth to the "naturalistic" school. There were Caravaggio's rivals, the brothers Annibale and Lodovico Carracci. And there was a progression of artists whose works would rise precipitously in value as the twentieth century progressed—Bernardo Strozzi, Guercino, Jusepe de Ribera, Salvator Rosa, Giovanni Paolo Panini, Francesco Guardi, Canaletto, Giovanni Battista Piranesi, Pietro Longhi, and the two Tiepolos, father and son.

With his flair for setting the scene, Chick added fine examples of Italian and French furniture to the galleries, including a set of doors from the Borghese family and a rare fifteen-foot-long panel, once used to screen the bed of Cardinal Richelieu's lascivious nephew, Louis François Armand du Plessis, from the eyes of his servants. Chick told the *Courant* that visitors who looked closely could see the initials of courtesans scratched into the surface of the panel.[49]

Those who entered the exhibition galleries were surrounded by oversize depictions of martyred saints, mythic heroes, and fleshy goddesses—most of them in various stages of rapture or agony and illuminated as if by a spotlight beyond the canvas. Chick hoped his audience would feel the glory and grandeur of a magnificent period. All skeptics were to be dismissed. As he later wrote, "the adverse critics of the Baroque find it over-theatrical and pretentious. They merely fail to comprehend its greatness. Theatrical it may be, for the first great rise of the theater coincides with its development, and it may be truly said that the seventeenth century conceived of even the Church's ritual as dramatic spectacles for all the senses. The world itself had become a vast and exciting stage."[50] Emphasizing this dramatic element, Chick mounted a small exhibition of baroque theatrical illustrations from Viennese collections as a pendant to the show.

The exhibition attracted immediate international interest and was reviewed by Chick's colleagues. An unprecedented number of museums, libraries, and dealers in Europe asked for catalogues. (Forbes even sent one to Berenson, though he did not expect it to change his mind.) Arthur McComb, who wrote the introduction for Chick, produced articles for *Art News* and *Parnassus*. He called the Hartford show "more ambitious" than his own earlier Fogg presentation and declared that "practically all the examples of Italian painting of this time in America outside of those in the larger Museums are here assembled to form a most significant showing."[51]

Charles Goodwin, though not likely to have fallen in love with the baroque, appreciated what Chick had done for the Atheneum's position in the art world.

Italian Painting of the Sei- and Settecento, *February 1930*

"The thing that especially pleases me," he told a reporter, "is that it gives Hartford people a chance to see paintings that are being universally discussed."[52] Although Chick suggested that the exhibition was "perhaps not so popular in the estimation of the public" compared with his eighteenth-century show the previous year, over twenty-seven thousand people came to see it during the two-week run, and the museum was kept open until ten o'clock two evenings a week to accommodate the crowds.[53]

Italian baroque art was newly defined for the public and the scholarly community because the exhibition gave Americans their first chance to see, together, nearly the whole range of schools represented within the style. The pioneering nature of the show was clear to Chick's colleagues in the art world. Russell Hitchcock predicted in the art journal *International Studio* that soon, as more Italian baroque paintings entered American collections, there would be other exhibitions on the period, "but they will not easily encroach upon this memory of Hartford."[54] Reviewing a similar show at Durlacher's in *The New York Times* two years after Chick's exhibition, Katharine Grant Sterne recalled that "the Hartford show was a revelation."[55] In 1934 Arthur McComb published the first scholarly book in English on the subject, *The Baroque Painters of Italy*, and in 1936, when Helen Gardner brought out the second edition of her text-book, students would find a new chapter: "Baroque Art in Italy in the Seventeenth Century."

After half a century, Chick's impact as a champion of the baroque had grown to epic proportions in the memories of old friends. "His influence was profound," said Agnes Mongan. "It was Chick who started a whole American generation looking at Guercino, Feti, Strozzi—all those people who had never even been regarded before—and he bought *brilliantly!*"[56]

Harold Parsons, self-serving though his enthusiasm was, accurately predicted the long-term effect of Chick's exhibition: "Your show gives one cause for a good deal of thought about acquiring fine Sei and Settecento things at this time. Evidently, a few of us are alive to the significance of these things; and a great many museum men are asleep, but will wake up when the dealers have cornered the best things and boosted the prices."[57]

Chick was well aware of his buying opportunities. Before the exhibition closed, Parsons told him that Bernardo Strozzi's *Saint Catherine of Alexandria,* belonging to the Venetian dealer Italico Brass, was for sale. It was not in Chick's show, but he had seen it at the Pitti Palace exhibition in 1922. Parsons said that Brass would accept $16,000 for it and congratulated Chick in advance on the purchase, which he called, with as much truth as dealer's hyperbole, "the finest Strozzi I have ever seen; and I think that your Trustees ought to feel that you have made a brilliant acquisition, considering the fact that we paid $18,000 for ours in Cleveland."[58]

To Chick's contemporaries, the painting's purchase was symbolic of his infallible eye. More than four decades later, art historian John McAndrew became rhapsodic as he described the moment when the painting arrived at the museum from Venice. Chick rushed down to the receiving room where it was about to be unpacked. "And they were pulling it out—this is absolutely true—they were pulling it out of the case, and he ripped the paper off, and before the picture was all out and in not a good light, he said, 'This is the wrong picture.' " McAndrew remembered that the museum had a "smoochy" photograph of the painting from the Pitti Palace exhibition catalogue and that everyone in the receiving room compared it with the picture and told Chick, "No, it's perfectly all right."

> And he said [McAndrew continued], "No, it's not the right picture. I know perfectly well the right picture. I saw it years ago. I know exactly what it looked like." And he cabled Brass, and the [dealer] said, "No, this is the replica, probably also by Strozzi's own hand, but the one that was in the Pitti is not available." And [Chick] said, "I don't want it. I will send it back." It was a duplicate by the actual master, but he

thought it wasn't as good, and he insisted on having it sent back. And a year or so later Brass said, "I can get the other one for you." And he said, "Fine." And they got it. And the picture is a *wow*. Oh, it's a *wonderful* picture. . . . That's a feat of connoisseurship you don't often match. He *knew*. . . .[59]

The tale, which almost certainly originated with Chick, instantly spread to his friends, who retold it in many versions.[60]

As with most myths, the real story turned out to be different. The Strozzi that Chick was expecting was not reproduced in the Pitti Palace catalogue. Instead, he had a photograph of it by Alinari, the preeminent Italian agency for fine-arts photography. When the duplicate picture arrived with its own photograph, Chick himself made it clear to Parsons that it was not difficult to tell the difference between the two versions: "I was under the impression, of course, that it was the original which Brass lent to the exhibition at the Pitti Gallery in 1922 and as photographed by Alinari and not the replica, which arrived day before yesterday. I never thought of there being two pictures of this same subject and a comparison of the photographs even, will show the differences in quality, which is very apparent."[61] Parsons replied that though he had known Brass had two versions, he had been confused about which picture the dealer was selling. When Brass heard about the mix-up, he generously sent the other painting to Hartford so that Chick could compare the two and choose his favorite at the original asking price. Chick chose the one he had seen eight years earlier, which his colleagues recognized, enviously, as one of Strozzi's masterpieces.[62] "When he bought that Strozzi," said Agnes Mongan, "he had all kinds of American museum directors saying, 'What can *I* buy that will be as beautiful as that?' "[63]

For most of the rest of 1930, Chick turned his attention to the modern. In the spring he began presenting selected loan shows from a precocious institution in Cambridge known as the Harvard Society for Contemporary Art. The Society was the brainchild of a brilliant and intense undergraduate in the fine-arts department named Lincoln Kirstein. The son of Louis Kirstein, a partner of Filene's Department Store in Boston, Kirstein had already founded, at the beginning of his sophomore year, a forward-looking literary magazine, *Hound & Horn,* inspired by T. S. Eliot's *Criterion. Hound & Horn* published pieces by an astounding roster of writers—Ezra Pound, William Carlos Williams, Katherine Anne Porter, W. B. Yeats, André Gide, T. S. Eliot, and Lewis Galantière—along with photographs by Walker Evans, Ralph Steiner, and Charles Sheeler, and works by contemporary painters.

In his Harvard Society enterprise, Kirstein was joined by two fellow students in the class of 1930, Edward M. M. Warburg, son of the prominent New York banker Felix Warburg, and John Walker III, of a wealthy Pittsburgh family. These three constituted the executive committee. Agnes Mongan, who as a graduate student at the Fogg became their close friend and associate, recalled that it was Kirstein who coined the often-repeated pronouncement that with his brains, John Walker's social connections, and Eddie Warburg's money, there was nothing they could not do.[64]

The Society had opened its galleries in February 1929 with an exhibition of modern American art. In its first year alone, it presented twelve shows, bringing to Boston a range of artists from Picasso, Matisse, Derain, and Prendergast to contemporary Japanese and English craftsmen, as well as the first showing of Alexander Calder's *Circus.*

Soon after he had accepted the job at the Atheneum, Chick met Kirstein through Forbes at Gerry's Landing. "We did not like each other for some time," Kirstein remembered many years later. "Probably competitive ambition."[65] He added that Chick "did not consider himself an intellectual and had contempt for the rather solemn group of young critic teachers-to-be that awed me. He was already playing quite hard; he made a business, or rather a professional career, of playing. . . . I was afraid of Chick's easy domestic familiarity, his family friendship with materials which belonged properly in photographic reproductions or bound in catalogued books."[66] Nevertheless, Kirstein and Austin each recognized the creative intelligence of the other. In the third issue of *Hound & Horn,* Spring 1928, Kirstein reproduced two of Chick's recent watercolors—views of Venice and Carcasonne. In June of the next year, he invited Chick to show two other watercolors in the Harvard Society's sixth exhibition, *Harvard Graduates.*

By January 1930, Chick had decided to borrow some of the Society's shows—both to take advantage of its forward-looking presentations and to help the fledgling organization by dividing the insurance costs. (The fact that Chick was then absorbed in building his house also made shows organized by others appealing.) As Edward Forbes was a trustee of the Harvard Society, Chick had little trouble convincing his board that its exhibitions could be safely borrowed.

The first came in March 1930, directly from its six-day appearance in Cambridge. This was Richard Buckminster Fuller, Jr.'s model of his Dymaxion House, an elevated hexagonal structure of steel and glass, suspended on a mast, that seemed to have carried French architect Le Corbusier's dictum about the house as a "machine for living" to its ultimate realization. Fuller would "do for houses," the Hartford press predicted, "what Henry Ford did for the automobile."[67] Fuller accompanied his model, which was set up in Tapestry Hall, and spoke for more than two hours to the small audience Chick had lured into the museum.

The Dymaxion House suggested to Americans that the Machine Age was upon them and that they might be on the brink of radical changes in their daily living. Fifty feet in diameter and weighing only 378 pounds, Fuller's strange module would be delivered by dirigible to any spot in the country. A small bomb would be dropped to clear a foundation, and the house would be suspended forty feet above the ground on a flexible mast attached to septic and water tanks. Air would be sucked in through the top and filtered before circulating through the house. The house would be earthquake- and storm-proof. Floors would move up and down pneumatically. Lights would be infinitely variable in their intensity and color. Doors would open automatically, triggered by photoelectric cells.

Fuller had promoted the Dymaxion House on a tour of the country the previous year, and the press had mostly ridiculed the idea. In Hartford, the newspapers were receptive, perhaps because Connecticut had been a home for inventors since the time of Eli Whitney. The *Hartford Times* reported that Fuller persuaded the audience at the Atheneum that the Dymaxion House was "not only possible but even necessary."[68] Others were more likely to have agreed with the American Institute of Architects. After Fuller offered them proprietary patent rights for the house in 1928, they adopted a resolution that they were "inherently opposed to any peas-in-a-pod-like reproducible designs."[69]

Chick presented the Harvard Society's next two exhibitions, *Modern Mexican Art* and *Modern German Art*, in April and May, again just after their showing in Cambridge. The Mexican show featured paintings, watercolors, drawings, woodcuts, lithographs, and "peasant pottery" by such artists as Jean Charlot, Diego Rivera, and José Clemente Orozco.[70] Mexico was becoming a haunt of adventurous Americans for its radical political climate and creative forces—a volatile mix of Mayan, Toltec, Aztec, Spanish, and nationalistic traditions. Though the *Hartford Courant* gamely ranked Rivera as "one of the half dozen best in the world," it felt that most of the paintings in the show revealed "a fondness for the horrible."[71] Solid Republicans like Charles Goodwin found pictures such as *The Peasant, the Workman and the Soldier; The Labor Leader; The Seventh of November, Moscow;* and *French Communists* abhorrent. Chick acknowledged that the show was criticized violently in some quarters, but he made a point of telling the trustees later in the year that many of the same paintings had been shown subsequently at the Metropolitan Museum of Art.[72]

On the heels of the Mexican show came *Modern German Art*, a nearly comprehensive exhibition of paintings, watercolors, drawings, and sculpture by seventeen artists, among them Paul Klee, Georg Grosz, Oskar Kokoschka, Ernst Ludwig Kirchner, Emil Nolde, and Wilhelm Lehmbruck. Most of the works came from the Detroit Institute of Arts and the personal collection of its German-born director, William Valentiner. The Hartford press appreciated the fact that many of them gave "profound and hideous expression" to the World

War and its aftermath in Germany.[73] A large selection of prints for sale from the Arnold Gallery in Dresden accompanied the exhibition, and Chick happily reported to Valentiner that seventeen of the prints had been sold. (He bought two.) "This, perhaps, would not be surprising in Detroit," he wrote, "but here it practically amounts to a miracle as there are few collectors of anything but early American furniture in the city."[74] Proud of the scope of his program that winter and spring, he told the press with only some exaggeration that "Hartford has been offered the opportunity to look at a greater variety of paintings since the first of the year than any other city in the country with the exception of New York."[75]

The fourth Harvard Society exhibition in Hartford opened in December—a pioneering look at international photography. In its Hartford incarnation (without prints by Alfred Stieglitz, which had to be returned to the Boston Museum of Fine Arts after the Cambridge showing), it covered the work of sixteen photographers from Eugène Atget to Berenice Abbott, Margaret Bourke-White, Walker Evans, Edward Steichen, Paul Strand, Tina Modotti, and Edward Weston. It also included aerial and astronomical views, press photographs and X rays ("A Bony Tumor Within the Frontal Sinus," for example, and "Skull Fractured by Baseball"). Many of the prints were for sale at bargain prices— Weston's later famous portrait of José Clemente Orozco could have been had for fifteen dollars—but there were no purchasers.

Emphasizing the legitimacy of the photographs as works of art, Chick told the press that he found the work of Eugène Atget, which had been seen in America for the first time only three years earlier, "distinctly super-realist" and thought that Edward Weston's close-ups of green peppers, pebbles, and kelp had made them into something "horrible and sinister and completely magnificent." Walker Evans, he said, had discovered "pictorial significance" in sewer gratings and clotheslines, and—straining the credulity of most of his readers— asserted that the medical X-ray photographs yielded "abstract designs of great sensitivity and delicate modulation."[76]

The aim of the Harvard Society had been to prove that "the photograph is worthy and capable of producing creative work entirely outside the limits of reproduction or imitation, equal in importance to original effort in painting and sculpture."[77] But committed as he was to photography, Chick disagreed. His Fogg training would not allow it. He told the public that "the camera cannot ever come up to the art of painting as there are so many elements such as design and color that are left out, and there is less of the quality of mind and creative intelligence. The imaginative element enters in the photograph only in the arrangement and choice of the subject."[78] Nevertheless, Chick would become one of the first American museum directors to promote the medium through his exhibitions.

Increasingly open about his commitment to modern art, he told the trustees soon after the Harvard shows: "It seems very important that a museum should exhibit as much contemporary art as possible if it is to be of real educational value, and a fair estimate of modern forms [must] include progressive as well as academic art. . . . In Hartford, the museum should be a Museum of Modern Art as well as a Metropolitan Museum."[79]

Early in November, as a trustee-pleasing antidote to all the new art, Chick offered another packaged show, *English Painting*—eighteen works, mostly eighteenth-century portraits, borrowed from the Robert C. Vose Galleries in Boston. Small as the installation was, Chick was proud of his elegant arrangement of the works, but the *Courant* article the day after the opening left him fuming. The entire text consisted of two sentences, the most memorable being that tea had been poured by Mrs. Charles A. Goodwin, Mrs. William B. Goodwin, Mrs. James Goodwin, and Mrs. C.L.F. Robinson.[80] "How can we accomplish anything in this town," Chick shouted, "with press coverage like this?" A friend overhearing this outburst convinced the paper's editor to run a long complementary review two days later, reproducing many of the works in its rotogravure section at the end of the week.[81]

At the time he borrowed the show, Chick bought from Vose, for over $12,000, what were erroneously believed to be three American colonial portraits. The acquisitions represented little more than a gesture to the trustees, as he had never expressed an interest in the field. His European bias was obvious in an article for the bulletin when he observed that the pictures were interesting for "the Venetian influence through Rubens" but that in their plainness they reflected "an underlying Protestant aversion to display." He asserted, presumably with unintentional humor, that the sitters' faces seemed "almost more ugly, often, than they actually were."[82]

A few days after the English show opened, Chick presented the first exhibition of paintings from the growing collection of modern art formed by a wealthy young man from West Hartford whom he had recently met, James Thrall Soby. Soby had built his already impressive collection in less than a year through purchases in New York and Paris. Included in the Atheneum show were works by such artists as Derain, Matisse, Lurçat, and Laurencin, artists Chick had exhibited as early as 1928. Soby was not shy about his own preference for European works, telling the *Hartford Times* that French painters were "the only true artists of the age," totally committed to their art, while most contemporary American artists "paint a picture, faint and then get up to drink tea." He added that although his collection stood out in "conservative Hartford," it would not be considered unusual in cities such as Munich, where many similar collections could be seen.[83]

As most of Soby's Hartford friends—and his own mother—were intensely skeptical of his collecting, he had turned to Chick for encouragement: "I had just bought in New York a figure piece by Matisse and a landscape by Derain," Soby remembered. "More than a little abashed by my temerity, I yearned for moral support from the Atheneum's Director. I got it instantly. When I mentioned my purchases to Chick, he grabbed me by the arm, bustled me to his car, and off we sped to see the Matisse and Derain at my West Hartford house. He could not have been more excited if the pictures had been his own."[84]

The emergence of Soby as a collector was profoundly important to Chick.[85] Though serious collecting of modern painting would not take hold in Hartford, Soby became Chick's lifelong friend and ally, as well as a trustee of the Atheneum. By then, however, he had left Hartford to join the staff of the Museum of Modern Art, where he was one of its most influential figures, both as curator and trustee.

Chick showed the Soby pictures with twenty-four oils and a gouache by Giorgio de Chirico, who was very much in vogue in New York art circles. The Balzac Gallery had given the artist a comprehensive exhibition in May, and the New York branch of Demotte, the Paris dealer, had just shown his most recent works in October and November. Having already borrowed the three de Chiricos from Lizzie Bliss for his controversial modern show, Chick was keen to bring Demotte's new selection to Hartford.

The pictures were easily identifiable for their recurrent themes—classical ruins; Roman gladiators; mannequins with blank, egglike heads; white horses, their manes streaming behind them as if frozen into sculpture; stark Mediterranean architectural landscapes—almost abstract in their dark and mysterious simplicity. The surrealists considered de Chirico a forebear, but he repudiated them, and in his nostalgic lyricism, he could just as easily be seen as an inspiration to the Neo-Romantics. The *Hartford Times* called de Chirico's work the "Height of Modernism," identifying the artist as "the leading figure of the neo-romantic movement" and asking questions that predicted the end of "modernism": "Has the modern school of painting turned literary and romantic? Has abstract painting had its day?"[86] The exhibition was a foretaste of Chick's introduction of both the Neo-Romantics and the surrealists to America the next year.

Before 1930 was out, Chick also presented a show of four promising Hartford artists. There were more than sixty oils and watercolors by Aaron Berkman, Russell Cheney of the silk family, Clinton O'Callahan, and Milton Avery, who had won first prize the previous year in the Atheneum's annual exhibition of the Connecticut Academy. It was Avery's first full-scale museum exposure.[87] The show marked the only time Chick himself organized a large exhibition focused on specific local contemporary artists.

More importantly, that December, Chick was preparing one of his most influential theme shows, *Landscape Painting*—the first comprehensive landscape show in the United States. With 143 pictures (only three of them drawings) loaned from forty-five collections in cities from New York to Boston, Chicago, and Minneapolis, the exhibition was almost three times the size of the baroque show. It ranged from the earliest stirrings of landscape painting in the background of religious and classical works, such as Sassetta's fifteenth-century *Procession of the Magi*, through every succeeding century up to the most advanced European and American painters of the twentieth. To provoke his viewers into pondering the question of what really constituted a landscape, Chick ended the installation with a Mondrian abstraction, lent by Philip Johnson.

Chick had high expectations for the show, telling J. P. Morgan, Jr., from whom he borrowed pictures by Claude Lorrain, Anthony van Dyck, and Thomas Gainsborough, that he hoped it "will surpass in importance any we have yet had." He said that with the baroque exhibition the previous year, "the prestige of the museum was considerably strengthened outside of Hartford." And he confided to Morgan that he saw some hope for Hartford's eventual enlightenment: "I don't think it is still quite so provincial in character as you felt that it was on the occasion of our conversation in New York, three years ago, but any change in Hartford pre-supposes a lengthy and hard struggle. Now, however, a growing interest in the Museum on the part of the public, begins to be encouraging."[88]

The number of loans Chick wanted for the landscape show made his preparations more frenetic than ever. A mountain of polite but urgent requests coaxing masterpieces out of collectors left his office in December. To scout out dealers' stock and private collections, he enlisted his friends, particularly Russell Hitchcock. When a severe case of the flu took Chick out of circulation early in January, Hitchcock chose many of the pictures to be borrowed from New York galleries; he also produced an introductory essay for the catalogue, one of his many unpaid writing assignments for the Atheneum. Often, with the printer's deadline dangerously close, Chick would sit Hitchcock down at the dining room table on Scarborough Street, a box of chocolates within easy reach, and the insightful texts would roll onto the paper as the pile of candy wrappers mounted.[89]

Chick continued asking for pictures until well into January. To Conger Goodyear, who lent a Gauguin to the landscape show, Chick noted with colossal understatement that he needed the work at least five days before the opening "as the exhibition will be a very difficult one to hang."[90]

By now, Chick's pattern of preparing for major shows was well established—the last-minute loan requests, the rush to put together a catalogue, the marathon installations on the eve of the opening. Long-range planning bored him. He always had confidence in his ability to produce something amazing, to pull the rabbit out of the hat. It left him exhausted, but the drama of it all, being in control while flirting with disaster, was intoxicating.

All day on January 16, a truck drove through Manhattan from dealer to dealer and house to house, loading up over sixty paintings, whose value would be practically incalculable by later standards. It then made the three-hour trip to Hartford. Four days later, nearly seven hundred formally dressed museum members walked into the huge exhibition, as a string orchestra played in the balcony above Tapestry Hall. Visitors could stroll through the five-hundred-year history of European landscape painting. As they proceeded—some asking loudly, "Where is the El Greco?"—the crowd encountered the opulence of the early Renaissance through Sassetta's *Magi* of 1450, sealed in a glass case; the seventeenth-century classicism of Claude and Poussin, and the Carracci brothers; the Flemish countryside of Rubens; Rembrandt's *Landscape with the Baptism of the Emperor*, reputedly one of the artist's two great landscapes in America; French eighteenth-century pastoral landscapes; the England of Gainsborough and Constable; Cézanne's southern France; Hopper's melancholy evocation of the contemporary American scene; and the whimsical chic of French painter Pierre Roy's *Electrification of the Countryside*, which the press noted was "said to be super-realistic." This work, its tall background of blue sky reaching down to a very low horizon, depicted a distant parade of high-tension wire stations waiting to be connected. In the foreground were two graceful glass goblets set on a wooden disk surrounded by four bamboo poles, with a fifth pole lying across the tops of the goblets and an egg suspended between them from a pink and red string.

Among modern pictures, the Roy vied for attention with the red, blue, and white stripes and squares of the nearby Mondrian, which expressed a concept in art that was entirely foreign to most museum-goers in Hartford. The press helpfully explained that it went "as far as a painting can into mathematics and still be a painting."[91]

The *Courant* reported in advance that the collection was so valuable (it was estimated to be worth four million dollars with the Rembrandt and the Gainsborough alone insured for a quarter of a million each) that police had been enlisted to help the two regular watchmen patrol the museum, that there were burglar alarms in every area of the building, and that the lights in the galleries would remain on throughout the night. The museum was particularly cautious, said the paper, after a recent theft of a Daumier from the Museum of Modern Art.[92] The aura of danger was excellent publicity.

Chick took the public on a tour through the exhibition on January 22, explaining the progression of landscape art and the surprising connections between works from different centuries. It was an accessible art history lesson that combined several themes. There was an analysis of composition learned at the Fogg in which Sassetta's *Magi* became "horsemen arranged on a diagonal slope and an arrangement of triangles forming the background landscape" and El Greco's *Agony in Garden* became "Christ against a landscape of geo-metrical design and acid tones."[93] Then there was the theme of the intercon-nectedness of art, one of Chick's greatest missions. "I am very anxious to draw analogies between ancient and modern forms," he had told Lizzie Bliss, who lent a Seurat to the show.[94] And so when he told his audience that El Greco had used tone to model his figures rather than light, he drew their attention to a similar technique in a picture painted by Cézanne three hundred years later. Discussing Gauguin's concern with composition rather than realism, Chick compared the artist's outlined figures and flatness of tone to ancient Egyptian painting. There were also Chick's more off-the-cuff remarks. He described a picture by the eighteenth-century French painter Hubert Robert as a Holly-wood set and summarily dismissed Monet: "He forgot his composition while his drawing got ever weaker." He ended the tour at the Roy, which he loved for its technical brilliance, telling his listeners that it was "painted with crafts-manship unparalleled in the present day."[95] Later he described it as "crystal-lized poetry."[96]

One New York art dealer wrote Chick that his show "was the big topic in the art circles here."[97] *Art News* gave it first-page coverage in January 1931 as an example of a new trend of theme shows in museums, but did find twentieth-century American landscape art "rather capriciously summarized" in three works by John Singer Sargent, Benjamin Kopman and Edward Hopper—an objection Chick would not have disputed.[98] When Cary Ross filled his request for Hopper's *House by the Railroad* from the Museum of Modern Art, he had teasingly told Chick that he and Barr had their doubts: "While we are not cer-tain that the picture is a landscape it has something that may be dirt in the fore-ground."[99]

The exhibition was groundbreaking nevertheless, and, as with the baroque show, museums and scholars in the United States and in Europe asked for the catalogue.[100] Three years later, the Metropolitan organized its first landscape show, but with just over eighty paintings, it was not nearly as extensive as Chick's.

The effort required to mount the exhibition took its toll on Chick and his small staff. Completely neglecting some of his public engagements in the mad rush, he received a well-deserved rebuke from a teacher at the Hartford Public High School:

I hope that you will not think me rude but I want you to know that we expected you on Monday. This is the third thing that you have promised with your own lips. Of course I suppose it is not important compared with all your appointments and your many other services. We are grateful for all that you have done for us "without money and

Michelangelo Merisi da Caravaggio, Ecstasy of Saint Francis, *c. 1594.*
Oil on canvas, 37 x 51 inches, purchased 1943

Piero di Cosimo, The Finding of Vulcan on Lemnos, *c. 1490.*
Oil and tempera on canvas, 61 x 68¾ inches, purchased 1932

Opposite top:
Workshop of Fra Angelico, Head of an Angel, *c. 1440.*
Tempera and oil on panel, 6⅞ x 5½ inches, purchased 1928

Opposite bottom:
Lucas Cranach the Elder, The Feast of Herod, *1531.*
Oil on panel, 32 x 47⅛ inches, purchased 1936

Bernardo Strozzi, Saint Catherine of Alexandria, *c. 1610–1615.*
Oil on canvas, 69 1/8 x 48 1/2 inches, purchased 1931

Opposite top:
Louis Le Nain, Peasants in a Landscape, *c. 1645–1650.*
Oil on canvas, 16 1/4 x 21 3/4 inches, purchased 1931

Opposite bottom:
Claude Gelée, called Claude Lorraine, St. George and the Dragon,
c. 1643. Oil on canvas, 44 x 58 1/2 inches, purchased 1937

Michiel Sweerts, Boy with Hat, *c. 1660. Oil on canvas, 14 1/2 x 11 5/8 inches, purchased 1940*

Jean-Baptiste Greuze, Indolence, *1756–1757. Oil on canvas, 25 1/2 x 19 1/4 inches, purchased 1934*

Juan de Valdés-Leal,
Vanitas, *1660 .*
Oil on canvas,
51 7/16 x 39 1/8 inches,
purchased 1939

Luis Eugenio Meléndez,
Still Life: Pigeons,
Onions, Bread, and
Kitchen Utensils,
c. 1772. Oil on canvas,
25 1/8 x 32 7/8 inches,
purchased 1938

Edgar Degas, Double Portrait: The Cousins of the Painter, *c. 1865–1868. Oil on canvas, 22 7/16 x 27 9/16 inches, purchased 1934*

Paul Gauguin, Nirvana: Portrait of Meyer de Haan, *c. 1889–1890. Gouache on silk or linen with touches of pencil and gold leaf, 8 1/4 x 11 3/8 inches, purchased 1943*

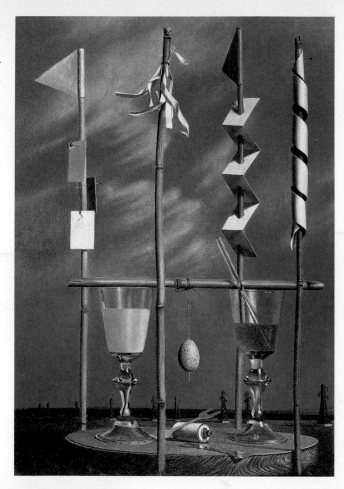

Pierre Roy, The Electrification of the Countryside,
*1930. Oil on canvas,
28 1/4 x 19 7/16 inches,
purchased 1931*

Joseph Cornell, Soap Bubble Set,
*1936. Construction, 15 3/4 x 14 1/4
inches, purchased 1938*

Piet Mondrian, Composition in Blue and White, *1935.*
Oil on canvas, 41 x 38 inches, purchased 1936

Léon Bakst, Costume Design for Vaslav Nijinsky as the Faun,
from L'Après-midi d'un faune, *1912. Graphite, tempera and/or watercolor,
gold paint on illustration board, 15 11/16 x 10 11/16 inches,
purchased 1935*

Giorgio de Chirico,
La Maladie du
Général, *1914–15.
Oil on canvas, 23 1/4
x 17 1/4 inches,
purchased 1937*

*Balthasar Klossowski
de Rola, called
Balthus,* Still Life
in Violence, *1937.
Oil on panel, 31 7/8
x 39 3/8 inches,
purchased 1938*

Joan Miró, Painting, *1933. Oil on canvas,*
51 3/8 x 64 1/2 inches, purchased 1934

Max Ernst, Europe After the Rain, *1940–1942.*
Oil on canvas, 21 9/16 x 58 3/16 inches, purchased 1942

Salvador Dalí, Apparition of a Face and a Fruit Dish on a Beach, *1938.*
Oil on canvas, 45 x 56⅝ inches, purchased 1939

Peter Paul Rubens, Portrait of the Archduke Ferdinand, *1635.*
Oil on canvas, 45¾ x 37 inches, purchased 1948

The Austin House, 1994. Photograph by the author

The Austin House dining room after restoration, 2000.
Photograph by Bruce Buck, courtesy of Elle Décor

without price" and always will be grateful but it does shake us to be promised so royally and disappointed so flatly, three times.[101]

Chick's secretary left him a note saying that she had telephoned the teacher and explained that he had been sick. "She seemed relieved, but you should explain further. I mentioned 'overdoing' and 'nervous breakdown.' "[102]

Between January and May that year, Chick went on a buying spree, spending over $80,000 on paintings for the Atheneum. Three were featured in the landscape show—Joachim Patinir's *Port on a Lake* for $5,500; Louis Le Nain's *Peasants in a Landscape* for $15,000 ("which would have otherwise have been bought by the Louvre," Chick told the trustees[103]); and Camille Corot's *Rouen from St. Catherine's Hill* for $15,200. (Chick and his group found Le Nain and Corot, with their spare realism, akin to the modernist sensibility, and Russell Hitchcock formally announced the rediscovery of Corot in the museum's bulletin.[104]) For $29,000, Chick bought from Durlacher a superb Giovanni Domenico Tiepolo from the late 1750s, depicting the Last Supper at the moment when Christ reveals that one of the disciples will betray him. Chick's intense reaction to drawing or painting on a flat surface was clear from his description of the Tiepolo in the bulletin: He saw in the work "the licentious careening of an imagination through a universe of violently agitated perspective, informing its occupants with enormous movement, swirling draperies of red and yellow into fugal patterns."[105] Meanwhile, the matchless Strozzi *Saint Catherine* arrived from Italico Brass.

But there was one other picture that Chick coveted—Pierre Roy's much-discussed *Electrification of the Countryside.* "I have gotten the Trustees quite interested in it," he wrote Joseph Brummer, the dealer who owned it, "and feel sure that if the price can be made attractive enough they will seriously consider its purchase."[106] It is surprising that he could have convinced his board to spend $2,100 for a surrealist work, which must have seemed much less accessible to them than, say, a comparably priced oil by Edward Hopper, but the public fascination with the picture, the fact that it was about to be published in *Vanity Fair,* and the success of the exhibition in linking contemporary works to the past—as well as Chick's powers of persuasion—carried the trustees along. Perhaps the vision of industrial progress that the painting conveyed warmed their capitalistic hearts. After all, the 1930s were the decade when electricity was brought to the vast farmlands of America for the first time.

Buying the Roy was a watershed in Chick's career, for he broke his rule about acquiring contemporary oil paintings. Less than a year earlier, he had dutifully told the press that it was "not the business of a museum to buy modern pictures."[107] Now he was opening the gates to ever more daring exhibitions and acquisitions of twentieth-century art, often in parallel with or even ahead of the

Museum of Modern Art. At the time of the purchase, Chick and Julien Levy, who would open his advanced New York art gallery in the fall of 1931, joked about the title, hoping it would be prophetic of the effect of modern art on America. "Although there were to be a few power failures," wrote Levy, "Austin's illumination would become an international glow long before most of his Connecticut countrymen saw the light."[108]

Tender Mysteries and
"The Ravings of Madmen"

> And then (as Alice afterwards described it) all sorts of
> things happened in a moment. The candles all grew up
> to the ceiling, looking something like a bed of rushes
> with fireworks at the top. As to the bottles, they each
> took a pair of plates, which they hastily fitted on as
> wings, and so, with forks for legs, went fluttering about
> in all directions: "and very like birds they look," Alice
> thought to herself, as well as she could in the dreadful
> confusion that was beginning.
>
> —Lewis Carroll, *Through the Looking-Glass*

Step by step, Chick led the insurance capital to the forward edge of modern art. So far the process had been remarkably painless. Whether Hartford had been looking at the *Contemporary French Paintings* exhibition of 1929 or the four shows Chick had borrowed from the Harvard Society for Contemporary Art in 1930, the local press had been enthusiastic. And except when the art was overtly political, as in the Mexican show, even the trustees seemed willing to tolerate exhibitions that projected a vision of the present for which they were congenitally unprepared.

Now, in 1931, Chick made plans to introduce American viewers to the newest artistic stirrings in Paris. He and his transatlantic friends thought they had discovered the next great shift in modern art. Picasso, Braque, and Matisse had redefined and dominated the contemporary scene since the early years of the century—long enough for them to have become "Modern Old Masters."[1] (Picasso would turn fifty later in the year.) But recently, a small group of artists in Chick's own generation had renounced the impersonal "painting as architecture" of the Cubists and had returned to portraying the natural world and the human figure through the traditional concepts of form, volume, and perspective. These were the Neo-Romantics, whose work Chick had just begun to notice.

When Virgil Thomson moved to Paris in 1925, he had singled out and befriended five of the painters: Christian "Bébé" Bérard, the only Frenchman in the group; Kristians Tonny, a Paris-born Dutchman; and three Russians— the brothers Leonid and Eugene Berman, and Pavel Tchelitchew. Their first group show, which included several other artists who remained obscure, had been held at the Galerie Druet in 1926.[2] Their works were lyric, nostalgic, and mysterious—Bérard's intense but delicate portraits, with their echoes of Degas and Modigliani; Leonid Berman's lonely Norman coastal scenes and fisherfolk; Eugene Berman's classical ruins, empty back streets, and interiors; Tchelitchew's melancholy acrobats and clowns; and Tonny's precise transfer drawings of tiny imaginary beasts and mythological figures, reminiscent of Bosch and Breugel. All found inspiration in the sentiment of Picasso's early blue and rose periods. The French art critic Waldemar George, in a review of the 1926 show, invented the term "Neo-Romantic" to describe them.

Thomson introduced Bérard, Eugene Berman, and Tonny to Gertrude Stein. She was already promoting Tchelitchew and took up the other Neo-Romantics, though her enthusiasm for them ebbed and flowed. Thomson covered the walls of his studio on the quai Voltaire with drawings by Bérard, and when the composer visited America at the end of 1928, he brought a stack of them to show friends. But it was Russell Hitchcock who became, as Thomson put it, "their earliest announcer" in the United States.[3] He met the Neo-Romantics through Thomson during a visit to Paris in 1928 and was attracted to the narrative quality of their pictures. They seemed to refute the modernist assertion that a painting could and should be judged as a composition, an image almost independent from its subject matter. As Hitchcock wrote in 1931, "subject matter is perhaps due to come into its own again and the absurd equation of apples and Madonnas need no longer appear axiomatic."[4] Hitchcock bought drawings by Eugene Berman in Paris and shared his discovery of the Neo-Romantics with close friends—Chick, James Soby, Kirk Askew, Agnes Rindge, and Julien Levy—who eagerly promoted the Neo-Romantics.[5]

Knowledge of the new movement was also reaching American art circles through international art journals like *Formes* and the New York branches of Paris dealers. In March 1931, when Bérard, Berman, Leonide, and Tchelitchew were exhibited together in Manhattan at the Balzac Galleries, *Art News* told its readers that they represented "the latest trends in School of Paris fashions."[6] At the same time, the Marie Harriman Gallery in New York organized a Tonny show. A few adventurous American collectors began acquiring these artists' works.

One of them was Duncan Phillips in Washington, D.C. Chick paid his first visit to the Phillips Gallery early in 1931, shortly after opening his landscape show. There he saw an oil by Eugene Berman, *Daybreak,* a dark picture of a young man sitting on the edge of a bed in an empty room, shrouded in some unknown sadness. It was, Chick wrote Phillips, "a marvel."[7] Phillips was delighted to find that "we have in common a great admiration for this unknown Russian painter" and told Chick that he wanted to see the works of Bérard and Tchelitchew, which he knew only through reproductions.[8]

By February, Chick had decided to produce an exhibition called *Five Young French Painters,* the first museum show devoted to the Neo-Romantics. With a new era apparently dawning, he retreated from his earlier stance that literary content diminished a work of art. In the spring of 1931 he announced that "ultra-modern art no longer offers to the public the seemingly incomprehensible qualities of the abstract."[9] Just six months earlier he had told an audience, "Let me repeat that you mustn't look at the subject. A painting must not tell a story. That is the role of literature."[10] Yet it was not surprising that he embraced the Neo-Romantics and, a few months later, the surrealists, the other artistic movement in revolt against the School of Paris. Chick always admired technically accomplished drawing, and the mysterious make-believe of both groups appealed to his love of the theater.

Working closely with Hitchcock, who knew about the few sources in the United States for pictures by the Neo-Romantics, Chick succeeded in assembling seventy-four paintings, drawings, and etchings, most of them from three New York galleries: Balzac (who had pictures on loan from Jean Bonjean, the Neo-Romantics' primary Paris dealer), Demotte, and Marie Harriman.[11] Demotte's representative, Maurice Sachs, tried to dissuade Chick from mounting an exhibition so quickly, as he expected to import many more works by the artists during the coming months, but postponement was not for Chick. He had to be ahead of the crowd.[12]

Private collectors, nearly all of them Chick's friends, filled out the rest of the show. There was the Museum of Modern Art contingent—Alfred and Marga Barr, Jere Abbott, and Cary Ross.[13] Hitchcock, Jim Soby, and the Askews also lent pictures. Drawings by Berman and Leonide came from Henry Francis at the Fogg. Sibley Watson in Rochester supplied works by Bérard and Berman. From Bernard Davis, the president of La France Industries in Philadelphia, Chick borrowed pictures by Leonid and Tchelitchew. A twenty-four-year-old photographer from New Jersey, George Platt Lynes, a friend of Gertrude Stein, lent drawings by Tchelitchew and Tonny. Carl Van Vechten—fashionable novelist, photographer, and a longtime promoter of Miss Stein—provided works by Tonny.

Hitchcock supplied the text of the slim catalogue. He dashed off biographical sketches of the artists and then presumptuously cabled Gertrude Stein in

Paris on March 18, asking her to produce a one- or two-page foreword, the manuscript to be mailed to Hartford five days later.[14] Gertrude Stein was not in the habit of writing on short notice, and in any case she did not consider the sometimes ponderous Russell Hitchcock one of Thomson's most congenial friends. She did, however, agree to lend two paintings by Tonny, one of them a portrait of her with her poodle, Basket. This was excitedly reported in the Hartford newspapers and was expected to give the exhibition a definite cachet.

Chaos again prevailed as the show was pulled together. On Monday, April 13, two days before the opening, Van Vechten notified Austin: "Saturday noon a Mr. Hitchcock telephoned me that you were sending for the Tonny pictures in half an hour! They have been wrapped and ready ever since then, but no one has called for them yet. If for any reason you have decided you don't want them, will you please notify me so that I can rehang them."[15] Chick managed to get them to Hartford in time.

To the public he explained that these works reflected a broad change in styles: "The new Romanticism, strongly expressed in the sudden changes of women's fashions two years ago [hems dropped, lines became more flowing] appears in literature, music and painting in the form of a reaction instituted by the younger creative artists against the ideas of their artistic forebears, Picasso, Matisse and Derain." But he cautioned his readers about jumping to conclusions: "This does not mean that such painting has become artistically invalidated, nor that the newer trends can be considered a return to something more conservative."

He simply wanted to give ordinary Americans the chance to see the new manifestations of art with their own eyes. "The painting of these young artists is not being offered to you with the assurance that it will eventually be great. . . . Each has an original and distinctive contribution to make to your artistic experience, a contribution which is life-communicating, at least four of them share at the moment the feelings which will possibly form the style of a new movement." Change was healthy. Otherwise modern painting would sink into what he described, melodramatically, as "a coma of sterility and stupidity."[16]

In the end, the artists would not seriously deflect the course of modern art from Cubism to Abstraction, though three of them—Bérard, Berman, and Tchelitchew—became brilliant stage designers. Gertrude Stein always had her doubts. Two years after Austin's show, she wrote of Bérard's pictures that "they are almost something and then they are just not."[17]

Chick, however, would be a lifelong friend and patron of the Neo-Romantics. At the Atheneum, he steadily built up a large collection of their works, beginning with a Berman oil in his show—a desert scene called *Nocturne*, acquired from the Harriman gallery for a hundred dollars. Visiting Paris that summer, Chick bought three drawings directly from Berman for a total of forty dollars. At these prices, the trustees could afford to indulge their director's taste for what seemed relatively innocuous contemporary works. On the same day that Chick bought the Berman painting, the museum paid $15,000 for Le Nain's *Peasants in a Landscape*.

Though a few Tonny drawings in the show were sold, Chick had little expectation of significant purchases by Hartford museum-goers. He was determined, however, to discover whether there was ever hope of encouraging the general public to collect art at any level. In conjunction with the Neo-Romantic exhibition, he set up a somewhat outlandish bazaar of contemporary works for sale at ten dollars or less to raise funds for the museum's slide library and to furnish a room for the children's educational program.[18] Oils could be had for ten dollars, watercolors for five, drawings for two, and reproductions for a dollar. Chick invited anyone with the least claim to be called an artist to submit works to the exhibition—from friends like Hitchcock and Jere Abbott to the faculty of the Hartford Art School, and even children in the Saturday art classes. Nearly three hundred items rained down on the museum. Chick donated seven of his own abstractions in oil, along with his costume designs for the Venetian Fete, and sketches from life.[19] The "One to Ten Dollar Show," as the press dubbed it, was extremely successful. More than a hundred works were purchased in the first twenty-four hours, and most of the others were sold within the first week.

Among the items for sale were about twenty photographs by George Platt Lynes. John McAndrew had shown Chick two examples of the photographer's work. Chick recognized their quality and asked permission to exhibit more of them. Pleased to have his first museum exposure, Lynes suggested that Chick price them at not less than five dollars each.[20] Within three years, Lynes would be considered one of the finest fashion and portrait photographers in New York. Later he would become the principal photographer for George Balanchine's American Ballet and the New York City Ballet, as well as the head of photography in Hollywood for *Vogue* magazine. None of his prints sold in Hartford in 1931.

Chick had barely caught his breath before he showed the other side of modern art. On May 15, he opened a modest exhibition of drawings and lithographs by Picasso, borrowed from the John Becker Gallery in New York. It was the first time Hartford had seen a show devoted entirely to the Spanish master, and the positive response from the press helped Chick convince the trustees to approve his only purchase of a Picasso oil, *The Bather* of 1922.[21] This depicted a sturdy nude woman holding a white drapery. The canvas was small—a mere seven and a half inches high—but monumental in its neoclassicism. It came through Wildenstein from the Samuel Kootz Collection and was a bargain at $2,500. Chick confided to the dealer that the purchase represented "an open-

Pablo Picasso, The Bather, *1922. Oil on canvas,
7⅜ × 5 inches, purchased 1931*

ing wedge" in developing a significant collection of modern art at the museum.[22] Before the year was out, he would contemplate producing the first comprehensive Picasso exhibition in the United States.

That summer, Chick was eager to return to Europe after a two-year absence to survey the art scene and to throw off his responsibilities. Telling Helen that they could afford passage for only one, he prepared to spend two months in Germany and France studying rococo art and architecture. He also planned to relax and devote as much time as possible to his own painting, perhaps enrolling in the Académie Moderne in Paris or the Dresden Kunstschule.

Not surprisingly, Helen felt left out. She was not convinced that an extra passage would be too expensive. It was clear to her that Chick wanted to wander through Europe as he used to, alone and fancy-free. She understood that he needed to unwind and renew his energies, but she, too, loved Europe and saw no reason why she should be deprived of a trip with Chick. She appealed to Laura Austin, who immediately paid for another ticket. Laura was not only helping Helen, whom she liked; she was also ensuring that her boy would have someone to look after him.[23]

Chick and Helen sailed from New York on the *Olympic* on June 6, stopping in Paris to see the latest exhibitions, visit dealers, and meet friends also traveling abroad. Helen gave Chick the chance to go off on his own adventures, while she accompanied Russell Hitchcock and Agnes Rindge to Germany. Chick took a more leisurely route, driving to Nancy and Strasbourg. He traveled through the Black Forest to Munich, where he bought a French stone bust of Saint John for a Gothic gallery he had installed in the museum. From Munich he went to Pommersfelden Castle, where, as he later told the press, he was delighted by a room furnished entirely in shells, including red stucco lobsters dusted with glittering mica.[24] He rejoined Helen, Russell, and Agnes in Stuttgart. Each morning at breakfast in their hotel, oblivious to the stares of waiters and other guests, Chick insisted that they join him in practicing movements in the traditional Bavarian dance called *Schuhplattler,* which he had picked up in Munich. "People in the hotel thought we were all crazy," Hitchcock remembered.[25]

They traveled to Wurzburg, seat of the Archepiscopal palace, one of the supreme examples of rococo architecture. Then it was on to Bayreuth, where Chick reveled in the theatrical decor of the Hermitage, a palace built by a sister of Frederick the Great. He particularly enjoyed its whimsical accessories, such as the decorative animal heads in one room, which, when a hidden control in the floor was activated, would squirt water on unsuspecting visitors.[26] They returned to Paris through Burgundy, sailing for New York on the *Majestic* at the end of July, and spent the rest of the summer at the senior Austins' cottage on Harpswell.

By the time he arrived back in Hartford that fall, Chick could hardly wait to produce his next exhibition. In June, at the Pierre Colle Gallery in Paris, he had seen twenty-four works by a young Spanish painter named Salvador Dalí. For Chick, they were pure magic. With all the finesse of some demonic cordon bleu chef, Dalí served up landscapes of "paranoiac" dreams—lurid, degenerate, and eerily beautiful. Chick wanted to show them to Hartford. He would make them the centerpiece of the first surrealist show in America.

Surrealism was the most tightly organized artistic movement of the century. Not simply a reaction against early modernism, it was also a philosophical movement, a way of looking at the world. It developed out of Dada, the anti-art movement generated in Switzerland in 1916 by Tristan Tzara. Despite sensational manifestos, public demonstrations, and festivals throughout Europe, Dada self-destructed in the early 1920s.

In 1924 André Breton, the "pope" of surrealism, issued the movement's first manifesto, decreeing that in the future the two seemingly contradictory states—dream and reality—would merge "into a sort of absolute reality, a *sur-*

reality."[27] The goal was to liberate the subconscious and portray dreams, hallu-cinations, madness even, in works of art. Sigmund Freud's theories of the sub-conscious—particularly the assertions that sexuality is the underlying motivator of human behavior and that repressed instincts and desires lead to neuroses—had already exerted a profound influence on contemporary culture, but they would find their most overt expression in the art of the surrealists. The surrealists' first group exhibition was held in Paris in 1925 at the Galerie Pierre, a show that included Miró, de Chirico, Roy, Man Ray, Arp, Klee, Ernst, and Picasso, but not Dalí. He, of course, soon became the most publicized of them all, both for his extraordinary technique and his outrageous persona.

In the summer of 1931, at the same time Chick was contemplating a surre-alist show, Julien Levy made his own plans. Levy knew Paris and its artistic milieu intimately through his beautiful and cosmopolitan wife, Joella, and her mother, the English surrealist poet Mina Loy, who had lived in the city for many years. He, too, had seen the Dalí exhibition and wanted to bring works by him and other surrealists to America for sale in the gallery he planned to open in New York. In his memoirs, written after Chick's death, Levy claimed credit for the Hartford show:

> I had arranged the group exhibition of Surrealism, and when he saw it, Chick asked me to lend it to him first, to give the Athenaeum [*sic*] the prestige of America's first exhibition of the kind. I agreed, considering that a museum show would carry more weight and give the artists pres-tige, enhancing the value of the pictures. I brought over the material from Europe, assembled it all, and Chick was able to supplement it. . . . Contemporary art historians will never convince me that the first American Surrealist show was not mine.[28]

Levy's claim has been accepted and disseminated widely, but it is far from the truth. The two shows, although related, were not at all the same; Chick bor-rowed directly from dealers and private collectors in France and the United States. Chick's correspondence makes it clear that Levy was keen to get many of those works in the Hartford show, scheduled to open in November, for his own exhibition in January. Answering one of Chick's queries about sources for pictures, Levy telegraphed: "COLL [*sic*] CARRIES BERARD HUGON JACOB MAS-SON DALI STOP MAY I BORROW SHOW AFTER YOU."[29]

Levy was also worried about the effect of Dalí's pictures on Manhattan because of their obvious sexual imagery. "Julien is not quite sure how much Dalí he dares show in the Gallery at once," wrote John McAndrew, then Levy's assistant, to Chick. Instead, Levy had originally intended to concentrate on Max Ernst in his exhibition: "He would, however, like very much to borrow from your show for one room to go with his room of Ernsts," McAndrew continued, "which he had planned for January, but would adjust to suit you."[30] McAndrew had no doubt about crediting the Atheneum for the first surrealist exhibition. In January 1932, he confided to Chick, "Our Super-Realist Show is going to be just a little stepchild of yours."[31]

Working with Jim Soby, who became one of America's earliest authorities on the movement, Chick tried to track down every surrealist collector in the country for his show and was especially keen to uncover pictures by Dalí, whose work was still practically unknown. When Chick wrote to Maude Dale, a trustee of the Museum of Modern Art and one of the greatest art collectors in New York, about borrowing a picture by the artist,[32] the name of the painter did not sound familiar to her secretary.[33] Chick clarified the request:

> The picture to which I referred was a painting by Salvador Dali, a new Super-Realist painter whose work occasioned some excitement at an exhibition in the Colle Galleries in Paris last summer.
>
> It was rumored in New York that Mrs. Dale had bought one, but this may not be true. Dali's technique is an exact and minute one similar to that of the early Flemish painters, and he likes to represent limp watches drooping over boards, and many ants and flies. Perhaps this will give you a clue to the picture.[34]

With that description, the light shone. The secretary responded, "Mrs. Dale does remember Dali now that you describe him, but whether she saw this exhibition or just recalled the excitement, I dont know. However, she didnt buy one and is sorry that she must refuse you."[35]

Chick's luck improved when he approached Conger Goodyear, who agreed to lend an oil and two drawings by Dalí. "I do not know what my Dali painting is called," he admitted jovially. "Give [it] some such name as 'Beach' or 'Sea Shore'. Of the drawings, one might be called 'Andromeda,' and the other 'Sun and Sand.' " He added that Chick could call them whatever he liked, but Goodyear's casual titles were printed in the catalogue.[36]

Even up to the final days before the opening, Chick was looking for more pictures. On November 10, he wired Mrs. John D. Rockefeller, Jr., for permission to borrow a work by Pierre Roy. "IF SO PLEASE INFORM MY WIFE AT MRS. JAMES GOODWINS 11 WEST 54TH STREET SHE COULD BRING THE PICTURE BACK WITH HER WEDNESDAY EVENING THE MUSEUM INSURING AGAINST ALL RISKS."[37] Mrs. Rockefeller replied that she was sending a smaller Roy (*Commice agricole*, a composition with wheat sheaves) because the one Chick wanted was too big for Helen Austin to manage.[38]

Chick finally assembled fifty works by eight artists: Giorgio de Chirico, Salvador Dalí, Max Ernst, André Masson, Joan Miró, Pablo Picasso, Pierre Roy, and Leopold Survage.

With the last arrivals barely affixed to the museum's walls, the exhibition opened on schedule, Sunday, November 15. Chick called it *Newer Super-Realism* because Breton had issued a second manifesto in 1929, and the art form now encompassed Dalí's "magic realism," which at times suggested glossy color photographs of the subconscious. Chick debated the title with Alfred Barr and Julien Levy, Barr opting for super-Realism and Levy holding out for the original French *surrealisme*. Translating it, Levy asserted, was "a very un-Surrealist thing to do—it was trying to be logical. Super-Realism, like Superman, was a vulgarization, I said. Surrealism was a French word invented by Apollinaire. As an invented word, it should exist in its own right." But Chick, as ever, wanted to sound ultra-up-to-date. "I remember his irrepressible laugh," wrote Levy, "as he said, 'The day will come, Guiliano, when you will find yourself talking again and again about that Little-Old-Newer-Super-Realism.' "[39]

The opening of the show was almost surreal in itself. Chick decided to combine the occasion with a celebration of Frank B. Gay's seventy-fifth birthday. Standing in the midst of Miró's floating amoebas and Dalí's viscous images of erotic decay, Frank Gay—who, only six years earlier, had presided over the installation of the Nutting Collection of Pilgrim furniture—must have felt like a traveler from another century. Chick presented his diminutive predecessor with a cake decorated in bright colors, and wished him well. A final Austin touch was a wooden sign he borrowed from another part of the museum and placed under Max Ernst's forbidding forests and their alarming feathered inhabitants. It read NATURAL HISTORY, BIRD ROOM.

The tiny catalogue ($4\frac{1}{2}'' \times 6\frac{1}{2}''$) seemed a very odd publication to Hartford. It sported on its cover a dark photograph by George Platt Lynes, *As a Wife Has a Cow*, which depicted a classical sculpture of a woman, superimposed on a small model of a cow that the woman seemed to be holding by one hoof above her shoulder—or, as a newspaper commentator described it, "the lady throwing the bull, just like some of the artists."[40] The catalogue offered an excerpt from Breton's prose piece, "Soluble Fish," to illustrate the automatic writing that was supposed to express the higher reality of the subconscious: "My yellow gloves with black clocks fall upon a plain. . . . The prostitute begins her song more roundabout than a cool rivulet in the country of the nailed Wing but it is only absence after all." This was accompanied by a poem called "Nothing" by Cary Ross, featuring such phrases as "gurgles of round bubbles blurp."[41] Also included in the catalogue were a chronology of surrealism and a selection from an essay, "The After-War Spirit in Literature" by Samuel Putnam, all about the refreshing liberation that came from "the spontaneous and uncontrolled play of the personality, unhampered by any of the fetters of civilization." Readers of the catalogue also learned that the "ideal surrealist act would be: 'to run down into the street, a revolver in each hand and start firing at random into the crowd.' "[42] It was not a text calculated to reassure the attorneys and insurance executives on Chick's board, but most of them probably dismissed it as the blathering of idiotic foreign artists.

Sounding a bit like a theatrical publicist, Chick announced that his exhibition would be "the outstanding novelty of the Hartford art season." The newspapers gave it massive coverage, alerting the public to its sensational qualities. The *Hartford Courant* called the artists "more daring than any of their predecessors" and singled out Dalí as the most disturbing of all: "it is the world of common sense which dies a sudden death in the pictures by Dali." Readers were warned about the erotic symbols they would see: "Spectators who know their Freud, or who have subtle understandings, will find much to be shocked at in these pictures."[43] No Hartford newspaper had ever previously suggested that visitors might be "shocked" by anything exhibited at the Wadsworth Atheneum.

Under the title "There's Method in the Madness of French Super-realists Whose Odd Works are Now on View Here," the *Courant* made one of the earliest attempts by an American newspaper to come to grips with surrealism. It was a mixture of good-natured banter and an honest effort to explain a disturbing new art that dared to probe the subconscious and expose thoughts and desires that many viewers would rather not admit to having:

You have been there. You have at least had a glimpse of the Super-Real World. You cannot say, "I'm from Missouri," because you have already seen, but you have probably forgotten. . . . Truly now, isn't there something familiar about those landscapes? Think way back, into your childhood if necessary. In these paintings, you see vast expanses of land, flat as a geometric plane and extending to a terrifying distance. The land looks something like a desert and something like a great floor, and on it is a single rock or tree. In one picture there is a stone wall extending directly backward into infinity. The foreground is occupied by some startling object, perhaps the ornate clock from your mantelpiece, or perhaps a vast, unnameable mass, like the ghost of a zeppelin. Now do you remember? All this is the stuff that dreams are made of. But dreams, you know, are but a door to the subconscious—to the greater mind. Now we see that the world of the superrealists is the world of the mind. Care and precision go into the painting of all objects in Dali's pictures, because he is painting a definite world. He seems to know what he is about when he puts in his clocks, watches, screws, keys and eggs, or even his purely imaginary objects, which sometimes serve as cabinets for his household hardware. But why all this stuff? And why the limp watches?

The reviewer saw the literary origins of surrealism in Lewis Carroll, the "Columbus" of the new art: "His 'Alice Through the Looking Glass' is the bible of the Super-Realists, and their book of psalms is 'The Hunting of the Snark.'" Edward Lear was their "geographer," he added, quoting the nonsense poem, "The Jumblies."

Ultimately, said the *Courant*, surrealism reflected the confusion, violence, and disillusionment of contemporary life, a theme already familiar to twentieth-century readers. The World War had prepared the way for surrealism. "Such tremendous evil, disrupting a world which the Victorians believed so good, made cynics of many young men in the countries hardest hit." Yet these artists were only a manifestation of "the sensationalism of the age, with its moving pictures, which make a direct attack on the emotions, sensational fiction, giant football spectacles and jazz music."[44]

In a similar article, the *Hartford Times* encouragedly urged readers to "look at the walls of the Morgan Memorial to see the wonderful intense blue of Dali, the queer figures of Picasso, the Chiricos, the Roys and all the others and try to come to some understanding of what often seems like child's play or the ravings of madmen."[45]

Chick was brilliantly disarming in defense of the show. Making light of potentially unpalatable experiences was his specialty. He told the *Hartford Times:*

Fashion in art is very much like fashion in dress. Most of our clothes are bought with the idea of ultimately discarding them and a few indeed with the idea that they will ultimately be acquired by museums, yet we do not hesitate to dress in fashion because we fear that next year the mode will alter. We know it will, but we can take pleasure in what we have on to-day. . . .

These pictures which you are going to see are chic. They are entertaining. They are of the moment. We do not have to take them too seriously to enjoy them. We need not demand necessarily that they be important. Many of them are humorous and we can laugh at them. Some of them are sinister and terrifying but so are the Tabloids. It is much more satisfying aesthetically to be amused, to be frightened even, than to be bored by a pompous and empty art which has become enfeebled through the constant reiteration of outmoded formulae.

I am being continually asked to explain super-realism. That is very difficult. It is essentially an attempt to exploit, in terms of paint, the more exquisite reality of the imagination, of the dream, even of the nightmare—the desire to push reality beyond the visual actualities of most painting. In it there is much of Freud, of our contemporary interest in the subconscious mind. . . . The artist seeks to create an effect of surprise and astonishment, made breathtaking by the juxtaposition of strange and disparate objects. Sensational, yes, but after all, the painting of our day must compete with the movie thriller and the scandal sheet. As a matter of fact, super-realism is not unknown in this country. We have all met it and some have recognized its spirit, more diluted and more popularized in "Mickey Mouse" and the "Silly Symphonies," which, for pure nonsense, imagination, and a sense of speed, remain in the field of the motion picture to be surpassed. Visitors have, in reality, a right to find excitement in a museum as well as in a movie theatre.[46]

Few other museum directors at that time would have tried to make modern art seem as entertaining. It is difficult to imagine Alfred Barr, for instance, comparing one of his exhibitions at the Museum of Modern Art with the scandal sheets or Walt Disney's cartoons. But telling ordinary museum-goers in a small American city—who were already self-conscious about their lack of knowledge—that they did not have to take the artists he showed "too seriously to enjoy them" was typical of Chick. It was a tactic he used repeatedly to take the intimidation out of the museum, to coax the public into visiting it, supporting it, and discovering the excitement that he himself found in it.

Of the fifty pictures on view, ten were by Dalí. Both Chick and Levy announced that they were introducing Dalí to America for the first time. In fact, three of his paintings had turned up in 1928 at the Carnegie Institute's annual international show in Pittsburgh, but they were not as overtly "surreal." It was the Hartford and New York shows that catapulted Dalí into the American consciousness. Both exhibitions included *The Persistence of Memory*, less than a year old and soon to become one of the twentieth century's best-known paintings. The Hartford papers recognized the vision of limp watches in an unearthly landscape as a quintessential surrealist image and reproduced it. Levy had bought it out of the Paris show for $250 and was offering it for $400. The "museum price" to Chick was $350. To the future regret of the Atheneum, he did not acquire it. Undoubtedly he felt that the picture was too bizarre to get past the art committee, which had already allowed him to spend $2,100 on a surrealist picture—the Pierre Roy—earlier in the year. He had to content himself with buying one of the exhibition's less controversial Dalís at the bargain price of $150 from the Pierre Colle Gallery: *La Solitude*, a small lyrical oil depicting a youth standing on a beach in the shadow of cliff, his face turned not toward the sea but to the rock wall. It was the first Dalí acquired by an American museum. Three years after Chick's show, *The Persistence of Memory* was given anonymously to the Museum of Modern Art by one of its trustees, Mrs.

Stanley Resor. Though Chick had not been able to capture surrealism's greatest icon, he was later able to buy two of Dalí's most important pictures.

Despite the "newer super-realism" of its title, the show included the older surrealists. There were four works by their reluctant forebear, de Chirico, including one of his most famous paintings, *La Famille de l'artiste*, which depicted a father mannequin and a mother mannequin holding a baby mannequin, each with a nearly blank egglike face. (De Chirico "thinks his family looks like this," said the *Courant*. "Crazy, isn't it?"[47]) Helen and Chick themselves were not above poking fun at such works. They doctored a photograph of Chick standing in front of the de Chirico and speaking through a WTIC-radio microphone, by pasting a snapshot of Helen's face onto one of the blank heads in the painting. This "family" group became their Christmas card for 1931.

Max Ernst, one of the earliest and most versatile surrealists, was represented by fourteen paintings, the largest single group in the show—three loaned by the photographer Berenice Abbott, three from the Société Anonyme, and the rest from the Julien Levy Gallery. The artist's bizarre birds and botanical lithographs reminded one journalist of pictures in "a textbook on unnatural history."[48] Eleven years later, after Ernst had escaped from a concentration camp and made his way to New York, Chick was among the first American museum leaders to welcome him and to purchase a new work—Ernst's supreme vision of the apocalypse, *Europe after the Rain*.

There were five examples of Miró's "biomorphic abstractions," in which lines and colored shapes float and sprout and metamorphose into curious figures and beasts. Among them was *Le Renversement* (now known as *The Upset*), which had become the first Miró to enter an American collection when the Société Anonyme bought it in 1927. Also shown was his later celebrated *Portrait of Mrs. Mills in Costume of 1750*, a whimsical deconstruction of an eighteenth-century English picture. It was loaned by the Valentine Gallery and soon purchased by Soby, who willed it to the Museum of Modern Art.[49] Masson, Roy, and Survage were represented by three works apiece.

There were seven pictures by Picasso: five from Wildenstein, one from Valentine, and one from Cary Ross. Picasso allowed himself to be informally associated with the surrealists for a short time, though it was always understood that an artist of such versatility could never be classified.

Picasso's works had been exhibited in the United States continuously since 1911, when they first appeared in Alfred Stieglitz's Photo-Secession Gallery in New York, but most of the other artists in the exhibition had been seen by the American public only since the mid-1920s—and even then on an extremely limited basis. De Chirico, Ernst, and Miró, for example, were all shown in America for the first time in 1926 in the Société Anonyme's International Exhibition of Modern Art at the Brooklyn Museum. André Masson's debut had

Chick and Helen's "family"
Christmas card, 1931

not come until 1930, at the Gallery of Living Art at New York University. When the press reported that Chick's show was intended to present "the most recent developments in Continental art so that the Hartford art-loving public may keep itself informed on strictly up-to-date artistic matters," it was no exaggeration.[50]

Again Chick demonstrated that modern compositional techniques and aesthetic aims were not entirely new. To illustrate how the double images of the surrealists could be found in works painted hundreds of years earlier, he installed with the show an anonymous sixteenth-century painting in the tradition of Arcimboldo, *Ambiguous Subject,* borrowed from Alfred and Marga Barr. At first glance it appeared to be an aerial view of a European town. If turned on its side, however, the landscape changed into the face of a bearded man. Chick wanted the public to make the connections that he naturally made. That was the joy of informed observation.

The surrealist show was by far the most sensational of Chick's exhibitions up to that time, and it clearly succeeded in stretching Hartford's sensibilities. He knew, of course, that most of the trustees found it baffling and absurd, but in reviewing the activities of 1931, he reminded them that *Newer Super-Realism* "notwithstanding its advanced nature, drew more interest and larger crowds than had yet come to any of the smaller exhibitions at the Memorial."[51]

A year or so after the show, Chick and Jim Soby decided to have a private showing of what Soby called "one of the finest and most scandalous films of its time," *L'Age d'Or,* which Dalí and Luis Buñuel had produced in 1930. Even in Paris, it had provoked such outrage that Charles de Noailles, who helped underwrite the film, barely escaped excommunication by the Roman Catholic Church. It combined sexual acts with sacrilege, and in one scene, priests clinging to a rocky wall metamorphose into praying mantises—one of Dalí's favorite obsessions because of the female's habit of killing and eating the male after mating. The screening took place in the Sobys' West Hartford living room because it was larger than the Austins', with introductory remarks on "the surrealist esthetic or anti-esthetic" by Russell Hitchcock. Although the projectionist lost his nerve as the film progressed, becoming terrified that they would all be arrested and his license revoked, and although a splinter group of Catholic friends who had retreated to the basement to drink began shouting that they would destroy the film if it were not stopped, *L'Age d'Or* was shown to the end, to loud applause by the throng of adventuresome viewers.[52]

Both surrealism and Neo-Romanticism remained Chick's particular favorites. The two groups were adamantly opposed to each other, however, and many of Chick's friends had strong preferences. Virgil Thomson asserted: "Just as the surrealists for their themes sought out the irrational, the subversive, and the cruel, the subjects of the neo-romantics were predominantly humane and tender, the feelings you have when you let your mind alone."[53] Always eclectic, Chick found the somber nostalgia of the one group and the bizarre dreams of the other equally enticing.

Chick's discovery of surrealism inspired him to return to the easel. He painted several oils reminiscent of Pierre Roy. In one, *Playing Paper Dolls*, disparate objects float on a blue-green background—a spool of thread, a tall wooden frame suggestive of a guillotine, and a pair of scissors in the act of slicing in half, at the waist, a paper cutout of a little girl dressed in the Victorian style, glued to canvas. Chick was not a stranger to the theme. Even as an adolescent, he had made exquisite paper dolls as presents to younger cousins.

Before the year was out, the Brummer Gallery in New York offered Chick his own three-week exhibition in February 1932, coinciding with Levy's surrealist show. Chick of course was one of the dealer's potential customers, but he had already exhibited his paintings with the Society of Independent Artists in Boston, the Harvard Society for Contemporary Art, and even at the Museum of Modern Art in a 1930 show dryly entitled *Forty-six Painters and Sculptors Under Thirty-five Years of Age*.

To fill out the exhibition with new work, Chick disappeared for a week in January. Helen wrote Agnes Rindge from Boston that they were "in seclusion at 110 Marlborough Street, while Chick paints a few dozen canvases for his February showing. It would be nigh impossible for me to dash off pictures to order (Yes, I know I couldn't dash off pictures anyway), but the feeling that he's only got a few days to paint an exhibition in doesn't seem to bother him at all."[54]

Helen was undoubtedly exaggerating Chick's output. The show included thirty-four pictures, many of them painted in the 1920s. Fifteen were oils, exploring traditional, abstract, and surrealist themes; nineteen were watercolors, eight of them Venetian scenes, along with views of Dresden, Antwerp, and Vienna. Hitchcock wrote a candid text for the accompanying six-page catalogue:

Chick becomes a surrealist. Playing Paper Dolls, *1931.*
Collage and oil on canvas, 20 × 16⅛ inches

Mr. Austin is not original nor profound. His pictures are, it is no dero-
gation to say, decorative. . . . He does not paint American subjects and
he is not developing continuously in any given direction. Upon a basis
of broad and daily familiarity with the art of the past and of the present,
he has erected in large part for his own amusement a delicate pavilion
of mirrors. The taste and the architecture are his own; the reflections
come from all the worthy sources of the twentieth century.[55]

The *Hartford Times* made much of the show, reproducing two of the oils.
Chick recounted his painting career to the paper, from the miniature stage set
he designed at age eight and the first oil he produced at eleven to his study of
tempera and fresco with Ioni in Siena. Venice was his favorite city for working
in watercolor, he said, adding that "Venice is not all color and light, and in my
paintings I have tried to bring out the stagnant and the tragic which I felt was

there beneath the surface."[56] The exhibition was briefly noted in *Art News,* which described Austin as "formerly connected with the Wadsworth Atheneum."[57] This was to be Chick's only one-man show.

Whatever the trustees thought of his excursions into contemporary art, and however outlandish they found the dreamscapes of *Newer Super-Realism,* Chick skillfully balanced it all with the purchase of a gilt-edged old master. The day before the surrealist show opened, Sir Joseph Duveen, at Chick's request, had a Florentine painting of the high Renaissance taken out of his Fifth Avenue gallery and put on a train to Hartford. This was Piero di Cosimo's late fifteenth-century canvas then called *Hylas and the Nymphs* but later known as *The Finding of Vulcan,* which Duveen had acquired from the Robert Benson collection in London. The huge image Chick paraded before the trustees—five feet high and nearly six feet across—showed half a dozen nymphs in filmy gowns, gathering around a long-haired youth, naked except for some strategically placed foliage, who had tumbled from the sky into a flowery meadow. These "dainty ravishers," as Chick called them, bring the young man flowers, fruits, and a fluffy white dog, and entice him with their own charms. Flowers, trees, grasses, and plants appear in meticulous detail. Birds swoop through the golden air. The figures are posed in a graceful frieze, as if floating in front of a theatrical backdrop. This one painting could stand as the touchstone for a great collection of European art. Furthermore, Chick observed in the museum's bulletin, Piero was a man of "merry sensual pleasure"; and he recommended the picture as a way for Hartford citizens "to share the spirit of joyous paganism which was the Renaissance."[58]

Like every Duveen picture, it came with a princely price tag—$100,000, far above any amount the Atheneum had ever paid for a single work of art. Edward Forbes, Chick's most trusted adviser on Renaissance pictures, was wary of Duveen's seductive salesmanship. Forbes felt that authorities closer to home should be consulted before he could endorse so momentous a purchase, and he asked Chick for photographs to show Paul Sachs, Chandler Post, and Arthur Pope at the Fogg "to see how much they warm up to it."[59] Apparently universal enthusiasm ensued, and the trustees agreed to buy it. As the Sumner Fund generated only about $70,000 annually, Duveen had to be paid in three installments in 1932 and 1933. For the next year and a half, Chick's acquisitive instincts would have to be curtailed. No matter; this painting was one of the very few by Piero di Cosimo in America. *Art News* featured it on the front page of its January 30 issue, and it was reproduced in art magazines from *Connoisseur* to *The Art Digest.*[60] It would be the only object Chick would buy for Hartford that was already so famous it was mentioned in the *Encyclopedia Britannica.*

Chick was at no loss for other counterweights to the surrealist show: a few weeks before it opened, he announced his plans for the rest of the winter—a survey of American art over four centuries. He promised to bring to Hartford some of the greatest paintings produced by Americans, along with furniture, silver, glass, and costumes. It would be, he said, a "pageant of American culture." Proposing this patriotic extravaganza just before installing the surrealist pictures was a brilliant tactic, which the local press fully understood.[61] Chick also may have thought of the exhibition as a complement to the opening of the Whitney Museum of American Art in New York, scheduled for November 17, much as his showing of artists of the School of Paris in 1929 had complemented the Museum of Modern Art's debut.

But even as he proposed the American show, Chick made it clear that the pendulum of exhibitions would continue to swing. He announced that in the spring of 1932 he would mount the world's first comprehensive Picasso exhibition. Though few of his trustees could say they understood or liked the Spaniard's work, at least they recognized him as the most famous of all modern artists. It would be an enormous coup for Hartford.

Finally, Chick reported that he hoped to make the city the third stop of a large seminal architecture exhibition that was being organized by Russell Hitchcock and Philip Johnson for the Museum of Modern Art. This was already expected to be a momentous event, said Chick, the presentation of a new aesthetic to the American public: "the international style in modern architecture." Following Chick's lead, the press declared that hosting such an exhibition would make Hartford the focus of national attention.[62] The city now aspired to a reputation as a leader of the arts, something that would have been inconceivable four years earlier.

As America entered 1932, the worst year of the Depression, Chick's ambitious exhibition plans had to be severely cut back. The trustees announced that the Atheneum's investments, though anchored securely in railroad stocks and utilities, were not generating enough operating income, and 1931 had ended with a deficit for the third consecutive year. All staff salaries, including Chick's, were cut by 10 percent. The museum circulated a public notice, clearly written by Chick, calling for more memberships. The Atheneum, it said, was as central to the life of the Hartford community as its schools and hospitals. It was essential that "the spirit of a people, whose major concern has been a struggle for bread and butter, be nurtured on the equally vital fare of the arts. Otherwise the spirit would perish and we should sink into the brutality and ignorance of the dark ages."[63]

It was obvious that Chick could not afford the American show he had announced in October, and his record of dazzling winter shows seemed about to be broken.

At that moment, Sir Joseph Duveen waved his profit-laden wand and made a hundred and twenty-six objects from the Italian Renaissance appear in Hartford. The loan was anonymous, and Duveen paid for all shipping and insurance—a courtesy he could well afford for such a good customer. And so on January 27, Chick opened another splendid exhibition, *Art of the Italian Renaissance*.

Long adept at cultivating clients, Duveen rounded out his favor by buying a picture from Chick's one-man show at the Brummer Gallery the next month, followed by a letter full of praise for the young director's artistry. Chick gratefully told the dealer that he had chosen the one work he was proudest of painting. Perhaps Chick was flattered enough not to think that it went straight to Duveen's basement, which was chock-full of such strategic purchases.[64]

The Renaissance exhibition was perfectly in line with what the trustees expected to see in their museum. There were nineteen paintings by such artists as Filippino Lippi, Cosimo Roselli, Andrea del Verrocchio, Giovanni Bellini, Lorenzo Lotto, and Dosso Dossi; and a dozen marble sculptures, along with bronzes, plaquettes, and medals. A larger than life-size bronze figure of Mercury by the sixteenth-century master Giovanni da Bologna dominated the gallery. Chick filled out the space with several pieces of Renaissance furniture. A local journalist expressed the wonder that Americans often felt in those years when brought face-to-face with European treasures: "Among the sculptures are figures so familiar that it hardly seems possible that these can be the originals." He added that "the Italians of Hartford will appreciate these masterpieces with something of the ardour with which they cheer an aria from Verdi."[65] It was a magnificent setting in which to unveil the Piero di Cosimo.

The Depression was by now so pervasive in Hartford, despite the relative insulation of the insurance industry, that Chick felt compelled to explain why the museum was spending so much on a single canvas at the same time that it was soliciting more public support:

> While the purchase of such a picture as the Piero di Cosimo, recently acquired by the Atheneum for the Sumner collection, may seem to some in questionable taste in such difficult times, it must be remembered that under the terms of the Sumner will the income from the fund can be applied only to the purchase of paintings, and at the present moment it is possible to invest such money most favorably. On the other hand this beautiful painting, I am certain, will give joy to many many persons at a time when the appreciation of works of art serves somewhat to allay for some moments the worry and anxiety in which all share.[66]

Privately, Chick had doubts about the purchase. He felt that he might have succumbed too easily to the temptation to get a famous Florentine picture, and he was bothered by the condition of the Piero.[67] As early as May 1932, a year before it was entirely paid for, he consulted a prominent New York conservator, who confirmed his suspicions. It had been overcleaned and clumsily over-painted.[68] As Chick and his friends liked to tell each other, it had been "Duveened." But whatever his misgivings, the masterly combination of realism and fantasy that had first attracted him was far from obliterated.

Duveen's intervention had turned the winter show into a triumph, but Chick knew there would be no angel for the vast, unprecedented Picasso exhibition he had wanted to produce. With great reluctance, he set the idea aside, keeping only the International Style show from MOMA on the museum's calendar.

Yet paradoxically, as the Depression deepened, Chick was presented with one of the most momentous opportunities of his life. On January 22, 1932, Charles Goodwin appointed a building committee to plan the construction of the long-delayed addition to the museum, the Avery Memorial.

CHAPTER NINE

International Style

> Brovik: They really liked what he wants to do. They thought it was completely new and different—that's what they said.
>
> Solness: Aha! New! Modern! None of the old-fashioned stuff I build!
>
> —Henrik Ibsen, *The Master Builder*

Even before he came to Hartford, Chick had known that more than half a million dollars was sitting in an account established by Samuel Avery, Jr., waiting to be spent. Avery had been a leading New York dealer in European paintings who had inherited the business from his father, a founder of the Metropolitan Museum of Art. In 1909 he gave up his Park Avenue house, retired with his mother to the serenity of Hartford, and began bestowing large sums on the city's worthiest institutions, particularly the Wadsworth Atheneum. Avery was soon a vice president of the museum's board, and in 1918, two years before his death, he presented the Atheneum with his collections of silver, bronzes, glass, and Chinese porcelains. At the same time he gave the museum forty-five hundred shares of Continental Fire Insurance Company stock, then worth $225,000, to be held for at least five years and used to build an addition to the Morgan Memorial or a separate building, in part to house the objects he had given. He stipulated that this addition should conform to the "general architectural effect" of the Morgan Memorial, designed in the Renaissance-Revival style.[1]

Chick knew that the choice of architect was a foregone conclusion. It was to be a family affair. For the earliest discussions about the building in 1928, Charles Goodwin had brought in his brother-in-law, New York architect Benjamin Wistar Morris. A product of the Ecole des Beaux Arts in Paris, he had built the Morgan Memorial under the close scrutiny of its donor, his wife's cousin, J. Pierpont Morgan.[2] Morris's success with the museum had brought other Hartford commissions, executed in a variety of historical styles.[3] To the Atheneum's trustees it was obvious that no one was more suited to produce an addition conforming to the architecture of the Morgan than the original architect himself. But at those first meetings in 1928, Morris had made it clear that he would defer to Chick, as the museum expert, in decisions about the character and function of the new building.[4]

Chick proposed an addition of palatial proportions, inspired not only by the Fogg, but also the Boston Museum of Fine Arts and the Isabella Stewart Gardner Museum. Each had a courtyard in a specific style. For Hartford, Chick saw no reason to settle for one when three would do. He proposed building a Renaissance court; a classical court, covered by a skylight; and an open-air Romanesque court. A gallery would be devoted to each of the principal European schools of painting, while American pictures would be combined with furniture and decorative arts. He would have an art library, a restaurant, a museum shop, and a lecture room equipped with projectors, seating at least four hundred people.

Eager to proceed, Chick followed up those first discussions with a field trip to the Fogg, the Gardner, and the Museum of Fine Arts, accompanied by an architect in Morris's firm, but the trustees hesitated. Building costs were high. There were unresolved questions about whether the other institutions housed in the Atheneum—the Hartford Public Library, the Connecticut Historical Society, and the Watkinson Library—would be allowed space in the new addition.[5] The board decided that postponement was the prudent course.

By the time discussions resumed three years later, at the end of 1931, Chick's ideas for a modern museum building had changed radically. Now they were very different from those of Morris, whom he addressed, from his new niche in the Goodwin family, as "My dear Uncle Ben." Chick had discovered the International Style. In the Avery Memorial he saw his one great chance to create the most advanced museum in America.

The International Style represented, at that time, perhaps the most abrupt change in living and working environments in the history of architecture. Its airy and immaculate spaces, defined and dramatized with primary colors on flat surfaces and bold lines that met at right angles, amounted to three-dimensional abstractions—a total rejection of the overstuffed and stylistically jumbled surroundings of nearly every European and American. The house, in Le Corbusier's words, would become "a machine for living."

The shift came in the wake of the First World War. In 1917 a group called *De Stijl* ("the Style") was formed in Holland by Piet Mondrian and his fellow abstract artists, the Neoplasticists; in 1919 the Bauhaus school was founded by Walter Gropius in Weimar, the capital of the new German republic. Rarely had

MAGICIAN OF THE MODERN / 172

the creative powers of artists, architects, and designers been so concentrated. During the five years from 1925 to 1930 alone, some of the most influential examples of the new architecture had been built in Europe: Gerrit Rietveld's Schroeder house at Utrecht; the famous Bauhaus complex itself, designed by Gropius for its second home at Dessau; J. J. P. Oud's housing estate in the Hook of Holland; Ludwig Mies van der Rohe's Weissenhof in Stuttgart; and Le Corbusier's Savoye House at Poissy, France. In 1929, only a few months after Chick had first proposed a traditional approach to the Avery addition for Ben Morris and the Atheneum's board, the German Pavilion designed by Mies van der Rohe for the Barcelona International Exhibition created enormous excitement in art circles. Henry-Russell Hitchcock later wrote that this luxuriously sleek and light-filled structure of steel, glass, marble, and travertine had "almost no other purpose than to be beautiful"[6] and called it "one of the few buildings by which the twentieth century might wish to be measured against the great ages of the past."[7]

Hitchcock was the American herald of the oncoming cultural currents. In his earliest published essay, "The Decline of Modern Architecture," which appeared in September 1927 in the first issue of Lincoln Kirstein's *Hound & Horn,* he had praised Le Corbusier, Oud, and Gropius, whose work was almost unknown in this country. A year later, also in *Hound & Horn,* he had described what he saw as two opposing modes of contemporary architecture—one based on borrowings from the architectural vocabulary of the past, the other free from traditional ornament, expressing itself through the function of the building and the properties of modern construction materials themselves. And in this essay of 1928 he had coined a new term: the advanced style was, he wrote, "very definitely not a French, nor a Dutch, nor a German, nor a Russian, but an international style."[8] He had transformed the title of Gropius's monograph of 1925, *Internationale Architektur,* from a purely descriptive phrase into the label for a new aesthetic.[9] In 1929, when he published *Modern Architecture: Romanticism and Reintegration,* the first comprehensive book in English on the subject, the twenty-six-year-old Hitchcock established his reputation as America's foremost authority on the new style. Expanding on the theme introduced in his essays, he christened the divergent strains of contemporary architecture "The New Tradition" and "The New Pioneers." With a breadth of vision similar to Chick's, he pointed to origins of modern architecture as far back as the thirteenth century.[10]

It was naturally the New Pioneers who captured Chick's imagination. As soon as Hitchcock's book appeared, Chick excitedly scribbled a review, apparently never published, on odd sheets of his mother's Boston stationery, noting that these trailblazers were "men like Le Corbusier of France, Walter Gropius of Germany and J. J. P. Oud of Holland, whose insistence on the house as a machine for living, on the facade as a function of the interior, on the interior, conceived as a volume rather than as mass, and on the negation of ornament reminiscent of the past, have produced solutions of utilitarian problems which are at the same time satisfying aesthetically."

Having promoted Art Deco design when he showed off his apartment in 1928, Chick now condemned it as passé. "That America is so long in accepting ideas of this sort is perhaps not so astonishing, especially in view of the confusion which exists in the popular mind in the use of the terms 'modern' and 'modernistic'. The former associates itself more properly with the work of the New Pioneers, whereas the latter describes more nearly the decorative degeneracies coming out of the Paris Exposition of 1925, which in its turn represented the decadence of the style of the new tradition." It was the International Style that represented the truly modern.

While he understood that the modernism he promoted was itself a style that would eventually be superseded, Chick feared it might not ever be given the chance to take hold in America. He would not be surprised, he wrote, if America, with "its sentimental subjection to the yoke of the past" and its "creative sterility," did not "have enough vitality to develop even the few directions which remain. It is this very ability to break with Romantic precedent which makes the New Pioneer work so stimulating in the vistas of progress which it opens."[11] For Chick and his confreres—Hitchcock, Barr, and Philip Johnson— vitality infused the Machine Age, and their mission was to let others know.

It was part of Chick's particular genius that he could put the new ideas into practice immediately. Early in 1930, just as he was supervising construction of his Scarborough Street house, with its dressing room inspired by the one in Gropius's house, he created a striking Bauhaus-style office for himself at the museum. This he opened to the public in the spring, ostensibly as a continuation of the period rooms he had installed at the end of 1929. Here he again made the point that modernism could be seen as a distinct era, one that was only beginning.

The walls and ceiling of his office were painted in different shades of the same color, ranging from deep reddish brown to pink. To dramatize the room's abstract qualities, Chick had a wide black band painted horizontally across one wall, continuing across a built-in shelf, up to the top of a bookcase at right angles to the wall and down along its side to the floor. The furniture consisted of a simple metal desk painted dark red and a tubular chrome table and tubular chairs designed by Marcel Breuer. A German lighting fixture made of vertical chrome and glass tubes was suspended from the ceiling. The office was an astonishing sight to visitors who wandered by it in the early 1930s.[12]

To introduce contemporary architecture more fully to Hartford, Chick asked Hitchcock to give a public lecture at the end of the year. With new

The director's office, Morgan Memorial, Wadsworth Atheneum, 1930.
Chair and table by Marcel Breuer

lantern slides from his summer in Europe flashing across a screen, Hitchcock illustrated the work of Le Corbusier, Oud, Gropius, and Mies van der Rohe, among others, with an emphasis on the recent Stockholm Exposition of contemporary design. His audience saw every kind of building in Europe that embodied the new aesthetic, from gas stations and churches to factories, houses, and museums.[13] Richard Neutra, on his way back to the West Coast from the International Congress of Modern Architecture in Zurich, made an unscheduled appearance at Hitchcock's lecture and described the radical buildings he had recently designed in Los Angeles.[14] The Hartford audience was thus among the first in the country to hear about the International Style directly—from the scholar who named it and the architect who first realized it in America.

As Chick's ideas of architecture were publicly evolving, Samuel Avery's money was quietly compounding. The trustees had converted his insurance stock into solid, conservative bonds—utilities, railroads, and government issues—which yielded a remarkably steady income. By the end of 1931 the fund had grown to more than $700,000. Few Hartford institutions had access to such a sum to employ the small army of contractors and skilled craftsmen which the Avery Memorial would require. In recalling the opportunity the new construction gave the city, Samuel Avery's niece, Amy Welcher, a pillar of the Congregational church, beheld the hand of Providence: "Building the Avery wing gave jobs to all those Hartford people. And I believe the Creator has plans of every kind for every kind of person. I think it would have pleased Uncle Sam greatly to know that when nobody had any money, they [could] come along and put up a wing—just like that."[15] The trustees undoubtedly agreed with Miss Welcher on Sunday morning, but during the week they recognized a bargain when they saw one: building costs were plunging to their lowest levels of the Depression.

The building committee Charles Goodwin appointed at the beginning of 1932 consisted of William Corson, Arthur Day, Edward Forbes, Frank Gay, Robert Huntington, Francis Parsons, Archibald Welch, and Goodwin himself. He formally urged all the trustees to comment on the design, but Frank Gay was the only one who did. He reminded the president that he had known Avery intimately and had spoken to him about the new wing. Avery, he wrote, "did not wish his future building to overshadow or detract in any way from the Morgan Memorial, which he greatly admired. I am sure that he hoped for a somewhat ornate and elegant structure both inside and out. Utility, solely, was not his first consideration. His tastes and beliefs were not modernistic."[16]

This was the last bit of advice Chick wanted to hear as he pushed for a totally modern design. He even dared to sound out Philip Goodwin on the possibility of dropping Ben Morris's firm altogether—a notion dismissed the moment Cousin Phil broached it to members of the building committee.[17] Morris suspected that Chick's conversion to the International Style might be a source of friction and diplomatically assigned his junior partner, Robert O'Connor, only five years older than Chick, to pilot the project. The fact that O'Connor happened to be Morris's son-in-law and Helen's "Cousin Bob" may or may not have smoothed the way for Chick.

O'Connor later said that he knew nothing about the International Style in those years and came to look on Chick as his teacher. He remembered how certain Chick had been about the general scheme: "The very first time I talked to him about the Avery, he said, 'I would like something like this.' He drew a rectangle with another rectangle inside of it, with the central court going up to the skylight."[18]

Chick's early notion of three courts in assorted historical styles had been abandoned in favor of one absolutely up-to-date space, rising three stories and painted white. Directly beneath the court would be a theater. This court would be the heart of the new building. The most original element of the design was the handling of the second- and third-floor galleries, which would run entirely around the court, projecting over the ground floor. Chick wanted no columns supporting them, no vertical interruptions of the court's sleek horizontal lines. O'Connor therefore designed the galleries to be cantilevered, held up by steel beams hidden under the flooring.

Those boldly conceived spaces on the second and third floors would contain a double row of galleries. One row would face out into the court over a half wall, with small projecting balconies at either end and a parallel row running around the outer walls of the building. Freestanding partitions would be used to vary the length of the galleries, particularly on the third floor, which was intended for changing exhibitions. As Chick preferred to show paintings in natural light whenever possible, skylights were to be set into the ceilings of the interior galleries. All surfaces and openings—walls, floors, ceilings, doors— would have the cleanest possible lines.

Morris seemed surprisingly receptive to Chick's concept of the interior design, perhaps because his own style was so eclectic. The preliminary drawings he presented to the trustees at the annual meeting early in 1932 incorporated Chick's latest suggestions.[19] Chick explained the functional look of the new addition to the board, saying that "there would be little elaborate architectural detail, the idea being to get away from the palace type of museum."[20]

For the first floor, Chick planned to have offices, print galleries, rooms for Samuel Avery's decorative arts collection, and an art library, with the two upper floors devoted to the Nutting furniture collection and the principal galleries for paintings. He had to forgo the restaurant he wanted; the depressed economy made such a venture too risky.

The architects also designed classrooms and studios on the second and third floors for the Hartford Art School. Helen Austin and her aunt Ruth Goodwin, both trustees of the school, had pushed to make it part of the Atheneum, much as the larger American art museums had their academic components, and Chick liked the idea, too.[21] Helen worked directly with Bob O'Connor, setting out the requirements of the school in detail, from the number of desks in each classroom to the couch needed "for possible fainting fits in the girls' room."[22]

Uncle Charlie Goodwin's special interests were accommodated on the second floor in a Marine Room, for ship models and other nautical artifacts. Chick's friends privately made fun of the idea—Russell Hitchcock always called it the "Shipping Room." Chick chose not to assign any space to the old natural history collection, despite a plea by Frank Gay, leaving it in a remote basement corner of the Morgan Memorial. Over succeeding decades, it was quietly dispersed.

Chick made certain that his own heart's desire found a place in the Avery Memorial. The lecture room he had proposed three years earlier was now to be a full-fledged theater with a proscenium arch, a stage, an orchestra pit, a cyclorama, dressing rooms, lights, a soundproof projection booth, and enough room to one side of the stage for moving scenery. His plans for 400 seats had to be scaled back to 299 to avoid having the space classified officially as a theater by the city of Hartford, which would have resulted in a multitude of building code requirements.

Chick later said that he wanted a theater because of the popularity of his film program of 1929: he hoped to attract people who were not especially interested in paintings but might be drawn to art museums by motion picture programs.[23] But there was more to it than that. Chick the impresario and, as the years went by, Chick the performer, had to have such a facility at his disposal. From the opening of the Avery to the end of his life, he was never without his own theater.

The Avery Memorial Auditorium, as it was originally called, was one of the first fully equipped theaters in an American art museum, but it had at least two predecessors: the round rococo theater later known as the Florence Gould Auditorium, at the Palace of the Legion of Honor in San Francisco, built in 1924; and the Kenneth Sawyer Goodman Memorial Theater at the Art Institute of Chicago, opened in 1925.[24]

Though the Atheneum's board was willing to give Chick a relatively free hand in the design of the interior of the Avery, he asked for more. He wanted an unadulterated expression of modernism on the outside as well. This neither Charles Goodwin nor Benjamin Wistar Morris could accept, as it would have violated Avery's clearly stated intentions. More importantly, though neither the senior architect nor the president was as sentimentally attached to old-fashioned decoration as Frank Gay, they were not prepared to tolerate the clash that a truly International Style façade would have made next to the Morgan Memorial.[25]

Attempting to end the discussion on the exterior, Goodwin asserted his own authority. In February 1932, he called a meeting of the building committee, which only four other trustees attended and which did not include Austin or Forbes. Those present unanimously resolved that all correspondence from Morris should be addressed to Goodwin, with only copies to Chick, and "that the original plan be adhered to and the architect be directed to go ahead."[26]

But Chick did not give up easily. He hated the thought of a bastardized modern exterior that would be outdated before it was built. If the architects were not inclined to design a Bauhaus building, he would create one himself and convince them. Winslow Ames, who had just been named the first director of the Lyman Allyn Museum in New London, Connecticut, remembered Chick's campaign to change their minds as "a furious affair" with much model-making going on in his office.[27]

As if to validate his pleas for the most contemporary design possible, Chick opened the Museum of Modern Art's traveling show, *Modern Architecture: Inter-*

national Exhibition, on April 30, 1932. Organized by Philip Johnson and Henry-Russell Hitchcock, the exhibition brought the term "International Style" into public consciousness across the country, visiting eleven cities in three years. It had opened in New York in February, and Hartford was the second stop on the circuit, just after the Pennsylvania Museum of Art (later the Philadelphia Museum of Art).

Tapestry Hall and its side galleries were filled with ten large scale-models, photographs, and drawings, representing the work of the most innovative American and European architects—Frank Lloyd Wright, Howe and Lescaze, Raymond Hood, the Bowman brothers, Richard Neutra, Le Corbusier, J. J. P. Oud, Otto Haesler, Walter Gropius, and Mies van der Rohe. Chick saturated Hartford with publicity extolling modern architecture. For readers of the Atheneum bulletin, he reprinted Alfred Barr's introduction to the exhibition catalogue and made certain that Barr and Philip Johnson were interviewed by the Hartford press. Barr said prophetically that "the stimulation and direction which an exhibition of this type can give to contemporary architectural thought and practice is incalculable."[28]

To one newspaper reporter, Chick dismissed those who failed to appreciate the aesthetics of the new architecture: "It is as if they rejected the automobile because it does not resemble the sedan chair."[29] The local press followed his lead. One journalist declared that the new architecture was "as much a part of the present mechanical age as were the log cabins of pioneer days."[30] Another saw in the vast apartment complexes in Europe a solution to the current economic crisis: "If the modern world comes to realize the need for bringing its housing up to date, the depression will be over."[31]

Chick and Hitchcock proselytized continuously for modernism during the month the exhibition was in town, offering conferences on the show every Friday and lectures on modern architecture every Sunday afternoon. An open forum for architects was held on May 11, at which Austin, Hitchcock, Johnson, and William Lescaze debated the merits of the new architecture with about eighty participants—local architects, contractors, even real estate agents.[32] Disarmingly, Lescaze said that he was surprised to hear people call modern architecture radical: "Modern architects are not trying to be radically original and have no other ambition than to apply a little common sense to their profession."[33] But many in the audience would have agreed with Theodate Pope Riddle—one of the few women architects in America—who chastised her male colleagues, saying that modern architecture failed because it was purely intellectual without regard to the emotions. She added that men who worked with machinery during the day might rather not sleep in a machine at night. And she defended the sentiments of ordinary home buyers: "These people are building nests. You can't take that out of human nature."[34]

The skepticism of some visitors was reflected in a satirical column in the *Courant* a few days later, in which a man visiting the International Style show observed to his wife: "Only remember, Phyllis, when you get a house like that never throw stones. You might break a neoplastic plane, and that would be terrible. . . . It's art and they say it's beautiful."[35]

As for Uncle Charlie Goodwin, the show did nothing to change his mind about the style of the Avery exterior. Chick had used every conceivable tactic to press for a relaxation of Samuel Avery's stipulation about "conforming to the Morgan Memorial," but this was one battle he could not win.

Benjamin Wistar Morris compromised as far as he could. He retreated from his original concept of an exterior in the Renaissance-Revival style.[36] After agreeing to a very functional interior, he knew that an ornate exterior would be incongruous. Instead, using the same Tennessee marble as the Morgan Memorial, he designed perfectly symmetrical facades in the Art Deco style. It was a restrained and handsome look, but modern only in the most superficial sense. Fluted pilasters were to be machined onto the stone in relief, along with inscriptions, entablatures, and medallions representing the arts. Chick was crestfallen and did not tire of reminding the trustees of his disappointment.[37]

He was forced to acquiesce, but by his own architectural sleight of hand, he had already created his International Style exterior. Avery Court was essentially the outside of a Bauhaus building turned inward.[38] To emphasize the impression of an exterior, Chick had first wanted the court to be a sculpture garden with a floor of white pebbles, trees, a pool, and a fountain. The pebbles and foliage were soon dropped from the design as impractical, but the pool and its sculptural fountain remained.

For this focal point of an immaculate twentieth-century space, he looked to the baroque. He sketched a rectangular rococo border with bowed ends for the pool. He already knew what he wanted for the fountain. This was a voluptuous eight-foot-high Mannerist sculpture of Venus, attended by a nymph and a satyr, standing between the heads of two large dolphins, which squirted jets of water into the pool. The work was signed by Pietro Francavilla and dated 1600, and was the most elaborate in a series of thirteen commissioned for the grounds of the Villa Bracci, outside Florence. Some of the statues were purchased in the eighteenth century by Frederick, Prince of Wales, and eventually installed on the East Terrace at Windsor Castle, but this piece had been lost in transit and was not rediscovered until 1919, buried in a garden near London. It now belonged to Durlacher Brothers and was on loan to the Fogg, where it was stored in the basement next to the men's room. Paul Sachs had wanted it for the Fogg's Renaissance court and had hoped to raise the money to purchase it. Edward Forbes, however, found the towering goddess quite improper, saying, "We cannot have that naked woman in the middle of a Harvard building."[39]

Sachs remained so attached to the sculpture that, in the summer of 1932 when he saw correspondence from Chick to Forbes inquiring about the weight of the piece, he impetuously dictated a note to Forbes and had it typed directly onto Chick's letter. That his former pupil was considering the purchase of the Francavilla, said Sachs, "is only another proof of what I felt for a long time, that Chick is a pretty wise boy. If that statue is set up in the central court of the Wadsworth Atheneum instead of in the central court of the Fogg Museum, you may look for me in Hartford sitting under the statue in a broken down condition and in tears."[40]

When Charles Goodwin found out that Harvard might still be interested in the sculpture, he insisted that Austin obtain an unqualified statement from the Fogg about its intentions. It was Sachs who replied graciously, relinquishing all claims the Fogg may have had on the work. Typically, having lost the prize for his own museum, Sachs gave Chick the strongest possible support to help him convince his board to acquire it: "I think it highly unlikely that any such object of comparable importance will in our time be again available. . . . I sincerely hope that you will promptly acquire it."[41]

For the better part of a year, the building committee remained timid about allowing the Venus such a prominent position in their museum. Goodwin asked both Chick and the architects for formal statements about the work. O'Connor sedately replied that "the size, scale, and general contour is admirable for this purpose."[42] Morris, however, wanted to invite extremely conventional sculptors, friends of his, to design something for the pool. Privately, he lobbied Philip Goodwin for support, but Goodwin, who sided with Chick, "exploded" at the suggestion.[43]

Chick insisted on getting the Francavilla, warning the board that

the lack of such a central and commanding group as the one under discussion would be extremely unfortunate.

Of the quality and importance of the sculpture itself there can be no doubt. It is without question the most beautiful object of its kind which I have ever seen in America and stands historically on the threshold of one of the very greatest epochs in the history of sculpture, the Baroque. Nor is there the slightest question of the genuineness of the object, the figure having been well known and mentioned often in critical writings of its period. The restorations are few and obvious.

As for the price, I consider it (possibly $12,000) extraordinarily reasonable, even at these times. In fact I think the sculpture is well worth the original asking price of over $30,000.[44]

Some members of the committee were convinced by Chick and the architects.[45] Other trustees were not as certain. Robert Huntington, head of the Connecticut General Life Insurance Company, was disquieted that pedestrians might glimpse the unclothed goddess from the street:

> I believe that the nude cannot be justly criticized inside of a museum. Nobody has to come in and see it if they don't want to. Whether we have reached the point of artistic appreciation in this country when the trustees can venture to put it where it will meet the gaze of the passer-by, I do not know. If the trustees think that the group is beautiful enough, I think I would be willing to take a chance, but I don't think that, without seeing it, we ought to be called on to vote.[46]

Representatives of the board visited the Fogg to look at the work early in 1933, but it was not until the spring that its purchase for $12,000 was finally approved. It was later recognized as the finest Italian Mannerist sculpture in America. Chick's placement of an elaborate baroque object in the midst of a Bauhaus court—combining the most florid style in the history of European art with the most unadorned—was a brilliant juxtaposition few other modernists would have contemplated.

While discussions of the Avery Memorial design were in their early stages in 1932, the Depression deepened. Building costs continued to sink, to the benefit of the Avery fund, but the general museum budget faltered. Among the programs facing cancellation that year were the popular children's summer art classes. Chick recognized kindred spirits among the troops of youngsters busily and messily working on their projects in the museum. He decided to raise the funds for children's education himself, announcing to the press that he would put on three magic shows in the Morgan Memorial. He called on his Trinity students, as well as a few adventuresome friends in the community, to help. Helen volunteered to play one of the two pianos that accompanied the act.

On April 14, 1932, dressed in white tie and tails, Chick made his first adult appearance as a magician. A bright yellow proscenium with a black velvet curtain was constructed at one end of Tapestry Hall. To drum beats, Chick stepped forward. He was then handcuffed, bound, and locked in a trunk, only to materialize moments later from behind the curtain. A West Hartford matron dressed as Fatima was levitated. An electric light moved mysteriously around the stage. Magic writing appeared on sealed slates. A fishing line that Chick cast out over the audience suddenly gyrated with a live goldfish. Pigeons, rabbits, and a canary were produced from nowhere. Chick's deft stagecraft and, above all, his sparkling patter were so popular that he added two more performances. For the next thirteen years he would entertain Hartford with increasingly elaborate magic productions, always for the benefit of the children's art classes. With his taste for the theater rekindled, Chick joined another group of

Trinity students in designing a set and painting backdrops for a production by the college players, the Jesters, called *Wings Over Europe*.

But reality kept intruding. Ben Morris's office in New York inundated Chick with questions, demanding immediate decisions on the minutiae of the Avery. Did he want a Spencer vacuum cleaning system piped throughout the building? Did he approve Deflex Glass #12? Should there be turnstiles at the theater entrance? Where should radiators be placed in the galleries? Should the fire-hose cabinets be built into the walls? The architects knew Chick wanted to be involved in every decision about the building but, as yet, they did not realize how intense that involvement would be.

As the summer of 1932 approached, Chick had more than a new building to anticipate. To his surprise, he was about to become a father. "Chick said when we were first married that we wouldn't be having children," Helen confessed long afterward. "He said we'd be too busy. But sometimes," she added, "things happen."[47]

Chick was both elated and anxious. The confusion and excitement of his upcoming role as a family man was added to the exhaustion from months of negotiations about the new building, the hectic teaching and lecturing schedule, the magic shows—even a stint as guest curator at the Slater Gallery in Norwich, Connecticut, where he produced a comprehensive show of modern art. He was eager to get out of town.

As his usual European trip seemed out of the question because of the Depression, Chick came up with an alternative escape. Encouraged by the success of his magic performances that spring, he invited his young assistants from Trinity to accompany him on a road show through New England for the summer. He invented a new stage name for himself, inspired by the German lightbulbs from the Osram company in the modern rooms of his house. He became "The Great Osram—Masked Master of Multiple Mysteries."[48] He called his troupe "the Little Osrams."

The promotional material about the Great Osram that Chick supplied to newspapers along the route accurately reflected how he saw himself:

> There is much mystery associated with the personality of the magician. Rumor has it that in private life he is an entirely different person, who holds an important position in an absolutely unrelated field. His manner is very much that of the man of the world, and it is said that he is even more familiar with Europe than with this country, and that this is the first summer for many years that he has spent in this country.[49]

In June, he and his troupe, his doves, and his rabbits, set off in a panel truck and a Ford Phaeton for northern New England.[50] The farm in Windham and the cottage in South Harpswell became their headquarters, depending on whether they were giving shows in small New Hampshire towns or along the coast of Maine. Chick kept Helen abreast of his arduous, and largely unprofitable, appearances at the kinds of places where he had performed in his childhood—town halls, churches, Grange and Redmen's Halls:

> I made the show at Orrs Island in plenty of time, which was a big surprise to me. We had a great success and made about thirty dollars which seems an enormous sum to us now. But last night we journeyed all the way to Bowdoinham only to make about two dollars. There was a terrific storm and we didnt get back until two A.M. drenched to the skin with the doves and rabbits in the same or worse condition.[51]

Nothing deterred him from presenting the two-hour performance, no matter what the turnout. One night in Dover, New Hampshire, though free tickets were handed out liberally, the audience consisted solely of the building custodian.[52]

When Chick and the Little Osrams finally returned to Hartford in August, he decided that he must make a quick trip to Europe after all. This would be his last chance to see the interior features and accessories of the new museums in Germany before plans for the Avery were completed. Without a word to Helen, he convinced Uncle Charlie to dole out $450 from the Avery fund for travel expenses.

On this trip Chick would be entirely free, for there was no chance of Helen's joining him. She was having a difficult pregnancy and had spent the summer in Hartford. To give her a change of scene during his still unannounced absence, he arranged for his aunt Sue Etnier, whom Helen adored, to invite them both to South Harpswell. Early in September, they drove to Maine. They had barely arrived when Chick confessed that he was about to sail for Germany. Helen was taken completely by surprise. After weeks away on his magic tour, he was leaving her again. She accused him of not wanting to spend time with her, of not caring about her. Chick was sorry, but he could not possibly give up the chance to get away to Europe. But from New York on September 14, hours before he sailed, he made an attempt to apologize:

> I feel dreadfully about going now and I think I should have given the whole thing up yesterday if it hadnt been for the ticket reposing in my pocket. It wont be long though till I'm back. I know you think that I'm always rushing off somewhere and that I never want to stay at home with you but it isnt that at all, Cunning. I couldnt ever love anyone else but you. I know it's dreadfully hard for you and I'm so sorry if it has made you unhappy. Please forgive me.

Yet he could not resist recounting his adventures, telling her that he had lunched at a favorite speakeasy with Odette Myrtil, the popular star of stage and screen, and that they had been joined by Paul Sachs, "who loved Odette and had such a merry time drinking cocktail after cocktail after cocktail and listening to story after story by Myrtil. Michels was filled with the art market all wishing to be remembered to you." He added that Charles Laughton's wife, Elsa Lanchester, was going over on the same boat and that "I am just bound for the Askews for cocktails and then to Joe Brewer's for a final party."[53] Helen was always his best audience, and, like a child, Chick had no idea that she could be anything but delighted to hear about his amusements. He sailed on the *Bremen* at midnight.

For two weeks he visited museums and the most modern suppliers of lighting and interior design in Germany. He was especially influenced by the Essen Museum for its movable partitions, lights, and almost invisible metal moldings for hanging pictures. And though the Sumner money was still being funneled to Duveen to pay for the Piero di Cosimo, he could not pass up the chance for a few smaller purchases. In Berlin he stopped by the Galerie Alfred Flechtheim and chose watercolors by Paul Klee to bring back to Hartford on approval, *Marionettes in a Storm* and *Mr. Pep and His Horse.* A few days later, Jim Soby visited the same dealer and also bought a work by Klee. Flechtheim told Soby of his amazement at Chick's perceptive eye: "Your friend Austin decided in ten minutes on two pictures which I myself, after months of study, had decided were perhaps the best in a top-quality group."[54]

When Chick returned to America on the *Europa* in the first week of October, he was bubbling with more ideas about interior design. Goodwin privately warned O'Connor to scrutinize Chick's suggestions, adding that he personally was expecting a museum that would be "permanently satisfying" rather than "predicated on transitory modes."[55]

But, of course, for Chick only the latest modes would do. He scoured New York for anything architecturally new. He inspected theater seats at Radio City Music Hall, marble in the Empire Trust Company Building, side walls in the Roxy Auditorium, and brass push bars on the doors of Bonwit Teller's Fifth Avenue store. He looked at samples of elevator switches and inspected linoleum for the museum's offices and the Hartford Art School.

Simultaneously, he continued his frenetic schedule of teaching, exhibitions, and programs. In December, under the auspices of the Hartford Art Society, he produced a show of the works of Thomas Hart Benton, aimed at local art students. Ten oil studies for murals and eleven watercolors and drawings were borrowed directly from Benton, who came to the museum on December 12 and explained his method of mural painting.

Earlier in the month, Chick invited Virgil Thomson to present a program to the Friends and Enemies of Modern Music, dormant during the 1931–32 sea-

Paul Klee, Mr. Pep and His Horse, *1925. Ink and watercolor, 18¾ × 21¹⁵⁄₁₆
inches, purchased 1933*

son. Thomson had just arrived in New York for a brief stay to raise money to pay
his rent in Paris and to promote an opera he had written four years earlier with
Gertrude Stein. It was called *Four Saints in Three Acts,* an almost indescribable
fantasy about fifteenth-century Spanish saints in Avila. Chick had heard about
the opera from Russell Hitchcock, whose enthusiasm had started him thinking
about giving the work its premiere.

Chick's unfamiliarity with the piece before Thomson came over, however,
was evident in the first draft of his letter inviting each "Friend or Enemy" to the
program: he described Thomson as "the distinguished young American composer . . . who is known in Paris for his opera 'Two or Three Saints' with Lyrics
by Gertrude Stein. . . . An unusual opportunity will be afforded the members to
become aware of the most recent developments of music in Europe, delightfully
explained, in the form of a lecture with many illustrations on the piano."[56] The
concert was held at the Austins' house on December 19, the day after Chick's
thirty-second birthday.

Thomson spent a good part of the winter of 1932–33 playing and singing
the piano version of *Four Saints* to friends and potential patrons throughout the
Northeast, hoping to find backing for a fully staged production. Once he had
actually heard the opera brought to life, Chick was extremely excited. Here was

Virgil Thomson and Gertrude Stein pose with the score of
Four Saints in Three Acts, *Paris, c. 1929.*

a jarring revolution in language wedded to delicate, tuneful, and wryly home-
spun music. It was an improbable amalgam of modernism, as though the
cubists and the Neo-Romantics had eloped.

Adding to the appeal of a possible production was the fact that, as early as
1929, Thomson had persuaded the reticent New York artist Florine Stettheimer
to design the sets and costumes in what promised to be a whimsical baroque
style. The painter Maurice Grosser, who had been Thomson's companion since
Harvard days (and had taken the Egg and Plaster course when Chick was
Forbes's assistant), had concocted a scenario that would give the work some
amusing stage business.

During this sojourn in America, Thomson had an inspiration about the
cast. He had gone to a Harlem café one night with some of his art history
friends, among them Russell Hitchcock. There he had heard the popular black
entertainer Jimmy Daniels, who was just beginning his career (and who became
what Philip Johnson later called "the first Mrs. Johnson"). "I turned to Russell," Thomson remembered, "realizing the impeccable enunciation of Jimmy's

speech-in-song, and said, 'I think I'll have my opera sung by Negroes.' "[57] The decision would not only make the opera even more of a novelty, it would have long-range effects on the history of the American theater.

Chick began scheming to find a way to give the opera its world premiere in Hartford under the auspices of the Friends and Enemies. Nothing else would do for the opening of his theater in the Avery Memorial, scheduled for the beginning of 1934. He promised Thomson that he would help raise enough money to get the orchestrated score professionally copied; negotiate contracts; and pay for the designer, director, choreographer, conductor, and the large cast the work required.

Chick did not bother the trustees overly about the project. He simply acted as the president of the Friends and Enemies of Modern Music, knowing that Uncle Charlie would not care about, much less understand, what he had in mind as long as it would not actually offend the public and he could figure out a way to pay for it. Deciding that there would be time for fund-raising later in the year, Chick turned his attention to his most pressing concerns—getting the inside of his new museum designed exactly to his taste and putting together one of his most original and provocative exhibitions.

In January, Chick began arranging his sixth winter show, *Literature and Poetry in Painting Since 1850.* Though Hitchcock and Soby helped produce it, the concept was pure Chick Austin. Julien Levy called it Chick's "first really personal exhibition."[58] For he was about to do something no other museum director, including his modernist friends, had thought of doing. He would hang Victorian pictures—many of them blatantly sentimental and academic—next to modern paintings of every ilk: cubism, futurism, Neo-Romanticism, and sur-realism. The seventy-six works he assembled from twenty-five lenders—museums, dealers, and private collectors—became another of Chick's lessons in juxtapositions of the old and the new.

"My purpose in gathering this exhibition," he told the *Courant,* "is to demonstrate that there is a close connection between such a modern painter as Dalí and a nineteenth century favorite such as Gerome." The pictures by the Pre-Raphaelites in the show, he said, such as Dante Gabriel Rossetti and Sir Edward Burne-Jones, and the French "story painters" like Jean-Léon Gérôme and William Bouguereau, "may again be appreciated through the eyes of neoromantics."[59] This was a clear affirmation of his announcement two years earlier that sentiment and narration, though tempered by postwar disillusion-ment and post-Freudian preoccupations, had returned to art. Soby later asserted that this show was "a more difficult and courageous venture" than even the surrealist exhibition, because here Chick was going well beyond both conventional notions and the modernist canon itself: "it was sheer heresy in 1933 to suggest that literature and poetry influenced painting after 1850, the approximate date when Courbet's realism had sought to outlaw all literary, religious and allegorical subjects in art."[60]

For an introduction to the catalogue, Chick tapped into the voluble flow of Hitchcock's intellect. With a dose of humor, Hitchcock wrote that much of nineteenth-century painting "is quite as bad as it seemed fifteen years ago, yet it is no longer to be considered bad for quite the same reasons." It was "a surprise and even a shock," he said, to discover that the obvious emotions expressed in works by the younger narrative painters, and even Picasso, could be linked with a supposedly outmoded tradition.

Accurately forecasting the next forty years of art history, Hitchcock insisted that figurative composition would continue to coexist with nonrepresentational art, no matter how radical the art of the future became: "A black circle on a black ground may be a possible ultimate of the art of painting, but so, also, is a mother and child. The unexpected pleasure of every new development in the arts is that it can open, not only new vistas into the future but new vistas into the past as well."[61] Here he articulated Chick's recurrent theme—the continuity and interconnectedness of art.

Visitors to the show that opened on January 24 saw William Bouguereau's saccharine *Sisters* of 1890 next to Picasso's jarring *Sisters* of 1921. ("What a metaphorical *coup d'etat!*" Julien Levy exclaimed.[62]) Beside Dalí's *Persistence of Memory* was Gérôme's *L'Eminence grise,* a scene from the seventeenth-century French court rendered with a photographic realism worthy of Metro-Goldwyn-Mayer. Monet's misty, glistening impression of Venice's Grand Canal was hung beside de Chirico's stark and sharply drawn view of a Mediterranean arcade, *Le Reve d'un poète.* Next to Jules Breton's *Song of the Lark,* Chick installed Eugène Zak's *Shepherd.* Breton's painting, depicting a peasant girl standing in a field, a sickle in her hand, was so familiar from illustrated calendars that it defined the word "cliché"—a point Chick emphasized by selling a puzzle of the work at the exhibition to pay for shipping it from the Art Institute of Chicago. Zak's shepherd kneeling beside a brook, reminiscent of Nijinsky's sinuous pose in *L'Apres-midi d'un faune,* seemed almost a continuation of the water flowing through the scene.

Chick asked visitors to vote for their favorite picture. Bouguereau's *Sisters* came in first, followed by Breton's *Song of the Lark.* Picasso's *The Blue Boy* was in third place—not surprising for a picture Alfred Barr once called "too pretty."[63] The least popular "favorite" was Dalí's *Persistence of Memory,* earning one vote.[64] Whatever the preferences, Chick felt the exercise had forced museum-goers to take the show personally, and he continued to distribute questionnaires at future exhibitions.

Another result, perhaps indirect, stemmed from the show. The single largest lender had been James Soby. Eleven works came from his collection, including pictures by Berman, Leonid, Klee, Masson, Picasso, Rousseau, Roy, Tchelitchew, and Tonny. Soby was quickly establishing a national reputation as an astute collector of modern art, and now even the Atheneum's trustees acknowledged it. At their annual meeting that January, by whatever powers of persuasion Chick summoned up, the board appointed Soby Honorary Curator of Modern Art. This was one of the first examples of such a title in an American museum.

A few days before the exhibition opened, as the paintings began arriving from all over the country and Chick prepared to race through another installation, Helen went into labor. Chick waited in his office for a call from the hospital, nearly beside himself with anticipation. "Don't go home," he told his secretary, Elinore Jaynes, at the end of the day. Miss Jaynes chatted with him while he chain-smoked and paced around the office until about eleven o'clock that night.[65] He was finally summoned to the hospital, and a healthy baby boy was safely delivered early on January 19, 1933. Chick and Helen named him David Etnier Austin, after two great-grandfathers: David Etnier and David Farnum Austin. As ecstatic as any new father, Chick spread the word to everyone he could think of calling. He telephoned Florence Berkman at six o'clock in the morning. "Florence!" he shouted into the phone, "I've just had a son!" She remembered him sounding "like a little boy himself. There was such *wonder* in his voice."[66]

Laura Austin rushed down to Hartford to join the jubilation. Arthur Austin characteristically kept his distance, but made his happiness clear to Helen:

> A thousand congratulations on the arrival of an heir to the Austin name, if not to the Austin fortune. . . . Take the best of care of yourself and rear the little one so that he will be at least 6 feet tall at maturity. . . . Laura came home last night and is so full of the great event that she can talk of nothing else. With oceans of love from Father.[67]

Chick was so excited about having a son that only a few months later, when he was visiting Helen's sister Lucy in Cambridge, Massachusetts, he asked impulsively, "Do you have a charge account at FAO Schwartz?" She did, and allowed him to use it to buy an electric train for David; he swore her to secrecy. "Can you imagine!" Helen informed Lucy a few days later. "Chick bought an electric train for David—and he's still a baby!"[68]

All may have been happiness on Scarborough Street, but at the Atheneum, tensions were rising again. To Benjamin Morris and Robert O'Connor, Chick seemed needlessly obsessed with the interior design of the Avery. For his part, Chick was determined that come what may, the finishes, fixtures, and furnishings would combine to make a great work of art. Morris began the new year by complaining to Charles Goodwin about a visit Chick had made to his office after Christmas. It was clear, he wrote, that his firm and the museum's director were in total disagreement about many artistic decisions. Whether it was the design of lintels over doorways or radiator grilles, Chick wanted to subtract the architects' traditional decoration in favor of the simple lines of the International Style. His good manners barely covering his annoyance, Morris asked his brother-in-law: "Will you kindly advise us how to proceed?"[69]

Goodwin felt he had promised Chick a free hand with the interior and advised Morris and O'Connor to defer to his judgment. The architects duly instructed their draftsmen to redraw the plans at the end of January. But Chick could not stop sending them a stream of alterations as he had new ideas. When they again protested, Chick asked Uncle Charlie to assemble the building committee, without the architects, to allow him to explain why he had to have his latest changes.

He took the uncharacteristic step of writing out his remarks so that he could make his strongest case to the committee. He was adamant. The architects obviously had never understood his artistic vision. He may have failed to get what he wanted for the outside of the building; he would not compromise on the interior. Daringly, he pointed directly to Uncle Ben Morris and Cousin Bob

Father and son: Chick and David Etnier Austin, 1933

O'Connor. The problems and delays were their fault, he said, a result of igno-rance:

> There is no reason why architects, unless they are especially inter-ested in the problem should understand completely the designing of the interior of a museum building—nor should they, for that matter try to combat the suggestions of a director whose last five years have been spent in the study of museum installation.

He insisted on having total control of the interior and began delving into details the committee did not want to hear—the balustrade for the circular staircase, the radiator grilles, the transoms over doors into the court: "I am absolutely opposed to the placing of a clock in a glass transom over a doorway." He wanted metal doors with wood veneers between one section of the building and another, instead of "bronze doors with chicken wire glass which are not only extremely ugly but give to the museum the appearance of a bank."

He urged the trustees to see the new building as an artistic achievement, a reflection of the best aesthetics of the present: "No building can be built which will be forever in good taste. It is quite sufficient to build in the best taste of one's own time. In ten years ideas will have changed but these changes cannot now be anticipated. Chartres Cathedral is a great piece of architecture because it embodies the best architectural practice of its own time of construction, though it by no means continued in fashion after the introduction of the later flamboyant style."

The design of the Avery interior should be entirely his, he felt, because he had the knowledge and discernment that others lacked. "I believe that I am competent as a critic and as a creative personality to establish my conception of contemporary beauty in a museum building—it is certainly not a very costly conception—and later the ornament I eschew for good reason because it is ugly, can be applied again at no great cost, if the taste for mediocrity and vul-garity persists in this country." As an example of bad taste, he pointed to Morris and O'Connor's design for the exterior, with its superfluous decoration: "I know that dignity is achieved in these days only through the utmost simplicity—columns and machine-edged garlands thrown in, are meaningless."

He concluded with both an oblique threat to resign and a plea for under-standing:

> If after five years, the trustees have no faith in me, then there is no point to my continuing as director—nor is there any point to these requests if the architects do not realize with how much thought and dif-ficulty our small, but I think distinguished, collection of paintings has

been built up and with what care I have tried to visualize the proper backgrounds and suitably harmonizing details for each group that they might have a distinguished setting.

. . . Perhaps I can be forgiven on the ground of my anxiety that the Avery building be as fine as I have tried to imagine it and excused for my insistence on details which may seem unimportant and irrelevant at the moment, but which are I am certain, vital to the ultimate success of the building.[70]

On behalf of the architects, Robert O'Connor met privately with Charles Goodwin at his house on February 20 to complain about the number of decisions that were being reversed. "We want to give the Museum Trustees the type of building they want," he said, "and if that means following Mr. Austin's desires well and good, but definiteness one way or the other is essential if demoralization of the architectural work is not to ensue." He warned the trustees that the time wasted on these changes, and the accounting required for cancellations and extra charges, had involved them "in a maze of contention and readjustment."[71]

Goodwin was out of patience. He ordered Chick to New York to make an end to the interior design. Early in March, Chick spent three days in the offices of Morris and O'Connor, reviewing every detail. He was incapable of stopping his torrent of new ideas about the interior. He was too afraid that he would get a detail wrong that would haunt him forever. Just as surely as the pyramids of Egypt were monuments to the pharaohs, this was to be his monument to himself. The result of his visit was an eight-page list of over fifty changes to the drawings—ranging from the kind of marble on the theater lobby staircase to the design of the letters in the word EXIT. And could the chromium lever door handles for his office be copied from samples designed by Mies van der Rohe, which Philip Johnson had loaned him? Could the brass numerals in the design of the clock over the entrance to the court be replaced with thin rectangular marks and hands like those on his wristwatch?[72]

O'Connor submitted these changes to Goodwin on March 13 with an angry cover letter. Chick's new suggestions, he wrote, reversed changes he had previously requested. Those had been submitted to the general contractor two months earlier, voiding most of the estimates the architects had already received. He acknowledged that the firm had lost any claim to be called the architects of the interior: "Mr. Austin is very definite as to his responsibility for the interior of the new building—which has now become his to a very large extent."[73] But O'Connor informed Goodwin that the changes Austin wanted would cost the Atheneum another $20,000.

Ignoring the maelstrom swirling in the drafting room on Park Avenue, Chick amended even these changes after returning to Hartford. He wrote to the architects on the very day that they dispatched their protest to Goodwin. For certain spaces he wanted to use an aluminum base molding he had seen at the Museum of Modern Art, and thought he might like window frames for his office similar to those he had just seen while walking past the Lexington Avenue side of the Chrysler building. This suggestion was accompanied by "a slight sketch."[74]

Two days later, frustrated past enduring, both Benjamin Morris and Robert O'Connor arrived in Hartford to confront Austin, Goodwin, and the building committee. Goodwin was in an awkward position. On the one hand, he reasoned, his brother-in-law was understandably exasperated with Chick's continual harping on the smallest details, refining them, changing them, throwing the architect's office into confusion. On the other hand, Chick had proven himself a master of taste—both traditional and modern—in the eyes of those who knew about such things. The changes he wanted would cost another $20,000, but the building committee had set aside $100,000 as a contingency fund. Chick claimed that these were his final changes. Overcoming his natural reluctance to spend money unnecessarily, Goodwin concluded that it would be easier for all concerned to give Chick what he wanted.[75]

Goodwin's willingness to part with $20,000 was perhaps also a gesture to a museum director whose salary had just been severely reduced for the second year in a row. In March 1933, because the value of the Morgan Memorial's maintenance fund had plummeted, the trustees decided that all staff salaries, cut by 10 percent in 1932, would be chopped by another 15 percent, beginning in April.[76] The Morgan Memorial would have to curtail its hours to save electricity and coal, and publication of the annual report and museum bulletins was suspended.

Unwilling to keep the galleries quiet, Chick brought two inexpensive exhibitions to Hartford that spring which reflected his own interests. In April, he borrowed a Pierre Roy show from the Brummer Gallery, and in May, he took another traveling exhibition from the Museum of Modern Art, *Early Modern Architecture: Chicago, 1870–1910*, organized by Johnson and Hitchcock. With large scale-models and photographs, the architecture show focused on the three greatest figures of the era: Henry Hobson Richardson, Louis Sullivan, and Frank Lloyd Wright. The exhibition documented the development of the first American skyscrapers after the Chicago Fire and provided a background for the contemporary architecture that had been explored in the International Style show.[77]

Chicago was very much on Chick's mind as summer approached. In May, he was elected to the Association of Art Museum Directors, whose annual meeting would be held in Chicago the following month. To help convince the board to pay for him to attend the meeting, Chick enlisted Mrs. Berger, who now doted on him. She informed Robert Huntington that membership in the association was "an honor which most Directors of museums covet" and that the

Atheneum had never before been represented.[78] (MOMA's Alfred Barr and Juliana Force, the Whitney's first director, would be elected at the June meeting.) Uncle Charlie took up a collection among the trustees to pay Chick's expenses, but cautioned them not to contribute more than fifteen dollars each.[79]

The meeting that year coincided with the Chicago World's Fair, called "A Century of Progress Exposition," which had opened on June 1. Here Chick could see marvels of industrial innovation—Chrysler's new streamlined Airflow automobiles; the dial telephone that Bell was about to introduce; the most lavish display of neon lights to date; and a bullet-shaped rocket ride that carried adventurous visitors, suspended from a wire twenty-five stories high, across a "lagoon" beside Lake Michigan—at five miles an hour. Even Hartford was represented. The Chamber of Commerce sent a giant aerial photograph of the city, labeled "300 Years of Progress," "The Home of Insurance," and "The Cradle of Industry."

The Art Institute of Chicago provided the official fine-arts component of the Exposition. With loans from thirty-two American museums and over a hundred and fifty private American collectors, the Institute mounted a gigantic exhibition of paintings and sculpture ranging from the mid-thirteenth century to the present. Chick was on the advisory committee for the show, which included nearly eight hundred pictures. Among them were the Atheneum's *Portrait of Mrs. Seymour Fort* by John Singleton Copley, a classic image of a wellborn elderly Englishwoman of the late eighteenth century. Also from Hartford came two works from the Soby collection—Picasso's *Seated Woman* and Derain's *The Bagpiper*. The exhibition was hailed as the finest display of art ever presented in the United States,[80] the *St. Louis Post-Dispatch* calling it "America's artistic declaration of independence."[81]

Again Chick saw the summer season as a chance to get away from his responsibilities. Squabbles over the building had been exhausting, the Depression had cramped his museum programs, and much as he delighted in his little son (whom he called "Cupid"), he no longer had Helen all to himself. He decided that he would drive to Chicago and then continue on to the West Coast. He wanted to visit Hollywood, which had entered its golden age.

As Chick always liked companionship, he invited his newest assistant at the museum, Paul Cooley, to accompany him. The son of a prominent Hartford bank executive, Cooley had joined the staff earlier in the year, fresh out of Yale, where he had studied art history with "Tubby" Sizer. His principal interests at that time were fine paintings and ballerinas.

The two of them set off for Chicago on June 11. The first night on the road, Chick wrote to Helen, reassuring her that he was being financially responsible—one of her perennial worries: "I am keeping a lovely log of the journey together with an expense account. . . . Kiss Cupid for me and lots and lots of love to you Cunning."[82]

A few days after arriving in Chicago, he told Helen that Robert Harshe, director of the Art Institute, escorted the museum directors through the paintings exhibition one day and "made all the Directors give gallery talks which was pretty funny especially mine which was too awful." Chick was asked to speak on both seventeenth-century Italian painting and Matisse and Picasso. At thirty-two, he was already well recognized for his expertise in the baroque and modern.

Chick added that "the various businesses of meetings, pictures and Exposition have been seriously exhausting. The Fair Grounds are so enormous that you have to go again and again and even now we havent succeeded in seeing half the show." He and Paul decided that they would return to the Exposition on their way back from California. But before leaving Chicago, Chick bought what he told Helen was "a very swell small Chirico at a bargain price" (*The Combat*, for $300) at the Chester Johnson Galleries and made arrangements to stay with Odette Myrtil in Hollywood.[83]

Heading westward, he and Paul traveled through Missouri to look at the St. Louis museum and then to Kansas City, where they were given a preview of the newly built Nelson-Atkins Museum, scheduled to open later that year.[84] From there they continued to the West Coast via Wyoming. Driving with terrifying speed across the broad spaces of the Midwest, Chick found the new American highway system made to order: "The roads are really marvelous," he wrote Helen, "so straight and smooth."[85] He urged her to join him on his return visit to the Exposition: "Please let me know in Hollywood that you have decided to come to Chicago. The Palmer house was so expensive that we will have to stay some where else."[86] He conveniently forgot that, with a new baby to care for, Helen was hardly in a position to run out to Chicago.

As Chick explored the west, Morris and O'Connor continued to work on drawings for the interior design of the Avery. When the firm wrote to Charles Goodwin asking permission to alter Austin's design for the pool in the central court, Goodwin was not about to get involved. With unintentional wordplay, he warned them: "You are getting into deep water as far as I am concerned. I would not know what to say and I would not want to make a determination of this until Mr. Austin returns. It is a matter where he is vitally concerned."[87] The architects sent their suggested design to Hollywood. Chick found that they were more attuned to the baroque style than they had been to the contemporary, and had successfully improved his own sketch. He cabled his approval ("POOL PEDESTAL DESIGN SWELL GO AHEAD")[88] and followed up with a friendly letter to one of O'Connor's deputies:

What excitement—I hardly get here before telegrams start flying—I thought everything was more or less settled before I left. However: I am very glad you sent on the design for the pool. I like its shape much better than that of the first one. I think it will be well worth changing it even if it is something extra. The pedestal too is very fine. I like especially the bowl part with dripping water. I think that <u>perhaps</u> the pedestal should be done in a stone more like that used for the statue. Too much travertine gives a sort of faked effect sometimes which might detract from the statue since the base is somewhat elaborate. I find it very hard to decide however. I'll leave it up to you.

Chick had mellowed under the palm trees: "I am having a swell rest," he added, "and Hollywood is exactly as you think it must be."[89]

He did want to make certain, however, that the proscenium of grained Brazilian rosewood framing the stage would *not* have mitered corners, but would meet at right angles in the approved International Style manner, and he sketched a design for the architects on Odette Myrtil's stationery.[90]

Unwinding in the lassitude of the southern California summer, Chick felt that Spartan Hartford and his squabbles with the museum administration were blessedly distant. On July 10, he wrote Helen:

I am sorry the time has slipped by without my writing—but then I waited a <u>long</u> time for a letter from you. I thought I never would get it. We stayed a week longer here than we planned—because Paul wanted to see a little bit of California and I felt much more tired than I thought I was when I arrived. I felt miserably for a while—depressed and feeling that I shouldnt have come—which isnt very restful.

However Ive been in the sun on a beach all day and every day and I feel much, much healthier. I hope I'll still have it when I get back.

I was so excited to hear that you had actually gotten off and though I havent heard, I suppose you all arrived safely. I cant wait to get back now and see you and David—which will be soon now—I'll come up to Castine a day or so after I arrive.

It has been really very nice here—I do wish I could get a job out here so we could move out for a while.

I'm still fed up with all the museum business. And I'm sure I'll never get any where in Hartford. They'll never pay me enough.[91]

He and Paul left Los Angeles that day, arriving at the Grand Canyon the next, July 11—Helen and Chick's fourth wedding anniversary. A quick telegram was dispatched to Castine: "MUCH LOVE TERRIBLY SORRY I CANT BE WITH YOU (SIGNED) CHICK."[92]

After taking another look at the World's Fair, Chick and Paul finally arrived back in Hartford at the end of July. They went straight to the museum to inspect the progress on the interiors of the Avery building and to go through the mail that had piled up in their absence. Then Chick expected to drive to Maine after more than six weeks away from Helen and his little son.

On his desk he found an envelope, postmarked London, from Lincoln Kirstein.

CHAPTER TEN

"We've Got to Get Them!"

Apollo in his own variation teaches the Muses the full
power of expressiveness that they must possess and
shows his own mastery after his initial tentativeness. He
chooses Terpsichore, his favorite, for a *pas de deux....*

—Peter Brinson and Clement Crisp, "Apollo
(Apollon Musagète)," *Ballet for All*

The letter Chick saw when he tore open the envelope was written on both
sides of four folio sheets of hotel stationery, making sixteen bulky
pages of small, neat, torrential handwriting.

BATT'S HOTEL,
DOVER STREET, W. 1
July 16: 1933.

Dear Chick:

This will be the most important letter I will ever write you as you
will see. My pen burns my hand as I write: words will not flow into the
ink fast enough. We have a real chance to have an American ballet
within 3 yrs. time. When I say ballet—I mean a trained company of
young dancers—not Russians—but Americans with Russian stars to
start with—a company superior to the dregs of the old Diaghilev Company which will come to N.Y. this winter and create an enormous success. purely because though they aren't much they are better than
anything New york will have seen since Nijinsky. Do you know
Georges Balanchine? If not he is a Georgian called Georgei Balan-
chavidze. He is, personally, enchanting—dark, very slight—a superb
dancer and the most ingenious technician in ballet I have ever seen.

For Diaghilev he composed The Cat, The Prodigal Son, Appollon Musagete, Le Bal of Chirico, Barabau of Utrillo, Neptune of the Sitwells, and many others. . . . He is 28 yrs. old—a product of the Imperial schools. He has split from the Prince de Monaco as he wants to proceed, with new ideas and young dancers instead of going on with the decadence of the Diaghilev troupe, which I assure you, although it possesses many good, if frightfully overworked dancers, is completely, worn out in artistic-commercial.[1]

Chick did know about Balanchine, Diaghilev's last ballet master. In 1931, two years after the great impresario's death, Balanchine had become ballet master and choreographer of Les Ballets Russes de Monte Carlo, when the company was formed from remnants of the original Ballets Russes by René Blum and the self-styled Colonel Wassily de Basil (Vassili Grigorievitch Vosskrezensky, a Cossack ex-military policeman) under the patronage of the Hereditary Princess of Monte Carlo. Boris Kochno, Diaghilev's secretary and librettist, was artistic adviser. Balanchine and Kochno broke with the company the next year when de Basil, a sly man more interested in commercial gain than artistic exploration, began to take complete control.

With financial backing from Edward James, the diminutive and immensely wealthy English aristocrat, Balanchine and Kochno had just produced a sensational series of ballets in London and Paris, known as Les Ballets 1933: *Songes, Mozartiana, The Seven Deadly Sins, Errante, Fastes,* and *Les Valses de Beethoven.* These were true successors of Diaghilev's productions. Balanchine chose music for his dances from a whole spectrum of composers—Milhaud and Mozart, Tchaikovsky and Weill, Liszt, Schubert, Sauguet, and Beethoven—and they were set against the novel decorative talents of Derain, Bérard, Tchelitchew, Caspar Neher, and Emilio Terry. Les Ballets 1933 were not a popular success, but they were so genuinely new, the choreography so much a marriage of movement with music rather than with story or spectacle, that artists and intellectuals applauded their originality. Among those most captivated was Lincoln Kirstein.

In the three years since he graduated from Harvard, Kirstein had pursued his multiple interests and had tried out a variety of roles. He was still editor of *Hound & Horn* and had published a roman à clef, *Flesh Is Heir,* about his experiences at boarding school and as an art history student and balletomane in Europe. He had been taken up during his sophomore year by Muriel Draper, the uninhibited hostess of New York's intellectual bohemia, who had introduced him to "high life, night life, and low life."[2] Her unvarnished tutoring in the realities of art and life continued after he had moved from Cambridge to Manhattan. There he had taken ballet lessons from Michel Fokine, one of

Diaghilev's earliest and most influential choreographers, and boxing lessons at the West Side YMCA. Now he was finishing work with Nijinsky's wife, Romola, on a biography of her husband—confined to a Swiss sanatorium—which would be published later in the year.

With Les Ballets 1933, Kirstein saw the way to realizing the dream he had contemplated and nurtured as early as undergraduate days—the creation of a preeminent American ballet company. That summer in Paris, he had the luxury of comparing Balanchine's work with two other choreographers who had come out of Diaghilev's company: Léonide Massine with the Ballets Russes de Monte Carlo, and Serge Lifar at the Paris Opera. Kirstein's friend Virgil Thomson and his new acquaintance Pavel Tchelitchew, who each understood the inner workings and intrigues of the theater, confirmed his growing belief that Balanchine represented the future: he was the only choreographer who could transplant the traditions of classical dancing to America and advance the art itself by creating new works in collaboration with contemporary artists and the greatest composers of the past and present. Although Kirstein had seen Balanchine in performance as early as 1926, he had not actually met him until Romola Nijinsky introduced them backstage at the Savoy Theatre in London, where the Ballets 1933 had moved after the Paris performances. Kirstein saw him again in the kitchen of Kirk and Constance Askew's rented house in Chelsea and arranged to meet him on July 16 at Batt's Hotel, where Kirstein was staying. There he poured out his proposal of an American ballet company, offering Chick's museum with its new theater as a possible home. Balanchine told Kirstein that he wanted to go to America. He was willing to hear more. Kirstein wrote the fateful letter that evening.

He said that Balanchine would bring two of his protégés with him. They would provide living proof of his choreographic genius:

Now Balanchine has with him Tamara Toumanova, the daughter of a General Toumanov, and a Circassian princess. She is 14 yrs. old. I enclose what the best Ballet critic in England says about her. Her technique is phenomenal. Preobrajinska, her teacher and Pavlova's great rival says she is unbelievable—in 3 yrs. a real phenomenon. Balanchine adores her—has really created her: made her Blossom out. Toumanova is so <u>photogenique</u> she has refused 2 movie contracts: she wants to dance above all. "Il faut danser." . . . Balanchine also has her partner Roman Jasinsky. He is a Pole from the Warsaw School. He is extremely beautiful—a superb body and by way of becoming a most remarkable dancer. He promises far more than Lifar who is absolutely spoiled and is artistically through. a terrible snob and cabotin. Jasinsky works all the time, is a fine mime modest, a bit dumb. but marvelous in an experts hand like Balanchine. . . . These 3 have <u>nothing</u> to do now.

Kirstein told Chick that Balanchine and the others were eager to accept his proposal of starting a ballet school in Hartford. Its distance from New York would give the choreographer "plenty of chance to work in an easy atmosphere" away from commercial distractions.

Balanchine is socially adorable—but he hates the atmosphere both of society, as such (Lifar loves it) and the professional Broadway Theatre. For the first he would take 4 white girls and 4 white boys—about sixteen yrs. old and 8 of the same, <u>negros</u>. They would be firmly taught in the classical Idiom—not only from <u>exercises</u> but he would start composing ballets at once so they would actually <u>learn</u> by doing. As time went on he would get younger children from 8 yrs. on. . . . He could start producing within 3 months. Now, if you could work it he could use your small theatre: a department of the museum a school of dancing could be started—entirely from the professional point of view. But since <u>no</u> tuition fee will be charged, the dancers will be picked for their <u>perfect</u> possibilities and they will have to sign contracts to prevent them from appearing anywhere else, except in the troupe for 5 years. This will obviate the danger of movies or Broadway snatching them up after they have been trained—better than anybody else in the country. In the meantime Balanchine and Jasinsky and Toumanova will serve as demonstrators and models. There you can already see in a girl not yet 15 and a boy of 20, finished dancers—artists of <u>conviction</u>. Now, Madame Nijinsky—her name is very important—has given me the rights to Sacre du Printemps, Jeux, Faun, Tyl Eulenspiegel and 4 unproduced ballets—the benefit of his <u>untried</u> system of training of dancers. She also volunteers to lecture with me—at these demonstrations where one could also see the dancing of Toumanova and Jasinsky . . .

He reiterated his conviction that the artistic integrity of the enterprise could be maintained only by keeping it in an educational setting like the Atheneum:

This will prepare the way for the company, which will give performances <u>not</u> at the theatres, but always kept on an educational level—with Museums. This takes us out of the competition class, obviates us from theatres—managers etc. It will be like a government art theatre. In the meantime Balanchine, Jasinsky, Toumanova and her mother must live, Toumanova can't go anywhere with out her ma. She is a nice woman, has starved for years and could keep house and cook for them which she has always done. It would be necessary to have $6000 to start it. That guarantees them for one year with passage back and forth. I count this sum as dead loss—though it won't be at all because by February you can have four performances of wholly new Ballets in Hartford. Balanchine is willing to devote all his time to this for 5 yrs. He believes the future of Ballet lies in America as do I. I see a great chance for you to do a hell of a lot here. The expense can be underwritten, say I glibly—but you must realize how much this means—so I have to be arrogant, by Phil Johnson, who is willing, myself, Jim Sobey, Jere [Abbott, director of the Smith Art Museum], the Lewisohns, the Cotters etc in N.Y. who are willing and I feel sure there are others. This school can be the basis of a national culture as intense as the great Russian Renaissance of Diaghilev. We must start small. But imagine it—we are exactly as if we were in 1910—offered a dancer only less good than an unformed Nijinsky, an incipient Karsavina—a maître de ballet as good as Fokine—who would also be delighted to cooperate. It will not be easy. It will be hard to get good young dancers willing to stand or fall by the company. No first dancers. No stars. A perfect esprit de corps.

He outlined his ideas for ballets on American themes—from *Pocohantas* to *Uncle Tom's Cabin*, *Moby Dick* and *Custer's Last Stand*—which would call on such talents as Katherine Anne Porter and e. e. cummings. But Kirstein knew that his plans depended entirely on Balanchine.

It is absolutely necessary to keep Balanchine to ourselves. Not let either Stokowski, The League of Composers, the Juillard [*sic*] or the Curtis Institute get a hold of him. He is an honest man, a serious artist and I'd stake my life on his talent. In two years, unhindered by petty intrigue by rows between Tchelitchev and Berard, between the Monte Carlo ballet, Lifar and the Paris Opera—unworried about how he could both live and call his soul his own which he has not done since Diaghilev died. He could achive a miracle—and right under our eyes: I feel this chance is too serious to be denied. It will mean a life work to all of us—incredible power in a few years. We can command whom we want. We will be developing new talent. It will not be a losing proposition. Conceived as an educational institution under the title of the American Ballet—or the School of Classical Dancing of America or something—it could travel, on small tours. at first, simply as a school and get a considerable return. We would have to do a little theatrical camouflage at first. A few leaps by Jasinsky or a few fouettés by the adorable Toumanova will lift a room full to their feet, cheering.

Kirstein desperately hoped that the scheme would appeal to Chick. He knew that Chick shared his passion for the dance—that he, too, revered the memory of Diaghilev's Ballets Russes as an almost miraculous achievement in the arts—and that Chick, more than anyone else he knew in America, could not only provide the setting for the enterprise, but would, if he believed in it, throw his whole being into bringing it to fruition.

I wish to God you were here: that you could know what I am writing is true—that I am not either over enthusiastic or visionary. Please, Please, Chick if you have any love for anything we do both adore—rack your brains and try to make this all come true. If not as I outline, then some other way must be feasible. We have both done harder things than to raise $6000. Hartford is a perfect place for it, I think. You will adore Balanchine. He is no trouble—i.e. not personally difficult in any way. He could come over in October or even sooner. when you have thought of this—considered it—talked it over with Russell [Hitchcock], Jere, Joe Marvell [Josiah Marvel, a lawyer friend from Harvard], even Winslow Ames and Francis Taylor [director of the Worcester Art Museum and later the Metropolitan]—talk to Muriel Draper too. She knows a lot about such things. but please wire me, give me some inkling as to how you will receive this letter. If not I can't sleep. I won't be able to hear from you for a week—but I wont sleep till I do. Just say Proceed or Impossible. If Impossible, I will try to think of something else—but as I see it—Hartford is perfect. It will involve no personal loss. The $6000. is just a gaurantee [sic]—for poor Balanchine—who is responsible for Toumanova and Jasinsky: He's been tricked so often.

We have the future in our hands. for christ's sweet sake let us honor it.

Yours devotedly

Lincoln.

Wire me here:[3]

Kirstein need not have lost sleep waiting for Chick's reaction to the letter. He was electrified. "I've seldom seen Chick so emotional," Paul Cooley remembered. "He said, 'My God! You just don't *know* what this *is*, what it *means*, the *possibilities!*' He was a madman, I mean he really was. He brushed everything off his desk and said, '*This* is the only thing that's of any importance! We've *got* to get them! We've *got* to get them!' "[4] At that, Chick started for the door, saying, "Paul, you've got to come with me." He burst out of his office, rushed through the museum and out onto Main Street. With Cooley keeping up as best he could, "he *ran, really ran*" to the office of Arthur Day in the Hartford-Connecticut Trust building one block away. He had to convince his most understanding trustee, first, not Uncle Charlie.[5]

Chick's eloquence was buoyed by firsthand knowledge of the ballet world. He knew about Les Ballets 1933. Everything Kirstein wrote about Balanchine rang true. Chick himself had lamented two years earlier, in program notes for the Bushnell Auditorium, that no successor to Diaghilev had emerged "who might be capable of carrying on that glorious tradition," which had "united . . . the creations of the very greatest of contemporary artists, not only in the field of painting and music but also in that of choreography and the dance."[6]

Here was the possibility of a new collaboration that would do just that. By February, Kirstein said, there could be ballet productions of the highest artistic quality on Chick's own stage, with two of the most promising young dancers in Europe in the troupe. What an extraordinary way to launch the theater. First Virgil's opera to open it, then the ballet. Perhaps Balanchine could choreograph *Four Saints in Three Acts*. Kirstein said that Balanchine had committed himself to the effort for the next five years. By then, a revolution in culture could have taken place. Even if Balanchine went off to New York in five years, the Atheneum would be recognized nationally as a great creative institution.

Chick was sure he could convince the trustees. He would point out that the scheme fell in beautifully with his goal of making the Atheneum a cultural center so alluring that it would draw even Europeans to Hartford. The venture would be financed outside the museum. He and Helen could contribute. Kirstein had money and rich, loyal friends like Eddie Warburg. Paul Cooley could afford to support it. Philip Johnson was bound to help. They would find the money. With Kirstein's ferocious intelligence and his proven abilities as the force behind the Harvard Society for Contemporary Art and *Hound & Horn*, it would happen. All of Chick's recent thoughts of abandoning Hartford and the Atheneum had vanished.

His enthusiasm swept over Arthur Day. The banker may have felt uncertain about so daring an idea, but as Chick assured him that the museum's budget could not possibly be affected, Day did not actually forbid the enterprise. That was all Chick felt he needed.

Later, Kirstein gave Chick the credit for being "the first person in America to think he could find institutional support for an endowed ballet company which would give in a museum performances equalling in intrinsic interest and excellence the important objects of a museum's permanent historic collection."[7]

On July 26, Chick cabled Kirstein to proceed. Two days later, Kirstein wired back from London, urging him on: "MAKE EVERY EFFORT GREAT CHANCES= LINCOLN."[8]

The most intense period of activity in Chick's life had begun. As if the ballet scheme were not enough, there was the completion of work on the Avery building, the organization of a winter exhibition for its opening—which must top all his previous shows—and, most daunting of all, the premiere of Virgil Thomson's new opera, which he had promised for the inauguration of the Avery auditorium.

How to produce *Four Saints* was a question he had to face soon, for Kirstein's was not the only letter waiting on his desk when he returned from California. On the strength of Chick's enthusiasm at the beginning of the year, Virgil had negotiated a contract with Gertrude Stein's agent (Thomson and Stein, in the midst of a four-year spat, were communicating only by letter) for the production of *Four Saints* in Hartford.

Writing from Paris on July 7, Virgil had dispatched three copies of the contract for Austin to sign. But Virgil was not happy. Chick had not responded to earlier communications, which had been arriving since at least early May:

Your complete silence in answer to my letters & my telegrams is of course not very comforting. Nor does it pay either my debts or my copyist. . . . If you dont want to go on with this opera, for God's sake wire at once. My own life is difficult enough without any money, and having to support a copyist is completely beyond my possibilities.

I understand you have been in Hollywood & having a nice time and I certainly hope so. Having no reply from you I was all for stopping everything, but I found that the copyist had given up everything else to do this job (at 50% reduction of commercial Paris prices) and I couldnt leave him in the lurch. . . . I ask you my darling I ask you is that any way to treat a guy. You should get this letter before the end of the month if you are anywhere near civilization. I beseech you to thereupon send me a cable containing either the word no, in which case I shall stop everything & pay the copyist for what is already done by what means God only knows, or else cable me $500. How on earth do you expect to put this opera on next winter if you cant raise more than $150 in all the six months that have passed since it was first informally agreed upon?

The score is advancing rapidly. So are my debts. I have given up my flat and pawned my silver.

Love & kisses
Virgil[9]

Despite delays, Chick would be astonishingly successful at finding money for both the opera and the ballet. Over the next few months, he would sound out close friends, trustees, and members of the Friends and Enemies of Modern Music. Much to their surprise, many in the insurance capital found themselves underwriting an opera by a strange middle-aged woman of puzzling, if not laughable, syntax and an unheard-of composer, as well as a nebulous plan for a ballet school that had nothing to do with a fine-arts museum. Chick was at his happiest persuading people to fall in with something solely on the basis of his imagination and vision.

But not everyone was easily convinced. Inevitably, Uncle Charlie Goodwin, once he realized how far Chick had already gone, demanded accountability. The day after Chick sent his encouraging cable to Kirstein, Goodwin dictated a formal warning:

July 27, 1933

Dear Chick:

I have been troubled a little bit about the rapid developments in connection with the opening of the new building, before it is finished. I do not wish you, or anyone else, to make any commitments involving [the] Wadsworth Atheneum without first consulting with me in detail, including some complete understanding as to the cost.

I, of course, have no power to commit the Atheneum on such matters, but I represent the Board and no one but the Board can finally approve any expenditure of money or any commitment as to the use of the building in connection with the opening or any ballet school, or any other enterprise.

As I am going away on my vacation I wanted to be clear about this matter.

Sincerely yours,
Charles A. Goodwin
PRESIDENT[10]

For Chick the operative part of Goodwin's letter was its last sentence. With Uncle Charlie away, there would be time to gather more allies and more money. Chick would be able to present overwhelming evidence that his plans were not only glorious, but well on their way to being paid for from sources outside the Atheneum. Then there would be no reason for his trustees to stop him. They might even thank him for a brilliant achievement.

Years later, both Thomson and Kirstein came to similar conclusions about the way Chick piloted his projects through obstacles that would have stopped most other museum directors in their tracks. "Chick went ahead with the opera plan in the same way that he accomplished other things," Thomson wrote, "not by seeing his way through from the beginning but merely by finding out, through talking of his plan in front of everyone, whether any person or group would try to stop him. Then once inside a project, he would rely entirely on instinct and improvisation. For he considered, and said so, that a museum's purpose was to entertain its director."[11]

Kirstein's insight was even more penetrating. He saw that Chick's success resulted from a deft touch, a magician's sleight of hand:

> He did it by his peculiar weaving of fact and fiction in which neither Jim Soby nor Paul Cooley, nor even Eddie Warburg or myself, knew exactly what was happening, how far commitments were committed, how far opinion was policy, if the official view was permissive, or if there was as yet an official policy. . . . If he accepted the validity of a vision he was not to be dissuaded by a mere structure of canonical precedent, and he persuaded museum trustees and immigration officials by the very lightness of his attack. Nothing was so important that it might ever be refused. Everything was so possible that there was much less resistance. His offhandedness insinuated itself into a surprisingly rapid achievement. He gave off no smell of failure.[12]

Kirstein also understood that what really drove Chick was the rush of adrenaline that came from being on the edge: "It was not the promise of success that excited him; it was the dazzle of immanence, the verge of discovery, the surprise in the package, the excitement in preparations and initiations. He had the energy to incite, which is creation."[13]

Priorities had to be set. The ballet scheme had to come first. The opening of the Avery was not scheduled to take place until the beginning of 1934; Virgil could be delayed a little longer. By telephone and telegram, friends were alerted and were sucked into the whirlwind that would bring Balanchine to America.

As Kirstein had expected, the first large contributor to the enterprise was Eddie Warburg, to whom he had written on the same day he wrote Austin. From New York on July 31, Philip Johnson, whose help Chick had immediately enlisted, telegraphed the good news: "ONE THOUSAND FROM EDDIE STOP MURIEL DRAPER ALSO WORKING STOP CANNOT COME BEFORE FRIDAY= PHILIP."[14] Johnson himself gave $500, and then bought two Corbusier beds from Cary Ross, so that Ross could contribute $50.[15] Paul Cooley and Jim Soby put in another $500 each. Jere Abbott sent $200. Chick gave $100 and extracted a token $25 from his mother. Helen's sister Lucy came forward with $50. Kirk and Constance Askew gave $50. Thomas Howard, whose New York firm was supplying fabrics for many of the walls of the new Avery galleries, contributed $100. Josiah Marvel put in $25, and even the Atheneum's business manager, Robert Drew-Bear, was persuaded to contribute $20. Lincoln Kirstein eventually headed the list, however, with $2,000. The total would exceed $5,000, more than enough to guarantee Balanchine and his associates round-trip passage to America.[16]

Chick cabled Kirstein on August 6 that $3,000 had already been pledged. This was enough to convince Uncle Charlie and the board that the enterprise would not be a drain on the museum. They gave Chick tentative approval to commit the Atheneum to sponsoring the immigration of the Russians, as long as a carefully worded contract was drawn up. On August 8, Chick again cabled Kirstein: "GO AHEAD, IRON-CLAD CONTRACT NECESSARY, BEGINNING OCTOBER 15. WHAT ABOUT ENTRY PERMITS? CAN YOU SETTLE AS MUCH AS POSSIBLE BEFORE LEAVING? BRING PHOTOS, PUBLICITY. MUSEUM WILLING. CAN'T WAIT."[17]

Kirstein worked feverishly to keep the momentum going in Europe. He followed Balanchine and his business manager, Vladimir Dimitriew, from England to France. On August 8, he cabled Chick from Paris: "POSTPONED SAILING CABLE HOTEL QUAI VOLTAIRE PARIS WILL ARRANGE EVERYTHING CAN I GUARANTEE LIVING EXPENSES BALANCHINE TOUMANOVA JASINSKY ONE YEAR NO SALARY NECESSARY SEND LETTERS OF MUSEUM RECOMMENDATION FOR ENTRY PERMITS AT ONCE MOST IMPORTANT THING ALL OF US WILL EVER DO CONGRATULATIONS = KIRSTEIN."[18]

The next day Chick wired his reply: "GUARANTEED LIVING EXPENSES UP TO $6,000."[19] He also drafted an official letter from the Wadsworth Atheneum to the State Department, promising to sponsor Balanchine and his dancers:

> As Director of the Morgan memorial in Hartford, Connecticut, I entirely approve and will support the project of bringing to America the Russian dance artists Balanchine, Toumanova and Jasinsky. This enterprise, designed to form the beginning [of] an American Ballet, will prove of inestimable, educational and cultural value to our own community and to the country at large.
>
> I hereby guarantee that the three artists mentioned above will not become public charges, nor will they be placed on a competitive basis with American artists in the same class.[20]

As Kirstein saw his improbable scheme actually taking shape, he became acutely conscious of the responsibilities he was heaping on himself and the pitfalls awaiting him. The realities of paying for the enterprise and the threat of competition for Balanchine's services set in more forcibly than ever. Three days after his cable, he wrote Chick another long letter asking about contractual arrangements with the museum. He suggested that a private corporation be formed "to be called The School of American Classical Dancing or some such Nationalist title" with Balanchine as its *chef d'école* and *maître de ballet*. He promised Chick that he could have at least three ballets by January 15, 1934— possibly the new Derain ballet, *Songes; Mozartiana,* originally designed by Bérard but perhaps newly conceived by Eugene Berman; Tchelitchew's *Errante;* or "Balanchine's masterpiece," *Apollon musagète.*

He told Chick that Balanchine had been offered work by the Royal Ballet in Copenhagen and the Paris Opera, but that he would not be swayed:

> He wants to come to the U.S. more than anything else. . . . Balanchine is willing to risk his whole future on the possibility that a more or less unobstructed future for dancing does exist in America—enormous material, enthusiasm and adaptability—everything but the proper Spirit of pure expression which classical dancing alone can give. . . . He wants to have a class for composition—that is a class for maître des ballets—a thing never before attempted. And we envisage a great National School—of state proportions rivalling the Imperial Schools under the Czars. . . . Its so marvelous in potential that I tremble for the economic accidents which may wreck it—a fall of the dollar—a revolution an earthquake, a shipwreck. . . .

Throughout his letter, Kirstein returned obsessively to the core of the enterprise:

> The School first of all. to feed the troupe. . . . It is the source, training, base and pillar of the whole idea. . . . the all important school, never for a second dear Chick, forget the school.

He concluded with another emotional surge:

> I hope we can suceed. I've promised to telegraph them yes or no—by September first—as they have to live. Such a chance as now presents itself comes but once in a life time. . . . When I think of the cash spent on the bushes and shrubbery of the Philadelphia Museum, of the people who collect stamps and matchboxes, I go mad. This will be no collection, but living art—and the chance for perfect creation.
>   May our dream come true
>   Lincoln[21]

Four supplementary sheets were enclosed, providing Kirstein's version of Balanchine's curriculum vitae, a list of projected expenses, and an outline of the structure of the school, which was described for the first time as the "School

of the American Ballet, Inc. (under the Auspices of the Morgan Memorial)."
Using a military metaphor that Kirstein favored all his life, one page was
headed: "Method of attack: importation of Balanchine."[22]

Within twenty-four hours of dispatching his letter, Kirstein had completed
arrangements for returning to the United States, cabling Chick:

EVERYTHING SETTLED HERE DONT DARE BRING BALANCHINE UNTIL YOU
AGREE SAIL SATURDAY DEGRASSE THEY CAN FOLLOW ANY TIME RIGHTS
SECRUED [sic] DERAIN BERARD TCHELITCHEN [sic] BALLETS CAN BE PRE-
SENTED HARTFORD BY JANUARY FULL OF NEW PLANS JUILLARD [sic] COPEN-
HAGEN PARIS BIDDING OR [sic] BALANCHINE BUT HE WANTS US ALONE
ANNOUNCE NOTHING YET DONT GET COLD FEET
                    LINCOLN.[23]

Far from getting cold feet, Chick frequently had one foot pressed to the
accelerator of his automobile during that frenetic August, as he made the ten-
hour drive between Castine and Hartford, spending half of each week at the
Atheneum. Though inevitably exceeding the speed limit, his car was not racing
nearly as fast as his mind. He finally answered Virgil Thomson's pleas from a
roadside stop on one of these travels. He had been careening through the days
so quickly that he had lost track of time, dating his letter "Tuesday the Some-
thingth":

Dear Virgil.—
    At last a letter—you're getting this because my car has just broken
down on a Maine road and its going to take hours to rescue me.
    Forgive me, darling, for all the time that elapsed before you heard
but if you were angry—I was worried as hell. I didnt know just where
the money was going to be got this summer and I was completely broke
or I would have sent it from my own meagre store—but this was impossible as you will learn more fully later.
    You see that business about the Russian Ballet in Hartford project
went through and it is under the auspices of the American Ballet, Inc.
that I hope to produce the opera—since money is more easily raised
for a more continuous plan like that. I cant explain it all until I see
you—but dont think that I at any time gave up the idea of the opera—
which comes first.
    I think that it will be a winter of fun for all, as I hope that you can
spend it mostly in Hartford (you have Russell's letter) first with the
opera—later orchestrating things for the new American ballets, writing some new scores perhaps and possibly conducting a permanent
orchestra which will serve all sorts of purposes. [Helen's brother Francis was forming an orchestra that would become the Hartford Sym-

phony.] I am hoping to raise some extra money to pay you some sort of salary.

Balanchine can do the ballet for the opera and I dont see why we cant all together do something of interest if not of importance.

Gertrude's book [*The Autobiography of Alice B. Toklas*] has been chosen by the book-of-the month club [it was the Literary Guild], which is no compliment but means a hell of a lot to us as far as public interest in the opera is concerned.

When can you come over and how much money is it going to take? (minimum please).

Please forgive my stinginess—I'm not a rich art patron. Im just a poor boy trying my damndest to get that opera produced. Come soon please. We have so much to discuss and to plan. When is Maurice [Grosser, Thomson's companion] coming? with you?

The building seems to be coming along well and the builders still insist that the theatre will be finished on December fifteenth.

My own summer has been fairly involved—Hollywood was swell I wish I could have stayed for a longer rest—but I had to get back to the building. Since then I have stayed half the week in Hartford and half in Maine with Helen and David who send all love to you.

Forgive me again for my delay and for this lousy and incoherent note.

> Fondly
> Chick[24]

As the *Degrasse* steamed toward New York, Kirstein wired Chick of his imminent arrival:

1933 AUG 26 pm 2 22
LAND TUESDAY FAMILY MEETING PLEASE IF POSSIBLE COME.[25]

Chick could not join him, but Kirstein immediately called Eddie Warburg and asked to visit the baronial Warburg estate, Woodlands, in White Plains. Warburg remembered: "[Kirstein] had an infectious way [of saying]: 'Come on, give me a hand. I've got a hell of an idea.' "[26] By the beginning of September, Warburg agreed to supply $5,000 a year to the company.[27] Unlike Chick, he had to take what Lincoln proposed entirely on faith. He had never seen a ballet.[28]

Then Kirstein met with Chick at the museum, cabling Balanchine on August 26: "HARTFORD SUPERB EQUIPMENT GREAT ENTHUSIASM."[29] On September 1, after engaging Arthur Shipman, Jr., a lawyer in Uncle Charlie's firm,

Chick wrote the American consul general in Paris to secure visas for Balanchine, Dimitriew, Jasinsky, and Toumanova and her mother. He informed the Consul that the Wadsworth Atheneum was "an Art Museum with an auditorium and stage and excellent equipment and has promised to place its equipment at the disposal of the group." He also stated that he would represent the museum on the board of trustees of an entity to be called The American Ballet, Incorporated, and that the other members of the corporation would be Lincoln Kirstein, James T. Soby, and E. M. M. Warburg. He added that they had deposited $3,000 in Balanchine's account at Lloyd's Bank to guarantee passage for the group to the United States and back to France.[30] Enclosed was a statement signed by each of the four guarantors, pledging that Balanchine and his associates would not become public charges.[31]

Throughout September, as arrangements for Balanchine's trip were completed, Kirstein and Balanchine communicated continuously by cable. Much to Kirstein's dismay, Balanchine wired that Toumanova and Jasinsky were not necessary to the enterprise and that he would sail alone with Dimitriew, arriving in mid-October. He would use American dancers and would bring in other Russian teachers like Pierre Vladimiroff. It was only later that Kirstein learned that de Basil had tricked Toumanova into joining the Ballets Russes de Monte Carlo, which was enjoying enormous success in London. Jasinsky was soon dancing with Lifar's company. Kirstein now felt he had raised false expectations among his backers and in Hartford, but he had to make the best of it. Chick remained committed to the project as long as Balanchine was coming.

Meanwhile, the machinery of the State Department rolled on, though somewhere in the bureaucratic labyrinth the case became that of "George St. Balanchini."[32] Hartford's congressional representative, Herman P. Kopplemann, shepherded the visa requests through the department for Chick. Kirstein sent one-year contracts for Balanchine and Dimitriew to the American consul in Paris to complete the procedures. In the second week of October, Balanchine and Dimitriew embarked on the White Star Line's old *Olympic*, sister ship of the *Titanic*.

On Tuesday, October 17, the day the *Olympic* was due in from Europe, Chick, Helen, and reporter Marian Murray met Kirstein for lunch in New York. In a story appearing in that morning's edition of the *Hartford Times*, datelined New York, Murray broke the news of the grand plan: "A slim, dark young man, still in his twenties, will step off the Olympic here late this afternoon on his way to Hartford to institute a project . . . which may well develop into one of the most important cultural movements of the decade."

The museum would move quickly to establish the school and prepare new productions: "Within a month, according to Mr. Austin, pupils will have been chosen by Balanchine, the school will have gone into rehearsal, a first ballet will have been chosen for presentation, and the American Ballet will have become reality."

Following what Kirstein had told him, Chick announced: "It is possible that we may be ready to present a ballet soon after the opening of the new Avery building. We shall use the lecture room at the memorial for practice, and the little theater in the Avery building will make a perfect setting for some one of the dance dramas which are at our disposal."

He emphasized the exclusiveness of the school. "The development of the scheme is in the hands of Balanchine. He will choose the pupils who are to be accepted for training. There will be no charge for tuition. Probably we shall use some sort of scholarship scheme. Only those pupils will be accepted who Balanchine feels are ballet material—who have the ability, the enthusiasm and the tenacity to become part of an organization which we hope will have very important results. They will get their experience both through training and by taking part in productions."[33]

The story was not picked up by the Associated Press, much to Kirstein's annoyance, and no New York paper reported it immediately. But John Martin, dance critic of *The New York Times*, wrote an encouraging article five days later, under the headline SCHOOL ESTABLISHED AT HARTFORD IS THE REALIZATION OF A LONG-CHERISHED DREAM. To the inevitable question "Why Hartford?" Martin replied that the school was to be a national organization that happened to be located in Hartford. The Atheneum, he explained, offered "excellent class rooms and a completely equipped auditorium, all new and ready for occupancy." The distance from New York would mean that the school would not be in competition "with the regular commercial schools" and that the company would not be tempted "to burst prematurely into performance."[34]

Such commercial ballet schools run by Russians were not new to the United States. Louis Chalif still directed the popular New York school he had founded in 1907. Adolph Bolm, once a dancer in Diaghilev's company, had started a school in Chicago during the First World War. In 1923 Fokine had taken up residence in New York, and the next year Mikhail Mordkin had also come there to live and teach.[35] But only the youthful Balanchine promised to move classical dancing in creative new directions.

At the end of that rainy Tuesday afternoon, the Austins, Kirstein, Warburg, Marian Murray, and photographer Ella Barnett watched the *Olympic* nose into the New York docks. They scanned the passengers as they walked down the gangplank, but neither Balanchine nor Dimitriew was among them. Kirstein finally spied them in tourist class. The immigration officer refused to let them land because they had a year's contract but only six-month visas. The welcoming party was told that the Russians might have to remain on the ship and return to Ellis Island.[36]

Helen Austin described the scene to Agnes Rindge a few days later:

Balanchine & Demitriew *did* arrive last Tues., were detained to be
taken to Ellis Island, & we could do nothing—not even get on board
the boat. All was despair for a half hour until we discovered our little
pal Eddie had quietly gone aboard & settled the whole business with
the magic name of Felix Warburg. We had given up all hope, & thought
Eddie had gone to a dinner engagement that was past due, when he
came bouncing off the boat followed by B. & D. All very dramatic.[37]

Looking slightly dazed, wearing a long, dark unbuttoned overcoat over a
pale double-breasted suit with a dark tie, holding a light-colored fedora in his
right hand and a square soft leather briefcase in his left, a raincoat slung over
his arm—Balanchine posed for a photograph with Dimitriew, Austin, Warburg,
and Kirstein.

It was a memorable day for European immigrants: Albert Einstein, fleeing
Nazi Germany, landed in New York on the *Westernland* and proceeded directly
to Princeton. The story and photograph of the famous physicist's arrival was on
the front page of the *Hartford Times;* the article about the little-known choreographer was relegated to page twenty-three.

Warburg departed for his dinner date, but the rest of the party accompanied
the two Russians to the Barbizon Plaza Hotel, where Kirstein had reserved a
two-bedroom suite on the thirty-fourth floor. Gazing down at Central Park and
the lights of Manhattan for the first time from a real American skyscraper, Balanchine and Dimitriew "gasped at the view," Kirstein wrote in his diary.[38]

Then they repaired to the hotel dining room. Peering at the menu through a
monocle in his right eye, Dimitriew was disappointed to discover that it was
written in French because he wanted "to know all about everything American."
Nevertheless, the dinner conversation was carried on in French until Dimitriew
ordered ice cream to accompany his melon and seafood. Hearing a familiar
phrase, Balanchine said, "Ah yes, ice cream is good. And ice cream soda."[39]

After dinner the party walked through the New York streets, the Americans
showing the Russians the illuminated skyscrapers and explaining the meaning
of a speakeasy they passed. They ended up at the brownstone of Kirk and Constance Askew, whom Balanchine had met in London. Conversation about future
plans continued long into the night, with Balanchine frequently answering
questions with another newly acquired phrase: "O.K. Kid."[40]

Balanchine's imminent arrival in Hartford was greeted excitedly by the
local press. An editorial in the *Courant* the day after the choreographer landed
in New York praised Chick for his foresight: "That the venture should be made
is one more of the many indications that in Mr. Everett Austin, Jr., the Morgan

Coming to Hartford to Direct Ballet

—[Ella Barnett Photo.
Georges Balanchine, famous ballet choreographer, and Vladimir Dimitriev,
teacher and manager, were met when the Olympic docked in New York

Balanchine arrives in America, New York, October 17, 1933.
Left to right, Vladimir Dimitriev, AEA, Edward M. M. Warburg,
George Balanchine, and Lincoln Kirstein, Hartford Times,
October 18, 1933

Memorial has as its director a man of initiative, imagination, energy and of very lively interest both in the art of the past, and in expression of contemporary life in art mediums." The editorial reminded readers that the enterprise would be essentially American. While "foreign ballet experts" were undoubtedly necessary to produce performances quickly and to train dancers in classical technique, it would remain "for the Americans themselves to add their contribution of national genius, if indeed the school is actually to achieve the high ambitions of its founders and become an expression of the American spirit in ballet."[41]

The next day, Chick explained to the press that ballet was more than a dance, but "a combination of all the arts and dependent for its success on composers, painters and costumers, as well as dancing. The scenery and costumes for the American ballet will be done entirely by Americans." In the same breath, however, he announced that the school would use sets and costumes for

Songes by André Derain and for *Mozartiana* by Christian Bérard.[42] As with the dancing masters, European artists would lead the way until American talent could be developed.

The news spread quickly. Local girls asked about auditions; telegrams and letters arrived at the museum, congratulating Austin on the proposed American Ballet. Chick imagined that soon Balanchine would be a magnet, drawing the most eminent musicians and artists in the world to Hartford. They would come because they would regard him as their equal.

But some votaries of Terpsichore already in town did not agree. The day before Balanchine arrived in Hartford, the curtain rose on a minor comic opera. The local dancing teachers, in high dudgeon, entered from the wings. Nearly twenty of them convened in the Farmington Avenue studio of Walter U. Soby (James Soby's cousin), secretary-treasurer of the Dancing Masters of America, who presided.[43] With one voice, they decried and denounced the establishment of a free ballet school under the auspices of the Wadsworth Atheneum.

The next morning, Thursday, October 19, as Balanchine, Dimitriew, and Kirstein prepared to leave New York, Walter Soby informed the *Hartford Times* that "all dancing teachers in the city should have been consulted and called into conference for advice and suggestions." Then the big guns were rolled forward. "If it is the plan of the proposed ballet school to give free tuition to the students of the school, Mr. Soby said to-day, the local teachers would regard it as unfair competition and a violation of the NRA [National Recovery Act] program. It is also the opinion of the teachers present that if an American ballet is to be organized that an American ballet master should have been employed." Furthermore, the museum was violating its purpose. With colossal irony, the teachers protested that their profession had nothing whatever to do with the fine arts: "the operating of a ballet school at the Morgan Memorial is placing an endowed institution on a commercial basis and is not in keeping with the purposes for which the building was erected."[44]

Among the most vocal of the lot were the Angelo sisters, Mary and Carmel, whose Church Street studio was a few blocks from the museum. They flew into what Kirstein described as "an Italian operatic rage," intimating that bread was being taken from their tables by Bolsheviks.[45] Years later, Paul Cooley concluded that their outburst was mostly "promotional"—and not merely for their studio: they sold ballet slippers on the side.[46] On the other hand, Cooley's assumption that their objections were purely self-serving did not take into account the historic realities of the moment. That week, the Hartford papers were full of President Roosevelt's forthcoming recognition of the Soviet Union. To many Americans this was legitimizing the godless Communists—and now Russians would be invading Hartford.

Chick and Jim Soby issued a statement countering the criticism while neatly putting the achievements of local practitioners in their place: "Quite the contrary to any desire to hamper the interests of dancing in Hartford, it is the purpose of the American ballet to stimulate interest in the art." As this would be a national school, very few students would be from Hartford.

> Those who have endowed the project have done so because of a belief that a true inauguration of an American ballet would give an opportunity to American composers and artists. Already several ballets on American themes are being created in an attempt to express through this art those native literary and artistic ideals which have never been developed to their fullest extent.
>
> Far from placing the Morgan Memorial on a commercial basis, this is a non-commercial and purely artistic venture, and one which is establishing the artistic prestige of Hartford, not only nationally but internationally.[47]

As Chick waited that day for Kirstein's car to pull up to the museum from New York, another of the batons he loved juggling flew into his hand. Just before lunch, an ominously succinct telegram arrived from Paris:

> PLEASE WIRE TODAY NO FOOLING
> VIRGIL.[48]

The testy composer of *Four Saints,* whose departure for New York to prepare the opera production was fast approaching, needed another infusion of cash. A month earlier, Austin had managed to procure five hundred dollars for Thomson from Jim Soby, Philip Johnson, and Jere Abbott. Now, from somewhere, he found fifty more to wire Thomson, though he did not manage to get to the telegraph office for three days.

That evening, Kirstein at last arrived in Hartford with Balanchine and Dimitriew. Jim Soby recalled that Balanchine politely requested accommodations in an eighteenth-century apartment. "It was rather difficult," Soby recalled, "to explain to him in French that people in Hartford did not build or live in apartments in the eighteenth century."[49] The Russians inspected the museum's new theater and rehearsal space and also toured the three-thousand-seat Bushnell Auditorium, whose modern facilities they pronounced superior to those in any European theater.[50]

Chick told the press that the next week would be taken up with meetings to discuss specific plans for the winter and that a formal announcement would be made the following Saturday, October 28. Meanwhile, he repeated strong assurances that the Russians would not take business from the local dancing teachers because students would be drawn form New York, Boston, and Philadelphia, as well as Hartford.[51]

Coached by Chick about the little tempest that was brewing, the Russians themselves tried to reassure the public. The *Courant* reported: "Both Balanchine and Dometriev [*sic*] reiterated that the school would in no way, be a competitor of the dancing schools, because it was to be a 'cathedral of ballet,' rather than a dancing school."[52] The Hartford teachers, despite their provincialism, could only have regarded such a description of the school as supremely condescending. Besides, they could point to the fact that their schools were already proven. They were not simply giving young ladies a chance to wear tutus and tiptoe around their studios. The week Balanchine arrived, for example, the Misses Angelo Studio of Dancing supplied twenty-two Hartford girls for the "ballet numbers" in the Columbia Opera Company's production of *Aida*— dances devised by the Angelo sisters themselves.[53]

The absurdity of the protest was obvious to those outside the local dancing set. One letter to the editor of the *Hartford Times* pointed out that "No musician has ever been foolish enough to plead for the abolition of grand opera and symphony orchestras on the grounds that they are often endowed institutions nor do grammar school teachers fly into a panic because someone endows a chair at a university." The complaint that the proposed school would be directed by foreigners was, the letter went on, "petty and irrelevant. In matters of art there should be one criterion, to get the best."[54]

But the protests were suddenly beside the point. A few days after Kirstein arrived with the Russians, he drove them to his parents' home near Springfield, Massachusetts. Balanchine and Dimitriew told him that they were not keen on Hartford. The Morgan Memorial, with its suggestion of the Morgan fortune, was not what they expected. The museum facilities were not ideal. The practice room was acceptable, but the ceiling of the stage was too low. Though Balanchine had said he wanted to be away from a large city, Hartford was too small and too far from the large population centers. He had lived and worked in some of the greatest cities in the world. After St. Petersburg, Paris, London, Copenhagen, and Monte Carlo, Hartford did not measure up. The ridiculous little storm stirred up by the local dancing teachers was still rumbling. They talked matters over with Lincoln's sister, Mina Curtiss, who agreed that Hartford was not a feasible location.

When Balanchine and Dimitriew returned to the museum a day or two later, they began talking about charging tuition, touring in commercial theaters, raising salaries. As Kirstein later wrote, they "flatly refused to have anything to do with a plan which involved non-profits. America was a rich country. This Museum bore the Morgan name. Was it not proper that an artist be allowed more than a mere pittance?"[55] Their apparent change of mind about the finances and their vagueness about plans for the winter made Chick suspicious. Kirstein, caught in the middle, seemed nervous and awkward.

On Sunday, Helen wrote to Agnes Rindge as the Hartford scheme disintegrated: "Horrible complications have been arising ever since [their arrival], & it is a great question whether they will be willing to start their damned old school in Hfd or not. Its all pretty awful & I don't know how its going to turn out. We really need you to convince them that the Hfd Museum is a swell place, & that its director really has taste & sense—He hasn't much of the last, but they needn't be told that."[56]

Balanchine and Dimitriew announced that they could not remain. Years later, Balanchine summed up the experience: "When we went to Hartford, it was a very little place and nobody wanted us there, and there were, you know, already three teachers there that were against us. And the reporters immediately came, you know, and began writing things like 'Why did he come here to spoil our life?' So, 'Lincoln,' I said, 'Let's go, because first of all it's too small. Let's go to New York.' "[57]

Kirstein had no choice. His leave-taking was brief and painful. Before the second week was out, he, Balanchine, and Dimitriew were on a train to New York. "I ran off to New York with my Russians," Kirstein wrote later, "leaving Austin to endure the consequences of ragged explanations, inconvenience, and humiliation." Shaken by the failure, Kirstein found the train ride "longer than that from Moscow to Vladivostock."[58]

Chick was bitterly disappointed. He knew intellectually that Balanchine and Dimitriew had made a rational, practical decision. But his months of hard work, his dreams about further transforming the museum, his passionate appreciation of the possibilities of a great American ballet company in the tradition of Diaghilev—and his public failure after a long string of amazing successes—left him temporarily but profoundly upset.

"Chick is in the deepest gloom of disappointment that his cherished ballet school is not to be in Hartford," Helen wrote Agnes Rindge. "You probably know all about it as you are in N.Y. now. Lincoln has acted in a very queer way about the whole thing, and has so enraged me that I can scarcely bear to see him again. He very likely has good reason on his side, but I can't see anything but Chick's at the moment."[59]

Though the necessity of returning to New York had become apparent, Kirstein was in what he later described as "an anguish of embarrassment having put everyone involved in a false position. . . . I obviously could never see Chick again."[60]

To save face, Chick announced to the press on Saturday, October 28, that he and James Soby had decided to abandon the project. He focused on whatever disagreements he may have had with Dimitriew and Balanchine over charging tuition and taking profits from future performances. "The flat refusal of A. Everett Austin, Jr., director of the Morgan Memorial," the *Hartford Times* reported, "to commercialize the proposed American ballet which was to have been established in Hartford, has resulted in a complete cancellation of the arrangements." Austin and Soby expressed their "extreme disappointment."[61]

Word of the unraveling of the Hartford scheme reached New York quickly. Philip Johnson wrote Chick, temporarily distancing himself from Kirstein ("I will be unable to contribute financially in any way to the new plan"), but pledging his loyalty to Chick: "Please believe that I am thoroughly in sympathy with anything which you attempt in Hartford and that I will do anything that is within my power to help you personally and your theater."[62] He and Jere Abbott had already jointly contributed $150 to *Four Saints* and would soon give more.

Early in November, still acutely uncomfortable about the turn of events, Kirstein sent Chick a letter of the utmost brevity—which he forgot to sign—noting that he had paid Arthur Shipman for legal advice in Hartford and asking: "Will you please send all my Ballet pictures and books here."[63] Chick did not reply.

A few weeks later, Kirstein wrote again:

Its too bad that everything turned out like it did. I miss not seeing you—but of course I understand how you feel. As in such cases always—the small talk about, around N.Y. has on successive Sunday afternoons [at the Askews'] done its best to elevate it into a feud between you and me. I hope there's nothing in this more than your justified resentment.

. . . I wish you'd send me what photos you have; also my two ballet books. Also the negatives for the slides.

Balanchine has been very ill and I don't know what will happen. Its possible nothing. He is not dying—but it may be difficult for him to work. My best to Helen:

Yours Lincoln[64]

Gone was the driving elation of Kirstein's first lines from London six months earlier. Instead there was an apology—subdued, anxious, uncertain—for what he would sometimes call, even half a century later, "the Hartford catastrophe."[65]

CHAPTER ELEVEN

Picasso and the Saints

They were much impressed by the thought of eternity, and they used to repeat often together, "For ever, for ever, for ever," admiring the victories of the saints and the everlasting glory which they possess.

—"St. Teresa of Avila," *Butler's Lives of the Saints*

C hick had no time to brood about Balanchine's departure from Hartford. On the very day he announced the cancellation of the ballet school, the *Ile de France* was steaming toward New York, bringing Virgil Thomson to prepare *Four Saints in Three Acts* for its world premiere in the still-unfinished Avery theater.

In September, Thomson had dispatched a detailed battle plan, assigning Chick tasks to lay the groundwork for the production. He should coax Florine Stettheimer into finishing her design for the decor ("some compliments and she will do wonders"); he should convince Alexander Smallens, Stokowski's assistant in Philadelphia, to conduct ("Lay the plans rather grandly before him. . . . Don't mention money unless he does"); he should confirm that Hubert Osborne, a friend of Virgil's in Cambridge, would direct; he should ask Mrs. W. Murray Crane, the Museum of Modern Art's great patron, about arranging subscription concerts in New York. "When I come," Thomson warned, "everybody should be ready to get at the dirty-work of scene-building & dress-making & rehearsing."

But Chick had been too busy. Except for the fifty dollars he had wired Virgil earlier in October, he had done almost nothing for the opera. Nor had he responded to the composer's plea for him to drum up performing engagements to pay his living expenses: "money, darling, money," Thomson had written, "is what keeps beer in the belly," adding that he would arrive "with nothing visible or invisible to feed fanny with."[1]

On October 31, Thomson disembarked in Manhattan, went first to Kirk and Constance Askew's guest room, then to a borrowed room with a piano at the

Hotel Leonori. It was obvious that if his opera were to happen at all, he would have to organize it himself, and he set to work with intense single-mindedness. Now Chick would have to do his part by concentrating on finding the money—through the Friends and Enemies of Modern Music and anyone else he could solicit.

Even as November began, the opera was only one of the schemes heating up Chick's imagination. Among the passengers stepping off the *Ile de France* with Thomson was Serge Lifar, Diaghilev's last favorite male dancer, now ballet master of the Paris Opera, who had arrived with a small troupe for his American debut at New York's Forrest Theatre followed by a tour.[2] But Lifar had brought something more precious to him than his troupe: an unparalleled collection of over 160 drawings, watercolors, and oils—most of them set and costume designs for Diaghilev's Ballets Russes.

The collection ranged from the gorgeous exoticism of the earliest "Russian Seasons," with works by artists like Alexandre Benois and Leon Bakst, to the astonishing provocations of Diaghilev's later productions, when the decor and costumes were created by the giants of the School of Paris—Matisse, Picasso, Braque and Derain, Léger, Miró, Gris, Modigliani, Rouault, Cocteau, and Laurencin. It also encompassed the surrealists, the Neo-Romantics, and the Russian avant-garde—Giorgio de Chirico, Leopold Survage, Max Ernst, Christian Bérard, Pavel Tchelitchew, Naum Gabo, and Nathalie Gontcharova. These pictures evoked the most memorable ballets of the era: *Le Pavillon d'Armide* of 1909, which had introduced Nijinsky and Karsavina to the West; Rimsky-Korsakov's *Schehérézade;* Stravinsky's *Petroushka, Firebird, Le Chant du rossignol, Les Noces*—the production that had captivated Chick in Paris ten years before—and *Apollon musagète,* Balanchine's early masterpiece; Ravel's *Daphnis and Cloë;* de Falla's *Le Tricorne;* Poulenc's *Les Biches;* Milhaud's *La Création du monde;* and Prokofiev's *Le Fils prodigue,* the company's last ballet.[3] Lifar had been amassing the works since 1923 and, at Diaghilev's death six years later, had inherited a cache of others from the impresario's own collection.[4]

Chick had known that the pictures were coming. Earlier in the fall, Julien Levy had arranged to give the Lifar Collection, which had been seen in London and Paris, its first American showing at his gallery before sending it out to selected museums around the country. Chick had immediately reserved the show for the Atheneum. He and Helen had also joined the sponsors of Levy's exhibition, which was produced as a benefit for the Architects' Emergency Committee in New York. Others on the list included familiar members of the Austin constellation—the Askews, the Sobys, Philip Goodwin, Lincoln Kirstein, and Eddie Warburg—as well as a sprinkling of Russian and French nobility.[5] The show was called *Twenty-Five Years of Russian Ballet* and opened on November 2, only three days after Lifar's arrival.

Chick buys the Lifar Collection. Alexandre Benois, Set Design for Petroushka, *1911. Graphite, tempera and/or watercolor and crayon on paper, 17¹¹/₁₆ × 24³/₁₆ inches, purchased 1933*

No one knew better than Chick that the Lifar Collection embodied the visual revolution of the twentieth century—all the strands of contemporary art, in fact, that he had been promoting since his arrival in Hartford. And at that moment his mind was still churning with thoughts of how close he had come to continuing the legacy of the Ballets Russes at the Atheneum. He wanted the collection. As Lifar's ballet tour quickly turned into a financial disaster, Levy negotiated, on Chick's behalf, a special museum price with the dancer for the entire hoard of pictures—$10,000.[6]

From Chick's point of view, the timing was perfect. The last payment had just been made to Duveen for the Piero di Cosimo, and the Sumner Fund was again generating income. The museum could afford the collection.

There was no doubt, however, that the trustees would balk at spending so large a sum on a stack of working drawings and watercolors, and, as with the American Ballet scheme, Chick was not about to approach Uncle Charlie first. Again, he rushed to see Arthur Day, who understood why he wanted the collection. But other board members were skeptical. Paul Cooley remembered their asking, with the Balanchine misadventure fresh in mind, "Well now, is it art or is it ballet? Are we an art museum or a dance emporium?" Arthur Day agreed that these sketches for costumes and stage sets were works of art by renowned twentieth-century artists. As he was head of the trust department in the bank that held the museum's funds, his polite "Well, I think we can find the money" was enough to induce the art committee to defer to his judgment.[7] Once again, Chick got his way. A check for $10,000 was made out to the Julien Levy Gallery on November 15, three days before the show closed in New York.

Levy described the startling aftermath of the sale:

> Chick was immensely pleased. Lifar was happy, too, since he was almost without fare for his return to Paris. We went together to my bank, the Central Hanover, just around a corner from my gallery at 602 Madison Avenue, to cash his check and buy Travelers'. This bank was of new design. The grilles and tellers' windows had been eliminated and the cashiers sat behind a marble counter the height of a man's chest. In one bound, after a pretty *entrechat*, Lifar was atop the counter by one of those leaps so famous in *Le Spectre de la Rose*. With half drawn revolvers the guards stared in amazement as Lifar flourished his check and bowed.[8]

Introducing the Lifar Collection to the public, Chick echoed his early prediction that he would turn Hartford into a cultural capital: "Nothing like it can be seen in any part of the world," he told the *Hartford Times*, "and it is not possible to form another of the same sort. These pictures will be a Mecca for art and ballet lovers."[9] Writing in the museum's bulletin, he called Diaghilev the "last of the great Baroque princes," who had "knit together the arts of painting, music, literature, acting and choreography into a brilliant pattern, a triumphal procession, and set against it the eternal beauty of youth." Recalling his own attendance at those performances, he was rhapsodic: "Forever fortunate are those who were privileged to see the creations of Diaghilew [*sic*]. To them the joyful pangs of memory will be a constant proof that the twentieth century has known splendor devoid of vulgarity and taste kept inviolate from commercial degradation."[10]

Such ardor may have seemed excessive, but it was based on Chick's absolute certainty of Diaghilev's achievement and therefore of the Lifar Collection's worth. Twenty-five years later, after the collection had been loaned to museums all over the world and reproduced many times over, Kirstein, as director of the New York City Ballet, noted that its value had soared to more than a hundred times what Chick paid for it and that, through its effect on later designers, it had become "one of the most influential and useful bodies of practical historic materials that exists."[11]

Chick bought the collection after little more than a cursory look before it went off to the first stop on its tour, the always adventuresome Arts Club of

Chicago. Late in November, on a day he was scheduled to lecture on contemporary painting at Hartford's Charter Oak Temple, glass slides of the works arrived at the museum. Chick went out the door to give his talk with the box of slides, a projector, and an assistant to operate it. He announced to the audience that he was changing his topic and instead would trace the history of design for the ballet in the twentieth century through the Lifar Collection, which he had just bought. "I'd like to show it to you and talk to you about it," he said merrily, "and see it myself!" The fact that he wore a pink shirt and a green tie made as much of an impression as the art.[12]

Even as he was pressing the trustees to buy the ballet designs, Chick had been plotting to assemble his long-intended Picasso exhibition to coincide with the opening of the Avery and the premiere of *Four Saints*, scheduled for the first week of February 1934. The Depression had stopped him from producing the world's first Picasso retrospective in March 1932, and in June of that year the Galeries Georges Petit in Paris took the honors by presenting a monumental exhibition, installed by Picasso himself.[13] Another version of the show appeared at the Zurich Kunsthaus that fall. But America had not yet seen the full range of Picasso's work—and Chick planned to set it off against the architecture of the Machine Age, a possibility open to no other museum director in the United States.

Not until November 9 did he formally ask the museum's building committee for permission to open the Avery with a Picasso show. Edward Forbes was down from Cambridge for the meeting and, despite his reticence about modern art, heartily agreed. Whatever the trustees thought of Picasso—which was not at all, if they could help it—they could not say no to Forbes. The exhibition was approved. Charles Goodwin warned the committee, however, to be careful to avoid "public criticism of too lavish expenditure of funds on an Opening at a time when it may be necessary to close the Morgan Memorial because of insufficient funds." Chick was advised not to spend much above $5,000 on the Picasso exhibition and catalogue, an additional catalogue of the museum's collection, the opening reception, and a commemorative bulletin about the building.[14]

Just at this time, Chick acquired a new secretary and a lifelong friend, Eleanor Howland. The only child of a Wall Street stockbroker, Nellie, as she was known, was twenty-eight, dark-haired, blue-eyed, and vivacious. She had graduated magna cum laude from Mount Holyoke College in the class of 1926, having taken every available art history course. She was among the few in Hartford who matched Chick's wit, his infectious humor, and his capacity for hard work. She was also accepted as an equal by Chick's inner circle in the New York art world. He soon changed her title from secretary to executive assistant. Forty years later, as a trustee and benefactor of the Wadsworth Atheneum, she was asked about working with him: "We worked late at night, we skipped lunch, or we'd have lunch at four in the afternoon, we all went out together and we laughed and we had a little relaxation and then went back and worked on and on."[15] Later, she reiterated, "We laughed all the time. I was paid to laugh."[16]

With his team of Nellie Howland, Paul Cooley, Jim Soby (in his new capacity as honorary curator of modern art), and Russell Hitchcock, Chick began his quest for Picassos. On November 16, he wrote to Gertrude Stein about lending some of her celebrated pictures to America for the first time. Warming her up for the appeal, he gave a glowing report of *Four Saints:*

> Preparations for the opera are going ahead very rapidly. Everybody concerned is delighted with the theatre, now almost complete, which has been incorporated in the new Museum Building. Miss Stettheimer has made the most enchanting models for both settings and costumes in a style which is entirely new and unique and singularly appropriate to the mood of the work as I understand it. I am extremely gratified at the prospect as I have dreamed for five years of seeing the opera on the stage. I am convinced that you have found the only literary solution for opera in English and that Virgil's music sets it off to perfection. That will be definitely proved, I think, by the production. I only wish that you and Miss Toklas could be persuaded to come and stay with Mrs. Austin and me for the première and for the opening of the New Museum. That too is something new in museum architecture and I am quite pleased with it.

Then he made his respectful pitch:

> At the same time as your opera I am planning to have also a retrospective exposition of Picasso's painting, an exposition which will include about sixty carefully chosen canvases and which will be particularly appropriate on this occasion. Until now no adequate selection of Picasso's work has been shown in this country and I feel that it is high time to exhibit the best of Picasso's work rather than the sweepings in dealers' hands on which up to now the American public has been forced to base its acquaintance.
>
> I am hoping therefore that you can be persuaded to lend me at least your portrait and La fille à la Corbeille plus several cubist pictures from your collection without which no fine exposition of Picasso is possible and which you might choose for me yourself.

He admitted that he was asking "a very important favor in requesting the loan of your pictures," and concluded with deference: "You have already conferred one high honor on the Wadsworth Atheneum in allowing us to produce your work and I wish you to believe me your grateful and sincere admirer."[17]

Miss Stein returned the compliments, thanking him for producing the opera: "I too have a great deal of belief in it and wish it every success. I am too very pleased in your belief in it. May it live long and prosper." She was not prepared, however, to deprive herself of enjoying her pictures. "About the Picasso show, I think your idea xcellent [sic] but alas I cannot find it in my heart to part with all my pictures just as I have returned to them after a seven months absence, and in any case quite frankly I do not like to lend them and certainly not any of them so very far away." With grand finesse, she added: "But you will understand." She softened the blow by assuring Austin of her "very genuine appreciation for all you are doing and the way you are doing it."[18]

Chick was thoroughly disappointed, but looked to an even more formidable source for pictures. Late in November, he wrote to the State Department for advice about borrowing the early Picassos in the Sergei Shchukin Collection in Moscow. Over fifty canvases had been confiscated by the Soviet state in 1918, but the collection had remained intact, in part because Picasso was Lenin's favorite modern painter. Alluding to President Roosevelt's recent recognition of the U.S.S.R., Chick suggested that such a loan would signal "the restoration of artistic as well as political relations between the United States and Russia."[19] His appeal was somewhat disingenuous, particularly for someone who was never known to vote in any election. The Shchukin collection would simply give his exhibition a dimension the two European Picasso shows had lacked. But Stalinist Russia was impenetrable.

In any case, Chick knew, despite what he told Miss Stein, that he could not pull off a large show without the help of well-placed dealers, whose stock had always been the backbone of his exhibitions. He turned first to Felix Wildenstein, head of the New York branch of the old-master firm that had supplied major works to Chick's shows and had sold him four canvases in the past three years, including Picasso's Bather in 1931. The dealer agreed to lend several paintings to Hartford and passed the word to his cousin Georges, director of the gallery's home office in Paris. From 1918 to 1932, Georges Wildenstein had represented Picasso in a more or less silent partnership with Paul Rosenberg, the artist's principal dealer. He was delighted to assist Chick. On November 29 he wrote to Picasso, urging him to cooperate.[20]

But it was Paul Rosenberg himself who made Chick's show happen. Rosenberg had been promoting American exhibitions of Picasso's art since 1923, when examples of the artist's dramatic shift to a neoclassic style were shown at Wildenstein's gallery and then at the Art Institute of Chicago through the Arts Club. It was Chick's good fortune that Rosenberg was visiting America under the auspices of the Louvre, soliciting loans for a Daumier retrospective the next year. He had sold Chick Les Saltimbanques in 1928, and came to Hartford to secure it for the show. He was extremely impressed by what Chick was planning for the opening of the new building. It was a surprise, he wrote at the time, "to see a curator of a museum capable of infusing so much life into his institute."[21] He offered to collaborate with the museum on the show, promising to supply the names of American collectors who could lend important pictures and to arrange for loans from illustrious Parisian collectors.

Rosenberg, of course, saw a golden opportunity in the making. On December 16 he wrote to Picasso from New York, reminding him that "the country remains very rich" and urging him to participate in Austin's exhibition. "You know that the museum in Hartford, which is in Connecticut, near Boston, wants to give you a show. I am lending them my most beautiful canvases and I recommend you contribute also. There is a great interest in the arts here, and there is a great market to conquer for you."[22] Chick was elated when Picasso agreed to lend several of his own canvases.

Not all was friendly cooperation among the Paris dealers, however. Paul Guillaume, who supplied the eccentric Philadelphia collector Albert Barnes with modern pictures, tried to control the scope of the show. When asked for two of his Picassos (of which he had forty), Guillaume agreed, but only if Chick promised not to borrow more than two from any other French dealer or collector—in order, he said, to protect the reputation of his collection.[23] This, Chick cabled Guillaume, was impossible.[24] With Rosenberg's commitment to the show, Chick could afford to dismiss such an attempt at commercial blackmail, and he was now in a position to solicit the leading American collectors for loans.

A batch of letters went out to collectors on December 19, only seven weeks before the opening. Recognizing that the show would be groundbreaking, most of them responded enthusiastically. Many lenders had strong connections with the Museum of Modern Art: Mrs. John D. Rockefeller, Jr., and Mrs. Cornelius Sullivan, two of the museum's three "founding mothers"; A. Conger Goodyear, the museum's president; Stephen Clark, a trustee and future president; Sam Lewisohn, secretary of the board; and James Johnson Sweeney, later head of the Modern's painting and sculpture department. Then there were such forward-thinking collectors as the W. Averell Harrimans, Adolph Lewisohn, and Albert Gallatin, founder of the Gallery of Living Art in New York, who sent a key work, Picasso's classic self-portrait of 1906.[25]

Only four museums provided oils—the Albright Art Gallery in Buffalo, the Art Institute of Chicago, the Smith College Art Museum, and the Worcester Art Museum—in part because so few of Picasso's paintings were held in American public institutions. Even the four-year-old Museum of Modern Art owned only one oil, *Seated Woman* of 1927, bought directly from Picasso in 1932.[26] Though the Modern did not lend the picture, it did contribute a gouache portrait head of 1909 to the show.

Chick's closest associates and friends also lent pictures—Paul Sachs, the Sobys, Julien Levy, Jere Abbott, Eddie Warburg—as did the one member of Helen's family who appreciated modern art, Philip Goodwin. Other dealer friends followed suit—Knoedler's, the Valentine Gallery, Marie Harriman, John Becker, Sidney Janowitz, and Pierre Matisse.

In the end, Rosenberg would be responsible for nearly half of the seventy-seven oils in the exhibition. Nineteen came from his personal collection alone. "All my dining room is spoiled as those fine paintings are taken from the wall," he wrote to Chick in January, after the pictures had been crated for shipment, "but it is worth [it] to please you."[27]

Several of these dealers benefited directly from their association with Chick that winter. From Rosenberg, for nearly $20,000, he bought a work of psychological complexity by Degas, *Double Portrait—The Cousins of the Painter*, in which one of the sitters is in focus while the other is diffused. Wildenstein sold him two major works, *Indolence* (*La Paresseuse italienne*) by the French eighteenth-century painter Jean-Baptiste Greuze, a genre scene dominated by a fat slovenly serving girl; and *Lictors Bring Back to Brutus the Bodies of His Sons*, believed to be by Jacques-Louis David, a smaller version of the great canvas at the Louvre, painted on the eve of the French Revolution. (The Greuze was $25,000; the David, $8,000.) From Pierre Matisse, for only $580, Chick purchased one of the first, and one of the most significant, works by Joan Miró to enter an American museum collection, his large *Composition* of 1933, in which finely drawn biomorphic figures float in a mysterious gray haze—a whimsical scene from the theater of the surreal.

All the time that Chick was rounding up pictures, he had been closely supervising the final work on the Avery. There were still decisions to be made about interior finishes. Though he wanted many of the exhibition spaces to be painted white, in keeping with the International Style, he decided that the walls in the galleries for the permanent collection should be covered with luxurious fabrics. He bought nearly fourteen hundred yards of raw cotton, silks, damasks, satins, and velvets, all of them dyed to his specifications—in mulberry, bright yellow, duck-egg blue, dark red, white, cream, and brown—to complement the works he planned to hang in each room.

For the furniture to be used throughout the building, he insisted on the most advanced designs available. From Thonet Brothers, the leading supplier of contemporary European furnishings, he ordered a huge shipment of chrome and canvas pieces, all designed by Marcel Breuer: fifty gallery stools, forty side chairs, half a dozen armchairs, glass-topped tubular chrome tables, and a two-tiered black-and-chrome desk. It was the first large-scale use of Bauhaus-style furniture in an American museum.

Chick made the final choices about the decor of his first-floor office, which opened onto the court and was meant to be a showcase of modern interior design. The floor was to be white rubber; two walls were to be paneled in rose-wood; another was to be painted white and would feature long wooden book-shelves suspended within chrome pipes, as in the New York apartment Mies van der Rohe had designed for Philip Johnson in 1930. Chick decided that the wall of windows behind his desk should be covered with swinging screens in the form of fifteen large rosewood rectangles that could be masked, floor to ceiling, with a plain dark curtain. He ordered two custom-made desks, each consisting of nothing more than a long slab of canaletta wood on chrome legs. To these he added Breuer chairs and two chrome pieces designed by Le Corbusier—a tubular chair, with a tilting canvas back and canvas straps for arms, and a chaise longue. (Later, Chick would be found lying on the chaise after particularly trying trustees meetings.[28]) As usual, no detail escaped him, down to the six chromium hooks which he bought from Philip Johnson for ninety cents apiece for his private bathroom. He also turned to Johnson, then in the midst of planning his *Machine Art* show at the Museum of Modern Art, for the design of gallery benches, which were upholstered in beige pigskin and supported by chrome legs.[29]

In mid-November the marble tiles were laid in the floor of the court, and the huge Francavilla Venus arrived from the Fogg. Pipe fitters connected her to the plumbing so that the two dolphins at her feet could spout water into the pool.

In December the theater equipment was installed, including a new sound film projector and a silver screen. The rare woods were polished, the apron of the orchestra pit grained to simulate the rosewood of the proscenium, and the walls inside the theater painted a light shell-pink. A deep blue velour curtain was hung, and seats upholstered in matching blue velour were secured into position. The theater was nearly ready for the opera.

Virgil Thomson had been busy in New York. Finding that Hubert Osborne, his Cambridge friend, could not direct *Four Saints* after all, he asked a young English dancer and choreographer named Freddie Ashton, whom he had met in London through the Askews, to take charge of the dances in the show as well as the overall movement of the large cast. The future Sir Frederick Ashton, later the director and choreographer of the Royal Ballet, was to come over in December and be paid ten dollars a week for the job, his first work in America. But Thomson also wanted a director who could draw up a budget, manage the production, and supervise rehearsals. It was at one of Kirk and Constance Askews' weekly salons that he found exactly the person he needed.

During most of the 1930s, the Askews' five-story brownstone on East Sixty-first Street drew one of the liveliest artistic and literary gatherings in the city. Every Sunday afternoon during the "R" months (September through April) when the Askews were in town, guests arrived at five for tea or six for cocktails.

A sophisticated crowd of about forty would circulate through the first floor. Among the regulars were the Austins, the Levys, the Barrs, Virgil Thomson, Russell Hitchcock, Lincoln Kirstein, Philip Johnson, Allen Porter, Jere Abbott, John McAndrew, Agnes Rindge, Muriel Draper, the Stettheimer sisters, Carl Van Vechten, and Henry McBride. Kirk Askew opened his house not only because it was good for business, but also because he liked to entertain and to show off his wife, who was commandingly beautiful and a great hostess. For Chick and his modernist friends, the Askew salon (or "saloon," as some of its habitués called it) was the epicenter of the art world.

Early in November, in the Askews' living room, Thomson met John Houseman and—after an hour's conversation followed by a two-hour solo performance of the opera by Thomson the next day—invited him to direct the show. Raised in Europe, Houseman had won and lost a fortune in the international grain market, moved to New York, and had just written a play with Lewis Galantière. Although he had not directed any kind of stage production, and although Thomson made it clear that there would be no salary involved, Houseman eagerly accepted the invitation. As he later confessed, only his naïveté allowed him to think that he could succeed. For at that point, he and Thomson had "nine and a half weeks in which to find a cast, coach and rehearse them in two hours of unfamiliar music and complicated stage action, execute scenery and costumes, rehearse a new score, move to Hartford into an unfinished theatre with an orchestra of twenty and a cast of forty-three, set up, light, dress rehearse and open cold before one of the world's most sophisticated audiences."[30]

Houseman's business experience quickly came to the fore. He arranged for auditions of the principals in the Askews' living room; engaged a prominent Negro choir, directed by Eva Jessye; secured rehearsal space in the basement of Saint Philip's Episcopal Church in Harlem; hired Abe Feder, the lighting wizard who would became a legend on Broadway; found a zealous press agent, Nathan Zatkin, and chose an alluring young photographer named Lee Miller (she had worked and lived with Man Ray in Paris) to make portraits of the cast and management for the program.[31]

He also developed a production budget of $8,970, which he rounded upward to $10,000. This was thought to be the bare minimum; the orchestra, chorus, scenery, and costumes alone would swallow up $6,000. But it was far more than the Friends and Enemies of Modern Music had in hand.[32]

Late in November, Chick finally began canvassing the most likely sources of cash. On the twenty-eighth, Eddie Warburg, after discussing the opera with Chick in New York, sent a check for $500, partly to ease the pain over the American Ballet's departure.[33]

On the day Warburg mailed his contribution, Chick felt confident enough to write to John Selby of the Associated Press, answering his persistent inquiries about rumors of a production of the opera in Hartford: "I think that we shall most definitely produce 'Four Saints in Three Acts' early in February. . . . I am so sorry that there has been so much delay, but after the ballet fiasco I did not want to announce anything until I was reasonably certain of it."[34]

Chick gave the news to the Hartford press at the same time. The "World Premiere" was announced for February 8, with an "Honorary Dress Rehearsal" for invited, but paying, guests to be given on the seventh, the day after the opening of the building and the Picasso show.

As usual, the prospect of another Austin extravaganza was hailed by both local papers. By now, the hometown art critics saw Chick as an emissary from the sophisticated worlds of New York and Europe—a peacock among the insurance capital's penguins—and they rarely missed an opportunity to boost his projects. Chick fed them his own brand of hyperbole about *Four Saints*, and they produced big spreads with pictures of Stein and Thomson. Writing in the *Courant*, T. H. Parker relayed Chick's assertion that all those involved in the production were leading figures in the art world. The unknown John Houseman, for instance, became "the noted English playwright," and Florine Stettheimer, whose only one-woman show had been in 1916, was billed as "one of the most brilliant of contemporary artists." Parker tried enumerating the scenes in the opera—which included a picnic, a maypole dance, and Saint Theresa painting Easter eggs while being photographed—but admitted that describing the action was impossible. He emphasized the fantasy of the work, but lest God-fearing Hartfordians become uneasy, assured his readers that *Four Saints* was "completely devout in spirit and religious in mood."[35]

In the *Hartford Times*, Chick's intrepid admirer Marian Murray declared that, by presenting the opera, Hartford would "add another cubit to its intellectual height." She offered an open-minded discussion of Miss Stein's work, with quotations from the recent best-selling *Autobiography of Alice B. Toklas* and from the libretto of the opera. Among the lines Mrs. Murray invited the public to ponder was the later-famous "Pigeons on the grass alas." She considered a few of Miss Stein's brain-twisting questions: "How many saints can remember a house which was built before they can remember," along with "Supposing she said that he had chosen all the miseries that he had observed in fifty of his years what had that to do with hats." Such a query, Murray candidly admitted, "has the effect of making you feel utterly mad."[36]

Having primed his local audience by a good splash in the press, Chick wrote to the Friends and Enemies, describing the opening of the building, the Picasso exhibition, and the opera, and asking for contributions to help support rehearsals.[37] In return, he promised choice seats at the honorary dress rehearsal and free admission to future concerts that season. Later in December, he sent out a blanket appeal—to New York art patrons, dealers, and museum professionals, enticing them with the chance to buy tickets before they went on public sale.

Chick also wrote to everyone of importance in his personal life, from childhood through Harvard—his parents (now living at separate Boston addresses); his Etnier relatives; Forbes and Sachs and their families; his other Harvard art professors; George Reisner and his family (this invitation was sent to the Harvard Camp at Giza); and even Harold Parsons, who had expressed so little faith in Chick's abilities.

Meanwhile, with Nathan Zatkin working overtime on publicity in New York, the novelty of a Gertrude Stein opera gave the national press an irresistible opportunity. From Ottumwa, Iowa, Manitowoc, Wisconsin, and Owatonna, Minnesota, to Great Falls, Montana, *Four Saints* became a welcome diversion in a Depression-weary world. "Come All, Ye Madcaps, Here's Gertrude Stein," headlined the *Philadelphia Record,* calling the opera "a fledgling, hatched under the Left Wing of the international modernist colony of Paris and now come home to roost."[38]

Gertrude Stein herself, as the only famous person connected with the production, took center stage. The *Boston Globe* called her "the high priestess of the cult of unintelligibility" and suggested that the opera be called "Four Saints and Two Ultra-Modernists."[39] In other cities, she was described as the "High Priestess in the temple of all the modern arts,"[40] "the Buddha of American revisionist literature,"[41] and "the Mahatma Gandhi of the Surrealists of letters."[42]

On January 20, Miss Stein consented to a rare interview with a journalist from the *Brooklyn Eagle,* which had an office in Paris. Responding to the charge that her libretto was not comprehensible, she answered testily: "Any one can understand if they do not try to understand. . . . We must get away from the highbrow complex. Outside of the first phrase, what do the words of the 'Star-Spangled Banner' mean? What do they mean!"[43]

Second only to Gertrude Stein as a favorite subject for the press was the all-black cast. *Four Saints* often appeared in headlines as a "Negro Opera" and was compared with the recent Broadway hit *Green Pastures.* In explaining his casting to reporters, much as he sincerely and emphatically praised the black singers, Thomson could not escape the prejudice ingrained in even the most enlightened of his contemporaries. Like most white intellectuals who were captivated by the Harlem Renaissance, he celebrated what were widely accepted as the "primitive" qualities of the Negro. He told the *New York World-Telegram* that

I have never heard a white singer with the perfect diction and sense of rhythm of a Negro.

Negroes objectify themselves very easily, and I think the explanation is all part of the "threshold of consciousness idea." Also they sing with more style, and can put themselves into the religious or fanciful moods of "Four Saints in Three Acts" a thousand times better than white singers.

The opera was written for white singers, but negroes will do it better, for when you're saying something that doesn't seem to mean anything much, you must say it with a great deal of authority. . . .

They're satisfied with the pure beauty of the words and the music, even though the words tell no story.[44]

Thomson also told the press, as he had told Gertrude Stein the previous year, that if the idea of blacks depicting saints proved too offensive to the public, he would have them perform in white face.[45] ("Paint 'Em White, Make 'Em Right!" ran a headline in the *Hartford Times*.[46]) As late as mid-January, Houseman told a reporter that "the cast itself, to give a certain uniformity, may be masked with white, silver or gold face paint."[47] Miss Stein was reportedly taken aback at the prospect of black singers, fearing that they would impart sexual overtones to her text.[48] And Florine Stettheimer fretted that their varied skin tones would disrupt her color scheme.[49] In spite of the racism that underlay these concerns, *Four Saints* was to be a watershed in the liberation of black performers from the traditional stereotypes they had been portraying.

The first weeks of 1934 did not bring in as many contributions as Chick had hoped. Except for Paul Cooley's banker father, who matched a $500 gift from Eddie Warburg, and the always strategically solvent Lord Duveen, who gave the Friends and Enemies $250, most of the wealthier prospects sent small contributions or none at all, reflecting the strain the Depression had placed on their resources. Mrs. John D. Rockefeller, Jr., who ordered tickets, could not bring herself to send the $25 that would have made her a patron, having "budgeted my resources very carefully this year."[50]

To help cover the production costs, which were rising to $12,000, ticket prices were set as high as $7.50 for the premiere—this when a good seat at a Broadway show went for less than $5.00. Paul Cooley apologized about the prices to one correspondent,[51] and had to remind Houseman that no one, no matter how prominent, should be promised free tickets: "Please tell Virgil that Chick says he absolutely cannot give tickets away. Chick and I and everyone else are buying our own. . . . Virgil told the Stettheimers they could have free ones. I think they can afford two tickets as well as the rest of us."[52]

Meanwhile, R. R. Burt of *The Mouthpiece Magazine,* a publication directed to the local African-American community, appealed to Chick to put on a special performance of *Four Saints* at a reduced ticket price of $1.50: "You will do a great honor to the colored population," he wrote.[53] A Friday afternoon performance was added at a lower rate for "students."

The level of tension at the museum rose precipitously on January 22 when Paul Rosenberg cabled Austin that Picasso had withdrawn his three promised loans. At the same time, news of violent political unrest in Paris brought fears that none of the French pictures could be moved safely out of the city. Chick knew that his exhibition would be decimated without them—and the catalogue was already at the printer. But Rosenberg solved the first problem by simply buying the paintings Picasso was going to lend—including the magnificent *Girl Before a Mirror*—and managed to get all the pictures loaded onto the *Ile de France* without incident. He sailed with them, landing in New York on the thirtieth, just eight days before the opening.

When the full complement of 137 Picassos had at last arrived at the museum—the seventy-seven oils were supplemented with sixty drawings, watercolors, gouaches, and prints—a desperate rush was on to get them up on the walls. A call for help went out to nearby museum directors.[54] Jere Abbott came from Northampton, Josiah Marvel from Springfield, and Winslow Ames from New London. Working until midnight right up to the opening, fortified by cigarettes and Scotch whiskey and humor, they entered into the heady, party-time atmosphere that Chick always created when he was approaching a deadline. After grouping the less figurative works by the painter in one gallery at the end of the top floor, he told Ames in a German accent that the room was his "Abstractus Kabinett."[55] When a crate of terra-cottas by Picasso proved to contain nothing but broken shards, Chick exclaimed gaily, "We've got *pots cassés de Picasso!*"[56]

At the same moment the Picassos were going up on the third floor, Russell Hitchcock supervised the placement of the Wallace Nutting Collection of seventeenth-century Pilgrim furniture on the second. Before Chick came to Hartford it had been installed in crowded approximations of period rooms in the basement of the Morgan Memorial. Now he and Hitchcock had decided to pull the objects out of their traditional context and force people to view them as sculpture rather than as historical artifacts. Spinning wheels were lined up along the white wall of the long gallery that looked out over the court. Hadley chests, tables, cradles, and kitchen utensils were set out on platforms in adjacent galleries. For Chick, part of the fun was knowing that the members of Hartford's venerable colonial societies, seeing these objects exposed in stark Bauhaus spaces, would have an experience bordering on the surreal.

Hitchcock also put together a small show of museum architecture from 1770 to 1850, with photographs and plans. This was one more way that he and Chick tried to remind the skeptics, as Hitchcock wrote in the exhibition catalogue, that the best museum architecture must provide distinctive settings entirely in the best contemporary style.[57]

In his compulsion to make the Avery opening as magnificent as possible,

Chick added even more work to an already staggering agenda. ("He was positively manic," Hitchcock remembered.[58]) He decided that the paintings collection he had been building since 1927 was not large enough to fill his new, richly decorated galleries or to stand up to the overwhelming impact of the Picasso installation. He therefore arranged for yet another loan exhibition of forty-nine paintings and sculptures, borrowed from Rosenberg, New York dealers, and private collectors, to run concurrently with the Picasso show. This bonus, ranging from the fourteenth century to the present, included a spectacular array of artists associated with France—Fragonard, Géricault, Delacroix, Ingres, Corot, Courbet, Cézanne, Gauguin, Degas, Toulouse-Lautrec, Renoir, van Gogh. Chick also borrowed seven modern sculptures for the court—works by Gauguin, Jacob Epstein, Gaston Lachaise, Wilhelm Lehmbruck, and Brancusi (his exquisite *Blond Negress* in polished brass, loaned by Philip Goodwin).

As the galleries were being readied, and as Chick's tiny staff coped with changing dates and seats for *Four Saints* ticket holders and reserving hotel rooms for out-of-towners, workmen still swarmed through the museum. During that last week they dealt with everything from installing telephone cables for the radio broadcast of the opera to adding a battery of extra spotlights in the theater, staining and waxing the platforms for the Nutting Collection, and replacing a faulty urinal on the first floor. On Saturday, February 3, the workmen were honored at a reception in the new building. Charles Goodwin thanked them, a local Catholic priest blessed them, and then Chick made an appearance in full costume as the Great Osram. After feats of magic, Chick screened two comic movies and provided a light meal.[59]

Meanwhile, the opera's cellophane sets and the two hundred lavish costumes designed by Miss Stettheimer had been arriving from New York piecemeal throughout January—but it was not until Sunday evening, three days before the honorary dress rehearsal, that John Houseman, Frederick Ashton, and the cast stepped out of a bus from New York. (Thomson had arrived a few days earlier.[60]) Greeted by a delegation from the Negro Chamber of Commerce, they posed for newspaper photographers and proceeded to the Hotel Avon on Asylum Street or to private homes which the city's black community provided for them.

Chick drove Thomson and Houseman to his house for dinner that night. Over brandy in the living room he told them, with a disarming smile ("He was the great charm boy of all time," said Houseman), that the Friends and Enemies had run out of money.[61] Although ticket sales were going well and the first three performances were nearly sold out, there would be very little cash on hand until after many of the out-of-towners arrived for the first performance. When Houseman replied that the performers and technicians had to be paid, Chick promised to see what he could do.[62]

On Monday morning, Alexander Smallens and the orchestra arrived, and a sixteen-hour rehearsal began. Although Smallens had conducted vocal run-throughs in New York, this was to be the first time the cast had sung with anything but a piano. As the rehearsal began, Thomson discovered to his horror and embarrassment that the orchestral parts had been badly copied when he and Maurice Grosser had worked on the score the previous summer. He had the grim task of correcting every mistake while the singers and musicians waited for hours, as the overtime expenses rose.[63]

At one-thirty in the morning, when the first rehearsal was finally over, Houseman gathered the cast together in Avery Court and said simply, "Well, look, we can't pay you this week. Sorry. We *will* pay you as soon as the tickets are sold, as soon as the money comes in, but you've got to have faith in us."[64] The cast, who had next to no money themselves, accepted the situation quietly.[65] They had little choice, of course, but they also knew that they were part of an artistic happening. As singer Thomas Anderson, who played Saint Giuseppe, remembered, "Everyone felt, 'We have something to bring. Don't know what it is'—no one saw way down the road—'but this is something.' As the old people would say, 'It's a *somethin'.*' "[66]

Later that morning, realizing that any demands for payment during the next thirty-six hours could jeopardize the premiere of the opera, Chick held an emergency meeting of the "incorporators and trustees" of the Friends and Enemies (consisting of himself, Helen, and his former secretary Peggy Parsons). After noting a $300 deficit in their treasury, they voted to authorize loans of $500 each from Paul Cooley and Jim Soby at 5 percent interest.[67]

During the day, the tension in the theater became extreme. After a disagreement with Freddie Ashton about the placement of the singers, Smallens became verbally abusive. Ashton ran for an exit in tears, calling out: "I have worked with Sir Thomas Beecham! A genius! And he never spoke to me as you have!" The lighting was inadequate and more equipment had to be trucked in from New York. Rehearsals for the cast and crew were so long and exhausting that Chick's local technical assistant, a former escape artist named Clevedore whom Chick used in his magic shows, was heard up in the fly gallery banging his head against the concrete wall to keep himself awake. Florine Stettheimer politely insisted that Abe Feder bathe the stage during the first act in nothing but pure white light, that the entire cast must use the same shade of medium-brown makeup so that their varied skin tone would not distract the audience from her color scheme, and—when she realized that the hands of the singers and dancers were bare—that a rush order of white gloves be sent from New York in time for the first performance.[68]

As Chick's friends in the art world awaited the Hartford events, they were only too aware of the superhuman effort he was making. Lincoln Kirstein could not or would not attend the opening, but had dispatched a letter of unabashed admiration: "I know next week will make you very happy indeed because you will open the most distinguished museum in the world—whose distinction comes entirely from the concentration of all your energies into courage and great taste." Apologizing for not being able to make good on a pledge of $100 toward the opera ("I've been absolutely broke since November"), he enclosed two drawings of nude figures by the sculptor Gaston Lachaise as a gift to the Atheneum in honor of the new building—"the only things I own which I think are fine enough to go into your museum." He asked Chick to "please believe me, in spite of mistrust and circumstance, your friend and admirer."[69] Alfred Barr wrote that "although I cannot give you much financial support, I would tell you again how much I admire your extraordinary initiative and courage in putting on this opera and this Picasso exhibition. Either one would be enough for any ordinary mortal museum director."[70]

At eight o'clock on Tuesday evening, February 6, 1934, with Chick apparently functioning on adrenaline alone, and with a brief suspension of the chaotic *Four Saints* rehearsals, the Avery Memorial and the exhibition, *Pablo Picasso*, opened to more than a thousand museum members, guests, public officials, and writers from the local and national press. Dressed in evening clothes, they entered the court and found themselves standing in a white, purely abstract space. Hovering horizontal planes rose three stories to a glass skylight overlaid with perfect squares. For nearly everyone, this was their first experience of the International Style. The forward-looking found it exhilarating. "Space, air, light, and color give an uplift to the spirits," declared the critic from *Art News*, which featured the Avery on the first page of its next issue. "Here is no vault shrouding the treasures of the past; nor yet a palace whose arcades of columns and flights of steps induce the feeling that the King may wake up and suddenly surprise you invading his sacred territory. At once you feel that this building stands for the freedom of the XXth century. It seems, indeed, to cast a spell of enthusiasm which it is hard to temper."[71] Punctuating and heightening the modernity of the space was the Francavilla Venus, with her clinging nymph and satyr and the spouting dolphins.

Guests flowed into side galleries and into Chick's gleaming futuristic office, where the newly purchased Miró was on view for the first time. They looked at the new library, at prints and drawings, at Samuel Avery's collection of silver, glass, brasses, and Oriental objects. They climbed the curved marble staircase a few steps beyond the court to the second floor to see the Nutting furniture, then continued to the top floor, where Chick had assembled the European pictures. Seen against the sumptuous fabrics, said the *Art News* critic, every painting looked like a masterpiece: "If I were purchasing a work of art from him, I should insist on seeing it first in some less glamorous surroundings.

Avery Court with Venus with Satyr and Nymph *of 1600*
by Pietro Francavilla, Wadsworth Atheneum, during the
Picasso exhibition, February 1934

Should Mr. Austin be disposed to take offence at this suggestion, I would ask
him whether he has ever heard the adjective 'glamorous' used in connection
with any museum other than his!"[72]

Moving out onto the balconies that surrounded the court, visitors came to
the Picassos. To eyes still unaccustomed to the explosions of modernism, the
Spaniard's forceful lines and audacious colors, presented against the white
walls, seemed to vibrate. Viewers could experience Picasso's entire career,
from an impressionistic portrait of a mother and child in 1895, painted when he
was in his teens, to three brazenly adventurous canvases from 1932.

Many of these works became icons of Picasso's genius. There was the
painfully bright *Au Moulin Rouge* of 1901—a jaded prostitute stares at the

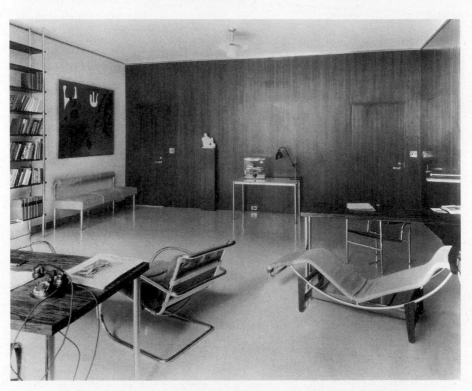

Director's office, Avery Memorial, Wadsworth Atheneum, 1934,
showing the newly acquired Joan Miró's Composition *and furniture by Marcel Breuer*
and Le Corbusier. Only the telephone shows its age.

viewer while cancan girls dance in the background—painted in thickly applied white, red, orange, and yellow, a work that looked back to Toulouse-Lautrec and van Gogh and forward to the Fauves. From the "blue period" came *The Old Guitarist* of 1903, the famous study of misery reduced to angles, loaned by the Art Institute of Chicago. From the "rose period" were such pictures as *The Girl with a Fan* of 1905—a figure stands in profile in the style of an Egyptian wall drawing; the tender *Harlequin's Family* of the same year; *La Toilette*, also from 1905, a work of delicate beauty, almost suggested rather than painted, in terracottas and blues, in which a nude woman gathers her hair over her head while her maid holds a mirror. Then there were such anomalies as the cleanly drawn *Sleeping Peasants* of 1919, in which a young man and woman, both round, fleshy, and partially undressed, sprawl on the ground, exhausted after a tumble in the hay.

There were the cubist pictures—from the *Seated Woman* of 1909 to *Vive La France* of 1914, *The Italian Woman* of 1917, and the culmination of synthetic Cubism, the *Three Musicians* (*Les Trois Masques*, as it was called in the cata-

America's first comprehensive Picasso exhibition, Avery Memorial,
Wadsworth Atheneum, February 1934

logue) of 1921. This large canvas from Rosenberg's collection—with its three
figures built up of multicolored planes that gave the illusion of movement and
volume, by turns comic, ominous, and festive—dominated the long side
gallery, confusing or enraging or fascinating the viewers. (Many years later, it
became one of the glories of the Museum of Modern Art. Another, equally
famous, version of the picture went from Gallatin's collection to the Philadelphia Museum of Art.) There were the neo-classic works, such as *La Légende de
la source* of 1921 and the Atheneum's own *Bather* (or *Femme nue*) of 1922, in
which Picasso turned his subjects into massive living sculptures, figures of
unmovable serenity. And as the artist moved forward in 1924, there was the
surprisingly accessible *The Red Table Cloth*, with its elegant drawing and
warm, enveloping colors. From 1927 was the *Seated Woman*, arresting in its
multiple profiles and bright red forms, from the Sobys' collection, which they
had lent the previous summer to the *Century of Progress* exposition in Chicago.
Perhaps most disturbing to those who allowed their imaginations to wander was
a 1929 surrealist *Composition* from Rosenberg, consisting of an organic form
with orifices and phallic shapes. For a grand climax there was one of Picasso's

greatest creations, *The Girl Before a Mirror*, painted in 1932 and never before seen in America. Alfred Barr compared this picture to Gothic stained glass with its sections of bright colors—red and acid green, yellow, blue, hot pink, lavender, and purple—its fecund circles and curves painted against a diamond pattern of latticework.

The show may have been hastily assembled, and it may have been uneven in its presentation of Picasso's periods, particularly as there were relatively few examples of the early cubist work before the First World War. It may have lacked the greater depth that loans from the collections of Gertrude Stein and Paul Guillaume would have given it. But it was an extraordinary achievement that gave viewers something never previously seen in America. Chick was offering the public the most stunning art history lesson of his career: the pictures were not only manifestations of Picasso's volcanic inner life and his insights into the human condition; they contained within them the evolution of twentieth-century art itself.

Yet to most of the insurance executives and the grande dames of Hartford society, the exhibition was unsettling in the extreme. They understood that Picasso was the world's most famous modern artist and that his art reflected, in some perverse way, the modern era. They saw that he could draw with an accuracy worthy of Ingres when he chose. A few of the sad blue figures were affecting, and the gentle Harlequins were charming. But so many of the pictures in the gallery, they felt, were simply distorted, garish, vulgar, and incomprehensible. Picasso was either laughing at a gullible public or he was a lunatic, and if his art represented the twentieth century, then something was seriously wrong, and Chick Austin and his ilk should not be encouraged. Though the leaders of Hartford society maintained a veneer of good manners, many were outraged. One prominent matron asked Helen Austin at a preview earlier in the day if she would like having Picasso's pictures in her own home. Helen said that she most definitely would, whereupon the woman departed with the words, "Every one to his taste!" At the opening, the same woman greeted Helen in the official receiving line with a double-edged complement: "Dear, loyal little woman!"[73] Another woman gestured to a fire hose curled up behind a sleek glass case in a hallway wall and remarked disgustedly: "And they call that art!"[74]

Sympathetic viewers, however, whether art critics or young people eager to embrace the visions of their own time, were uplifted. Henry McBride, *The New York Sun*'s perennial champion of innovation, announced that the show was "the most important event of its kind anywhere in the world."[75] *Art News* told its readers that the exhibition was "not to be missed at any cost" and that the American setting made it easier to assess Picasso's achievement than either of the European shows had allowed.[76] Edward Forbes's daughter, Rosamond, pouring out her feelings in her diary, captured the impact of the exhibition on the younger

The Picasso exhibition, showing The Girl Before the Mirror *from Paul Rosenberg and*
Seated Woman *from the Soby collection*

generation: "the most magnificent—thrilling—inspiring—upsetting show of
Picasso! . . . We looked + looked till we were exhausted."[77] Nathaniel Salton-
stall, an architect and a trustee of the Museum of Fine Arts in Boston who
accompanied Agnes Mongan to the opening events, was so inspired that he conceived of the Boston Museum of Modern Art (later the Institute of Contemporary
Art) on the ride home.[78]

At nine-thirty that night there was a brief dedication ceremony, though
many in the enormous crowd continued to wander through the galleries, and the
speeches were difficult to hear over the din. From a second-floor balcony overlooking the court, Charles Goodwin introduced each of the speakers—Governor
Wilbur Cross, the mayor of Hartford, Robert O'Connor (appearing for the absent
Benjamin Wistar Morris), and Edward Forbes. Forbes credited Chick with the
conception of the building, which he called one of the finest museums in
the world. Then Goodwin urged Chick to speak, and the crowd below him
applauded loudly in anticipation of his remarks. But they were not delivered.
The months of struggling to fulfill his vision of this new house of art, a monument to his imagination and taste—a vision now so triumphantly realized—had

finally overwhelmed him. As the *Hartford Courant* put it, "Mr. Austin was unable to comply due to indisposition resulting from the great strain from pressure of work on the museum during recent weeks."[79] In fact, for the first and only time in his life, words would not come—only tears.

On the morning of February 7, those recovering from the parties after the opening of the Picasso show awoke to arctic weather. The mercury stood at four degrees at eight a.m. and, after rising to twenty-nine in the afternoon, would plummet to fifteen below zero overnight. Prominent guests from New York, Boston, and overseas were entertained at a lavish luncheon at the Prospect Avenue manse of the Charles Cooleys. There, Paul Rosenberg turned to Henry McBride and announced: "At last there is one genuinely modern museum in the world."[80]

The arbiters of taste in art, music, and literature—those whom the popular press called "the streamlined intelligentsia"—continued to arrive in Hartford during the day, by every possible conveyance. The previous day, some of Chick's friends had been frankly skeptical that he could pull off the exhibition and the opera. In the lavatory of the Heublein Hotel, as they changed into evening clothes after arriving by train from New York, Julien Levy overheard Francis Henry Taylor comment about the "unfeasibility of Chick."[81] But they had all come to see what would happen.

As the audience arrived from dinner parties hosted by the Austins and the museum's trustees and friends, John Houseman found himself in a state of panic brought on by the chaotic rehearsals. He went out into the icy clear night and was dumbfounded by the sight of a black object, shaped like a teardrop, that looked as if it had come from outer space. It pulled up to the theater door, and out stepped a small man, two beautiful young women, and their escorts. The vehicle was in fact the second version of the famous Dymaxion Car, recently invented by Buckminster Fuller, who had driven it to Hartford from New York.[82] His passengers were actress and playwright Clare Boothe (soon to be Luce), socialite Dorothy Hale, *New Yorker* cover artist Constantin Alajalov, and the young Japanese-American sculptor Isamu Noguchi.

The audience went through the Picasso show and made their way down into the theater lobby, its curving polished walls and bright brass railings suggesting more an elegant salon in a brand-new luxury liner than the interior of an art museum. Politely jostling one another were Alfred and Marga Barr, Philip Johnson, Russell Hitchcock, Maurice Grosser, the Edward Forbeses, the Paul Sachses, Agnes and Betty Mongan ("the Mongan sisters, A. and B.," as they were known), Julien and Joella Levy, Mr. and Mrs. John D. Rockefeller, Jr., Mrs. W. Murray Crane, the three Stettheimer sisters, Kirk and Constance Askew, Agnes Rindge, the James Sobys, Paul Rosenberg, New York columnists Henry McBride and Lucius Beebe, Carl Van Vechten and his wife, Fania Marinoff, Muriel Draper, Société Anonyme founder Katherine Dreier, novelist Eleanor Shaler, art dealer Sidney Janowitz, and sculptor Alexander Calder and his wife, Louisa. The Calders had arrived in a open car from their home in Roxbury, Connecticut, wearing mountainous layers to protect them from the weather. Sandy Calder's attire consisted of a red lumberman's shirt, a tweed coat, and dusty boots.

Just before nine o'clock, as everyone finally settled into the deep-blue velour seats of the Avery Theater, there was a sharp roll of timpani and the lilting whine of an accordion, and Florine Stettheimer's bright red inner curtains parted on a tableau of black singers, dressed in silks, satins, gold and silver lamé, motionless in a cellophane world—all in shades of pink, white, green, and blue. Two huge orange and yellow cloth lions sat under cellophane trees with dark orange velvet trunks and fronds made of ostrich plumes. The cyclorama added a luminous blue to the blue-green cellophane sheets draped in swags across the back of the stage. The Gothic arch representing the entrance to the cathedral at Avila was made of crumpled balls of white cellophane. Under the white lights Stettheimer had insisted upon, the scene was dazzling.

The stage looked like an enchanting baroque candy box. The dignified bearing of the black singers gave the opera a whimsical gravity as they began the opening chorus: "To know to know to know her well four saints prepare for saints it makes it well fish it makes it well well fish four saints prepare for saints." Thomson's robust and tuneful music, which he later described as a "total recall of my Southern Baptist childhood in Missouri," won the plaudits of most critics.[83] *The New Yorker* later asserted that the composer "has something like genius for setting words so that they 'come out,'" adding that Thomson "apparently can set to attractive music a theatre program, from the fire notice to the liquid-soap credits."[84]

Miss Stein's text, immediately enshrined in the popular imagination with the line "Pigeons on the grass alas," did not fare as well. It was found to be a kind of cubist romp through the English language—playful, irreverent, and tender, but mystifying. But whatever its underlying meanings, it *worked* as theater.

By the first intermission, Chick's friends knew that he and Thomson and Houseman had pulled off a gigantic success. Lucius Beebe, between sips from a pocket flask, noted that young aesthetes (Julien Levy and Kirk Askew) wept for beauty, telling each other that they "didn't know that anything so beautiful could be done in America."[85]

At the end of Act IV, after the saints pointed to the audience and shouted, "Which is a fact," the curtain closed and half an hour of cheering erupted. Russell Hitchcock tore open his collar and dress shirt and bashed his top hat, screaming "Bravo! Bravo!" and "Bis! Bis!" Chick was propelled onto the stage

The audience settles down in the Avery Theater for the first performance of
Four Saints in Three Acts, *Hartford, February 7, 1934. At left, Chick Austin,
on the aisle in the fifth row, looks over his shoulder. Next to him are Helen Austin,
Kirk and Constance Askew, John McAndrew, Agnes Rindge, and Julien and
Joella Levy.* Hartford Courant, *February 8, 1934*

by his delirious friends. From Hartford's Heublein Hotel that night, Carl Van
Vechten wrote to Gertrude Stein that he had not witnessed such excitement
since the Paris premiere of Stravinsky's *Sacre du printemps* in 1913: "The difference was that they were pleasurably excited."[86] Thomson thought that his
opera's notoriety could only be compared with the showing of Marcel
Duchamp's cubist icon, *Nude Descending a Staircase,* at the New York Armory
Show.[87] To a local reporter, Chick said the opera was "beautiful beyond my
wildest hope."[88] He told Virgil that it was "an opera about a group of people
who loved one another very much."[89]

A riotous celebration followed at Chick and Helen's house. Champagne
and other libations were copiously consumed, precipitating an incident that
was recorded in the memoirs of both Julien Levy and Alexander Calder. Levy
recalled attempting to congratulate Virgil Thomson on the opera when the suddenly self-conscious composer said, "Oh dear, Julien, didn't you notice that the

Four Saints in Three Acts, *Hartford, 1934*

trumpets came in a beat late at the beginning of the second act?" With that, Levy replied, "Oh Virgil, don't split hairs!" and playfully poked Thomson, who fell backward, splintering a gilded eighteenth-century chair. Calder then wrapped his arms around Levy, asked him if he was drunk, picked him up, and deposited him on an upstairs bed. Levy returned to the party a few minutes later. He concluded that he and Calder had been "overly considerate, each of the other."[90] According to Calder, an intoxicated Julien Levy was blocking the stairs to Chick's basement bar and, at Louisa Calder's suggestion, he and Jim Soby put Levy to bed. "He came down shortly after," wrote Calder, "very indignant that we should have called attention to his inebriety, and remained in that state of indignation for about twenty years."[91]

Tributes poured into Chick's office. Katherine Dreier, who met Chick for the first time after the lights had gone down in the theater, wrote that the occasion had "something of the flavor of the early days of the Société Anonyme when Duchamp, Man Ray and I had such fun in just what we were doing."[92] From the Museum of Modern Art the next day, Philip Johnson told Chick that the Atheneum's new architecture, the exhibition, and the galleries "made the Museum here look very drab and dull. I know what trouble and anguish it must have been for you to get the kind of a place you wanted, but the success of it was surely worth it."[93] Count Raoul de Roussy de Sales, whose Beekman Place apartment in New York was known as the unofficial French embassy, wrote Chick about what he perceived as a "Hartford movement" and told him that his work in bringing all the arts together was "one of the rare efforts of its kind, either in this country or elsewhere."[94] Years later, remembering *Four Saints*, Pierre Matisse said, "Chick was the only one who could shake us out of the gloom of the Depression."[95]

The next night, February 8, was the official world premiere. Many of Chick's friends from New York saw the show a second time. And more out-of-towners came to Hartford. But that evening, the city embodied the difference between highbrow and popular entertainment in America. At six o'clock, a caravan of second-string movie stars who had been touring the East to promote the movie musical *Moulin Rouge*, starring Constance Bennett and Franchot Tone, drove into Hartford with a police escort. Among the entertainers were Anna Q. Nilsson, Ben Turpin, and Antonio Moreno, along with a dozen lithesome "chorines" from the picture, and such was the allure of live Hollywood stars that no fewer than six thousand screaming fans, mostly women, turned out in the zero-degree weather to see them arrive at Poli's Capitol Theater, directly across Main Street from the Atheneum. Despite the presence of twenty-five policemen, pandemonium broke out, glass poster cases in the theater lobby were smashed, and buttons and badges were torn off the officers' uniforms. By the time the sophisticates pulled up to the Avery door for the eight-thirty performance, the streets were relatively calm, and they could experience a more rarefied form of entertainment.

After six performances in Hartford, *Four Saints in Three Acts* went on to New York, first to the Forty-fourth Street Theatre for a month, then to the Empire for two more weeks.[96] This was the longest run of any American opera on Broadway before *Porgy and Bess*. (The Gershwin masterpiece appeared the next year, also with the Eva Jessye Choir and Alexander Smallens conducting.) The novelty of the opera attracted the fashionable, the cosmopolitan, and the merely curious. Even Arturo Toscanini was seen applauding enthusiastically at one performance. The opera became the most publicized cultural event of the year, inspiring one of Al Hirschfeld's early drawings in the *New York Herald Tribune*,[97] as well as a cartoon by Barbara Shermund in *The New Yorker*. "This picture ought to give you a pretty foggy idea of what Gertrude Stein and Virgil Thomson have been up to," ran *The New Yorker* caption. "The dark lady on the cellophane throne is St. Theresa I, who isn't interested in the idea of electrocuting fifty thousand Chinamen by pushing a button. The two large heads in the foreground belong to St. Ignatius and St. Theresa II. The people leaning against the trees are Compere and Commere, who explain things with lucy-lucidity as you go along. St. Settlement and St. Plan, among others, are mixed up in that bunch in the back. Clear is?"[98]

The Avery family, whose name was carved on the outside of the new building, expressed little amusement at the whole enterprise. "Gertrude Stein had not won our admiration completely, in spite of twelve pigeons on the grass, alas," said Samuel Avery's niece, Amy Welcher, half a century after the opening. Nor did she think that the modern interior of the Avery Memorial was at all what her uncle had in mind. "Chick Austin was very, very busy with people who spoke his language," she observed. "We knew very little about the plans that were being made for the Avery Court. . . . If that's what they wanted, that's all right, they got it." She added pointedly that the director of the museum liked having "lots of cocktail parties and things—and *we weren't cocktail people.*"[99]

But for those with any interest in learning about the art of the present, Chick never tired of sharing his knowledge and enthusiasm. Often he would walk through the galleries, strike up conversations with visitors, and ask them how they liked his shows. One afternoon he ran into a young woman from Hartford's "Little Italy," who came often to his programs and exhibitions. She told him that she simply did not understand most of Picasso's paintings. At that, Chick guided her through the entire show, talking nonstop, making sweeping gestures at the works as he moved along. "Art precedes civilization," he told her, explaining that Picasso's works were not only great studies in line, color, composition, and human psychology, but also visions of the future—the stresses and fragmentations and excitements of twentieth-century life. Like so many visitors who met Chick Austin, she marveled at the way he spoke to her, as if she were an important person. "He didn't have a class distinction. There was so much of that in Connecticut when I grew up—being the child of immigrants, you know. But it didn't seem to touch him. He would associate with anybody or anything. He had that great elegance that he was born with, his manner, and of course his looks. But he was so down-to-earth, he never spoke down to anybody—never."[100]

The artistic aspirations Chick had brought to fruition in February 1934 put the museum on the national map for weeks afterward. For the first time in its history, the Wadsworth Atheneum was the subject of articles in *Time* and *Newsweek*, which both published photographs of *Four Saints*.[101] And Francis Henry Taylor, throwing off his earlier skepticism about Chick's "unfeasibility" declared in print that Chick and his collaborators "have not only scored a bull's eye on every count, but have indicated the paths that the coming generation must inevitably follow."[102]

Over twenty thousand people came to see the Picasso show during its short four-week run. Though Chick had privately wished for even more visitors, such an attendance figure for an exhibition of modern art in Hartford in the 1930s was extraordinary.[103]

After the show closed, Paul Rosenberg, who, more than anyone else, had helped make Chick's vision come true, wrote formally from New York: "The

Picasso show is also a 'tour de force,' & gives a much better impression of his genius than the one in Paris. I regret that we have not at the head of our Museum a man like you, who is the perfect type of a director of a great Museum."[104] Hearing of the high attendance, he wrote again, perhaps with a dealer's flattering hyperbole, but also with genuine admiration: "I think it is a just reward to your efforts, & of your daring to have presented such fine manifestations. . . . I am sailing very soon back to my country, where I shall tell to the curators of our Museums, what can be done, with courage and faith."[105]

The cost of America's first Picasso retrospective, including insurance, freight, travel expenses, the catalogue, advertising, invitations, and postage, was $2,665.[106]

With what seemed to be his own personal art institution, Chick was, as Alfred Barr had suggested before the opening, no longer an "ordinary mortal museum director." He was an impresario of the arts.

CHAPTER TWELVE

"Nobody's Business"

Another Athens shall arise,
And to remoter time
Bequeath, like sunset to the skies,
The splendour of its prime.

—Percy Bysshe Shelley,
"Hellas"

"You appear to forget, sir, that *Connecticut is not Athens.*"

—Governor Jonathan Trumbull, Sr., to his son,
John Trumbull

After his triumph with *Four Saints,* Chick felt he had license to do exactly as he liked, and what he liked was the theater. Before February was out, the Great Osram had insinuated a magic review, as an entr'acte, into one of the amateur drama productions that quickly found a home in the Avery Theater. And soon he was concocting a magic show with fully constructed sets, elaborate costumes, dramatic lighting, and a team of assistants.

He also announced three "Sunday Cinema Soirees." Each focused on a recent advanced European film, beginning on March 11 with René Clair's *À nous la liberté* of 1931, which Chick advertised with a dash of populism as "The French Film Masterpiece That You Can Understand."[1] This light satire of the Machine Age was followed by Sergei Eisenstein's powerful *Thunder Over Mexico* of 1933, depicting the last day of a brutally oppressed Mexican peasant. A local critic called it "the furthest step yet from the idiocies of corn-fed Hollywood," and the public seemed to appreciate that.[2] The film's two showings were sold out. Third in the series was Jean Cocteau's 1930 *Le Sang d'un poète,* which Chick screened with *Lot in Sodom,* another experimental film by James Sibley Watson, whose *Fall of the House of Usher* had been so popular when he showed it in 1929. *Le Sang*, Cocteau's first attempt at filmmaking, soon became one of the most famous products of the avant-garde cinema. In the poet's dream world, a man struggles through a hallway filled with wind; a child is killed during a snowball fight; a hermaphrodite holds, in its crotch, a sign warning of death. Many in the audience must have agreed with a reviewer who called the film "almost too much to bear," but Chick was carrying out his mission to show the art of the present to his constituents.[3] Both the Eisenstein and Cocteau films had been given their New York premieres only a few months before.

Chick by no means neglected his galleries. In March, just five days after the Picasso show closed, he offered a light counterpoint to modern painting: *Castles in the Air and Houses on the Ground*, an exhibition of the work of Emilio Terry, a French architect and interior designer. It featured over a hundred items—drawings, projects and plans, models and photographs—which suggested that there might be a place for fantasy in modern architecture. Julien Levy had organized it for his gallery in January and had sent it to Agnes Rindge at Vassar, and it was an easy show for Chick to drop into the schedule while he recovered from the Avery opening.

Terry's buildings and architectural caprices included bridges, fountains, follies, and grottoes. Cracked and broken walls were set in ruined classical landscapes like those in Eugene Berman's drawings. Yet they were meant to be built of modern materials—ornamental swags and even palm trees were to be cast in concrete. Terry was Neo-Romanticism's answer to the Bauhaus: instead of Le Corbusier's "machine for living," the house as envisioned by Terry would be a "machine for dreaming." He shared Chick's eclecticism and liked nothing so much as placing a painted and gilded eighteenth-century commode in a stark modern interior. Two years later, Alfred Barr would include Terry in one of the Museum of Modern Art's most influential exhibitions, *Fantastic Art, Dada, and Surrealism.*

The eighteenth century mingled with the Neo-Romantic musically as well as architecturally that month, when Chick produced another event for the Friends and Enemies of Modern Music, in part to give Virgil Thomson some badly needed income. Thomson devised the program, which consisted of Mozart and Handel arias sung by Philip Johnson's sister Theodate, and piano works by Mozart and contemporary French composer Henri Sauguet played by John Kirkpatrick, just beginning his international career. Kirkpatrick also performed the American premiere of Thomson's first piano sonata. Saying he was reviving an eighteenth-century practice, Chick designed and executed three backdrops for the music—a draped baroque doorway, a series of arched walls painted red and set against a dark blue sky, and a large shell, painted pink.

Expanding his theatrical activities, Chick presented his first fully staged magic show, again given to benefit the children's art classes. With the affection local journalists felt for Chick, the *Hartford Times* informed the public that a "stupendous, miraculous, unique and altogether astounding magic show" would be given on April 14, in the Avery Theater, "by that arch-magician and apparent prestidigitator, A. Everett Austin, Jr., who in his more conservative moments is director of the museum."[4]

This time Chick had a troupe of nine costumed assistants, music, sets, and special lighting effects provided by a technician from the Yale Drama School. After treating spectators to sleight-of-hand tricks with cards, coins, pigeons, and rabbits, Chick was tied and shackled and locked into a cabinet while members of the audience circled it to the accompaniment of bells, horns, tambourines, and other noisemakers. The cabinet opened—and it was empty! The last and best part of the evening was the Executioner's Dream, an illusion Chick had just perfected. As the condemned prisoner, he mounted a scaffold and was covered from head to foot with a dark cloth. A rope was placed around his neck. At a signal from the Lord High Executioner, the trap was sprung, and the prisoner dropped to the stage below. The executioner descended from the platform and inspected the body, which was revealed to be nothing but an empty cloth. Then the executioner turned grimly toward the audience. He was Chick himself.

That spring, in the interest of "influencing and guiding" public taste, Chick inaugurated a small changing exhibition of commercial objects of "good" and "bad" design, displayed in the first-floor windows of the Avery building, facing the sidewalk. As he loved to shop, especially for luxury goods, the concept offered him unlimited possibilities. The first show opened on April 19 and featured ultra-modern items from the German jeweler Margraf of Berlin. Against a background of purple herringbone fabric, Chick installed a chrome and glass clock with black hands, a platinum ring set with jade and diamonds, a crystal and emerald pin, a platinum wristwatch with only the number twelve and a dot for the number six visible on the face, and a silver cigarette case with heavily machine-cut horizontal and vertical lines. To emphasize the splendor of these pieces, he set out similar objects of what he considered bad design, clearly labeled so that passersby would have no doubt about the difference.

He claimed that this show was the first of its kind in any museum; in fact, progressive art institutions had already come up with similar displays. As early as 1928, the Newark Museum, under its foresighted director John Cotton Dana, had presented exhibitions such as *Inexpensive Articles of Good Design;* and Philip Johnson's pioneering *Machine Art* had just opened at the Museum of Modern Art in March, with three floors of gallery space filled with American products of good design. But only Chick had the nerve to contrast such items with objects of so-called bad design.

A cloud appeared on the horizon when he chose, for inclusion in his second presentation, a wristwatch manufactured by the Ingraham Company as an example of bad design. He later claimed he had no idea that the company was based in nearby Bristol, Connecticut, and that its vice president, Dudley Ingraham, was the nephew of George Dudley Seymour, one of America's most distinguished collectors of colonial furniture and a trustee of the Atheneum since 1918. Chick's label for the Ingraham watch was relentless: "The excess of unnecessary and badly drawn ornamentation, the unfunctional shape of the dial, the ugly trade name, and the badly designed and not very legible numerals, in addition to the ugly projecting stem, as well as the thick ungainly shape of the whole, can be contrasted to the adjoining example."[5] A five-month correspondence ensued, involving Ingraham, Seymour, the Atheneum's trustees, Chick, and Paul Cooley. Ingraham was full of irate questions: How could the museum criticize a Connecticut company? Why was the manufacturer's name not erased from the watch? What could be wrong with a watch that was extremely popular? And, by the way, how could the museum state in its recent display of lighting fixtures that a German model was superior to an American design?[6]

Chick was conveniently unavailable for weeks while Paul Cooley covered for him. Eventually, Ingraham progressed from railing against the museum's window display to attacking Chick's efforts to promote contemporary art. The Atheneum had plummeted in the public eye, he wrote, because of its promotion of Picasso and its concentration on "so-called modern art." The museum was "no longer an Art Institute but a Propaganda Institute." Instead, it should be showing Connecticut impressionists from the turn of the century.[7]

Board member Robert Huntington finally put the matter to rest by apologizing to Ingraham while defending Austin. His letter perfectly captured the feelings of most trustees about their director—paternal, appreciative of his eye for "old pictures," and unable to see any value in his promotion of contemporary art but willing to indulge him because of the attention it brought the museum:

> With the hopefulness of youth, I think that Mr. Austin started his campaign with the idea that he might do something towards educating the public taste in this way. I suspect that he has received a good many protests, and I notice that there are no exhibitions of the sort being made at present, and I suspect it is another experiment which hasn't got much of anywhere except to rile up certain people.
>
> . . . As far as the modern things that we have bought go, I am not particularly in sympathy with them, and I have made a very earnest attempt, for instance, to appreciate Picasso, Matisse, Derain and others of the modern French school without any particular success. I cannot see, however, that there is anything to be severely criticized in having an exhibition of this sort of thing, which is the vogue at present

among the dealers and the very rich, and I am inclined to believe that it is possible that the opposition that these exhibitions have stirred up has at any rate served to concentrate attention on the Atheneum and make it a live place instead of a dead one, as it used to be.

Huntington suggested that the public criticism of the Picasso show was misleading: "When we have a Picasso exhibition, the whole world is mad, and undue emphasis is put on the modern tendencies of the museum."[8]

Chick reported to a trustee at the end of the affair that he had offered, outrageously, to send Dudley Ingraham the watch he considered superior to the Ingraham model "with my permission for him to copy any of the features."[9]

Early in May, he again presented the ever-expanding Soby collection in an exhibition called *Modern French Paintings, Drawings and Sculpture*, which he kept on view for six months. With forty-two pictures, this was the most complete showing of the collection to date. By now it included Degas, Rousseau, Matisse, Picasso, Gris, Derain, Bonnard, Rouault, Laurencin, Léger, Klee, Roy, as well as the Neo-Romantics—Tchelitchew, Bérard, Tonny, Leonide, and a whole room full of Bermans. Showing the collection regularly was not only Chick's way of keeping the latest artistic manifestations from Paris in the consciousness of his audience, but also of demonstrating that an important collection of modern art could be assembled in a small American city like Hartford. Chick supplemented the show with a Braque and several Dalís borrowed from New York dealers.

The profusion of contemporary art at the Atheneum during the first five months of 1934 played into the hands of a *Hartford Courant* book reviewer named George Brooks Armstead. On May 20, under a banner headline— "Notes On Belated Demise of Modernism Movement In Art / Current Deflation of Picasso, Stein and Vacuous Bohemia"—Armstead reviewed a new monograph, *Modern Art* by Thomas Craven, a prolific art commentator of aggressively conservative taste. Craven's book was a scathing indictment of the School of Paris—and the influence of Harvard and the Fogg Art Museum to boot. Armstead described Picasso and his ilk as "an aberration, something no more permanent than the rise of Rudy Vallee, or the blatancy of jazz."

Modernism was dying, wrote Armstead, but it was far from over. "There still are Picasso exhibits in America; and volatile young men of pretentious claims to authority are lecturing to women in search of diversion, on the hidden meanings and the elusive glories or exotic designs in gaudy colors." He heartily agreed with Craven that Picasso's pictures were "framed rubbish" and that American museums were now "directed by soft little fellows from the Fogg factory who use pictures to titillate mischievous erotic appetites. Some of them support little communities of retainers, trades, esthetes. They cater to tall coats,

*The swanky young modernist:
Chick as drawn by Sam Berman,
c. 1931*

bored women and kept radicals."
During the last few years, "under
strong influences from foreign quarters," the Wadsworth Atheneum
itself had succumbed to the worst of
contemporary culture.[10]

This article was the most blatant assault on Chick ever published by a Hartford paper. Robert
Huntington had defended him
against an irate watch manufacturer
by private letter. Now Chick wanted
the board to defend him publicly.
He got Russell Hitchcock to draft a
letter from the president and the
board of trustees, which condemned Armstead, Craven, and the *Courant*. But
Charles Goodwin declined to involve the board in a public debate.

Winslow Ames, director of the Lyman Allyn Museum, took it on himself to
send a strong and reasoned rejoinder to the *Courant*. Calling the review "a
thinly-veiled attack upon the director of the Wadsworth Atheneum," Ames
described Craven as a "fanatic" and asserted that Armstead had essentially
suggested "that young museum directors are pimping for dirty peep-shows." As
for the Atheneum, "although the admirable Morgan and Nutting collections
were already in place when Mr. Austin arrived, the bulk of the paintings of
quality and importance in the collection have been acquired during his directorship and upon his advice. And the museum is a far livelier place than it was
two years ago."[11] While most of the trustees would have agreed with this
defense, the perception of Chick as too provocative was spreading.

Ames's phrase about museum directors "pimping for dirty peep-shows"
was unfortunate. Two days before his letter was printed, a front-page headline
in the Hartford edition of the *Bridgeport Sunday Herald,* something of a scandal
sheet, proclaimed "Nude Movie at Avery Memorial / Seeking Art, Elite Watch
Banned Show." Chick's curiosity had been piqued when a "naughty nudie
movie" called *Elysia* had been outlawed by the Hartford police vice and liquor
squad after a single showing at the local Rivoli Theater. Chick screened the
film a few days later so the museum staff and a few friends could see what the
guardians of public morality had found offensive. When the *Herald* found out

that the movie had been shown "within the chaste portals of Hartford's new art museum," it sent a reporter to Scarborough Street to interview the wayward director. Chick was happy to oblige. "I was looking for a good movie," he said. He was always looking for a good movie, he added, and this one was neither vulgar nor particularly good. The *Herald* concluded that "the alluring curves of the steaming movie mamas" were apparently too risqué for ordinary citizens but not for the upper crust.[12]

In June, in the midst of such journalistic barbs aimed at the museum, Frank Gay, the Atheneum's first director, died at seventy-five. He had joined the staff in 1876, when the picture gallery was one of Hartford's quietest precincts. The long obituaries that ensued were reminders of the changes in the museum in the seven years since his retirement—and of a time when the artistic revolutions of the twentieth century were unimaginable to the American museum-going public.

That same month, Chick and Helen went to Woodlands, the estate of Eddie Warburg's parents in White Plains, New York, for an evening of ballet that was part of those modern revolutions. (Having brought Kirstein to the Avery Theater in April to lecture on dance from the ancient Greeks to Diaghilev and Balanchine, Chick had already made it clear that as far as "the Hartford catastrophe" went, all was forgiven, if not forgotten.) The School of American Ballet had opened in New York in December 1933, and Balanchine's choreography and the results of his teaching now would be seen by a select group from the art world, ostensibly invited to celebrate Eddie Warburg's twenty-sixth birthday. The Saturday evening program, presented on an outdoor platform, was to consist of the American premiere of two works from Les Ballets 1933—*Mozartiana* and *Les Songes* (later entitled *Dreams*)—and one new ballet called *Serenade*. Torrential rain stopped the performance, but when it was presented in full the next day, the young American dancers, though dressed in their practice clothes on the makeshift stage, brought Balanchine's extraordinary gifts to life. "Sorry you couldn't make it the second night," Warburg reported to Chick, who had not returned the next day. "It looked damned impressive!"[13] It had been eleven months since Kirstein's first letter about "a real chance for an American ballet."

With summer's arrival, Chick wanted nothing more than to take a deep breath. Since his return from California the previous July, he had careened through a year that included one frenetic failure and several frenetic triumphs. Now he wanted to escape from the museum and a growing pile of bills at home, among them one for a picture he had bought from Arnold Seligmann & Rey for more than $1,600. Chick told the dealer that he had been "in drastic financial difficulties for the last year. However, we are now on a new basis and I think that I can see my way clear to make payment of the bill at the end of the summer. I am very sorry to keep you waiting so long but up to now, I have not even been able to keep up with my household expenses."[14]

He and Helen were not living on a shoestring, however. Chick's combined annual earnings from the Atheneum and Trinity College was about $5,000. This was supplemented by dividends of nearly $800 from the irrevocable trust his mother had set up in 1931 and by Helen's income of over $5,100 from personal investments and her grandfather Goodwin's estate, giving them a total income of about $11,000—a handsome sum for a family of three during the Depression. Because money meant very little to Chick, he relied on Helen to take their financial obligations seriously. She paid the bills, kept meticulous records of expenditures, and allotted him a monthly allowance of $100, which he always exceeded.[15]

Despite his professed poverty, Chick thought at first that he might go abroad and, to finance the trip, managed to persuade his mother, then pursuing her mad genealogical research in Washington, D.C., to let him have the remains of proceeds from the sale of family land in Mount Union. When the money was slow in coming, he gave up the idea in favor of repeating his road show of 1932 as the Great Osram. He saw no problem in leaving his wife and two-year-old son with his in-laws in Castine. Late in June, he packed up his tricks, pigeons, and rabbits, rallied his youthful assistants, and set off for the granges and meeting halls of New Hampshire and Maine, again using the farm in Windham and the cottage in South Harpswell as home bases.

The travels of the Great Osram and the Little Osrams were cut short by a more attractive prospect. John Houseman had taken over the President Theater in New York, changed its name to the Phoenix, and planned to open with Euripides' *Medea*, translated by the Harlem poet Countee Cullen. Rose McClendon, the original Bess in the 1927 stage play *Porgy* by Dorothy and DuBose Heyward, would head a multiracial cast; Chick was invited to design the show; and Virgil Thomson promised to set the choruses to music. Chick spent two weeks in New York at the Askews' in August, turning out drawings of Minoan costumes and a set in the style of de Chirico. The play was supposed to open in New York that fall, and Chick considered having it presented in Hartford by the Friends and Enemies, but the project was abandoned before it ever reached the production stage.

On August 27, Paul Cooley wrote to Chick in New York, gently reminding him that he was still a museum director and that the exhibition season would be starting soon: "We are wondering if you have made any definite plans for the fall as some announcements might be useful . . . and we are also interested." He added that Chick's bank account was overdrawn.[16]

By the last week in September, when the Austins finally arrived back in Hartford from Maine, Chick and Helen knew that they were expecting their second child in the spring. Buoyed by the thought of an expanding family, and refreshed from his time away, Chick radiated infectious enthusiasm. He was just in time to resume his teaching schedule at Trinity and plan an artistic season packed with novel artistic offerings. There would be an exhibition devoted to Man Ray, the leading surrealist photographer; a ten-week retrospective of the motion picture; a lecture by Salvador Dalí, who was scheduled to visit the United States for the first time in November; the first public performances of Balanchine's company from the School of American Ballet; and a personal appearance by Gertrude Stein, who had been persuaded to return to America for the first time in thirty years to give a lecture tour. That fall, museum members received a calendar of events emblazoned with the scope of Chick's ambitions: EXHIBITIONS MUSIC DRAMA LECTURES BALLET CINEMA.[17] At that moment, he had arrived at the point he had dreamed of reaching as a museum director. He had brought all the arts into the Atheneum—and, by example, he was setting the course for American museums.

The Man Ray show that opened on October 15 was a product of Chick's network. Julien Levy was Man Ray's American dealer, and Jim Soby had underwritten the first complete published survey of his work: *Photographs, 1920–1934*. Raised in Brooklyn, Man Ray had founded the Société Anonyme in 1920 with his mentor, Marcel Duchamp, and Katherine Dreier. He moved to Paris, developed the "rayograph" and, with his lover, Lee Miller, the solarized print. In April 1932, Julien Levy had given him a one-man show in New York, but Chick's exhibition, which consisted of Soby's collection of the one hundred prints he had used for his book, was the first thorough survey of Man Ray's work in any museum.

Chick's second program that fall was another innovation—the first film retrospective held in an American museum: *The Motion Picture, 1914–1934*. Months earlier, probably at the Askew's, he had hatched the idea with the librarian of the Museum of Modern Art, Iris Barry. Her knowledge of motion pictures was formidable. Through her reviews in *The Spectator* and the *Daily Mail* and her pioneering book of 1926, *Let's Go to the Movies*, she was already known as one of the most astute film critics in England. Charles Laughton and his wife, Elsa Lanchester, had brought her to New York and introduced her to the Askews, who welcomed her as a regular member of their salon. In the summer of 1933, Philip Johnson had hired her as the Modern's first librarian.

Like Alfred Barr, Iris Barry believed that a true museum of modern art ought to have its own film department. Having cofounded a film association in London in 1925, she joined Julien Levy, Nelson Rockefeller, and Count Raoul de Roussy de Sales in starting the New York Film Society. During its short life, the society showed hard-to-get historic and foreign films in rented spaces. In 1933 a committee consisting of Eddie Warburg as chairman, Iris Barry, and

John Hay Whitney was formed to develop plans for a department of film at the Modern. With Chick's backing, this committee encouraged Barry to put together a film series that would be shown in Hartford to enhance the museum's program but also to convince the trustees at the Modern, who were invited to attend, that a permanent film program was a worthy goal for their museum.

Chick and Iris Barry chose twenty-three films, to be shown at the Atheneum on ten consecutive Sunday evenings, from October 28 to December 30. The series was to begin with D. W. Griffith's *The Birth of a Nation,* as the first major American film, and each subsequent presentation would have a theme—"Charles Chaplin Films," "The German Film," "The Russian Film," "The French Film," "The Slapstick and the Western," "The Documentary Film," "The Experimental, Amateur, Abstract Films and The Animated Cartoon," "The Sociological Film," and finally, "The Justification of the Talkies." Chick supplemented the program with a Saturday film series for children, which included an early *Alice in Wonderland,* Jackie Cooper's *Skippy,* and Walt Disney cartoons. He also made the theater available for a showing of amateur films by members of the Hartford Cinema Club.

No sooner had Chick announced that he would show *The Birth of Nation* than voices of protests were raised. A local minister charged that the film was so prejudiced against Negroes that it should not appear in Hartford; he and a citizens' group put pressure on the mayor to keep the museum from screening it. Three days before the program was to be presented, Chick was forced to announce that only six non-controversial reels (out of the total twelve) of *Birth of a Nation* would be shown and that the rest of the evening would be devoted to Griffith's later film, *Way Down East.* Chick did not hide his anger from the press: "I am surprised that one of the greatest historical documents the motion picture industry has produced should still be capable of arousing such criticism. Its importance in the development of film technique was the only reason for showing it." He doubted whether "such a great work of art can be mutilated with satisfactory results."[18]

Despite the initial controversy, the series was greeted with enthusiasm during its ten-week run. Less than a year later, Chick discussed the significance of the art form and his presentation of *The Motion Picture:*

> In the present century the film has so far taken the place of the novel as the chief popular art that no proper understanding of the culture of the past generation is possible without the ability to review at least the epoch-making motion pictures. Cultural scholarship alone requires the preservation and the study of these important documents. But the primitives of the cinema, like the primitives of any art, have an appeal of their own. The movies have already been in existence long enough so that a list of generally accepted masterpieces would include many pictures long withdrawn from the commercial repertory.

Moreover, if we are ever to have intelligent and influential criticism of the films, public and critics alike must know the classics in the field and without effort and institutional support that is quite impossible. In some respects it is easier to acquaint oneself at second hand with the beginnings of any other art than with that of the movies.

He noted that the retrospective that he and Iris Barry had developed had culminated in a grant from the Rockefeller Foundation for the creation of a film library at the Museum of Modern Art.[19]

A few days after the film series began, Chick formally opened the Lifar Collection, timed to occur on the same day that the Ballet Russe de Monte Carlo gave their first performance in the Bushnell Auditorium. The entire ballet company, including its director, Colonel de Basil, Alexandra Danilova, Tamara Toumanova, and Léonide Massine, came to the Avery Memorial on the afternoon before their performance to see the exhibition, sip tea, and listen to chamber music. Massine was excited to see de Chirico's original sketch of the settings for *Le Bal* in the museum's collection because the ballet was in the company's repertoire and part of the scenery had been lost. Chick arranged to have a watercolor copy made on the spot and delivered it to Boston himself.

At the end of the same week, he spoke at a luncheon for Gertrude Stein at the Ritz Tower in New York. Organized by soprano Eva Gauthier (another regular at the Askew salon) for the benefit of the New York Christmas and Relief Fund, the program was devoted entirely to *Four Saints*.

With the unexpected success of *The Autobiography of Alice B. Toklas*, Miss Stein had been persuaded by American friends to make a six-month lecture tour of the United States. It was her first trip to America since 1904, and her presence made headlines from the moment she and Miss Toklas arrived in New York on October 24. Virgil Thomson finally had something of a reconciliation with his famous collaborator, telling Chick: "Gertrude & I have kissed. I wouldnt quite say made up, but kissed anyway."[20] On November 7 she and Miss Toklas flew to Chicago with Carl Van Vechten in a plane he filled with roses for the opening of a week's run of *Four Saints* at the Auditorium Theater.

The New York luncheon took place a few days after the Chicago performances. Chick described his role in producing the opera and formally introduced Miss Stein. Eva Gauthier joined the many who were captivated by Chick's elegantly offhand stage presence: "You must develop your talent," she wrote him that evening, "as you are most gifted & you are too modest about it— I am not joking."[21]

His own theater consumed him. Always generous with the museum's facilities, he offered the stage that fall to a twenty-two-year-old woman who had acted and directed the apprentices in Eva Le Galliene's Civic Repertory Company in New York. She was May Sarton, the Belgian-born daughter of a distinguished Harvard professor. When the Depression forced Le Gallienne's company to disband in the spring of 1933, Sarton formed the Apprentice Players and presented a season of modern European plays in Manhattan. Sarton was looking for a theater outside New York for her company when she met Chick. He immediately suggested the Avery Theater, transforming her enthusiasm into fantasies about full houses and high box-office returns.

In October, Chick announced that the Apprentice Players would establish themselves permanently in Hartford. "We decided to come to Hartford," Sarton told local journalists, "because we feel that it is one of the outstanding cultural centers of the east, and that the people are in sympathy with creative effort and with the more advanced movements in the arts." She said that the company would devote itself solely to American plays, both classic and modern, to interpret the American scene just as the Abby Theater in Dublin expressed the Irish perspective.[22] But after reading through hundreds of scripts, Sarton found no new American plays she wanted to stage. Instead, the company produced a French farce, a lackluster adaptation of a novel, and a well-received version of Henrik Ibsen's *Master Builder*, with Sarton herself appearing to great effect as Hilda. But a large professional company was too expensive to maintain in a small theater in a small city during the Depression. Sarton said many years later that she had misjudged Hartford, which she found "tremendously Republican" and full of "stodgy insurance people. . . . I felt we were misfits in the city."[23]

Hoping to keep the Apprentice Players alive, Sarton moved the company to Boston, but after one production, she abandoned the enterprise and turned to writing novels and poetry. But she maintained a lasting friendship with Chick, whom she later compared to Ariel in *The Tempest*. "I say that almost with a double meaning," she explained; "I mean the *air* in it, the airiness of this man, the wonderful spontaneous brilliance of him. It was very fascinating. And then, he was very kind, and very human. And I think this was one reason he attracted certain kinds of people—that he had both brilliance and kindness. This doesn't come together very often. He was willing to invest in adventures in the arts."[24] Chick would offer the theater to countless companies and performers throughout his tenure, from mimes and dancers to singers, jazz musicians, and the Connecticut branch of the W.P.A. Federal Theater.[25]

By far Chick's greatest adventure in the theater at the end of 1934 was the return of Lincoln Kirstein and George Balanchine to Hartford. When they proposed having the public debut of their young company in the Avery, Chick seized the chance to host another first for his museum. Late in November he sent out Lincoln Kirstein's press release that on December 6, 7, and 8, the producing company of the School of American Ballet would present four Balanchine ballets in Hartford. Three would be world premieres: *Alma Mater, Transcendence,* and *Serenade;* the fourth, *Mozartiana,* which had been produced for Les Ballets 1933, would be an American premiere. While the last two works had been tried out at the Warburg estate, the other two were entirely new.

Kirstein himself had developed the scenario for *Transcendence,* based on music by Franz Liszt that had been orchestrated by George Antheil. Philadelphia artist Franklin Watkins provided a backdrop—his first work as a set designer. *Alma Mater* was the brainchild of Eddie Warburg. Originally to be called *Touchdown,* it was a surreal parody of college life, and featured flappers in tweed tutus, undergraduates in leopard-skin bloomers and raccoon coats, and a Salvation Army girl. George Gershwin, one of Warburg's friends, had been approached to compose the score but was busy writing *Porgy and Bess.* Instead, his mistress, Kay Swift, composer of the recent Broadway musical *Fine and Dandy,* took the job, enlisting Morton Gould to arrange her score. Cartoonist John Held, Jr., known from *Vanity Fair* and *The New Yorker,* designed the sets and costumes. The ballet was the first of Balanchine's many excursions into the American idiom. There was consternation in Hartford when it was learned that the Salvation Army girl—who did a mild striptease during a rumba—would be wearing cancan panties and a ruby garter, but Chick would not think of censoring the performance.

For The American Ballet, as the School's company was then called, the Hartford appearance was a chance to present itself to the public in a nonunion theater with the aura of a progressive art museum, as its founders had originally intended. Chick could justify to the world his original faith in the ballet scheme. In encouraging his friends to support the production, Chick spoke only of Eddie Warburg, the School's director and chief underwriter, not Kirstein. "This is our most exciting event of the winter," he told Edward Forbes, "and I think we should do all we can to help further the Warburg scheme, since, as far as I am concerned, it is far more important to have it established than to consider my earlier personal feelings about the matter."[26]

Chick, of course, was eager to participate in the preparations and, by the first week of November, had made a model of the stage so that he could test various decorating and color schemes for *Transcendence* and *Mozartiana.* He personally executed the decor for both works from the artists' designs.

On Tuesday afternoon, December 4, following in the wake of truckloads of scenery and costumes, Balanchine, Dimitriew, and Eddie Warburg arrived by bus from New York with their troupe of twenty-three dancers—sixteen girls and seven boys, whose average age was seventeen. Three of those boys were to be among America's first famous male dancers—Charles Laskey, Erick Hawkins, and William Dollar, whose name seemed delightfully American to Balanchine in its inverted form, "Dollar Bill." Several of the ballerinas would also become famous in the dance world: Ruthanna Boris, Elise Reiman, Annabelle Lyon, Marie Jeanne, and Gisella Caccialanza. As carpenters worked on the sets and lighting technicians experimented with colored gelatins, Balanchine supervised the long rehearsals.

Franklin Watkins arrived to add the finishing touches to Chick's translation of his Corot-like design for the full-scale backdrop, which was then lying on the marble floor of the Tapestry Hall in the Morgan Memorial. Meanwhile, Chick could not keep away from the theater. A young woman escorting a photographer backstage glanced into a dressing room and saw the director of the museum in what looked like the costume of a French courtier, posing on a tabletop in front of a mirror. He turned to her nonchalantly and said, "You know, I've always thought of myself as something of a dilettante."[27]

In an interview with the *Hartford Times,* Warburg said that the company's first public performances were being given at the museum "because Hartford is fast becoming a place where experiments in all the arts may have their debuts and look for intelligent appreciation."[28] Among Chick's New York friends, Hartford was going by a new, only partly facetious name: "The New Athens."[29] And the Wadsworth Atheneum had become "Chick's museum," or, simply, "Chick's."[30]

Remembering the excitement of *Four Saints,* prominent leaders in the arts again made the trip to Hartford for the premiere of the American Ballet on Thursday, December 6. That afternoon a Pullman car left Grand Central Station, decorated with a sign proclaiming it the "Ballet Special" and filled with prominent New Yorkers, including George Gershwin. (He was standing in for Kay Swift, who was off in Reno getting a divorce.) Before the train reached New Haven, Gershwin opened a hamper of champagne. As the train steamed into the Connecticut Valley, men struggled into boiled shirts and white ties and women transformed themselves. One socialite "bloomed with sudden magnificence into a sort of grass mat of tan orchids," Lucius Beebe reported to his readers, "and the neatest trick of the week was accomplished by Mrs. Wallace Harrison [wife of the New York architect], who had evidently heard about Peter Arno's combination sport and dinner suit, and who by merely turning her street dress inside out became socked out in an evening gown of platinum lamé."[31]

Among the other guests at the first performance were the Sam Lewisohns, A. Conger Goodyear, Mrs. Nelson Rockefeller, Sol Hurok, Eddie Warburg and his parents, Lincoln Kirstein and his parents, the three American designers of the ballets, the George Antheils, and Boston neurosurgeon Harvey Cushing with his wife and two of their three famously attractive daughters, Barbara (the future Mrs. William Paley) and Betsy with her husband, James Roosevelt. Lending the occasion a decidedly Continental luster were Salvador Dalí and Pavel Tchelitchew, both of whom had arrived in America for the first time just a

Salvador Dali and Mrs. Dali talking to Allan Porter of New York. Dali is that famous modern painter, best known in this country for the little picture, "Persistence of Memory," sometimes known as "The Wet Watches," which was shown at the Morgan memorial with several others in his canvasses.

Paul W. Cooley of Hartford and Miss Eleanor Shaler, musician and actress of New York.

John Held, jr., talkin

American Ballet Wins Plaudits in Premiere

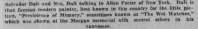

Large Audience at Avery Thrilled by Balanchine's Choreography Expressed by New Group of Dancers.

BY MARIAN MURRAY.

A gayly enthusiastic, excited audience, clapping for the cast to return again and again, and finally bursting into bravas and calls for "Balanchine," greeted the world premiere of the American Ballet last evening, at the Avery memorial, proclaiming the success of the ballet and all it connotes. Choreography, dancing, scenery, costumes, music met with an approval that portends triumph for the

—[Photos by The Hartford Times.
GEORGE GERSHWIN.

Another glamorous opening in Hartford. The Salvador Dalís and George Gershwin attend Balanchine's ballets, 1934.

few weeks earlier, as well as Nicholas Nabokoff, composer of the ballet *Ode*, which Tchelitchew had designed for Diaghilev in 1928. And, of course, Chick's Harvard–New York art constellation who had attended the opening of the theater returned to Hartford.

The audience arrived late from the pre-performance dinner parties. Again, as at *Four Saints*, fashionable ladies—a "tidal wave of sable," as Beebe wrote—made multiple entrances into the theater lobby for the benefit of the photographers. When Lincoln Kirstein's towering form was finally seen rushing into the lobby, with a huge sandwich of ham on rye in one hand, ticket holders burst into applause, recognizing him as the moving force behind the occasion. They entered the theater with much bowing and waving of handkerchiefs.[32]

The curtain did not open on the first ballet, *Mozartiana*, until nine-fifteen, forty-five minutes behind schedule. Against the backdrop of a bright Italian town square (Chick's version of Christian Berard's original design), a *pas de trois* brought three dancers leaping to the very edge of the small stage. Dressed in brilliant attire as gypsies and children, Balanchine's full company, stretched to their limits, negotiated his sophisticated choreography for Tchaikovsky's orchestration of four Mozart dances, which had been a vehicle for Tamara Toumanova in Paris the previous year. Next came the boisterous *Alma Mater*, with its outrageous costumes and swirling music, a mélange of college songs, ragtime, and jazz. Both Hartford critics pronounced it highly entertaining but more like a Broadway musical than a ballet. The final work of the evening was *Transcendence*. With its haunting forest backdrop, it was acclaimed a master-piece. "It is all so very tender," wrote T. H. Parker in the *Courant*, "so very thrilling, so deeply appealing just from its very visual content, so filled with exquisite figures, patterns and rhythms, that 'what it means' seems rather unimportant indeed."[33] The *Hartford Times* called *Transcendence* "the embodi-ment of the subconscious."[34]

Throughout the evening, the two pianos in the orchestra pit were drowned out by applause and cheering. At the end, Russell Hitchcock, who had been so ebullient at the opening of *Four Saints*, again danced in the aisle, calling "Bis!" and "Encore!" in his booming voice.[35] There were many shouts for Balanchine, but it was not until the last of the dozen curtain calls that the diminutive chore-ographer was persuaded to make a shy bow.[36]

Most of the elated audience piled into cars and taxis and set out for the Sobys' house in West Hartford, where the triumph was celebrated far into the morning. At a basement piano sat Gershwin, smoking a cigar and playing selections from his forthcoming opera, *Porgy and Bess*. Salvador Dalí settled into a living room love seat with Nellie Howland, "looking raptly and not too chastely," as John Houseman put it, at the large buttons down the bosom of her evening dress.[37] In his guttural Catalán-accented French, Dalí asked, *"Madame, ces boutons—sont-ils comestibles?"* ("Madame, those buttons—are they edible?"[38]) Years later, she commented, "Dalí would have eaten any-thing."[39]

The American Ballet appeared again the next two evenings, giving a Satur-day matinee performance as well. On Saturday night—taking the place of *Mozartiana*—*Serenade* made its public debut.

Ten days before Christmas, as if December had not been busy enough in this, the most eventful year of Chick's career, the Friends and Enemies of Mod-ern Music presented its first concert of the 1934–35 season. After the debut of a scene from a new opera, *Hester Prynne*, by composer Avery Claflin, under the direction of John Houseman, there was a performance of a Haydn string quartet and the premiere of Virgil Thomson's Quartet No. 2, with a backdrop that Chick commissioned from Tchelitchew—the painter's first work in America. Against the blue of the theater's cyclorama was a screen consisting of three panels, framed by what appeared to be a wrought-iron arch. The score of the first three pages of the score were painted in white by Maurice Grosser, who also reproduced the cello part in black paint on twenty yards of white tulle, draped over the arch. The four musicians sat on a black platform in front of the screens. Thomson found Tchelitchew's decor "in just that spirit of fluffy Baroque that Chick loved."[40] But the theater was just over half full. Less than two weeks after Balanchine's ballets, most of Chick's out-of-town friends did not want to make another trip to Hartford.

This program, however, was only meant to be a warm-up for an extremely ambitious musical season. Having asked Virgil Thomson to come up with ideas for programs, Chick had already announced to the Friends and Enemies that he was considering presenting Stravinsky's *Symphony in Memory of Debussy*, anthems by Henry Purcell performed by an African-American chorus, and the American premieres of both Erik Satie's symphonic drama, *Socrate*, and the Kurt Weill / Bertoldt Brecht "operatic morality play" *The Rise and Fall of the City of Mahagonny.*[41]

Meanwhile, Hartford was invited to contemplate something entirely beyond its ken. On December 18, Chick's thirty-fourth birthday, Salvador Dalí spoke in the Avery Theater. There were rumors that he would appear with a loaf of bread on his head, but instead the audience saw a slim young man in a suit with sleek black hair and a thin mustache—in those days barely beginning to curl up at the ends. In introducing the program, Chick seemed, according to *New York Herald Tribune* columnist Joseph W. Alsop, Jr., "more apprehensive than at any of his previous efforts to make Hartford the new American Athens." Chick reminded the audience that before Dalí appeared, the surrealist film that he and Luis Buñuel had made in 1928, *Un Chien andalou*, would be screened. Chick asked the spectators "not to be upset by the forthcoming motion picture."[42] Then the film began. It later became notorious for the opening scene, in which a young woman's eyeball appears to be sliced in half by a razor blade, but other images created through free association by the codirectors (who appeared on screen) were also disturbing to more sensitive viewers. Live ants swarmed on a cyclist's hand, hair suddenly appeared over his mouth after it disappeared from a woman's armpit, and dead and decaying donkeys adorned grand pianos.

When the film was over, Dalí spoke in French about how his goal was always to make "the fantastic, paranoiac idea of dreams a reality in paint." Double images could be the vehicle of the subconscious. He showed a slide of a postcard of an African village with people standing in front of a hut. Then he turned the picture on its side and said that it reminded him of some of Picasso's drawings of the human head. He projected surrealist constructions by Picasso, and a detail of a vulture in a painting of a Madonna and child by Leonardo da Vinci, which he claimed was a manifestation of Leonardo's subconscious mind. Even the "sex appeal" of the modern streamlined car, he said, came from the subconscious of the designer. Explaining the evolution of the concept of space, Dalí declared that for the father of geometry, Euclid, space was essentially a flat surface; for Newton, it took on anthropomorphic qualities; and in the present day, space was being "devoured" by "huge mandibles." The *Courant* translated his concluding remarks as "Only those who can see these subconscious ideas behind all matter can attain the 'liberty' which hyper-realism imparts and which may later [become] a religion."[43] He also uttered, apparently for the first time, his famous dictum: "The only difference between me and a madman is that I am not a madman."[44] Many in Hartford might have disputed that pronouncement, particularly Charles Goodwin and the museum's trustees. But it is unlikely that he, or many of the board members, attended Dalí's program. The theater was two-thirds empty.

In honor of Dalí's visit, Chick opened a small three-week exhibition of the artist's recent paintings, taken from a one-man show at the Julien Levy Gallery. The pictures were on display in Chick's office, again exemplifying his tendency to open his personal spaces, whether his apartment or his house, to the public—and perhaps to suggest that such works, which were even more bizarre and salacious than those in the 1931 show, should not have to be seen by the casual visitor. Among the pictures was *The Specter of Sex Appeal*, in which a child in a sailor suit, holding a hoop, stares at what a Hartford critic described as "a gigantic diseased figure propped up by forked sticks."[45] This was in fact a deformed and decaying nude woman. The viewer saw in *Skull and Its Lyrical Appendage Leaning on a Night Table Which Has the Temperature of a Cardinal Bird's Nest* an elongated grand piano whose keyboard wound down into a skull. One local critic said that the museum visitor quickly becomes convinced that "either the artist is insane or he (the spectator) is—or soon will be."[46]

Another work was called *Paranoiac-Astral Image*, a small lyrical oil on a wood panel painted just months earlier, which Chick bought for the Atheneum for $720. Evoking Dalí's troubled childhood, the picture portrays the empty beach at Rosas—the Spanish fishing village on the Mediterranean where Dalí spent his summers as a youth. At the left, a man in a suit, presumably Dalí's father, walks toward the viewer, his head in shadow and his hands clasped behind him. In the background is the tiny figure of a woman, probably Dalí's nurse, Llucia. At the right is an open boat resting in the sand, in which a small boy in a sailor suit sits with a second woman, undoubtedly Dalí and his mother. In the foreground a broken two-handled jug suggests a shell or a skull. The effect of this carefully balanced composition, all in gray-blues and greens with a hint of yellow, is one of dreamlike disconnectedness. Levy always felt that the picture was one of Dalí's finest works.[47]

Unlike most of the other paintings in the show, *Paranoiac-Astral Image* had none of the artist's blatant grotesqueries, so Chick had no difficulty getting it approved by the Atheneum's board. Nevertheless, he had to draw a hundred dollars from a small allocation the art committee had recently made available to allow him some leeway in his purchases. He understood that he could use the money for modern art that the trustees might not necessarily like but would tolerate. Mrs. Berger, as general curator, always noted in the acquisition ledger when payment was made from the "Modern Art Allocation." Modestly priced new works began entering the collection, many drawings or watercolors, so that Chick could buy contemporary pictures of high quality while staying within the minuscule amount allowed.

Chick also had to please his employers, of course, and his most expensive purchases at that time were much more to the board's taste—a thirteenth-century Tuscan crucifixion; Salvator Rosa's turbulent and romantic *Tobias and the Angel;* an intimate Dutch genre scene by Jacob Ochtervelt, *The Dancing Dog;* and a Hopper watercolor, *Coal Box,* which Chick later said was his favorite among the Hoppers he bought.

Just two days after Dalí's appearance, Chick opened a modest exhibition of women artists, which had been assembled by Katherine Dreier for the Société Anonyme. At the opening, the formidable Dreier gave a joint gallery talk with the equally formidable Madame Annot Krigar-Menzel Jacobs, a German-born painter and lecturer, founder of the Annot Art School in Berlin, and the only woman admitted to the avant-garde artists' association called the Berlin Secession. With the seemingly unending parade of events, the audience for yet another conference on modern art had dwindled to thirty-five, although the remarks were reported fully in the press. Annot and Dreier expressed the view Chick had often promoted—that great art was not necessarily pleasant and familiar. As for those who complained that they did not understand modern painting, Madame Annot said, "then they don't understand the old kind either. And when they look at a thing and say, 'I couldn't live with that,' I know they have no concept of the meaning of art. For, after all, a painting isn't a coffee pot!" Dreier elaborated on the theme in no uncertain terms: "We reject truth, too often, when it is expressed too strongly and it interferes with our taste. Taste is concerned with comfortable, livable things, that often are pretty. Truth may deal with ugliness, and still be truth." She explained that, in the case of works in her exhibition, the viewer should be able to "feel beauty through ugliness."[48]

Chick himself drew a far larger crowd than either Dalí or Dreier when he metamorphosed into the Great Osram on December 22 for his Christmas magic show to benefit the children's art classes. His two performances, with exotic costumes and dramatic sets and lighting, led the *Hartford Times* to call him a "modern Aladdin."[49]

His public program for 1934 ended with the last installment of the film retrospective—"The Justification of the Talkies," through the recent comedy *The Thin Man* and the original German version of Josef von Sternberg's *Blue Angel*, which had launched the international film career of Marlene Dietrich five years earlier. The subtlety of the film was lost on many in the audience. Throughout the screening, there were loud conversations about the fact that the film was not in English and shouts when a familiar word came through.[50] But Chick expected such reactions from Americans who were, from his point of view, still relatively unsophisticated.

He entered 1935 with undimmed energy, for the Hartford public was about to see and hear the woman whose opera had begun the miraculous year that had just ended. The notion of Gertrude Stein actually stepping onto a stage in Hartford was fascinating even to the skeptics on the Atheneum's board. The American public clearly enjoyed her feisty pronouncements like the one published in *The New York Times* from a question-and-answer session in Paris early in 1934: "Present day geniuses can no more help doing what they are doing than you can help not understanding it, but if you think we do it for effect and to make a sensation, you're crazy."[51]

On January 18, 1935, the Avery Theater was overflowing beyond its 299-seat capacity. Settling into their seats, several in the audience noticed a small woman sitting with Nellie Howland. She had a mustache and short dark hair covered by what looked like a baby's bonnet, all in silver, tied under her chin with a silver string. She peered at the local citizenry through a lorgnette. She was Alice B. Toklas.

Miss Stein, looking like someone's kindly grandmother in a long, dark blue silk dress with a yellow shawl over her shoulders, walked onstage without an introduction, as she insisted for all her appearances, sat down at a table equipped only with an electric light and a glass of water, and put on tortoise-rimmed glasses. She started reading the lecture Chick had chosen from her repertoire. It was the one she had given at the Colony Club in New York in November for the Museum of Modern Art, the first stop on her tour: "Pictures and What They Are."

To the surprise of many, she spoke in clear sentences in a beautifully modulated voice, beginning: "It is natural that I should tell about pictures, that is, about paintings. Everybody must like something and I like seeing painted pictures." She intimated that a museum should have plenty of places to sit down, or preferably lie down and take a nap. Paintings must be contemplated for long periods of time. The key to understanding modern pictures, especially, was familiarity: "I like familiarity. It does not in me breed contempt it just breeds familiarity. And the more familiar a thing is the more there is to be familiar with."

She then articulated modernism's central doctrine of the visual arts. Her years of contemplating pictures, she said, had led her to a simple discovery: "The relation between the oil painting and the thing painted was really nobody's business. It could be the oil painting's business but actually for the purpose of the oil painting after the oil painting was painted it was not the oil painting's business and so it was nobody's business."

During a short question-and-answer period, in a curious echo of Chick Austin's attempts to promote collecting in Hartford, she asserted that "six bad oil paintings in the home are better than good ones in a museum, because they give casual people a chance to look at paintings."[52]

Just when many in the audience were deciding that being in the presence of this sibyl of modernism was easier than they had expected, Miss Stein began reading excerpts from her portraits of modern artists—Matisse, Picasso, and Gris. Some found her long repetitions mind-numbing, while others could not restrain their guffaws.[53] Of Picasso, she said: "Would he like it if Napoleon if I told him. If I told him if Napoleon if Napoleon if I told him."[54] One critic gave her credit for meeting "with apparently unruffled equanimity the repeated laughter of the audience in what was surely the wrong places."[55] Whatever they thought of her, Hartford citizens had to acknowledge that Chick Austin had made their city a destination for leading figures in the international art world.

It had been just under a year since Chick had opened the Avery Memorial with its revolutionary interior design, the Picasso show, and *Four Saints*. Now, in 1935, after a string of triumphs in the eyes of his fellow modernists, he ignored signs of discontent among the trustees and the public. With the local press cheering him on, Chick prepared to push his avant-garde agenda forward.

CHAPTER THIRTEEN

"Number One!"

One must be absolutely modern.

—Arthur Rimbaud, *Adieu*

The year 1935 was the three-hundredth anniversary of the founding of Connecticut, and Chick had been appointed to the Connecticut Tercentenary Commission. But the historical pageants, memorial tablets, and commemorative exhibitions that were part of this jubilee could not have interested him less. Because the museum owned the Wallace Nutting Collection, he was required to present the state's official furniture show, *Three Centuries of Connecticut Furniture*, that summer. And because there were complaints from his trustees that he had never given American art its due, he agreed to produce an exhibition called *Three Centuries of American Painting and Sculpture* early in the year. This show, however, would be done on his terms.

Once again, he did not get around to sending out requests for loans to the paintings show until January 9—twenty days before the members' opening. But Chick knew exactly what he wanted—his standard line to museums and collectors was that he had "always particularly admired" whatever he hoped to borrow—and despite the incredibly short notice, pictures were shipped to Hartford from the Metropolitan, the Modern, the Boston Museum, the Whitney, the Corcoran, the Art Institute of Chicago, the Nelson Gallery in Kansas City; collectors like Abby Aldrich Rockefeller and the Sam Lewisohns; dealers like Knoedler and Julien Levy; and the artists themselves.

Chick made no attempt to present a balanced survey of American art; he chose works that appealed to him personally. There were familiar painters—from Copley and Stuart to Cole and Homer, Cassatt, Whistler, Sargent, and Hassam. But fifty-seven of the ninety-six pictures in the show were from the twentieth century, many of these by contemporary artists who reflected a new view of American art—John Marin, Arthur Dove, Charles Demuth, Maurice Prendergast, Georgia O'Keeffe, and Florine Stettheimer.

Of the twenty sculptures on view, none was from the eighteenth century, and the few nineteenth-century works were typified by a bronze figure of Lincoln. But from the twentieth century came pieces by Alexander Calder and Joseph Cornell (his first museum showing), Jacob Epstein, Gaston Lachaise (not convincingly American), Paul Manship, Isamu Noguchi, and William Zorach.

While Chick's show appeared intent on promoting modern trends in American art, the essays that he and Russell Hitchcock supplied for the catalogue seemed, amazingly, to denigrate the national school itself. With the European bias of his generation of Fogg Museum students, Chick wrote that "there have been few powerfully original American painters. This should be no cause for shame since it is quite possible that the Anglo-Saxon mind is pictorially and musically unimaginative—that the written word is for us a more powerful exciter of the mind than the painted picture or the heard sound." Realism was "the true American metier" because realism was "what the greater part of our public wants and is most capable of enjoying." This was the fault of bourgeois American society, he added, "since materialistic periods most unusually demand realism as a mode of artistic expression."[1]

Chick continued to voice his low opinion of most American art during a gallery talk after the show opened: "To some extent I feel that all American art is 'provincial art' in that in all periods it has been so largely derivative, and has its origins in so many other sources than the native soil." Folk art, he said, such as a nineteenth-century wooden figurehead in the show, was the kind of American art that was "least dependent" on outside influences.[2] This condescension toward the traditional art that his trustees held dear was extraordinarily impolitic, but he did not seem to care.

It was not that Chick was unaware that members of the public and the museum's board thought they had seen more than enough of contemporary works. He simply felt that his judgment was more fully developed than theirs. In presenting his annual report for 1934 to the board a few days before the American exhibition opened, he fiercely defended the Picasso show, calling the artist "one of the most provocative, if not the greatest, genius[es] of our time" and declaring that "no more fitting artist could have been chosen for the dedication of a museum building which represents the first successful breaking away, at least in America, from the dusty, dingy, and outworn museum tradition of the nineteenth century." As for his other programs, he painted them in red, white, and blue: "Altogether it has been a great year. We have served the causes of European and local art well, and especially American art, with an American opera, an American ballet, and the important exhibition of Three Centuries of American Painting."[3] Considering how he had dismissed much of American art even as he presented it, this was at least a disingenuous claim, if not an outright insult to the trustees' intelligence.

At the opening of the show on January 29, he spent his time drawing attention to the most modern work on view. It was a strange object suspended from the ceiling over the tea table in Avery Court. This, the local press explained, was a new kind of sculpture devised by Alexander Calder. It consisted of wires and spheres, balanced so that its components could move in different patterns. Readers were informed that these new sculptures were called "mobiles." Chick kept the piece in constant motion throughout the evening by prodding it with a stick. Calder had made his first mobiles in 1931 (Marcel Duchamp coined the term) and showed them publicly for the first time in Paris a year later at the Galerie Vignon and in New York at the Julien Levy Gallery. Chick had placed another Calder mobile, this one electrically powered, upstairs in the sculpture section of the show. Nearby was the "Charter Oak Cradle," fashioned in 1857 for Elizabeth and Samuel Colt from pieces of Connecticut's fabled Charter Oak, the symbol of the state, which had blown down a year earlier. Chick told the press that the object was actually "an early wooden sculpture,"[4] and in order to make the connection between the old and the new (or so he claimed), he had attached an electric motor to the famous relic so that it rocked back and forth continuously. Such a sacrilege was guaranteed to give the antiquarians of Hartford apoplexy.

Much as he enjoyed challenging viewers, Chick thrived on being in touch with his audience. He distributed a questionnaire asking the public six questions about the show:

"Which picture in this exhibition would you prefer to have in your home?"
"Which picture do you like best?"
"Which picture or sculpture do you dislike most?"
"Which do you think is the most American painting and sculpture in the exhibition?"
"What American painters do you regret the *absence* of most in this exhibition?"
"What American painters do you regret the *presence* of most in this exhibition?"

Not surprisingly, the results published in the *Courant* and the *Times* showed that the public taste for pleasant realism remained strong and that modernism was actively disliked. The favorite work was Rockwell Kent's *Winter,* a rocky northeastern coastal scene, painted in 1907. Also popular were nineteenth-century works by Sully and Eakins, an impressionist canvas by Childe Hassam, and Charles Sheeler's recognizable *Yachts and Pertaining to Yachting.*

The most disliked work was *The Crucifixion* by Franklin Watkins, who had designed Balanchine's *Transcendence*. It depicted the moment when a spear is thrust into the side of Christ, the figures on the crosses distended almost to the point of caricature. But Chick defended it: "I like the vitality, the fine color, and the rare emotional intensity." Also high on the list of "hates" was Florine Stettheimer's *Birthday Bouquet* of 1931, an eccentric two-dimensional arrangement suggesting a homemade valentine. "It is rather vulgar, as a matter of fact," said Chick disarmingly. "But that is its strength."[5]

One irate respondent to the questionnaire probably represented the opinion of the majority of viewers:

> You can't force the public to like this modern jazz art. 90% of the people detest it! 9% more follow like a bunch of sheep because someone has said it is "Ot" and they want to appear intelligent and sophisticated so they sacrifice all common sense and backbone and fall in line with the remaining 1% who are either laughing up their sleeve at the public or else they failed to learn to draw when in school so turned to modernism. The balance of the last 1% are undoubtly [*sic*] insane.[6]

But Chick staunchly echoed Gertrude Stein, telling the *Hartford Times:* "The recognition of subject matter is not really related to aesthetic pleasure."[7]

Even while he put the American show together, Chick was concentrating on a subject far closer to his own obsessions. On January 21, at the Whitney Museum in New York, he gave the first version of a lecture he would repeat and refine for the rest of his life: "The Romantic Agony in Paint." The topic had fascinated him from the moment in 1933 when Jim Soby introduced him to a new book by the Italian art critic Mario Praz, *The Romantic Agony*. Soby had frequently chided Chick about his neglect of serious reading, and Chick himself often said, "I'm no intellectual. I only read *The Saturday Evening Post*."[8] "He was too restless to read much," Soby remembered, "though he was constantly poring over the illustrations in art books." Chick's bedtime reading consisted almost exclusively of cookbooks; but he read *The Romantic Agony* from cover to cover.[9]

Praz examined the erotic sensibility of nineteenth-century Romanticism and its antecedents in the seventeenth century. He saw in the poetry of Byron and the novels of the Marquis de Sade critical sources for the pervasive fascination with the beautiful and the bizarre, as well as the connection between sensuality and pain, in the art and literature of England, France and Italy. He delved into literary treatments of sadism, masochism, and sexual perversion. The Romantic period could be seen as a precursor to the Freudian world of the modernists, who brought the dark complexity of the human psyche out into the open and even celebrated it.

The Modern romantic:
Chick with a sculpture
by Henri Gaudier-Brzeska,
by George Platt Lynes, 1936

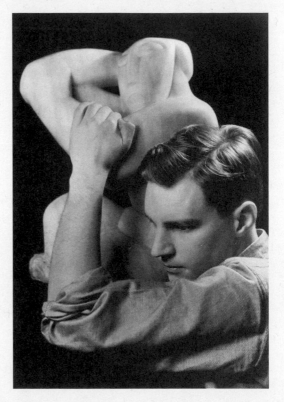

Chick's exploration of Romanticism's somber side—lighter and wittier than Praz's approach—followed the themes of beauty and agony from "the emotional violence" of the baroque painters to the grandiose drama of the Gothic Revival in the late eighteenth century and on to the surrealists such as Dalí, who, said Chick, sought to "freeze the nightmare." Like Praz, he saw the artist as the defining influence on the sensibilities of a culture. For Chick, this included the cinematic artist as well, and in a later version of the lecture, his last slide was the enigmatic image of Greta Garbo, her luminous hair covering half her face, an indication, he said, that "romanticism is not yet altogether dead."[10]

For the rest of 1935 Chick kept his spotlight on contemporary art. On March 12 he opened two new exhibitions: the first, from the Museum of Modern Art, on the art of George Caleb Bingham, the popular nineteenth-century painter who had just been "rediscovered" as a precursor of modern American realism. The show was a reassuring oasis for the conservative members of the board. The second exhibition was more provocative—Pavel Tchelitchew's first one-man museum show. It consisted of seventeen paintings and fifty-one drawings, mostly new works that Tchelitchew had brought with him from Europe. It had been presented at the Julien Levy Gallery in December 1934 and at the Arts Club of Chicago. Tchelitchew's colors had brightened almost painfully since Chick's Neo-Romantic show of 1931, and many of his paintings displayed such an elongation of perspective that critics felt he was skating on the surface of surrealism without the psychological depth.[11] Certain images were bound to raise the eyebrows of some Hartfordites. There were several portraits of Tchelitchew's young companion, Charles Henri Ford, a handsome Mississippian who became a poet and novelist. One depicted him staring at the viewer with a lurid red wheat field behind him; another showed him in blue armor. There were also three oils from Tchelitchew's bullfight series. The bulls and matadors were seen mostly in a low perspective from the rear, and the portrayal was anatomically graphic. But Chick's own enthusiasm for Tchelitchew was so warm that the artist later declared that "Hartford was the first U.SA town to be a great friend to me" and that the Atheneum "[k]new more about me than I know myself."[12]

In the mid-1930s, the Neo-Romantics, the surrealists, and other emerging European artists were beginning to visit America in unprecedented numbers, both to develop the market for their works and to experience the creative energy to be found in New York, Chicago, Hollywood—and Hartford. Indeed, early in March, as the Tchelitchew show was being prepared, Eugene Berman also came to the Atheneum, only a few days after setting foot in the United States for the first time. (Through Julien Levy, Chick mounted a Berman exhibition of seventy-five recent drawings, all for sale, beginning at the end of March.) Many years later, Berman left the most telling account of the attraction European artists felt to the museum Chick had created:

> No sooner had I landed in New York than I was whisked away on my first week end to see the Hartford museum and to meet the almost legendary man behind it: Chick Austin.
>
> This immediate visit to Hartford was not just an exceptional occurrence. It was a must with every newcomer to the American shores, with every new artist or leader in the plastic arts or music. It must be remembered that at the time the famous Museum of Modern Art was only in the process of becoming what it is now and had a rather nomadic life moving from and rapidly outgrowing successive narrow and temporary headquarters. Hartford was then the big, new attraction, the museum to be seen and admired for a completely new style and approach to buying, exhibiting and displaying art.[13]

Also in March, Chick presented the season's second concert from the Friends and Enemies—a program combining eighteenth-century arias and modern songs performed by soprano Eva Gauthier against a backdrop designed by Chick.[14] Billed as a celebration of the 250th anniversary of the births of Handel, Scarlatti, and Bach, the concert was devoted mostly to pieces by such composers as Debussy, Ravel, Schoenberg, and Berg. Speaking between numbers about the twentieth-century pieces, which the press had described in advance as esoteric, Mme. Gauthier repeated an injunction that was becoming familiar to Chick's audiences: "Whether you like them or not, you should hear them."[15]

That spring, Chick's domestic life was enlarged. Late in the night of April 22, Helen delivered a baby girl, whom she and Chick named Sarah Goodwin

At home in Hartford with the children: Helen with
David and Sally, c. 1938

Austin after Helen's great-aunt Sallie Goodwin. Laura Austin communicated
her pleasure to Helen by telegram at four o'clock in the morning:

WITH LOVE AND THANKS FOR MY PRECIOUS EASTER GIFT MY GRAND-
DAUGHTER LITTLE SALLY . . . CONGRATULATE FATHER I KNOW HE WILL LOVE
HER & POPPA BE BOUND RIGHT ROUND HER LITTLE FINGER WHAT WILL BE
LEFT FOR GRAND MA[16]

"You *two* seem to get just what you want," she added by letter the same day.[17] It did seem in 1935 that at home and at his museum Chick had everything he could want.

In the beginning of May, through the Marie Harriman Gallery, he exhibited another art collection with ties to the Ballets Russes. Choreographer Léonide Massine had assembled a huge group of cubist and futurist paintings and had already shown them in several American cities. Among the artists represented in the show were Picasso, Matisse, Braque, and Derain, along with the Russian artists associated with Diaghilev.[18] All of the pictures were for sale, and Chick bought two that supplemented the Lifar Collection: Bakst's sinuous watercolor and gouache in blue and gold depicting Nijinsky in Debussy's *L'Après midi d'un faune,* produced by Diaghilev in 1912, perhaps the most famous painted image of the dancer; and a set design by André Derain for the Rossini / Resphigi *Boutique fantastique* of 1919.

Soon after the Massine show opened, Chick came down with a debilitating case of chicken pox, was in bed for two weeks, and the whole family was quarantined. This forced him to miss the visit of the American Museum Directors Association, whose members toured the new museum building on May 19. Edward Forbes reported to him that Paul Sachs "was so perfectly delighted that he almost blew up with enthusiasm over your work." Describing the visit to Chick afterward, Alfred Barr wrote that he had arrived late at the museum and climbed the circular staircase to the third floor of the Avery. The balcony in front of him commanded an impressive view of the court below. There he saw Paul Sachs:

He was in a frenzy of excitement and avuncular pride—rushed up to me—put his arm around my waist and announced in a voice of thunder NUMBER ONE! . . . "Chick Austin is the number one museum director of America! You can't beat this! Number one I tell you, Alfred—Number one!"

In two postscripts, Barr not only confirmed his admiration for Chick, but also revealed how much Chick's friends knew about the chance Edward Forbes took when he recommended him as director of a museum:

"P.S. I agree with Sachs[.]
"P.P.S P.J.S. [Sachs] gave full credit to Forbes for his original act of faith."[19]

The chicken pox had postponed the last concert of the season from the Friends and Enemies of Modern Music, but it was finally held on June 2 at

A party in the "Venetian Lagoon." Helen (with cigarette) and Chick
flank Helen's mother, Fanny Goodwin, seated.

Chick and Helen's house. Four American composers—Virgil Thomson, Aaron Copland, George Antheil, and Paul Bowles—came to play the Austins' piano. Copland performed his *Variations* and music by Thomson. Thomson offered his own musical portraits of people in attendance and then, in his high reedy voice, sang songs by Antheil and by Bowles, including a letter from Gertrude Stein that Bowles had set to music. Antheil performed a suite and played duets with Thomson, and Bowles played his Sonatina as well as portraits of Copland, Thomson, and Antheil.[20] The affair, like most parties at Chick's house, lasted into the early hours of the next day, and the atmosphere blurred into an alcoholic haze. Bowles remembered that, "in the general drunkenness," his suitcase disappeared. "I could not very well go back to New York in white tie and tails; Austin had to lend me suit, shirt, tie, and socks in order for me to get out of Hartford."[21]

During the first five months of the year, Chick had continued to expand the museum's permanent collection. His major purchase was a splendid, moody view of the Piazzetta in Venice by Francesco Guardi, done in

*William Harnett,
The Faithful Colt,
1890. Oil on canvas,
22½ × 18½ inches,
purchased 1935*

the 1770s, bought from Kirk Askew for $3,000. Chick always preferred Guardi to the eighteenth century's most popular painter of Venetian scenes, Canaletto, because Guardi left more to the imagination, hinting that there was a dark side to Chick's favorite city. Most of the other purchases were from the twentieth century, but only for extremely modest sums, such as a Calder mobile for $100.[22]

That spring, Chick made one of his most important American acquisitions, William Harnett's *The Faithful Colt*, painted in 1890. Harnett had been a popular artist in the late nineteenth century, but had fallen into near oblivion in the four decades since his death. This picture, in the trompe l'oeil style that fascinated Chick, shows an aging Colt revolver hanging by its trigger guard on a nail, against a dark green, battered wooden door. A bright scrap of newspaper, partially peeled away from the door, balances the composition. New York dealer Edith Gregor Halpert offered it to Chick the day after she acquired the work from one of her "scouts," knowing that its illusionism and its anticipation of surrealism would appeal to him. She suggested that it could be hung in Hartford next to Pierre Roy's *Electrification of the Countryside*.[23] Naturally, Chick wanted it because it was a masterful work of art by an artist on the edge of rediscovery. He might have expected to get the picture approved on the strength of its historical ties to Hartford's most successful industry, to say nothing of the Atheneum's huge firearms collection, but the trustees would consent to the purchase only after he persuaded Halpert to reduce the price from $475 to $300.[24] "Despite what appears at first glance to be an approach to supreme realism in Harnett," Chick wrote of the painting, "and notwithstanding the commonplaceness of the subject matter, an antirealistic and almost fantastic result is achieved. For, as in the Flemish Primitive, the eye is enabled to experience in the picture what it is not permitted to do in actuality, that is, to focus on one detail at a time."[25] This was the first Harnett bought by any museum, and its subsequent exhibition in the United States and Europe helped to make his works among the most coveted of all American paintings and to revive interest in the trompe l'oeil genre.

The purchase that caused the greatest stir during the summer of 1935, however, was Jean-Baptiste Greuze's *La Paresseuse* (or *Indolence*), which Chick had bought the previous year. He featured the painting of the servant on the cover of the museum's combined annual report and bulletin, accompanied by an essay by novelist Glenway Wescott, who had just returned to America after living in Europe for several years. His article was entitled "Poor Greuze" and was unlike anything Atheneum members had ever seen in their bulletin. In describing the artist's promiscuous wife, Wescott observed that "[Greuze's] conjugal ardour lasted longer than his respect for her" and that he projected his lust onto his canvases through a series of voluptuous models. Wescott suggested that "if civilization, then as now, had not frowned upon the rendering of the fevers and chills of sex," Greuze might have turned "to thoroughly erotic art." Greuze often hinted in his pictures at "animal bliss," he said, "matrimonial pleasantness, budding femininity's fever, the worm in the bud," but never went far enough. Wescott called the woman in the Atheneum's new painting "the Hartford slattern" and "the slattern of slatterns," and described one particular flesh tone in Greuze's palette as "the colour that the French call excited-nymph's-thigh." He referred to the "fragrant-looking breasts" in Greuze's pictures as being "so motherly and mother-of-pearly." When Greuze painted well, Wescott explained, all the elements in his pictures came together in a "penetrating and penetrable felicity."[26]

Readers were appalled. How could anything so coyly suggestive be sanctioned by the Wadsworth Atheneum? One infuriated museum member warned the trustees:

> More articles by Glenway Westcott [*sic*] will undoubtedly cause some of your contributors to ask you to stop sending your magazine into their homes and also stop their contributions.
> Admittedly clever but utterly disgusting, it takes first prize as a complete give-away of its author's decadent character.
> Just silly little bad boy stuff but most offensive to decent people and perhaps especially nauseating as an amusing example of immaturity strutting around in the small boy's way of showing off and of trying to prove how smart he is in knowing so many, many naughty words. Bah!
> A hair brush used to cure it![27]

Reporting to Chick about reaction to the article in July, Nellie Howland jauntily alluded to the federal laws about sending indecent material through the mail and the possible protests by members of the board: "So far no word from Uncle Sam as to whether the remaining copies of the Bulletin should be destroyed. And so far no resignations."[28] But Chick's habit of making light of the criticism of the conservatives was more dangerous than he realized.

In June, after installing the *Three Centuries of Connecticut Furniture* show (doing everything he could to take the objects out of context by placing them on platforms like pieces of sculpture), Chick looked for a way to get out of Hartford and even America. It had been three years since his last trip abroad, but his finances were so tight that crossing the Atlantic seemed out of the question. (It may not have been a coincidence that he also had a new baby to escape, just as he had done on his last trip to Europe, the year David was born.) Melodramatically, he told Edward Forbes, "I am afraid that we are not able to afford any thought of Europe ever again."[29] He evidently made the same statement more than once: Philip Goodwin took the hint and invited Chick to accompany him to Europe as his guest on the *Bremen,* which was sailing for Cherbourg on July 6. Despite his plea of poverty, Chick immediately wrote to Stafford & Rand on Saville Row, ordering a tailcoat, a dinner jacket, a gray flannel double-breasted suit, a blue overcoat, a white serge coat, and several pairs of trousers. Just before heading for New York, Chick visited the Austin cottage on Harpswell for a rare family reunion: "Mother was well and Father was there too," he wrote Helen, "and everything seemed very calm."[30]

On the crossing, Chick and Philip Goodwin got to know each other better than ever, though as Chick reported to Helen, "Philip and I are so polite to each other that it takes at least ten minutes to get through each door but I think he hasnt minded me too much and I've really enjoyed him a lot. . . . We eat—sometimes drink—play shuffleboard go to the movies and swim every day at six and the time on board which I've discovered Phil hates even more than I do—has gone more swiftly than ever."

They also mingled with what Chick called "the other museum racketeers," from Conger Goodyear to Mrs. Charles (Bobsy) Goodspeed, whom Chick dubbed "Mrs. Chicago Goodspeed." The stylish president of the Chicago Arts Club had known about Chick from the time she had played hostess to Gertrude Stein during the Chicago performances of *Four Saints* and, before the ship docked, she and Chick had agreed to collaborate on at least one contemporary exhibition that fall.[31] From Cherbourg on July 11, he cabled Helen: SAFELY ARRIVED LOVE ON OUR DAY.[32] For the second time during their six years of married life, he was far away on their anniversary.

Writing from Paris the next week, Chick told Helen that he had decided to return on a later boat and would not be in New York until August 11 or 12: "I hate to be so late getting back I miss you so much, but I have never had the chance to do the things in Paris that have been arranged for me." This was his first trip to Europe since his recent fame, and doors opened as never before. In that first week he dined with the dealer René Gimpel, who arranged for him to meet Marie Laurencin. He made the rounds in Paris with Pierre and Teeny Matisse, who took him to a gallery that sold furniture by Bérard, Giacometti, and Dalí. (The Dalís invited him to dinner, but he had promised to dine with Jere Abbott and accompany him to the Paris Opera.) He lunched with Paul Rosenberg. He went to tea at Monroe Wheeler's apartment, where he saw Joella Levy's mother Mina Loy, the painters Pierre Roy, Jean Lurçat, and Kristians Tonny (from whom he bought a drawing for the Atheneum for $18), and the Barrs. On one day alone, Bobsy Goodspeed arranged for the two of them to visit Bérard, Mondrian, Braque, Giacometti, and Brancusi in their studios. "All this is very valuable," he told Helen. "I think that together we can get very good shows reasonably for both Hartford and Chicago."[33]

Chick was very much affected by his meeting with the great Dutch abstract painter: "I went to Mondrian's studio," he told Soby on his return to Hartford, "and there were all those arrangements of rectangular and square forms in primary colors. They had always seemed limited in scope and meaning. But the longer I stayed, the more convinced I became that Mondrian was a true artist, intense, dedicated and on the track of enduring discoveries."[34] He decided that he must buy one of Mondrian's latest abstractions for Hartford and tentatively committed the museum to an immaculate composition of intersecting black lines that formed white squares and rectangles and enclosed one small blue square. The price was 6,000 francs, or $399.65.[35]

Chick and Bobsy Goodspeed decided to produce a small exhibition of abstract art to open in Hartford in October and at the Arts Club in January 1936. The Whitney had already mounted an exhibition of American abstract painting in February 1935, and Alfred Barr was planning a comprehensive show of cubism and abstract art for the spring of 1936, but Chick's exhibition would offer a more focused look at "pure" abstraction. It would include works by Mondrian (several still in progress when Chick saw them), the Russian constructivists Naum Gabo and his brother Antoine Pevsner, and the Dutch Neo-Plasticist painter and constructivist César Domela. Gabo and Pevsner were especially interesting to Chick, as they had designed the sensational futuristic sets and costumes for Sauguet's ballet La Chat, which Balanchine had choreographed for Diaghilev in 1927.[36]

The other side of Chick, the side that relished the opulence of old masters, could not get enough of the milestone exhibition of Italian art at the Petit Palais, which included three hundred masterpieces, from Cimabue to Tiepolo, gathered under one roof for the first time: "The Italian show would have been criminal not to see," he wrote Helen. "I go almost every day even though it costs 70 c—enormous crowds theyve taken over 4 million francs."

In Paris Chick joined Helen's mother and her sister Lucy and motored with them to Brussels, ("such a relief—everything so cheap and the food marvelous—" he told Helen, "Chesterfields only 15 c and they were 50 c in Paris") where he visited the World's Fair. There he saw the unprecedented exhibition covering five hundred years of Flemish art, from 1400 to 1900, which he told Helen contained "several swell numbers." He asked her to deposit his "August allowance" (the one hundred dollars that was allotted to him monthly in their household budget) in their checking account, so that he could buy books and photographs for the Atheneum.[37]

Arriving back in America in mid-August, Chick continued to confer with Bobsy Goodspeed about arrangements for the abstract show. At first there was some fear that Naum Gabo would be unable to send anything out of France. "Because he is behind in his rent," wrote Mrs. Goodspeed, who remained in Europe for another month, "his landlord has seized his works, & he cant send anything to America."[38] But the impoverished sculptor managed to get around the problem, and on September 24, six containers of paintings and sculptures (so fragile that they were packed in fitted cases within cases) by Mondrian, Gabo, Pevsner, and Domela were loaded onto the *Lafayette* for shipment to New York.

Chick supplemented the show with other works by the artists. Katherine Dreier lent Pevsner's *Torso;* Jere Abbott lent a Domela from Smith College; one Mondrian came from James Johnson Sweeney's collection and another from the Museum of Modern Art. MOMA still had only the one on loan from Philip Johnson, which Chick had borrowed for his landscape show in 1931. These artists were so little-known that, six days before the opening, Chick had to ask Barr for "any dope you may have as far as dates and birthplaces are concerned on Gabo and Domela. Is Gabo's first name Nicolas?" Attaching such completely abstract works to their titles turned out to be no easy task, either.[39] When the Arts Club was at a loss to figure out which Domela belonged to the Atheneum, Nellie Howland replied that it was "the black one with the buttons on it that look like cough drops."[40] But the works were sorted out, and Chick took extraordinary care in their installation. Although there were only nineteen pieces in the show, they were so skillfully placed in Avery Court that they appeared to have been created for the abstract space they occupied.

Visitors entering the court on October 22 saw the cool forms of transparent celluloid and metal, their gleaming curves and planes rising in space, almost as if Chick had installed models of buildings from some distant future time. Widely spaced along the white walls were nine paintings by Mondrian. Two Calder mobiles were added to the show at the last moment and did not appear in the catalogue.[41] Two large placards on the walls offered unimpeachable endorsements of abstract art, which Chick took directly from Philip Johnson's catalogue for the Modern's *Machine Art* exhibition of 1934. The first was from

Plato (in the voice of Socrates): "By beauty of shapes I do not mean, as most people would suppose, the beauty of living figures or of pictures, but, to make my point clear, I mean straight lines and circles, and shapes, plane or solid, made from them by lathe, ruler and square. These are not, like other things, beautiful relatively, but always and absolutely." The other statement was from Saint Thomas Aquinas: "For beauty three things are required. First, then, integrity or perfection: those things which are broken are bad for this very reason. And also a due proportion or harmony. And again clarity: when those things which have a shining color are called beautiful."[42]

In his review of the show, T. H. Parker of the *Courant* teased Chick about his favorite new lecture, declaring that the trend toward abstraction would be "a relief and a refuge" for those who "have been unable to grow old along with Dalí" in the short time since surrealism had "reared its gory head and began to shake its Medusa locks in romantic agony." Chick had wisely limited the scope of the exhibition, Parker said, because he had "realized that Abstractions cannot be taken in large doses."[43]

Alfred Barr visited the show in November and gave Chick his own assessment. He felt that the works were all "very handsome," except, curiously enough, the Mondrians, "which as Russell [Hitchcock] pointed out looked rather as if they needed typographical additions." He did register a complaint about the checklist, which Chick had printed in gold ink on celluloid: "I had to make a copy of it before I could take any notes."[44]

Barr's own abstract show the next year, *Cubism and Abstract Act,* was the antithesis of Chick's exhibition, including nearly four hundred objects that filled all four floors of the exhibition space at the Museum of Modern Art. It encompassed every form of art—painting, sculpture, constructions, furniture, architecture, theatrical designs, costumes, photography, and motion pictures—and was accompanied by Barr's erudite catalogue of nearly two hundred and fifty pages. By contrast, Chick had nineteen well-chosen and elegantly displayed works. He felt that his abstract show was "one of the most beautiful installations yet achieved by the museum."[45] It was itself an abstract work of art.

Most of the objects in Chick's show were for sale. Katherine Dreier bought a Mondrian in gray and red, and Chick reserved for Atheneum the one in white and blue that he had seen in the artist's studio, although he still had not discussed it with the museum's trustees. He told the Arts Club that he had already bought a sculpture by Gabo and another by Pevsner—each $200—but not to attribute them to the Atheneum's collection in their catalogue of the show, as he was not ready to announce the purchases.[46] In fact, he could not get the money out of the trustees for another four months.

These works were approved only because they were inexpensive and because at this time the art committee gave Chick a relatively free hand with

Abstract Act, *Avery Court, October 1935*

the tiny annual modern art allocation. Not long after *Composition in Blue and White* was grudgingly accepted, Charles Goodwin fumed, "Look at that damn thing. Just crossed lines."[47]

Chick himself was profoundly affected by the implications of abstract art. His cousin Emily Hall von Romberg (later Emily Tremaine, an astute collector of modern art up through the 1980s), remembered seeing the Mondrian in Chick's office soon after he bought it. "That picture is having a very radical effect on my life," he told her. "I'm going to stop being a director. Where does Western art go from here?"[48] On the other hand, he valued the work as a powerfully calm icon of the modern, as far from the writhing neuroses of the surrealists as it was possible to go. He even claimed that its analgesic powers were better than aspirin. When his head was pounding, he told a friend, he had only to lie on his Le Corbusier chaise longue and gaze at the Mondrian, and his headache would disappear.

Buying the Mondrian was considered insignificant compared with his purchases that year of two sumptuous old masters: a sixteenth-century School of Burgundy diptych on wood, *Saint Gregory Celebrating Mass*, obtained from Wildenstein for $27,000, and Nicholas Poussin's huge dark *Crucifixion* of 1645–46—already a widely recognized masterpiece—bought from Arnold Seligmann & Rey for $12,500.

But the modern remained the focus of Chick's public programs. On October 25, three days after the abstract show opened, Le Corbusier, one of the greatest proponents of the abstract in architecture, appeared at the Avery Theater, the second stop on his first American tour. Philip Goodwin had arranged for him to speak extensively in the United States under the auspices of the Museum of Modern Art, the site of his first lecture, on October 24. The Modern had hastily assembled a small display of Le Corbusier's furniture to coincide with his arrival, and Chick lent the chaise longue from his office and a small table, delivering them to the museum himself.[49] He later assured the staff that "it was a pleasure to have a few legs for company on the ride."[50]

In Hartford, after screening a film of his work by René Clair, Le Corbusier came onstage clutching a handful of pastels. Speaking in French as his translator, future architect Robert Jacobs, unwound a four-foot roll of paper around the stage, Le Corbusier drew elegant plans and diagrams and explained his theories of housing. He described houses he had built, and set forth his vision of the city of the future—a fast, efficient, airy urban center of tall buildings on stilts with glass walls, flat roofs for aerial gardens, elevated expressways, pedestrian walkways, and underground parking garages—a vision that, to more than a few, was unimaginable. Even Philip Goodwin, who paid for Le Corbusier's visit to Hartford, confided to Austin: "I admire the new ideas, and think we are going toward them, but to live in one of his two hundred and twenty thousand human-being-honeycombs—or one of his chairs—would be hell!"[51]

Le Corbusier was captivated by Chick's new museum in every way, from the interior architecture to the exquisitely austere display of abstract art in the court and the newly conserved old masters on the gallery walls. Writing about the museum in his book on the American trip, *When the Cathedrals Were White*, the architect marveled at what Chick and his inner circle had made of Hartford: "This Hartford museum, with its youthful architecture, its joyous enlightenment, is only valuable because its director, Mr. Austin, and his two great friends, Messrs. Soby and Hitchcock, have a lively and optimistic spirit. . . . Thus Hartford, a small city far up in Connecticut, has become a spiritual center of America, a place where the lamp of the spirit burns."[52]

Telling Chick in 1936 that "you and the Museum of Modern Art have organized the most important exhibitions of modern art in the world," Le Corbusier proposed a grand collaboration among his fellow artists in Paris—Picasso, Léger, Braque, Laurens, Lipchitz, and Brancusi—for the construction and decoration of a villa or an office building in Hartford, sponsored by the Atheneum. He promised that he could convince his renowned friends to lower their usual high fees.[53] But Chick never pursued the scheme because there was no money and no interest in Hartford for a monument to modern art.

Earlier in the year, he had had his own grand inspiration and had sounded out Virgil Thomson and others about the possibility of presenting a gigantic music festival in the Avery Theater. By October, Chick felt ready to propose a week-long "Hartford Festival" to the trustees. There would be concerts, ballets, movies, and the American premiere of Erik Satie's symphonic drama *Socrate* with a mobile set by Calder. But the centerpiece of the festival would be the American premiere of Kurt Weill's opera *Mahagonny*. It was, he said, possible to do the work because Weill had just arrived in America with his wife, Lotte Lenya, "the only soprano who can interpret his music with the greatest degree of understanding and style."

To justify to his conservative overseers the production of so many new musical works, Chick reiterated his mission with a cutting implication about the general state of American culture: "It is our duty to do all we can to keep the stream of creative effort alive, else what shall we have to offer the generations who come after us as proof that we are not entirely sterile?"

The festival would culminate in a spectacular "paper ball" in Avery Court, he told the board, which would include extravagant decorations and costumes, all made of paper, to be designed by Pavel Tchelitchew and other contemporary artists at very little expense. Tchelitchew had always wanted to create a grand ragpicker's ball, something reminiscent of the elegant Paris soirees in *le style pauvre* that the Neo-Romantic artists were naturally attracted to. "Thus although costing nothing," said Chick, "the costumes, in the hands of persons of experience would be beautiful and fantastic in the extreme." Mrs. Richard Bissell had agreed to organize the ball as she had the Venetian Fête eight years earlier. The profits from the ball would go to the Atheneum: "Although it would probably be impossible to clear the sum of 3500 dollars again," Chick cautioned, "even a much smaller amount would help us considerably in getting through the year." On a final persuasive note, reflecting the growing feeling that, after three years of the New Deal, the country was at last beginning to recover, he told the board that "the end of the depression could at no other time be so appropriately and joyfully celebrated as now. It is time to have a ball."[54]

CHAPTER FOURTEEN

Fusion of the Arts

"Astonish me!"

—Serge Diaghilev to Jean Cocteau

N o costume was more appropriate for Chick to wear at the Paper Ball of 1936 than the one Tchelitchew designed for him. He was to be the Ringmaster. With a top hat and a red coat, he would lead a procession of fantastically bedecked merrymakers through his museum, cracking a whip. As it turned out, the Hartford Festival was more of a three-ring circus than anything Chick had ever undertaken.

When he announced the program to the press on October 25, Chick compared his plans to the famous European festival of opera and music that Max Reinhardt had founded: "We hope that eventually the idea may develop into something larger, like the Salzburg Festival, which attracts outside talent, and in which composers, designers and directors all collaborate."[1]

Chick felt certain that his production of *The Rise and Fall of the City of Mahagonny* by Kurt Weill and Bertolt Brecht would focus national attention on the festival. Weill had originally composed a shorter version of the work, based on six of Brecht's poems, which depicted a future American metropolis—a city of gold, set in a steamy bayou, where all was empty self-gratification, leading ultimately to self-destruction. This work, a "Songspiel," as Brecht called it, was first performed at the Baden-Baden Festival of 1927 and was recognized as a searing indictment of bourgeois capitalism in a sensational new style. Two years later, Weill and Brecht expanded *Mahagonny* into a full opera, which had its premiere in Leipzig in 1930. A riot had broken out on the first night, fomented by members of the Nazi Party, who excoriated the work as degenerate Bolshevism. But the opera was soon produced in Paris, London, and Rome with great success.

Through reports from friends like Virgil Thomson who had seen the opera, and through German recordings, Chick knew enough about *Mahagonny* to want to be the first to present it in the United States. As early as January 1935, he had asked Thomson to look into securing performance rights for the Friends and Enemies of Modern Music, possibly for a production that spring.[2] As the opera required a thirty-five-piece orchestra and a cast of singers especially suited to contemporary music, Chick decided to wait until the next season, when he might present it as part of the festival that was already taking shape in his mind.

On September 10, Weill and Lotte Lenya had arrived in New York, their first trip to America. Weill was finishing the music for Franz Werfel's saga of the Old Testament, *The Eternal Road*, which Max Reinhardt expected to produce in New York early in 1936, with Lenya as a principal singer. The composer's presence in the United States seemed a stroke of luck for Chick, who met the Weills at John Houseman's apartment in New York and discussed his proposed American premiere of *Mahagonny*. Weill showed great interest in supervising the performances, with Thomson as conductor and "Director of the First Hartford Music Festival," Houseman as director, and Lenya to recreate her role from the original production.[3]

Early in November, with the permission of the museum trustees and what he thought was the blessing of the composer, Chick began writing to the Friends and Enemies, along with his out-of-town supporters, asking each of them to be a patroness or patron of the festival for a donation of twenty-five dollars, which would give them a subscription to all the events except the ball. To Helen's cousin, Elizabeth Sage Hare, in Colorado Springs, Chick was open about his growing frustration with provincial Hartford: "I always swear that each of these Hartford doings will be the last, as there is little support to be had in the vicinity. But I am so fond of *Mahagonny* that I couldn't give up making this one last crack."[4]

After the success of *Four Saints* two years earlier, prompt support did come from Chick's varied constituency. Representing the sympathetic members of Hartford's old guard—they did exist, though Chick downplayed them—was Miss Anne Eliot Trumbull. This elderly descendant of the ancient Connecticut family of Revolutionary War fame wrote to "Everett" a bit stiffly that she was "not unappreciative of the much that you do to render the atmosphere of Hartford piquant and alert."[5] Rather more enthusiastic was Janice Loeb, a young graduate student at the Fogg and an ardent fan of Weill's music, who told Chick that his myth was growing at Harvard: "Your shade haunts Mr. Forbes—violently. You are brought into every sentence—becoming an historical personage, at least worthy [of] a 'Beato,' if not [a] Saint to wide-eyed and starry-gazed museum course disciples."[6] And there were Chick's contemporaries, the established highbrows of arts and letters, like Lincoln Kirstein's sister Mina Curtiss. She sent a check with the declaration that "I have such admiration for your achievements and for what you are trying to do that even if my house isn't painted this year I send you my twenty-five dollars."[7]

Yet such encouragement did not mitigate Chick's feeling that he was not valued or understood by the local elite. When Mr. and Mrs. Morris Joseloff, wealthy Hartford art patrons, agreed to contribute a prize of $200 for the best new musical composition by a Connecticut Valley composer, Chick told them that they had given him "new courage to go on with the Festival project."[8]

On November 19, Chick, as president of the Friends and Enemies of Modern Music, and Nellie Howland, as treasurer, signed a contract with Weill's New York publisher for the exclusive American rights to *Mahagonny*, guaranteed up to February 15, 1936. He returned the contract with a check for $300 from the Friends and Enemies.[9]

Almost immediately, a series of miscommunications transpired between the composer and the museum. After arranging a meeting of the collaborators, including Virgil Thomson, in Hartford, Chick drove to New York to pick up Weill, who had accepted a radio engagement for that evening without telling him or Thomson. The meeting took place without him.

A few days later, Weill's publisher informed Chick that he was "surprised and frankly embarrassed" when the composer himself appeared at their West Forty-fifth Street offices and told them "that he had no connection whatever with the production and that, in fact, you were not proposing even to consult him about certain artistic matters in which he felt he had a right to be consulted."[10] Appalled, Chick immediately invited Weill and Lenya to Hartford for the weekend of November 30 to clear the air. (The fact that he spoke German helped, as Lenya's English was minimal at that time.) Chick turned up his charm to full strength, and Weill was won over by his enthusiasm and the models he had made of the stage, with modernist constructions for the decor.[11] "Everything is again running smoothly," Chick assured the publisher, attributing the problem to "the occasional upsets of composers."[12]

But Lenya would not commit to singing in his production because she was worried that the Hartford premiere might conflict with the opening date of *The Eternal Road*, which was still not scheduled. By December 9, Chick had moved the Hartford Festival forward by a week to accommodate her, but he confessed that he was "getting extremely anxious" because he felt he could not go ahead with the opera without her participation.[13] To his relief, Lenya cabled him on December 12 that *The Eternal Road* would open by January 27 and that she would have two or three days off to appear in Hartford as long as Chick publicized the New York production.[14]

During these negotiations, other elements of the festival had to be addressed and artists had to be entertained. In November, Eugene Berman turned Chick's office into a temporary studio, where he designed a set for a

*Alexander and Louisa Calder, Mme Simone Herman, and Fernand Léger
visit "Chick's Museum," December 1935.*

"Mantinee Musicale" that would conclude the festival—Berman's first theatrical commission in a long career that would take him to the Metropolitan Opera.
And one morning early in December, Alexander Calder arrived at the museum
to confer about his part in the festival. In addition to designing a mobile set for
Satie's *Socrate*, he had agreed to make costumes for one of the groups that
would process through the museum at the start of the Paper Ball. The fact that
Calder had unexpectedly brought Fernand Léger with him reflected the exciting atmosphere of the new museum by that time. Chick bounded into Nellie
Howland's office that morning, saying, "Léger's here! Come and meet him." She
found the famous French painter standing in Avery Court, looking at remnants
of Chick's *Abstract Art* exhibition while a photographer who had rushed across
the street from the *Hartford Times* took pictures.[15]

Swamped by the plans for the Hartford Festival, Chick decided to schedule
two shows in January that would require little work on his part. The first was
The Paintings of Paul Klee, a group of fifty oils and watercolors borrowed en
masse from J. B. Neumann's New Art Circle Gallery in New York. The second
show, *Paintings in Hartford Collections*, was meant to mollify some of his

trustees who felt that he paid no attention to local collectors of more traditional art. This would be the museum's major winter exhibition, and for the first time since coming to Hartford, Chick handed its organization over to someone else, a young Hartford real estate broker named Henry Kneeland, who had begun collecting significant contemporary art and a few old masters.

Meanwhile, publicity for the festival rolled along. On December 20, Tchelitchew spoke to a *Hartford Times* reporter in New York, in company with Virgil Thomson, about his plans for the "Ragpicker's Circus"—"in torrents of English, French, and a mixture of the two." There will be "t'ousands and t'ousands of yards of paper arrange with originality supreme," said Tchelitchew.

> Each lady will want, you see, to have a costume design for her own personality. It will be stupendous! There will be draperies and garlands and vases of paper between the boxes, some of them with flowers, and some with feathers. I am tired of columns. I am sick of Greece and Rome, and all that foolishness. We will have vases—oh so very gay! And very, very, very much paper hanging down from all around.

Demonstrating with scissors and paper, he said, "This is the court, and here the boxes. And from here, and all over, come the streamers, cut like zis, and on them will be all sorts of spot lights, to change the colors. Oh, it will be very gay. Like a valentine!"[16]

The next day, Chick announced that the festival would be postponed a week.[17] A few days later, Henry McBride told readers of the *New York Sun* that the festival would be one of the high points of 1936. "I am most titillated, naturally, by the King Ludwiggian revelries promised us by Chick Austin at the Wadsworth Atheneum in Hartford." He mentioned the novel music events and the ball, which he had heard would be designed by Tchelitchew and Cecil Beaton, and of course the chance to see "all of Chick's extraordinary new pictures in the museum." The Paper Ball would have "all the museum's moral resources" behind it, said McBride, "just as they were for the immortal premiere of 'Four Saints.' "[18]

However entertaining such stories were to the public, resentment of all the attention paid to foreign emissaries of the avant-garde was building among local artists. January 1936 began with a letter to the *Hartford Times* from artist Aaron Berkman, a former resident now living in New York, whom Chick had featured in a show with Milton Avery and others in 1930. The Atheneum, Berkman claimed, had become "a playground for experimentalists." A European visitor to the museum "could get no more idea of contemporary American art than if he were in France. In fact, in the Hartford Museum he would get a better representation of certain cliques of Paris than he would in Paris itself, where fashion changes upon the moment and vogues are picked up by Americans long after they have become obsolete over there." It was "tragic and humiliating" that local artists were cut off from the "cultural center of the city." Attacking Chick directly, he suggested that the museum needed a new "directorship" with "a deeply rooted social, cultural and democratic outlook—utterly devoid of snobbery. This spirit appears to be totally lacking at present."[19]

Fueling the fires of dissent a few weeks later were excerpts from Chick's annual report for 1935, published in the *Hartford Times* under the headline "Austin Raises Question over Art Interest." Chick had not hidden his annoyance at earlier criticism, from inside and outside the museum, that he was too modern and did not pay enough attention to American art. Referring to *Three Centuries of American Painting and Sculpture,* he told the board: "Curiously enough, although there had been considerable clamor for American painting, this exhibition was less well attended than any held in the past." He had also tweaked the trustees about the success of his modernist activities: "It is most unfortunate that, as we have found, so few people seem interested in the occasional lectures offered during the season. In fact, the only well attended lecture of the year was that given by Miss Gertrude Stein."[20]

Chick's comments unleashed a flurry of letters to the editor right up to the beginning of the Festival, most of the correspondents signing themselves with such monikers as "Uneducated," "Vox Populi," and "Another Art Lover." One said that Chick had filled the museum with "clashing, dissonant compositions that might be products of the nursery or the asylum (or someone laughing up his sleeve)."[21] Another wrote that the public wanted the kind of pictures "that perhaps Mr. Austin does not designate as art at all."[22] An "Art Lover" called the pictures in Chick's recent exhibitions "trash" that was "thrust upon us."[23]

Offensive, and even ominous, as this barrage was, Chick was hardly alone among the museum directors of his day in having to cope with public attacks. That same January, there was a furious outcry in Chicago when Robert Harshe, director of the Art Institute, relegated Jules Breton's sentimental *Song of the Lark* to a storage vault. Ironically, Chick had shown the work three years earlier in his *Literature and Poetry* exhibition, where it had been voted the second most popular picture. Harshe's response to the criticism was uncompromising: "It's not good enough. That's why it's not hanging. In a weak moment during the World's Fair we showed it because it was voted the 'most popular picture[']. That shows the low taste of America."[24] Still, the timing of the Hartford controversy was bad for Chick's festival.

By January, he realized that the full-length *Mahagonny* would be too expensive and complicated, and so decided to produce a one-act version, which would require less than twenty musicians and would take only forty-five minutes to perform.[25] To fill out the evening, Chick would add *The Seven Deadly Sins,* a mimed cantata by Weill and Brecht, first produced for Les Ballets 1933 in Paris, with dancing by Tilly Losch and singing by Lenya and a male quartet. Lenya would sing again for the Hartford production, Balanchine's company would dance, and Tchelitchew would design the decor. (The tentative budget was $3,725, much more than the Friends and Enemies had on hand.) Chick hired Nathan Zatkin, who had handled publicity for *Four Saints,* to drum up an audience, and he also engaged New York agent Mata Roudin to secure a conductor and whatever special instrumentalists might be needed. She was also to act as a go-between with Weill, who immediately expressed doubts that a Hartford orchestra would be capable of doing the one-act *Mahagonny* and said that unless each instrumentalist was up to his standard, he would not permit the production.[26]

To guarantee the hiring of outside musicians, Chick sent a check for $1,500 to Mata Roudin on January 6. Nellie explained to her that this left the Friends and Enemies with $200 in their treasury, "so please make it go miles."[27] On January 10, Roudin held an audition of singers for the Weills at her house in New York. Chick obtained permission from the publisher to broadcast one of the performances of *Mahagonny.*[28] On January 11, Nellie reported to Roudin that "a TERRIBLE complication" had arisen with *The Seven Deadly Sins.* Tchelitchew had telephoned to say that the American Ballet could not do the performance: "Not enough time, not enough money, Balanchine won't, and so on. We are going crazy as the tickets are being printed, the announcements are practically in the mail."[29] The next day, Tchelitchew arrived in Hartford and declared he was too busy designing the Paper Ball to do the sets and costumes for the Weill ballet. Word also came that Fritz Kitzinger, the conductor Weill had finally agreed upon, demanded six weeks of rehearsals, well beyond the new dates for the festival.

On January 14, thoroughly alarmed, Chick took a train to New York to meet with the composer and spent the day vainly trying to track him down. From Grand Central Terminal, as he was leaving for Hartford, he sent a telegram to Weill at the Hotel St. Moritz, canceling the production. The next morning, he informed Mata Roudin that the whole thing was off, saying that he was so caught up in his other projects that he could no longer think of spending any more time on the opera. Despite his bitter disappointment, he had to begin installing the galleries immediately for his two paintings shows, scheduled to open in less than a week. He now had nothing except Satie's short *Socrate* for the big second weekend of the festival. "We are too busy to be low in our minds," he told Roudin, "but I would give practically anything to know what goes on in the Avery Memorial just one month from tonight."[30]

That same day, Weill wrote to Chick, accusing him of never making the nature of the Festival clear and claiming that Chick had misled him into thinking that Balanchine's company would do the ballet. "I am terribly disappointed of the way you have handeled this whole affair and you have treated Mrs. Lenja and me. I have done my best to help you, but nor you yourself nor the singelst one of your friends has shown interest in bringing about this evening. This is the only and real reason of your difficulties."[31]

Chick answered in kind, reminding Weill that he and Lenya had repeatedly refused to commit themselves to a contract: "You cannot for a moment think that, as a busy man, I can spend all my time in New York to [attend to] details that are never settled." He concluded that "the truth of the matter is that, with the exception of myself and a few of my friends, nobody wants to do it, not even you, I fear."[32] Nellie's reaction was more succinct. In her scrapbook for 1936, under a photograph of Lenya that she had cut out of *Town and Country,* she inscribed "Biche."[33]

Except for Balanchine's abandonment of Hartford in 1933, which had been mitigated when his company returned for their first public performances, this was one of Chick's very few failures. *Mahagonny* would not have its American premiere until many years after Weill's death.

For several feverish days, Chick concentrated on supervising the hanging of *Paintings in Hartford Collections,* the largest show he would ever present. Working on his behalf, Henry Kneeland had rounded up nearly four hundred oils, drawings, lithographs, and etchings from the seventeenth century to the present—so many, in fact, that they had to be broken into groups and displayed throughout the Avery building. Then there were the pictures by Paul Klee to be hung in the court.

Somehow the exhibitions were ready in time for the opening on the evening of January 21. As members of the Hartford Civic Symphony played in the court, three hundred museum members wandered through a vast hodgepodge of art. The European pictures in the *Hartford Collections* show included a fifteenth-century portrait by Hans Memling and a drawing by Albrecht Dürer as well as oils by Magnasco, Bronzino, Constable, Gainsborough, Turner, Degas, Renoir, Toulouse-Lautrec, de Chirico, Dalí, Miró, Berman, Tchelitchew, and Picasso. There were works from Japan, China, Russia, and Mexico. But more than half the pictures in the show were by American artists—beginning with an anonymous *Portrait of Miss Eggington* of 1664, one of the earliest dated American portraits, and continuing through the best-known history and landscape painters to impressionists and the more conventional of contemporary artists. Setting an example, Chick and Helen had lent ten works: drawings by Jan Breughel the Elder, Renoir, Miró, and Charles Despiau; an eighteenth-century design for a stage set; a watercolor by Marie Laurencin; some seventeenth-century oils; and a pastel portrait of three-year-old David Austin by Tchelitchew. The show demonstrated that there were, after all, paintings of surprising quality in private hands in the region.

The large group of works by Paul Klee, however, did not sit well with the trustees. A few days after the exhibition opened, Aunt Ruth Goodwin made a point of saying to Helen, "Helen dear, you know how your Uncle Charlie loathes the modern art Chick buys. This Klee fellow is really the living end."[34]

But Chick always had something ready to counteract the criticism of the anti-modernists. That night, he unveiled the School of Burgundy altar panel he had just bought from Wildenstein; Marian Murray in the *Times* found it suggestive of surrealism because of the small, disparate, and meticulously rendered objects on a wall in the background.[35]

A newspaper photographer snapped a picture of the Austins and their friends in Chick's office at the opening, looking at Berman designs for the Hartford Festival. Everyone in the room appeared relaxed, without a care in the world, But the photograph was misleading, for the event was frighteningly close. In late January, when Agnes Rindge sent a check for the festival, it was obvious that all was confusion around the upcoming program in the wake of the Weills' defection: "Enclosed please find—but *for what,* I wonder?"[36] Chick told her three days after the opening of his exhibition that he was "rushing off to New York" and would give her more details "about what is going on as soon as I know myself."[37] As he reported to another correspondent, his plans had

Left to right: *Chick, Jim Soby, Mimi Soby, Henry Kneeland, Beatrice Kneeland, Nellie Howland, Eugene Berman, Henry-Russell Hitchcock, Helen Austin, Paul Cooley, and Mrs. Edward Stimpson seem carefree as they peruse Berman's sketches at the opening of* Paintings in Hartford Collections, *January 21, 1936.*

"reached an unbelievable state of complication," and it looked as though the festival might culminate in disaster.[38]

On January 22, with nerve-racking irony, *Variety* trumpeted Chick's program under a blazing headline: "America's New Salzburg . . . CULTURE CAPITAL OF U.S. IN CONN.?" Citing *Four Saints in Three Acts* and the first public performances of Balanchine's company as examples of the museum's brilliant success, the newspaper announced, to Chick's embarrassment, the American premiere of the now canceled *Mahagonny*.[39]

Desperately enlisting the help of Virgil Thomson and Lincoln Kirstein, Chick finally filled the gap in his program with the opera-oratorio version of Stravinsky's *Les Noces,* which he had seen in Paris as a ballet thirteen years earlier. For $1,250, a New York group called "The Art of Musical Russia" agreed to perform it during the second weekend of the festival. As Chick had Gontcharova's original set design for the ballet in the Lifar Collection, he decided to copy it for the backdrop at this performance, as usual doing the painting himself—a welcome distraction.

He also announced that he had commissioned Balanchine to do a new "ballet divertissement" for the same program. It was to be a short piece called *Serenata,* with music by Mozart, featuring magical illusions. This subject captured Tchelitchew's imagination, and he suddenly found that, despite the pressure of decorating the Paper Ball, he would have time to design a set and costumes for a Balanchine production after all. As Balanchine and Tchelitchew had been inspired by watching Chick do sleight-of-hand tricks in one of his magic shows, the work became a salute to Chick as the Great Osram and was subtitled "Magic" in the program.

Dancing the principal role (and making her American debut) would be Felia Doubrovska, one of the last of Diaghilev's great prima ballerinas, whom Chick had seen in the original *Les Noces* and who was now teaching at the School of American Ballet. (When Eugene Berman heard that Chick was considering using the famous dancer, he warned: "you must control carefully the choice of dances presented by Doubrovska. Like all ballerinas, she has a naturally bad taste and not sufficient culture."[40]) Ironically, this debut would be her last public performance; visa problems soon forced her to return to Europe. The male lead was to be taken by Lew Christensen, making his professional debut.

The third work on the bill for Friday and Saturday was the American premiere of Erik Satie's *Socrate,* with a mobile set by Calder, as originally advertised. Considered Satie's masterpiece, *Socrate* was first performed in 1919. Satie had set three passages from Plato's *Dialogues* to music. The score called for a soprano, strings, a single woodwind, horn, trumpet, harp, and timpani. Thomson gave the single vocal part to two singers, soprano Eva Gauthier and tenor Colin O'More.

Calder of course had also been commissioned to design one of the entrées for the ball, and he chose the theme of "A Nightmare Side Show," for which he would design circus animals. Writing in early February to Nellie, who by now had taken on the role of Chick's second self at the museum, Calder said that he would bring the materials he needed to Hartford and make everything there. He would, however, need the help of a local blacksmith shop, which he asked her to track down. On the eve of his departure, with the opening of the festival only a few days away, he feared that he might be at the museum too early in the morning. Nellie told him that this would not be a problem: "Don't worry about there being no one at the Atheneum when you arrive, particularly if you leave New York early. We all live here now."[41]

As Berman worked on his set for the final concert, Chick decided that he wanted him to dress up the theater lobby, too. Berman improvised a Neo-Romantic fantasy world. Colorful fabrics festooned the walls, and pedestals displayed casts of historic portrait heads belonging to the museum, which Chick sacrificed for the sake of the theatrical effect. Berman remembered:

I used whatever plaster heads of American statesmen I could lay my hands on in the cellars of the museum. By smashing in a few noses and other features which betrayed too clearly the American origin of the model, by freely dousing them with running colors to achieve astonishing effects of real marble and painting in some cracks and characteristic features, I was able to transform them into Roman Emperors, Matrons or Baroque heroes. The effect of this last minute improvisation was immensely effective. . . .

Many of Chick's activities and productions verged at times on the brink of disaster because too few people had to do too many things at once or were lacking in the necessary professional help and advice— yet, in the end everything that Chick planned and showed to the public had that quality of taste, elegance and professional competence which belied the desperation and exhaustion which so often gripped him and his collaborators behind the scenes.[42]

The festival did not begin auspiciously. A blizzard struck Hartford on Sunday, February 9, the opening day, and few ticket holders braved the weather to hear the afternoon concert of "Music of Today from the Connecticut Valley"—a tedious two-hour program that critic Carl Lindstrom of the *Hartford Times* declared was "dedicated to the cultural drainage of the Connecticut Valley" and amounted to nothing more than "a series of fussy and unrewarding scores."[43]

The theater was just over half full that night for the film festival that Iris Barry had created, "Early Masterpieces of Cinematographic Art," which ran the gamut of movie-making, from Georges Melies's whimsical *A Trip to the Moon of* 1902 to *Queen Elizabeth* of 1911 with the tottering but still brilliant Sarah Bernhardt; *A Fool There Was* of 1914 with Theda Bara as the original "vamp"; two fragments from *The Whirl of Life,* featuring ballroom favorites Irene and Vernon Castle, also of 1914; and René Clair's *Entr'acte* of 1924, a surrealist work with a scenario by artist Francis Picabia.[44]

During the week before the next series of events, Chick closed Avery Court to the public, removing the Klee pictures to make way for Tchelitchew's decorations. Chick, Paul Cooley, and other staff members worked alongside "Pavlik" and Charles Henri Ford to help transform the space into a dream world with bundles of newspapers that had been collected from all over the city.

There was a crisis when Richard Bissell, the husband of Chick's social chairman and the head of the Hartford Insurance Group, warned that the decorations and costumes would present a monumental fire danger and had to be investigated. Inspectors reported their findings to one of the company's vice presidents, later known more for his poetry than his insurance work—Wallace Stevens. The firm decided that the ball could go on if there was absolutely no smoking anywhere in the museum except an undecorated room on the first floor; if buckets of water were placed inside each of the boxes; if firemen with extinguishers were posted throughout the public areas; and if the paper costumes were sprayed with a fire retardant before the procession of revelers.

On Friday night, Valentine's Day, Chick and Helen hosted a dinner for their friends in the art world. Then they and a glamorous crowd made up of trustees, museum members, out-of-town music critics, and a large New York contingent arrived at the Avery Theater. In the lobby, they encountered Berman's Neo-Romantic fantasy—the pseudo-Roman plaster heads, streaked with purple and green, set on tall pedestals placed about fifteen feet apart on three sides, each one backed by swags of gold fabric lined with scarlet.

At eight-thirty, the curtains opened on the "Grand Concert Spectacle," Chick's last-minute replacement program—nearly three and a half hours of music and ballet, with Alexander Smallens conducting "the Hartford Festival Orchestra." First came Stravinksy's *Les Noces.* Ranged in front of Chick's huge blue, black, and white backdrop—copied from Gontcharova's design—four soloists and a chorus, all Russians, sang the stark percussive music, based on both church modes and barbaric Russian folk tunes. One critic suggested that the Avery Theater was too small for such an explosive work.[45]

This was followed by Satie's *Socrate.* The contemplative and transparent score was such a contrast to *Les Noces* that some found it monotonous,[46] but Calder's set was recognized as unique and exceptionally well matched to the philosophical character of the composition. On the right side of the stage, against the sky-blue background of the cyclorama, were two steel hoops, one set within the other at right angles, suggesting lines of longitude on a globe, but a globe on its side, for the hoops were attached to an axis parallel to the stage, suspended on invisible wires like the bar of a trapeze. facing the audience. Then, connected to a wire strung across the stage, not far below the proscenium, was a huge red disk, first seen hanging just to the left of center. On the audience's left was a tall rectangle (ten feet high), painted white, suspended on wires so that it hung just above the stage.

During the first section of the music, with mesmerizing stillness, the red disc began moving across the top of the stage to the right, then to the far left, then back to its original position. Then the steel hoops started rotating toward the audience, moving down toward the stage until they stopped, reversed their rotation, and moved up to the proscenium. During the final part of the work, the tall white rectangle fell slowly onto its side, then tilted backward until it rested on the stage, only to rise again from its outward edge so that its other side, which was black, was visible. It stood up vertically and moved across the stage to the right. As the music ended, the red disc slowly traveled away to the left. "The whole thing was very gentle," wrote Calder, "and subservient to the music and words."[47] Here was a new dimension to *Socrate,* a ballet danced by shapes and colors. Calder had fulfilled what his friend Léger had suggested in 1931: "Satie illustrated by Calder, why not? He is serious without seeming to be."[48] Decades later, Virgil Thomson, by then a veteran of thousands of musical performances, both as conductor and critic, thought the Hartford *Socrate* was "one of our century's major achievements in stage investiture."[49]

The long program ended with Balanchine's *Serenata.* With its walls made of three layers of white chiffon lighted from behind in shades of violet and mauve, Tchelitchew's decor made a dramatic contrast with Calder's abstract set. A black door, suspended by red and green ropes, was hung in front of each of the three walls. Two chairs and a table were hung high above the stage on invisible wires. Dancers, first seen in silhouette as they approached the doors from behind the white fabric, made an eerie entrance, wearing blue greasepaint masks. Later in the performance, they created a sensation when they appeared onstage balancing lighted candelabra on their heads, disappearing again into walls through the visual magic Chick and Tchelitchew had devised. Firemen stood in the wings with extinguishers, as they did during the Paper Ball the next day.[50]

That evening, a series of dinner parties was given in Hartford and surrounding towns. In Farmington, Marie Bissell and her husband entertained the Archibald MacLeishes and their close friends Fernand Léger and Sara Murphy. Jim Soby and his wife hosted a party at their new Farmington house for members of their entrée, Calder's "Nightmare Side Show."[51] Calder intended to create his costumes for the ball out of brown paper at the dinner party. He and Louisa Calder were late arriving, making some of his guests so "jittery," Soby remembered, that they settled their nerves with large infusions of alcohol. The

Calders finally appeared, bearing, as Soby recorded, "huge sheets of brown wrapping paper, scissors, needles and strong thread. Yet it seemed to me that at one moment I looked around at old friends, at the next to see the house swarming with tigers, elephants and other jungle beasts." Soby remarked that their group was aptly named "A Nightmare Side Show" as "none of us was exactly sober, and our paper shrouds were starting to give at the seams."[52]

Tchelitchew had originally proposed dressing Russell Hitchcock in a collection of false breasts as Diana of the Ephesians,[53] but instead he came as "Architecture" in a multicolored ensemble with a cape, breeches, white hose, buckled shoes, and a picture of the interior of a Romanesque cathedral on his chest. The costume revealed what Helen Austin once called his "perfectly repellent" knees.[54] For "A Nightmare Side Show," Calder covered Hitchcock, architecture costume and all, with a brown paper elephant costume.

Beginning at nine-thirty, nearly five hundred guests entered the museum through the Morgan Memorial, as they had eight years earlier for Chick's Venetian Fete, then moved through Tapestry Hall and into Avery Court. They found themselves in Tchelitchew's breathtaking world. The skylight was spread with newspapers of different hues—pale pink, blue, green, and white. Forming a sort of canopy, long, brightly colored daisy chains hung down from the center of the skylight, their ends attached to the top edge of the balconies that ran along all four sides of the third floor. More daisy chains connected the third- and second-floor balconies. The outer walls of the balconies were entirely covered with newspapers that had been painted in black and white to resemble boxes in a theater, curtained with swags of newspapers edged with paper fringe, each box separated by striped pillars and peopled by dozens of strange faces of every race (a few suspiciously reminiscent of the museum's trustees), gaping down at the visitors. As at the Venetian Fete, Chick had arranged for changing colored lights, controlled by *Four Saints* veteran Abe Feder, to play over the painted surfaces and the party-goers, enhancing the make-believe atmosphere. Despite the extreme fragility of Tchelitchew's decorations, they were unforgettable. Henry McBride declared in the *New York Sun:* "No words will give you the richness of the decoration achieved by this Russian artist with a few hundred tons of abandoned newspapers. . . . Sir Philip Sasso[o]n's ball-room in London, with paintings on mirrored walls by Sert, was not more splendid, I assure you, than the Wadsworth Atheneum's entrance court on the night of February 15, 1936."[55] Chick later called the effect Tchelitchew had achieved "a sort of newspaper heaven of incredible delicacy, shimmering with extraordinary color." This was not mere decoration, he said, but "one of the most beautiful exhibitions that the museum has ever held."[56]

From a corner of the room, an orchestra began an hour-long concert as the party-goers gazed at the novel setting, marveled at each other's costumes, and sipped strong punch. By ten-thirty, members of the twelve costume groups had

*Avery Court as transformed by Tchelitchew for the
Paper Ball, February 15, 1936*

assembled in the Morgan Memorial. They paused to have their costumes
sprayed with the allegedly fire-retarding mist, then the orchestra struck up
musical selections especially composed by George Antheil, Nicholas Nabokoff,
and other contemporary composers. To the sound of trumpets, Paul Cooley and
Robert Drew-Bear, dressed as heralds, began the procession through Tapestry
Hall, past a whirring movie camera, and into Avery Court. Behind them came
"the Committee and Attendants," all in costumes designed by Tchelitchew: six
men and six women dressed as prancing circus horses, with pink and black
heads of papier-mâché and colorful paper equine bodies, driven by Chick as
the Ringmaster in his red, white, and black paper costume and Marie Bissell,
Chick's social chairman, dressed in a black satin riding outfit—each holding
reins and cracking whips.

Stranger sights came into view: Helen Austin, garlanded with paper flowers as Summer, next to Agnes Rindge as Winter; the Archibald MacLeishes, dressed as black and white horses; Ruth and Charles Goodwin as principals in "Mae West and the Boys," then Calder's "Nightmare Side Show," the brown paper shapes looking like something out of a surrealist children's book; "A Calendar of Trees," a troupe of older Hartford ladies holding branches of paper flowers; and "Modern Art," in which the director and students of the Hartford Art School dressed in bright cardboard and paper constructions of works by artists Chick had shown who had been singled out by critics as part of the outrage he was perpetrating on the public—Picasso, de Chirico, Brancusi. A group of broken pillars and other architectural remnants walked by, designed and led by Eugene Berman and undoubtedly named by Chick, "Les Ruines de Hartford, 3095." To the strains of Nabokoff's music, came "Beggars," led by George Balanchine, with Lincoln Kirstein and Eddie Warburg, ballerina Lucia Davidova, and a smattering of minor European nobility—covered with glimmering, shroudlike layers of gauzy veils.

But the most talked-about entrée of the party was "Poets." To the report of blanks fired from six-shooters and loud whoops, Charles Henri Ford appeared with six very handsome young men—among them Chick's old friend John McAndrew and Parker Tyler, future biographer of Tchelitchew and Florine Stettheimer. Some were cowboys, some bare-chested Indians with feather skirts. To the horror of Hartford patrons, they were all wearing makeup and false eyelashes. Tchelitchew called them "the children," but to Marie Bissell's daughter, Mrs. Hector Prud'homme, they were simply "nasty young men . . . kind of gay cowboys with false eyelashes, who did *not* go down well with me and my friends."[57] "The children" carried with them, on a litter, Charles Henri's beautiful young sister, Ruth Ford, an aspiring actress whom Tchelitchew painted and sketched many times. She was the Muse of Poetry. Over a black sheath, as she recounted decades later, she wore "a cellophane dress which was covered with letters of the alphabet cut out from all the newspapers, which I pasted on. Pavlik told me to do this, you see." Her headdress consisted of wires adorned with more letters of the alphabet. She sang a song written for the occasion by Vernon Duke, already well known as the composer of "April in Paris."[58] Bringing up the rear after this apparition was the twelfth and final entrée, "Perseus and Andromeda," with the Viennese dancer Tilly Losch.

Tchelitchew himself was not in the procession; he could be seen in the background, watching with arms folded, playing the simple artisan in a dark denim jumpsuit with a dark shirt.

After a midnight supper, the orchestra played popular tunes, and the revelers—some still in their costumes, others now changed into evening clothes—danced around the court, while Abe Feder continued directing colored lights

*Ruth Ford appears at the Paper Ball on a litter with the "Poets." Left to right:
Parker Tyler, Blanchard Kennedy, Charles Henri Ford,
Peter Linda-Mood, and Steve E. Cole*

across the scene. By four in the morning, the orchestra stopped playing, but some of the die-hard party-goers lingered until dawn, many in an extremely disoriented condition. At about this time, some of the students and the "nasty boys" from New York began frolicking in the pool. Then Calder, in what Soby called "one of his chronic fits of playfulness," pushed Chick into the pool. Dye from his Ringmaster's jacket ran in blood-red streaks onto the marble floor.[59] The last stragglers finally left the building at six-thirty in the morning.

It was no wonder that two thirds of the seats were empty for the final offering of the Hartford Festival on Sunday afternoon, a "Matinee Musicale." But the absent ticket holders missed a special occasion. This concert of "ancient and modern music," conducted by Virgil Thomson, was played on original instruments, an innovation decades ahead of its time, against Berman's architectural set, reminiscent of classical ruins. Among the performers was the great Viennese harpsichordist Alice Ehlers, who would make her New York debut ten days later.

It was of course the Paper Ball that most dazzled the attendees. "Your weekend was a triumph!!!" raved Alma Clayburgh to Chick from her perch in the Ritz Tower. "The seeing and hearing have done me in."[60] Agnes Rindge rhapsodized that "a rosy glow is still suffusing the landscape. . . . I continue to esteem you as the Impresario Glorious and now you've added a mandorla to the nimbus."[61]

But the gargantuan effort prostrated Chick, his staff, and even Marie Bissell. They all came down with severe cases of "la grippe" and took to their beds until well into March.[62] In some ways, Chick never entirely recovered from the Hartford Festival. For although his friends and admirers in the arts saw the festival and the Paper Ball as beacons of artistic daring, the trustees of the Atheneum were not happy. Instead of raising funds for the museum as promised, and as the Venetian Fête had done, the Paper Ball had lost a thousand dollars, an unacceptable sum to the board, particularly to Charles Goodwin, who still doubled as president and treasurer. He asked Mrs. Bissell, as chairman of the ball committee, to explain the deficit and relay to him any comments on the party that she may have heard. She sent a detailed, apologetic report and tried to emphasize the enthusiastic responses of guests. Goodwin took these into consideration, but the bills had to be paid, and he made it absolutely clear to Mrs. Bissell and to Chick that not one cent would come from the Wadsworth Atheneum. For nearly a year, at every meeting of the trustees' executive committee, there was a report on the amount unpaid, down to the last nine dollars.[63]

Goodwin and his colleagues on the board looked askance at the Paper Ball, not simply because of the cost. Tchelitchew and his "poets" did not go unobserved. Discussing the occasion decades later, Eddie Warburg observed: "Really, it's asking a hell of a lot of an old bunch of moneybags, who are the trustees of a museum, to take the loose-wristed boys who were around the place."[64]

By now, Chick's disregard of the board's preferences had eroded their reserves of goodwill. Goodwin finally imposed controls on museum finances, informing Chick that there would be no more outside exhibitions that year, that it was "imperative" that the museum not exceed its budget, and therefore "all contemplated commitments as well as purchases" would be presented to the business manager and the building superintendent for approval. He directed Chick to "see that a system of this kind is installed immediately."[65] Chick replied (on April Fool's Day) that he was not planning to have any other exhibitions that year, "at least," he added, leaving the door open, "none that will cost money."[66]

One of Chick's Hartford sympathizers vividly recalled Goodwin at this time: "He was a handsome man, but *cold* and *mean.* I'd see him when he'd leave Chick's office after a little discussion. He scared the hell out of me."[67]

The displeasure of Uncle Charlie and the trustees made Chick fear for his future at the museum. Late in March, he wrote to Julien Levy, who, as Tchelitchew's dealer, was pressing for payment to the artist for work on the ball. Chick confessed his consternation at the financial disaster:

The ball lost about a thousand dollars which annoyed everyone especially the President. A great deal of the blame fell on me. I suggested that the deficit could be lowered as we had no money to pay for it by paying Pavlik out of the picture funds. Pavlik was very much blamed for the Poets episode especially as they all had free tickets to the ball /and in return behaved badly/ as well as supper tickets into the bargain which lost money for us. In fact almost all of the New York contingent expected and got free tickets to everything.

Marie Bissell, he said, had spent hundreds of dollars of her own money in ball-related expenses, and he personally had paid $200 to produce Tchelitchew's design for the festival program in color because he wanted to be sure that it had the best possible reproduction. He listed the costume sketches by Tchelitchew that he thought he could get past the trustees, but warned Levy:

> It's going to be hard as hell to get the money anyway as everyone is so down on Pavlik, and because there is a very strong rumour going around that the whole festival was just a way of getting money for my friends. . . . We did not ask him to try to lure New York to Hartford which is what he spent most of his time on. . . . I know that he put far more into the ball than was expected, yet Hartford and especially the museum which is now very definitely anti-New York cant see that point and it is definitely better not to bring it up. I should like to buy a serious picture by Pavlik as we have so many of his theatrical things, but I think in justice to him and to me we should wait until things blow over a but [bit] because I am definitely seriously worried about my job here.

Wryly he sent "Love to all from the flood," as torrential rains that March had caused the worst flood in Hartford's history, adding to the general mood of dissolution.[68]

Levy managed to placate Tchelitchew, but fanned the flames of resentment that Chick felt toward the trustees: "some time you must put your foot down against Hartford using you for their own prestige, not adequately supporting you, and scolding you after the fait accompli. By taking all the blame you lose your own shirt, without gaining their respect. Rich people really respect only those who can pursuade [sic] them to spend money, and never those who try to save them their money."[69] Despite the advice, Chick had to turn down an offer from the Museum of Modern Art to lend the Atheneum a reduced version of its *Abstract Art* exhibition, explaining that "at the moment we are so out of funds, and modern art seems to be so unpopular here."[70]

Instead, at the request of Helen's cousin Elizabeth Sage Hare, Chick helped to arrange the festival marking the opening of the new Art Center in

Colorado Springs in April. He engaged Eva Gauthier and Colin O'More to repeat their performance of *Socrate* with the Calder set, and contracted for harpsichordist John Kirkpatrick to play music by Francis Poulenc and for Remo Bufano and his puppeteers to perform Manuel de Falla's puppet opera *El retablo de Maese Pedro*, based on a chapter from Cervantes's *Don Quixote*. Helen and Chick attended the opening, and Chick spoke publicly about making the modern museum a place for all the arts. The trip was above all a chance to distract himself with something outside the Atheneum, as he wrote to Elizabeth Hare: "You must know what a godsend it was for me to get away from Hartford just at that time, so that I could recover a little from the depression which followed the winter undertaking here."[71]

Chick was frequently away from the museum that spring, teaching at Trinity, presenting magic shows, and lecturing at the Metropolitan, the Cooper Union, and at Connecticut art institutions. On one of those occasions, feeling more keenly than ever that much of what he was doing was not appreciated, he explained his mission as a museum director more eloquently than ever—but almost as if he were looking back on his career: "I have tried to make of the Avery Memorial in Hartford a museum of living things—pictures, sculpture, architecture, decorative arts, even movies and music—as well as of fine examples of the past. For we must have the great things of the past to enjoy and to study, but with that valuable experience and pleasure as guide and criterion, we must surely seek to live in the present and to try to create the new forms which are to be our legacy to the future."[72]

For most of the summer, he, Helen, and the children retreated to the farm in Windham, where they entertained New York friends, including Joella and Julien Levy and Alan Porter. They saw a good deal of Laura Austin, who was ensconced at Uncle John's down the road.

Laura was a favorite topic among Chick's intimates. They all knew the story that demonstrated her faith in Helen: once, when she was traveling with Helen on a train, Laura got her red wig stuck in the window of the Pullman car and could not get it out. Helen asked her, "Why in the world do you wear that? You look so much nicer with your own hair." "I believe you're right," said Laura and threw the wig out of the train.[73] Virgil Thomson called her "nicely cukoo,"[74] but Joella did not see her appeal: "She was mad as a hatter. . . . She had a husband to have a child, like certain animals. . . . But what Helen told me about her was really shocking . . . that Chick would go and see her in the morning. She had him come into bed with her and have breakfast. . . . [Helen] said: 'What am I supposed to do? She comes to visit us and they get into bed together and he thinks it's all right.' "[75]

Chick was restless in Windham, busying himself with decorating a cabin on Cobbett's Pond that his mother owned, announcing that he was going on a crash diet and then sneaking off to a nearby store to cheer himself up with chocolate bars.

In September, soon after returning to Hartford, Chick received the final blow of this difficult year. Nellie Howland told him that she had to move to New York to be closer to her mother, who was seriously ill. Chick burst into tears at the news. He was losing his right hand. Julien Levy knew what the loss meant to him: "Lovely for New York," he wrote, "but I should think terrifying for you."[76] Little more than a month later, Alfred Barr hired her as his personal assistant at the Museum of Modern Art. It was not until long afterward that Nellie learned Chick had secretly arranged the job.[77]

In retrospect, Nellie's move to New York was symbolic. By now, the Museum of Modern Art, though it still needed a permanent building, had become the dominant exponent of contemporary aesthetics, mounting exhibitions like the comprehensive *Abstract Art* show the previous spring. Wealthy trustees of the Modern—the Rockefellers, the Lewisohns, the Goodyears— were serious collectors of modern art and were donating important paintings or funding high-priced purchases. Finally, there was a much larger and more sophisticated audience in New York than Chick could ever hope to have in Hartford. At the same time, by 1936 his ability to be an innovator was diminishing. There were few threads of modern art that Chick had not explored and almost no form of art that he had not already introduced into his museum.

More ominously, in circumventing the criticism of the local audience and the entrenched powers that governed the museum, he had begun to undermine the very freedom that had made his innovations possible.

CHAPTER FIFTEEN

After the Ball

Dancing time
May seem sublime
But it is ended all too soon,
The thrill is gone,
To linger on
Would spoil it anyhow,
Let's creep away from the day
For the party's over now.

—Noël Coward

Although the trustees had placed controls on Chick's power to initiate new programs, he still had the Sumner Fund. It continued to generate large sums; and with it, he could concentrate on the connoisseurship that had put him at the top of his profession. Throughout the rest of the 1930s, he bought scores of pictures, and he bought well. As the great majority of them were painted before 1800, the trustees were usually delighted.

Chick relied on a few close friends in the art market for his great purchases, whether baroque or modern. Most of the principal old-master acquisitions were supplied by Kirk Askew at Durlacher. Through Askew, Chick purchased Lucas Cranach's *The Feast of Herod* for $19,000, a panel painting of 1531 that was one of the most important examples of sixteenth-century German painting to enter an American collection.[1] The earliest known and finest version of Cranach's treatment of this theme, it depicts the moment Salome appears before Herod, his queen, and their dinner guests, bearing John the Baptist's head on a serving tray. With what Chick called "an extraordinarily naive sense of humor of most refreshing character," Cranach drew attention to necks and collars, particularly Salome's high gold and jewel choke collar with dangling pearls.[2]

The art crowd at a party in the Soby house, Farmington, c. 1939.
Left to right: *Iris Barry, Thomas Howard, Helen Austin, Pierre Matisse,*
Jane Cooley, Constance Askew, Henry-Russell Hitchcock, Chick, Leila Wittler,
Paul Cooley. Seated: *Teeny Matisse and Kirk Askew*

One of Chick's greatest buys in French seventeenth-century pictures also
came from Durlacher—Claude Lorrain's *Saint George and the Dragon* of about
1640, acquired in 1937 for just over $17,000 and immediately described by
The New York Times as a masterpiece.[3] This work was a splendid example of the
classical side of the baroque, a picture in which a serene landscape, rather than
the tiny galloping saint and the diminutive dragon, becomes the subject of the
canvas.

In 1938 Askew provided Chick with *The Return of the Holy Family from
Egypt* by Peter Paul Rubens, one of his few old-master acquisitions by an artist
of universal fame. The big opulent picture of Mary, Joseph, the young Jesus,
and their donkey, much of it the product of the painter's busy workshop, cost
$35,000, the second most expensive work Chick purchased for Hartford.

The next year, for a modest $3,000, Askew supplied an image that was
much closer to Chick's particular fascinations. A spectacular example of virtuoso baroque painting wedded to devout Spanish sensibility, Juan de Valdés
Leal's *Vanitas* of 1660 depicts a table strewn with symbols of worldly vanities—
books, flowers, cards, dice, coins, jewelry, a crown and scepter, a bishop's

mitre, and a globe. A cherub mindlessly blows a bubble beside a human skull crowned with laurel leaves, while behind the table an angel looks at the viewer as he lifts a curtain over a painting of Christ at the Last Judgment. The meticulously dazzling rendition of every kind of texture, combined with the fearful drama of the subject, made the picture irresistible to Chick.

In 1937 from Knoedler, another favorite old-master gallery in New York, Chick bought a rediscovered Magnasco, *A Stag Hunt in a Forest* (later called *A Medici Hunting Party*), painted around 1705, for $3,500. Well known from an early biography of the artist but out of sight for more than a century, the work illustrated an actual incident in which hunters had pretended to mistake a court jester, who had retired to the bushes to relieve himself, for their quarry. The combination of an amusing subject with the thrill of finding a lost picture by the baroque master who bridged the gap between the seventeenth and eighteenth centuries was a quintessential Austin acquisition.[4]

As the 1930s progressed, an increasing number of purchases came through Paul Byk at Arnold, Seligmann, & Rey. A jolly, heavyset German, Byk was relentless in pressing Chick to consider certain pictures, sometimes writing him two letters a day. He appeared in Hartford so often during the next six years that the Austin children called him "Uncle Sink-So" because he repeatedly expressed his agreement with Chick by exclaiming, "I sink so!"

Cornelis van Poelenbergh, Feast of the Gods, *c. 1630.*
Oil on panel, 12½ × 19 inches, purchased 1940

Perhaps the most entertaining picture from Byk, and touching upon Chick's love of theater, was a small full-length portrait of the famous eighteenth-century Italian opera singer Scalzi, by Charles Joseph Flipart, bought for $2,000 in 1937. The singer, showing off his slender legs, appears almost to be an exotic bird in his rococo version of a Persian nobleman's tailcoat, the tail raised stiffly, as if it were part of his own feathers.

In the years ahead, Chick would come to rely more and more on the suggestions of this persistent dealer. Two exquisite Dutch pictures came from Byk: *Boy with a Hat,* painted in the 1650s by Michael Sweerts, for $3,000—with an enamel-like surface and a luscious rendering of the face; and, for $1,500, *Feast of the Gods,* of about 1630, by Cornelis van Poelenbergh. The generous display of food, drink, and fleshy buttocks, as dainty cherubs strew flowers on the party at a banquet table in the clouds, conveys an almost illicit delight in sensual pleasure. Hitchcock observed that Byk "had a peculiar knack for turning up pictures that were of special personal interest to Chick."[5]

Despite the many acquisitions of European pictures from earlier centuries, Chick did not curb his efforts to add contemporary works to the collection. Most of them were available at absurdly low prices compared with their future value, but it was often difficult to convince the art committee of their merit. Usually, he took the money from his small and somewhat nebulous modern art allocation. Among the greatest bargains was surrealist Jean Arp's *Objects Placed on Three Planes Like Writing* of 1928. This was a framed wood relief consisting of three white biomorphic shapes, reminiscent of Miró. Chick bought it for a token $67.50 through the Museum of Modern Art, which was importing it from Europe with other objects for its own collection.[6] In 1937 he acquired Giorgio de Chirico's *La Maladie du général* from the Pierre Matisse Gallery for $400. Painted in 1914 and 1915, the image of an empty quarter of an Italian city, seen as if through an upper window, exemplifies de Chirico's anguished response to the First World War.[7]

But Julien Levy was Chick's primary source for modern art. Like Askew, he was a trusted intimate who could supply the best of what Chick wanted. From Levy in 1938 came a box construction by the then obscure American surrealist Joseph Cornell, called *Soap Bubble Set,* which featured a nineteenth-century astronomical map showing the moon, a white clay pipe, and a small wineglass containing a green egg. Levy told Chick that the box had taken Cornell a whole summer to make and that he had originally wanted to sell it for $300, "as he is a madman," but in the end Chick got it for $60.[8] It was the first work by Cornell to enter a museum.

At the same time, Levy sold Chick a powerful picture by the Polish-born artist Balthus, *Still Life in Violence,* for $600. It was a disturbing image of objects lying on a table, apparently after a terrible encounter: a smashed glass

Russell and Chick pose in front of The Street *by Balthus in the Soby house, Farmington, February 1940.*

decanter, a potato stabbed by a fork, and a loaf of bread with a large knife driven into it. This was evidently the first purchase of a Balthus by an American museum. Earlier in 1937 Soby had bought one of the artist's most monumental works, *The Street*, for himself from the Pierre Matisse gallery, which had presented the first Balthus exhibition outside of France that year. *The Street*, which was said to be the first painting by Balthus to enter a private collection in the United States, later went to the Museum of Modern Art. Here was the modernist network in action—Chick, Soby, Levy, and Matisse all working simultaneously to promote a contemporary European artist in America.[9]

But selling a modern work to the Atheneum was not always the same as getting paid for it. Chick invariably had trouble securing approval for these newer paintings, driving Levy at one point to implore Chick: "I *must* have some consideration given to our bill or I'll take an overdose of Luminol."[10]

In 1939 Chick made his most visually striking modern purchase—Salvador Dalí's *Apparition of Face and Fruit Dish on a Beach*, painted a year earlier. He bought it from Julien Levy for $1,750 at the same time he acquired Valdés-Leal's *Vanitas*. Like that baroque masterpiece, it was a tour de force of technical virtuosity, a supreme example of Dalí's "metamorphic dislocation" in which one image dissolves into another. In the center, a fruit dish on a pedestal seems to be a white face, or a mask, superimposed over a white tablecloth that becomes a beach. One eye of the face turns out to be the opening of a jug, lying on its side, while the other eye is the head of a dead child. The upper part of the fruit dish becomes the body of a brown dog, wearing a thick collar. The dog's back changes into brown pears, its collar a section of a Roman aqueduct. Among other smaller figures in the work are a nude black man facing the spectator, a peasant woman with her head bowed, and a tiny version of the face–fruit dish itself. Chick was probably able to persuade the art committee to approve a modern painting that cost nearly $2,000 because it was an intriguing picture puzzle and less overtly sexual than other Dalís they had seen.

As he had with Mondrian, Chick bought an important work directly from Calder. In 1938, for $350, he acquired *The Praying Mantis*, a "stabile" on a stand, which Calder told Chick was "about the best thing I've done."[11] It had been featured in the Museum of Modern Art's landmark exhibition, *Fantastic Art, Dada, and Surrealism*, and was one of Calder's biggest and most compli-

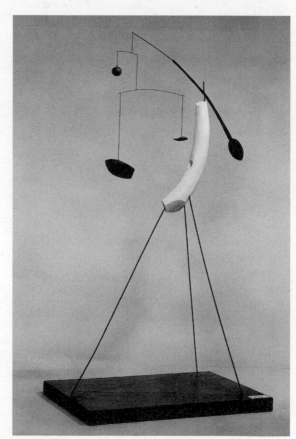

Alexander Calder, The Praying Mantis, 1936. Wood rod, wire, string, and paint, 78 × 51 × 40 inches, purchased 1938

cated works up to that time—an excursion into "surreal abstraction" reminiscent of Miró.[12] Like Mondrian and the dealers, Calder had trouble collecting his payment. A series of increasingly impatient requests, written in larger and larger letters, to be paid "PRONTO" came from Calder until a check was dispatched.[13]

The trustees allowed Chick to make such purchases not because they liked most of them, but because there was a tacit understanding that he could use his own discretion in buying a few contemporary works every year if they did not cost very much. When pictures had very low price tags, Chick felt free to buy on his own authority even those his trustees would find revolting. Such was a work like *The Clinic*, which cost $85, by American surrealist and political radical Walter Quirt. Here a black man is shown strapped to a board in a government-run medical facility, while satanic doctors perform experiments on him.

James Soby, as honorary curator of modern art, was a member of the art committee and recalled the trustee resistance when contemporary works were proposed for acquisition. "Occasionally there were rather stormy-polite sessions when Chick and I, with help from Mr. Day's saintly patience and sympathy, were trying to persuade our elders to approve some of the more advanced paintings and sculptures we admired."[14] Soby recorded that by the mid-1930s, he, Russell Hitchcock, and Paul Cooley had become Chick's "principal allies in the struggle to convert the Atheneum into an important museum and a brilliant showplace for the allied arts," a situation strongly resented by some of the trustees:

> I remember that one day two of the Atheneum's elder statesmen tried to break up this unholy alliance by carting me off to luncheon in New York. I had known both men and liked them for years, their sons having been classmates of mine at school. But when they tried the old, tired technique of telling me that I had been behaving like Chick's stooge, I could only reply, "You flatter me." The luncheon broke up in a morose silence.[15]

To counter the attacks on Chick for acquiring too much modern art, Robert Huntington, chairman of the art committee, tried to put these purchases into perspective for his fellow trustees. In 1936 he reported that of the $527,000 Chick had spent on pictures since he arrived in Hartford, only $4,500 had been disbursed for works by "the modernistic school,"[16] which should have silenced his critics. However, even Huntington grew testy, and during the next few years, he and Chick got into repeated arguments about whether or not the modern art allocation existed at all. Chick believed that he had $2,000 to spend as he saw fit. In June 1938, Huntington formally wrote to Chick, citing a trustees' resolution of 1935 that $2,000 a year be appropriated to the director for "emergencies"—situations "where an instant decision is necessary." He added that he did not consider the fund an appropriation for modern art and that "no purchases should be made out of this $2,000 that you do not think the Trustees would approve of."[17] A year later, when Chick brought back pictures from a trip to Mexico, Huntington objected to the notation, "Modern Art Allocation," attached to the bill. He informed Chick, "I think you did nobly on buying these things, but let's get this 'Modern Art Allocation' thing clear. There isn't any."[18]

It was just this sort of blunt assertion, well intentioned as it was, on the part of the trustees that frustrated and infuriated Chick. He could read the trustees' records as well as they, such as the minutes of an executive committee in 1937 in which Huntington reported that the art committee had authorized "the purchase of the drawing by Kristians Tonny from the Modern Art Allocation Fund."[19] The official records of the full board that year included a list of recent acquisitions by artists such as de Chirico and Arp with the notation "Modern Art Allocation" typed beside each of them.[20]

The battle continued into the next decade, until Huntington finally allocated each member of the art committee $2,000 to spend at his own discretion. "Chick and I at once went off to New York," Soby remembered, "he to buy pictures by Campigli, Jimmy Ernst, Clyde Singer, Tchelitchew, John Atherton, Corrado Cagli, Max Ernst and Leon Kelly, among others; I to buy paintings by Max Ernst, Yves Tanguy, Tchelitchew and Matta." Soby later acknowledged that the Atheneum "did acquire *avant-garde* works which most acquisitions committees in this country would have rejected impatiently at that time."[21] To Chick, the board's approval of a relatively few inexpensive purchases of modern art was not enough.

Chick's major winter exhibitions for the rest of the decade represented a return to the thematic surveys of earlier years. By this time, his reputation in the art world was such that he could borrow priceless paintings for Hartford and have the satisfaction of amazing the trustees and the public alike with the value and quality of the works. And his installations were always visually stunning.

Before 1936 was over, he managed to fit in two small exhibitions that did not affect the museum's budget. They reflected the art of Chick's two favorite centuries. The first, *Abstract Painting*, came from his admirer Katherine Dreier of the Société Anonyme, who paid all the shipping expenses as a contribution to the museum.[22] The show, notable for its early showing of the subtle geometric studies by former Bauhaus teacher Josef Albers, opened on December 11, just after it had closed at the Delphi Studio in New York.

The second exhibition looked back to the seventeenth century. For just two days, Chick borrowed one of the year's most influential traveling exhibitions, *George de la Tour and the Brothers Le Nain*, organized by Knoedler, which included loans from the Louvre, the Kaiser-Friedrich Museum, and the

Rijksmuseum. There was special excitement about seeing La Tour, the master of mystical candlelight scenes, who had been rediscovered only two years earlier through an exhibition in Paris. *Art News* editor Alfred Frankfurter called La Tour's technique "impersonal, abstract and expressionist" and pointed to connections between the art of the seventeenth and twentieth centuries, a correlation Chick had been demonstrating for some time.[23] He rightly promoted the show as a once-in-a-lifetime chance to see European masterpieces, and over a thousand visitors came through the museum on December 16 and 17.

At the end of December 1936, Chick decided to make his winter exhibition an exploration of portraiture, and with manic speed, he assembled a major retrospective. The opening was scheduled for January 26, but his first letter requesting loans did not go out until December 29—after his Christmas magic shows. He scribbled notes to himself on odd pieces of paper as the exhibition formed in his mind: "write Dalí about portrait of Gala," "get a Goya—Holbein," "elaborate Catalogue, all Wildenstein pictures to be illustrated," "will not need Velasquez as we have Cincinnati."[24]

He began sending telegrams to museums, galleries, and collectors on January 6. Many institutions were not able to comply on such short notice, but twenty-five lenders (ten of them dealers) sent extremely important pictures. Six centuries were represented in the show, which Chick called *43 Portraits*—from an oil on panel lent by J. P. Morgan, Jr.; to Hans Memling's *A Man Holding a Carnation* of about 1470; to Salvador Dalí's portrait of his wife, Gala, called *Geodesical,* an unusually modest view of the back of her head. In between, there were famous pictures by Titian, Velásquez, van Dyck, Rembrandt, Hals, David, Courbet, Renoir, and van Gogh. A characteristic Austin touch was the inclusion of an anonymous sixteenth-century optically distorted, or "anamorphic," portrait of Charles V, which had just been shown in the Modern's exhibition *Fantastic Art, Dada, and Surrealism.*

The traditional content of the show pleased the trustees, but the point of view Chick expressed in his introduction to the catalogue was distinctly modernist and harked back to Gertrude Stein's lecture about an oil painting being an oil painting. Pleasure from looking at portraits, as at landscapes, he said, was not related to the recognition of subject matter. He had made no attempt to present a collection of portraits that was "historically balanced," but to gather together "a group of very beautiful paintings all of which happen to be portraits." He found similarities between the earliest work in the show, the fifteenth-century Memling, and the most recent, by Salvador Dalí.

Great interest surrounded this exhibition because of the high number of famous and valuable pictures. The newspapers were quick to announce that the collection Chick had brought to Hartford was worth five million dollars. The local press declared sweepingly that the show was "perhaps the most spectacu-

Old Masters meet modernist elegance: Chick's installation of
43 Portraits *in Avery Court, January 1938.*

lar in the history of the Wadsworth Atheneum."[25] Chick had proven again that
he could please the trustees as well as himself.

His installation was inspired. He hung the pictures on the first-floor walls
of Avery Court and on both sides of freestanding panels, which he covered with
brightly striped fabric. Florence Blumenthal, Chick's new secretary, wrote to
Nellie Howland that "the court is actually transformed again—I could have
sworn that after the paper ball, it could never be done again—wonderful colored panels—coming out at you at all angles—subtle theatrical lightings—and
no paper!"[26]

For the next three summers, Chick traveled widely to find both new acquisitions and inspiration for his major exhibitions. The trustees were supportive
of this kind of museum business, and in the summer of 1937, Charles Goodwin
advanced Chick fifty dollars for traveling expenses in Europe and a hundred
dollars to buy lantern slides and photographs for the museum. For the first time
since 1931, Helen planned to join him on a European holiday. David was four
and Sally two, and Helen's mother had offered to take care of them in Castine.

Chick arranged to leave before Helen in order to travel by car through Italy.
With him were Jim Soby, recently divorced, and Nellie Howland, who would

become Soby's second wife. They were joined by Tchelitchew and Charles Henri Ford on visits to Venice, Rome, Naples, and Pompeii, and many locations along the way. Nellie acted as navigator, a road map on her lap, as Chick drove with abandon through the countryside, talking nonstop with a cigarette permanently dangling from his lower lip, Tchelitchew and Ford alternately laughing and shrieking with fright in the backseat, and Soby remaining his quietly amused self.

Far from Hartford, Chick felt free to indulge his sensual impulses. One day, as he and Charlie Ford strolled through Naples, Chick proposed hiring a prostitute and a sailor to make love. Sitting across a room, as the couple became engrossed in their activity, he was "poker-faced," silently contemplating the scene. "Chick was very intellectual in his eroticism," Ford explained.[27] By this time Chick had apparently resumed some homosexual adventuring as well, though only in New York or abroad, and Helen was still entirely unaware of it. "We knew it," Joella Levy recalled, "Alan Porter and Julien and I." But she was warned by Philip Claflin: "You ever tell Agnes Rindge or Helen about the boys, and we'll *lynch* you." "I was very discreet," Joella remarked. "I never talked to

Chick and Pavlik, Pompeii, June 1937

the women. I knew that they would be terribly upset. . . . It's too bad [Helen] was so unsophisticated. She was very inexperienced. . . . But she was a great lady."[28]

Traveling with Agnes Rindge, Helen arrived in Europe early in July and, after staying in Paris and Strasbourg, met up with Chick in Vienna on July 16. From then on, as she told her mother, "I can truthfully say I have never had such a good time in my life before. . . . it was so wonderful to be together again." Helen and Chick spent three mornings at the vast Kunsthistoriches Museum, visited innumerable private collections, toured Schönbrunn Palace, and dined at the Hotel Sacher before moving on to Salzburg, where harpsichordist Alice Ehlers arranged for them to stay in a sumptuous apartment. The city looked especially beautiful on their first night, Helen wrote, with "candles in *every* window in Salzburg, & the surrounding hills." But these lights were not festive. They marked the third anniversary of the assassination of Austria's president, Engelbert Dollfuss, by Austrian Nazis.

Chick and Helen went on a musical marathon, beginning with the opening performance of the Salzburg Festival, *Fidelio*, with Elisabeth Schumann— "but Toscannini [*sic*] certainly walked away with the show," Helen wrote.[29] They went to a performance of Verdi's *Falstaff* and heard masses by Bach, Brahms, and Mozart in Salzburg Cathedral. So appealing was the magnificent lake outside Salzburg, the Wolfgangsee, that they talked of renting a house and bringing the children over the next summer.

Extravagantly, they took the Orient Express to Paris, where their breakneck pace continued with hours spent together at dealers and exhibitions in France, Belgium, Holland, and England, to say nothing of nights of theater and music and reunions with close friends in the art world who were also circulating throughout Europe that summer—the Cooleys, the Matisses, the Askews, Jere Abbott, and Agnes Rindge. After a quick trip to Scotland, they sailed from London on August 20.[30]

But it was the thousands of paintings that dominated Chick's memory when they returned to Hartford. "We lived in galleries," he told a reporter. "I think we saw every picture in Europe."[31]

On this European holiday, Chick's various worlds were beginning to intersect. With Jim Soby and Nellie, Pavlik and Charlie, he was at his least inhibited. Helen saw the inexhaustible enthusiast, a companion who loved sharing as many moments of art and music and fun with her as they could pack into a day. The time Chick had spent with dealers was productive. He returned with twelve oil paintings for the museum, the largest haul he had made during any excursion to Europe. Four were from the Galerie Sanct Lucas in Vienna, a gallery Chick and Agnes Rindge considered a great discovery, as it was a source for better-known dealers. The other pictures were from galleries in

*Nellie, Chick,
and Leonid
unwind at
Cesenatico,
Italy, June
1937.*

Amsterdam. Six were outstanding still lifes, and by the time he had finished his buying spree, Chick had the germ of his next winter exhibition—*The Painters of Still Life.*

In the first week of September, soon after he and Helen arrived back in Hartford, Chick was interviewed by the press about the changes in Europe since his last trip, in 1935. He was struck by the powerful effects of Fascism. In Germany, he saw "thousands of children about ten years old" wearing "man-sized knapsacks on their backs, like businesslike Boy Scouts, and there is a great show of military efficiency. In Rome there seem to be as many soldiers as civilians." He reported that he had never seen so many first-rate pictures on the market in Europe, but that they were being sold quickly. This in itself was a sign of disruption in the political and social fabric.[32]

Before organizing the still-life show, Chick busied himself with another project. Back in March, he had approached the trustees with the suggestion that Kristians Tonny, the Dutch Neo-Romantic artist whose works he had first shown in 1931, should decorate the side walls of the Avery Theater. He felt that the theater would be enhanced with lyric, representational images that would entertain future audiences. Mural paintings were in vogue during the Depression, the Works Progress Administration having commissioned artists to paint many for public buildings. As Tonny's style was not too modern, Chick was able to convince the trustees to hire the artist for the project, which could be paid for from the Sumner Fund. In mid-October, Tonny and his wife, Marie Claire, arrived in Hartford from Mexico, where they had been living in near poverty. Having already prepared cartoons for the works, Tonny set to work to cover the walls of the theater from the proscenium arch to the lobby doors.

It was a small step from the approval of murals for the theater to Chick's proposal that the museum should unveil the works, scheduled for completion in January, in conjunction with some kind of theatrical performance. He had bided his time for many months since the Hartford Festival. He had bought splendid pictures and mounted a magnificent exhibition that had made the trustees happy. But he had never stopped dreaming of new artistic collaborations. In September, he found just what he wanted, in the form of Ballet Caravan.

Lincoln Kirstein had created the company in the spring of 1936, after Balanchine had begun doing choreography for Radio City Music Hall and Hollywood movies. For four years, Ballet Caravan would give leading dancers from the School of American Ballet enormous experience, both as performers and choreographers, as they traveled the country presenting commissioned ballets on American themes by young American composers and designers. The company had actually appeared in Hartford the previous December, but as Chick was still paying for the Paper Ball, they had performed in the auditorium of their sponsor, the Hartford Women's Club. Now Kirstein offered Chick three premieres to be given at the museum in the beginning of 1938. Chick saw the makings of another milestone.

Approaching the trustees, he argued that he would not be producing or designing the show as he had during the Hartford Festival. Furthermore, the ballets all had American themes that should please a general audience, and the performances could be paid for by ticket sales supplemented with a few donations from the Friends and Enemies. He was allowed to proceed. But once he saw the door opening, his ambitions grew. In a letter to the Friends and Enemies at the end of December 1937, he not only described the upcoming Ballet Caravan performances in conjunction with the unveiling of the Tonny "decorations," but also announced the premiere later that season of a new production of John Webster's Jacobean drama, *The Duchess of Malfi*, "directed and acted by Orson Welles whose 'Julius Caesar' is currently a New York sensation," with sets and costumes by Tchelitchew, which were already in progress. He asked for money to support both the ballet and the Webster play, "which will be certain to continue Hartford's prestige as a center of interest in music."[33] As far as Chick was concerned, despite the setback from the Paper Ball, the "Hartford movement" that he had talked about after *Four Saints* was still alive.

The opening night of Ballet Caravan on January 6, 1938, seemed to revive some of the glamour of his other triumphs. Once again, friends in the New York art world came to Hartford, expecting more Austin magic. They entered the theater before the eight-thirty curtain time, and draperies covering the side walls were swept away to reveal the new murals. They conjured up a mythological vision of chase and pursuit, a horizontal rush of graceful primitive figures—horses with naked riders, bulls, dogs—to and from the proscenium arch, reminiscent of ancient cave paintings. In one corner, a futurist city arises in clouds; in another, a hayrick burns while monkeys escape the flames. Asked to interpret these images, Tonny replied that there was no meaning. All he would say was that the figures were "a series of rhythmical arabesques without a formal composition. I think the best kind of composition comes without consciousness." Chick found the enigmatic quality of the works a refreshing escape from clichés of municipal wall-painting: "We have gone through a period of literature and political subject matter in mural painting. We are sick of Mexican Communist preachments and of ladies representing the civic virtues and the pastoral vices. Here we have no story, no propaganda, no symbolism, merely a dreamy space peopled with rushing figures."[34]

Minutes after the audience had their chance to scan the paintings, the lights dimmed, and the curtains opened on the first of the three ballets, *Show Piece*, a "Ballet Work-Out in One Act." A single piano struck up Robert McBride's lively score and the dancers demonstrated their virtuosity in a circuslike atmosphere, with such pieces as "strut," "jig," "pizzicato," "bolero," "waltz," and "nightmare," choreographed by dancer Erick Hawkins.[35] The second was *Filling Station*, a "Ballet-Document in One Act," with a jazzy score by Virgil Thomson, choreography by Lew Christensen—who danced the principal role of the gas station attendant—and sets and costumes by Kirstein's future brother-in-law, painter Paul Cadmus. The Cadmus decor—his only design for a theatrical production—evoked a comic-strip world, symbolic of the day-to-day life of the American "Everyman," in which the fates of a gangster, a policeman, and a young couple converge at the quintessential American stopping place. Recognized as one of the first significant American works of classical dancing, *Filling Station* found a place in the repertoire of dance companies for decades. The last ballet on the program, *Yankee Clipper*, a "Ballet-Voyage in One Act," with music by Paul Bowles and costumes by Charles Rain, told the story of the Farm Boy turned sailor, danced by its choreographer, Eugene Loring, who travels to the South Seas, Japan, Indochina, and West Africa, and comes of age. Hartford critics praised Ballet Caravan, asserting with questionable accuracy that there had not been such sustained applause in Chick's theater since the opening of *Four Saints*—the standard by which his theatrical productions in Hartford were always measured.[36]

Avery Theater with the newly installed murals by Kristians Tonny, 1938

The ballets behind him, Chick now charged ahead with the still-life exhibition and in just three weeks assembled eighty-nine pictures of the highest quality, covering six centuries, from twenty-six lenders. (The most generous of these was the ever-eager Paul Byk at Seligmann, who supplied eight, telling Chick soothingly that "your worries are partly my worries."[37]) Chick hung the works according to seven schools of painting—Italian, Spanish, Dutch, Flemish, German, French, and American. Artists ranged from Caravaggio and Zurbarán to Chardin and Delacroix, Cézanne, Picasso, Braque and Matisse, Miró and Dalí, with a few favored Americans, such as Raphaelle Peale, William Harnett, and Georgia O'Keeffe. Five recent acquisitions were on view for the first time, including a tour de force by eighteenth-century Spain's greatest master of the still life, Luis Egidio Meléndez: *Pigeons, Onions, Bread, and Kitchen Utensils,* for which Chick had paid $950 in Amsterdam. It was a larger and more balanced presentation than *43 Portraits.* As with the landscape show, he claimed that this was the first comprehensive still-life exhibition ever held in an American museum.[38]

Tracing the concept of the still life in European art in another of their joint introductions for the catalogue, Chick and Hitchcock asserted that the increased interest in Dutch still lifes reflected a return to accurate representation in painting, as seen in works by artists like Tchelitchew and Dalí: "For contemporary art has always a double importance. Besides its own intrinsic interest, it is perpetually leading us into some new part of the past which has been forgotten." Chick's enthusiasm for these works burst through the art-historical prose: "What exquisite surfaces are to be enjoyed in these seventeenth century pictures! What simple purity of craftsmanship! They are not at all like the still-lifes of the art schools, those *natures mortes* as the academic term so well has it. Rather these insects, these shells, these hams, seem to live with something of the mysterious double-life to which the Surrealists have called our attention."[39]

In his two most recent winter exhibitions, Chick had presented elegant retrospectives of a major genre of art, heavily weighted toward old masters but given a pinch of controversy with a recent work by Dalí. Among the trustees and members of the public, Chick seemed to have succeeded in calming the waters he had stirred up with his large doses of modern art. But the exhibitions impressed his fellow museum directors as well. Alfred Barr, not given to superlatives, told Chick that he thought the still-life exhibition was "one of the most distinguished and interesting shows ever put on in America."[40]

During the next two months, however, Chick felt he had to remind the public of their own era. In late February, just a week and a half after the still-life exhibition closed, he installed a show of nearly thirty paintings in Avery Court, calling it *Modern European Art, 1900–1937*. Two thirds of the works came from Jim Soby, and they were probably exhibited as a courtesy to a friend. Jim and Nellie Howland had been married in New York on February 12, and the removal of their pictures to the Atheneum was a convenient security measure during their honeymoon.

Chick also invited one of the heroes of modernism, Bauhaus founder Walter Gropius, to speak in the Avery Theater in February about "The New Horizon in Architecture." Having seen the Bauhaus School condemned by the Nazis, he, his wife, and his young daughter had emigrated first to London in 1934 and then in 1937 to the United States, where he had accepted a lifetime teaching position at Harvard's Graduate School of Design. In Hartford, Gropius spoke about the need for low-cost housing, multistoried and undecorated, declaring that "ornament is doomed to failure" because it "originates in harmonious periods," which the twentieth century presumably was not.[41] Dining at the Austin house that evening, Gropius saw the dressing room Chick had modeled on the one in the architect's house near the original Bauhaus in Dessau, a reminder of how drastically life had changed in Europe.

Chick's third look at modernism that season came in late March with *Constructions in Space*, sculptor Naum Gabo's first one-man show in any museum. Julien Levy had brought the objects over from the London Gallery for exhibition in his new gallery on Fifty-seventh Street, but gave Chick the chance to show them first. Gabo and his American-born wife, the painter Miriam Israels, came to the United States from London to unpack and prepare twelve delicate constructions, mostly made of thin plastic components, for exhibition.[42] The futuristic installation sent a message to the community that Chick was not going to allow contemporary art to slip into the background. After the show, Chick bought Gabo's *Construction on a Line in Space,* and emphasized the museum's commitment to abstract art by creating a gallery on the second floor of the Avery for this and other works from the permanent collection by such artists as Calder, Mondrian, Arp, and Miró, along with a Negro mask, an oceanic figure, as well as the Brancusi *Blonde Negress* on loan from Philip Goodwin.

Throughout the spring of 1938, Chick had been distracted by his father's worsening health. In April, from the Veteran's Hospital in Chelsea, Massachusetts, Arthur Austin wrote to Laura as he might have reported to a casual acquaintance: "I had a birthday last Monday and got some ice cream and candy for the nurses which they seemed to enjoy very much."[43] By June, he was well enough to go to the farm in Windham, where Helen, Chick, and the children joined him and Laura for two weeks. He died on August 23 at the age of seventy-seven at Uncle John's, and was buried with the Austin family in Belgrade, Maine. Chick later told his children, "My greatest regret is that I never really knew my father."[44]

At the end of the summer, Chick decided to return to Europe. Although the Germans had annexed Austria in March and tensions were rising in Europe, he hoped to find more bargains among the dealers and to secure loans for an ambitious new exhibition he was planning for the next winter—America's first comprehensive exhibition of paintings by Nicholas Poussin. Chick had already bought the great *Crucifixion* by this most influential of French seventeenth-century artists. Now he wanted to do for Poussin in 1939 what he had done for Picasso five years earlier. Chick asked Jere Abbott to help him organize the show, promising that Abbott could borrow it for Smith College after its Hartford run. On September 9, the two of them sailed for Europe on the *Bremen.*

After stopping in Hamburg, his favorite source for magic paraphernalia, Chick went on with Jere Abbott to the Netherlands, England, and France. They arrived in Paris just before the Munich Crisis, precipitated by Hitler's mobilization of the German army in preparation for an invasion of the Sudetenland in Czechoslovakia. On September 28, France came within two hours of mobilization, on the report that Germany was actually marching on the Czech republic. As Chick told the *Courant* ten days later,

the report was, of course, absolutely unfounded, but the war scare was so bad that no one wanted to sell or show pictures. The paintings in

The Louvre had been removed. The French people who hadn't believed war possible suddenly decided that it might just be something they would have to go through. They didn't get excited but their faces were solemn. There was no laughter on the streets. They didn't want war. Nobody seems to want war.

Chick watched as Paris was transformed into a state of readiness. The streetlights were all fitted with blue bulbs, invisible to invading airplanes. Sand was piled up on street corners to help prevent the spread of fire in case buildings were bombed. It was almost impossible for him to find a taxi; they had been commandeered to transport men called up for service. Instructions for evacuating the city within thirty-six hours were issued. For five days, Chick reported, no one could talk of anything but war. "When a picture dealer won't show you a picture," he added wryly, "something is pretty serious."[45]

At the height of the tension, Chick boarded the boat train from Paris to Le Havre, where he expected to embark on the German liner *Europa* for New York. Five miles outside the city, word came that the ship had been ordered back to a German port, so the train returned to Paris. On September 30, when British Prime Minister Neville Chamberlain and French President Édouard Daladier signed an agreement with Hitler, pledging peaceful intentions, the *Europa* returned to Le Havre, and on October 1, Chick finally sailed. Nine days later, Germany marched into the Sudetenland.

Despite the crisis, Chick successfully negotiated loans from important European collections, including the Louvre, for the Poussin show. Soon after his return, he secured permission from the Atheneum's trustees and, on November 19, told the press that the French ambassador to the United States, Count René Doynel de St. Quentin, would head an honorary committee for the exhibition, which would open in February.[46]

As these plans developed, Chick gave Hartford a look at contemporary art in three forms. First, in October, he opened a six-week series of foreign films—German, Russian, French, British, Czech, and Mexican—which by now had a local following. Then, in November, he jolted the public with the outer limits of Neo-Romantic painting by showing one of Tchelitchew's most complex and shocking works: *Phenomena*. Seven feet high and nine feet wide, the picture was a grotesque tapestry in distorted perspectives, peopled by circus freaks and public figures like Hitler and Mussolini, Tchelitchew himself, and his friends and enemies in the art world. Gertrude Stein was depicted as Sitting Bull with Alice Toklas as a knitting maniac, while the pudgy and unkempt Bébé Bérard had been transformed into a bearded lady. Joella Levy appeared as a woman with multiple breasts. Many of these creatures were nude and engaging in bizarre or obscene activities. *Art News* had hated it when it was shown at Julien Levy's gallery the previous month, telling its readers that similar works "are to be found in profusion on the walls of the public toilets of the city."[47] With Tchelitchew verging on the suicidal after such reviews, Chick welcomed the chance to encourage him and felt secure enough to stir up the Hartford bourgeoisie. But exhibiting the painting—which his trustees could only regard as hideous—by the perpetrator of the Paper Ball seemed like a deliberate attempt to thumb his nose at the board. At best, Chick had been dangerously impolitic.

Early in December, he offered the first of what he billed as "concerts intimes," sponsored jointly by the Friends and Enemies of Modern Music and the museum. Austrian-born composer Ernst Krenek, best known for his opera *Jonny Spielt Auf*, gave a lecture-concert on "Why Modern Music is Unpopular." The previous March, shortly after the German takeover of Austria, Krenek had written Chick from Amsterdam, telling him that "my situation is very serious after the tragic events in my country. . . . I am more than grateful for every kind of support in these most painful circumstances."[48] Chick not only gave him a choice of lecture dates, but suggested that Krenek participate in a larger project in 1939.[49] Krenek fled Europe at the end of August to take up residence in the United States.

Speaking to a half-empty theater, Chick used his introduction of the composer to explain his aims in founding the Friends and Enemies of Modern Music a decade earlier. He had hoped, he said, that the Hartford audience would gradually develop an appreciation of modern composers and that the society's name would be changed to "the Friends of Modern Music." He said that he had not yet found any reason to make the change.[50] Krenek then gave a formidable discourse on the differences between conventional music and the atonal music he was then writing. In addition to his own compositions, he played works by Arnold Schoenberg, illustrating his points by drawing diagrams on a blackboard. The *Hartford Times* reported that Krenek's diagrams were at least easier to comprehend than the official graphs showing the relief given to the indigent of Connecticut each year—which probably summed up the feelings of the audience. (Even Chick understood how the composer's music sounded to the uninitiated. He joked to a friend that there were two ways to remember the pronunciation of the composer's name: "It's either 'Creaks for Krenek' or 'Shrieks for Shrenek.' "[51])

As soon as 1939 began, Chick concentrated on the Poussin show. He and Jere Abbott had arranged for the eminent art historian Walter Friedlaender to write the catalogue essay. They had contacted a long list of museums, dealers, and collectors in America, England, France, Sweden, Denmark, and Ireland. This time, however, Chick stumbled, but not because of his usual last-minute rush. The political situation in Europe was so precarious that potential lenders were afraid to send their pictures. Furthermore, the San Francisco World's Fair had already preempted many of the pictures he wanted from American collections. On January 20, Chick had to cancel the show, though he hoped to go abroad that summer and secure additional paintings and drawings in order to produce it the following year.[52]

For the first time, Chick was left without an exhibition for the annual meeting and had to turn to friends to help him fill in his schedule with smaller shows. From Julien Levy came *Documents of Cubism*, consisting of pictures owned by a Paris collector, Ladislas Szecsi, which opened in January. Artists included Picasso, Braque, and Léger. In February, Chick borrowed seventeenth-century prints, among them works by Rembrandt and van Dyck, from an exhibition assembled by Russell Hitchcock for Wesleyan University. To liven up the show, Chick turned set designer again and transformed Tapestry Hall in the Morgan building into "an ormolu Victorian fantasia" for the opening tea on February 18. But he missed the opening when he came down with his perennial winter respiratory illness, not helped by his chain-smoking.[53]

Chick produced three significant programs for the Friends and Enemies early in 1939—Brazilian soprano Elsie Houston singing contemporary French and Brazilian art songs and Latin-American folk music; the pioneering modern dancers Doris Humphrey and Charles Weidman performing with their troupe; and the young American dancer and mime, Angna Enters, in a tour de force of character sketches from the comic to the horrific. These events were not well attended, and Chick was overheard on the telephone saying to Albert Coote, managing director of the Bushnell Auditorium: "The trouble is, Al, Hartford needs your oatmeal and can pass up my caviar."[54]

But Chick had high hopes for the culmination of his theater season that spring. For a modest four hundred dollars, Ernst Krenek had agreed to compose and conduct the music for a new ballet in exchange for retaining the orchestral parts as his property. Aware, even in Europe, of the success of *Four Saints*, he asked Chick to promote his ballet as a continuation of the "extraordinary Hartford performances of the last years."[55] Chick's friend Truda Kaschmann, a gifted modern dancer trained in Germany by one of the pioneers of the art, Mary Wigman, would collaborate on choreography with her young protégé, Connecticut-born dancer Alwin Nikolais. Chick would design the sets and costumes. He somehow persuaded Charles Goodwin and the trustees to join the Friends and Enemies in sponsoring the production, perhaps because it was tangible support for a refugee artist. Like Krenek, Truda Kaschmann was a sophisticated German-speaking European, and she approached the advanced atonal music with unusual sympathy and imagination. Kaschmann and Nikolais worked out a scenario on an anti-Fascist theme. The ballet told the story of how peace and harmony, portrayed by Kaschmann, is disrupted and subdued by intimidation and ultimately megalomania, personified by Nikolais. At intervals, a newsboy appears, leaping across the stage as if announcing these ominous developments. The ballet was called *Eight-Column Line:* newspaper language for a headline spread across a full page.[56]

In mid-April, in a letter asking for support from the Friends and Enemies, Chick announced the world premiere of the ballet and made it clear that this was the most significant undertaking since the Hartford Festival three years earlier.[57] His "Committee of Honor" included Alfred Barr, Lincoln Kirstein, and Leonide Massine, and more than two dozen of Chick's friends contributed to the production. But most of his former New York patrons declined because of increased demands on their resources as the political situation in Europe worsened. Mrs. Murray Crane said that she had "never had so many appeals for destitute Chinese, Spanish, Czechs, etc., etc."[58]

The performances on May 19 and 20 attracted large audiences, including the Salvador Dalís. Critics praised Chick's abstract sets and costumes, and the choreography was considered an excellent match to the music, even though audiences were not yet used to modern dance and certainly not to atonal music. Chick was given credit for once again bringing together creative artists to present a serious program of new music and a new form of expression. But the event could not compare with his earlier successes. The premiere did not grab the attention of a glamorous New York contingent, and the ballet was not taken up by other companies or dancers.

Although the luster of Chick's offerings in the performing arts was dimmed, the visibility of the Atheneum as a repository of art increased dramatically that spring. Wilhelm Valentiner of the Detroit Institute, acting as director-general of the "Exhibition of Masterpieces" at the New York World's Fair, borrowed eleven of Chick's acquisitions, all painted before 1800, for the show.

Chick supplemented the Atheneum's collection in a new way that year by traveling to Mexico. With the threat of war increasing daily in Europe, an overseas trip was too risky in the summer of 1939. Interest in Mexico had grown during the decade, with the emergence of the artists who had been represented in the *Modern Mexican Art* exhibition that Chick had borrowed in 1930. The subsequent show at the Metropolitan and the murals José Clemente Orozco and Diego Rivera had executed in American public buildings focused enormous attention on the region. Chick's friend John McAndrew, now head of the architecture department at the Museum of Modern Art, was preparing a large exhibition of Mexican art for the spring of 1940 and was going to Mexico to scout out works for the show.

With Helen and the children in Castine for the summer, Chick decided to drive to Mexico, meet up with his museum pals, and look for works of art. He asked a young Hartford dancer, Tommy Hughes, to go with him. Hughes had

Curtain call at the premiere of Eight-Column Line, *May 19, 1939. Left to right:* Ernst Krenek, Truda Kaschmann, and Alwin Nikolais. *Set by AEA*

been an assistant in Chick's magic extravaganza of 1938 and had taken the role of the Newsboy in *Eight-Column Line.* Much as Chick always hated being alone on his travels, his interest in Hughes went beyond having company. A recent high school graduate, Hughes looked like a younger version of Chick. They became close companions for the next two or three years. Chick later told a friend that he believed everyone wanted to make a replica of himself. "And my God, he did," the friend went on. "Thomas Hughes looked like Chick, he talked like Chick, he acted like Chick."[59]

What Helen thought of the relationship was kept entirely private, although Joella Levy remembered that it was at this time that Chick confessed to Helen that he was in love with a man.[60] Helen never said or did anything to indicate that she was not steadfast in her love for Chick. From Joella Levy's viewpoint, "he wasn't being untrue to her. He never had other women and he always considered her feelings."[61] The fact that Chick went to Mexico with a young man from his theatrical productions was not regarded as unusual in that more innocent era. In announcing that Chick would leave for Mexico on August 4 to meet friends in Mexican cities and to look at paintings in museums and galleries, the *Hartford Times* noted that he would be accompanied by Hughes.[62]

Chick kept the museum staff supplied with postcards documenting his journey. On one from Nashville that showed a "perfect replica" of the

Tommy Hughes as the Paper Boy in Eight-Column Line

Parthenon at Centennial Park, he announced: "MAKING GOOD TIME—ALREADY IN ATHENS[.]"[63]

Julien Levy, who had recently taken up with a young American painter, Muriel Streeter, thought he might join Chick in Mexico. Clearly knowing Chick's interests, Julien sent along "a few tips from having pioneered the way. . . . In Norfolk the Navy Yard hangout is East Main St. near Church Street and the Negro hangout is Church St. near East Main."[64] Chick got word from Julien in New Orleans that he and Muriel had given up Mexico: "too far, too hot, too old, too dear."[65]

As soon as Chick arrived in Mexico City, he ran into his old Harvard friend George Valliant, now assistant curator of Mexican art at the American Museum of Natural History, who conveyed Chick to the local archaeological sites, as he reported to Helen, "in his papa-in-laws giant Packard—we examined every ruin and George even threw in a few Baroqueries for good measure. What with George for the earlier and John McAndrew for the later monuments I feel very well educated."[66] Despite the fact that Chick was dizzy from the altitude, he took in all the entertainments available—a bullfight, operas, dance halls, and a performance by the sensational singer Carmen Amaya.

Chick bought a dozen inexpensive pictures in Mexico, including nineteenth-century portraits, a still life, and religious images for the Atheneum's collection, along with examples of Mexican crafts to sell at the Atheneum in

December for the benefit of the children's art classes.[67] His most significant modern purchases included Guerrero Galván's *La vigornia,* later regarded as the artist's greatest early oil, for $175; and, for $620, Diego Rivera's *Girl with a Mask,* a portrait of a little peasant girl holding a papier-mâché mask of a human skull, a popular symbol in Mexico during the festival of the Day of the Dead.[68]

Chick arrived back in Hartford on September 6, three days after Britain and France declared war on Germany.

The Atheneum's board approved the paintings he had bought, but did not agree to underwrite his purchase of Mexican crafts for the children's program. Chick did not let that stop him and personally ordered two hundred dollars' worth of additional material for the fund-raiser, complaining openly to a Mexican dealer about his trustees' lack of cooperation.[69]

The exhibition and marketplace were extremely successful. Writing in the *Courant,* T. H. Parker called it Chick's "one-man fiesta," an apt description of the opening on December 5. Blazing candles filled Avery Court, which was imaginatively crammed with colorful objects and enough long swags of brightly painted tissue to give any fire marshal pause. The newly acquired Mexican paintings further improved the ambience. Parker pointed to the reputation for innovation that Chick had developed in the museum world by the late 1930s: "In planting the banner of the Wadsworth Atheneum among the Mexican popular arts, Mr. Austin once more displays his legendary enterprise. Having beaten the Museum of Modern Art at Picasso by five years' margin, he is keeping the Avery out in front by a three months' nose, as the New York rival encampment is not planning to discover Mexico until some time around February."[70]

For his first exhibition of 1940, Chick accepted Katharine Dreier's invitation to show seventy-one abstract paintings from the twentieth-anniversary show of the Société Anonyme, *Some New Forms of Beauty, 1909–1936,* which had opened at the Phillips in Washington and came to Hartford by way of the art museum in Springfield, Massachusetts. She was most offended, however, when she visited the show in Hartford and discovered that Chick had hung five of the paintings sideways. Dreier let him know that

> I admired you too much to mention this to anyone and I made my two young friends promise me that they would not for I felt how frightfully embarrassing it must be to you not to recognize the construction of a painting. . . . You can imagine my surprise when it was told in Springfield by someone from your Museum as a good joke!!! Frankly I do not understand such an attitude either towards you or towards art.[71]

Chick was not fazed by Dreier's ruffled feathers. "I intentionally hung the five paintings vertically rather than horizontally," he replied, "since I felt that the installation was much better, and I knew that only one or two persons would know the difference. Also, I often feel that if an abstract picture is fine enough, its balance is satisfactory no matter how the picture is hung." He added, however, that perhaps "it would be wiser in the future for you to avoid tempting me with exhibitions."[72] This was the last of their collaborations.

On January 16, while the abstract exhibition was still up, Chick opened a small show of the surrealist paintings of Yves Tanguy, which came from the Pierre Matisse Gallery, as an example of the opposite end of the modern spectrum. The show included a Tanguy he had recently acquired for the Atheneum, along with works lent by Paul Cooley and Jim Soby. The pictures from the gallery were all on sale for the benefit of artists working in Paris during those early months of the war, but none were sold.[73]

Making up for the fact that Chick had failed to produce a major exhibition the previous year, his show for 1940 was one of his most mysterious and beautiful. The war in Europe forced him to abandon the comprehensive Poussin exhibition, but the Poussin *Crucifixion* he had bought had suggested a theme, *Night Scenes.* He had received trustee approval for the show in November, but waited until mid-January to request loans. Once again, his fellow museum directors were generous, along with private collectors and his usual dealer friends. Chick assembled eighty paintings, from the fourteenth century to the twentieth, in time to have a catalogue printed and to open the exhibition on February 15.

Among the stunning works in the show were pictures he had acquired for Hartford—Giovanni Battista Caracciolo's *Annunciation;* the mysterious Monsù Desiderio's *The Feast of Nebuchadnezzar;* and Bernard van Orley's *Crucifixion.* Loans ranged from Rembrandt's *Christ Washing the Feet of the Disciples* from Chicago; one of the finest versions of El Greco's *Spanish Proverb* from Durlacher, showing a man lighting a candle held by a woman as a monkey peers over her shoulder; Whistler's *Nocturne—Blue and Silver* from Dumbarton Oaks; Winslow Homer's *The Lookout—All's Well* from the Boston Museum of Fine Arts; and Orozco's *The Cemetery* from the Museum of Modern Art. There were two images of *St. Francis in Ecstasy,* one attributed to George de la Tour, on loan from Durlacher, which Chick bought for $4,800; the other, a sublime work by Caravaggio, then owned by Arnold Seligmann, Rey and available for $50,000, too high for Chick's acquisition budget.

In his introduction to the exhibition catalogue Chick traced the history of the night scene, noting its predominance in baroque painting, which he linked to the rise of the theater with its dramatic stage lighting. "Night was never again to stimulate so universally and so faithfully the imagination of painters as it did in the seventeenth century," he wrote. He also pointed with obvious delight to the "gayety and disarming superficiality" of candlelit ballrooms and masquerades depicted in the rococo works of the next century.[74]

Word of the quality of the show traveled quickly in the American museum world. Francis Waring Robinson, curator of European Art at the Detroit Institute, told Chick that his reputation for innovative ideas was still thriving out of town: "Your current Exhibition of Night scenes appears to be another stroke of genius characteristic of your museum."[75] On February 18, five of the paintings in the show were reproduced in a rotogravure spread in the Sunday *New York Times.*

Aside from mounting a small show of George Platt Lynes photographs in April, Chick drifted through the spring, continuing his Trinity College teaching schedule, outside lectures, and occasional trips to New York galleries to scout out new acquisitions. That summer he, Helen, and the children spent several weeks at Laura's cottage in South Harpswell, where Chick painted watercolors and presented a magic show at Centennial Hall in West Harpswell in August. He made a brief excursion to Canada to explore the art market in Quebec and Montreal, returning to Hartford with a few minor nineteenth-century paintings.

In October, the New England Conference of the American Association of Museums held its annual meeting in Hartford, and, as host, Chick entertained them in a way no other museum director would have contemplated. In the guise of demonstrating varieties of museum programs, he presented an exhibition of models, sets, and costume designs from productions in his theater, from *Four Saints* to Balanchine's ballet, the Hartford Festival, *Eight-Column Line,* and the plays and ballets he had designed, along with the sketches for the Tonny murals. He also produced for the museum professionals a short magic show by the Great Osram, modern dances by Truda Kaschmann and her troupe, a ballet by Carmel Angelo for which he had designed the sets and costumes, and, to add a scholarly component to this kaleidoscope of theatrical activities, a lecture on Gothic art in the Renaissance by the eminent German art historian, Erwin Panofsky.

As the 1930s came to an end, Chick more than ever saw his trustees as hopelessly reactionary—unsympathetic, unappreciative, and tightfisted. In many ways he was right. Several of them had only the most superficial knowledge of art and had come to look on him as an annoyance. Walter Goodwin, the president's cousin, called him "Squirt Austin." Uncle Charlie obviously had no deep love of the arts, and his wife openly sneered at modern art and those who collected it. One evening, arriving for a reception at the Sobys' Farmington house—its rooms filled with works by de Chirico, Berard, Berman, Dalí, and Calder—she remarked to a friend as she came through the front door: "This is nothing but a surrealist stunt."[76] For his part, Chick walked away from gatherings of old Hartford whenever possible. One afternoon, the seamstress in an upper floor at one of the Goodwin houses, seated at her sewing machine and eating her lunch from a tray, looked up to see Chick. "Mrs. O'Connell," he said, "do you mind if I join you for lunch?" "Why no, Mr. Austin," she answered, surprised. Then he explained: "I don't want to eat with all those stuffed shirts downstairs."[77]

Inevitably, Chick looked for new ways to express himself and find a release for his powerful energies and inclinations, and just as inevitably, he found them in the Avery Theater. Back in June 1938, he had appeared for the first time on the Avery's stage as an actor for an amateur group called the Little Theater of Hartford, playing Commander Peter Gilpin in Noël Coward's one-act comedy *Hands Across the Sea*. Chick also designed the sets and committed himself to the decor for the Little Theater's next six productions, including *Tovarich*, in which he portrayed Charles Dupont. He made sketches for *Idiot's Delight*—scheduled to open in November 1938—on the boat to Europe, mailing them back to Connecticut from Hamburg. In December, Chick appeared onstage as Alan Howard for three performances of the Little Theater's production of *French Without Tears*, the recent comedy by Terrence Rattigan. Laura Austin came to stay with Helen and Chick for the weekend in order to see her boy perform in his own theater.

For one of the plays, Chick wanted a pair of console tables, so he simply borrowed an elaborately carved Italian center table from Helen's mother without telling her what it was for. He then sawed it in half and installed the two pieces on the stage. When the curtains opened one night, there was a loud

Chick designs the set for the Little Theater's production of Tovarich, *1940.*

shriek from the audience as Mrs. Goodwin recognized the two pieces of her table. (She was generally so proper that she would say of a comedy: "It was so funny I almost laughed out loud."[78]) Chick spoke soothingly to her after the show, persuading her that she would really prefer having two consoles.[79]

Strangely, while Chick always welcomed Helen and the children to all his performances onstage, he adamantly refused to let them hear him lecture, when, by all accounts, he was at his most impressive. He simply felt too vulnerable to appear in front of them as his public self.

In December 1938, Chick began rehearsals for his Christmas magic production, "Around the World in Eighty Tricks," which surpassed anything he had done before. In addition to his own large group of assistants, Chick enlisted actors from the Little Theater, along with Truda Kaschmann and Alwin Nikolais. He created six sets, built on revolving stages—a New York nightclub, a baroque variety theater in Vienna, and scenes in Egypt, India, China, and Japan. The costumes, which Chick designed, were sewn from seven hundred yards of fabric, much of it specially woven from silk and metal strands. Most of his routines, including his escape, bound and gagged, from a locked trunk, were new, requiring hours of practice.[80] Actress Elsa Lanchester, Charles Laughton's wife, attended the first performance on December 29. Chick told the *Hartford Times* that if autograph hunters bothered her, he would make her disappear during the show.[81] The production was impressive enough for Chick to recreate it in March as part of a benefit at the three-thousand-seat Bushnell Auditorium.

Chick spent more and more time preparing for the annual magic show. The production for December 1939, "Magic on Parade," required a huge company, drawn from both the Little Theater of Hartford and the Angelo School of the Ballet. The seven sets ranged from ancient Egypt to seventeenth-century Italy, Versailles before the Revolution, Paris in 1849 and 1900, Hartford in 1939 and "Anywhere, 1995." In this last sequence, anticipating the digital age, Chick identified the magicians and dancers only by numbers, some as long as fifteen digits, except for "A Visitor from Mars." To the accompaniment of music from Shostakovich's brutal *Age of Gold* ballet, they whirled about in bizarre futuristic costumes. Chick wore a cloth helmet designed by Salvador Dalí and executed by Elsa Schaiparelli, giving him the appearance of a surrealist space traveler. In the program notes for this sequence, Chick asked the audience to try to imagine the magic of the 1990s: "What will it be like? Who can tell[?]" He hoped it would give pleasure to the audience of the future, "as it did to those who are gone, who enjoyed it and were deceived by it."[82]

At the first of these magic performances, he unveiled his newest acquisition—five large eighteenth-century painted panels, known as *The Carnival in Venice*. Tiring of the plain walls of his Art Deco lobby, he had the panels nailed into the exotic wood. Painted by the German artist Johann Joseph Scheubel II, they were cartoons for tapestries woven for the Residenz Palace in Würzburg and depicted characters from the commedia dell'arte eating, drinking, flirting, and generally making merry, with some of Chick's favorite sights—the Piazza San Marco, the church of Santa Maria della Salute—as a backdrop for their revels.

By the end of 1940, despite the success of his *Night Scenes* exhibition, Chick found himself increasingly hemmed in by circumstances. The year had seen the defeat of France in June, and European travel was out of the question indefinitely. He had already gone south to Mexico and north to Canada during his restless summers. The possibility of producing exciting new exhibitions seemed small. The stage became more enticing than ever.

He began taking dancing lessons, first with Truda Kaschmann, then with the Angelo sisters, and he actually appeared in one of their productions as a dancer. "It was absolutely dreadful," said Alwin Nikolais, "but of course everybody went that could get into the theater." Nikolais saw a change in Chick: "I don't think he wanted to be head of the Wadsworth Atheneum. What he really wanted was to be a performer."[83]

CHAPTER SIXTEEN

Turning Awry

> He stooped down to drink, and saw his own image in the
> water; he thought it was some beautiful water-spirit liv-
> ing in the fountain. He stood gazing with admiration at
> those bright eyes, those locks curled like the locks of
> Bacchus or Apollo, the rounded cheeks, the ivory neck,
> the parted lips, and the glow of health and exercise over
> all. He fell in love with himself. . . . He cherished the
> flame that consumed him, so that by degrees he lost his
> color, his vigor, and the beauty which formerly had so
> charmed the nymph Echo.
>
> —Thomas Bulfinch, "Echo and Narcissus," *Mythology*

One afternoon in the late 1930s a young artist, newly arrived in
Hartford, came to the Avery Memorial in hopes of introducing herself to Chick Austin. She had been teaching art at New York's Pratt
Institute, whose director told her that Austin was a genius and she
should meet him. As she entered the empty court, a voice shouted: "Hartford is
dead! dead! dead!" Then, from behind a partition, an apparition dressed in a
Renaissance costume—tights and a slashed velvet doublet—appeared and
introduced itself as "A. Everett Austin, director of this mausoleum." Afraid of
intruding, she blurted out, "Oh, I shouldn't be here." He said, "No, I'm beginning to think that *I'm* the one who shouldn't be here." When she mentioned the
director of the Pratt, he accepted her immediately as a friend and said, "Call
me Chick." He confided that he had just come from a trustees' meeting. He had
been summoned from the dress rehearsal of a magic show to be informed that
one of his projects had been vetoed. He then produced two tickets to the show
from inside the doublet and handed them to her. "If you're interested," he said.[1]

Chick's magic shows had become a favorite part of Hartford's Christmas
season. "Santa Claus himself is looked forward to with scarcely less excited

curiosity than is the Great Osram," declared the *Hartford Times* in December 1940.[2] His offering that year, "Magical Merry-Go-Round, An Extravaganza in Two Acts," was planned around three painted carousel horses he had bought for the museum's collection while passing through Albany the previous summer. Chick brought in two dance companies—Truda Kaschmann's troupe and the Angelo sisters' Hartford Ballet—and designed four sets and forty-seven costumes. He began the show as the Tricky Hussar by leaping from a moving carousel in the Vienna of the 1880s. Cards, flowers, milk, fish, and a quacking duck appeared and disappeared, and the scene changed to the Enchanted Nursery. There, in an oversized set, toys danced and the Children entered, carrying in their newest toy: Chick dressed as a large doll in a black, gold, and turquoise costume. He was Dr. Mirakle, the Automaton Magician, who jerkily came to life and amazed the children with his illusions. Then Chick was a couturier in an elegant dress shop, the House of Osram, transforming models and society matrons. In the grand finale, the Incredible Circus, to the strains of Saint-Saens's *Carnival of the Animals,* he jumped out to crack his whip as the Ringmaster, and barely controlled mayhem ensued. Wild animals sprang from cages, ponies galloped around the ring, and tightrope walkers and trapeze artists cavorted. When the Freaks entered to help the Ringmaster—the Blue Man, the Tattooed Man, and Emma, the Fat Girl—some observers may have recognized the references to the Paper Ball and the bizarre figures in Tchelitchew's *Phenomena.*[3] During one scene in the show, as Chick contemplated a jar filled with a murky liquid and an unidentified object, he mused, "This reminds me—Someone said that I should leave my brain to Harvard, but they didn't want it when they had it!"[4]

To prepare such productions, Chick rented a studio on Temple Street, a few blocks from the museum. There, as he chain-smoked and played records, he could teach his assistants new tricks, spread out his art supplies, build his models, paint his designs, and supervise the making of costumes, sewing some of them himself on his portable Singer. Occasionally, he would wander into the Angelo sisters' studio in the same building and help with the costumes for their ballets. A dancer named Sylvia was astonished to see the director of the Wadsworth Atheneum on his knees in front of her one day, measuring, pinning fabric, and, when he discovered her name, quietly singing Schubert's "Who is Sylvia?"[5]

Chick recruited a legion of young volunteers, some still in high school, to help with every aspect of his magic shows and plays, from building and painting sets to performing onstage. Among them was Wallace Stevens's teenage daughter Holly, who felt such a bond with Chick during a lonely adolescence that she called him her surrogate father.[6] Chick's three most devoted disciples, however, were Tommy Hughes, Jim Hellyar, a former Trinity student, and Elena

Longo, who ran the children's educational program at the museum. The trio were such constant companions that they became the focus of local gossip. When Chick was spotted buying Elena Longo expensive clothes in Hartford's best department store, some speculated, quite erroneously, that they were having an affair. Years later, she said,

> A lot of people thought that Mr. Austin and I were something that we weren't. It's not true. He required a lot of women. He needed a woman at home to be the mother of his children, the best woman in the world. He needed somebody at the office, a good secretary. He needed somebody to take care of the magic. I was in charge of it. And [Helen] understood that. And I don't think she was ever jealous. And this didn't mean that she didn't love him as much as she did. She knew what his needs, what his demands were, and she just rode the wave.[7]

It was in fact Tommy Hughes and, later, Jim Hellyar who were the objects of his desire. Ironically, Elena Longo later married Tommy Hughes, and when they had a son, gossip in Hartford turned, absurdly, to whether or not Chick was the actual father.[8]

Sometimes Chick would take his assistants out to dinner at an Italian restaurant near his studio, Mickey's Villanova, or invite them home to Scarborough Street, where he would prepare an elegant meal. Helen was invariably gracious when Chick turned up on the spur of the moment with his "gang."[9] His young friends were only too glad to follow the pied piper, and their parents felt that working long hours with the Atheneum's director was educational. Elena Longo remembered that although he would keep them at the museum until midnight or one o'clock in the morning, "he would take us home very properly, and he would get to know our parents, and he wouldn't forget them at Christmas."[10]

By the beginning of 1941, Chick was so engrossed in theater that he decided to create his first independent dramatic production. On January 9, he announced that for the benefit of the children's art classes, the Wadsworth Atheneum would present Shakespeare's *Hamlet*. He would not only design the sets and costumes in a style he called "Delacroix-Neo-Romantic," but would appear in the title role. Virgil Thomson would supply the incidental music he had composed for John Houseman's 1936 New York production with Leslie Howard.[11]

It was an idea Chick had considered since the previous August, when he was elected president of the Hartford Players,[12] and by November, he had invited the other principal Hartford theater groups to take part in the production.[13] Somehow he convinced the trustees to assume partial financial responsi-

Chick at his slimmest in Hamlet, *February 1941*

bility for it. What could be more appropriate for Hartford's leading cultural institution than an illustrious drama presented in cooperation with other Hartford organizations? It was certainly more appealing to them than the nonsensical opera by Gertrude Stein or the grandiose hodgepodge of modern pieces and paper costumes of the Hartford Festival.

Chick told the press that he was "tired of the constant reiteration of Broadway successes by our theater groups, and I feel that once a year we might do something a little more serious." Anticipating criticism of his tackling one of the world's greatest dramas, he asserted that "no matter how often it is repeated, or perhaps how badly played, there is always something new that gets across to the audience. . . . Even though the undertaking may turn out to be over-ambitious, it is better than if the attempt had not been made at all."[14]

Preparations for *Hamlet* became so consuming that Chick did not think of mounting a large winter exhibition. (Instead, he borrowed a collection of watercolors by the little-known Spanish painter Arturo Souto, and scheduled a continuous succession of programs in the theater.) Chick turned out fifty costume designs and ordered truckloads of luxurious fabrics from New York—along with yards of tarnished gold braid and piles of weapons and jeweled accessories. Some of the costumes were made in New York, but many more were fabricated in the Atheneum's basement, with Chick and an army of women measuring, cutting, and stitching through the night. And wherever Chick went, his script was in hand. Even during photography sessions for publicity portraits of the principals, he paced back and forth as the lights and camera were adjusted, trying to memorize the monumental role. To help him perfect his delivery, he also bought a machine that made 78 rpm records.

In order to fit into the elegant black doublet he had designed for himself, Chick cut out all the rich foods he relished. This deprivation was not new to him. "Between theatrical events," said Russell Hitchcock, "he would eat a great deal and get very fat, and then he would wish to thin down, and he would go on some perfectly crazy diet of eating only bananas, and he would be down and sylphlike again."[15] The waist of his Hamlet costume measured twenty-seven inches.

Chick sent his New York friends personal invitations to the show, promising parties at Nellie and Jim Soby's house and at his Scarborough Street house.[16] Headlines before the opening announced the "Social Audience" arriving for the festivities, and T. H. Parker wrote in the *Courant:* "Veterans of 'Four Saints,' the Paper Ball and other local Arabian Nights, who had been recovering ever since in the quiet of New York" were returning "to take up their old stations among an audience including our own best-appointed families."[17] But in fact many of Chick's intimates were worried about what they might witness and found excuses to stay away.

At eight o'clock on the evening of Wednesday, February 26, as his new record-making machine was turned on in the wings to capture the occasion, the curtains opened on the first of Chick's dozen sets, all giving the illusion of massive architecture extending beyond the small stage. As the play progressed, Chick's costumes created a sumptuous picture. Thomson's music amounted to little more than cues and sound effects, rather heavy on trumpets, except for an eerie duet between a French horn and a recorder during the Dumb Show, when Truda Kaschmann's dancers combined gestures taken from medieval paintings with the abstract movements of modern dance.

With his slimmed-down figure and handsome profile, Chick had never looked better onstage. His silvery tones and aristocratic accent heightened the impression. The *Hartford Times* drama critic, Julian Tuthill, who happened to be vice president of the Hartford Players, was too eager in his praise, asserting that Chick's interpretation "far exceeds Barrymore's dashing delineation and Gielgud's weak and ineffectual portrayal" and was "far more sympathetic than was Maurice Evans."[18] Tuthill chose to overlook, or did not notice, the small bits of paper that Chick had hidden in his costume and placed around the set to

The glamorous museum director and his wife arrive at the trustees' annual reception, March 1941.

remind him of the lines. A more objective T. H. Parker noticed the nervous speed of Chick's delivery, which could be heard on the records he made. Parker felt that the only time the poetry of Shakespeare's lines came through was in the bedroom scene when the prince was alone with his mother, though Chick handled the role "capably."[19]

To some in the audience, Chick's constant emoting, the earnestness of the young amateurs in the cast, and above all the interminable breaks for scene changes were hard to endure. Several husbands who had been dragged to the theater to see Chick's *Hamlet* left the performance in search of a drink. When they returned to escort their wives home, they discovered the play was still in progress. The curtain did not close on the final act until after midnight. Years later, even one of Chick's most vocal admirers in Hartford admitted, "We were embarrassed for him."[20] To Alwin Nikolais, *Hamlet* "was about the limit. It was the last straw. The only thing he could play after that was the Virgin Mary."[21] Some of the trustees began to find such performances self-indulgent and too much of a distraction for the director of their museum.

Chick, however, thought his sets and costumes were so splendid that, after his performance, he had his stage crew install many of them in Tapestry Hall with framed sketches of his designs, which he sold to benefit the museum. This, along with a selection of recent acquisitions, became his exhibition for the annual reception for trustees and members later in March. It was a noticeably weak offering compared with his earlier winter exhibitions. The trustees could see that there had been a shift in Chick's energy and creativity.

Worst of all, *Hamlet* had increased an already high deficit in the museum's auditorium account. In April, the executive committee called for a detailed examination of expenditures for the theater and a month later announced a new

policy for its use. The board's earlier directive instructing him to present proposed expenditures to the business manager and the building superintendent
had not been effective. Now there would be no outside programs in the theater
without payment of the full established fees, and no museum use of the theater
beyond public lectures without a vote of both the executive committee and the
auditorium committee. Chick was more constricted than ever.[22]

The trustees had greater worries than Chick's reaction to their control over
the theater. In June, with the war devastating much of Europe and the transfer
of American military ships and equipment to Britain through President Roosevelt's lend-lease program, the possibility of the United States' entering the
conflict was mentioned for the first time at a meeting of the trustees. They discussed the removal of paintings from the museum to protect them from air
raids. Chick suggested that the Atheneum could save money by eliminating the
1942 winter exhibition and substituting a loan show exclusively from dealers,
who would underwrite the cost, he said, with the expectation that some of the
pictures would be bought by individuals and given to the museum. He also
requested and received money to finance a trip to California that summer to
scout out new acquisitions.[23]

This time, Helen joined him. Her sister Mary and her husband, Willie
Graff, were living in Los Angeles, and Helen was as eager as Chick to get away
from Hartford. With Chick's contacts, he and Helen had little trouble entering
the artistic world in Hollywood and Los Angeles, now increased by recent
European émigrés. Among their new friends was composer Darius Milhaud.
Never missing an opportunity, and ignoring the new controls on his theater,
Chick told Milhaud that he wanted to commission a work from him to be per-
formed at the museum in the spring of 1942.

Such projects were soon to be more difficult, for after Chick and Helen
returned home in September, America's entry into the war seemed imminent.
American ships had actually fired on German submarines in the Atlantic, and
the Roosevelt administration was maintaining an uncertain peace with Japan in
the Pacific. In October, Charles Goodwin reported to the board that he had a
commitment from the Connecticut Commissioner of Motor Vehicles to provide
transportation for the removal of all art treasures in an emergency, adding that
Wesleyan University had offered storage space in case bombing seemed likely.[24]

Goodwin continued to have concerns about the museum's finances and the
way Chick was using museum funds. At an executive meeting at the end of
November, the board voted to form a committee to consult Alfred Terry, a partner in the accounting firm of Bennett & Terry, "to coordinate the activities of
the Wadsworth Atheneum"—that is, to review Chick's expenditures, including
his theatrical ventures, during his entire tenure.[25] To the trustees, this was an
exercise in fiscal responsibility; to Chick, it felt like a threat.

Two weeks later, on December 7, the Japanese air force made its massive surprise attack on the American naval base at Pearl Harbor.

The entry of the United States into the Second World War affected Chick profoundly, but for personal reasons. Although he was as shaken as anyone at the prospect of joining the global conflict, he saw most clearly that his own activities and his freedom of movement would be severely curtailed, perhaps for years to come. He was acutely aware that the European treasures he had known since his childhood and whose existence underlay his career, his mission in life, were in danger of destruction or at least removal from the great museums and churches and palaces to some unimaginable Nazi repository. Only a few weeks before Pearl Harbor, Chick had spoken to a visiting Dutch scholar and collector whom the Nazis had forced to flee Holland; they then had taken over his house and sent his art collection to Germany.[26] And now, the best of what Chick had purchased for the Atheneum, those paintings that had remade the museum in his image, were being removed to Jim Soby's storage vault in Farmington. Pictures too large to send there were put into the cellar of the Avery Memorial. Chick had to rehang the galleries with lesser works.

Added to that was his dread that the report of the budget committee would result in such restraints on his programs that the life would be squeezed out of the Atheneum. His anxiety and his long-held resentment of the "stuffed shirts" who had never understood or appreciated him—or so he thought—took him beyond the bounds of discretion. On January 17, 1942, he presented an emotional and accusatory annual report to the trustees, demanding resolutions that would guarantee their support of him and the staff. He declared that "in this moment of extreme crisis" it was necessary to clarify "the situation of the Wadsworth Atheneum." He said that during the past several years, "the purposes and aims of the museum have been increasingly clouded by the defeatism, timidity and lethargy which have in general been symptomatic of the decadence of our time. . . . The world of art exists in identical terms with the world of politics, of economies and all the other worlds of ideas, and is equally important, if not more so." He read out a catalog of negative factors in American society during the past two decades:

the pedestalling of mediocrity, the fear of offending by conviction or definite statement, the cult of compromise, the marked suspicion of enthusiasm, the many false values engendered by the racket of advertising, the mesmerism exerted by numbers, tables, polls, efficiency as such, and, finally and most dangerously, the almost total lack of imagination, have all been the ingredients of these weakened years in increasing force.

Chick's reference to numbers and efficiency—and lack of imagination—seemed a direct response to the upcoming budget report.

He called on the trustees to remember that the mission of the museum was to serve as a safe repository for works of art and "as the vigilant guardian of the spiritual values in a time when there is every indication that materialist concepts will continue to be over-extolled, for it will not really be the guns and ships, important as they are, that will eventually conquer, but the spirit which animates them."

Paraphrasing Hamlet, he warned that "we cannot succumb to the sugared dangers of a fatal lethargy—To Sleep, To Dream, Ay there's the rub. The Museum must remain alive and awake. . . ."

Feeling that his authority as director was about to be undermined, he made a series of "demands" in language he had never used in any address to the trustees: "I must demand therefore that the Trustees first make clear their feelings and intentions in this matter. I must demand that they define the duties of the museum in the support of public morale during war-time, and finally that they define the duties of the Director of that museum."

With a mixture of anger, frustration, and pride, he looked back on his career at the museum:

> When I first came to Hartford fifteen years ago, my sole instructions were to make the Wadsworth Atheneum a lively institution, to make it take its place with other museums of comparable size in the country. I do no[t] think that anyone can deny that I have done so. At that time, it was a provincial museum. From that time, I do not believe that it has been. . . . With what I have done you may not always have entirely agreed. No definite statements have ever enjoyed universal acceptance or acclaim. . . . But things got done, and done on an amount of money that would have seemed laughable to any other American museum of this size in a city of comparable wealth.

Referring to the budget as well as the moral support he felt he lacked, Chick claimed that during recent years, "the cancer of defeatism" had spread through the museum. "Gentlemen, I plead for the staff, for the morale of the whole museum which is now seriously endangered. We must be paid. Not exclusively in the material sense . . . but paid in the more significant currency of appreciation and enthusiasm."

He expressed his conviction that his contribution to the arts would be more valued in some future time:

> Do you believe, furthermore, that museums, as practically the sole guardians of the highest standards of taste and quality, at a time when

mediocrity is constantly confused with those standards, should preserve them for possible use by the generations who are to come, and
who will perhaps be more understanding of them?

He spoke as if he were defending the survival of everything he had stood
for as a disciple of Forbes and Sachs, as a connoisseur of paintings, and as a
creative personality: "The record of the great culture of Western civilization
must not be imperilled . . . if our new world is to live, it will not live because we
have sold it electric refrigerators, but because we will have provided it with the
means for a more spiritual existence.

Concluding this impassioned plea, he reminded the board members

that beauty is not a luxury—that intangibles cannot be measured by a
monetary yardstick. Remember, too, that the shell of a building, like
the shell of a country, is no stronger, no matter how well kept in repair,
than the mortar and brick of its inner life, its vitality, its ability to imagine, its enthusiasms, its hopes and its fears. . . .

Our museums have given up being mere cemeteries of the past.
Will they now give up the possibility of becoming one of the wombs of
the future?[27]

The stunned trustees passed polite resolutions in favor of most of Chick's
"demands," but these did not resolve the tension between Chick and the board.
His report was sent to all trustees and, surprisingly, considering its critical
tone, published in its entirety by the *Hartford Times*.

J. P. Morgan, Jr., was not pleased when he received his copy, as he told
Cousin Charlie Goodwin:

There is a curious tone of exculpation about it which strikes me very
unfavorably—a sort of an idea that he has wanted to do things and has
not been allowed to do anything except under compromise which does
not suit him, although in the view of the Trustees, who are responsible,
it is a necessary thing to do; in fact, the whole thing reads to me like
the wail of a disappointed person, or of a very young man who feels
himself held back by the older ones—perhaps *both* in this case: I do
not know!

With an evenhandedness that might have surprised Chick, Morgan added
that he had "a good deal of sympathy with many of Austin's ideas, but I realize
from long experience that all that kind of idea is very expensive to carry out—
and in these times may be impossible." Chick's report had focused Morgan's

attention on his own role as a trustee of the Wadsworth Atheneum, and he suggested to Goodwin that he step down from the board.[28]

The idea of losing Cousin Jack Morgan as a trustee was unthinkable, and Goodwin replied instantly. Family ties and fiscal responsibilities were paramount to him. "Don't please resign," he wrote. "We both of us have many other things to do but this is one thing that is hereditary. I think you know that the solvency of the foundation will be protected just as long as the present management is able to remain on the job."

Goodwin professed sympathy with Chick's worries: "Austin's statement was the result of just exactly what you had surmised—a revolt against the steadily closing in of events over which none of us have any control whatever, not even Mr. Hitler, but I think since writing that paper Austin has come to a different attitude and has realized that we are really trying to help him and not just bother him."

He assured Morgan that the board was "thoroughly in sympathy with Austin's real objective, namely, the creation of a *small* provincial museum that will still on *quality* challenge any museum."

Goodwin did see a problem with Chick's extracurricular activities:

We have had all sorts of entertainments, plays, etc. in the auditorium and it is the curtailment of these which added to Austin's agitation. . . . During the years immediately ahead we feel that the activities of the museum should be confined to those which are necessary to meet the demands of a people under a war emergency—that is we have a contribution to make towards the maintenance of the morale of the community but it is not necessary for us to bankrupt ourselves to do it.[29]

The budget committee's report was released to the board in mid-February. It was a thorough and reasoned look at the evolution of the Atheneum, reporting on the history and current value of the endowment funds, the income and expenditures for the last decade, the annual membership since 1930, and attendance and budget figures for the Avery Theater since its opening. There was a proposed budget for 1942 with recommendations for making the Atheneum's operations more efficient and less expensive, including the elimination of the stage manager and tighter controls on expenditures in this area.[30] A month later, Chick received a memorandum from the trustees announcing that he would have a new "assistant," who would "confer with the Director in determination of activities, . . . check allocations of expenditures, . . . systematize work in Museum so as to avoid confusion and waste, . . . make frequent visits to the Museum to the end of keeping in touch with what goes on." Most demoralizing from Chick's point of view, he would "eliminate, with approval of

Trustees, unproductive and costly activities where not essential to best interests of museum."[31] The new operating system went into effect on April 16.
Chick's so-called assistant was Alfred Terry, who was appointed the museum's
comptroller.

Despite Goodwin's assurances to Morgan, Chick refused to "come to a different attitude." When the board's auditorium committee informed him that
"there was absolutely no money" for a talk by Vittorio Rieti, the composer of *Le
Bal,* one of Diaghilev's last ballets, Chick hosted the lecture at his own house
and charged a small admission fee. Explaining the new venue to Rieti, he said
that he would probably get a larger turnout "as the lecture audiences at the
museum are always pathetically small."[32] Rieti gave his lecture, entitled "The
Features of Bad Music," on February 10, and before the composer left Hartford, Chick audaciously proposed commissioning him to write a ballet for Truda
Kaschmann and her troupe.[33]

Chick followed through on the exhibition he had suggested to the board in
the fall, *In Memoriam.* With the help of his dealer friends, particularly Paul
Byk, he gathered 119 paintings and drawings that could be bought for less than
$1,000 each and given to the museum in memory of a loved one—or taken
home by the purchaser. Describing these works as "chamber music rather than
a full symphonic performance," Chick reminded his audience that "quality can
be perfectly compatible with modesty in price." He felt that "one of the most
sinister influences the American museum has exerted on the public is the
implication that works of art are priceless, that they can therefore be afforded
only by museums and millionaires, that original art can have nothing whatso-
ever to do with the private home." Every one of the pictures, he said, would be
welcome in the Atheneum's collection, but they would also be "a source of
constant enjoyment to the private collector."[34]

The works Chick chose covered six centuries—an amazing range, consid-
ering the prices—and included eleven national schools. Visitors to the exhibition could acquire oils by such artists as Salvator Rosa, Benjamin West,
Rubens Peale, John Kensett, Childe Hassam, Maurice Utrillo, Miró, Picasso,
Chagall, Tanguy, Balthus, and Tchelitchew. Among the drawings were works by
Goya, Delacroix, Matisse, and, for under $200, Domenico and Giovanni Bat-
tista Tiepolo. The exhibition opened at the end of February and ran for a month.
No one bought a picture to give to the museum. Chick used the Sumner Fund to
acquire three works Paul Byk had lent to the show.

As for Chick's museum purchases that spring, by far the most important
was Max Ernst's *Europe After the Rain* for $1,400 from Pierre Matisse. Despite
feeling beleaguered, Chick had not lost his touch. Ernst's image of a mon-
strously melted and twisted landscape—a world that had destroyed itself—was
one of the great surrealist works of the twentieth century. Like many of the contemporary masterpieces Chick bought, it had just been painted. As Ernst

recounted, he had begun the picture at his country house two months before the fall of France, was "interrupted by an involuntary stay in french concentration camps" and finished it in New York in January 1942.[35] Pierre Matisse showed it at his gallery in March in an exhibition called *Artists in Exile,* where Chick saw it.

This show gave Chick the idea for an small but important exhibition he planned for the end of May, *Painters in Attendance.* He proposed bringing to Hartford, for one week, works by distinguished European exiles, some of whom would come to the museum for the opening. Drawing on dealers, collectors, the artists themselves, and the collections of the Museum of Modern Art and the Atheneum, he assembled twenty-one works by Breton, Chagall, Ernst, Masson, Matta, Miró, Tanguy, and, as an exception to the theme, Joseph Cornell.

In need of more personal projects, Chick decided to combine the opening of this exhibition with another magic show, to be produced by a group he invented, the Friends of the Arts in Wartime. This "Compendium of the Arts in 4 Parts" was called "The Elements of Magic," with scenes based on the themes of earth, water, fire, and air.

Chick wanted the show to be more theatrical than the "Magical Merry-Go-Round" of the previous December. For the water sequence, he found money to commission a dramatization of Hans Christian Andersen's story, "The Young Siren," from a new friend of his, an aspiring Belgian-born writer named Marguerite Yourcenar. Still almost a decade away from her fame as the author of *Memoirs of Hadrian,* and forty years away from becoming the first woman elected to the French Academy, Yourcenar had moved to Hartford to live with her future translator, Grace Frick, then dean of Hartford College for Women. Yourcenar found the Atheneum an unexpected oasis of European culture in a small American city, and she distinctly remembered her first sight of Chick Austin: "It was one of those occasions when he had a quarrel with his trustees," she recounted. "He was lying [in] his office with a towel on his head and declaring he had a very strong headache and he seemed discouraged with the world."

They became close friends, and long after Chick's death, the serenely intellectual Yourcenar was rhapsodic when describing him: "There is a line of Shakespeare. It's Cleopatra who says it in Shakespeare: 'I am air and fire.' Well, Chick Austin *was* air and fire. [He had] great enthusiasm, a great facility to respond to the moment, the excitation of the moment. He had a great *gaîeté,* great lightness of mind. . . . He was of course a prince."[36]

Chick knew he was living dangerously by putting on an extravagant magic show that would again require him to spend weeks designing costumes and sets, building and painting scenery, rehearsing his magic and now his dancing. But from his point of view, the theater was the only thing that kept him sane. In urging Peggy Guggenheim, who had just married Max Ernst, to whip up excitement among the artists in New York, Chick said, "I am so anxious to have the various painters who have not seen the museum get a look at it before I collapse totally. . . . Hartford has begun to depress me so this winter that I shall go mad I am afraid if there is not at least a temporary influx of human beings to cheer me up!"[37] To May Sarton, he wrote:

> I am doing my last show in two weeks which I wish very much that you could see. It is my last I am certain because I am sure to be out of a job after it is over but I am still determined to do it. The Trustees have become increasingly maddened at my antics yet they give me no money for exhibitions or other museum activities so I am forced to keep going in some way or other.[38]

Sarton replied sympathetically that she was "furious" with Chick's trustees:

> Why *are* Trustees always such doddering old tyrants—the Trustees or whatever they're called of the London Zoo have just fired Julian Huxley, who had made the Zoo almost as exciting as the Wadsworth Ath—so what is the world coming to? I feel life closing down everywhere. It gives me the creeps. . . . The only solution I can see is for us to become Trustees, call ourselves Trustees Inc. and cash in on their easy lives.[39]

Philip Johnson brushed aside all thought of Chick's leaving the Atheneum: "What nonsense about your swan song. You are better than ever and I have never seen you look younger or healthier. . . ."[40]

Most of the artists represented in the exhibition did not appear at the opening. Max Ernst was in Chicago; André Breton was "*désolé*" that he could not come.[41] Yves Tanguy did come with his wife, the artist Kay Sage Tanguy, so at least Chick could say that there were "painters in attendance." Many of his close friends were unable to attend: Virgil Thomson was rehearsing a performance of *Four Saints;* even Paul Byk cabled that he was "under the weather."[42]

But "The Elements of Magic" gave Chick the diversion he needed. He played the Prince in Yourcenar's *Young Siren* and appeared as Lucifer in a *Satanale.* In the finale, a classical ballet by Carmel Angelo, Chick again put on his ballet slippers and danced the leading role of Jupiter—assisted by dancers pretending to be clouds, continents, and mythological creatures—all to music by Rameau provided by a pianist and a string quartet.

Most members of the audience could not know the level of defiance and desperation that lay beneath Chick's performance. Yourcenar's note at the end of the program had a subtle undercurrent that might have been applied to him: "Magic is the oldest method evolved by man in the attempt to transform his environment," she wrote, "and acquire power over the universe."[43]

As his performances did not result in a call for his dismissal, Chick went ahead with a large exhibition in honor of the museum's hundredth anniversary: paintings from the original nineteenth-century American collection, thirty-five pictures acquired through the Sumner Fund, *A Short History of the Chair*, and a display of stage sets and designs called *Contribution to the Theatre*.

In a provocative gesture to those who were trying to curtail his performing arts activities, Chick devoted more space in the exhibition brochure to an essay on the Avery Theater than he gave to any other part of the show, observing: "To the Puritans and the conscience which is their legacy to us, the theatre has more often than not seemed a wicked place which offered merely useless and extravagant, if not actually immoral 'entertainment.' But then, too, to the Puritan way of thinking, paintings themselves appear often as unnecessary luxuries, smacking a good deal even still of the counter-reformation." He pointed out that many of the programs in the theater had been produced by so-called amateurs (like himself), but that "it is now forgotten that the word 'amateur' is one who loves his art so much that he practices it without recompense, and not one who is not a professional in pursuing it." The exhibition, he concluded, was "a reminder that beauty is not alone imprisoned in the gold frames on gallery walls."[44]

Knowing that his scope was limited for the duration of the war, Chick left for the summer with Helen and the children with no particular plans. Mostly he painted watercolors, moving restlessly from Castine to South Harpswell to Windham. One Sunday morning during a brief stay at the farm, Chick and Helen left Sally and David alone with Laura Austin. While they were gone, she invited David into her bed and read him the funny papers while Sally sat outside the locked bedroom door feeling frightened and rejected. Eventually hearing about the incident from Sally, Helen told her, "Daddy and I were very bad to have left you alone with Grandmama."[45]

In the fall, Chick resumed his teaching schedule at Trinity, but mounting interesting exhibitions at the Atheneum was difficult. In September, he put up a small show of artists he had championed, *Painters of Fantasy*, which included both the surrealists and Neo-Romantics—de Chirico, Dalí, Ernst, Tchelitchew, and Berman—all from Julien Levy. For his Christmas entertainment, Chick offered a revised version of "The Elements of Magic," without *The Young Siren*. For the water scene, he played Signor Homard, the Crustacean Conjuror, and did tricks with mermaids and Sea-Dwarfs. Although Elena Longo and Bea Ganz appeared in the show, the cast had dwindled. Tommy Hughes was now in the army, and Jim Hellyar did not participate.

By the beginning of 1943, Chick had recovered himself enough to create a magnificent exhibition on the theme of war: *Men in Arms*. He presented images of warfare through eighty paintings spanning seven centuries from the fifteenth to the twentieth, most of them borrowed from dealers. (Fourteen alone came from Paul Byk.) Unlike museums, dealers still hoped to sell pictures and had not removed them to storage. Chick did not write an introduction to the catalogue and offhandedly told the press that "there is no particular aesthetic rhyme nor historical reason for the exhibition." He simply wanted to show the changing styles and subjects associated with war over the centuries, demonstrating that history and painting were inseparable.[46] Visually, the show had the scope and taste of his earlier explorations of grand themes in art history. But few in Chick's inner circle found they could make it: "I don't know how we can practicably get up to Hartford," wrote Julien Levy. Kirk Askew told him, "All the arrangements seemed so difficult, what with heat and gas rationing."[47]

War was making inroads into the old network. Jim Soby managed to combine curatorial work with a contribution to the war effort as director of the Armed Services Program at the Museum of Modern Art. But most of Chick's friends joined the armed forces or took on war-related jobs. Lincoln Kirstein was drafted soon after Pearl Harbor and served in the European campaign. Julien Levy entered the army for a brief stint in 1942, and Russell Hitchcock went to work for Pratt & Whitney, the East Hartford aircraft engine manufacturer. Even Marie Bissell, Chick's champion and the hostess of his great entertainments, was soon on her way to head up the Red Cross in Washington. But Chick was too old to be drafted and was psychologically incapable of attempting any kind of war work. The closest he came to it was giving a few magic shows at army camps.

As the war began to dominate all aspects of life, another of Chick's central activities was taken away. In January 1943, as part of converting the college to a reduced wartime schedule, Trinity suspended his teaching duties after fifteen years. Chick saw the Avery Theater as the only outlet left for his energies.

He resolved to produce something absolutely new to Hartford: John Ford's Jacobean tragedy 'Tis Pity She's a Whore, written about 1627. This would be only the second public presentation of the play in the United States; the Lenox Hill Players had staged it in New York in 1926. This tale of incest and death—in which the protagonist, Giovanni, impregnates and then murders his sister Annabella to save her from shame—was a classic baroque drama that appealed to Chick's attraction to the dark side of art, "the Romantic agony." In its probing of forbidden recesses of the human psyche, its attempt to release demonic forces in the imagination of the spectator, 'Tis Pity She's a Whore could be regarded as a precursor of surrealism.

Again Chick would design the sets and costumes and play the leading role. He commissioned Paul Bowles to compose incidental music (he had just written a score for a recent New York production of Twelfth Night) and hired Elizabeth McCormick, a veteran of local theater groups, to direct. It was a testament to Chick's powers of persuasion that he could obtain permission from the trustees to put on another large-scale production.

To head off the potential shock and criticism that he knew the play would engender, Chick rounded up as many honorary patrons to list on the title page of the program as he could, among them Iris Barry, John Houseman, Carl Van Vechten, George Platt Lynes, the Sobys, the Cooleys, Beatrice Fox Auerbach—Hartford's department store magnate and philanthropist—Helen's brother, Francis, and her mother. Chick also got professors at Harvard, Yale, Williams, and Trinity to endorse the production.[48]

But this was Hartford, 1943. None of the advertising and no newspaper writer used the full title of the play. Those who settled into their seats in the Avery Theater on May 18, however, had only to open the program to see a reproduction of the title page of the first edition: "TIS Pitty Shee's a Whore / Acted by the *Queenes* Majesties *Servants, at The Phoenix in Drury-Lane."*

In her program notes, Elizabeth McCormick wrote that the play addressed psychological problems that were still difficult to face in twentieth century because "frightened backward-thinking" people preferred "to hide behind outmoded rules and traditions."[49] But many in Hartford did not consider their rules and traditions outmoded at all. McCormick had also written, in an article for the *Hartford Times* a few days before the opening, that Giovanni was "the daring individual thinker up against the forces of reaction." He "must either submit to death to his spirit, or break all the taboos set up by society."[50] This characterization of the play's protagonist could be read as a defense of creative spirits like Chick. But the public was not disposed to see the play as an allegory of artistic independence.

Chick's sets may have been his most imaginative and detailed, with architectural backdrops and constructions depicting the streets of Parma in the tradition of seventeenth- and eighteenth-century scenic design. His costumes may have been as rich and luxurious as those in *Hamlet* two years earlier. His acting may have matured, as some commentators said. And he may have been applauded by some English professors.[51] But the reaction of the audience when they grasped the true nature of the drama—when they saw the director of the Atheneum as Giovanni delighting in having taken his sister's virginity ("I marvel why the chaster of your sex / Should think this pretty toy called maidenhead / So strange a loss"), when they saw him enter in the last scene declaring he had Annabella's heart impaled on his dagger ("I vow 'tis hers: this dagger's point ploughed up / Her fruitful womb, and left me the fame / Of a most glorious executioner")—was, at the very least, distaste.[52]

Reviewers from both Hartford papers, while too sophisticated to be offended by the play itself, found the production lacking. T. H. Parker felt that Chick had gone too far. There were "enough costumes to clothe all the charac-

Chick as Giovanni in 'Tis Pity She's a Whore, *Avery Theater, May 1943.
Set and costumes by AEA*

ters in all the plays Ford ever wrote," and the scene changes were interminable. He dismissed Paul Bowles's music as a parody of Scarlatti. The acting gave "the general effect of two hours of stereopticon slides." In sum, Parker agreed with a comment he overheard from one audience member: "'Tis pity it's a Bore."[53]

In the public mind, however, the play itself was the issue.[54] More letters were addressed to the editors of the local press than for any other program or exhibition Chick undertook, continuing for days after the production closed. They fairly shrieked about what they considered a diseased excuse for a play. Some saw it as an attack on the Roman Catholic Church and thus a slap in the face of the Irish and Italian communities in Hartford.[55] *The Catholic Transcript* condemned the play as a "monstrosity"—a product of "Tudor totalitarianism"—and deplored the fact that "in an hour when there is no time for the nonessential and the nonsensical, when every penny not required for necessities is supposed to be put into war bonds, there are people who have time enough and money enough to stage an elaborate production of a tedious dramatization of degeneracy." Indeed, putting on *'Tis Pity* when "scores of Hartford Catholic men" had gone to war represented "the negation of all they are fighting and suffering and dying for, the smirching of all that they love and prize." And as for McCormick calling the play's hero "a daring individual thinker," she might as well have applied that phrase to Hitler and Tojo. The *Transcript* concluded with an enraged *"Heil and Bonzai!"*[56]

For the most part, the public stayed away. To Chick, the reason was clear: "Any intelligent person," he told the wife of a New York dealer, "must have realized the obstacles that were put in the way of the performances by a smug and destructive community." Once again, he said, he felt "the heartache and frustration that attends any attempt to enliven the provincial New England Culture." Chick had been motivated also by a compulsion to provoke. In that he had succeeded too well, stirring up unprecedented public antagonism and embarrassing his trustees.[57]

But he had already taken action to free himself from any possible consequences. A week before the opening of *'Tis Pity*, exhausted and depressed, Chick could no longer stand the thought of trying to function at the Atheneum. He scrawled a note to Charles Goodwin, resigning as director, effective October 1, 1943. He said only that "for the past years the situation at the museum" had become "increasingly unsatisfactory to me for a variety of reasons." He did not specify those reasons, adding that "I should prefer not to discuss my position in this situation for another three weeks, that is, until after the performances of 'Tis Pity."[58] Honoring the request, Goodwin did not reply, nor did he talk to the other trustees.

Nothing more was said until the morning of June 11. Chick had been talking about his future plans with Helen and a few old friends. After the tension of *'Tis Pity* had died down, he decided that, instead of resigning, he should ask for a year's leave of absence. This would give him time to assess his career, away from the Atheneum. With his love for the movies, he now thought he might try working in Hollywood, perhaps as a set designer, producer, or even an actor. He mentioned the idea privately to the *Hartford Courant*'s T. H. Parker on June 8. Three days later, Chick opened the morning paper and saw a photograph of himself over the headline: "A. E. Austin Will Request Year Leave." To his horror, the story of his intention to approach the trustees had been made public before he had said a word to Uncle Charlie.

Seizing pages of Helen's stationery of different sizes and colors, Chick wrote to Goodwin in anguish:

My dear Uncle Charlie:

I am deeply disturbed by the Courants unwarranted and treacherous publication of the leave-of-absence story this morning.

As you know—I have felt more and more in need of some kind of retirement from Hartford to attempt to bring my whole situation at the museum back into some kind of perspective which will work for me. I have felt increasingly frustrated for the last years—a frustration which finally led to my resignation which I sent to you some weeks ago. This apparently was not brought by you to the attention of the Trustees and on thinking the matter over it occurred to me that what I needed most was a sabbatical leave such as is commonly granted in museums and colleges. It appeared to be appropriate at the moment since due to the war my connections with Trinity have been severed.

Chick explained that he had talked informally with Arthur Day and Charles Seaverns, who were sympathetic to the idea. He had been about to write a formal request to the trustees when the *Courant* got wind of it and Parker came to his office:

I have known him for sixteen years and I regarded him always as a friend. I told him that such an announcement could come only from the Trustees—that there was nothing in any way definite—that it was completely nebulous and of no importance to anyone but myself and the trustees and he agreed to say nothing about it.

It was therefor with the most complete surprise and anguish that I saw the Courant this morning.

You must be aware of the fact that the Courant has been opposed to all my policies in the museum since I have come here. They have repeatedly distorted my intentions as to the museum by publishing unimportant items and holding back important ones. I regard this as their final stab in the back not only directed at me as a person but far more dangerously at the museum as an alive institution. The Courant has repeatedly sought to destroy all indiginous efforts to increase the cultural prestige of this city, whereas I and many others have fought with our last breaths to raise standards of taste and appreciation.

The fight however is much bigger than we are—and the issues are clearly fundamental—the progressive vision leading to the future vs. the reactionary manacles chaining us to the past. But clarification of all of this at least and at last is here.

The Courant statement is a piece of cultural perfidy which has been most subtly engineered. I am sorry indeed that my naivete has allowed me to be trapped by the arch conspirators against everything in which I believe—I should have fought harder—but the fact that I am not wholly a Yankee has made me only half as shrewd.

I want you to believe however that despite the unfortunate fact that apparently I have done many things "behind your back" this was most certainly not one of them.

Yours faithfully

Chick[59]

Charles Goodwin responded to this outpouring with kindness: "I gather that our friends at the Courant had discovered a slight leak and instead of doing what the Dutch boy did, they blew the dike wide open, but it doesn't matter and I think it will more easily open the subject for discussion when the Trustees meet on the 24th."[60]

Chick asked for a year's leave of absence with full pay, but the executive committee granted him six months' paid leave beginning on July first. Mrs. Berger was appointed acting director. Writing to Goodwin from his summer home in Maine, Robert Huntington reported that he had told Chick he hoped he would return to the museum. Chick had responded that what he wanted to do was "not so much the theatre but to write and paint and to discover how much the Atheneum and he do really need each other. . . . It is astounding what a blank the thought of his not being there creates."[61] Goodwin replied bluntly that many trustees felt that the museum's purpose was to please the public and slip in "as much education as is possible by the way. Chick always believes in administering the drug raw with sometimes unforeseen and unpleasant results. . . . A limited amount of controversy and unpleasantness help an institution but the amount is limited."[62] In describing the problems with Chick to Edward Forbes that summer, Goodwin was more specific. Chick's attempt to create a "little theater" program at the museum was not compatible with the size of the theater and was "in direct competition with the Bushnell Memorial. . . . His preoccupation with other than museum business has definitely interfered with the growth and usefulness of the museum proper."[63]

Chick was vague about his plans, simply explaining to the press that he was tired. To carry on his work, he needed "fresh ideas," which he had formerly found in Europe. Now, he said, "I just want to wander."[64] There had been many times when Chick felt that he had to retreat from Hartford. Now, under the greatest stress of his career, this need was overwhelming. Helen, angry at Uncle Charlie and always loyal to Chick, understood. She would remain at home with the children. She could not "wander"; she could only let him go.

Before he left for California, Chick made a plea to Huntington as head of the art committee for one more addition to the collection. It was a picture he had been contemplating since he had shown it in the *Night Scenes* exhibition of 1940: *Saint Francis in Ecstasy* by Caravaggio. Because Chick usually spoke extemporaneously to the art committee, his letter to Huntington was one of the few examples of how he argued the case for a purchase. Its calm reason in the midst of a personal crisis reflected his clarity of mind when judging a work of art.

Chick explained that Paul Byk at Arnold Seligmann, Rey & Company had first offered the painting to him for $50,000. "It is the only authentic Caravaggio in America and yet at that time I did not feel, important as the picture was, that we should spend that much money on it as the whole question of Caravaggio is a pretty mysterious one and it is difficult to get a consensus of opinion among the various scholars on the matter." But by the end of 1942, to straighten out a tax problem, the gallery had lowered the price to $17,000.

In the meanwhile I have thought a great deal about the painting and have asked many scholars about their feelings in connection with the work. They have all admired it very much and all agree that it is by Caravaggio. . . .

Now as you know the greatest strength of the Atheneum collections lies in the field of seventeenth century art which have now become I am sure the greatest in this country. Both in Italy and in the other countries of Western Europe Caravaggio was the greatest single influence on that century and for that reason it has always been most essential that we have a work by this great master as a pivot to the many wonderful pictures we have bought. But since the purchase many years ago from Wildenstein of the so called Caravaggio Head of a Boy (which is almost certainly a French picture and a very handsome one but not by the master) I wanted to be quite certain in my own mind that our next essay should be undisputed. Of this I am now convinced. At seventeen thousand the price not only represents a sensational buy for a Caravaggio but as well protects us in the future against any reversal of judgment as to the authorship since the painting is a very beautiful one and would be worth that amount in any case.

I hope that I have made all of this clear to you. That Caravaggio is one of the greatest masters in the history of art no one would deny. That we need an authentic and beautiful picture by him is obvious. That this is the time to get it is very clear as no others, as far as is now known, can come on the market.[65]

The purchase was approved, and Chick assembled an exhibition in Avery Court around the *Saint Francis*, which he called *Caravaggio and the 17th Century*, using pictures he had bought for the museum supplemented with a few loans from dealers. The show was scheduled to remain on view until he returned in December.

Chick gave himself a huge send-off at the Scarborough Street house, with free-flowing liquor. He later apologized to Truda Kaschmann for his overindulgence: "I was sorry that at my 'farewell' party I hadnt been in condition to say farewell to anybody. But from what I am told our final scene was played not without a certain tenderness. It must have been the Pernod. It always gives me an attack of combined amnesia and lethargy." He headed for Hollywood by way of an army camp in Gatesville, Texas, where Tommy Hughes was stationed; he stayed for a week, planning each day, he told Kaschmann, by figuring out "how to get through it with the least possible pain."[66]

When Chick arrived in Los Angeles, he was Paul Byk's guest in one of the poolside cottages at the Garden of Allah, the former residence of the Russian actress and silent film star Alla Nazimova. It had become a popular resort hotel for writers like Robert Benchley, Dorothy Parker, Christopher Isherwood, and W. H. Auden, along with artists, musicians, and movie stars.

In 1943 Hollywood and New York were the two most stimulating places to be for anyone involved in the arts, and the Garden was a prime location for a meeting place. Chick already had friends in the film world—John Houseman, Virgil Thomson, Ruth Ford, Tonio Selwart, and George Balanchine among them—and Helen's brother-in-law Willie Graff was in the movies. Chick soon had a large circle of acquaintances. Bette Davis, with her New England background, developed an immediate rapport with him. He got to know Vincent Price because of the actor's art collection. He became a favorite of the pioneering decorator Elsie de Wolfe (also known as Lady Mendl). Virgil Thomson introduced him to Joan Fontaine. He introduced himself to Vera and Igor Stravinsky at the Brown Derby one evening, and they became so friendly that later he prepared a Russian Easter dinner for them. They applauded and licked their plates as a Russian compliment.

The Graffs introduced him to the newly arrived Anglo-Irish actress of great distinction, Moyna MacGill, and her three teenage children, Angela, Edgar, and Bruce Lansbury. Chick and Miss MacGill, who were about the same age and had the same mad sense of humor, got along "like a house on fire," Angela Lansbury recalled. (Chick was especially delighted to learn that Miss MacGill had played Annabella in a London production of 'Tis Pity.) Angela Lansbury's first sight of Chick arriving at their house in Hollywood remained vivid decades later: "He was in a pair of old gray bags [slacks], sneakers, a navy blue- and red-striped shirt, his hair disheveled, no hat, and a cigarette hanging out of his mouth, the inevitable cigarette that always had the bit of spit dribbling down . . . because he couldn't stop talking long enough to take it out of his mouth." Her assessment of Chick as seen in those years was astute:

He had so much class, he had so much behind him always. All his life. He really was a very fortunate person, I think. Obviously his mother exposed him to the world at such a tender age that nothing really impressed Chick. But Chick to me was a very good example of somebody who had all of that extraordinary knowledge and taste and sensitivity and selectivity and eclecticism, but he was still bowled over by the romance of the movies.

Like everyone who remembered Chick from that time, she never knew what his goal was in Hollywood. "Perhaps indeed he did come to California to act. I don't know. I wasn't aware of that, I really wasn't. He was just this fascinating top that never stopped spinning."

Chick soon bought a house on Miller Drive in the Hollywood hills overlooking the city, where he could throw his own parties. "It was always an event if you went to Chick's," Angela Lansbury remembered. "He always had an incredible mixture of people."[67] He reverted to his premarital habit of using every dish in the house and never cleaning up. When a friend asked him how he coped with the mess, he replied: "Oh, Bette Davis comes in once a week and does the dishes."[68] His old dealer friend from Venice, Adolf Loewi, lived nearby, having moved his business to Los Angeles to escape persecution in Italy, and Chick purchased or borrowed eighteenth-century furniture and other objects from him to decorate his house. Among them were two terra-cotta sphinxes in his garden. One night, producer Sam Goldwyn asked if he could rent the sphinxes to use in a movie, offering a ridiculously high monthly rate. Chick agreed and was delighted when, through some oversight in the studio's accounting department, checks continued to arrive long after the shooting was finished.[69] Tonio Selwart, a German stage and film actor Chick had known through the Askews, recalled that another of these newly acquired items was a beautiful seventeenth-century painted bidet—from which Chick served cauliflower and celery at his cocktail parties.

Deciding that he needed a maid, he asked Selwart for advice. Selwart had an African-American maid named Evelyn who offered the services of a cousin for Chick. She supplied what seemed to be a very handsome young woman with painted toenails and hair covering one eye, suggesting a black Veronica Lake. But when Evelyn referred to her cousin as "he," Selwart was confused and asked her whether this cousin was a man or a woman. Matter-of-factly, she replied, "He could be both." Chick was delighted. "Tonio," he said a few days later, "that is absolutely wonderful what you sent me! I call him 'the couple.' Because he can be the butler, and he can be the maid. So Bette Davis is coming tomorrow, and you're coming, too—and *he* can open the door and so on until the food is done, and *she* can dress and serve!"[70]

Sober reality intruded in October when an unregistered picture was discovered in the basement of the Wadsworth Atheneum. It had been sent to Chick on approval six years earlier and had never been presented to the art committee. This prompted Robert Huntington to ask Mrs. Berger for an inventory of all the paintings on loan from dealers. She came up with an astounding thirty pictures, worth nearly $70,000. "Needless to say," Huntington wrote Chick, enclosing the list, "I am considerably disturbed by this situation and want it to be cleared up and settled entirely and promptly."[71] He insisted that Chick choose a few of the works for immediate purchase as a good-faith gesture to the dealers. Explaining the discovery to Forbes, Charles Goodwin said that "these pictures were apparently taken in by Chick and laid away in dark corners" with "nothing to show under what arrangement they were received by him." As a man for whom fiscal responsibility was a sacred duty, Goodwin was acutely embarrassed because "some of the pictures are in bad condition and for four we are now receiving overdue bills (some of them overdue as much as four years)."[72]

Chick treated the matter lightly. The dealers were all his friends, especially Byk, who had lent twenty of the canvases. "That business about the pictures," he wrote to Helen, "is really a tempest in a teapot and I told him [Huntington] that I refused to be made to feel guilty long distance."

He checked off a handful of paintings valued at over $30,000 to be purchased from the list Huntington had sent, among them Paul Gauguin's sinister depiction of his friend and patron, *Nirvana: Portrait of Meyer de Haan* of 1889–90, which came from Wildenstein for $2,200. He also chose an enchanting picture by Giovanni Battista Piazzetta, *Boy with a Pear in His Hand* of about 1740, from Adolf Loewi for $2,600; and an extremely fleshy seventeenth-century work, *Daedalus and Icarus* by Orazio Riminaldi (then attributed to Bernardo Cavallino), from Seligmann for $5,000. The three paintings were significant additions to the collection, and as Chick had suggested to Helen, none of the dealers seemed concerned about the delay.

But all of his resentments had been stirred up by the tone of Huntington's letter. "Why should I have guardians always appointed for me by Uncle C which is what [Alfred] Terry essentially is[?]" Chick asked Helen. "It still makes me so mad to think of those younger stupids like Britton and Gross [trustees John Britton and Spencer Gross] saying that I had never done anything for the museum to warrant such generosity on their part. I'm going to tell Uncle Charlie that it is pointless for me to return if the younger men feel that I am no good at the job." Having just heard that Alfred Barr was resigning from the Museum of Modern Art under pressure, Chick told Helen, "It sounds as though he had been eased out and that as apparently happens in many museums after the director has done all the spade work the trustees begin to think that they can run it better themselves."[73] (Barr was fired as director in October, but refused to leave and was given a small office and, in 1947, the title of Director of Collections. In December, Chick sent him a hand-decorated sheet with the message: "A very merry Christmas To The Resigned From The Resigned."[74])

Late in November, the board extended his leave of absence for another six months. Goodwin wrote pointedly to Chick:

While Chick ponders his future in Hollywood, the Goodwins assemble at the museum to celebrate the installation of the parlor from Woodlands, the recently dismantled family mansion in Hartford, February 1, 1944. Left to right: Charles Goodwin, Mrs. Walter Goodwin, Helen Austin, James Goodwin, Mrs. Charles Goodwin, Mrs. James Goodwin, and Philip Goodwin

The feeling of the trustees also was unanimous that you ought not to try to resume your duties as Director of the Wadsworth unless the psychological situation could be such that you could offer and exact warm, mutual cooperation. This means, of course, that you accept the city which is served by the museum with its strengths and its shortcomings and make the museum as acceptable to the city as your own high standards permit and you will also without in the least lowering those standards work willingly and cheerfully with your Trustees in accordance with the usual forms of management in building up the museum and increasing its usefulness.[75]

It was probably Robert Huntington who followed Uncle Charlie's letter with an assurance that, at the trustees' meeting granting him leave, "there was no expression in the matter which would cause you to feel other than pleased." He urged Chick to "stick to your career in the field in which you were so well trained under Mr. Forbes" and to "remember, you are yet young and recognition of your ability will surely come to you. . . . Put your pride in your pocket and—come back to us."[76]

Chick had not made up his mind. He used the extended leave to try to enter the Hollywood theatrical scene. He made a model for a theater redecorating business ("my work will at least be seen by producers," he told Helen). He helped found a small theater company, the Gate Theatre Studio, inspired by The Gate in Dublin, with movie stars Edgar Bergen, Charles Coburn, Walter Huston, and others. This offered him possibilities of designing and performing.[77] Jim Hellyar, furloughed from the army after a nervous breakdown, stayed with Chick in Hollywood and helped build the set for at least one production of the Gate. By then, Chick was well connected in the studios and took Jim to watch Balanchine rehearse with Tamara Toumanova for a film and to meet Bette Davis for lunch at Warner Brothers. But he found no lasting work for himself in show business.

At Uncle Charlie's request, Chick returned to Hartford in May to discuss his future at the museum with the trustees. He met with Goodwin, Huntington, and Arthur Day. They explained their requirements for a more positive attitude toward Hartford and for exhibitions that would have more appeal to the local audience. Chick then spoke for an hour and a half, reminding them of what he had done for Hartford. A few days later, on May 25, the board of trustees unanimously decided, as Goodwin reported to Edward Forbes, "that it would be a mistake to attempt to revive the old relationship." The board extended Chick's leave through the end of the year to give him time to make new arrangements. "I think the decision was welcomed by him and is a great relief," Goodwin concluded.[78]

But for Chick, leaving the museum he had virtually created was far more traumatic than Goodwin claimed. After the trustees' meeting, he returned to his office. He asked Mrs. Berger and his secretary, Mary Blasi, to join him. When they came in, he said simply: "Well, I've been fired." The two women did not know what to say. After a brief silence, he said, "Everything happens for the best." A few days later, he returned and began emptying the office.[79]

His "resignation" was not announced publicly, as he was still officially the director until the end of the year, but the word spread quickly to his friends in the art world. They offered what comfort they could. None was more heartfelt than the letter from Alfred Barr, who for so long had been Chick's friendly competitor in the exploration of contemporary art:

> Perhaps it was an impasse and you feel well out of it—with the last dust shaking from your feet. But I think we're all the poorer (not that I have the least concern for Hartford or the Atheneum which gained distinction *only* through you. They deserve now a perpetual mediocrity

which I'm sure they'll contrive with no trouble.) But you did things sooner and more brilliantly than anyone. You made us gay—and envious and no one can replace you.

I've always felt a bit shy of you and inarticulate. . . . But now I must confirm my admiration for you and my regret and grief (no matter how *you* feel) for what has happened and how you've been treated.[80]

Jim Soby, then functioning as the Modern's unofficial acting director after Barr's demotion, sent Goodwin a polite letter, resigning from the Atheneum's board of trustees: "My interest in the Atheneum has always centered on Mr. Austin's activities there. Our sympathies have been so close that I think it better both for the Atheneum and for us if we leave at the same time."[81]

Less than two weeks after the board accepted Chick's resignation, Goodwin opened a major exhibition in the Tapesty Hall of the Morgan Memorial. It was devoted entirely to marine architecture, with paintings, prints, plans, ship models, and an actual seventeen-foot two-masted sailing dinghy commissioned by Goodwin the year before Chick came to Hartford.[82]

Chick spent most of the summer of 1944 with Helen and the children[83] until restlessness overcame him, and he returned to Hollywood at the end of August with a vague idea that he might be wanted for a screen test.[84] No sooner had he arrived than he learned that his mother, who had turned eighty in April, was near death from cancer. He set out for New Hampshire, but Laura died on September 3, before he could reach her. At her instructions, she was laid out in her favorite burgundy red velvet evening dress—her "traveling clothes," she had told Herb Crucius, the longtime caretaker of her property in Windham. The coffin was then brought back to Uncle John's and placed on the dining room table. Chick could manage to enter the room and take a quick look inside the casket only after having several drinks in the kitchen.[85] He, Helen, and David accompanied her body to Mount Union, Pennsylvania, where she was buried near Uncle John in the Morrison family plot. Her death, just after his dismissal from the museum, left him doubly adrift.

To give Chick some kind of income and to take advantage of his expertise, the trustees commissioned him to prepare a catalogue of all the pictures he had bought with the Sumner Fund. In December, though the catalogue work dragged on for two years, he installed the paintings in the Morgan Memorial. Just after Christmas, he returned to the stage of the Avery Theater as the Great Osram for his last magic show as director of the Wadsworth Atheneum.

The Sumner Collection went on view for the first time as a group on January 1, 1945, the day his resignation took effect.

There was no public announcement of his stepping down as director, no article in the *Hartford Times* or the *Courant*. By then, the cataclysm of war, as the Allies smashed into Germany and battled to drive the Japanese from the

The Great Osram as "The Sea-God of Magic" in Chick's
final magic show as director, Avery Theater, December 1944.
Set and costumes by AEA

South Pacific, dominated the news. Every day the Hartford papers published photographs of servicemen killed in action, and of young brides beside their smiling grooms in uniform.

And no grateful resolution was adopted by the museum's board of trustees. Indeed, Chick's departure was not ever recorded in the official trustees' records, the volumes that had chronicled every important event in the Atheneum's long history. Chick simply ceased to be mentioned in the minutes.

The news finally filtered down to the public at the beginning of February. Letters to the editors of both Hartford papers reflected a genuine appreciation for what the city was losing. "Art lovers in Connecticut are appalled," wrote one correspondent; another expressed "shock and real grief"; Chick's resignation was, wrote still another, "a catastrophe for Hartford."[86] Of all the personal statements printed in the press, one from Peggy Parsons Robinson, Helen's childhood friend and Chick's secretary early in his career, most tellingly put his leave-taking in perspective. It represented, she told the *Courant*, nothing less than the end of an epoch: "It was an era in which national attention was focused upon Hartford as in the days of Mark Twain. . . . The people of Hartford will be eternally grateful to the man who brought great art so close to us and who made it live."[87]

Chick wandered from Hartford to Windham to New York. He had not come to terms with the reality that he was no longer director of the Atheneum. One evening early in the year, at a cocktail party in New York given by a collector of pre-Columbian art, Chick struck up a conversation with an attractive young woman who had lived in Mexico and now wrote for *Vogue*. Then known as Peggy Riley, she was later to become an editor, writer, and lecturer on the arts under another name, Rosamond Bernier. She and Chick shared such enthusiasm for the artifacts at the party and got on so well that she accepted his invitation to come to Hartford for the weekend before she even knew his name. A short time later, arriving at the Hartford train station, she was met on the platform by a magnificent figure in a silk mandarin's costume, complete with an embroidered Chinese hat and a pigtail. It was Chick, of course. Ignoring the stares of passersby, he explained breezily that he was on his way to give a magic show, but that he would drive her to his house, where his wife was expecting her. In the evening, he took her alone to dinner, apparently with Helen's blessing.

"He confided that he had been fired from the museum," said Madame Bernier, "and it was clear that he was heartbroken. His eyes brimmed with tears as he described how he had built the Atheneum's collection from nearly nothing to an extraordinary group of baroque and modern masterpieces only to be unappreciated by the trustees." She was so moved that she reached into her purse and handed him a tiny bronze pre-Columbian figure with a conical hat that she always kept with her as a good luck charm. "Here, keep this," she said. He took it, and to reciprocate in some way, blurted out, "Let me show you the museum." It was close to midnight, but Chick still had his keys to the building. When they arrived, the night watchman stepped aside. "So Austin took me into the galleries, turning on the lights himself as we passed from one to another." He showed her scores of pictures that he had bought—from Fra Angelico's *Angel* to Dalí's *Apparition,* the masterpieces by Piero di Cosimo and Cranach, Caravaggio and Strozzi, Valdés Leal, Murillo, Poussin, Le Nain, Claude Lorrain, Sweerts, Tiepolo, Guardi, Greuze, Goya, Degas, Ernst, Arp, Balthus, de Chirico, Miró, Mondrian, Picasso—"his children, so to speak," said Madame Bernier. "And it was the most poignant, extraordinary experience."[88] She never saw him again.

Only one possibility seemed to give Chick a sense of purpose that year. Soon after his mother's death, while walking around her property in Windham with Laura's loyal Herb Crucius, Chick had pointed to the barn, built in the 1830s, next to the house Laura had given him and Helen as a wedding present. He said that he thought it would make a wonderful theater. To his amazement, Crucius replied, "Hey, Everett. Your mother said you were going to make that a playhouse." He added that Laura had instructed him to store three old wooden sleighs up on the hay lofts, telling him, "Sometime he's going to use them for boxes or something."[89]

The theater Chick now began planning could take the place of his unfulfilled Hollywood ambitions. Here he could be the producer, the designer, and even the star. He lined up old friends from the magic shows at the museum—Bea Ganz to take on leading roles and her husband, Harry, to be the business manager—and started the conversion of the barn. He expected that, by the following July, he could open the "Windham Playhouse."

The war, which had changed everything for everyone, including those on its periphery like Chick, came to an end in Europe on May 8 and in the Pacific on August 14.

Throughout the rest of 1945, Chick made little effort to find a new job, instead dabbling at the Sumner catalogue and driving back and forth to the farm in Windham and his house in Hollywood. After Christmas, in the Avery Theater, he made a second, and final, "farewell" appearance as the Great Osram. By this time, it was a sad anticlimax, and Chick's future was still uncertain.

But once again, in a curious repetition of history, Edward Forbes had been quietly working on his behalf behind the scenes.

CHAPTER SEVENTEEN

The Baroque and the Big Top

Everything will be *new*. The exhibition will contain more startling and entirely novel Wonders of *Creation* than were ever before seen in one collection, as I expect to make this the CROWNING SUCCESS OF MY MAN-AGERIAL LIFE.

—P. T. Barnum

Wintering in Florida in 1946, Edward Forbes was approached by Governor Millard Caldwell for advice about finding the first director of the pink and white palace on Sarasota Bay known as the John and Mable Ringling Museum of Art. Ten years after the Circus King's death, the State of Florida had finally won title to his legacy—the museum, its collections, and Ca' d'Zan, the extravagant mansion he and his wife had built on the property. The choice of someone qualified to take charge of a museum with the largest collection of baroque pictures in America was obvious to Forbes. The governor's committee, which had been overseeing the Ringling, authorized him to invite Chick Austin to Florida to consider the position.[1]

Forbes had opened the way for Chick to return to the museum world where he could exercise his greatest talents, the connoisseurship and the mission to educate that had been born and nurtured at the Fogg. By now, he knew that he could never reach the same heights in the theater or in Hollywood that he had achieved in the fine arts.

In mid-March, Chick met with Governor Caldwell and his committee in Tallahassee. They offered him the job on the spot and agreed to his one stipulation—that he would work only seven and a half months of the year and be paid accordingly. He wanted to keep the summer and fall free. Florida was practically dead during that time (these were the days before widespread air-conditioning), and he had already decided to start the summer theater in New Hampshire. In a strange echo of his appointment to the Atheneum as "acting director," he was hired for a six-month trial period, beginning on October 15.

"All went smoothly as clockwork and—I had so many ideas it knocked them over," he wrote to Helen from St. Petersburg on March 17. He was elated at having a compelling new project after more than three years in the doldrums:

> Its really a wonderful short order job and I know I can do it very show-ily—just my style—you should see the warehouses of 1870 Baroque—I'm going to exhibit it—with circus wagons etc—and shows in the patio and with the performers during the winter—a circus museum which shocked Edward [Forbes] Im afraid but entranced the board. They take in $500 a day in paid admissions—(25c) always an audience. I feel in clover—at last an audience—it will be fun. . . . love to the kids—Im still in a daze.[2]

From Hartford, thirteen-year-old David wrote: "Glad to hear you got the good job. . . . Thank you for the postcard. I hope I can see the museum sometime. . . . I wish you were here more and I am looking forward to your coming back."[3]

There was no thought of Helen and the children moving to Florida. Even under conventional circumstances, it would have been difficult. Chick had no intention of living there year-round, the job seemed to be a short-term proposition, and David and Sally were happy in their Hartford schools. Also Helen and Chick could never sell the house on Scarborough Street; it was the symbol of their existence as a family and of Chick's artistic achievements. But beyond these reasons, Helen and Chick's relationship had already evolved into a long-distance marriage. Chick had spent years in a restless pursuit of personal and professional fulfillment—and Helen had come to appreciate a less tumultuous existence without him. At the same time, a part of her wanted Chick to be with her and the children. Helen and Chick loved each other; they were confidants and best friends. Yet she realized that if he returned, his bisexuality would pose problems. She also knew that Chick needed to be in a place where he could have an outlet for his creative energies. So she was strong, patient, and forgiving, holding the family together and hoping that Chick could someday rejoin them.

His appointment was confirmed in April. He sent new photographs of himself to Marian Murray at the *Hartford Times*, urging her, as he told Helen, "to cut loose on publicity. . . . I do want it known that I am respectably occupied again."[4] Like the Atheneum in 1927, the Ringling awaited transformation into a modern museum. But this time, instead of building an extraordinary paintings collection, Chick would be rescuing one; and now, in his mid-forties, he was a seasoned professional with an international reputation and a whole repertoire of programs up his sleeve.

The Sarasota Chick saw in 1946 was still imbued with the presence of the man who had created the museum. There was Ringling Boulevard, the Ringling causeway, the Ringling Hotel. The city had been the winter quarters of Ringling Brothers and Barnum & Bailey since 1927. Throughout the "season," circus people, including giants and midgets, went about their business without being treated as out of the ordinary. Many of the midgets still lived in Lilliputian housing that Ringling had built for them in one part of town.

Like Chick, John Ringling was a man of vision and flair with an instinct for the theatrical. The youngest of the six Ringling brothers who had started the circus in the 1880s, he was the genius behind the complex logistics of moving it around the country. Eventually, he ran the whole lucrative operation. He invested in railroads, oil wells, real estate, and theaters, becoming one of the richest men in America, known simply as "Mr. John." He and his wife, Mable Burton Ringling, visited Sarasota for the first time in 1911, soon after the first influx of wealthy winter vacationers to the Gulf Coast of Florida. They bought a home on the bay with over a thousand feet of shoreline, where they moored their 125-foot steam yacht. Over the next decade, Ringling became the city's prime real estate developer, buying property that was measured in square miles instead of acres.

The house that he and Mable began building in 1924, Ca' d'Zan, or "John's house" in the Venetian dialect, was exactly the kind of theatrical setting Chick loved. It was a thirty-one-room villa based on the Doge's Palace in Venice, but made even grander with the addition of a sixty-one-foot-high tower inspired by the one atop Madison Square Garden. Its pale rose stucco exterior was ornamented with terra-cotta; its roofs were covered with sixteenth-century Spanish tiles. Visitors entered through twelve-foot carved walnut doors that led into a huge living room, fifty by sixty-five feet, two and a half stories high. A crystal chandelier from the original Waldorf-Astoria was suspended over the black-and-white marble floor. Across the room from the giant fireplace was an Aeolian organ, constructed in the house, its four thousand pipes hidden by tapestries on the second-floor balcony. The dining room, with a table that could seat forty people, was paneled in black Italian walnut. Its ceiling was decorated with cameos that had once adorned the Gothic Room of Marble House in Newport. The house was filled with European furnishings and decorative objects from the seventeenth through the nineteenth centuries. Ca' d'Zan was finished in time for Christmas, 1926, at a cost of $1,500,000. It was said that from his

Ca' d'Zan at the John and Mable Ringling Museum of Art, Sarasota

two-hundred-foot polished terra-cotta-and-marble dock, where six Venetian gondolas were tied up, Ringling could see no land that he did not own. Chick immediately envisioned the entertainments and public programs that he could create at Ca' d'Zan.

But what had attracted him most to the job was of course the enormous collection of European paintings. Ringling had developed a discerning eye for art during his annual trips to Europe in search of new circus acts. While building the house, he began buying baroque paintings with the advice of the German art dealer Julius Böhler. In just ten years, he amassed over six hundred canvases, including works by Velásquez, van Dyck, Hals, Veronese, Giordano, El Greco, Ribera, Poussin, Reynolds, and Gainsborough. Among the most spectacular were Piero di Cosimo's *Building of the Palace* and four huge oils (one of them sixteen feet high) by Peter Paul Rubens and his workshop—cartoons for a great tapestry series, *The Triumph of the Eucharist*. It was by far the most valuable collection of European pictures in the South.

In 1927, after a section of the property was drained and the water moccasins and alligators were removed, Ringling started construction of a museum to house the art—a monument to his wife and himself that he promised to leave to the State of Florida. The Italian Renaissance-style building, consisting of

Chick at the Ringling Museum, Look, *October 26, 1948*

twenty-two galleries and a private burial crypt, incorporated elements that recalled the fifteenth through the eighteenth centuries. Seventy-six life-size cast-stone replicas of antique Italian statues were stationed along the three sides of the roofline. The terraced garden court was dominated by twentieth-century copies of monumental Italian Renaissance sculpture, among them a bronze cast of Michelangelo's *David.* The museum appeared to be either a palazzo that had grown over several centuries or a Hollywood set constructed by Cecil B. DeMille. It was finished just before Mable's death in the summer of 1929, but the paintings were not fully installed until the next year. When Ringling invited the public to visit the museum for a single day in 1930, fifteen thousand people—more than Sarasota's entire population—swarmed over the property.

The Depression brought Ringling severe financial reversals. In 1932 he opened the museum free to the public but charged a twenty-five-cent parking fee, which his butler collected at the door. This was rumored to be Ringling's only income. Four years later, he died in New York at the age of seventy. Though he had willed his house, the museum, and its contents to the State of Florida, creditors tied up the estate, and relatives tried to break the will. The tangled legal battles went on for a decade until the title to the property passed unencumbered to the State.

The museum Chick found was not the pristine temple of art that John Ringling had completed in 1930. Set on thirty-seven acres and invisible to anyone traveling on any main thoroughfare, the Ringling was in a frightful state of neglect. The grounds—though lush with palms, native pines, banyan trees, bougainvillea, and hibiscus—were wildly overgrown. Ca' d'Zan had been closed up for a decade. Nothing seemed to have been touched since Ringling's death. His clothes still hung in his bedroom, and his razor lay on his shaving stand in front of his personal barber chair. The interiors had faded and were in serious need of refurbishing.

The art collection itself was in a precarious condition. It was true that the opulent, oversize baroque canvases remained intact—some in storerooms, some still in the massive galleries, for despite his financial problems, Ringling had not sold any of the hundreds of pictures he had acquired. But a decade of subtropical climate could have been a century in a more temperate zone. Many of the paintings stood on the floor, leaning against the walls. Surfaces had cracked, and mold and mildew grew on them, and when it rained, water ran down the gallery walls and dripped across the canvases.

The museum had no amenities. There were no administrative offices, workrooms, or even public toilets. There was no professional staff. When Chick was named director, there was a doorman who had been hired by the Ringlings, a superintendent of the estate who was once the captain of their yacht, a business manager brought in by the State of Florida, a guide who took tips for his tours, and a few laborers. Chick later recalled that the Ringling had "something of the aroma of the circus with its various concessionaires. Four hundred dollars in a cardboard shoebox represented the net assets of the museum."[5]

Chick knew he would need strong support in dealing with the State of Florida as he set about bringing the museum to life. Among the first to welcome his appointment was one of John Ringling's friends, Karl Bickel. A former president of United Press International, Bickel was a retired journalist who had settled in Sarasota after a career that had taken him all over the world. Ringling had made him a member of the museum's original board of trustees, and he had been a moving force on the governor's committee. Supported by another enlightened Floridian, Hollis Rinehart, Bickel became Chick's greatest advocate in the state.

Though he was invigorated by the familiar rush of adrenaline as he contemplated the Ringling, Chick had not entirely regained his bearings. After only a brief stop in Hartford, he dashed back to Hollywood to give a birthday party for Bette Davis. When he found out that one of the actors from 'Tis Pity, Paul Geissler, was planning to visit a friend in Mexico, he invited Geissler to accom-

*AEA, Jr., with Hollis Rhinehart and Carl Bickel on the grounds
of the Ringling Museum, 1948*

pany him to Hollywood first to help with the party. Chick decided that nothing
less than a total redecoration of his house would do. He borrowed paintings,
furniture, and silver from Adolf Loewi to create a perfect setting for his guest of
honor, and the party was one of his most dazzling. But when the guests were
gone, Geissler saw a very different side of Chick: "Chick hated to be alone. He
didn't want to be alone for one second . . . and if he was he would drink himself
to unconsciousness practically. . . . He said he could never accept his mortality. . . . He needed support constantly with somebody he could fall back on."
When Geissler decided to leave for Mexico, Chick protested strenuously, and
then telephoned another friend in Hartford, asking him to come out immediately.[6]

He was back in Sarasota by May 4 for his first press conference. Dressed
informally in a blue-and-white-striped sport shirt, Chick, who now called himself Everett, escorted reporters through the buildings and warehouses where
the museum's collections were stored. He announced that he would open Ca'
d'Zan to the public in six months. The museum itself would take longer
because of the condition of the galleries and pictures. Repairs and a massive
conservation program, he said, would have to take place before the public
could see the collection.[7]

The Florida legislature put the museum under the jurisdiction of the State Board of Control, which also oversaw state universities. That summer the board approved an emergency appropriation making it possible for Chick to deliver over twenty paintings to dealer Julius Weitzner in New York for restoration. He wrote to Jim Soby, again expressing relief and joy at emerging from his darkest period: "I am really in a delirium about life again after those miserable fallow years and having been afraid for a while that I COULDN'T work again, I now find that I can do more than ever and much more sensibly."[8]

By coincidence, earlier that year, the Wadsworth Atheneum had finally hired a new director as well—also on the recommendation of Edward Forbes— Charles C. Cunningham. He was everything Charles Goodwin could have asked for—a naval officer, an athlete, and a yachtsman. He was trained at the Fogg, descended from James Russell Lowell, and married to Eleanor Lamont, the daughter of the chairman of J. P. Morgan and Company. Different as the two men were, Cunningham admired Chick tremendously and went out of his way to lend paintings to his exhibitions in Sarasota.

Chick's excitement as he left Florida for the summer came not only from the challenge of the Ringling, but also from the prospect of transforming his mother's barn into a theater. "I can't wait to get to the farm to commence summer doings," he confided to Mrs. Berger.[9] As usual, he called on old friends from Hartford to help him: in addition to Harry and Bea Ganz, he was joined by Mary Blasi, Elena Longo, Harry Overend (the Atheneum's carpenter), and, as chief scenic artist, Jim Hellyar.

Hellyar had replaced Tommy Hughes as Chick's companion. He had first met Chick in 1934 when he was a junior in high school and came to the museum to see the Picasso show, and ran into him again during his freshman year at Trinity. When Chick discovered that Jim was so strapped for money that he was subsisting on lunches of peanut butter crackers and Coca-Cola, he obtained a small stipend for him in return for operating the slide projector in the art history course. As another kindness, Chick and Helen invited him to a formal dinner for three on Scarborough Street at which, as Jim later recalled, only a gentle movement by Helen stopped him from serving the dessert into his finger bowl. He soon became one of Chick's scene painters and magic assistants and was a veteran of *Hamlet* and *'Tis Pity*. Hellyar accepted his role gratefully. As he said years later, "I was always the one that was just around."[10]

Jim's devotion was characteristic of Chick's other followers in the theater, but different from that of his equals in the art world, whether Jim Soby, Julien Levy, or Nellie Howland. Bea Ganz, who became a perennial star of the Windham Playhouse, was still ecstatic thirty years after Chick's death: "What he exuded—I tell you, it was like a magnet. You couldn't help but just adore him, and I think everybody felt that way, men or women, it made no difference. He was a man that you had to *see*, you had to *feel*. Oh, he was gorgeous. . . . And not

Jim Hellyar works on Chick's set for The Elements of Magic,
Hartford, May 1942.

only that, he enlarged my life so. I learned so much from him."[11] (Even if she and Chick did get into an occasional squabble, he would find a way to mollify her quickly. Shortly after one noisy tiff, he was seen walking cheerily with her down by Cobbett's Pond. Explaining the rapprochement to an observer, Chick said, "Oh, I decided to let by-Ganz be by-Ganz."[12])

As soon as Chick arrived in New Hampshire, his team of carpenters and volunteers tore out the rear wall of the barn, erected a thirty-foot-high fly gallery and built a stage twenty-four feet deep and fifty feet wide, supported by beams from an abandoned railroad trestle. The proscenium arch was fifteen feet high and twenty-eight feet wide. Full theatrical lighting was installed. Chick salvaged 220 seats from a movie house in Connecticut that was being demolished and acquired a collection of nineteenth-century sets and back-drops from the old Goodspeed Opera House in East Haddam. As Laura Austin had predicted, her brightly enameled sleighs served as box seats. Chick deco-rated the lobby and the rest rooms with his own set and costume designs from times past. And in huge black letters painted across the front wall of the white barn was the name WINDHAM PLAYHOUSE.

Chick and Beatrice Ganz in Private Lives, *Windham Playhouse, 1953*

In an announcement to attract subscribers, Chick was ever the ambitious promoter: "Our aim is to serve you with a summer entertainment artistically on the highest level and with your assistance we can in a short time build a national reputation."[13] He asked Edward Forbes's daughter, Marla, a director for the Players of Sarasota, to direct for the summer. He recruited professional actors through his theatrical network. But Chick intended to be not only the owner and producer of this enterprise; he cast himself in the leading role of Charles in the first production, Noël Coward's *Blithe Spirit.* He supplied the local press with copy in keeping with his mother's promotion of "Professor Marvel" in Windham three decades earlier: "Mr. Austin's acting talents have carried him from coast to coast, being seen in many shows both in the East and in Hollywood. His roles have been varied and his interpretation of the melancholy Dane in 'Hamlet' was compared to Barrymore's."[14]

The Windham Playhouse was an immediate success, in part because there was little else to do during the evenings in rural New Hampshire, but mostly because of the quality of the productions. The professionalism of the young actors, who welcomed relief from steamy New York City, was high. A few, like Rod Steiger, Jack Carter, Jason Robards, and Broderick Crawford, became famous. Most of the actors were housed in Uncle John's, sometimes four or five

The Windham Playhouse in winter, newly painted barn red, c. 1955

beds to a room, while Chick lived next door at Barn Manor with the principal actors. He was usually up at six in the morning, and when he felt it was time for others to arise, he would play a particularly raucous popular record so loudly that, as one assistant recalled, "it could get you out of bed in order to wring his neck."[15] At the end of each play, which meant every week, he gave a party with superb food and a punch into which he poured champagne and every kind of alcohol close at hand.[16]

A young woman from York, Pennsylvania, Bertha Love, came to audition for Chick that first summer on the recommendation of his aunt Sue Etnier. Miss Love arrived at Barn Manor and sat nervously on a couch, waiting to meet Mr. Austin. Suddenly a door flew open: Chick made a ballet leap into the room, pirouetted, knelt gracefully at her feet, took her hand, kissed it, and said, "You must be my Bertha." He and Tonio Selwart decided that her stage name should be Judith, and she happily changed it permanently. "I was very innocent," she explained, "and he took me under his wing." She became a favorite at the Playhouse, returning for three more summers to do ingenue roles. One season, she contracted a bad case of poison ivy, and arriving back the next summer, she discovered that the room she always occupied had been completely repapered in ivy wallpaper. "This is just a reminder," said Chick, laughing. "Stay out of the woods!"[17]

As he had done in Hartford, Chick took infinite pains over the sets and costumes, bringing in the furniture and pictures that filled his mother's houses as well as objects he bought at local antiques barns. (Laura Austin had 321 side

The Windham Playhouse, 1947. The set for Rebecca, *with Chick at right as Maxim de Winter. Laura Austin's portrait collection has been put to good use.*

chairs from many periods stored in her attic when she died.[18]) There were also trunks of her clothes, and actresses found themselves wearing Laura's turn-of-the-century dresses from Worth in Paris. Chick did much of the set work himself and could marbleize a mantelpiece so expertly that it looked genuine from five feet away. If assistants said that a scenic effect he wanted could not be done, his response was always "Do it. Nothing is impossible." When a play required an oak tree, Chick sent his crew into the woods to cut a full-grown oak into sections, which they reconstructed on the stage.[19] He was so insistent about making the stage look its best that, on more than one opening night, he held the curtain while a different shade of paint was applied or Herb Crucius ran to Uncle John's to retrieve a painting Chick had decided would improve the set.

Crucius recalled that the opening of that first season was delayed a week because a truck delivering sand to cover the manure in the cow stalls under the theater backed into the barn and fell through the floor.[20] Tonio Selwart had a further explanation. Having seen the dress rehearsal of *Blithe Spirit,* he told Chick that he was so unprepared for his role that he had to postpone the opening to avoid embarrassment. The only way Selwart could get Chick to work on his lines was to have him drive around the nearby lakes with Selwart beside him, feeding Chick his cues. The curtain finally went up on July 30 to a full house—mostly Chick's artist and theater friends from Hartford, Boston, and New York. Even after the opening, Chick asked Selwart to sit in the front row every night to give him confidence. When Selwart slipped out one evening, Chick began the second act with his lines from the third act.[21]

Each summer season, Chick presented recent Broadway plays as well as popular revivals and musicals. With remarkable speed, he had solidly established his own professional theater. And he was accountable to no one but himself. Windham became Chick's best haven, with memories that went back to a time before he had thought of Harvard, the Wadsworth Atheneum, or the Ringling. He could live a simple life in the woods of New Hampshire, where the amenities were primitive—the power and the plumbing failed regularly—while enjoying his mother's antiques, paintings, even her gold-washed plates and flatware. And to look after the property year-round, he had Rose and Herb Crucius, who had been devoted to his mother and treated him as family.

Helen never felt at home in Windham, and she and the children spent the summer of 1946 as usual in Castine with her mother. Chick ran over to visit for a few days at a time when he could. Many of their discussions that year were centered around the fact that he and Helen found themselves temporarily short of cash. Chick had not had a salary for a year and a half and was embroiled in arguments with lawyers and bankers about getting the full income from his mother's trust fund. He and Helen also owed Fanny Goodwin money. Although Helen had not considered moving to Sarasota, she and Chick decided that in the fall she, David, and Sally should go out to the Brentwood house for a year. This would allow them to lease the Scarborough Street house and supplement the income from the smaller of Chick's two Hollywood houses, currently rented to actor Norman Lloyd and his wife. Southern California appealed to Helen far more than Florida. Her favorite sister, Mary, was there, Chick's friends in the film community would welcome her, and the schools were good. Chick promised that he could easily visit them on his holiday breaks.

Late that summer, Helen and the children took the train to Los Angeles. Soon afterward, when his theater season ended, Chick drove out with their maid in his 1938 Packard. When he discovered that hotels in the South would not provide a room for a "colored" woman, Chick slept in the car with her for several nights. He was in Brentwood only a few weeks before leaving for Florida to start work in mid-October. The trip was not easy. "Two blow-outs in Texas which were difficult and costly," he reported to Helen, "and then to cap the climax the differential went to pieces in Alabama." Low on cash, he paid the garage with his mother's diamond ring.[22]

Chick convinced Mary Blasi to take a leave of absence from the Atheneum for a few months to help him get started and then asked Jim Hellyar to join them. They moved into a small house Chick had rented. Mrs. Berger worried about the propriety of Mary Blasi's living with Chick and Jim, so she boarded a train to Florida at the beginning of October and appeared on their doorstep.

Chick introduced her to all his new friends as if she were a favorite aunt, but when she stayed on for weeks, his feelings changed. On Thanksgiving day, he reported to Helen: "Mrs. B is still here and driving me nuts. . . . We wait on her hand and foot and I have been getting crosser and crosser."[23] Finally satisfied that all was well, Mrs. Berger returned to her post at the Atheneum.

Operating out of a nook on the third floor of the museum, Chick attacked every conceivable task, from planning the opening of the Ringling house to pasting newspaper clippings into scrapbooks. By the end of November, he had finished painting about half the museum galleries in colors he mixed himself. Inside other galleries, to protect the pictures from the dampness of the plaster and to give the interior an appropriate sumptuousness, he began the process of overlaying the walls with wood furring, which he covered with brocades. He divided the larger spaces into bays to increase the surface area for hanging pictures, then reinstalled the collection more spaciously, relegating paintings he identified as copies or inferior works to the basement. The manager of the Ringling Hotel found the museum walls so beautiful that he asked Chick to choose new paint colors for the hotel's principal rooms. Seldom able to resist the role of decorator, Chick did the job for free, but asked Helen ruefully, "When will I ever be able to cash in on my talents(?)."[24] Chick also welcomed the chance to redecorate Ca' d'Zan, and for months he was seen in the public rooms of the residence with his portable Singer, cutting and stitching brocade for the walls on the second floor—even after tourists began to visit the house.

The mansion opened to the public for the first time, along with half the museum, on December 15, 1946. More than ten thousand people descended on the Ringling property that day. Cars approaching the grounds were snarled in a gigantic traffic jam. The long line of visitors waiting to see Ca' d'Zan was eight abreast in places. An astounding 3,485 people filed through the house; the rest had to be satisfied with the museum only. Despite the presence of state policemen, objects were stolen and furniture was damaged. One woman was observed in the gardens pulling up an exotic shrub and tucking it under her arm.[25]

Chick now had his first taste of a type of criticism that he had never experienced—politically motivated rather than in reaction to the art he showed. He told Helen that "there have been paid advertisements in the papers asking people to protest everything from the colors on the walls to the way in which the house was opened."[26] The Tampa press, which had connections to rivals of the state officials who controlled the Ringling, took aim at him personally: "There was a terrific attack on me and what I had done to the hanging which I will send you when I can get another copy. . . . I imagine that it will make a great deal of trouble but it would be silly to answer it in any way at least until [Karl] Bickel arrives. There are so many political aspects to the job that I shall have to go very carefully."[27] Early in January 1947, he was hearing "ugly rumors that the museum is really nothing and filled with fakes and that I was a big fool to touch it."[28] Inflammatory charges and half-truths ran like a leitmotif through Chick's career in Sarasota, and he found it nerve-racking. He never knew, he told Helen during one of the attacks, whether he would "get it in the neck or not. This round of uncertainty about everything will land me in the nut-house I am sure."[29] But in the coming years, Chick managed to keep such criticism at arm's length unless the Board of Control made a decision that actually threatened the museum.

He moved ahead with his plans, among them the circus museum. A building on the grounds of the Ringling that was jammed with circus objects and memorabilia could be converted into an exhibition space. He knew that other relics—circus wagons, vintage clown costumes—were stored by Ringling Brothers and Barnum & Bailey at their winter quarters. By February 1947, he had convinced the Board of Control to approve funds for his plan to remodel the existing building to resemble a circus tent, complete with sawdust on the floor.

At the same time, the state agreed to improve the grounds of the Ringling by acquiring thirteen acres between the museum's entrance and the Tamiami Trail, which would be turned into an esplanade with a grand new public road lined with royal palms. A garden plaza would be laid out by the director of the Florida State Park Department, and Chick told the press that he would decorate it with a multitude of sculptures, which had been found in out-of-the-way places on the property. There were "herds" of stone lions, he said, a bronze copy of the famous *Discus Thrower,* metal sphinxes, and small whimsical figures. Newspaper photographers recorded Chick contemplating a fallen statue of Neptune, while one of the circus midgets, "Miss Daisy Doll, world famous Lilliputian," pretended to ride a sphinx. Chick arranged for Ringling circus elephants (assisted by power cranes) to move the sculptures to the site of the new plaza in front of the museum.[30]

Busy as he was, he could not stay away from the performing arts. Early in the year, he joined the city's leading amateur drama group, the Players of Sarasota. He landed the role of Maxim de Winter in the dramatization of Daphne du Maurier's *Rebecca.* With amazing candor, considering what was expected of him at the Ringling, he told a local reporter, "I get bored with buying pictures painted by others for someone else. To me the joy of living is active participation."[31]

He also resumed his role as impresario. Advancing the money himself, he engaged the celebrated organist E. Power Biggs to play John Ringling's Aeolian organ in Ca' d'Zan. Chick declared that although technically "a recital," the event would be "a spectacle which will live in people's minds for years to come."[32] He made a profit for the museum and began booking concerts and speakers for the house.

Chick gazes at a fallen sculpture of Neptune, Ringling Museum, 1947.

Chick was settling into Sarasota. "I do like this job immensely," he wrote Helen.[33] It was becoming clearer that he would continue to live apart from Helen and his growing children. He had not spent Christmas in Hollywood as he had planned. (Through bureaucratic confusion, he had not received a paycheck, so he sent Helen his travel money for presents instead.) He wrote often and telephoned, but the years apart were adding up. That spring, he bought a two-story 1920s stucco house at 320 Delmar Avenue, in the Whitfield Estates, a block from the ocean and less than two miles from the museum. Jim Hellyar moved into a guest house in the back. He and Chick undertook a complete renovation program. "We called it 'Termite Towers,' " Hellyar remembered. "It was really a shambles. We tore all the inside out, the bedrooms and all that, but most of the walls we covered with fabric."[34] Over the next decade, Chick embellished it with money from the sale of some of his mother's paintings, the cottage on South Harpswell, and, eventually, his trust fund. Guests entered another of his stage sets, with gilded console tables, painted Italian chests, Renaissance dining chairs set with tiny mirrors, chandeliers of crystal or bronze, an impossibly gaudy rococo clock, trompe l'oeil faience dishes offering faience pears or pistachio nuts, and the occasional modern surprise, like an exotic drum used as a table in the sitting room.

Chick also had enough—or almost enough—money to indulge his love of fast and elegant cars. In the late 1940s, he bought one of the first Porsches available in the United States. This was followed by other cars, including a Jaguar and, eventually, a Rolls-Royce. Jim Hellyar observed that to Chick a new car "was like a wristwatch. He loved the looks of it. He would only keep these cars probably about a year and then he would want something else."[35] One spring, after Helen and the children had returned to Hartford, Chick arrived at the Scarborough Street house in a silver-gray Mercedes, the new "gull-wing" 300SL, one of a handful that had just been delivered to America. "Daddy knows he shouldn't get it, & I think he may sell it to a man in Sarasota," wrote Helen hopefully to Sally at boarding school.[36] He did sell the Mercedes in Florida, but when he and Jim Hellyar stopped in Hartford two months later on their way to Windham, Chick was driving a Bentley.

For her part, Helen liked being in southern California, and friends like Moyna MacGill and the Lansbury children were kind to her. She and Chick decided that the family would remain in Los Angeles another year. David and Sally were Helen's greatest concerns. As Angela Lansbury observed, "Helen was very, very shy and for her to be plunged into that milieu I think must have been quite a shock for her. She carried it off very, very well because she tended

Chick's bedroom at "Termite Towers," Sarasota

At home in Hollywood with the children: Helen, Sally, and David, 1947

to her business of looking after the children, and she was totally *there* for them. And she adored Chick and she stood behind everything and anything that he did."[37] Helen told the children repeatedly about the wonderful things "Daddy" was doing, and she involved him in even minor decisions. When Chick sent David a large check for his fourteenth birthday, his son wrote back to thank him "ever so much for the lavish birthday present" and, obviously at Helen's prompting, to suggest a way of spending it: "I sort of had my eye on a diesel engine for $18.75. . . . Would you please drop me a post card and tell me what you think? I don't want to get it unless you approve."[38] David accepted his absentee father as he was. Many years later, he said with complete conviction: "He did what he had to do."[39] But Sally, at eleven, saw the separation as a personal injustice. She was always torn between feeling cheated of her father and delighting in his occasional company.

Hartford heard about Chick's rapid success early in 1947 when Carl Lindstrom, the veteran music critic at the *Hartford Times,* visited Sarasota. He told his readers that in a matter of months Chick had transformed a neglected American museum into a lively gallery of art. Chick clearly wanted the Hartford public to know that though he may have departed from their city under a cloud, he was triumphing in Sarasota: "When I left Hartford I thought I would never take another museum job. This is the only one in the world to interest me." He added that the State Board of Control had been generous, that he hoped the annual budget would reach $100,000, and that since July 1946 over fifty thousand people had visited the museum.[40] But no matter how buoyant he sounded from time to time, Chick was still ambivalent about Florida, telling Mrs. Berger that spring that he preferred California: "It is far nicer than here between you and me but I guess I am stuck with this for a while at least."[41]

One drawback of the job was being beholden to the official bureaucracy of the State of Florida. Long procedural directives came down to him from Tallahassee almost as soon as he arrived. When he bought postage stamps with his own money for museum business, he was admonished by a communication from the Board of Control that made Uncle Charlie Goodwin's administrative requirements at the Atheneum seem amiable:

> In the future when it becomes necessary to buy postage stamps, please send to this office about ten days before the stamps are needed, a voucher payable to the postmaster at Sarasota, giving his full name and title in the voucher. This voucher will be approved and delivered to the Comptroller. The Comptroller will then issue a state warrant payable to the postmaster at Sarasota. You can then take the warrant to the postmaster and purchase stamps. This is the way all state departments purchase stamps. They are not permitted to mix their own funds with state business.[42]

Chick was also required to sign a loyalty oath stating that he was not a member of any organization that advocated the subversion of the United States government.

At the end of March 1947, Chick announced a five-year plan to restore a hundred pictures annually. He had already cleaned a few himself: "Its not such a mystery after all," he told Helen, "and they have come out very well."[43] That spring, Chick hired an Italian restorer based in New York, Cesar Diorio, to conserve the pictures. In the museum's auditorium he set up a five-month exhibition of sixteen of the most significant restored works; as he told Helen, "to try to answer the constant attacks that we are doing nothing about repairing the damages to the paintings."[44] Just after hanging the show, he put the finishing touches on his own catalogue of the Atheneum's Sumner Collection and sent it to Mrs. Berger on May 26, saying that he was "shaking with fatigue and still have to prepare an annual report tonight."[45] In the report he dashed off, he declared that "a pulsating life has returned to the dreams of John Ringling."[46]

Then he left with Mary Blasi and Jim Hellyar for New Hampshire. The second season of the Windham Playhouse began far more smoothly than the first. Moyna MacGill came to take the lead in one of Tennessee Williams's earliest plays, *Portrait of a Madonna*, which she performed with great sensitivity. Edgar and Bruce Lansbury, who had graduated from the Choate School in Connecticut in June and were touring the United States in a secondhand car, stopped at Windham to see their mother. Chick offered them jobs as stagehands, building sets, which helped point them toward their long careers as producers. "It was my first experience and my brother's first experience in a professional theater company," Edgar recalled.

> It kind of got under our skin. . . . In 1947, when I was there, it was really the quintessential summer stock theater. . . . It was very, very quaint, and the lights would go out during the thunderstorms, and we'd open the big barn doors and let the cars shine headlights in, and we'd use candles and Coleman lanterns. And all the scenery was stored downstairs in the barn—in the stalls—the cow stalls, with a dirt floor. Of course it rotted very quickly, so every time we brought a piece of scenery out, it had to be recovered or repainted.[47]

Chick also gave the Lansbury twins a joint walk-on part in *The Drunkard,* so that when the drunkard came in, he thought he was seeing double. Later, Chick brought Moyna MacGill to the Ringling to perform a series of dramatic readings.

Chick borrowed money to get the Playhouse started each summer, and he suspected that some of Helen's family, and perhaps even Helen herself, saw the Playhouse as just another of his self-indulgences. He explained to her later in the year that he was running the theater to amuse himself, to keep working, to lower his income tax, and to make a profit. "I know that what is called my extravagance is always in the forefront of everyones mind but I am trying to take a long range view of things and I can very easily from now on make the theater pay around $5000 / year if I want to."[48] (It never did.) He implied that the income was to be shared with his family, but in fact, when he had money, he spent it. After the 1950 season, he wrote gleefully to Nellie and Jim Soby: "The theater was a financial success at last though very wearing. I was cooking for seven as well as acting and doing everything else but I have fifteen hundred smackers in my jeans for my trouble and it wont take a moment to exchange it for some 18th century fripperies I suppose."[49]

At the beginning of 1948, Chick sounded exhilarated on arriving back in Sarasota after Christmas in Los Angeles with his family. "The circus folk are getting out their biceps and aerial trapezes again and its just like old times," he wrote to Ruth Ford, noting the imminent arrival of her brother Charlie with Pavel Tchelitchew, Bette Davis, Tonio Selwart, and his wife, Isa.[50] And for Chick, entertaining always meant working overtime in his kitchen or going out to dinner. Sarasota restaurateurs were among his closest friends, and once, when he took Jim Soby and his third wife, Melissa, to one of the city's finest restaurants, Chick disappeared into the kitchen and prepared the entire meal himself. After dinner, as they were leaving, the manager said, in an aside to Soby, "If I could hire him I'd make a fortune."[51]

Many of Chick's New York friends assumed that he had withdrawn from an active role in the art world when he went to Sarasota, which they looked on as a kind of Siberia. Philip Johnson said that "he was like a retired man" in Florida.[52] But that was not true. By the winter and spring of 1948, after a year and a half on the job, with the income of the museum secured, Chick launched many programs simultaneously. In February, he brought in harpsichordist Sylvia Marlow for a recital of baroque music at Ca' d'Zan. (During this period, as a kindness to an old friend, he hired Marian Murray, who had lost her job as art critic at the *Hartford Times*, to be the Ringling's first publicity director.) He finished installing the new galleries of the Museum of the American Circus, which opened in March, full of objects ranging from gilded and painted circus wagons to costumes, vintage circus posters, and other ephemera. It was touted as the first museum of its kind in the United States.[53]

In April, he organized a three-week seminar in conjunction with Florida State University. As he had done with his first exhibition in Hartford, Chick chose "The History of Art" as the theme for this first seminar. He brought to Sarasota a roster of national authorities, most of them his friends—Russell Hitchcock, John McAndrew, Agnes Mongan, Julien Levy, and Iris Barry. The topics ranged from Rubens to contemporary painters, modern architecture, and the surrealist cinema. For students at the university, visiting scholars, and the members of the public who attended the lectures, this was art education at an extremely high level.

To coincide with the seminar, Chick produced the Ringling's first major loan exhibition. The show presented the greatest possible contrast with the museum's baroque collection: *Masterpieces of Modern Painting*. It was the first comprehensive exhibition of twentieth-century art ever held in Florida. With his well-established contacts, Chick had little trouble assembling two dozen important modern pictures, including three of his greatest twentieth-century purchases for the Atheneum: Dalí's *Apparition of a Face and a Fruit Dish on a Beach*, Miró's *Composition*, and Mondrian's *Composition in Blue and White*. He also brought in Tchelitchew's *Phenomena*, which had jolted Hartford in 1938. When the show opened on April 3, Sarasotans could see nearly every style of twentieth-century art: fauvism, cubism, Neo-Romanticism, surrealism, and abstraction. Though

Julien Levy and Chick discuss twentieth-century art with students in the first annual seminar at the Masterpieces of Modern Art *exhibition, April 1948. Behind Chick is Dalí's* Apparition of a Face and a Fruit Dish on a Beach, *bought for the Wadsworth Atheneum from Levy in 1939.*

the exhibition did not contain the very latest aesthetic—abstract expression-ism—Chick had returned to teaching a relatively unenlightened public about the art of their own era. "The confusion, the hopes, the despair, the cruelty and the violence of our moment," he wrote in the catalogue, "are the materials from which our beauty must be wrought by our creative interpreters."[54]

He correctly predicted that the exhibition would be "startling for Florida." Under the headline "This Is Kind of Thing That Gives Art Bad Name," a col-umn in the *Tampa Morning Tribune* called the show "a grave disappointment" and declared that "at least eight of the paintings are either unintelligible, unin-teresting or repulsive." The Dalí and the Tchelitchew reminded the writer of "the anatomical subjects usually found in medical text books." Mondrian was no better than someone who was "working out a geometrical design for bath-room tile."[55] Chick paid no attention to such remarks. He had heard them all at least fifteen years earlier in Hartford, and he would continue the pattern of a seminar and a major exhibition throughout his tenure.

The Ringling's reputation was rising rapidly. In an article on the museum in the 1948 summer issue of *Art News*, Metropolitan Museum curator A. Hyatt Mayor declared that "no collection outside Europe gives so rich an idea of taste from 1600 to 1800" and that the grand setting showed off the baroque master-pieces "better than any other in North America."[56] *Look* magazine sent a writer with the young Stanley Kubrick as photographer to produce a spread on the museum and its handsome forty-seven-year-old director posing throughout the grounds and galleries.[57]

Chick offered the public a self-assessment in an article for a local paper:

> I have been described by the Florida press as a "Renaissance Man in the Mid-Twentieth Century" for recreating the splendor of the Renais-sance in the Ringling Art Museums of Sarasota. However fantastic that description may be, it is true that I derive an excitement from partici-pating in all phases of the fine arts. Furthermore, my avant-garde activities seem to me to highlight rather than shadow my status as a classicist. I imagine that I understand the past. I certainly revel in the present and surely regard the art of living as the greatest of the arts.[58]

He was now more of a celebrity in the museum world than ever, but as soon as Bette Davis told him she would attend the opening of *Laura* at the Windham Playhouse that summer, he became once again the starstruck movie fan. He rushed to Boston to buy designer clothes for the leading lady and went all out on the set. At the last moment, Chick's idol sent word that she could not come after all, but would attend the opening of the next play, *Voice of the Turtle*. Chick was so determined to impress her that, two days after *Voice of the Turtle* started rehearsal, he announced that he was bringing in a professional company from New York to perform it. The summer actors were incensed, but when Miss Davis did appear, radiating charm, they all sat at her feet at Chick's party in Uncle John's.[59]

His fondness for Bette Davis led him to further excesses a year later. Her husband, William Grant Sherry, painted inconsequential landscapes and pro-duced competent medical drawings. Chick gave Sherry his first solo exhibition at the Ringling. He admitted to Helen that this was only a "publicity gag,"[60] and even Jim Hellyar, who helped with all the installations, said, "I felt a little bit guilty about doing that for such a bad artist." But Chick relished the chance to show off Bette Davis to the five hundred Sarasotans who mobbed the museum for the opening.[61]

He brought celebrities to the Ringling as often as he could, entertaining them at home with a mix of the show people and movie stars who happened to be in town. His dinner guests one January alone included Dame Edith and Sir

Osbert Sitwell, who gave poetry readings at Ca' d'Zan, Dorothy Lamour, and Gypsy Rose Lee.

At the end of 1948, Chick made his first acquisition for the Ringling. The previous year, through the efforts of Governor Caldwell and Karl Bickel, the state had agreed to allocate the full sum of $1,250,000 that had been received from Ringling's estate for the purchase of works of art. It was thought that maintenance costs could be covered by admission income and that any future building programs would be eligible for special appropriations from the state. After five years away from the art market, Chick could go shopping for pictures. At Knoedler, for $30,000, he found a masterpiece: Peter Paul Rubens's *Portrait of the Archduke Ferdinand,* painted in 1635. Ironically, the portrait came from the collection of Helen's cousin and the Atheneum's great benefactor, J. Pierpont Morgan.[62]

In 1948 attendance had jumped to eighty-two thousand from sixty-six thousand the previous year. "My success is far beyond anything I managed in Hartford," he told Helen that year. "I have the town at my feet."[63] But his success owed much to his Hartford career. His exhibitions were engaging, ingenious even, and as visually captivating as ever, but most would be echoes of themes he had explored in the past. His next winter show, *American Paintings—3 Centuries,* was a version of his Connecticut Tercentenary exhibition, brought up to date with an abstract expressionist work by Robert Motherwell. The basis for a later exhibition called *Harnett and His School* was that artist's *Faithful Colt,* which Chick had bought for Hartford in 1935. He featured art from local collections in another show, as he had in 1936. In *Designed to Live With,* he offered "well designed objects available in Florida shops"—a more palatable version of his *Objects of Good and Bad Design* in Hartford.[64] And there would be a modest survey of Picasso's graphic art. Only a handful of his exhibitions had either novel subject matter or an unusual twist to the familiar. Chick was no longer the innovator he had been before World War II, in part because the 1920s and '30s had been a more revolutionary period. His primary mission in Sarasota was to educate.

Helen and the children moved back to Hartford from California in the summer of 1948 and Chick spent that Christmas with them, as he would every year thereafter. His arrival was always timed for his birthday, December 18. He would drop Jim Hellyar off at his family's home before appearing on Scarborough Street. Christmas was Chick's favorite holiday, and in 1948 he and Helen prepared the scene in the living room for the first time in five years. While David and Sally slept, a huge tree was brought in and decorated. In the morning, the big rococo doors were opened as Helen played "Once in Royal David's City" on the piano, and the children saw a glittering tree with presents piled high underneath. Chick returned to other Hartford rituals—the Goodwin Christmas dinner and, at Charles Cunningham's invitation, the staff Christmas party at the Atheneum. But old friends recalled that an embrace at a party or in a theater lobby would bring tears to his eyes.[65] In little more than a week after Christmas, Chick was gone. For much of the year he was accessible to Helen only through telephone calls and the letters that began "Dearest Cunning." The pattern of brief Christmas visits and long absences continued for the rest of his life.

Jim Hellyar, too, was an inevitable part of the routine. One summer Helen and David stayed with Chick in Windham to attend the first play of the season. They arrived with Nera, a black Labrador retriever that Chick had found in Florida, and the dog recognized Jim as her favorite family member. "She went nearly wild with joy," wrote Helen to Sally, "& jumped up & licked his face, & would not leave him alone." She added that she and "Daddy" had decided Nera should stay in Windham for the summer and that Jim would take care of her.[66] Helen, and even Chick, seemed to treat Jim as if he were a young nephew for whom they had affection, but who was obviously not their equal, socially or intellectually. It was as if Jim were part of a play in which his role changed according to the scene. In Sarasota, he was the assistant who lived in the guest house; in Windham, when Helen was not there, he moved in with Chick; in Hartford, he exited into the wings.

Chick began his third year in Sarasota, 1949, with a tribute to the origins of the Ringling: *Art, Carnival and the Circus.* Though the catalogue lacked an introductory essay, Chick characteristically linked four centuries of art history through his selection of forty-seven pictures of harlequins, mountebanks, clowns, animals, and acrobats by such artists as Carlevaris, Tiepolo, Daumier, Toulouse-Lautrec, Gris, Chagall, Walt Kuhn, and Reginald Marsh.

His next show would be more scholarly. In the fall of 1949—ignoring the endless political intrigue in Sarasota ("the whole museum is split apart and the war of the factions is still raging," he told Helen[67])—Chick planned an annual film festival with the help of Iris Barry (another echo of his past) and prepared an exhibition of the shadowy seventeenth-century artist known as Monsù Desiderio. His work had intrigued Chick since 1937 when he purchased *Balshazzar's Feast* for the Atheneum. He had also bought a view of Naples by Desiderio for himself. In 1949 his second acquisition for the Ringling had been Desiderio's *The Martyrdom of a Bishop Saint*, later called *The Martyrdom of Saint Januarius*, depicting the beheading of a bishop in an open square surrounded by architectural ruins.

Borrowing from museums and collectors in England, France, Italy, Sweden, and the United States, Chick assembled about thirty works by Desiderio, half his known paintings—aerial views of Naples and unsettling architectural fantasies. The exhibition that opened early in February 1950, *The Fantastic Visions of Monsù Desiderio*, was Chick's only groundbreaking show in Sarasota.

The exhibition catalogue became the first monograph on Desiderio. In his

François de Nomé (Monsù Desiderio), Martyrdom of Saint Januarius, c. 1630.
Oil on canvas, 17 × 38⅛ inches, purchased 1949

commentary, Desiderio scholar and collector Alfred Scharf discussed the shadowy identity of the artist, whose career was thought to span the years from about 1617 to 1631. He was named Monsù, the Neapolitan word for a foreign gentleman, in 1742 by Bernardo de' Dominici, the earliest art historian to mention him, but no one had yet uncovered his true identity. In his foreword to the catalogue, Chick explained what rediscovering the artists of the seventeenth century during the past twenty years had meant to him. One of the great satisfactions in art history, he said, was isolating "an occasional personality who, often neglected and even forgotten during the intervening years, emerges once more as a significant artist whose pictorial statements become valid again for a generation he could not possibly have envisaged." Chick became almost surreal in describing the turbulent and frightening world of Desiderio's imagination, filled with cities, palaces, churches, and ruins: "These infinite vistas of richly jeweled facades, eclectic and hallucinatory in the extreme, dissolve in unbelievable variety before our eyes, swallowed up in a sulphurous atmosphere heavily charged with the premonition of an ultimate or actual drama of destruction."[68] For Chick, the artist was one of the great exponents of architectural fantasy in paint whose influence could be traced to the eighteenth-century Gothic-Revival, then to the Romanticism of the early nineteenth century, and on up to his favorite modern movements, Neo-Romanticism and surrealism.

The exhibition attracted international attention for its novelty and Desiderio's surprising connections to twentieth-century art; *Art News* named it the most important old master show in the United States in 1950, and it reopened inquiry that eventually led to the discovery that Desiderio was the pseudonym of a French artist living in Naples, François de Nomé—though his works are still confused with those of the French topographical artist Didier Barra.

Chick and David in Windham with Nera, July 1949

On the day the Desiderio show opened to the public, Chick wrote to Helen in great excitement about another inspiration. He had been contemplating a new wing for the Ringling, and he had just "thought up a wonderful scheme to include the Loewi eighteenth century Italian theater which he will now sell very cheaply as the core of the structure. In this way we can consider most of the building as part of the art collection and pay for the installation of the theater out of the Ringling fund."[69]

This theater was a tiny rococo structure that had been built between 1796 and 1798 in the castle at Asolo, the picturesque hill town about twenty miles northwest of Venice. Chick had been coveting it since the early 1930s, when Adolf Loewi had "told me about a jewel-like little theater that he had just acquired, and showed me pictures of it. I yearned to own it, and never forgot how beautiful it was." It had been dismantled in 1930 to make room for a movie theater, but Loewi had bought the interior and kept it in a warehouse in Venice for two decades. Chick had once toyed with the idea of bringing it to Hartford, but the Second World War had intervened. He had continued to discuss the theater with Loewi, who now agreed to sell it to the Ringling for a mere eight thousand dollars.[70]

The Asolo Theater was imbued with the lore of its original home—the thirteenth-century castle that had been given to Caterina Cornaro, the exiled queen of Cyprus, when her island was made a Venetian dependency in 1489. During her twenty-year reign, she made Asolo a center for artists and poets. Great painters recorded her likeness—Bellini, Georgione, and Titian. Three hundred years later, when the theater was installed on the second floor of the castle's banqueting hall, a new portrait of Caterina was attached to the front of the central box in the first balcony to honor her patronage of the arts. The arts flourished again in Asolo during the nineteenth century, and the theater was refurbished in 1857, when most of the remaining decorations were added. Italian actors like the great tragedienne Elenora Duse performed on its stage.

Having persuaded Loewi to offer him the theater for a bargain price, Chick asked the Board of Control to give him the funds to buy it. He asserted that the Ringling's original auditorium had poor acoustics and was not sufficient for his expanding programs. Acquiring the theater, he said, was in the spirit of John Ringling himself, who had incorporated both the salon and the library from the John Jacob Astor residence into the galleries. But what Chick really wanted was to bring the dramatic arts into the museum. "The function of a museum is more than merely showing pictures," he had told a Sarasota reporter two years earlier. "The museum is the place to integrate the arts and bring them alive."[71] The board was convinced. The Asolo Theater would be shipped that summer. In March, as if in anticipation of its arrival, Chick produced the first play ever performed at the Ringling, Moliere's *School for Husbands*, in the museum's outdoor courtyard.

While Chick was making arrangements for the theater, Helen went to California to be with her sister Mary, who was dying of cancer. Chick wrote sympathetically to Helen, but did not consider accompanying her. Instead, he continued his end-of-season entertainments, with parties every night, including a spaghetti dinner given by John Ringling's sister, Ida Ringling North, for Cecil B. DeMille, who was in Sarasota to prepare for his film *The Greatest Show on Earth*.[72]

Chick made two important acquisitions in the spring of 1950. The first was Bernardo Strozzi's *The Prophet Elijah and the Widow of Zarephath* (later called *An Act of Mercy*), painted when the artist was under the influence of Caravaggio. It was the first work by Strozzi to enter the Ringling's collection and came from the great Oscar Bondy collection in Vienna, which had been stolen by the Nazis and then recovered after the war. His other prize for the year was a series of fifteen decorative paintings depicting the disguises of Harlequin. Originally attributed to an "Eighteenth-Century Venetian Master," the pictures were later identified as the work of Giovanni Ferretti. Not only did they represent the Italian Comedy, which Chick loved, but they came from the estate of one of his heroes, Max Reinhardt, and had hung in his castle, Schloss Leopoldskron, in Salzburg. Chick told the Board of Control that Reinhardt had once considered buying the Asolo Theater and hanging the Harlequin series in its lobby.[73] Chick intended to do so himself.

Citing the necessity of scouting out European dealers for future acquisitions, he got the state to give him two months off with pay to visit his contacts in Europe for the first time in twelve years. After a profitable season at the Windham Playhouse, Chick sailed at the end of August and reported to the Board of Control that he had "managed to cover rather thoroughly" twenty cities, among them London, Paris, Amsterdam, Munich, Florence, and Rome. He took a special interest in visiting theaters, particularly the Fenice in Venice, which was a model for the Asolo.[74]

He told the board that while decorative objects could still be had for reasonable prices in Europe, the American market had the best selection of paintings. At the end of 1950, he bought a monumental work from Adolph Loewi, an allegorical fresco by Giovanni Battista Tiepolo (executed by his son, Domenico, about 1758 and later transferred to canvas) called *Glory and Magnanimity of Princes.* Done in grisaille (monochrome painting mostly in shades of gray), it features a tall pyramid, in which Glory is personified by a standing woman wearing a gold belt while Magnanimity is represented by a lion and a cornucopia beside the seated figure of Alexander the Great. At $10,500, it used up more than half the 1950–51 allocation of $18,000 for acquisitions, but it became one of the Ringling's treasures.

In January 1951, Chick presented two small exhibitions closely linked to his own taste. The first, *Reflections of the Italian Comedy,* centered around his purchase of the Harlequin series. It also included loans of seventeenth- and eighteenth-century paintings, prints, and drawings, along with decorative objects depicting characters from the commedia dell'arte. In the catalogue he reminded viewers that the influence of the Italian comedy carried through to the abstract Harlequins of Picasso and to the modern circus; he hoped that his show would "recall to our technological world, perhaps, the mercurial and witching universe of the all but lost art of improvisation."[75] The second show was *Drawings by Tchelitchew,* which consisted of recent studies of heads done in an abstract style as if they were made of concentric circles of neon light, and Chick coaxed his Russian friend into giving a lecture on his relationship to Gertrude Stein. The talk was "swamped," said Chick. Tchelitchew and Charlie Ford stayed with him for a week, unrestrainedly trying to charm everyone they saw, paying special attention to John Ringling North because Tchelitchew hoped (in vain) to be commissioned to do designs for the circus.[76]

When Chick submitted his operating budget in Tallahassee that April, he was met with a hostile reaction from a new political faction. He wrote to Helen:

Chick's costume design for
Bastien from Bastien et Bas-
tienne, *1952. Graphite, water-*
color, and gouache on paper,
19¾ × 13⅞ inches

The museum was vio-
lently attacked by the
new economy block and
I have great fears that
the budget will be dras-
tically cut. The commit-
tee was very insulting to
me and about my salary
so heaven knows what
will happen. . . . It has
turned very hot here and
I am longing to get out.
I feel so discouraged
about the political turn
of events, that I am
almost ready to resign
but there is so much
going on. The theater is progressing very well and looks so attractive
and exciting.[77]

Much of Chick's time in 1951 was taken up with the temporary installation
of the Asolo Theater in the Ringling's auditorium, and now he planned a splendid opening for February 1952. There would be a double bill of two short
eighteenth-century operas, *La Serva Padrona* by Pergolesi and *Bastien et Bas-
tienne,* written by Mozart at the age of twelve. Eugene Berman, by now one of the
most successful opera designers in the United States, agreed to do the sets and
costumes for the Pergolesi, while Chick did those for the Mozart opera. Laszlo
Halasz produced and conducted the productions, using singers from the New
York City Center. Chick urged Helen to come to Florida for the opening. She felt
unsure about it at first but was convinced when Nellie Soby, now separated from
Jim Soby, said she would go, too. "I think he's glad I'm coming," Helen timidly
wrote to Sally.[78] As it happened, a whole contingent from Hartford made the trip
to Sarasota to witness what seemed certain to be another Austin triumph.

On the night of February 26, Helen entered the museum on Chick's arm, as

The Asolo Theater, 1952

she had at so many openings at the Wadsworth Atheneum. Their entourage recalled earlier times: Helen's brother, Francis, Marie Bissell, and Nellie. The audience reached the Asolo through the museum, and as they stepped into a tiny foyer decorated with the *Disguises of Harlequin*, they entered a world that Chick had carefully contrived. The exquisite interior of the theater had been masterfully reassembled, cleaned, and retouched. The walls and boxes were painted in pale green and cream, and gilded. Light green draperies with gold fringe framed the tops of the boxes on all three tiers, creating a continuous scalloped effect all around the theater. The portrait of Caterina Cornaro on the face of the first balcony was flanked by profiles of famous Italian writers, including Dante and Petrarch, painted on the outside of each box, alternating with brightly lit wall candelabra. All along the face of the second tier were large raised medallions painted in red and green to look like jewels. A delicate crystal chandelier hung from the ceiling, which was covered with small painted gold stars. Chick had placed a pink carnation and a mask covered with gold glitter on each seat. When the lights dimmed, the curtain rose on the Mozart opera. This and *La Serva Padrona* were performed in English, and there was a tremendous response from the audience. Back at the house that night, Helen and Chick gave a party for a hundred and fifty people which lasted far into the morning. As Nellie told Chick later, "I felt that we were right back in the golden period when every day was full of excitement and beautiful things."[79]

The Sarasota press reached for superlatives, declaring that the opening of the Asolo "leaves no doubt in one's mind concerning the genius of A. Everett Austin, Jr., the director of the Ringling Museum. It was by all odds the most artistic, most interesting and most colorful, gala night in the history of Florida as well as Sarasota."[80] A few days later, Virgil Thomson, now music critic at the *New York Herald Tribune,* proclaimed Chick's success to the rest of the country on the front page of the paper's Sunday arts section. In addition to describing the theater and its opening program, Thomson reminded his readers of Chick's many theatrical achievements in Hartford, noting that he "has long played roles (including Hamlet), designed sets and costumes, painted scenery, sewn seams; and he has organized some of the most distinguished productions of the last two decades." He commended Chick for importing the Asolo, predicting that the theater would be "a model to other institutions."[81]

Helen stayed in Sarasota another week, long enough to attend a dinner with playwright Thornton Wilder in John Ringling North's magnificently appointed railway car. "I hated to leave," she wrote to Sally after returning home.[82] Chick loved sharing his adventures with Helen because he knew that she understood and appreciated him more than anyone ever had. But when she was in Hartford, their telephone calls and their letters were enough for him. He was working compulsively, surrounded by admirers, and doted on by a live-in companion. Helen had the children and her civic and social activities, but these could not entirely fill the void that Chick's absence left in her life.

Yet Helen's visit in 1952 had renewed the bonds between them, and they decided to take a long European holiday that summer with Sally and David, who was entering Harvard in September. Keeping the Windham Playhouse dark for the first time, Chick preceded them, leaving in May on the *Queen Elizabeth* to attend the European premiere of *Four Saints in Three Acts* in Paris, conducted by Virgil Thomson. He reported to Helen that "4 Saints was a great success among the Americans. The French were shocked and called it an operetta— however it was all very gala and I went with Virgil to a sumptuous party at Schaperelli's [*sic*] house after—the whole cast plus Matta and a few others. Marvelous food and champagne."[83] He ran into Marguerite Yourcenar and Grace Frick at the opening and lunched with them before leaving by train on the first of June for the south of France. In Provence, he visited Iris Barry in the hill town of Fayence. After leaving the Museum of Modern Art the previous year, she had bought a small farm "and tills the soil." She had taken up with a Breton sailor named Pierre Kerroux, formerly of the French Resistance, whom she had met in a bar. "Life is cheap," Chick told Helen, "and the country beautiful."[84]

*Traveling together: the Austin family in Europe with their
rented Renault, 1952*

From there he went to Italy, back to Paris, and then to Sweden. Arriving in
Stockholm on June 20, he headed for Drottningholm, the palace of Gustav III,
with its famous fully working eighteenth-century theater. He spent a day as a
guest of the director, exploring the theater, the exquisitely restored residence,
the rococo Chinese Pavilion with its original furniture and decorations, and the
baroque gardens. To be in a place that combined such graceful fantasy and luxurious elegance was Chick's idea of heaven.[85]

Turning to more practical matters, he advised Helen to buy fifteen cartons
of Pall Malls on the boat, as they were a fraction of the price in France, and to
hide a few more packs in her luggage, also suggesting that she "bring a couple
of bottles of scotch as it is too expensive to buy in France or Italy and it is rather
nice for you to have a cup after a long day's driving and sightseeing. The ladies
from Texas put theirs in Thermos Bottles."[86]

On July 12, Helen, Sally, and David joined him in Paris, where they watched
the Bastille Day parade from a balcony in Yourcenar's hotel. Then they began a
trip of nearly five weeks, which took them through France, Italy, Switzerland,
Germany, Holland, Belgium, and back to Paris. With Chick's energy spurring
them on, they visited countless museums, monuments, palaces, churches, and

galleries. Chick took them to elegant small hotels and insisted they
sample prodigious amounts of the
local cuisine. With a new Rollei-
flex he had bought in Switzerland,
David captured his well-fed father
posing in front of the window of an
expensive furniture dealer in
Paris. The picture, given to Chick
from "the firm of Austin, Austin
and Austin" that Christmas, had a
warm, bantering inscription by
Sally.[87]

During this trip, Chick spent
nearly every waking moment with Helen, nineteen-year-old David, and seventeen-year-old Sally. He came back into his children's lives more intimately than
ever, at a time when they were old enough to appreciate his knowledge and his
irrepressible humor. But he did not return with them on the boat. He wanted to
spend another two weeks looking at museums in Switzerland, France, and Holland and visiting Iris Barry again in Fayence. Still, he asked Helen to meet him
at the boat in New York, and the two of them drove Sally to school at the Concord Academy outside of Boston. From there he went on to Cambridge to see
David as he began his freshman year at Harvard.[88]

When he finally arrived back in Sarasota in mid-October, Chick discovered that bids for the new wing for the Asolo Theater were higher than expected
and that the state had put the project on hold. Hollis Rhinehart, then chairman
of the Board of Control, came up with a clever plan to convince the legislature
to give Chick more money and to combat the recurrent criticism of the museum.
He persuaded the state to appoint a national committee of museum professionals to report on the operations of the Ringling. It was headed by Chick's old
friend Francis Henry Taylor from the Metropolitan.

In January 1953, the committee visited the Ringling and met with the
Board of Control. Francis Taylor told the Board point-blank, "I hope you realize
how fortunate you are to have A. Everett Austin, Jr. here."[89] After thoroughly
studying the Ringling's evolution as an art museum, the Taylor Committee pre-

sented an extremely favorable report. Calling Chick's program "brilliant," it declared, "One cannot fail to be impressed with the prodigious accomplishment performed by Mr. Austin and his staff in transforming, during this six-year period, this woefully neglected private collection into a great public museum." It warned the state that the need to preserve, maintain, and use the collections properly for public education "places grave responsibility upon the people of Florida." It recommended an increase in staff, including a full-time paintings conservator and a director of education. It suggested that the Ringling house be used both as a museum of Venetian art and as a site for educational activities. And it endorsed Chick's plea for a thorough inspection and improvement of the buildings, along with his proposed administrative wing that would house offices, a conservation studio, and the Asolo Theater.[90]

During the Taylor Committee's visit, one of Chick's most personal exhibitions was on view, *The Artful Rococo,* the period he concentrated on in his own collecting. There was sculpture, furniture, decorative arts, and paintings and drawings by such artists as Boucher, Nattier, Watteau, Crespi, Guardi, Canaletto, Longhi, and Tiepolo. The Wadsworth Atheneum and the Smith College Art Museum were the only museums that lent paintings; the rest came from Chick's favorite dealers. He himself anonymously lent an array of unusual objects he had recently acquired, including most of the porcelain and faience pottery in the show.

In the catalogue Chick expressed his love of the period: "The utmost richness of texture was attained by all of the arts on a scale which, since it was always intimate, could never err on the side of pomposity or pretension." He admitted that the period had its limitations: "No profound truth was perhaps expressed by the art of the Rococo," but with that style, "a model of tremendous refinement of taste was created for the future. . . ."[91]

The show's exquisite treasures attracted more than seventeen thousand people during its three-week run, making it the most popular loan exhibition yet presented by the Ringling. Chick followed the theme of the show and bought several eighteenth-century paintings for the collection, including Pierre Goudreaux's *Lover's Pilgrimage,* an amorous work that Kirk Askew called, approvingly, "that enchantingly pretty, frivolous picture." Askew further observed, "Like all basically serious men, the really profound moved him as deeply as the really frivolous completely delighted him."[92]

Helen flew down for the opening, and she and Chick gave a dinner for the Taylor Committee. "The party went off very well," Helen told Sally; "Daddy does all these things so much more easily than I do, as you know, that it seems very simple."[93] Chick wanted Helen to stay longer, but for once she turned the tables on him, telling him that she had to return to see Sally and do volunteer work for the Hartford Symphony.[94]

Chick's life in 1953 followed a predictable pattern. He presented programs in the Asolo; he appeared with the Players of Sarasota in Jean-Paul Sartre's *No Exit;* and he organized his sixth seminar, "Rubens and the Flemish Tradition." That summer, he reopened the Windham Playhouse, and among the plays was *Private Lives,* with Chick playing Noël Coward to Bea Ganz's Gertrude Lawrence. Then there were the rushed visits to Helen and the children in Castine, their excursions to Windham, the stops at home on Scarborough Street in transit, the birthday and Christmas reunion, and the return to Sarasota. As one of David's classmates, Woody Eitel, later said, it seemed almost as if Chick were a busy college student who was occasionally home for the holidays.[95]

That year the Board of Control allowed him to institute some of the recommendations of the Taylor Committee. Cesar Diorio's connection with the Ringling was severed—with acrimony on both sides, for Diorio was vocal about Chick's informality around works of art—to pave the way for a full-time conservator in June. In the fall of that year, Chick hired an assistant director, Henri Dorra, and a curatorial librarian, Kenneth Donahue, both promising art historians, who relieved him of the burden of running the entire operation. Donahue had been offered a coveted teaching post at the University of Chicago, but turned it down for the opportunity to work with Chick.

Years later, Donahue recounted some of the Sarasota myths about Chick: that he had bought the Asolo Theater the day he was hired by making a long-distance call to Adolf Loewi from the governor's office;[96] that when one of Chick's cars ran out of gas, he simply bought another; and that he smoked more than any other mortal, a story Donahue believed himself. "He smoked a carton of cigarettes a day, not a pack a day, but a carton of cigarettes a day," said Donahue. "When he came to our house—he finally brought us an ashtray that was big enough for him."[97]

Helen came to Sarasota in the beginning of 1954 for the opening of Chick's winter show of American trompe l'oeil pictures, *Harnett and His School.* Chick told her he had decided to stay on at the Ringling for at least another year because state support was improving.[98] That spring, the legislature finally approved nearly $200,000—which they would later increase—for the building to house the Asolo Theater, the restoration laboratory, a darkroom, workshops, storage space for paintings, children's classrooms, and offices. With Chick's blessing, Florida architect Marion Manley designed a simple modern structure in pink and white to match the museum, with a nod to the Renaissance in its decorative details.

But Chick had been looking around for an escape route. He had seen how easy the living was for Iris Barry and her lover in Fayence. On the family trip in 1952, he had looked at a house in the nearby town of Saint-Pol as a possible base for his European travels. He finally settled on a property in Fayence itself.

The view from Chick's balcony in Fayence, c. 1955

At the top of the hill in the town, near the hotel de ville and the local café, was a four-story medieval house that had been rebuilt in the seventeenth century. It was something of a ruin, but it was solid, and there was a commanding view of the valley from its rear windows—an irresistible redecorating project. It was also a bargain. For $1,600, Chick bought it and the property across the street, finalizing the sale by letter in the early part of 1954. He now owned six houses. "He always had houses," said Hitchcock. "That was a bad habit he had inherited from his mother."[99]

During the next two autumns, Chick scoured local antique dealers for inexpensive but charming objects, mostly eighteenth-century furniture, paintings, and pottery, to embellish his villa. He created a small balcony on the fourth floor, where he and a few friends could have a drink and contemplate the view. Word spread in that part of Provence that Chick Austin was turning an ancient house into something special, and he and Jim Hellyar got used to finding anyone from Christian Dior to visiting British matrons on their doorstep.

As Chick planned the new building for the Asolo Theater in the fall of 1954, he had to contend with an attempt by the Board of Control to undermine his authority by giving the museum's business manager greatly increased powers. Chick found the appointment of such an overseer intolerable, ominously reminiscent of his denouement in Hartford, and he told the board in January 1955 that unless these decisions were reversed, he would resign. "This threw them into a tizzy," Helen reported to Sally, who was then studying art history in Florence, "& almost immediately they gave him what he wanted in the way of authority."[100] Chick had won a victory, but the episode made him anxious about the future.

He produced two exhibitions early in 1955, works from Sarasota collections and *Directors' Choice:* thirty-three museum directors throughout the country each lent a favorite object from their collections, a show that ranged from ancient Greek sculpture to modern paintings. He noted with delight that the only duplications were three views of Venice by Francesco Guardi. This fondness for the rococo among museum directors, said Chick coyly, "may be significant."[101]

Helen arrived in Sarasota at the beginning of February for the *Directors* exhibition and, at Chick's insistence, stayed for more than a month. He talked with her about returning to Hartford. She had mixed emotions, finally telling him, wisely, that he should not leave Sarasota until he found something else to do that was worthy of his energy and talent. She knew that nothing would be more demoralizing for him than to return to the city where he had seen such triumphs—and ultimately rejection—with nothing to do.[102]

In October, Ken Donahue, now assistant director at the Ringling, told Chick that he had an offer to become chief curator at the Los Angeles County Museum. Chick answered that he did not expect to be director much longer. "You know I'm getting pretty fed up with the place," he said, "and all the political problems and the difficulty of working in a public institution. If you leave, I think I'll leave too." Donahue decided to stay. Chick told him that he had been considering buying a small museum in Saint-Pol, near Fayence. He had already discussed renovating it with the local authorities and had promised to will it to the city at his death.[103] At last he would be entirely in charge of his own museum, with no trustees, no Board of Control, and no politicians.

But he wanted to see the Asolo Theater installed first. Groundbreaking for the new building had taken place the previous summer, and construction was under way. So Chick kept going. Early in 1956, he presented a small loan show of graphic art from the Museum of Modern Art that recalled an earlier triumph, *A Half Century of Picasso.* And he continued to appear onstage with the Sarasota Players—this time in *Dear Charles,* a comedy he had recently produced in Windham.

Chick and Helen at Sally's graduation from the
Concord Academy, 1954

For his big exhibition that year, Chick chose a theme that expressed one of his greatest pleasures, *The Art of Eating.* He invited Sally to come down from Hartford to stay with him and do research for the catalogue. She was just twenty-one and had her father to herself for the first time. She had grown into an attractive and sophisticated young woman and Chick loved introducing her to friends. However, he would not relax his rule about never allowing family members to hear him lecture, and one evening when he was about to speak on eighteenth-century porcelain in the Asolo Theater, he instructed her to wait in his office. Only after she resorted to tears did Chick change his mind. She said that it was the best lecture she ever heard.[104]

The Art of Eating had a good deal of Chick's old flair for looking at tradi-tional art in new ways. This aesthetic journey through culinary images spanned six centuries in thirty-one paintings from the Italian, French, Flemish, Dutch, Austrian, and American Schools—along with a nineteenth-century copy of a sixth-dynasty Egyptian relief from Giza. Visitors could look at Biblical meals in such works as Desiderio's *Balshazzar's Feast,* back again from the Atheneum, along with sumptuous secular spreads like Ferretti's *Harlequin the Glutton* from

Entertaining in Sarasota. Left to right: *Karl Bickel, Helen Austin, Mrs. LeRoy Collins, Governor LeRoy Collins, and Chick, February 1956*

the Ringling, and Pierre Bonnard's casual *Luncheon* from the Museum of Modern Art. In the catalogue Chick traced holy repasts and licentious feasts from the time of the Egyptians through those favorite rococo meals that, like Chick himself, sought to combine the arts—with music, theater, "and amorous dalliance" accompanying the food—and ending with the informality of the modern lunch. He noted with a certain nostalgia that "the magnificent set-pieces that adorned Roman, Baroque, even Victorian banquet tables are now seen rarely, and only at the wedding breakfast or on the French Line."[105] Perhaps it was not entirely inappropriate that he and Sally ate and drank too well with old Sarasota friends at one of Chick's favorite restaurants before the opening of the show, arriving in an unsteady but genial condition, two hours late.

That spring, as the shell of the building for the Asolo Theater rose near the Ringling's courtyard, some members of the Board of Control began talking about reviewing the museum's administration again. Chick knew from experience that complaints about wasting taxpayers' money to house the remnants of an old rococo theater would only grow louder. But he refused to allow those voices to stop him. Whatever the opposition, he would produce a magnificent reopening of his "priceless and incomparable" setting for the performing arts.

CHAPTER EIGHTEEN

Home to Helen

My Ariel, chick,
That is thy charge: then to the elements
Be free, and fare thou well!

—William Shakespeare, *The Tempest*

n June, Chick returned to Windham with Jim Hellyar, relieved to step back into the roles of theatrical producer and actor. Walking back and forth in Rose Crucius's kitchen every morning, helping himself to whatever she was baking as it came out of the oven, sipping coffee or the eggnog she made to ease his persistent cough, Chick outlined grandiose schemes for his theater and his future career. Often she and Herb would hear him say, almost to himself, "I just need a million. . . ."[1]

The 1956 season was sophisticated and up to date. Among the eight plays were *The Rainmaker* ("Soon on Screen—See Original Play," said Chick's advertising), *Tea and Sympathy* ("Adult Play for Mature Audience"), and *Anastasia* ("From the pages of Life Magazine"), in which Chick played Prince Bounine. Marble fireplaces and French doors appeared onstage in the barn, and his mother's pictures and antiques once again began migrating down to the Playhouse. By now, Chick's loyal and eager audience was well established. Attendance was high, and he would have money to spend on his European holiday.

Chick was only fifty-five, but he was feeling old. Although he did not seem to be seriously ill, he talked to Rose and Herb Crucius about his death, a subject he had always avoided. Once, at a party in Sarasota, when the discussion turned to wills, Chick announced, in front of Helen and Jim, that he did not have a will and never would have a will. "When I go," he added, "you're all going to have to fight over it." "With that," said Jim, "we all had another martini."[2] But that summer, he gave a parcel of land between the Playhouse and the old cemetery to the town of Windham, reserving a large plot near Range Road

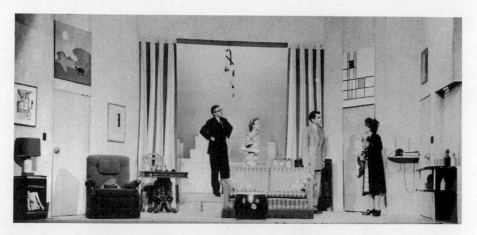

*Chick in a modernist set (including a "Mondrian") at the
Windham Playhouse, mid-1950s*

for himself, Helen, and the children, which he intended to enclose in a
wrought-iron fence fifty feet square. When Sally visited the Playhouse, she
found that he had sketched monuments for each of their graves and had tacked
them up in the box office. They were all Egyptian obelisks.

He talked more openly about quitting the Ringling. He asked Jim what he
thought about retiring to the south of France. He would go ahead with his
scheme of buying the small museum in Saint-Pol. And he would finish decorating his villa in Fayence. Iris Barry and Pierre Kerroux would have to find other
quarters. He would spend most of the year in Provence as the independent
museum proprietor; in summer he would return to the Playhouse. He never
quite considered the repercussions of such plans on his domestic life; he took it
for granted that Helen would be as supportive as ever.

As in the past, Chick kept in touch with her by telephone and letter, but his
visits to Maine were brief. On the first Wednesday in August, he drove to Castine, but it was, as Helen wrote Sally, "one of his usual one-night visits. It's better than nothing, though," she added resignedly. While her life consisted of the
usual summer routine of shopping, sailing, cocktail parties, and church every
Sunday, Chick's was the theater with all its demands day and night, followed by
late dinners and camaraderie with the actors and actresses.

He was eager to get back to Europe. He had ordered a new Rolls-Royce (to
be paid for in installments), the car he had talked about owning since his teens.
The 1956 Silver Cloud represented the second year of the most dramatic
styling change in the company's history. His was a green and tan version, which
he had arranged to pick up in Cherbourg when he arrived on the *Queen Mary* on
August 27.

Chick on his balcony in Fayence, September 1956

By the time he sailed, however, he was not feeling well. He felt weak on the boat, and his vision was occasionally blurred. He thought he was having mild strokes. He developed severe pain in his lower back. "I don't know why I feel so awful," he told friends.[3]

Disembarking at Cherbourg, Chick took possession of his luxurious car and drove to Paris. He checked into a hotel and went to bed. Jim Hellyar flew into Paris a few days later, but Chick did not feel well enough to meet him at the airport as planned. When Jim reached their hotel and saw Chick's condition, he convinced him to see a doctor, who concluded that Chick was suffering from fatigue and recommended a few more days of bed rest before the trip to the south of France.[4] This seemed to give Chick more strength, and he managed to visit the shops in Paris and buy a few luxury items for himself and Helen. Then he and Jim drove to Fayence, where Iris and Pierre welcomed them home with alcoholic enthusiasm.

That fall, Chick concentrated on completing the renovations and redecorating at the house. The warm weather eased his back pain. Late in September, he wrote Helen, "I am feeling better if anyone at my age ever can feel better. But somehow my heart isnt in my work anymore. Have managed, however, to get the house almost finished and at least in pretty liveable shape. It has been quite a struggle what with Iris in quite a drinking state and trying to keep Pierre from doing much work."

Chick felt he was finally settling into the house: "The weather has been quite warm up to a few days ago," he wrote, "when the equinoxial rains began to come down. Now summer seems to have ended and the days are warm but the nights quite chilly. Iris cooked sweetbreads last night which were delicious and we decided to light a fireplace in the dining room. It was quite cozy and the first time I had ever seen any fire lit here in the house."

Chick had agreed to chauffeur his old Sarasota pal Olga McLeod and a woman friend through southern France and into Italy in early October. He was skeptical about what he had taken on, however, and found their taste well below his standards. "The ladies wish to see Vallauris where the horrible pottery is made. I sincerely hope that they dont try to buy any. We will also get a look at the Matisse chapel on the way back which I havent seen for some time."[5]

When they reached Florence, Chick walked into a restaurant, and to his amazement saw Nellie Howland Soby with her third husband, Jack Bunce. Chick insisted that they all bring their drinks out to the Rolls for a private cocktail party. They promised to meet again in Venice.

Arriving in Rome a few days later, Chick felt drained of energy. He reported to Helen, "I have been rushing around trying to see as much as possible but have not managed all that I intended as I get very tired after a bit." Nevertheless, his schedule was hectic. They went on to Naples, Pompeii, and Capri—Chick's first visit to the island—where they found Ruth Ford and her second husband, actor Zachary Scott, who was filming a movie near the piazza. Then it was on to Assisi, Perugia, Bologna, and Venice. His traveling companions began to weary him, as they complained about the food and were afraid to do anything on their own until he forcibly instituted what he called "I.A.," independent activity.

Chick always bought Helen and the children presents when he was in Europe, and he indulged himself as well. He ran into Tonio Selwart, who introduced him to his favorite tailor in Rome, "and after all these years," Chick told Helen, "I have a new not ready made suit. It is very handsome and cost less than the off the rack numbers at Lord & T. I was so encouraged that I ordered a tuxedo to be sent to Venice. Hope it fits with no fittings, which he assures me it will. Thought it might be nice for Xmas dinner."[6]

From Venice, Chick and his two charges returned to Paris via Geneva. On October 31, he wrote Helen his last letter from Europe. His five-month holiday away from the Ringling and its problems was nearly over. The tourists had mostly departed, the winter was coming on, and even Paris seemed somber. "I now have contracted my usual Paris cold and feel a bit on the miserable side. It is cold and rainy and very gloomy but there are so many things that still have to be done today as tomorrow is a holiday. And we start for Cherbourg right after lunch as the car has to be on the dock by noon Friday."

He filled his last day in Paris with activity. "Paris is hopping with theatrical energy," he told Helen. "I still hope I can make the Faulkner Requiem for a Nun which is supposed to have been written for Ruth Ford and has not been performed in the USA. Here it is the rage of the city." And there was always the lure of shopping, despite his professions of fiscal responsibility: "The shops are jammed with sumptuous goods. I dare not look in the windows any more, everything is so tempting. I have noted what you have said about David's preferences and will try to get an old book on Palladio or at least architecture this afternoon when I have to pass by Mons. Bernard to pick up a magic lantern which I am getting for the museum."[7]

On November 2, Chick and Jim sailed on the *Queen Elizabeth* with the Rolls, arriving in New York on the seventh. From there they drove to Hartford to see their families before making the trip to Sarasota. When Chick reached the house on Scarborough Street, both his cold and his back pain were worse. Feeling that he must find some way of getting rid of the pain and his overall exhaustion, he made a quick run up to the farm in Windham. There he ransacked the medicine cabinets for some of his mother's old remedies—including morphine and laudanum—in the hope that one of them would help him. Returning to Hartford, he consulted the doctor who had treated Helen's mother in the 1940s, one of the few he trusted. He was told that he merely had bronchitis and that his recurrent back pain was due either to arthritis or a slipped disk.

Chick and Jim drove to Florida in the Rolls, arriving in mid-November to find the mood in Sarasota subdued after the demise of the debt-ridden Ringling Brothers circus in July.

Controversy was still smoldering over Chick's projects, especially the new building for the Asolo Theater. In part to head off criticism that winter, Chick wrote two articles for Sarasota papers, the first attempting to stir up excitement about the reopening of the theater, which he planned for the spring of 1957, the second—with Chick at his highbrow best—about the need for art critics to avoid "vituperation, shallow sarcasm, or the unjustified assumption of unassailable omniscience."[8]

On December 2, the same day Chick's second article appeared, the *Tampa Morning Tribune* launched a relentless campaign against him and his administration. Sam Mase, a feature writer at the paper, had ingratiated himself with the Ringling staff, including Chick, in the guise of writing a comprehensive story on the Ringling's operations. Then, for five consecutive days, Mase produced a series of inflammatory articles bringing up every issue he could find that would make Chick look extravagant and elitist. Under one headline, "State Funds go to Theater While Museum Deteriorates," he asserted that the Asolo was nothing more than "trappings of an ancient Italian theater" for which Chick had paid only $8,000 but was spending $274,000 of the taxpayers' money on a building to house it.[9] He claimed that a local sideshow "museum" gave the public better value than the Ringling's circus museum.[10] Another attack was more personal: "Wealthy Austin Paid $9000 For Part-Time Job," announced the headline.[11] Chick had explained his abbreviated schedule by stating that he had come to Sarasota "with the understanding that I work seven and one-half months each year." But when Mase pursued him on the details of his income, Chick had responded dismissively: "Salary is not a question with me." Mase latched on to this, using Chick's offhand remark to insinuate that he was a man of independent means.[12] Chick came off as aristocratic and condescending.[13]

When Karl Bickel and George Higgins, a former president of the Sarasota Chamber of Commerce, publicly condemned Mase for spreading falsehoods, even the *Tampa Morning Tribune* had to report the story. Bickel praised the Asolo Theater as a great work of art and vehemently defended Chick in words reminiscent of some of the more sympathetic Hartford trustees: "We almost had to kidnap Austin to get him to take over the museum, which was dead, like a morgue. . . . Do you want a great art center or a roadside attraction? Austin knows art and he has been working like a dog to achieve an artistic and museum miracle."[14]

It was clear not only to Bickel, but to newspaper writers outside Tampa— and eventually to the public—that Mase had been put up to the job by petty politicians and a few people on the Board of Control who resented Chick Austin and wanted to force him out. Suspicion that Chick was not quite "normal" in his private life undoubtedly fueled their enmity. To them he was an outsider, a rich Harvard-educated northerner. With his multiple talents, his four languages, and his cosmopolitanism, he intimidated the anti-intellectuals. And what infuriated them most of all was that he had succeeded, despite many obstacles, in getting large sums of money from the state legislature for his highbrow activities. They wanted to discredit him both to promote their populist notion of an art museum as public entertainment and to get control of the Ringling for their own political ends. As an editorial in *The News* of Sarasota put it, the series of articles was "obviously inspired by the Tallahassee boys who know about as much about art as your goldfish."[15]

Nevertheless, the *Tampa Morning Tribune* gleefully reported on December 7 that "Board Head Lauds Tribune Stories on Ringling Museum." Ralph Miller of Orlando, chairman of the Board of Control, called Mase's articles "accurate and fair." He announced that the board would undertake a thorough investigation of the museum's operation and that they would ask the Florida legislature to transfer governance of the museum to some other state agency. He added that the Ringling should be "put on a paying basis if possible"—an almost unheard-of suggestion for an art museum.

In reaction to this ominous turn of events, letters protesting the Mase articles inundated the Tampa paper, which felt obliged to publish a few of them. One Sarasota art collector described the Ringling before Chick arrived as "nothing but a morgue of art, untended, unappreciated and practically unvisited." Another correspondent astutely noted that "the unending battle of the Ringling Museum and all state owned cultural institutions is to prevent them from being used to take care of super-annuated politicians."[16]

Hostile members of the Board of Control went ahead with their pressure on the state government, and Governor LeRoy Collins appointed a committee to review Chick's administration. Unlike the 1952 investigation, however, his judges would not be distinguished museum directors, but were likely to be a mix of a few enlightened people and unsympathetic, untutored bureaucrats.

Depressed by what he saw as the ingratitude of the community, Chick spent the last few days in Florida before his Christmas holiday concentrating on final details of the new building for the Asolo Theater. Then, less than a month after they had returned to Florida, he and Jim prepared to drive to Hartford. Chick had put the Rolls in a friend's garage because the Tamiami Trail was torn up by road construction, and he thought it would damage the car. He decided that they would make the trip back to Connecticut in a small German Borgward he had bought at the beginning of the year. Chick's back pain was now so severe that he felt he would not have the strength to honor an engagement to lecture at the Museum of Fine Arts in Boston on December 20, and he asked Ken Donahue to fly to Boston and fill in for him.[17]

Chick called Helen twice on the trip home, saying that he was in terrible pain and that he did not know how he was going to make it. When they reached Washington, Jim urged Chick to call his cousin Virginia, who lived nearby, to see what could be done, but Chick said, "We'll wait until the morning." The next day he decided to continue: "We'll drive to Hartford."[18] They arrived there on the eighteenth, in time for his fifty-sixth birthday. His arrival was extremely upsetting to Helen and Sally. He could hardly get out of the car. They had to help him into the house and onto a sofa in the living room.[19]

He was in too much pain to decorate the tree on Christmas Eve. He could only lie on a settee and watch as Helen, David, and Sally attached the ornaments and tinsel. Nor did he feel well enough to attend the annual Christmas dinner at Jim and Tulie Goodwin's house a few blocks away. For the first time in seven years, Helen and the children went without him.[20]

Back in Florida, on December 23, Lawrence Dane of the *Sarasota Herald-Tribune* had published a long and thorough rebuttal of the attacks in the Tampa press.[21] And Bickel sent Chick a stream of reassuring communications, telling him that "the Mase series was so blatantly bad that the reaction is getting better all the time"[22] and enclosing favorable newspaper clippings. In a note to Chick on Christmas Day, Bickel said, "This situation here is going to be a big dividend for you Everett..it had to be because, after all, the facts, the decencies and the right were all on your side but we had to get the Devil to throw a bolt to illuminate the scene...and Sam did it for us."[23]

On the day after Christmas, Chick's condition worsened, and he was admitted to Hartford Hospital. Doctors noted on his chart that his back pain had been "acutely precipitated by a long drive home from Florida in a small car" and told him to remain in the hospital for twenty days of bed rest and observation.[24]

Then, as the kettle of ignorance and envy boiled in Florida, the voice of a national art authority was raised on the subject of Chick Austin. In the January 5 issue of *The Saturday Review*, Jim Soby published a resounding tribute to an old friend. He declared that Chick had brought "to the task of restoring and expanding the Ringling collection one of the most perceptive and courageous eyes in the international museum world and long curatorial experiences, especially at Hartford's Wadsworth Atheneum." Thanks to him, the Ringling could now be regarded as "one of the most exciting public art galleries" in the United States. And as for the Asolo Theater, it was "not only one of the most important architectural documents ever brought to this country, but a thoroughly rewarding work of art in its own right."[25] Bickel bought up piles of the magazine to send to state legislators and the heads of executive departments. Ken Donahue forwarded copies to the Board of Education, the governor, and members of his cabinet.

Chick's proposed budget for the next fiscal year was about to be considered by the legislative committee, and that always made Bickel nervous. "Its not the Mase stuff," he told Chick, "but just the general bull headed cow minded standards of most members of the legislature that I fear and always will." He added that he expected that *Life* would cover the opening of the Asolo in its new building that spring.[26]

On January 16, concluding that Chick's distress was caused by "Lumbosacral strain,"[27] his doctor discharged him from the hospital in a back brace. Chick was too weak to climb the stairs at home, so Helen had a hospital bed placed in the rococo bed niche in the dining room and had a ramp installed on the steps up to the bathroom in the back hall. She and Sally supplied him with whatever he wanted, including the chocolate that he loved.[28]

A few days later, Bickel briefed Chick on the machinations surrounding a possible new entity to take over the museum from the Board of Control. Fred Kent, who wanted his own people in charge, was the enemy, a man who, said Bickel, "just from the limitations of his mentality and the sort of back ground he has been brought up in hates the Ringling." But Bickel was confident of his personal influence with Governor Collins. "The Governor, who thank God, is intelligent and understanding, will not, I am sure, go for the plundering of the Museum by any pig snouted gang such as Kent would normally propose." Bickel contemplated forming a separate board of those who really appreciated the museum.[29] Ken Donahue wrote to assure Chick that the Ringling could profit from having such a board or committee as a buffer between the museum and the Board of Control. And he tried to counteract Chick's increasing discouragement: "You have been so extremely skeptical on the phone about the appreciation of your work in Florida and the admiration and affection which people here have for you as a person. . . . I do ask you to accept my word . . . that there is a real and great admiration for both you and your work here.

"We are all eager to have you back."[30]

Bickel wrote delightedly to Chick at the end of January that the tide was turning in their favor, encouraging him to return soon. "There is a big hole in the local atmosphere that only you will fit. How about it, chum, better pick up Helen and come on down."[31]

At that same moment, on January 31, Chick was readmitted to Hartford Hospital with a recurrence of back pain that was too severe to be managed at home. A myelogram showed a mass in his lower back. Five days later, exploratory surgery was performed on his spine. The doctors found an inoperable cancerous tumor that had spread to a vertebra from his lungs. They severed a nerve root that had been compressed by the tumor, and the pain disappeared.

On February 4, the day of Chick's surgery, under the headline "A Better Boss for the Museum?" an editorial in the *Tampa Morning Tribune* advocated transferring control of the museum to the state university system under a new director, repeating all of Mase's criticisms and saying that no institution—"art museum or pickle factory—can operate efficiently when the head man is out of reach nearly half the time." The Ringling Museum was "neither the private hobby of Director Austin nor the exclusive ward of Sarasota's art colony."[32]

To counter the attacks and dramatize the accomplishments of his absent, ailing director, Ken Donahue organized a large retrospective exhibition to commemorate the Ringling's first decade as a public art museum. *Acquisitions and Achievements: The Ringling Museum, 1946 to 1956*, which opened on February 10, was in fact a tribute to Chick, featuring his greatest purchases—the Rubens portrait of Archduke Ferdinand, the Strozzi, the Tiepolo, the Magnasco, the Harlequin series by Giovanni Ferretti, and Poussin's *Ecstasy of Saint Paul,* along with the eighteenth-century furniture and decorative arts and the Asolo Theater itself. Chick's programs were also celebrated—whether his massive conservation efforts, the visits of the Dublin Players, or the Wednesday-night foreign films. As the *Sarasota Herald-Tribune* put it, the show "will renew your pride in the museum, in Sarasota, and in the state which has vision enough to try to support properly such a museum and such a director, A. Everett Austin, Jr., who is now recovering from an operation in Connecticut and who will probably return here in March."[33]

In Hartford, Helen kept the true nature of Chick's affliction entirely to herself at first. "Daddy doesn't feel very well" was all she would say to Sally and David after the surgery. In mid-February, David came down from the Harvard Architecture School for a weekend visit. Just as he, Sally, and their mother had finished dinner in the kitchen, Helen said, with a strange formality, "I'd like to speak to both of you in the living room." Once they had all sat down, Helen said, "Daddy's dying." She told them to tell no one. David burst into tears, and at that moment the telephone rang. Sally answered it. It was their old family friend Peggy Robinson, one of Chick's first secretaries, who had attended his wedding in Paris. "How's your father?" she asked. Sally said, *"Fine."*[34]

Helen could not bear to tell Chick himself. And she did not tell Jim Hellyar. Chick asked Jim to return to Florida to help install the Asolo Theater in the new building, as he was among the few who really understood how the interior pieces should be reassembled. After Jim left, Chick told Helen, "I don't ever want to see Jim Hellyar again."[35] He had come home to Helen.[36]

No one in Sarasota was told about the seriousness of Chick's illness. "They all expected him to come back," Jim remembered, "which I did, too. . . . I always thought he was going to get better. I never knew."[37]

Chick was afraid. "What's wrong with me?" he asked repeatedly. "What's wrong with me?" Helen tried to reassure him, rarely leaving his bedside.[38]

She allowed few visitors into his hospital room. David's old school friend Woody Eitel managed to see Chick and hand him a box of chocolates. Eitel remembered that he "gave off that same charisma that he always had. It's hard to describe. He had a certain kind of inflection in his voice. . . . He sparkled and glittered, even in the hospital."[39] Another visitor brought him marzipan, a favorite from his trips to Europe as a child. Chick immediately responded, with a laugh, "If things get really bad, I'll put some kind of pill in this, and then they'll say I died of marzipan."[40] While reading some obituaries in a Hartford newspaper one day, Chick saw the notice "Please omit flowers." He turned to Helen and said, "Don't put that in. I want everything I can get."[41]

At the end of February, Bickel reported to Chick that, working behind the scenes, he had masterminded the composition of the governor's museum committee, which would be announced soon. It would be a shock to the Tampa paper, he added. He told Chick not to worry about opening the Asolo in the spring as he had planned. "I'd take all the time I needed and open it up late next November with a lot of glitter and gloss. . . . Get yourself well, Everett and all the other problems will skid away."[42]

Although the *Tribune* made yet another attempt to criticize Chick for wasting taxpayers' money, it was running out of steam. The atmosphere had changed completely. Bickel had managed to choose most of the ten members of the citizens' committee appointed by the Board of Control to consider Chick's performance and to address the future administration of the Ringling Museum. On March 12, the committee met with members of the board for the first time. A report was expected within a month, and all signs pointed to a favorable outcome for Chick.

On March 18, Bickel wrote with the good news that the meeting of the new museum committee had gone exactly as he would have wanted. The Ringling's independence of political agencies was assured, and, as for the Asolo Theater, "It sold itself." The crisis was as good as resolved. "It won't be long now that the 'season' will be over, and I'll be glad..and that the weather will be warm and regular and things will beat as usual. We are looking forward to it and to you."[43]

At the same time, impersonally following its regulations, the Board of Control informed Helen that her husband's sick time had run out and that his salary would not be paid.

But that no longer mattered.

After being given nitrogen mustard, an early form of chemotherapy, and a series of cobalt treatments, Chick had developed a severe infection and fever. He was intermittently delirious. One day he imagined that he had dropped an art book, which Helen pretended to pick up for him. Then he thought his mother had come into the room. Then Chick saw an angel, not animated and beckoning, but conjured out of the thousands of paintings he had looked at all his life. "An extremely fragile and mystic beauty," the twenty-seven-year-old Chick Austin had written about one angel in the bulletin of the Wadsworth Atheneum, "lost in the contemplation of timeless and spaceless existence." On another day he reached out to Sally and said something that she thought she had never heard from him before: "Sally, I love you very much." A mass of confused emotions, she rushed from the room without saying a word. He never was able to speak to her again.[44]

On March 27, he went into a coma. Helen remained beside the bed, talking to him and holding his hand. On the evening of Friday, March 29, while she and the children were having dinner at her brother Francis's house, the hospital called to tell her that Chick might not last through the night. David and Sally drove her to the hospital. After sitting beside him for some time, she decided to rest in an unoccupied room, telling the nurse that she must be awakened if anything changed. She did not want Chick to die alone. But five minutes before midnight, as Helen slept, Chick quietly stopped breathing.

The next morning at the Ringling, the staff, having been kept almost entirely in the dark, was staggered at the news. "All members of the staff are desperately shocked," a spokesman told the press, "and although we knew Mr. Austin had been ill we didn't realize it was as serious as this." Even Ken Donahue did not know the truth until the day before Chick died.[45]

Though a few of his intimates outside Florida had hints during the last weeks that he was much sicker than anyone had thought, his death came like an unexpected hammer blow to his closest friends in the art world. The old network flashed into life one last time. Constance Askew, who had remained Helen's steadfast confidante all through the years, was devastated. Like so many of those who had helped shape the modern cultural scene, she saw the end of an era. She told Helen:

> I've had many people I loved, die—but none that has shaken me like this—It's impossible for me to say the conventional things—Chick himself won't let me,—I can see him—now—this minute—come in the room,—the laugh,—the gesture with his hands,—all the mannerisms—and the wonderful divine nonsense about what had happened to him five minutes before,—I simply can't go on, Helen,—a whole part of our life has died,—a whole period in time. . . . There was no one like him,—and God knows, there's no one in our lives about whom one can even say, "He's like Chick."[46]

Constance immediately cabled Virgil Thomson, who was in Caracas, Venezuela. "I still cant believe it," he wrote Helen. "Because Chick in my mythology was immortal. I still cant quite believe he isnt there. But of course he is because he has always been there whether we were with him or not. His reality was unerasable."[47] It was, as Tonio Selwart said, "so *unlike* Chick to die."[48]

Julien Levy scrawled an anguished note to Helen: "a piece has been cut out of my heart."[49] An emotional Lincoln Kirstein told her, "Chick knew what everything good was—*first*—before everyone else. They knew what was good through his discovery which became a revelation—an education—then a fact in their lives—like the ballet."[50] Jim Soby wrote her that "none of us has ever known anyone more brilliant or vital or generous."[51]

Edward Forbes, more fatherly to Chick than Arthur Austin was able to be, was too self-effacing to be effusive. He concentrated into a short sentence more than thirty years of admiration and affection for the unformed student and the great museum director whose career he had guided and protected: "He was a rare human being."[52]

Alfred Frankfurter, editor of *Art News*, was vacationing in Sarasota and had just visited the Ringling on Friday. He was still on Longboat Key when he was tracked down by a Sarasota reporter the next day: "I have known him for almost 30 years," Frankfurter said, "and from the vantage point of editor of the oldest U.S. art magazine, which gives a unique opportunity for scanning the entire field. . . . A. Everett Austin was perhaps the most creative and original of art museum directors in the century since such institutions came into being."[53] Later, in a full-page editorial in *Art News*, he wrote: "It is true that today's generation of art historians specializes with a precise focus, in a way that Austin's never could have—but it is equally true that there are certain sparks of originality that fly off only from forerunners and originators."[54]

The funeral was held on Monday, April 1, at Hartford's Christ Church Cathedral, Helen's church from childhood, where her father had preached and where his own funeral had taken place forty years earlier. Lincoln Kirstein described the day with razor-sharp acuity to Tchelitchew, far away in Rome, who himself was very ill and would not live through the summer:

> Chick's funeral was a triste reunion . . . there were tons of white flowers; Helen was really marvelous, do write her; the little boy David looked exactly like Chick & Helen combined, very pretty but angular, with beautiful manners, and very manly and the girl was sweet too; Lelia Wittler; Genia, Leonide? Julien Levi fat with a black moustache; Nelly Soby who is married again; very sweet . . . old Edward Forbes and a lot of the Goodwin's; somehow it was inexpressibly sad to me; the whole ballet started through Chick in Hartford; his house, like the Brenta villas, but paper and cardboard; the memories of the Paper Ball and Four Saints and the Ballet Caravan. A whole life. But Chick was not in pain, and did not realize what was the matter until very late.
>
> . . . [Helen] was heroic; her whole life, too, which must have been a kind of hell, but always adoring Chick no matter how long his absence, whatever his affairs, and she knew everything and forgave everything. God knows what will happen to Jim whom no one can bear; and what will happen at Sarasota because Chick was the only one who could hold the horrible State Legislature together; and the Barnum, Ringling circus is bankrupt, but whatever he touched, he did with great distinction. He was certainly an arbiter elegantarium.[55]

At the reception in the Austin house after the funeral, Kirstein sat down on a settee in the living room and broke down sobbing. Ten minutes later, he rushed out of the house and disappeared.

Tchelitchew did write to Helen: "I find it unbelievable that someone, who was the image of life, boiling life, all interest, understanding, discovery, excel-

lant taste—all this is gone like in Fire! . . . He was allways ready to do something new, something in which he saw a new possibility to promote art and to
give it new life."[56]

All of Chick's old friends understood Helen's role in allowing him to be who
he was. Adolph Loewi told her directly: "You stood by Chick even when as I
well know it was not always easy to live with a genius, and I know that he himself admired you & loved you for it."[57] Speaking to an old Hartford friend,
Helen said simply, lest anyone pity her for Chick's behavior: "But he ennobled
my life."[58]

On the morning after the funeral, through a steady rain, the hearse, followed by Helen and the children and a few friends, took Chick back to Windham. Herb Crucius had helped dig the grave in the plot of land Chick had given
to the town the previous summer. It was on a little rise, just inside the old stone
wall along Range Road. The red barn, with the huge letters WINDHAM PLAY-
HOUSE, could be seen through the bare trees. It was three o'clock when the burial service began.

At that moment in Sarasota, art lovers, museum members, artists, actors,
writers, and restaurateurs, along with the staff of the Ringling, gathered in the
museum's vast Rubens Room for a memorial concert. There, in the gallery,
the audience could see Chick's first purchase, the great Rubens portrait of the
Archduke Ferdinand, and one of his last, Poussin's dramatic *Ecstasy of Saint
Paul*. Ken Donahue, who would soon be named Chick's successor, rose to
speak. "He not only perfected what had been begun by John Ringling in Sarasota," he said, "but he fought for ten years against the Philistine who wished to
make of this museum something less."[59] A string quartet, made up of four members of the West Coast Symphony, two women and two men, all friends of Chick,
started to play. The hour's program consisted of music he had especially
liked—Haydn's Opus 20 quartet, the Andante Cantabile from Tchaikovsky's
Quartet No. 1, the Andante from Schubert's *Rosamunde,* and the Adagio from
Mozart's Quartet No. 17. A Sarasota radio station scheduled a broadcast of
Mozart's *Requiem* for late that night.

Back in Windham, the rain stopped as the casket was lowered into the
ground. (Herb Crucius later had trouble securing the stone to the cement foundation at the head of the grave. To finish the job, he gathered up a large variety
of theatrical screws from the Playhouse that had once attached Chick's elaborate sets to the stage.) When the short service was over, the sun came out and
the skies cleared.

Chick never got the obelisk he had designed. Instead, Helen chose a polished slab of gray granite from Maine.[60] But his monument was elsewhere.

At noon in Hartford, on that same April day, the doors of the Avery Memorial opened to the public as they had for the past twenty-three years. Visitors
entered the immaculate Machine Age court, its sleek floating planes so dar-

ingly combined with the spiraling curves of the baroque Venus on her pedestal above the ornamental pool, her two dolphins spouting playfully. Then they made their way to an upstairs gallery to see an exhibition of modern paintings, just opening that day. And in the evening, others arrived at the museum for the first Hartford performance of a new play. They came down the two staircases to the lobby with its curved walls of exotic wood, and its festive painted panels of the Carnival of Venice. At eight-thirty, they settled into the deep-blue velour seats of the theater. The house lights dimmed, and the curtains began to open.

ACKNOWLEDGMENTS

The encouragement, enthusiasm, and trust of the family of A. Everett Austin, Jr., made this book possible.

I first saw the Austin House on Scarborough Street in 1973 on an early visit to Hartford. I wondered who had built a Palladian villa that looked like a stage set in the midst of conventional Neo-Colonial and Tudor Revival houses. After moving to the Hartford area three years later, I occasionally returned to Scarborough Street to photograph the house, still not aware of its owner. In 1980 the Wadsworth Atheneum's librarian, Elizabeth Hoke, and its development director, Christopher Cox, invited me to come as a consultant for a week to advise the museum on the feasibility of organizing and preserving its archival material. Among the scattered papers in basements, vaults, and closets were more than twenty thousand pages of Chick Austin's correspondence. I learned that it was he who had built the house on Scarborough Street, that he had died in 1957, and that his widow still lived in the house.

My survey led to my joining the staff of the museum as its first archivist. This would not have happened without the help of my friend and mentor, William G. DeLana, one of the Atheneum's most effective and best-loved trustees, who sustained my work at the Atheneum until his untimely death in 1987.

I soon met Helen Austin and her children, Sally and David, who were surprised and happy to know that Chick Austin's papers had survived. I frequently visited Mrs. Austin, describing the latest discoveries in the archives and talking with her about her husband's achievements. She was unfailingly gracious and kind. Sally Austin, an artist in New York, came to see her mother often; she began to appear at the museum, delivering boxes from the attic in the Scarborough Street house. I would find letters from Calder and Le Corbusier, postcards from Dalí, and photographs of Chick Austin in costume. Sally's brother, David, was equally excited about the rediscovery of his father's career. In 1984, after events celebrating the fiftieth anniversary of the opening of the Avery Memorial wing, the Atheneum's trustees asked the Austin family to donate the Scarborough Street house and most of its contents to the museum. They agreed, and with extraordinary generosity, Helen's cousin Genevieve Harlow Goodwin promised to provide funds to restore, preserve, and operate the house in perpetuity. The house was subsequently designated a National Historic Landmark. In 1994 Sally Austin died of cancer at the age of fifty-eight. She had followed the restoration of the house and the progress of the book every step of the way and had become one of my best friends. David Austin, his wife, Sandy, and his children, Laura Etnier Austin Allyn and Donald Munro Austin, have provided unflagging support for my work.

Other members of the Austin, Etnier, and Goodwin families have been most generous with their time and recollections: Nancy Goodwin Cobb, Stephen Etnier, Dorothy Goodwin, Henry Sage Goodwin, Jacqueline James Goodwin, Jane Fenwick Goodwin, Mary Madden House, Virginia House, Lucy McNeece, Mary Wistar Morris O'Connor, Robert O'Connor, Virginia Etnier Ragsdale, Nancy Goodwin Graff Short, Lucy Goodwin Stone, Emily Hall Tremaine, and Rosamund Stone Zander.

I had the good fortune of getting to know many of Chick Austin's friends in the art world. I owe a profound debt of gratitude to the late Eleanor Howland Bunce. She was Austin's assistant from 1933 to 1936, a close friend of his family, a vital member of the modernist art circle in New York in the 1930s and 1940s, and a benefactor of the Wadsworth Atheneum. Through her generosity and that of her late husband, John Lee Bunce, Nellie helped make the archives program and the restoration of the house possible. Her gifts to the archives of letters, books, and period photographs relating to the Austin era, as well as her intimate knowledge of the period, were invaluable to this biography.

Many of Austin's other close associates shared their memories with me. I am immensely grateful to Mrs. Alfred H. Barr, Jr., Joella Levy Bayer, Paul Cadmus, Helen and Elliott Carter, Philip Claflin, John Coolidge, Charles Henri Ford, Ruth Ford, Henry Sayles Francis, Henry-Russell Hitchcock, John Houseman, Philip Johnson, Truda Kaschmann, Lincoln Kirstein, Angela Lansbury, Bruce Lansbury, Edgar Lansbury, Mildred and Russell Lynes, Pierre Matisse, Agnes Mongan, Alwin Nikolais, May Sarton, Tonio Selwart, Theodate Johnson Severns, Holly Stevens, Muriel Streeter, Virgil Thomson, Edward M. M. Warburg, and Marguerite Yourcenar. Chick Austin's friend and longtime champion, Florence Berkman, former art critic of the *Hartford Times,* whose memory and acuity are undimmed after more than nine decades, has been unfailingly helpful.

A number of people were interviewed in 1974 and 1975 by the Atheneum's chief curator, Peter O. Marlow, and Jill Silverman. Their contribution in preserving the memories of many important figures in the arts who knew Chick Austin has been invaluable.

I want to thank the following individuals with whom I spoke: Louisa Adelson, Thomas Anderson, Pamela Askew, Harry Balf, Arlene Johnson Baum, Rosamond Bernier, Richard M. Bissell, Jr., Hugh Campbell, Elizabeth Capen, Ralph D. Childs, Susanna Coggishall, Robert Cole, Elizabeth Creamer, John Crockett, Rose and Herbert Crucius, Elizabeth de Kantor, Meta de Macarté,

Walter Woody Eitel, Alice and Ostrom Enders, Isabel Fairchild, Mary Blasi
Forchelli, Miriam Gabo, Dr. Michael Ganz, Paul Geissler, Brendan Gill, Alden
Gordon, Charles Gulick, Julius S. Held, Helen Hellyar, James Hellyar, Betty
Henritze, Katharine Hepburn, Mrs. James Howard, Robert Jacobs, Sheldon
Kahn, Beatrice Kneeland, Mrs. Horace Learned, Kenneth Lee, Norman Lloyd,
Judith Love, Clare Boothe Luce, William McDougall, Dr. Currier McEwen,
J. Bard McNulty, Jack Melanos, Bryce Muir, Barbara and Howard Norris, Reata
Overman, John Parsons, Rosamond Forbes Pickhardt, James Plaut, Elizabeth
Prentiss, Noel Preston, Ann Carolyn Bissell Prud'homme, Gladys Richards,
Mrs. William Robertson, Mary Parsons Robinson, Elinore Jaynes Safford,
Robert Schutz, Walter Schwinn, Mary and Arthur L. Shipman, Jr., Millie Sil-
vestri, Janet Smith, Ann and Sid Solomon, Philip Stapp, Dr. George Starkey,
Donald Starr, Rod Steiger, Elizabeth Tafford, Mary Thomas, Francis Thompson,
Robert Thorndike, Herbert Todd, Robert Tollett, Edwina Urann, Lillian
Scataregia Varol, Phyllis Alsop Ward, Amy Welcher, Jeanne Welcher, Harry
Wiley, and Beatrice Ganz Williams.

Others who helped with this book include Melanie Anderson, Mardges
Bacon, Madeleine Fidell Beaufort, the heirs of Agnes Rindge Claflin, Priscilla
Cunningham, James Dowell, Michael Duncan, Wilson Faude, Michael
FitzGerald, Lorraine Gagnon, Robin Green, Kay Hoffman, Robert Irving, Lisa
Jacobs, Jeanne Welcher Kleinfield, Michael Mahoney, Francis Mason, Joseph
Panitch, James Parker, Stephen Robeson-Miller, Colin Rowe, Nancy Rubin-
stein, Nancy Savin, Ingrid Schaffner, Charlie Scheips, Alexander Schouvaloff,
Robert Sitton, Martha Smith, Jeanne Strouse, Joel Thome, Katherine Warwick,
Richard Guy Wilson, David W. Wright, and Deborah Zlotsky. Mr. and Mrs.
Peter A. Soby gave me permission to quote from the unpublished memoirs of
James Thrall Soby. Psychiatrist Dr. James Black provided valuable insight into
Austin's childhood. Peter Griffin has long been helpful for research assistance
and knowledge of his native Windham, New Hampshire. Steven Watson, one of
the finest writers on modernism in America, has been endlessly generous with
his research materials and support. As ever, Robert H. Smith, Jr., former president of the Wadsworth Atheneum, has been a sage adviser and friend.

This book has benefited from the kindness of several people who read all or
portions of the manuscript: Joan Acocella, Florence Berkman, Coleman H.
Casey, Arlene Croce, Mildred Gaddis, Krystyn Hastings-Silver, Laurie Lane-
Reticker, Kathleen Marr, Robert R. McQuilken, Jr., Andrea Miller-Keller,
Kristen Mortimer, Elizabeth Northey, Helen Searing, Melinda Martin Sullivan,
Wilda Van Dusen, Steven Watson, and Eric M. Zafran. Linda Ayres read many
of the early chapters with a keen eye for stylistic and interpretative accuracy.
The incomparable Alice M. DeLana read the manuscript twice in its last
stages, making meticulous corrections to the text.

For support of my work in the museum's archives and related research on Chick Austin, I would like to express my thanks for generous grants from the Connecticut Humanities Council, the Henry Luce Fund for the Scholarship in American Art, the Howard and Bush Foundation, the J. Walton Bissell Foundation, the National Endowment for the Humanities, the National Historical Publications and Records Commission, Eleanor Howland Bunce and John Lee Bunce, and James B. Lyon.

Essential to this study were the careful organization of the Austin Papers by Margaret Atwood and nearly twenty years of additional work in all areas of the archives by Doris Lederer. Many museum interns have worked on projects that have contributed to this biography. Robert R. McQuilken, Jr., was an inspiration both at the start as I prepared chapter summaries and years later when the manuscript was complete. Nancy Frazier reviewed correspondence and documents at the Atheneum relating to Austin's tenure at the Ringling Museum. Sara Bodinson organized and annotated the extensive materials provided by the Ringling and carried out research on Austin's exhibitions in Sarasota. I am also grateful to Alexandra Blau, Jad DeQuattro, Robyn Deutscher, Maureen Fenton, Joseph Ferrucci, Christopher Fox, Thomas Hermes, Ingrid Lederhaas, Shannon Lucas, Rachel Robbins, and Gabrielle Sellei.

For important research on the construction, design, and social history of the Austin House, I wish to thank Gillian Bucky and Jane Catler. Architect Jared Edwards, who was instrumental in the Atheneum's acquisition of the Austin House, gave me the benefit of his wide-ranging knowledge of historic preservation.

The Atheneum's Austin House Committee has been extremely supportive of this biography. In particular, I wish to acknowledge the four chairmen of the committee since its establishment in 1985, James B. Lyon, Clare Cooley Edwards, Melinda Martin Sullivan, and Kathleen Colville Marr, along with Alan Barton, the museum's associate director of properties and information systems, and Krystyn Hastings-Silver, our peerless restoration project manager.

The staffs of numerous institutions have been generous with their time and expertise. For assistance in the research on Austin's ancestry and early life, I wish to acknowledge Erik Jorgensen, director of the Pejebscot Historical Society; Elin L. Wolfe, archivist at the Francis A. Countway Library of Medicine; Donna Shermeyer of the Historical Society of York County; Elizabeth Goodman of the Mount Union Area Historical Society; the staff of the Juniata College Library; the staff of the Huntington County Historical Society; Joyce K. Bibber; and Mrs. John S. Rand. The Fogg Art Museum Archives and the Harvard University Archives are the best source for Austin's academic and early professional career, and I am especially grateful to James Cuno, the Elizabeth and

John Moors Cabot Director of the Harvard Art Museums. I would also like to thank L. Fred Jewett, dean of Harvard College; Harley Holden, the longtime curator of the Harvard University Archives; and Christopher Wolff, dean of the Graduate School of Arts and Sciences at Harvard University; and above all, Abigail G. Smith, archivist of the Harvard University Art Museums. For their astute insights into Austin's archaeological work with George Reisner, I thank the staff of the Department of Ancient Egyptian, Nubian, and Near Eastern Art at the Museum of Fine Arts in Boston, especially its curator, Rita Freed, as well as Peter Manuelian and Timothy Kendall. For information about archaeological work in the Yucatan, I am grateful to John Strom, archivist at the Carnegie Institution of Washington, D.C. At the Museum of Modern Art, Rona Roob, the museum's founding archivist, and her staff were enormously helpful over many years of research. I would also like to thank the staff of the Archives of American Art–Smithsonian Institution; the staff of the Dance Collection at the New York Public Library at Lincoln Center, particularly Genevieve Oswald and Madeleine Nichols; the staff of the archives of the Vassar College Art Gallery; the staff of the Collection of American Literature at Yale University's Beinecke Rare Book and Manuscript Library, especially curator David Schoonover; and the staff of the Yale Music Library, particularly librarians Victor Cardell and Suzanne Eggleston.

For photographic work, I am ever appreciative of my friends at the Camera Bar and Kula Photo in Hartford, along with Color and Design, Lasting Image Video, and TFG Film and Video.

The staff at the John and Mable Ringling Museum of Art in Sarasota, Florida, provided unlimited access to the voluminous material on Austin's tenure as director, particularly my friend and colleague, Deborah W. Walk, curator of the Circus Museum and Historical Resources. I also thank David Ebitz, director; Lynell A. Morr, museum librarian; Edward Amatore, registrar; Ronald McCarty, associate registrar; Rebecca Englehardt of Photographic Services; and Heidi Anderson, Marian Coker, and Beatrice Warfield.

I am profoundly grateful to the board of trustees and the entire staff of the Wadsworth Atheneum, from the volunteers at the information desk to the presidents of the museum. For nearly twenty years, this wonderful institutional family has supported and nurtured the process of rediscovering Chick Austin. I would like to thank the three directors under whom I have served. Tracy Atkinson encouraged me in my work as archivist and curator of the Austin House and supported the exhibition and events surrounding the fiftieth anniversary of the Avery Memorial and *Four Saints in Three Acts*. Patrick McCaughey enthusiastically endorsed my undertaking this book, allowed me to take a leave of absence to do much of the writing, read many of the early chapters, and gave me the benefit of his insight into the art that Chick Austin promoted and the human story that he represented. Peter Sutton's keen and continuous support of the book enabled me to bring it to fruition. The Atheneum's curatorial staff, past and present, has been unfailingly helpful, beginning with chief curator Gregory Hedberg, deputy director and chief curator Kristen Mortimer, and chief curator Elizabeth Mankin Kornhauser (who also assisted me in her capacities of acting director and Krieble curator of American paintings, sculpture and drawings), along with the Atheneum's librarians, Elizabeth Hoke and John Teahan, and our wonderful curatorial administrator, Gertrud Pfister Bourgoyne. Jean K. Cadogan and Eric M. Zafran, successive curators of European painting, as well as Andrea Miller-Keller, the museum's former Emily Hall Tremaine curator of contemporary art, gave me the benefit of their scholarship and deep understanding of the art that Chick Austin acquired and exhibited. Also especially helpful were Thomas Denenberg, Richard Koopman associate curator of American decorative arts, and William N. Hosley, Jr., former Richard Koopman curator of American decorative arts; Carol Dean Krute, curator of costume and textiles; Linda Roth, Charles C. and Eleanor Lamont curator of European decorative arts; Deirdre Bibby, curator of African American art and executive director of The Amistad Foundation; registrars David Parrish, Mary Ellen Goeke, Martha Small, and Matthew Siegal and their staff; Lynn Mervosh, rights and reproductions coordinator; Cecil Adams, head of exhibitions; Jeremy R. Barrows, marketing manager; and Susan Hood, public relations officer. Every other department, in its own way, has contributed to this book.

I would like to acknowledge, as well, my close friends and mentors, the late Albert E. Van Dusen and his wife, Wilda, who introduced me to Connecticut's history and taught me essential lessons about the art of historical research.

I am deeply grateful to Melinda Martin Sullivan and her husband, Dr. Paul R. C. Sullivan, for generously providing the color plates of the Austin House and many of the masterpieces Chick Austin acquired during his career. Melinda Sullivan has been unswerving in her belief in the significance of the Austin House as an American cultural landmark. For more than a decade, her support of its restoration has been unequaled.

Judith Jones, my distinguished editor at Knopf, had faith that an untested author could sustain a narrative about the life of Chick Austin. I cannot thank her sufficiently for her kindness, patience, and wisdom. I am extremely grateful to her step-daughter, Bronwyn Dunne, who, after an hour's conversation one afternoon at the museum, brought me to Judith's attention. Working with the staff at Knopf—particularly editorial assistant Kenneth Schneider, production editor Kevin Bourke, designers Virginia Tan and Steven Amsterdam, publicity director Nicholas Latimer, associate publicity director Kathryn Zuckerman, and subscription rights director Sean Yule—has been a joy.

My dear friend Ann Brandwein, assistant archivist at the Wadsworth

Atheneum, has been the principal research assistant on this biography, working by my side for many years. With patience and good cheer, she has been involved in every phase of the thinking and writing. She has offered insightful editorial comments and has been a continuous source of moral support. This book could not have been written without her help.

Finally, I thank my family, whose encouragement and patience have sustained me. My wife, Alison Lane-Reticker, tirelessly read and reread the manuscript, offering astute editorial suggestions. David, Jonathan, and Elizabeth have put up with ten years of constant references to Chick with good humor.

I have made every effort to use original sources wherever possible and to check the accuracy of all statements. All errors, however, are solely my responsibility.

Eugene R. Gaddis,
Hartford,
April 22, 2000

ABBREVIATIONS

AEA	A. Everett Austin, Jr.
AP	Austin Papers, WAA
Building Recs.	Building Records, WAA
DEA	David Etnier Austin
Director's Taste	*A. Everett Austin, Jr.: A Director's Taste and Achievement* (Hartford: Wadsworth Atheneum, 1958)
HC	*Hartford Courant*
HGA	Helen Goodwin Austin
HT	*Hartford Times*
LEA	Laura Etnier Austin
LEA Paps.	Laura Etnier Austin Papers, WAA
Object Files	Object Files, Registrar's Office, Wadsworth Atheneum
SGA	Sarah Goodwin Austin
Special File	Special File, WAA
Trustees Recs.	Trustee Records, WAA
WAA	Wadsworth Atheneum Archives
Year Files	Year Files, WAA

PROLOGUE

1. Edward M. M. Warburg in conversation, Jan. 7, 1983.

2. Le Corbusier, *Quand les cathédrales étaient blanches: voyage au pays des timides* (Paris: Librairie Plon, 1937), pp. 129–30.

3. Alfred Barr to AEA, [June] 1944, AP.

4. Philip Johnson, recorded lecture, Avery Theater, Wadsworth Atheneum, Feb. 25, 1984.

CHAPTER 1

1. Marguerite Yourcenar, recorded interview, Aug. 2, 1982.

2. Funeral Address by the Rev. J. R. Davies, quoted in "Genealogy of the Families Etnier, Etnire, Etnyre, Itneyer, Itnyer, Itnyre: Descendants of Johannes Eydne(?)er," ed. Oliver L. Etnier, 1935, LEA Papers.

3. Ruth Vuille Stewart, recorded interview, May 17, 1993.

4. Arthur Everett Austin, Sr., to Francis H. Brown, Jan. 17, 1896, Brown Catalog of Harvard Medical School, Francis A. Countway Library of Medicine, Boston, Mass.

5. LEA, Draft of Will, Nov. 26, 1900, LEA Papers.

6. LEA, "Baby Days," 1900–29, AP.

7. LEA, "Physicians Diary," 1901, AP.

8. Ralph Childs, recorded interview, May 1986.

9. Virginia Etnier House to AEA, July 4, 1906, "Baby Days."

10. AEA to LEA, Feb. 16, 1906, Ibid.

11. Faculty Minutes, Oct. 2, 1908, Tufts University Archives, Boston, Mass.

12. LEA, "Uncle John's," c. 1913–15, LEA Papers.

13. AEA, April 28, 1910, "Baby Days."

14. Bradford Sprout, recorded interview, Jan. 21, 1993; Henry Sayles Francis, recorded interview, March 12, 1992.

15. Bradford Sprout, recorded interview, Jan. 21, 1993.

16. AEA to LEA, Oct. 3, 1912, AP.

17. Ibid., Oct. 4, 1912, AP.

18. Ibid., Oct. 10, 1912, AP.

19. Ibid., Oct. 16, 1912, AP.

20. AEA, "A Great Wreck," c. 1912–13, AP.

21. AEA, "Our Doctor," c. 1913–14, AP.

22. Paul Geissler, recorded interview, Jan. 4, 1991.

23. LEA, Uncle John's.

24. Ibid.

25. Ibid.

26. Newspaper article, "Baby Days."

27. Stephen Etnier, recorded interview, Aug. 1983.

28. Ralph Childs, recorded interview, May 1986.

29. SGA, recorded interview, April 15, 1986.

30. Once, in the late 1930s, Austin drove to Boston with a magic assistant, Arlene Johnson, in his newest car, an English Swallow. She remembered: "Chick parked a few blocks from his house and said, 'Now we're going to walk the rest of the way. Don't mention the automobile to my mother.' I thought, 'Isn't this weird? This head of a museum—and yet he couldn't tell his mother about the English Swallow.'" Arlene Johnson Baum, in conversation, April 10, 1992.

31. Newspaper article, "Baby Days."

CHAPTER 2

1. LEA to Chester N. Greenough, May 17, 1920, AEA, Undergraduate File, Harvard University Archives, Cambridge, Mass.

2. Richard Collier, The Plague of the Spanish Lady (Forge Village, Mass.: Murray Printing Co., 1974), p. 80.

3. Harvard Class of 1922: Twenty-fifth Anniversary Report (Cambridge, Mass.: Harvard University, 1947), pp. 361–2, 451.

4. The Harvard Freshman Red Book: The Year Book of the Class of 1922 (Cambridge, Mass.: Harvard University, 1919), pp. 182–5; Harvard 1921 Class Album (Cambridge, Mass.: Harvard University, 1921), p. 143.

5. AEA, "The Undergraduate Library," n.d., AP.

6. Kenneth B. Murdock to Arthur Everett Austin, Sr., April 14, 1919, AEA, Undergraduate File.

7. AEA, Transcript, 1918–24, AEA, Undergraduate File.

8. Murdock to AEA, July 2, 1919, AEA, Undergraduate File.

9. LEA to Chester N. Greenough, May 17, 1920.

10. AEA to the Gentlemen of the Faculty, Aug. 28, 1919, AEA, Undergraduate File.

11. Arthur Pope, "Report on Courses," Fine Arts 2c, April 24, 1920, AEA, Undergraduate File.

12. LEA to Chester N. Greenough, May 17, 1920.

13. Arthur Everett Austin, Sr., to LEA, June 2, 1920, AP.

14. Donald C. Starr, recorded interview, April 9, 1991.

15. HT, Feb. 11, 1932.

16. Warren R. Dawson and Eric P. Uphill, Who Was Who in Egyptology (London: Egypt Exploration Society, 1972), pp. 244–5.

17. Bill Pronzini, Tales of the Dead (New York: Bonanza Books, 1986), pp. 295–6; Donald C. Willis, Horror and Science Fiction Films: A Checklist (Metuchen, N.J.: Scarecrow Press, 1972), pp. 151, 334.

18. SGA, recorded interview, Feb. 17, 1992.

19. LEA, n.d., in untitled notebook, AP.

20. Sir E. A. Wallis Budge, Cook's Handbook for Egypt and the Sûdân (London: Thomas Cook & Son, 1921), p. 11.

21. Chandler R. Post, "Painting of St. Jerome, by Ribera," Fogg Art Museum, Harvard University, Notes, Vol. I, No. 2 (June 1922), pp. 15–21.

22. AEA to Edward R. Gay [Oct. 1922], AEA, Undergraduate File.

23. Budge, p. 948.

24. George A. Reisner, "Confidential Report," [Dec. 1921], Reisner File, 1922,

Boston Museum of Fine Arts, Egyptology Department, Boston, Mass.

25. T. H. Parker, "Austin and the Theater," *Director's Taste,* p. 54.

26. Reisner, "Confidential Report."

27. More than two thousand years before Christ, there had been continuous traffic between Egypt and Ethiopia by caravan. The Egyptians traded faience beads, stone vessels, and other manufactured goods with the Ethiopians in return for slaves, leopard skins, resins, ebony, ivory, and gold from the mines in the eastern deserts. Around 900 B.C., as the Egyptian empire weakened, a family originating in southern Libya established itself as a power at Napata near the fourth cataract of the Nile. Two centuries later, a king of Kush moved north and conquered all of Egypt. Though driven back to ancient Ethiopia by the Assyrians in the next century, the kings of Kush remained powerful in Napata until about 300 B.C., when a branch of the royal family moved the capital of Ethiopia to Meroë, where they reigned for over six centuries. Weakened by the Romans in the first century A.D., the Meroitic kingdom was finally destroyed around 350 A.D. by the Abyssinians. After that the ancient sites fell into ruin and near oblivion.

28. *HT,* Oct. 25, 1927.

29. John A. Wilson, *Signs and Wonders upon Pharaoh* (Chicago: University of Chicago Press, 1964), p. 148.

30. Dows Dunham, *Recollections of an Egyptologist* (Boston: Museum of Fine Arts, 1972), p. 27.

31. Mrs. M. T. Symonds to George A. Reisner, March 1923, Correspondence, 1921–3, Boston Museum of Fine Arts, Egyptology Department, Boston, Mass.

32. Richard Buckle, *Diaghilev* (New York: Atheneum, 1979), p. 412. Of Picasso's set for *Pulcinella,* Buckle wrote that it was "one of the most beautiful stage settings ever made." Ibid. p. 362.

33. *HC,* Nov. 21, 1934.

34. AEA to Edward R. Gay, Sept. 21, 1923, AEA, Undergraduate File.

35. Ibid.

36. LEA to Lloyd Scott Etnier, April 15, 1940, LEA Papers.

37. Oliver Etnier to LEA, April 7, 1929, LEA Papers.

38. LEA to Stephen Etnier, April 20, 1940, LEA Papers.

39. LEA to Lloyd Scott Etnier, April 15, 1940, LEA Papers.

40. John Coolidge, "Foreword," *Edward Waldo Forbes, Yankee Visionary,* (Cambridge, Mass.: Fogg Art Museum, Harvard University, 1971), p. 3.

41. Edward W. Forbes, "The Campaign for a New Museum," *Fogg Art Museum, Harvard University, Notes,* Vol. II, No. 1 (April 1925), p. 21.

42. Rosamond Forbes Pickhardt, recorded interview, March 16, 1992.

43. Agnes Mongan, "Introduction," *Edward Waldo Forbes, Yankee Visionary,* p. viii.

44. LEA to Edward W. Forbes [June 1924], Forbes Files, Fogg Art Museum Archives, Harvard University, Cambridge, Mass.

CHAPTER 3

1. Daniel V. Thomson, *The Materials of Medieval Painting* (New Haven, Conn.: Yale University Press, 1936), p. 9. Thompson's brother was the composer Randall Thompson.

2. Thompson to Edward W. Forbes, Oct. 12, 1924, Forbes Papers, Fogg Art Museum Archives, Harvard University, Cambridge, Mass.

3. Forbes to AEA, Sept. 9, 1924, Forbes Papers.

4. Thompson to Forbes, Sept. 24, 1924, Forbes Papers.

5. Ibid., Oct. 12, 1924.

6. AEA to Forbes, Oct. 17, 1924, Forbes Papers.

7. Ibid., Nov. 23, 1924.

8. Ibid.

9. Forbes to AEA, Oct. 28, 1924, Forbes Papers.

10. AEA to Forbes, Nov. 23, 1924, Forbes Papers.

11. Edward W. Forbes, "A. Everett Austin, Jr.," *Director's Taste*, p. 17.

12. Howard M. Nixon, "Binding Forgeries," *International Association of Bibliophiles, Proceedings* (1977), p. 69.

13. A few years after Chick met him, Ioni described his shady practices in an autobiography known in the English translation as *Affairs of a Painter*. He blithely admitted that sometimes he saturated the market with fakes. At the same time, Ioni denied that he was guilty of forgery. "An artist who creates a work of art of his own, in imitation of the style of an old master, is not a forger; he is at worst an imitator, and he is creating something of his own." J. F. Ioni, *Affairs of a Painter* (London: Faber and Faber Limited, 1936), pp. 338–9.

14. Ibid., p. 343.

15. Forbes to AEA, Jan. 6, 1925, Forbes Papers.

16. Edward W. Forbes, *Fogg Art Museum, Harvard University, Collection of Mediaeval and Renaissance Paintings* (Cambridge, Mass.: Harvard University Press, 1927), pp. ix–x.

17. Edward W. Forbes, "The Campaign for a New Museum," *Fogg Art Museum, Harvard University, Notes*, Vol. II, No. 1 (April 1925), pp. 22, 26–7.

18. Agnes Mongan, recorded interview, Nov. 24, 1974.

19. John Coolidge, recorded interview, March 14, 1990.

20. Agnes Mongan, "Introduction," *Edward Waldo Forbes, Yankee Visionary*, p. vii.

21. John Coolidge, recorded interview, March 14, 1990.

22. Forbes, "The Campaign for a New Museum," pp. 23–4, 28.

23. Paul Sachs, "The New Fogg Art Museum," *The Arts*, Vol. XII, No. 1 (July 1927), pp. 10–11.

24. Paul Sachs, "Tales of an Epoch," Vol. II, unpublished typescript, 1958, Fogg Art Museum Archives, p. 169.

25. Ironically, it was the self-effacing Forbes who seemed the most difficult to resist when he came to call. After years of experience, J. P. Morgan, Jr., said that he found it much simpler to reach for his checkbook than to try to explain to Forbes why he could not really afford to give him a gift right at that moment. John Coolidge, recorded interview, March 14, 1990.

26. Forbes, "The Campaign for a New Museum," p. 32.

27. Julien Levy, *Memoirs of an Art Gallery* (New York: G. P. Putnam's Sons, 1977), p. 135.

28. John McAndrew, recorded interview, Nov. 4, 1974.

29. Henry-Russell Hitchcock, recorded interview, Dec. 9, 1974.

30. Philip Johnson, recorded interview, Nov. 30, 1982.

31. Virgil Thomson, *Virgil Thomson* (New York: Alfred A. Knopf, 1966), p. 214.

32. Virgil Thomson, "The Friends and Enemies of Modern Music," *Director's Taste*, p. 61.

33. Philip Johnson, recorded interview, Nov. 30, 1982.

34. Paul Cadmus, recorded interview, July 8, 1996.

35. AEA to George Edgell, Nov. 9, 1925, Harvard University Archives, Cambridge, Mass.

36. Forbes to AEA, Oct. 29, 1925, Forbes Papers.

37. Ibid., Nov. 25, 1925.

38. Ibid., Jan. 13, 1926.

39. Harold W. Parsons to Paul Sachs, May 16, 1926, Paul Sachs Papers, Fogg Art Museum Archives, Harvard University, Cambridge, Mass.

40. Sachs to Parsons, June 4, 1926, Sachs Papers.

41. Parsons to Sachs, Aug. 22, 1926, Sachs Papers.

42. Ibid., Sept. 26, 1926.

43. AEA to Forbes, Aug. 17, 1926, Forbes Papers.

44. Ibid.

45. Agnes Rindge, recorded interview, Nov. 18, 1974.

46. AEA to Forbes, Aug. 17, 1926, Forbes Papers.

47. Virgil Thomson, videotaped interview, May 17, 1988.

48. AEA to Forbes, Aug. 17, 1926, Forbes Papers.

49. Forbes to AEA, Sept. 8, 1926, Forbes Papers.

50. Paul Sachs, "Tales of an Epoch," Vol. III, p. 214.

51. Agnes Mongan, recorded interview, Nov. 24, 1974.

52. John Coolidge, recorded interview, March 14, 1990.

53. AEA, "A Study of Technique," *The Arts,* Vol. XII, No. 1 (July 1927), p. 20.

CHAPTER 4

1. Goodwin preferred nautical subjects. On a family trip to the British Isles, he spent most of his time afloat, exploring the coasts. At Falmouth, he snapped forty-eight well-focused photographs of *Cutty Sark,* but his few ventures into English art museums were remembered by his children as a blur. Dorothy Goodwin, recorded interview, March 16, 1990.

2. "Director's Report for 1927," Trustees Recs.

3. Edward W. Forbes to Charles A. Goodwin, Jan. 19, 1927, Special File.

4. Goodwin to Theodore Sizer, March 15, 1927, Special File.

5. Goodwin to Forbes, May 9, 1927, Special File.

6. Paul J. Sachs to Goodwin, March 31, 1927, Sachs Papers, Fogg Art Museum Archives; Goodwin to Forbes, May 9, 1927, Special File.

7. Forbes to Goodwin, May 13, 1927, Special File.

8. Goodwin to Forbes, May 18, 1927; Forbes to Goodwin, May 20, 1927, Special File.

9. William B. Goodwin, "Notes on Primitive Furniture in New England," *Bulletin of the Wadsworth Atheneum* (April 1925), p. 21.

10. LEA to AEA, [1927], AP.

11. Goodwin to Forbes, June 9, 1927, Special File.

12. Forbes to Goodwin, June 14, 1927, Special File.

13. *HC,* June 29, 1927.

14. Frank Gay to Forbes, Aug. 16, 1927, Special File.

15. "Report of the Treasurer for the Year 1928," Financial Recs., WAA.

16. Forbes to Goodwin, Sept. 20, 1927, Special File.

17. Goodwin to Forbes, Sept. 26, 1927, Special File.

18. Florence Berkman in conversation, Jan. 2, 1991.

19. Kenneth Lee, recorded interview, Sept. 26, 1989.

20. *Hartford Directory,* 1928.

21. Ann Carolyn (Bissell) Prud'homme, recorded interview, Feb. 14, 1985.

22. LEA to AEA, Nov. 4, 1927, AP.

23. Ibid., [1927].

24. Susan Etnier to AEA, [Nov. 1927], AP.

25. *HC,* Oct. 25, 1927.

26. Ibid., Oct. 30, 1927.

27. *HT,* Nov. 12, 1927.

28. Francis Goodwin II, recorded interview, Jan. 9, 1975.

CHAPTER 5

1. They were Robert W. Huntington, president of the Connecticut General Life Insurance Company; Arthur P. Day, vice chairman of the Hartford-Connecticut Trust Company; William R. C. Corson, president and treasurer of the Hartford Steam Boiler and Inspection Insurance Company; Francis Parsons, vice-chairman of the Hartford National Bank and Trust Company; and Henry W. Erving, vice president of the Connecticut River Banking Company and a nationally known collector of American colonial furniture.

2. Edward W. Forbes, notes, [Oct. 1927], Special File.

3. Wadsworth Atheneum, Trustees' Minutes, Vol. 2, p. 71.

4. Forbes to AEA, Dec. 5, 1927, Special File.

5. Bernard Berenson to Forbes, Dec. 30, 1927, Object File. Jean K. Cadogan, editor, *Wadsworth Atheneum Paintings II: Italy and Spain: Fourteenth Through Nineteenth Centuries* (Hartford: Wadsworth Atheneum, 1991), pp. 247–8. A few years later, the eminent Italian scholar Lionello Venturi also attributed the painting to Tintoretto.

6. AEA, "A Painting by Tintoretto," *Bulletin of the Wadsworth Atheneum,* [Vol. VI, No. 1] (Jan. 1928), pp. 2–4.

7. *HT,* March 17, 1928.

8. AEA to Adam Paff, Dec. 15, 1927, Object File.

9. AEA to Forbes, Dec. 15 and Dec. 22, 1927, Special File.

10. Ibid., Dec. 31.

11. AEA to Rolf H. Waegen, Feb. 16, 1928, AP.

12. Forbes to Paul J. Sachs, Jan. 24?, 1928, Sachs Papers, Fogg Archives.

13. *HT,* Jan. 25, 1928.

14. *Art News,* Jan. 21, 1928; *The Christian Science Monitor,* Jan. 23, 1928.

15. *HT,* Jan. 17, 1928; *HC,* Jan. 19, 1928.

16. Dorothy Goodwin, recorded interview, March 16, 1990.

17. *HT,* Jan. 25, 1928.

18. Ibid., Feb. 3, 1928.

19. Cadogan, pp. 247–8.

20. *HT,* Jan. 28, 1928.

21. AEA to James L. McConaughy, Jan. 25, 1928.

22. AEA to Forbes, Dec. 15, 1927, Special File.

23. George Starkey, recorded interview, Nov. 27, 1991; Bard McNulty, recorded interview, Feb. 1983; Hugh Campbell, recorded interview, Dec. 15, 1982.

24. Hugh Campbell, recorded interview, Dec. 15, 1982.

25. Bard McNulty, recorded interview, Feb. 1982.

26. Ibid.

27. AEA, Lecture notes of History of Art course given at Wesleyan University, [Jan. 1928], AP.

28. *HC,* May 11, 1928.

29. Ibid., May 17, 1928.

30. *HT,* Feb. 3, 1928.

31. *HT,* March 17, 1928.

32. Ibid., April 20, 1928.

33. LEA to AEA, March 18, 1928, AP.

34. Charles A. Goodwin to Garrett J. Farrell, April 19, 1928.

35. *HT,* April 21, 1928.

36. Ibid.

37. *Silhouettes,* May 1928, p. 15.

38. *HT,* April 21, 1928.

39. AEA to Sachs, May 24, 1928; Sachs to AEA, May 28, 1928; AEA to Forbes, June 5, 1928.

40. *HC,* April 21, 1928. Parker was the son of the famous Boston music critic, H. T. Parker.

41. *Wadsworth Atheneum Bulletin,* Vol. VI, No. 2 (April 1928), p. 16.

42. Duncan Phillips, "A Collection Still in the Making," *Formes* (Nov. 1930), p. 7.

43. *HC,* May 4, 1928.

44. Ibid., May 11, 1928.

45. Russell Lynes, *Good Old Modern* (New York: Atheneum, 1973), p. 65.

46. AEA to Mrs. John Alden Carpenter, May 24, 1928, AP.

47. AEA to Paul Vanderbilt, May 26, 1928, AP.

48. Florence Paull Berger to E. Wyhe, Aug. 28, 1929, Berger Papers, WAA.

49. Forbes to AEA, May 4, 1928; AEA to Forbes, June 5, 1928, AP.

50. AEA to Forbes, June 5, 1928, AP.

51. Abandoning his law office as usual for the cockpit of his yacht, Charles Goodwin headed north with his nephew Francis Goodwin to take his brother Spencer's new seventy-eight-foot German sloop, *Waiandance,* on her maiden voyage from New Foundland to Connecticut. The trip proved

as arduous as any Goodwin could have wished. Caught in a tremendous gale, the boat lost all her sails and drifted for days off the Grand Banks.

52. Forbes to AEA, May 4, 1928, AP.

53. Citing the sale that summer of a Raphael *Madonna and Child* to Sir Joseph Duveen for an unprecedented $875,000, Chick warned of a rapid escalation in prices and predicted that "in five to ten years, the mediocre and second-class pictures will take the places of many objects still to be obtained." *HT,* Aug. 24, 1928.

54. AEA, "A Small Tempera Panel by Fra Angelico," *Wadsworth Atheneum Bulletin* (Jan. 1929), pp. 2–3.

55. AEA, "A Water Color by Daumier," *Wadsworth Atheneum Bulletin* (Oct. 1928), pp. 28–9.

56. AEA to Sachs, Aug. 28, 1928, Object File.

57. Sachs to AEA, Aug. 30, 1928, Object File.

58. Sachs to Forbes, [c. Sept. 12, 1928], copy with Forbes to AEA, Sept. 12, 1928, Object File.

59. *HT,* Oct. 20, 1928.

60. Forbes to AEA, Dec. 5, 1928, AP.

61. AEA to Frank M. Rehn, Dec. 5, 1928, AP.

62. AEA, Introduction of Ernst Krenek, Dec. 13, 1938, typescript, AP.

63. Mary Edwards, recorded interview, Jan. 30, 1991.

64. Walter Schwinn, recorded interview, Jan. 23, 1991.

65. Elliott Carter, recorded interview, May 19, 1989.

66. Philip Johnson, recorded interview, Nov. 30, 1982.

67. Clifton J. Furness to AEA, Nov. 25, 1928, AP.

68. S. F. Westbrook to AEA, Dec. 19, 1932, AP.

69. AEA to S. W. Reyburn, March 3, 1928; S. W. Reyburn to AEA, March 1 and 13, 1928.

70. *HT,* Aug. 24, 1928.

71. Ibid., Dec. 19, 1928.

72. Ibid., Dec. 12, 1928.

73. Ibid.

74. Hugh Campbell, recorded interview, Dec. 15, 1982.

75. *HC,* Jan. 6, 1929.

76. Hugh Campbell, recorded interview, Dec. 15, 1982.

CHAPTER 6

1. Henry-Russell Hitchcock, recorded interview, Dec. 9, 1974.

2. HGA to Frances Goodwin, July 9, 1927, AP.

3. Ruth Goodwin to HGA, May 28, 1928, AP.

4. Francis Goodwin II, recorded interview, January 9, 1975.

5. HGA in conversation, May 12, 1982.

6. *HC,* Jan. 4, 1917.

7. Mary Alsop Goodwin to HGA, March 21, 1920, AP.

8. HGA, "My Trip Abroad," travel diary, 1921, AP.

9. HGA to Frances Goodwin, Feb. 2, 1924, AP.

10. HGA to Mary and Wilton Graff, July 7, 1927, AP.

11. HGA to Frances Goodwin, July 19, 1927, AP.

12. HGA to Miss Harris, June 18, 1928, AP.

13. Ruth Ford, recorded interview, May 17, 1983.

14. Francis Goodwin II, recorded interview, Jan. 9, 1975.

15. Lucy Goodwin Stone, recorded interview, Nov. 9, 1989.

16. Susan Etnier to HGA, [March] 1929, AP.

17. Lucy Goodwin Stone, recorded interview, Nov. 9, 1989.

18. Joella Levy Bayer, recorded interview, July 5, 1991.

19. Virgil Thomson, recorded interview, May 17, 1988.

20. Lucy Goodwin Stone, recorded interview, Nov. 9, 1989.

21. Virgil Thomson, recorded interview, Nov. 1974.

22. Ibid.

23. AEA to HGA, Jan. 27, 1929, AP.

24. Ibid., Feb. 10, 1929, AP.

25. Virgil Thomson, recorded interview, May 17, 1988.

26. Henry-Russell Hitchcock, recorded interview, Dec. 9, 1974.

27. AEA to HGA, Feb. 10, 1929, AP.

28. Ibid., Feb. 16, 1929, AP.

29. Winslow Ames, recorded interview, Oct. 25, 1974.

30. Josephine Lippincott Goodwin to HGA, March 23, 1929, AP.

31. Philip Goodwin to HGA, March 24, 1929.

32. Philip Goodwin to AEA, March 25, 1929, AP.

33. Susan Etnier to HGA, [March] 1929, AP.

34. Remsen Ogilby to AEA, March 27, 1929, AP.

35. *HC*, c. 1965, AP.

36. AEA to HGA, April 15, 1929, AP.

37. Lucy Goodwin Stone, recorded interview, Nov. 9, 1989.

38. LEA to AEA, May 20, 1929, AP.

39. Ibid., June 9, 1929, AP.

40. Lucy Goodwin Stone, recorded interview, Oct. 31, 1989.

41. Mary Parsons Robinson, recorded interview, Feb. 1982.

42. Francis Goodwin II, recorded interview, Jan. 9, 1975.

43. Lucy Goodwin Stone, recorded interview, Oct. 31, 1989.

44. The brocatelle was later determined to be a nineteenth-century copy of an earlier pattern.

45. Adolf Loewi to AEA, Sept. 26, 1929, AP.

46. Jared Edwards in conversation, 1983.

47. Jaqueline Goodwin in conversation, Jan. 9, 1991.

48. Lucy Goodwin Stone, recorded interview, Nov. 9, 1989.

49. Henry-Russell Hitchcock, recorded interview, Dec. 9, 1974.

50. Adolf Loewi to AEA, Nov. 14, 1929, AP.

51. AEA to Adolf Loewi, March 23, 1932, AP.

52. Robert Cole in conversation, Sept. 18, 1989.

53. Comparing the house to the outrageously gaudy brick mansion that Edward Tuckerman Potter built in Hartford for Samuel Clemens, Virgil Thomson remarked that "if anybody thought Chick's new house was odd, I don't know what the hell they thought of the Mark Twain house, which had been there for some time. . . . [At least] everybody could recognize that Chick's house was neo-something-or-other." Virgil Thomson, recorded interview, May 17, 1988.

54. Winslow Ames, recorded interview, Oct. 25, 1974.

55. The Austin house soon became the subject of folklore in Hartford. It was said that the house was part of a movie set that was never taken down, or that it was only a false front erected to camouflage electrical equipment or a water tower or a much smaller house that was not in keeping with its grander neighbors.

56. Friend of Hugh Campbell, in conversation, ca. 1986.

57. *HC*, March 10, 1930.

58. Ibid., Dec. 17, 1930.

59. Henry-Russell Hitchcock, "A. Everett Austin, Jr. and Architecture," *Director's Taste*, p. 40.

60. Henry-Russell Hitchcock, recorded interview, Dec. 9, 1974.

61. Philip Johnson, lecture at WA, Feb. 25, 1984.

62. Lincoln Kirstein to ERG, June 20, 1985; Jan. 11, 1985, ERG Correspondence.

63. Philip Johnson, lecture at WA, Feb. 25, 1984.

64. Ralph Childs, recorded interview, May 1986.

CHAPTER 7

1. *Wadsworth Atheneum and Morgan Memorial, Fourth Annual Report,* 1928, p. 4.

2. Bryce Muir, recorded interview, Aug. 3, 1987.

3. AEA to HGA, n.d. [1929], AP.

4. AEA to Grace L. Hoadley, March 13, 1929, AP.

5. AEA, "Last Week of Important Loan Show of French Eighteenth Century Paintings," 1929, typescript, AP.

6. *HT,* Jan. 16, 1929.

7. In 1925 the Arts Club of Chicago mounted a show of eighteenth-century French paintings, furniture, and decorative arts, drawn from Felix Wildenstein, who had apparently sent the works directly from an exhibition in their New York gallery. The next year, the Detroit Institute of Arts presented a major exhibition of French paintings (with nearly three times the number of oils as in Chick's show), claiming to illustrate "for the first time in any single exhibition, the rich resources of eighteenth-century French painting in America." Josephine Walther, "Foreword," *A Loan Exhibition of French Paintings* (Detroit: Detroit Institute of Arts, 1926), [p. 1].

8. Paul Sachs to AEA, Jan. 4, 1929, AP.

9. *Loan Exhibition of French Art of the Eighteenth-Century* (Hartford: Wadsworth Atheneum, 1929), p. 2.

10. *HC,* Jan. 12, 1929.

11. Ibid., Jan. 24, 1929.

12. Goodwin to AEA, Jan. 24, 1929, AP.

13. Forbes to Goodwin, May 7, 1929; Goodwin to Forbes, May 8, 1929; Forbes to Goodwin, May 10, 1929, Special File.

14. *HC,* Jan. 26, 1929.

15. AEA to S. R. Bertron, Jan. 4, 1929, AP.

16. AEA to Wildenstein, Nov. 16, 1927, AP.

17. Ibid., Oct. 26 and Oct. 31, 1928, AP.

18. *Bulletin of the Wadsworth Atheneum,* Vol. VII, No. 1 (Jan. 1929), pp. 4–5.

19. Kirk Askew to AEA, March 21, 1929, AP.

20. *HC,* April 14, 1929.

21. AEA to HGA, April 14, 1929, AP.

22. *The Arts,* Vol. XIII, No. 6 (June 1928), pp. 391–2; Vol. XIV, No. 5 (Nov. 1928), pp. 289–90; Vol. XV, No. 1 (Jan. 1929), pp. 56–9; Vol. XV, No. 3 (March 1929), pp. 204–5.

23. Julien Levy, *Memoir of an Art Gallery* (New York: G. P. Putnam's Sons, 1977), p. 11.

24. Vachel Lindsay, *The Art of the Moving Picture* (New York: Liveright Publishing Corp., 1970), p. 28.

25. Russell Lynes, *Good Old Modern* (New York: Atheneum, 1973), p. 110.

26. AEA to Jay Leyda, Oct. 7, 1929, AP.

27. AEA to J. Croteau, May 17, 1929, AP.

28. *HC,* April 17, 1929.

29. *HT,* May 8, 1929.

30. AEA to A. Croteau, May 17, 1929, AP.

31. Ibid.

32. AEA to Lizzie Bliss, Dec. 14, 1929, AP.

33. Askew to AEA, Nov. 20, 1929, AP.

34. *HT,* Nov. 30, 1929.

35. *New Britain Herald,* Dec. 7, 1929.

36. Ibid., Dec. 9, 1929.

37. Ibid., Dec. 19, 1929.

38. *Art News,* Vol. 28, No. 13 (Dec. 28, 1929), p. 14.

39. AEA to Lizzie Bliss, Dec. 14, 1929, AP.

40. John Ruskin, *Lectures on Architecture and Painting* (New York: Merrill and Baker, n.d.), p. 303.

41. Agnes Mongan, recorded interview, July 21, 1983.

42. Bernhard Berenson, *The Italian Painters of the Renaissance* (London: Oxford University Press, 1930), p. 337.

43. Martin Green, *Children of the Sun* (New York: Basic Books, 1976), p. 155.

44. Sir Osbert Sitwell, "Foreword," *Director's Taste*, p. 15.

45. The Fogg's show was recognized abroad as "the first of its kind in America," but it was not nearly as comprehensive, nor did it have the same impact, as the Hartford exhibition. *Burlington Mazagine*, Vol. 55 (Aug. 1929), p. 105.

46. As early as the nineteenth century, the Detroit Institute of Arts was given a significant collection of pictures by seventeenth-century Italian artists. Three decades later, Detroit's German-born director, William Valentiner, keenly interested in the period, presented a series of exhibitions focusing on art from the Netherlands: *Seventeenth-Century Dutch Art* in 1925; the largest van Dyck show in the United States in 1929; and, in 1930, a loan exhibition of Rembrandt's works. In 1928 the Art Institute of Chicago organized a small show of Venetian paintings from the sixteenth through the eighteenth centuries.

47. *Burlington Magazine*, Vol. LV (Aug. 1929), p. 105.

48. AEA to John Ringling, Nov. 19, 1929, AP.

49. *HC*, Jan. 20, 1930.

50. AEA, "The Baroque," *1950 Art News Annual*, Vol. XIX, p. 12.

51. Arthur McComb, "Exhibition of Italian Paintings and Drawings of the Sei- and Settecento," *Parnassus*, Vol. II, No. 2 (Feb. 1930), p. 8.

52. *HC*, Jan. 20, 1930.

53. *Wadsworth Atheneum and Morgan Memorial, Sixth Annual Report*, 1930, p. 4. Attendance figures at this time were not necessarily accurate. The number of visitors recorded in the museum's door diary during the two weeks of the exhibition amounted to just under eight thousand.

54. Henry-Russell Hitchcock, *International Studio*, April 1930, p. 24.

55. Sterne reflected the usual metropolitan prejudice against small cities outside a certain radius of Manhattan. She noted that the early impact of the Hartford show was limited by "its inaccessibility." *New York Times*, Jan. 31, 1932.

56. Agnes Mongan, recorded interview, July 21, 1983.

57. Harold Woodbury Parsons, to AEA, [Feb. 1930], Object File.

58. Ibid.

59. John McAndrew, recorded interview, Oct. 15, 1974.

60. Agnes Mongan, recorded interview, Nov. 4, 1974.

61. AEA to Parsons, July 25, 1930, Object File.

62. Current scholarship identifies five versions of the picture. The first one Brass sent to Austin is now in the Buhler Collection in Zurich. See Jean K. Cadogan, ed., *Wadsworth Atheneum Paintings II: Italy and Spain: Fourteenth through Nineteenth Centuries* (Hartford: Wadsworth Atheneum, 1991), pp. 229–33.

63. Agnes Mongan, recorded interview, July 21, 1983.

64. Ibid., Nov. 24, 1974.

65. Lincoln Kirstein to ERG, Nov. 5, 1982.

66. Lincoln Kirstein, "The Ballet in Hartford," *Director's Taste*, p. 64.

67. *HT*, March 13, 1930.

68. Ibid., March 18, 1930.

69. R. Buckminster Fuller and Robert Marks, *The Dymaxion World of Buckminster Fuller* (Garden City, New York: Anchor Books, 1973), p. 20.

70. Katherine Anne Porter, then living in Mexico, lent three drawings by Xavier Guerrero. Pleased that Chick had taken the exhibition, she wrote him of her conviction "that Mexican painting, even with its prodigious faults, may be praised before any other for its energy and integrity" though it had been "overclouded by floods of amateur appreciation." Porter to AEA, July 1, 1930, Special File.

71. *HC*, April 22, 1930.

72. *Wadsworth Atheneum and Morgan Memorial, Sixth Annual Report*, 1930, p. 4.

73. *HT*, May 17, 1930.

74. AEA to W. R. Valentiner, June 7, 1930, AP.

75. *HT,* May 17, 1930.

76. Ibid., Dec. 13, 1930.

77. "Introductory Note," *Photography* (Hartford: Wadsworth Atheneum, 1930 [Cambridge: Harvard Society for Contemporary Art, 1930]).

78. *HT,* Dec. 13, 1930.

79. *Wadsworth Atheneum and Morgan Memorial, Sixth Annual Report,* 1930, p. 5.

80. *HC,* Nov. 13, 1930.

81. Florence Berkman in conversation, Sept. 17, 1992; *HC,* Nov. 15, 1930.

82. *Bulletin of the Wadsworth Atheneum,* Vol. VIII, No. 4 (Oct. 1930), pp. 38–9. Ironically, thirty years later, the portraits attributed to Smibert and Theus were found to be English pictures with false signatures, dates, and documentation. The mortified Robert Vose, who had been hoodwinked by his New York source, took them back and refunded the purchase price.

83. *HT,* Nov. 18, 1930.

84. James T. Soby, "A. Everett Austin, Jr. and Modern Art," *Director's Taste,* p. 32.

85. Austin's earliest known reference to Soby came in December 1930 in a letter to Duncan Phillips in Washington: "We have one collector of modern art in Hartford, a young one, who has bought nine or ten pictures during the last year, and this encourages me to hope that collecting in Hartford may develop [*sic*]." AEA to Phillips, Dec. 20, 1930, AP.

86. *HT,* Nov. 22, 1930.

87. *HC,* Jan. 12, 1931.

88. AEA to J. P. Morgan, Jr., Dec. 20, 1930, AP.

89. Florence Berkman in conversation, July 29, 1992.

90. AEA to Conger Goodyear, Jan. 5, 1931.

91. *HC,* Jan. 21, 1931.

92. Ibid., Jan. 18, 1931.

93. Ibid., Jan. 23, 1931.

94. AEA to Lizzie P. Bliss, Dec. 31, 1930.

95. *HC,* Jan. 23, 1931.

96. AEA, unpublished text for the Sumner Collection catalogue, c. 1946, Object File.

97. A. Silberman to AEA, Feb. 18, 1931, AP.

98. *Art News,* Vol. XXIX, No. 18 (Jan. 24, 1931), p. 20.

99. Cary Ross to AEA, Jan. 14, 1931, AP.

100. With the Depression entering its worst days, the Atheneum donated proceeds from catalogue sales to Hartford's unemployment fund.

101. Frances Bacheler to AEA, May 27, 1931, AP.

102. Secretary to AEA, note on Frances Bacheler to AEA, May 27, 1931, AP.

103. *Wadsworth Atheneum Annual Report,* 1931, p. 5.

104. *Bulletin of the Wadsworth Atheneum, Junius Spencer Morgan Memorial,* Vol. IX, No. 1 (Jan 1931), p. 3.

105. *Bulletin of the Wadsworth Atheneum, Junius Spencer Morgan Memorial,* Vol. IX, No. 3 (July 1931), p. 23.

106. AEA to Joseph Brummer, Feb. 17, 1931, AP.

107. *HT,* Nov. 19, 1930.

108. Julien Levy, "Dealing with A. Everett Austin, Jr.," *Director's Taste,* p. 33.

CHAPTER 8

1. Virgil Thomson, *Virgil Thomson* (New York: DeCapo Press, 1966), p. 165.

2. The other artists in the 1926 Paris group show were Pierre Charbonnier, J.-F. Laglenne, Therese Debains, and L. de Angelis.

3. Thomson, p. 164.

4. Hitchcock, "New Painters of Sentiment and Mystery," typescript, [1931], AP.

5. "As these things often are," Hitchcock explained later, "it was a matter of certain people who happened to know each other." Hitchcock, recorded interview, Dec. 9, 1974.

6. *Art News,* March 28, 1931, p. 13.

7. AEA to Duncan Phillips, Feb. 17, 1931, AP.

8. Phillips to AEA, Feb. 20, 1931, AP.

9. *HC,* April 4, 1931.

10. *HT,* Nov. 21, 1930.

11. AEA to Henry S. Francis, March 20, 1931, AP.

12. Maurice Sachs to AEA, March 2, 1931, AP.

13. Ever the impish commentator, Ross wished Austin success with his "trick exhibitions." Cary Ross to AEA, April 10, 1931, AP.

14. Notes by Henry-Russell Hitchcock, [March 1931], AP.

15. Van Vechten to AEA, April 13, 1931, AP.

16. *HC,* April 4, 1931.

17. Gertrude Stein, *The Autobiography of Alice B. Toklas,* pp. 280–3. From the distance of thirty years, Thomson admitted that "as draftsmen, all were strong; in painting it is doubtful whether any ever grew to be a master." They failed to produce a great advance for painting as they had few followers strong enough to overcome what he called "the Picasso marketeers." The Museum of Modern Art, in particular, had neglected them, he claimed, by canonizing the painters of the School of Paris, in part to legitimize the collections of its founders and trustees—a minority view shared by a few other prominent adherents of the Neo-Romantics. For them, these artists were keeping alive the art of fine drawing that was the legacy of centuries. Virgil Thomson, *Virgil Thomson,* pp. 93, 165.

18. Three hundred children were enrolled in the Saturday drawing class, where fifty at a time worked to the sound of Russian ballet music on the electrola. According to the *Courant,* the teacher Austin had just hired, Helen Henley, was "planning experiments with slow, languorous [sic] strains of Viennese waltzes, the cacophonies of jass and the buoyant airs of grand opera, to see if various effects can be produced." Soon the children had branched out into painting watercolors, carving linoleum, and weaving tapestries. *HC,* May 16, 1931.

19. Sixty years later, a small abstraction of 1927 that was probably one of his ten-dollar paintings was offered by the Richard York Gallery in New York for $12,000.

20. George Platt Lynes to AEA, April 11, 1931, AP.

21. *HC,* May 16, 1931.

22. AEA to Felix Wildenstein, June 3, 1931, AP.

23. SGA in conversation, 1983.

24. *HC,* July 30, 1931.

25. Henry-Russell Hitchcock, recorded interview, Dec. 9, 1974.

26. *HC,* June 7, 1931.

27. Marcel Jean, ed., *The Autobiography of Surrealism* (New York: Viking, 1980), pp. 120–1.

28. Julien Levy, *Memoir of an Art Gallery,* pp. 136–7.

29. Levy to AEA, Oct. 14, 1931, AP.

30. John McAndrew to AEA, Oct. 14, 1931, AP.

31. McAndrew to AEA, Jan. 6, 1932, AP.

32. AEA to Mrs. Chester Dale, Oct. 14, 1931, AP.

33. Mary Bullard to AEA, [Oct. 1931], AP.

34. AEA to Bullard, Oct. 20, 1931, AP.

35. Bullard to AEA, [Oct. 1931], AP. Chick also wrote, in care of Scribners, to Ernest Hemingway—who had been encouraged to collect by Gertrude Stein—asking him to lend works by André Masson, Max Ernst, and Paul Klee, but the novelist did not respond. AEA to Hemingway, Oct. 14, 1931, AP.

36. Conger Goodyear to AEA, Oct. 19, 1931, AP. Because of the uncertainty of the titles of pictures, many of the works in the exhibition are now difficult to identify.

37. AEA to Mrs. John D. Rockefeller, Nov. 10, 1931, AP.

38. Anna L. Kelly [for Mrs. John D. Rockefeller, Jr.] to HGA, Nov. 11, 1931, AP.

A telegram from Cary Ross noted that Mrs. Rockefeller was giving Roy's *Danger on the Staircase* to Helen Austin, rather than *Commice agricole*, which had already been listed in the catalogue. Ross to AEA, Nov. 11, 1931, AP. But *Commice agricole* came after all.

39. Julien Levy, "Dealing with A. Everett Austin, Jr.," *Director's Taste*, p. 34.

40. *HC*, undated newspaper clipping [Nov. 1931], WA scrapbook, p. 55, WAA.

41. *Newer Super-Realism* (Hartford; Wadsworth Atheneum, 1931), [p. 1]. Cary Ross sent Austin three poems for the catalogue, describing them as "almost completely super-realistic, although of course I have never understood what super-realism is." Ross to AEA, Nov. 9, 1931, AP.

42. Samuel Putnam, "The After-War Spirit in Literature," printed in an insert, "Notes on Surrealisme," in *Newer Super-Realism* catalogue.

43. *HC*, Nov. 16, 1931.

44. Ibid., Nov. 22, 1931.

45. *HT*, Nov. 19, 1931.

46. Ibid., Nov. 7, 1931.

47. *HC*, Undated newspaper clipping, WA scrapbook, p. 59.

48. *HC*, Nov. 22, 1931.

49. The work is now entitled *Portrait of Mistress Mills in 1750.*

50. *HT*, Nov. 7, 1931.

51. *Wadsworth Atheneum and Morgan Memorial, Seventh Annual Report*, 1931, p. 5.

52. James Thrall Soby, unpublished memoir, Chapter 4, pp. 7–10, copy in WAA.

53. Thomson, *Virgil Thomson*, p. 164.

54. HGA to Agnes Rindge, [Jan. 1932], Vassar College Archives, Rindge Papers.

55. Henry-Russell Hitchcock, [Introductory Note], *A. Everett Austin, Jr.* (New York: Brummer Gallery, 1932).

56. *HT*, Feb. 11, 1932.

57. *Art News*, Feb. 13, 1932, p. 10.

58. *Bulletin of the Wadsworth Atheneum, Junius Spencer Morgan Memorial*, Vol. X, No. 1 (Jan. 1932), pp. 3–6.

59. Forbes to AEA, Nov. 12, 1931, AP.

60. *Art Digest*, Feb. 15, 1932, p. 8.

61. *HT*, Nov. 9, 1931.

62. Ibid., Nov. 7, 1931. The show came with a high fee because of the scale models involved, but Austin explained that the sum was being donated by "certain Hartford and New York individuals"—who turned out to be Theodate Pope Riddle, Jim and Mimi Soby, and Philip Goodwin.

63. Wadsworth Atheneum Circular, [January] 1932.

64. AEA to Duveen, Feb. 23, 1932, Object File.

65. *HC*, Jan. 28, 1932.

66. *HT*, Jan. 16, 1932.

67. John McAndrew, recorded interview, Nov. 4, 1974.

68. C. F. Louis de Wild to AEA, May 24, 1932, Object File.

CHAPTER 9

1. WA Trustees Minutes, Vol. 1, [p. 126].

2. Morris graduated from the Columbia School of Architecture and continued his studies at the Ecole des Beaux Arts. In 1901 he married Alice Fenwick Goodwin, daughter of the Reverend Francis Goodwin, making him Helen Austin's uncle.

3. In 1909 Morris designed the Hartford Armory, whose massive, rough-cut stones and tiny windows suggested a medieval fortress. Ten years later, he built the Italianate Phoenix Mutual Life Insurance building, with its heavily ornamented flat roof and stately rows of arched windows. Then came the Hartford Connecticut Trust building of 1920, a redbrick skyscraper in the Georgian style, topped with a miniature Roman temple; and in 1924, the Mechanics Savings Bank, a solemn imitation of a Greek temple.

4. "Mr. Austin," Morris explained to the trustees, "hopes to create an Art Museum in Hartford which will combine the sheer functional character of the Galleries, Working Spaces and Store Rooms of the Fogg

Museum at Cambridge with the informality successfully achieved in certain museums here and abroad by the use of period rooms." B. W. Morris, Memorandum, Oct. 11, 1928, Building Recs.

5. Individual galleries would be devoted to Flemish, Dutch, Italian, and Spanish pictures from the fifteenth through the seventeenth centuries. American paintings would be displayed with furniture and decorative arts in period rooms. There would be an exhibition space for local contemporary artists. Prints, photographs, and textiles would have separate galleries and examining rooms. B. W. Morris, Memoranda, Oct. 11 and 15, 1928, Building Recs.

6. Henry-Russell Hitchcock, *The Pelican History of Art: Nineteenth and Twentieth Centuries* (Baltimore: Penguin Books, 1958), p. 379.

7. Ibid., p. 376.

8. Hitchcock, "Four Harvard Architects," *Hound & Horn*, Vol. II, No. 1 (Sept. 1928), p. 47.

9. See Helen Searing, "Henry-Russell Hitchcock: Architectura et Amicitia," *In Search of Modern Architecture: A Tribute to Henry-Russell Hitchcock*, Helen Searing, ed. (Cambridge, Mass.: MIT Press, 1982), p. 4.

10. Alfred Barr enthusiastically reviewed *Modern Architecture* in *Hound & Horn* in the spring of 1930. In praising Hitchcock, Barr expressed the disdain for contemporary American culture that was common to the young modernists: "American books on modern architecture, with the exception of Lewis Mumford's, have been as provincial, as ill-informed, as complacent and as reactionary as are most American architects and American schools of architecture." Hitchcock's new volume was, on the other hand, "a scholarly and critical achievement of the greatest originality and distinction. Unfortunately this will be more thoroughly appreciated in Europe than in America." Barr, *Hound & Horn*, ibid., p. 435.

11. AEA, [Review of *Modern Architecture*], handwritten manuscript, c. 1929, AP.

12. Interpreting the office in the museum's bulletin, Hitchcock proclaimed it "one of the most complete demonstrations of the contemporary European style of decoration to be found in America." Hitchcock, "An Office in the Contemporary Style," *Bulletin of the Wadsworth Atheneum*, Vol. 8 (April 1930), p. 27.

13. *HT*, Dec. 13, 1930.

14. *HC*, Dec. 15, 1930.

15. Amy Welcher, recorded interview, April 28, 1983.

16. Frank B. Gay to Charles A. Goodwin, Feb. 2, 1932, Building Recs.

17. Philip Goodwin to AEA, Dec. 29, 1931, AP.

18. Robert B. O'Connor, recorded interview, Dec. 13, 1974.

19. B. W. Morris, Memorandum, Jan. 16, 1932, Building Recs.

20. WA Trustees Recs., Vol. 2, p. 111.

21. The Hartford Art School had a long connection with the Atheneum, going back to the 1880s, when Mrs. Samuel Colt and the Reverend Francis Goodwin arranged for its parent organization, the Hartford Art Society, to use the original picture gallery for art classes. In years prior to the Avery addition, the school had been housed in a building across town, but its board seized the chance to be part of an expanded art museum.

22. Helen Austin to Robert B. O'Connor, [received Jan. 4, 1932], Building Recs.

23. AEA, "Innovations in Activities Offered by the Wadsworth Atheneum," radio broadcast, WAAB, mimeographed typescript, March 5, 1936, AP.

24. The Goodman Theater was especially advanced, presenting such works as George Kaiser's expressionist play *Gas*, with music by Hamilton Forest and scenic design by Louis Lozowick, in 1926; and, in 1929, Sean O'Casey's *The Shadow of a Gunman* and the first English-language production of *The Golem*, originally performed in Moscow in Hebrew by the Habima Players. In 1931 the theater staged the American premiere of Pirandello's *Lazzaro*.

25. Robert B. O'Connor, recorded interview, Dec. 13, 1974.

26. Memorandum of a Meeting of the Building Committee of Wadsworth Atheneum, Feb. 26, 1932, Building Recs.

27. Winslow Ames, recorded interview, Oct. 25, 1974.

28. *HT,* April 21, 1932.

29. *HC,* April 22, 1932.

30. Ibid., April 21, 1932.

31. Ibid., April 29, 1932.

32. *HT,* May 12, 1932.

33. *HC,* May 12, 1932.

34. *HT,* May 12, 1932. Florence Berkman vividly remembered Mrs. Riddle on that occasion: "She was standing there, upright, like a general. And Chick was having an awfully good time because he loved controversy." Florence Berkman in conversation, Sept. 11, 1997.

35. *HC,* May 13, 1932.

36. Eldredge Snyder, Memorandum, Oct. 11, 1928, p. 8, Building Recs.

37. Philip Johnson agreed with Chick, calling the exterior "scraped classical." Philip Johnson, recorded lecture, WA, Feb. 25, 1984.

38. See Helen Searing, "From the Fogg to the Bauhaus: A Museum for the Machine Age," *Avery Memorial: The First Modern Museum,* Eugene R. Gaddis, ed. (Hartford: Wadsworth Atheneum, 1984), p. 27.

39. John McAndrew, recorded interview, Nov. 4, 1974. Agnes Mongan confirmed Forbes's reticence: "When we inherited the Winthrop collection and I hung up Ingres *Odalisque,* Mr. Forbes carefully averted his gaze as he went by it, so as not to have to look at a nude." Agnes Mongan, recorded interview, Nov. 24, 1974.

40. Sachs to Forbes, [July 1932], written on AEA to Forbes, July 11, 1932, Object File. Chick knew what the effect of his interest in the sculpture might be at the Fogg. In June, Morris and O'Connor noted that Austin "prefers not to have us write the Fogg Museum in this connection as he does not want them to know he is seriously considering purchasing the statue."

Morris and O'Connor, Memorandum, June 22, 1932.

41. Sachs to AEA, [May? 1932], Object File. The first page of the letter is missing.

42. O'Connor to Charles A. Goodwin, Dec. 7, 1932, Building Recs.

43. Philip Goodwin to AEA, Dec. 12, 1932, AP. Goodwin refers to Carl Paul Jennewein and Allan Clark. In 1926 the Atheneum had bought a bronze by Jennewein, depicting a boy on a stork.

44. AEA to Charles A. Goodwin, Dec. 22, 1932, Object File.

45. W. R. Corson to Charles A. Goodwin, Dec. 23, 1932, Object File.

46. Robert W. Huntington to Charles A. Goodwin, Dec. 23, 1932, Object File.

47. HGA in conversation with ERG, 1983.

48. Robert T. Stumpf, "Fond Recollections of 'The Great Osram,' " *Trinity Alumni Magazine,* Vol. 8, No. 3 (Spring 1967), p. 6.

49. AEA, press release, [June 1932], AP.

50. Stumpf, p. 6

51. AEA to HGA, Aug. 4, 1932, AP.

52. Stumpf.

53. AEA to HGA, Sept. 14, 1932.

54. James T. Soby, "A. Everett Austin, Jr. and Modern Art," *Director's Taste,* p. 28. Chick brought back five Klee watercolors in total. Presumably all five were among the best examples of the artist's work. Galerie Alfred Flechtheim to AEA, Dec. 12, 1932, Object File.

55. O'Connor, Memorandum, Oct. 25, 1932, Building Recs.

56. AEA, Draft of invitation to the Friends and Enemies concert, Dec. 19, 1932, AP.

57. Virgil Thomson, *Virgil Thomson,* p. 217.

58. Julien Levy, "Dealing with A. Everett Austin, Jr.," *Director's Taste,* p. 35.

59. *HC,* Jan. 11, 1933.

60. James Thrall Soby, Unpublished memoirs, 4–13, copy in WAA.

61. Henry-Russell Hitchcock, "Explanation," *An Exhibition of Literature and*

Poetry in Painting Since 1850 (Hartford: Wadsworth Atheneum, 1933), pp. 5–8.

62. Levy, *Director's Taste,* p. 35.

63. Edward M. M. Warburg, *As I Recall* (Privately printed), p. 50.

64. *HC,* Feb. 16, 1933.

65. Elinor Jaynes Safford, recorded interview, Feb. 1, 1991.

66. Florence Berkman in conversation, March 3, 1993.

67. Arthur Everett Austin, Sr., to HGA, Jan. 24, 1933, AP.

68. Lucy Goodwin Stone, recorded interview, Oct. 31, 1989.

69. B. W. Morris to Charles A. Goodwin, Jan. 4, 1933, Building Recs.

70. AEA, Notes for a discussion with the building committee, typed manuscript, [Feb.? 1933], AP.

71. Robert B. O'Connor, Memorandum, Feb. 20, 1933, Building Recs.

72. Ibid., March 8, 1933.

73. B. W. Morris and Robert B. O'Connor to Charles A. Goodwin, March 13, 1933, Building Recs.

74. AEA to C. A. Cochran, March 13, 1933, Building Recs.

75. Charles A. Goodwin to Building Committee, March 15, 1933, Building Recs.

76. The maintenance fund was tied to a large block of the preferred stock of U.S. Steel, donated by Pierpont Morgan in 1910, and the company had slashed its dividend from $7 to $2 a share. The museum's annual income was instantly reduced by $11,000. *HC,* February 2, 1933.

77. Ibid., May 7, 1933.

78. Florence Berger to Robert W. Huntington, May 13, 1933.

79. Charles A. Goodwin to the Trustees of the Wadsworth Atheneum, May 23, 1933, Financial Recs., WAA.

80. *Bulletin of the Art Institute of Chicago,* Vol. 27, No. 5 (Sept.–Oct. 1933), p. 82.

81. Ibid., p. 87.

82. AEA to HGA, June 11, 1933, AP.

83. Ibid., [June 17, 1933], AP.

84. The museum was then known as the William Rockhill Nelson Gallery of Art and the Mary Atkins Museum of Fine Arts.

85. AEA to HGA, [June 17, 1933], AP.

86. Ibid., June 19, 1933, AP.

87. Charles A. Goodwin to C. A. Cochran, June 22, 1933, Building Recs..

88. AEA to Morris and O'Connor, June 28, 1933, Building Recs.

89. AEA to L. B. Wamnes, [June 28], 1933, Building Recs.

90. Ibid., c. June 8, 1933.

91. AEA to HGA, July 10, 1933, AP.

92. Ibid., July 11, 1933, AP.

CHAPTER 10

1. Lincoln Kirstein to AEA, July 16, 1933, Special File.

2. Lincoln Kirstein, *The New York City Ballet* (New York: Alfred A. Knopf, 1973), p. 16.

3. Kirstein to AEA, July 16, 1933, Special File.

4. Paul Cooley, recorded interview, Nov. 1, 1974.

5. Ibid.

6. AEA, "Strawinsky, Prokofieff and Stokowski," *The Prompter* (Hartford: Bushnell Auditorium), May 1931, p. 3.

7. Kirstein, "The Ballet in Hartford," *Director's Taste,* p. 65.

8. Kirstein to AEA, July 28, 1933, Special File.

9. Virgil Thomson to AEA, July 7, 1933, Special File.

10. Charles A. Goodwin to AEA, July 27, 1933, AP.

11. Thomson, *Virgil Thomson,* p. 219.

12. Kirstein, "The Ballet in Hartford," *Director's Taste,* p. 66.

13. Ibid.

14. Philip Johnson to AEA, July 31, 1933, AP.

15. Johnson to AEA, Sept. 28, 1933, Special File.

16. "Contributions to the American Ballet," typescript, n.d. [c. Sept. 1933], AP.

17. Richard Buckle and John Taras,

George Balanchine: Ballet Master (New York: Random House, 1988), p. 69.

18. Kirstein to AEA, Aug. 8, 1933, Special File.

19. Buckle and Taras, *George Balanchine*, p. 70.

20. AEA to whom it may concern/State Department, Aug. 9, 1933, AP.

21. Kirstein to AEA, Aug. 11, 1933, Special File.

22. Ibid.

23. Ibid., Aug. 12, 1933.

24. AEA to Thomson, [c. August 1933], Special File.

25. Kirstein to AEA, Aug. 26, 1933, Special File.

26. Edward M. M. Warburg, recorded interview, Jan. 10, 1983.

27. Buckle and Taras, *George Balanchine*, p. 71. There is some disagreement about this. Edward Warburg remembered that he merely wrote checks to help sustain the ballet for the next few years, rather than agreeing to underwrite the enterprise for any set length of time. See Nicholas Fox Weber, *Patron Saints* (New York: Alfred A. Knopf, 1992), p. 372.

28. Edward M. M. Warburg, recorded interview, Jan. 10, 1983.

29. Buckle and Taras, *George Balanchine*, p. 71.

30. Kirstein, Austin, Soby, and Warburg to American consul general, Paris, Sept. 1, 1933, AP.

31. Guarantee by Kirstein, Austin, Soby, and Warburg to American consul general, Paris, Sept. 1, 1933, AP.

32. Secretary of State to Herman P. Kopplemann, Oct. 9, 1933, AP.

33. *HT,* Oct. 17, 1933.

34. *New York Times,* Oct. 22, 1933.

35. Buckle and Taras, *George Balanchine*, p. 78.

36. *HT,* Oct. 18, 1933.

37. HGA to Agnes Rindge, Sunday [Oct. 22, 1933], Rindge Papers, Vassar College Archives.

38. Buckle and Taras, *George Balanchine*, p. 77.

39. *HT,* Oct. 18, 1933.

40. Ibid.

41. *HC,* Oct. 18, 1933.

42. Ibid., Oct. 19, 1933.

43. Ibid.

44. *HT,* Oct. 19, 1933.

45. Kirstein, "The Ballet in Hartford," *Director's Taste,* p. 67.

46. Paul Cooley, recorded interview, Nov. 1, 1974.

47. *HT,* Oct. 19, 1933.

48. Thomson to AEA, Oct. 19, 1933, Special File.

49. James T. Soby, unpublished memoirs, Vol. 1, Chapter 4, p. 16.

50. *HT,* Oct. 21, 1933.

51. Ibid.

52. *HC,* Oct. 20, 1933.

53. Ibid., Oct. 18, 1933.

54. Ibid., Oct. 23, 1933.

55. Kirstein, "The Ballet in Hartford," *Director's Taste,* p. 67.

56. HGA to Agnes Rindge, Sunday [Oct. 22, 1933], Rindge Papers, Vassar College Archives.

57. W. McNeil Lowry, "Our Local Correspondents: Conversations with Balanchine," *The New Yorker,* Sept. 12, 1983, p. 54.

58. Kirstein, "The Ballet in Hartford," *Director's Taste,* p. 67.

59. HGA to Agnes Rindge, Saturday [Oct. 28, 1933], Rindge Papers, Vassar College Archives.

60. Kirstein, "The Ballet in Hartford," *Director's Taste,* pp. 66–7.

61. *HT,* Oct. 28, 1933.

62. Johnson to AEA, Oct. 26, 1933, Special File.

63. Kirstein to AEA, Nov. 4, 1933, Special File.

64. Ibid., [Dec. 1933?].

65. Kirstein to ERG, Aug. 30, 1982, ERG Correspondence, WAA.

CHAPTER 11

1. VT to AEA, Sept. 25, 1933, Special File, AP.

2. He was accompanied by eight

dancers, including Toumanova's erstwhile partner, Roman Jasinsky, who had been part of Kirstein's original ballet plan. The *Ile de France* also carried one of the great progenitors of modernism on that particular crossing: Marcel Duchamp.

3. Julien Levy exhibited sixty-eight works from the Lifar Collection in his gallery. The Arts Club of Chicago, which showed the collection next, displayed 167 works.

4. Lifar seems to have helped himself to Diaghilev's collection. In 1965 Levy wrote, with tactful delicacy, that "Lifar was heir to much of what was left of Diaghilev's small estate, partly through propinquity" and "partly through affection." Julien Levy, "The Lifar Collection," *The Serge Lifar Collection of Ballet Set and Costume Designs* (Hartford: Wadsworth Atheneum, 1965), p. 7.

5. Her Imperial Highness the Grand Duchess Marie of Russia headed the roster, which included Prince and Princess Chavchavadze, Vicomte and Vicomtesse de Forceville, Prince and Princess Alexis Obolensky, the Marquise de Polignac, and the Comte and Comtesse Raoul de Roussy de Salles—the latter having brought the collection to Levy's attention.

6. Levy, "The Lifar Collection," p. 7. Levy wrote that Lifar and his dancers appeared at the Metropolitan Opera, but in fact they performed at the Forrest Theatre in New York.

7. Paul Cooley, recorded interview, Nov. 1, 1974.

8. Levy, "The Lifar Collection," p. 7. Lifar later decided that he had practically given away the collection. At a luncheon at the Atheneum in 1980, he told Helen Austin that she should get the trustees to pay him more for it. Jean K. Cadogan in conversation, 1983.

9. *HT*, Dec. 2, 1933.

10. AEA, "The Lifar Collection," *Report for 1933 and Bulletin*, Vol. XII, No. 2 (Oct.–Dec. 1934), pp. 30–2.

11. Lincoln Kirstein, "The Ballet in Hartford," *Director's Taste*, p. 69.

12. Sheldon Kahn, recorded interview, Oct. 19, 1994; *HC*, Nov. 30, 1933.

13. *Art News*, July 16, 1932, pp. 3–4.

14. Building Committee Minutes, Nov. 9, 1933, Building Recs.

15. Eleanor Howland Bunce, recorded interview, Jan. 1975.

16. Ibid., Jan. 28, 1993.

17. AEA to Gertrude Stein, Nov. 16, 1933, Gertrude Stein Papers, Beinecke Library, Yale University.

18. Gertrude Stein to AEA, [Nov.? 1933], AP.

19. AEA to William C. Bullit, Nov. 25, 1933, AP.

20. Georges Wildenstein to Picasso, quoted in Michael C. FitzGerald, *Making Modernism: Picasso and the Creation of the Market for Twentieth-Century Art* (New York: Farrar, Straus and Giroux, 1995), p. 220.

21. Paul Rosenberg to AEA, Dec. 23, 1933, AP.

22. Quoted in FitzGerald, p. 216.

23. Paul Guillaume to AEA, Dec. 23, 1933.

24. AEA to Paul Guillaume, Dec. 19, 1933.

25. Gallatin told Chick that this was Picasso's only self-portrait, but knowledge of Picasso's work was fragmentary in 1933. There were actually several self-portraits, including the revolutionary abstract head of 1907. A. E. Gallatin to AEA, Dec. 26, 1933, AP.

26. Two other canvases came into MOMA's collection in the spring of 1934, when, after a three-year delay, the Lillie P. Bliss bequest was released to the museum.

27. Paul Rosenberg to AEA, Jan. 16, 1934, AP.

28. Marguerite Yourcenar, recorded interview, Aug. 2, 1982.

29. Morris and O'Connor, Memoranda, Dec. 12–13, 21, 1933, Building Recs.

30. John Houseman, *Run-Through* (New York: Simon & Schuster, 1980), p. 101.

31. Houseman, *Run-Through*, p. 96.

32. Eventually another $2,000 would be needed, and Chick, Houseman, and Constance Askew would lend it to the production. Thomson, *Virgil Thomson*, p. 244.

33. Edward M. M. Warburg to AEA, Nov. 28, 1933, AP.

34. AEA to John Selby, Nov. 28, 1933, AP.

35. *HC*, Nov. 29, 1933.

36. *HT*, Nov. 29, 1933.

37. AEA to Mr. and Mrs. Lorenz, Dec. 22, 1933, AP.

38. *Philadelphia Record*, Dec. 17, 1933.

39. *Boston Globe*, Feb. 4, 1934.

40. *Philadelphia Record*, Dec. 17, 1933.

41. *Brooklyn Eagle*, Jan. 29, 1934.

42. Ottawa *Citizen*, January 27, 1934.

43. *Brooklyn Eagle*, Jan. 29, 1934.

44. *New York World-Telegram*, Dec. 16, 1933.

45. *New York Times*, Dec. 31, 1933.

46. *HT*, Jan. 6, 1934.

47. *New York Herald Tribune*, undated newspaper clipping [after Jan. 17, 1934], WA scrapbook, WA.

48. Gertrude Stein quoted in William A. Bradly to Virgil Thomson, May 15, 1933, Virgil Thomson Collection, Yale Music Library.

49. David Harris, "The Original *Four Saints in Three Acts* (1934)," *The Drama Review*, Vol. 29, no. 1 (Spring 1982), p. 110.

50. Mrs. John D. Rockefeller, Jr., to AEA, Dec. 18, 1933, AP.

51. Cooley to Gerdt A. Wagner, January 23, 1934, AP. Thomson later wrote that $4.40 was standard for a Broadway show. Thomson, *Virgil Thomson*, p. 242.

52. Paul Cooley to John Houseman, [c. Jan. 1934], AP.

53. R. R. Burt to AEA, Jan. 22, 1934, AP.

54. Paul Cooley to Jere Abbott, Jan. 19, 1934, AP.

55. Winslow Ames, recorded interview, Oct. 25, 1974.

56. Levy, *Memoir of an Art Gallery*, p.

141. This is the only known reference to Chick's intention to show this kind of material by Picasso at this exhibition. Levy may have been thinking of a later incident.

57. Henry-Russell Hitchcock, *Museum Architecture, 1770–1850*, Wesleyan University Architectural Exhibitions, Hartford, 1934, p. 2.

58. Henry-Russell Hitchcock, recorded interview, Dec. 9, 1974. Of Austin's ceaseless drive to be occupied, Virgil Thomson observed that "as soon as he finished one thing . . . he'd lie on the floor and writhe in boredom trying to think of what to do." Thomson, recorded interview, Nov. 1974.

59. *The Standard Diary*, 1934, WAA.

60. The *New York Times* (Feb. 7, 1934) reported that Houseman and Ashton arrived in Hartford with the cast on Sunday night. The *Hartford Times* (Feb. 6, 1934) concurred. The *Hartford Courant* (Feb. 5, 1934), however, reported that Thomson was also with Houseman and Ashton when they arrived. In their memoirs, both Houseman and Thomson reported arriving together in Hartford by automobile on Thursday, February 1. This seems unlikely, because they were rehearsing with the cast every day for weeks. On the other hand, it is possible that they came to Hartford to confer with Austin and look over the theater on Thursday and that Houseman returned to New York on Friday, while Thomson remained in Hartford.

61. John Houseman, lecture, Kingswood-Oxford School, West Hartford, Connecticut, Oct. 29, 1982, audiotape copy in WAA.

62. Houseman, *Run-Through*, p. 112. This conversation may have taken place on Thursday, February 1, if Houseman and Thomson arrived together that day.

63. Houseman recounts this devastating discovery as happening on the first night of rehearsals in Hartford. This may be inaccurate, as Smallens had been conducting vocal rehearsals with the cast in New York during the last week in January. As he had also recruited the orchestra and presumably had

been rehearsing separately with them, he would have noticed the discrepancy between the vocal and orchestral scores long before the first Hartford rehearsal.

64. John Houseman, lecture, Kingswood-Oxford School, West Hartford, Connecticut, Oct. 29, 1982, audiotape copy in WAA.

65. Houseman, *Run-Through*, p. 115.

66. Thomas Anderson, recorded interview, Jan. 31, 1989.

67. Minutes of the Friends and Enemies of Modern Music, Feb. 6, 1934, AP.

68. Houseman, *Run-Through*, pp. 114–15.

69. Lincoln Kirstein to AEA, Jan. 20, 1934, AP.

70. Alfred Barr to AEA, Jan. 18, 1934, Special File.

71. Laurie Eglington, "Avery Memorial Unique Example of Modern Style," *Art News*, Feb. 10, 1934, p. 3. Enthusiasm was not universal among the locals. The day before the opening, one amateur critic of architecture, wrote to the editor of the *Hartford Times*, claiming that after spending a few minutes in Avery Court, he had a desperate urge "to escape before all that unsupported mass collapsed on me." (*HT*, Feb. 5, 1934.)

72. Eglington, "Avery Memorial," *Art News*, Feb. 10, 1934, p. 4.

73. *New York Sun*, Feb. 10, 1934.

74. Florence Berkman, recorded interview and in conversation, December 27, 1996. The woman was Gertrude Robinson, a leader of Hartford society.

75. *New York Sun*, Feb. 10, 1934.

76. *Art News*, Feb. 10, 1934, p. 3.

77. Rosamond Forbes Pickhardt, Diary, Feb. 1934, transcript of excerpts in WAA, courtesy of Rosamond Forbes Pickhardt.

78. Agnes Mongan, recorded interview, Nov. 24, 1974.

79. *HC*, Feb. 7, 1934.

80. *New York Sun*, Feb. 1934.

81. Levy, *Memoir of an Art Gallery*, p. 141.

82. Houseman, lecture, Kingswood-Oxford School, West Hartford, Conn., Oct. 29, 1982.

83. Virgil Thomson, "About 'Four Saints' " record liner notes in *Four Saints in Three Acts*, Orchestra of Our Time, Joel Thome cond., Nonesuch 79035.

84. *The New Yorker*, March 3, 1934.

85. Lucius Beebe, *Snoot If You Must* (New York: D. Appelton-Century Co., 1948), p. 169.

86. Carl Van Vechten to Gertrude Stein, Feb. 8, 1934, in Bruce Hellner, ed., *The Letters of Carl Van Vechten* (New Haven: Yale University Press, 1987), p. 134.

87. Thomson, *Virgil Thomson*, p. 243.

88. *HC*, Feb. 11, 1934.

89. Quoted by Thomson in his inscription on the title page of Austin's copy of *Four Saints in Three Acts* (New York: Random House, 1934). The other inscriptions read: "Haussmann"; "To Chick, With admiration and sentiments more baroque / Maurice Grosser"; "For Chick Austin who made this opera come off—with many thanks from Carl Van Vechten / February 20, 1934 / NYCity." Julien Levy remembered Austin's irrepressible affection for his friends: " 'Let's everyone love everybody, Guiliano,' he would shout, 'Jim and Iris, and Mrs. Berger, and Kirk and Virgil and Gertrude and Pavlik, and Gypsy Rose Lee and . . .' So Chick disarmed and encircled his friends, and seduced them into unexpected achievement." Levy, "Dealing with A. Everett Austin, Jr.," *Director's Taste*, pp. 34–5.

90. Levy, *Memoir of an Art Gallery*, p. 142.

91. Alexander Calder and Jean Davidson, *Calder: An Autobiography with Pictures* (Boston: Beacon Press, 1969), p. 146.

92. Katherine Dreier to AEA, Feb. 14, 1934, AP.

93. Philip Johnson to AEA, Feb. 8, 1934. Johnson soon wrote again to ask for the retrieval of his top hat, or twenty dollars for a new one. "In the meantime I shall go

bare-headed to parties." Johnson to AEA, Feb. 13, 1934, AP. The hat was sent back to him.

94. Raoul de Roussy de Sales to AEA, Feb. 15, 1934, AP.

95. Pierre Matisse in a telephone conversation with ERG, 1982.

96. Thomson states that "we gave six shows in Hartford," although he inaccurately quotes the top ticket price as ten dollars. Thomson, *Virgil Thomson*, p. 242. The museum's official door diaries confirm the six performances, from February 7 to February 10, including Friday and Saturday matinees. *The Standard Diary* (Cambridge, Mass., 1934), WAA.

97. *New York Herald Tribune*, April 1, 1934.

98. *The New Yorker*, Feb. 7, 1934. Drawing by Shev Munch.

99. Amy Welcher, recorded interview, April 28, 1983.

100. Lillian Scataregia Varol, recorded interview, Aug. 24, 1993.

101. *Time*, Feb. 19, 1934, p. 35; *Newsweek*, Feb. 17, p. 37.

102. Francis Henry Taylor, "African Baroque in Hartford," *Parnassus*, Vol. VI, No. III (March 1934), p. 11.

103. Levy, "Dealing with A. Everett Austin, Jr.," *Director's Taste*, p. 38.

104. Rosenberg to AEA, Feb. 9, 1934, AP.

105. Rosenberg to AEA, March 14, 1934, AP.

106. The total exhibition budget was $2,815, which included $150 for the exhibition of museum architecture.

CHAPTER 12

1. *HC*, March 11, 1934.

2. *HT*, March 7, 1934.

3. Ibid., April 16, 1934.

4. Ibid., April 7, 1934.

5. AEA, exhibition label, [May 1934], AP.

6. Dudley S. Ingraham to AEA, May 7, 1934; Ingraham to Paul Cooley, May 18, 1934, AP.

7. Ingraham to Francis Parsons, Sept. 29, 1934, AP.

8. Robert W. Huntington to Ingraham, Oct. 2, 1934, AP.

9. AEA to Parsons, Sept. 18, 1934, AP.

10. *HC*, May 20, 1934.

11. Ibid., May 29, 1934.

12. Bridgeport *Sunday Herald* [Hartford Edition], May 27, 1934.

13. Edward M. M. Warburg to AEA, June 20, 1934, AP. Warburg's note to Chick implies that he was present the first night. As Chick had patched things up with Kirstein by April, and as all of his and Helen's New York friends were coming to the performance, it is highly unlikely that he and Helen stayed away.

14. AEA to Paul Byk, April 16, 1934, AP.

15. HGA, account book, AP. The only extant income figures during this period are from 1935, but the amounts budgeted in 1934 were similar compared with those in 1935, indicating that the Austins' income remained relatively stable.

16. Cooley to AEA, Aug. 27, 1934, AP.

17. "Calendar, 1934–1935," Wadsworth Atheneum, Hartford, Conn., Year Files.

18. *HC*, Oct. 25, 1934.

19. *HT*, Oct. 9, 1935.

20. Virgil Thomson to AEA, Nov. 2 [1934], AP.

21. Eva Gauthier to AEA, [Nov. 16, 1934], AP.

22. *HT*, Oct. 20, 1934.

23. May Sarton, recorded interview, June 15, 1987.

24. Ibid.

25. Among those appearing in the Avery Theater during Austin's tenure were Martha Graham, Erick Hawkins, and Pearl Lang, Yurek Shabelevsky and his company, Doris Humphrey and Charles Weidman, Anna Sokolow, Paul Nordoff, Paul Vellucci, Agna Enters, the Chinese Cultural Theater, Iris

Barry, Muriel Draper, Nadia Boulanger, Erwin Panofsky, and local theater groups including the Little Theater of Hartford, the Jitney Players, the Hartford Players, the Mark Twain Masquers, the Trinity Jesters, the Amherst College Masquers, and the Wesleyan Paint and Powder Club. The W.P.A. Federal Theater was in residence from 1937 to 1939 and consisted of a "White Unit" and a "Negro Unit." The latter, which was one of only five in the country, presented the first all-black version of Eugene O'Neill's *The Emperor Jones* in 1937.

26. AEA to Edward W. Forbes, Nov. 30, 1934, AP.

27. Elizabeth Prentiss, recorded interview, Oct. 26, 1986.

28. *HT,* Dec. 5, 1934.

29. Agnes Rindge, recorded interview, Oct. 22, 1974; Allen Porter, recorded interview, Oct. 30, 1974.

30. Russell Lynes, *Good Old Modern: An Intimate Portrait of the Museum of Modern Art* (New York: Atheneum, 1973), p. 122.

31. *New York Herald Tribune,* Dec. 9, 1934.

32. Ibid.

33. *HC,* Dec. 7, 1934.

34. *HT,* Dec. 7, 1934.

35. *New York Herald Tribune,* Dec. 9, 1934.

36. *HT,* Dec. 7, 1934.

37. Houseman, lecture, Kingswood-Oxford School, West Hartford, Connecticut, Oct. 29, 1982, audiotape copy in WAA.

38. Houseman, *Run-Through,* p. 118. Houseman recounted the exchange between Dalí and Nellie Howland as having taken place at the party at Chick's house after the opening of *Four Saints.* Dalí, however, did not arrive in America for the first time until November 1934. He was definitely at the premiere of Balanchine's company. Houseman was also in town, about to prepare the premiere of an act from Avery Claflin's new opera *Hester Prynne,* which he was directing

at the museum the next weekend. The Austins did give a party at their house on Saturday night, December 8, after the final performance of Balanchine's company, but there is no evidence that Dalí had remained in Hartford after December 7.

39. Eleanor Howland Bunce, recorded interview, May 23, 1994.

40. Thomson, *Virgil Thomson,* p. 250–1.

41. "The Friends and Enemies of Modern Music, Inc., Seventh Season 1934–1935, Work in Preparation," AP.

42. *New York Herald Tribune,* Dec. 20, 1934.

43. *HC,* Dec. 19, 1934.

44. *New York Herald Tribune,* Dec. 20, 1934.

45. *HT,* Dec. 18, 1934.

46. Ibid., Jan. 1, 1935.

47. Julien Levy, "Dealing with A. Everett Austin, Jr.," *Director's Taste,* p. 37.

48. *HT,* Dec. 21, 1934.

49. Ibid., Dec. 23, 1934.

50. Ibid., Jan. 1, 1935.

51. James R. Mellow, *Charmed Circle: Gertrude Stein & Company* (New York: Praeger, 1974), p. 371.

52. Gertrude Stein, *Lectures in America* (Boston: Beacon Press, 1985), pp. 59, 78, 79.

53. *HT,* Jan. 19, 1935.

54. Stein, *Lectures,* p. 81.

55. *HT,* Jan. 19, 1935.

CHAPTER 13

1. AEA, "Foreword," *American Painting and Sculpture of the 18th, 19th & 20th Centuries* (Hartford: Wadsworth Atheneum, 1935), pp. 3–4.

2. *HC,* Feb. 15, 1935.

3. AEA, Director's Report, 1934, typescript draft, WAA.

4. *HT,* Jan. 25 and Jan. 30, 1935.

5. Ibid., Feb. 22, 1935.

6. Wadsworth Atheneum, "Ballot," 1935, [filled out by D. D. Newton of Hartford], AP.

7. *HT,* Feb. 22, 1935.

8. Florence Berkman in conversation, 1983.

9. James Thrall Soby, unpublished memoir, Chapter 4, p. 4, copy in WAA.

10. Joyce Blum, "A. E. Austin, Museum Head, at Art Center," unidentified newspaper article, c. May 1955, enclosed in letter from HGA to SGA, May 18, 1955.

11. *HC,* March 13, 1935.

12. Pavel Tchelitchew to Charles C. Cunningham, Oct. 3, 1946, Special File.

13. Eugene Berman, "Legendary Chick," *Director's Taste,* p. 48.

14. AEA to Eva Gauthier, Feb. 16, 1935, AP.

15. *HC,* March 5, 1935.

16. Laura Austin to Mr. and Mrs. AEA, April 23, 1935, AP.

17. Ibid., April 23, 1935.

18. *HT,* May 2, 1935.

19. Paul Sachs to AEA, [May 1935], AP.

20. Thomson, *Virgil Thomson,* p. 251.

21. Paul Bowles, *Without Stopping* (New York: Ecco Press, 1985), p. 190.

22. This was one of the first Calder mobiles to enter an America museum; Abby Aldrich Rockefeller had given the Museum of Modern Art its first one a year earlier.

23. "This is the most extraordinary canvas we have located in all these years, aside from the Peale, with which it can be favorably compared. 'The Faithful Colt' can well be hung next to a Pierre Roy." Edith Gregor Halpert to AEA, April 13, 1935, AP.

24. AEA to Halpert, May 24, 1935, AP.

25. AEA, unpublished Sumner Fund catalogue, Object File.

26. Glenway Wescott, "Poor Greuze," *Report for 1934 and Bulletin* (Jan.–June 1935), pp. 2–8.

27. Unsigned note to "The Directors of the Wadsworth Atheneum," [July? 1935], AP.

28. Eleanor Howland to AEA, July 8, 1935, AP.

29. AEA to Edward Forbes, May 22, 1935, AP.

30. AEA to HGA, [July 5, 1935], AP.

31. Ibid., July 6, 1935.

32. Ibid., July 11, 1935.

33. Ibid., [July 18, 1935].

34. James T. Soby, "A. Everett Austin, Jr. and Modern Art," *Director's Taste,* p. 27.

35. Piet Mondrian to AEA, April 18, 1936, AP. Mondrian also asked that the payment be sent in banknotes or a letter of credit, as he did not have a bank account. Mondrian to AEA, Jan. 19, 1936, Special File.

36. Except for one element of the set, Gabo was the real designer of *La Chatte,* but insisted that his brother share the credit.

37. AEA to HGA, [c. July 18, 1935], AP.

38. Mrs. Charles Goodspeed to AEA, Aug. 25, 1935, AP.

39. AEA to Alfred Barr, Oct. 16, 1935, AP. Austin was perhaps thinking of Nikolaus Pevsner, the historian of art and architecture.

40. Eleanor Howland to Isabel Jarvis, Jan. 13, 1936, AP.

41. [AEA], *Abstract Art* wall label, 1935, AP.

42. *HC,* Oct. 25, 1935.

43. Ibid.

44. Alfred Barr to AEA, Nov. 21, 1935, AP.

45. AEA, Director's Annual Report for 1935, typescript, Trustees Recs.

46. Eleanor Howland to Alice Roullier, Nov. 18, 1935, AP.

47. Ostrom Enders, recorded interview, Jan. 28, 1991.

48. Mrs. Burton Tremaine, Sr. (Emily Hall Tremaine), interview by Paul Cummings, Jan. 24, 1973, Archives of American Art–Smithsonian Institute, Washington, D.C.

49. Ernestine Fantl at the Modern reported to Chick that the little display of objects "pleases everybody but the Maestro himself who seems surprised to find that he

designed them." Fantl to AEA, Oct. 26, 1935, AP.

50. AEA to Ernestine Fantl, Nov. 1, 1935, AP.

51. Philip Goodwin to AEA, Oct. 25, 1935, AP.

52. Le Corbusier, *Quand les cathédrales étaient blanches*, pp. 129–30.

53. Le Corbusier to AEA, Oct. 1, 1936, AP.

54. AEA, Notes for presentation of the Hartford Festival to the Wadsworth Atheneum's board of trustees, [Oct. 1935], AP.

CHAPTER 14

1. *HT,* Oct. 25, 1935.

2. M. E. Tompkins to Virgil Thomson, Jan. 9 and March 5, 1935, Special File.

3. Thomson to AEA, [October 1935]. Special File.

4. AEA to Elizabeth Sage Hare, Nov. 5, 1935, AP.

5. Anne E. Trumbull to AEA, Nov. [14], 1935, AP.

6. Janice Loeb to AEA, Nov. 20, 1935, AP.

7. Mina Curtiss to AEA, Nov. 26, 1935, AP.

8. AEA to Mrs. Morris Joseloff, Nov. 27, 1935, AP.

9. AEA to Ernest R. Voigt, Nov. 19, 1935, AP.

10. Voigt to AEA, Nov. 27, 1935, AP.

11. Katherine Dreier had suggested that German expressionist artist Heinrich Campendonk design *Mahagonny,* but Chick told her that "the opera is going to cost us more money than we had expected and that importing anything would be absolutely out of the question." Dreier to AEA, Nov. 5 and Nov. 30, 1935; AEA to Dreier, Dec. 3, 1935, Special File.

12. AEA to Voigt, Dec. 4, 1935, AP.

13. AEA to Lotte Lenya, Dec. 9, 1935, Special File.

14. Lenya to AEA, Dec. 12, 1935, Special File.

15. Eleanor Howland Bunce, in conversation, Feb. 14, 1986.

16. *HT,* Dec. 21, 1935.

17. Ibid.

18. *New York Sun,* Dec. 28, 1935.

19. *HT,* Jan. 1, 1936.

20. Ibid., Jan. 20, 1936.

21. Ibid., Feb. 4, 1936.

22. Ibid., Feb. 6, 1936.

23. Ibid., Jan. 31, 1936.

24. *New York American,* [Jan. 18?, 1936], newspaper clipping attached to letter from Dudley Seymour Ingraham to Henry Tracy Kneeland, Jan. 20, 1936, AP.

25. Thomson to AEA, Sept. 26, 1935, Special File.

26. Mata Roudin to AEA, [January 1936], AP.

27. Eleanor Howland to Roudin, Jan. 6, 1936, AP.

28. Voigt to AEA, Jan. 10, 1936, AP.

29. Howland to Roudin, Jan. 11, 1936, AP.

30. AEA to Roudin, Jan. 15, 1936, AP.

31. Kurt Weill to AEA, Jan. 15, 1936, Special File.

32. AEA to Weill, Jan. 29, 1936, Special File. As was usual with Chick, peace and even friendship were eventually restored, and he later invited Lenya to sing some of her old songs for the Friends and Enemies. Although she declined, feeling that this repertoire was tired, she wrote, "Kurt sends his love and so do I." Lenya to AEA, Oct. 25, 1938, Special File.

33. Howland Scrapbook, 1936, Howland Paps, WAA.

34. HGA in conversation with Coleman Casey, 1983.

35. *HT,* Jan. 22, 1936.

36. Agnes Rindge to AEA, Jan. [22?], 1936, AP.

37. AEA to Rindge, Jan. 24, 1936, AP.

38. AEA to Mrs. Morris Joseloff, Jan. 19, 1936, AP.

39. *Variety,* Jan. 22, 1936.

40. Eugene Berman to AEA, [Jan. 1936], Special File.

41. Howland to Alexander Calder, Feb. 10, 1936, AP.

42. Eugene Berman, "Legendary Chick," *Director's Taste*, p. 47.

43. *HT*, Feb. 10, 1936.

44. Ibid., Feb. 10, 1936.

45. Ibid., Feb. 15, 1936.

46. *HC*, Feb. 15, 1936.

47. Jean Lipman, *Calder's Universe* (New York: Viking Press, 1976), pp. 172–4.

48. James Johnson Sweeney, *Alexander Calder* (New York: Museum of Modern Art, 1943), p. 30.

49. Virgil Thomson, "The Friends and Enemies of Modern Music," *Director's Taste*, p. 61.

50. Kirstein, "The Ballet in Hartford," *Director's Taste*, p. 73. Kirstein claimed that the fire department interrupted the dance at this point, but that did not happen.

51. Others in the entrée were Pierre and Teeny Matisse, Allen Porter, Russell Hitchcock, Kirk Askew, the Winslow Ameses, and the Calders.

52. James Thrall Soby, "My Life in the Art World," unpublished memoirs, Chapter 7, pp. 5–6, copy in WAA.

53. Winslow Ames, recorded interview, Oct. 25, 1974.

54. Ann Carolyn Prud'homme, recorded interview, Feb. 14, 1985.

55. *New York Sun*, Feb. 22, 1936.

56. AEA, typescript of radio broadcast, WAAB Boston, March 5, 1936, AP.

57. Ann Carolyn Prud'homme, recorded interview, Feb. 14, 1985.

58. Ruth Ford, recorded interview, May 17, 1983.

59. Soby, unpublished memoirs, Chapter 7, p. 7, copy in WAA.

60. Alma Clayburgh to AEA, Feb. 18, 1936, AP.

61. Rindge to AEA, [Feb. 19, 1936], AP.

62. "The excitement hasn't yet died down," Nellie Howland reported to Tchelitchew, "although most of the people have." Feb. 20, 1936, AP.

63. Executive Committee Minutes, Wadsworth Atheneum Board of Trustees, Nov. 24, 1936, Trustees Recs.

64. Edward M. M. Warburg, recorded interview, Jan. 10, 1983.

65. Charles A. Goodwin to AEA, March 27, 1936, AP.

66. AEA to Goodwin, April 1, 1936, AP.

67. Florence Berkman, in conversation, July 8, 1997.

68. AEA to Julien Levy, [March 1936], from Michael Duncan, Sept. 19, 1996.

69. Levy to AEA, March 25, 1936, AP.

70. AEA to Thomas Dabney Mabry, Jr., March 27, 1936, AP.

71. AEA to Hare, July 8, 1936, AP.

72. AEA, fragment of a typescript, [1936], AP.

73. Mrs. Baxter Ragsdale, recorded interview, Nov. 12, 1992; SGA in conversation, 1983.

74. Virgil Thomson, recorded interview, Nov. 1974.

75. Joella Levy Bayer, recorded interview, July 5, 1991.

76. Levy to AEA, [Sept. 1936], AP.

77. That Eleanor Howland had the unique distinction of working side by side with the two most innovative American museum directors during an extraordinarily eventful time in their careers was a testimony to her talents.

CHAPTER 15

1. Egbert Havercamp-Begemann, "Introduction," *Wadsworth Atheneum Paintings: The Netherlands and the German-Speaking Countries, Fifteenth–Nineteenth Centuries* (Hartford: Wadsworth Atheneum, 1978), p. 12.

2. AEA, unpublished Sumner Collection catalogue, Object File.

3. *New York Times*, Jan. 18, 1937.

4. The discovery was chronicled in Egbert Havercamp-Begemann, "Introduction," p. 12.

5. Henry-Russell Hitchcock, recorded interview, Dec. 9, 1974, AP.

6. Dorothy H. Dudley to Florence N. Blumenthal, Feb. 11, 1937.

7. AEA, unpublished Sumner Collection catalogue, c. 1946, Object File.

8. Julien Levy to AEA, [c. Feb. 1938], AP.

9. Chick bought a second major oil by Balthus, *The Bernese Hat*, in 1940 from Pierre Matisse for $1,200. The work had just been finished the previous year; in it, a young woman turns in her chair to gaze with sad intensity at the viewer. Except for the bright mustard-yellow hat with its red and white flowers, the picture is subdued and somber, evoking Courbet.

10. Julien Levy to AEA, [Dec. 1937?], AP.

11. Alexander Calder to AEA, March 31, 1938.

12. Patrick McCaughey, "Joan Miró, *Painting*," "*The Spirit of Genius*": *Art at the Wadsworth Atheneum* (New York: Hudson Hills, 1992), p. 90.

13. Calder to AEA, May 18, 1938, AP.

14. James T. Soby, "A. Everett Austin, Jr., and Modern Art," *Director's Taste*, p. 32.

15. James Thrall Soby, unpublished memoirs, Chapter 4, p. 4–3, copy in WAA.

16. Wadsworth Atheneum Trustees Minutes, Vol. 2, 1923–43, p. 144, WAA.

17. Robert W. Huntington to AEA, June 20, 1938, AP.

18. Huntington to AEA, Dec. 26, 1939, AP.

19. Wadsworth Atheneum Executive Committee Minutes, March 24, 1937, WAA.

20. Wadsworth Atheneum Trustees Minutes, Vol. 2, 1923–43, pp. 148–9.

21. James Thrall Soby, "A. Everett Austin, Jr. and Modern Art," *Director's Taste*, p. 32.

22. Katherine Dreier to AEA, Aug. 13, 1936, Special File.

23. Alfred M. Frankfurter, "George de la Tour and the Le Nains," *Art News*, Nov. 28, 1936, p. 24.

24. AEA, exhibition notes, [Dec. 1935].

25. *HC*, Jan. 29, 1937.

26. [Florence Blumenthal] to Eleanor Howland, January 26, 1937, AP.

27. Charles Henri Ford, recorded interview, April 22, 1991. Julien Levy remembered going in late 1936 to a sailor bar in the Bowery in New York one night with Chick and Giorgio de Chirico. This was during an unusual tour of the city Levy was giving the painter, who had just come to America for the first time. Chick and Julien entered into the spirit of the place as "the dancers threw themselves about in a kind of agony that was neither pleasurable nor simulated. Giorgio was really frightened. Chick and I were having fun. . . ." Levy, *Memoir of an Art Gallery*, pp. 187–90.

28. Joella Levy Bayer, recorded interview, July 5, 1991.

29. HGA to Frances Goodwin, July 30, 1937, AP. Other sources state that Lotte Lehman was the singer.

30. Ibid.

31. Ibid., Sept. 7, 1937.

32. *HT*, Sept. 7, 1937.

33. AEA to Friends and Enemies of Modern Music, Dec. 31, 1937, AP.

34. *HT*, Jan. 6, 1938.

35. Kirstein, *The New York City Ballet*, p. 50.

36. *HT*, Jan. 7, 1938. Kirstein wrote Chick a few days later in an unexpectedly playful mood, suggesting that Ballet Caravan's next production would be "made especially for Hartford, with the scene of a composite decor of the lobbies of the Bond and the Heublein. You would figure largely with the magic act. . . . The Hartford Police and Fire Department will be pressed to use in the finale." Kirstein to AEA, Jan. 11, 1938, Special File.

37. Paul Byk to AEA, Jan. 6, 1938, AP.

38. Unidentified Hartford newspaper article, Jan. 22, 1938, Wadsworth Atheneum newspaper scrapbook, p. 110.

39. "jrs." [A. Everett Austin, Jr., and Henry-Russell Hitchcock, Jr.], "Foreword," *The Painters of Still Life* (Hartford: Wadsworth Atheneum, 1938), [p. 2].

40. Alfred H. Barr to AEA, Feb. 28, 1938, Special File.

41. *HT*, Feb. 9, 1938.

42. The show also contained a photograph of the set Naum Gabo and his brother, Antoine Pevsner, had designed for Diaghilev's ballet *La Chatte* of 1927, which Balanchine had choreographed; a sculptural interpretation of an "airdrome"; and recent drawings for constructions.

43. Arthur E. Austin to LEA, April 17, 1938, LEA Paps.

44. SGA, recorded interview, April 25, 1986.

45. *HC*, Oct. 9, 1938.

46. *HT*, Nov. 19, 1938.

47. Levy, *Memoir of an Art Gallery*, pp. 232–3.

48. Ernst Krenek to AEA, March 28, 1938, Special File.

49. AEA to Ernst Krenek, April 13, 1938, AP.

50. "AEA's introduction [of] Mr. E. Krenek Dec. 12 [*sic*], 1938," AP.

51. Alwin Nikolais, recorded interview, Oct. 23, 1992.

52. AEA to Daniel Catton Rich, Jan. 29, 1939, AP. As it happened, Chick was not to return to Europe for twelve years, and in March 1940, Kirk Askew opened the first Poussin exhibition in the United States at Durlacher's.

53. *HC*, Feb. 19, 1939.

54. John Crockett, recorded interview, March 6, 1990; John Crockett to HGA, March 31, 1957. In the letter, Crockett wrote "hor d'oeuvres" instead of "caviar."

55. Ernst Krenek to AEA, Dec. 26, 1938, Special File.

56. Since Krenek was traveling throughout the United States that spring, the choreography and the music were connected through the mail. Though this was modern dance in the Wigman tradition of improvisation, Nikolais wrote out a rhythmic score of the choreography as he and Kaschmann developed it, and then sent it to Krenek. Back would come a piano score for those sections of dance.

57. AEA to Friends and Enemies, April 18 and 24, 1939, AP.

58. Mrs. W. Murray Crane to AEA, April 19, 1939, AP.

59. Paul Geissler, recorded interview, Jan. 4, 1991.

60. Joella Levy Bayer, recorded interview, Dec. 6, 1990.

61. Ibid., July 5, 1991.

62. *HT*, Aug. 4, 1939.

63. AEA to Staff, Aug. 8, 1939, AP.

64. Julien Levy to AEA, [Aug. 1939], AP.

65. Ibid.

66. AEA to HGA, [Aug 1939], AP.

67. Ibid.

68. MacKinley Helm, *Modern Mexican Painters* (New York: Harper & Brothers, 1941), p. 121.

69. AEA to Humberto Arellano, Oct. 11, 1939, AP.

70. *HC*, Dec. 6, 1939.

71. Katherine Dreier to AEA, Feb. 26, 1940, Special File.

72. AEA to Dreier, March 6, 1940, Special File.

73. *HC*, Jan. 16, 1940.

74. AEA, "Introduction," *Night Scenes* (Hartford: Wadsworth Atheneum, 1940), p. 3.

75. Francis Waring Robinson to AEA, Feb. 26, 1940, AP.

76. Eleanor Howland Bunce in conversation, 1983.

77. Reata Overman, recorded interview, May 5, 1992.

78. Nancy Goodwin Graff, recorded interview, Jan. 25, 1990.

79. Bryce Muir, recorded interview, Aug. 3, 1987.

80. *HT*, Dec. 23, 1938.

81. Ibid., Dec. 30, 1938.

82. [AEA], "Magic on Parade," program, December 28, 29, 30, [1939].

83. Alwin Nikolais, recorded interview, Oct. 23, 1992.

CHAPTER 16

1. Isabel Fairchild to ERG, Feb. 4, 1986; recorded interview, Feb. 28, 1986.

2. *HT,* Dec. 28, 1940.

3. *HC* and *HT,* Dec. 28, 1940.

4. Fairchild to ERG, Feb. 4, 1986, ERG Papers, WAA.

5. Lillian Scata Varol to ERG, Jan. 6, 1994, ERG Papers, WAA.

6. Holly Stevens, Memorandum, April 20, 1990, WAA.

7. Elena Longo Hughes, recorded interview, Nov. 25, 1974.

8. Florence Berkman in conversation with the author, 1982.

9. Alwin Nikolais, recorded interview, Oct. 23, 1992; Edwina Urann, recorded interview, March 5, 1990.

10. Elena Longo Hughes, recorded interview, Dec. 12, 1974.

11. *HC,* Jan. 10, 1940.

12. Ibid., Aug. 25, 1940.

13. AEA to Merril Joels, Nov. 7, 1940.

14. *HC,* Jan. 10, 1941.

15. Henry-Russell Hitchcock, recorded interview, Dec. 12, 1974.

16. AEA to Julien Levy, Feb. 21, 1941, AP.

17. *HC,* Feb. 27, 1940.

18. *HT,* Feb. 27, 1940.

19. *HC,* Feb. 26, 1940.

20. Florence Berkman, recorded interview, Oct. 14, 1981.

21. Alwin Nikolais, recorded interview, Oct. 23, 1992.

22. Wadsworth Atheneum Trustees Minutes, April 14, 1941, Vol. II, p. 178.

23. Ibid., June 26, 1941, p. 180.

24. Ibid., Oct. 23, 1941, p. 181.

25. Ibid.

26. Wadsworth Atheneum Executive Committee Minutes, Nov. 27, 1941; Clerk of the Executive Committee to John M. K. Davis, Nov. 27, 1941, Executive Committee Files, WAA.

27. AEA, "Annual Report of the Director, January, 1942," Trustees Recs.

28. J. P. Morgan, Jr. to Charles A. Goodwin, Feb. 13, 1942, Charles A. Goodwin Papers, WAA.

29. Goodwin to Morgan, Feb. 16, 1942, Charles A. Goodwin Papers, WAA.

30. "Wadsworth Atheneum, Report of Budget Committee," February 19, 1942, Trustees Recs.

31. "Wadsworth Atheneum—Conference, Memorandum," March 25, 1942.

32. AEA to Vittorio Rieti, Jan. 9, 1942, AP.

33. Rieti to AEA, Feb. 16, 1942, AP.

34. AEA, "Foreword," *In Memoriam* (Hartford: Wadsworth Atheneum, 1942).

35. Max Ernst to Charles C. Cunningham, Oct. 10, 1946, Charles C. Cunningham Papers, WAA.

36. Marguerite Yourcenar, recorded interview, Aug. 4, 1982.

37. AEA to Peggy Guggenheim, [May 1942], AP.

38. AEA to May Sarton, [May 1942], AP.

39. Sarton to AEA, May 12, 1942, AP.

40. Philip Johnson to AEA, [May 1942], AP.

41. André Breton to AEA, May 23, 1942, AP.

42. Paul Byk to AEA, May 22, 1942, AP.

43. Yourcenar, program note, "The Elements of Magic," 1942.

44. AEA, "The Contribution of the Avery to the Theatrical Arts of Hartford," *100th Anniversary of the Founding of the Wadsworth Atheneum,* 1942.

45. SGA in conversation, 1983.

46. AEA, note on *Men in Arms,* typescript, [c. Feb. 1943], AP.

47. Julien Levy to AEA, Jan. 25, 1943, AP; Kirk Askew to AEA, Jan. 25, 1943, AP.

48. These men were nothing but encouraging. Chauncey Brewster Tinker, a distinguished retired professor of English at Yale, told Chick: "I entirely share your admiration of Ford's play, and should be glad to be mentioned on your list of 'patrons,' even if you advertised the play by its full title." Tinker to AEA, March 4, 1943, AP.

49. Elizabeth McCormick, "Notes on the Play," *'Tis Pity,* Avery Memorial Auditorium, 1943.

50. *HT,* May 14, 1943.

51. "But you, sir, *were* the play, and have contributed another to that series of artistic productions which is once again making the name of Hartford known for something besides premiums and prosperous gentility." Morse Allen [Trinity College] to AEA, May 22, 1943, AP.

52. For this production, Chick kept the dagger bare; earlier productions featuring a pig's heart, or some other grisly counterfeit, often required the summoning of physicians to revive the squeamish. See William Lloyd Phelps, "Esquire's Five-Minute Shelf," *Esquire*, Sept. 1944, p. 126.

53. *HC*, May 19, 1943. Typically, Chick found Parker's line about the play being a bore amusing and often quoted it. Sarah G. Austin in conversation, 1983.

54. *HT*, May 17, 1943.

55. *HC*, May 31 and June 10, 1943.

56. *Catholic Transcript*, May 1943, newspaper clipping in WA Scrapbook, p. 149.

57. AEA to Berte Mondschein, [May 1943], AP. Mrs. Mondschein was the wife of A. F. Mondschein.

58. AEA to Goodwin, May 11, 1943, Charles A. Goodwin Papers, WAA.

59. Ibid., [June 11, 1943].

60. Goodwin to AEA, June 12, 1943, Charles A. Goodwin Papers, WAA.

61. Robert W. Huntington to Goodwin, June 29, 1943, Charles A. Goodwin Papers, WAA.

62. Goodwin to Huntington, July 1, 1943, Charles A. Goodwin Papers, WAA.

63. Goodwin to Forbes, August 3, 1943, Charles A. Goodwin Papers, WAA.

64. *HT*, June 11, 1943.

65. AEA to Huntington, July 1, 1943, Object File.

66. AEA to Truda Kaschmann, [Aug. 13, 1943], AP.

67. Angela Lansbury, recorded interview, April 26, 1983.

68. Henry-Russell Hitchcock, recorded interview, Dec. 9, 1974.

69. Nancy Goodwin Graff, recorded interview, Jan. 25, 1990.

70. Tonio Selwart, recorded interview, Dec. 8, 1986.

71. Huntington to AEA, Nov. 1, 1943, Charles A. Goodwin Papers, WAA.

72. Goodwin to Forbes, Nov. 10, 1943, Charles A. Goodwin Papers, WAA.

73. AEA to HGA, Dec. 10, 1943, AP.

74. AEA to Alfred Barr, [Dec.] 1943, Alfred Barr Papers, Museum of Modern Art Archives.

75. Goodwin to AEA, Nov. 23, 1943, Charles A. Goodwin Papers, WAA.

76. [Robert W. Huntington? to AEA, Nov.? 1943], unsigned copy in Charles A. Goodwin Papers, WAA.

77. AEA to HGA, Dec. 10, 1943, AP. The Hartford press reported that he had recently designed the sets for a production of the play *Maya* for the Gate Theatre Studio in which Wilton Graff appeared. *HC*, Feb. 11, 1944; *HT*, Feb. 10, 1944. The *Times* listed the other founders of the theater as Edgar Bergen, Charles Coburn, Elizabeth Dickenson, Dr. T. E. Hanley, Walter Huston, Arlington Kane, Martin Kosleck, and Max Laemmle.

78. Goodwin to Edward Forbes, May 25, 1944, Charles A. Goodwin Papers, WAA.

79. Mary Blasi Forchelli, recorded interview, March 8, 1990.

80. Alfred H. Barr, Jr. to AEA, [June 1944], AP.

81. James Thrall Soby to Charles A. Goodwin, June 2, 1944, Charles A. Goodwin Papers, WAA.

82. *HT*, May 22, 1944. The exhibition focused on the work of yacht designer and builder Nathaniel Greene Herreshoff.

83. That summer was traumatic for nine-year-old Sally Austin. On July 6, she went to a performance of the Ringling Brothers, Barnum & Bailey Circus with friends. Partway through the show, the main tent caught on fire and was soon engulfed in flames. Sally managed to crawl through the pandemonium to safety, but 168 men, women, and children died. It was the worst disaster in the history of the Ringling Brothers circus. Chick tried to downplay the

tragedy with Sally—he did not want her to have an aversion to a form of entertainment he had loved since his own childhood—but it was not something his daughter ever overcame.

84. Truda Kaschmann to AEA, Sept. 8, 1944, AP.

85. Herbert O. Crucius, recorded interview, Jan. 1, 1989.

86. HC, Feb. 17, 1945; Feb. 5, 1945.

87. Ibid., Feb. 1, 1945.

88. Rosamond Bernier, "Remembering Chick Austin," unpublished typescript, Feb. 1994, WAA; see also recording of Madame Bernier's account of the story at a luncheon in her honor at the Wadsworth Atheneum, Sept. 18, 1997, WAA.

89. Herbert Crucius, recorded interview, Jan. 1, 1989.

CHAPTER 17

1. Edward W. Forbes, "A. Everett Austin, Jr.," Director's Taste, p. 18.

2. AEA to HGA, March 17, 1946, AP.

3. DEA to AEA, [March 1946], AP.

4. AEA to HGA, April 9, 1946, AP.

5. AEA, "Report Submitted to the Committee by A. Everett Austin, Jr.," Report of Chairman of Board, Taylor Committee, 1953, pp. 36–7.

6. Paul Geissler, recorded interview, Jan. 4, 1991.

7. Sarasota Herald-Tribune, May 5, 1946.

8. AEA to James Thrall Soby, May 31, 1946, Soby Papers, Museum of Modern Art Archives.

9. AEA to Florence Berger, [May 30, 1946], Berger Papers, WAA.

10. James Hellyar, recorded interview, March 21, 1985.

11. Beatrice Ganz Williams, recorded interview, Jan. 30, 1986.

12. Tonio Selwart, recorded interview, Dec. 8, 1986.

13. AEA, Windham Playhouse announcement, [July] 1946.

14. Lawrence Evening Tribune, July 20, 1946.

15. Susanna Coggishall, recorded interview, Feb. 15, 1990. One year, Chick's favorite wake-up song was "Hernando's Hideaway."

16. Gladys Richards, recorded interview, March 7, 1996.

17. Judith Love, recorded interview, April 25, 1997.

18. Kirk Askew, "The Old Master Acquisitions of A. Everett Austin, Jr.," Director's Taste, p. 19.

19. "Rural Oasis," The Record, March 31, 1998.

20. Herbert Crucius, in conversation, July 29, 1999.

21. Tonio Selwart, recorded interview, Dec. 8, 1986.

22. AEA to HGA, [Oct. 1946], AP.

23. Ibid., [Nov. 21, 1946], AP.

24. Ibid.

25. Sarasota Herald-Tribune, newspaper clipping in AEA scrapbook, Dec. 18? 1946.

26. AEA to HGA, Dec. 26, 1946, AP.

27. Ibid., [Oct. 1946], AP.

28. Ibid., Jan. 5, 1947, AP.

29. Ibid., March 30, 1950, AP.

30. Sarasota Herald-Tribune, Jan. 26, 1947.

31. "The Spotlight Gallery," undated typescript for radio spot, AEA scrapbook, [Jan. 1947].

32. Sarasota Herald-Tribune, Feb. 16, 1947.

33. AEA to HGA, Feb. 10, 1947, AP.

34. James Hellyar, recorded interview, Feb. 28, 1989.

35. Ibid.

36. HGA to SGA, March 27, 1955, AP.

37. Angela Lansbury, recorded interview, April 26, 1983.

38. David Austin to AEA, [Feb. 27, 1947], AP.

39. David Austin in conversation, Sept. 21, 1995.

40. *HT,* April 14, 1947.

41. AEA to Florence Berger, May 26, 1947, Berger Paps., WAA.

42. J. T. Diamond (secretary, Board of Control) to AEA, April 21, 1947.

43. AEA to HGA, [Nov. ? 1946], AP.

44. Ibid., [May] 1947, AP.

45. AEA to Florence Berger, May 26, 1947, AP.

46. AEA, Annual Report, May 1947.

47. Edgar Lansbury, recorded interview, Feb. 25, 1987. Moyna MacGill appeared at the Playhouse for several seasons, and Chick brought her to Sarasota in April 1954 to present "My Favorite Readings" in the Asolo Theater.

48. AEA to HGA, Oct. 20, 1947, AP.

49. AEA to Nellie and Jim Soby, Sept. 2, 1950, AP.

50. AEA to Ruth Ford, Jan. 21, 1948, AP.

51. James Thrall Soby, unpublished memoirs, Chapter 4, p. 3.

52. Philip Johnson, recorded interview, Nov. 30, 1982.

53. A few years later, when one of the greatest collections of magic memorabilia in America was given to the Ringling, Chick placed it in the circus museum, saying that magic was closely related to the circus. This collection came from Thomas Chew Worthington III of Baltimore, an intimate friend of the well-known magician Howard Thurston. The collection included the apparatuses of many famous performers, going back as far as Robert-Houdin, along with sixty-seven wands by illustrious prestidigitators. These were to be put on display in the circus museum along with Chick's own magic collection, which he donated to the Ringling.

54. AEA, "Foreword," *Masterpieces of Modern Painting* (Sarasota: John and Mable Ringling Museum of Art, 1948).

55. *Tampa Morning Tribune,* April 16, 1948.

56. A. Hyatt Mayor, "The Greatest Show Down South," *Art News,* June–July–August 1948, p. 61.

57. *Look,* Oct. 26, 1948, p. 89.

58. Unidentified newspaper clipping in AEA scrapbook, c. 1948.

59. Judith Love, recorded interview, April 25, 1997; Jack McDougal, recorded interview, April 25, 1997. The change of cast could not have been too traumatic, as there were only three characters in the play. Chick himself later made the incident into an amusing story for a Sarasota reporter, noting that he had prepared a crown roast of lamb for Miss Davis's first scheduled visit, which the actors devoured in her absence, but that he had saved a bouquet of orchids for her in his refrigerator. These he presented to her a week later, he said, but the moment the actress took them out of their transparent box, they fell apart, leaving her with nothing in her hand but a ribbon and a pin. "Main Street Reporter," unidentified newspaper clipping (c. Nov. 1948) in AEA scrapbook, WAA.

60. AEA to HGA, Feb. 25, 1949, AP.

61. James Hellyar, recorded interview, March 21, 1985.

62. By another curious coincidence, the other picture he considered for his first purchase, Tiepolo's *Building of the Trojan Horse,* was bought by Charles Cunningham for the Atheneum.

63. AEA to HGA, [Feb.? 1948], AP.

64. "Calendar, 1955 / 1956," John and Mable Ringling Museum of Art.

65. Florence Berkman, recorded interview, Feb. 27, 1990.

66. HGA to SGA, July 7, 1949, AP.

67. AEA to HGA, Oct. 25, 1949, AP.

68. AEA, "Foreword," *The Fantastic Visions of Monsu Desiderio* (Sarasota: John and Mable Ringling Museum of Art), 1950, p. 4.

69. AEA to HGA, Feb. 10, 1950, AP.

70. *Sarasota Herald-Tribune,* Nov. 11, 1956.

71. Ibid., Oct. 19, 1947.

72. AEA to HGA, March 27, 1950, AP.

73. "Annual Report of the Director, 1949–1950," p. 4, Ringling Museum Archives.

74. "Report of the Director, October 20, 1950," p. 1, Ringling Museum Archives.

75. AEA, "Foreword," *Reflections of the Italian Comedy* (Sarasota: John and Mable Ringling Museum of Art, 1951), pp. 3, 5.

76. AEA to HGA, March 13, 1951, AP.

77. Ibid., April 24, 1951, AP.

78. HGA to SGA, Feb. [23?] 1952, AP.

79. Eleanor Howland Soby to AEA, March 7, 1952, AP.

80. *Sarasota Herald-Tribune*, March 2, 1952.

81. *New York Herald Tribune*, March 9, 1952. In the coming years, Chick would bring to the Asolo such performers as the Dublin Players and the National Grass Roots Opera Company, mime Agna Enters, and musicians Sylvia Marlow, Bernard Greenhouse, and Andres Segovia, along with distinguished lecturers and an annual film series.

82. HGA to SGA, March 9, 1952, AP.

83. AEA to HGA, June 1, 1952, AP.

84. Ibid., [June 1952], AP.

85. Ibid., June 21, 1952, AP; Marguerite Yourcenar, recorded interview, Aug. 2, 1982.

86. Ibid., June 21 and 25, 1952, AP.

87. "FAT MEN CAN'T WIN! THIS LARGE GEN-TLEMAN, FULLY SATISFIED WITH THE TEN THOU-SAND FRANC MEAL WHICH HE HAS JUST CONSUMED, IS STANDING OUTSIDE AN ANTIQUE SHOP ABOUT READY TO SPEND HIS REMAINING FRANCS WHICH HE IS SO FEVERISHLY CLUTCH-ING IN HIS LEFT HAND." DEA, photograph, Paris, 1952, annotated by SGA, Dec. 1952.

88. AEA to HGA, [Sept. 2, 1952], AP.

89. *Sarasota Herald-Tribune*, Jan. 30, 1953.

90. "Report of the Committee," in "Biennial Report of the Board of Control, 1952–1954," pp. 34–44, Ringling Museum Archives.

91. AEA, *The Artful Rococo* (Sarasota: John and Mable Ringling Museum of Art, 1954), [pp. 2–3].

92. Kirk Askew, "The Old Master Acquisitions of A. Everett Austin, Jr.," *Director's Taste*, p. 24.

93. HGA to SGA, Feb. 1, 1953, AP.

94. Ibid., Feb. 13, 1953, AP.

95. Woody Eitel, recorded interview, April 29, 1997.

96. Kenneth Donahue, transcript of oral history, May 1985, p. 93, Ringing Museum Archives.

97. Ibid., pp. 94–5.

98. HGA to SGA, Feb. 26, 1954, AP.

99. Henry-Russell Hitchcock, recorded interview, Dec. 9, 1974.

100. HGA to SGA, Jan. 9, 1955, AP.

101. AEA, "Foreword," *Directors' Choice* (Sarasota: John and Mable Ringling Museum of Art, 1955), [p. 2].

102. SGA in conversation, 1983.

103. Kenneth Donahue, transcript of oral history, May 1985, pp. 124–5, Ringling Museum Archives.

104. SGA to HGA, [Jan. 23, 1956], AP; SGA in conversation, 1983.

105. AEA, "Foreword," *The Art of Eating* (Sarasota: John and Mable Ringling Museum of Art, 1956), [pp. 4–5]. In assembling the show, Chick looked back to his first, formative experience with art. He wrote to Dows Dunham, George Reisner's assistant in Egypt and the Sudan in the winter of 1922–23, asking for an offering table scene with an invocation that he remembered from the expedition. Dunham, now curator of Egyptian Art at the Museum of Fine Arts in Boston, dispatched a cordial letter, promising a picture from a tomb at Giza, with the required invocation to Anubis, the god of embalming. He supplied both the hieroglyphics and the English translation: "A boon which the kind gives (and) a boon which Anubis gives, (he who is) upon his mountain, Foremost in the Divine Booth, he who is in bandages, Lord of Ta-Djeser, invocation-offerings of bread

and beer. . . ." Dunham to AEA, Dec. 20, 1955, Austin Correspondence, Ringling Museum Archives.

CHAPTER 18

1. Rose Crucius, recorded interview, Jan. 29, 1989.

2. James Hellyar, recorded interview, Feb. 28, 1989.

3. SGA, recorded interview, Feb. 17, 1992.

4. James Hellyar, recorded interview, March 21, 1985.

5. AEA to HGA, Sept. 28, 1956, AP.

6. Ibid., Oct. 13, 1956, AP.

7. Ibid., Oct. 31, 1956, AP.

8. *Sarasota Herald-Tribune*, Nov. 11, 1956; *The News*, Dec. 2, 1956.

9. *Tampa Sunday Tribune*, Dec. 2, 1956.

10. *Tampa Morning Tribune*, Dec. 3, 1956.

11. Ibid., Dec. 5, 1956.

12. Ibid.

13. Mase also took Chick to task for petty infractions such as hanging the new Poussin in his office until its appearance in *Art News* and hiring "Northern residents" as maintenance men and carpenters. *Tampa Morning Tribune*, Dec. 5, 1956.

14. Ibid.

15. *The News* (Sarasota), Dec. 6, 1956.

16. *Tampa Sunday Tribune*, Dec. 9, 1956.

17. Donahue's talk was ostensibly on John Ringling, but he addressed the complexities involved in state ownership of an art museum, praising Chick for opposing those who wanted to make the Ringling "a political spoil or honky-tonk attraction." *The News*, Dec. 20, 1956. The Florida press reported Donahue's remarks in detail, noting that Chick's absence was due to a back problem, but that he was "not seriously ill." *Sarasota Herald-Tribune*, Dec. 19, 1956.

18. James Hellyar, recorded interview, Feb. 28, 1989.

19. SGA, recorded interview, Feb. 17, 1992.

20. James L. Goodwin, Diary, Dec. 15, 1956.

21. Dane called Sam Mase's articles an "unfair knife-in-the-back assault." The Asolo Theater was "an unheard of bargain," he said. "If Austin had never done anything else, this acquisition would bolster his standing throughout art history in Florida." Quoting Karl Bickel, he characterized Chick as a "museum genius" and reminded readers that "He could move out as quickly as he pleased, and into a better paid, more nationally influential position. But he's going to stick—and one inducement is the fact that his contract calls for seven and a half months work only, with time to travel." He pointed out that Chick was "meticulous about not accepting salary for work not done, and he has made many anonymous gifts to the museum. He is a connoisseur without rivals in this field." *Sarasota Herald-Tribune*, Dec. 23, 1956.

22. Karl Bickel to AEA, Dec. 20, 1956, AP.

23. Ibid., Dec. 25, 1956, AP.

24. Hartford Hospital, Discharge Summary, Jan. 16, 1957, copy in AP.

25. Soby's article was immediately reported in the Sarasota press. *Sarasota Herald-Tribune*, Jan. 6, 1957.

26. Karl Bickel to AEA, Jan. 14, 1956, AP.

27. Hartford Hospital, Discharge Summary, Jan. 16, 1957, copy in AP.

28. SGA, recorded interview, Feb. 17, 1992.

29. Bickel to AEA, Jan. 19, 1957, AP.

30. Kenneth Donahue to AEA, January 25, 1957, AP.

31. Bickel to AEA, Jan. 31, 1957, AP.

32. *Tampa Morning Tribune*, Feb. 4, 1957.

33. *Sarasota Herald-Tribune*, Feb. 17, 1957.

34. SGA, recorded interview, Feb. 17, 1992.

35. Ibid.

36. A. L. Rowse, the distinguished Shakespearean scholar, wrote a poem, "Chick Austin," after visiting Helen in the Hartford house in the early 1970s. Acutely aware of the complexities of Austin's life, he wrote: "Having received your *congé*, taking off / For Sarasota and the gay Gulf, a world away / From Puritan New England of your birth . . . / Still finding no haven for your life of dream / And ardour, pursuing the mirage of love / In vain—until at last, stricken still young, / When you came home to die you came home to Helen. . . ." A. L. Rowse, *A Life, Collected Poems* (Edinburgh: William Blackwood, 1981), pp. 260–1.

37. James Hellyar, recorded interview, Feb. 28, 1989. Hellyar remained in Sarasota for the rest of his life. He worked for a men's clothing store and died in 1990.

38. SGA, recorded interview, Feb. 17, 1992.

39. Woody Eitel in conversation, May 10, 1993.

40. Leigh Westbrook in conversation, 1990.

41. Allen Porter, recorded interview, Oct. 30, 1974.

42. Bickel to AEA, Feb. 25, 1957, AP.

43. Ibid., March 18, 1957.

44. SGA, recorded interview, Feb. 17, 1992.

45. *The News* (Sarasota), March 31, 1957.

46. Constance Askew to HGA, April 2, 1957, AP.

47. Virgil Thomson to HGA, April 1, 1957, AP.

48. Tonio Selwart to HGA, March 31, 1957, AP.

49. Julien Levy to HGA, March 29, 1957, AP.

50. Lincoln Kirstein to HGA, April 2, 1957, AP.

51. James T. Soby to HGA, March 30, 1957, AP.

52. Edward W. Forbes, "A. Everett Austin, Jr.," *Director's Taste*, p. 18.

53. *Sarasota Herald-Tribune*, March 31, 1957.

54. Alfred Frankfurter, "Austin of Hartford and Sarasota," *Art News*, Vol. 56, No. 3 (May 1957), p. 25.

55. Lincoln Kirstein to Pavel Tchelitchew, April 2, 1957 (Michael Duncan to ERG, Sept. 19, 1996, p. 5.)

56. Pavel Tchelitchew to HGA, April 7, 1957, AP.

57. Adolph (later spelling) Loewi to HGA, April 5, 1957, AP.

58. Florence Berkman, recorded interview, March 27, 1990.

59. *Sarasota Herald-Tribune*, April 3, 1957.

60. In the year 2000, Austin, who could not bear to be without company throughout his life, remains alone in his family plot in Windham, New Hampshire. Arthur Austin is buried in Belgrade, Maine. Laura Austin lies in Mount Union, Pennsylvania, with the Etniers and Morrisons. Helen Austin and Sally Austin are buried in the Goodwin family plot at Cedar Hill Cemetery in Hartford.

SELECTED BIBLIOGRAPHY

A. Everett Austin, Jr.: A Director's Taste and Achievement. Hartford, Conn.: Wadsworth Atheneum, 1958.

Ades, Dawn, ed. *Dalí's Optical Illusions.* Hartford, Conn.: Wadsworth Atheneum Museum of Art; New Haven and London: Yale University Press, 2000.

Ayres, Linda, ed. *"The Spirit of Genius," Art at the Wadsworth Atheneum.* New York: Hudson Hills Press, 1992.

Barr, Alfred H., ed. *Fantastic Art, Dada, Surrealism.* New York: The Museum of Modern Art, 1936.

Beebe, Lucius. *Snoot If You Must.* New York: D. Appleton-Century Company, 1943.

Berman, Leonid. *The Three Worlds of Leonid.* New York: Basic Books, 1978.

Bowles, Paul. *Without Stopping: An Autobiography.* New York: The Ecco Press, 1972.

Brazeau, Peter. *Parts of a World: Wallace Stevens Remembered.* New York: Random House, 1983.

Buck, Patricia Ringling. *The John and Mable Ringling Museum of Art.* Sarasota, Fla.: The John and Mable Ringling Museum of Art, 1988.

Buckle, Richard. *Diaghilev.* New York: Atheneum, 1979.

Budge, Sir E. A. Wallis. *Cook's Handbook for Egypt and the Egyptian Sûdân.* London: Thos. Cook & Son, 1921.

Cadogan, Jean, ed. *Wadsworth Atheneum Paintings II: Italy and Spain: Fourteenth through Nineteenth Centuries.* Hartford, Conn.: Wadsworth Atheneum, 1991.

Calder, Alexander, and Jean Davidson. *Calder: An Autobiography With Pictures.* Boston: Beacon Press, 1969.

Calloway, Stephen. *Baroque Baroque: The Culture of Excess.* London: Phaidon Press, 1994.

Chauncey, George. *Gay New York: Gender, Urban Culture, and the Makings of the Gay Male World, 1890–1940.* New York: Basic Books, 1994.

Coote, Albert W. *Four Vintage Decades: The Performing Arts in Hartford, 1930–1970.* Hartford, Conn.: Huntington, 1970.

Dawson, Warren R., and Eric P. Uphill. *Who Was Who in Egyptology.* London: Egypt Exploration Society, 1972.

De Jong, Frida, and Laurens Vancrevel. *Kristians Tonny: Monografie.* Amsterdam: Meulenhoff, 1979.

Dunham, Dows. *Recollections of an Egyptologist.* Boston: Museum of Fine Arts, 1972.

Dunning, Jennifer. *"But First A School"; The First Fifty Years of the School of American Ballet.* New York: Viking Penguin, 1985.

Edward Waldo Forbes: Yankee Visionary. Cambridge, Mass.: Fogg Art Museum, Harvard University, 1971.

Elderfield, John. *The Museum of Modern Art at Mid-Century: Continuity and Change.* New York: The Museum of Modern Art, 1995.

Ellis, Havelock, ed. *The Mermaid Series: John Ford.* London: T. Fisher Unwin, [1888].

FitzGerald, Michael C. *Making Modernism: Picasso and the Creation of the Market for Twentieth-Century Art.* New York: Farrar, Straus and Giroux, 1995.

Fogg Art Museum, Harvard University, Collection of Mediaeval and Renaissance Paintings. Cambridge, Mass.: Harvard University Press, 1927.

Fogg Art Museum, Harvard University, Hand-Book. Cambridge, Mass.: Harvard University Press, 1927.

Fuller, R. Buckminster, and Robert Marks. *The Dymaxion World of Buckminster Fuller.* Garden City, N.Y.: Anchor Books, 1973.

Gaddis, Eugene R., ed. *Avery Memorial: The First Modern Museum.* Hartford, Conn.: Wadsworth Atheneum, 1984.

García-Márquez, Vincente. *The Ballets Russes: Colonel de Basil's Ballets Russes De Monte Carlo, 1932–1952.* New York: Alfred A. Knopf, 1990.

Gill, Brendan. *Happy Times.* New York. Harcourt Brace Jovanovich, 1973.

———. *A New York Life: Of Friends and Others.* New York: Poseidon Press, 1990.

Graham, Sheilah. *The Garden of Allah.* New York: Crown Publishers, 1970.

Green, Martin. *Children of the Sun.* New York: Basic Books, 1976.

Harvard Class of 1922: Twenty-fifth Anniversary Report. Cambridge, Mass.: Harvard University Press, 1947.

The Harvard Freshman Red Book: The Year Book of the Class of 1922. Cambridge, Mass.: Harvard University, 1919.

Haskell, Barbara. *Milton Avery.* New York: Harper & Row, 1982.

Haverkamp-Begemann, Egbert. *Wadsworth Atheneum Paintings: Catalogue I: The Netherlands and the German-speaking Countries: Fifteenth–Nineteenth Centuries.* Hartford, Conn.: Wadsworth Atheneum, 1978.

Hellner, Bruce, ed. *The Letters of Carl Van Vechten.* New Haven, Conn.: Yale University Press, 1987.

Helm, MacKinley. *Modern Mexican Painters.* New York: Harper & Brothers, 1941.

Hitchcock, Henry-Russell, Jr. *Modern Architecture: Romanticism and Reintegration.* New York: Payson & Clarke, 1929.

———. *The Pelican History of Art: Nineteenth and Twentieth Centuries.* Baltimore: Penguin Books, 1958.

Houseman, John. *Run-Through.* New York: Simon & Schuster, 1980.

Ioni, J. F. *Affairs of a Painter.* London: Faber and Faber, 1936.

Janis, Sidney. *Abstract & Surrealist Art in America.* New York: Reynal & Hitchcock, [1944].

Janson, Anthony F. *Great Paintings from the John and Mable Ringling Museum of Art.* Sarasota, Fla.: The John and Mable Ringling Museum of Art; New York: Harry N. Abrams, 1986.

Jean, Marcel. *The Autobiography of Surrealism.* New York: Viking, 1980.

John Ringling: Dreamer, Builder, Collector: Legacy of the Circus King. Sarasota, Fla.: The John & Mable Ringling Museum of Art, 1997.

Jones, Caroline A. *Modern Art at Harvard: The Formation of the Nineteenth- and Twentieth-Century Collections of the Harvard University Art Museums.* New York: Abbeville Press, 1985.

Kirstein, Lincoln. *Mosaic: Memoirs.* New York: Farrar, Straus & Giroux, 1994.

———. *The New York City Ballet.* New York: Alfred A. Knopf, 1973.

———. *Tchelitchev.* Santa Fe, N. Mex.: Twelvetrees Press, 1994.

Kornhauser, Elizabeth Mankin. *American Paintings Before 1945 in the Wadsworth Atheneum.* Hartford, Conn.: Wadsworth Atheneum; New Haven and London: Yale University Press, 1996.

Le Corbusier. *Quand les cathédrals étaient blanches: Voyage au pays de timides.* Paris: Librarie Plon, 1937.

Leonid and His Friends: Tchelitchew, Berman, Bérard. New York: The New York Cultural Center, 1974.

Levin, Gail. *Edward Hopper: The Art and the Artist.* New York: W. W. Norton and Company, 1980.

Levy, Julien. *Memoirs of an Art Gallery.* New York: G. P. Putnam's Sons, 1977.

Lindsay, Vachel. *The Art of the Motion Picture.* New York: Liveright, 1970.

Lipman, Jean. *Calder's Universe.* New York: Viking Press, 1976.

Lynes, Russell. *Good Old Modern: An Intimate Portrait of the Museum of Modern Art.* New York: Atheneum, 1973.

———. *The Lively Audience: A Social History of the Visual and Performing Arts In America, 1890–1950.* New York: Harper & Row, 1985.

Marquis, Alice Goldfarb. *Alfred H. Barr, Jr.: Missionary for the Modern.* Chicago: Contemporary Books, 1989.

Martin, John Rupert. *Baroque.* London: Allen Lane, Penguin Books, 1977.

Mellow, James R. *Charmed Circle: Gertrude Stein & Company.* New York: Praeger, 1974.

Murray, Marian. *CIRCUS: From Rome to Ringling.* New York: Appleton-Century-Crofts, 1956.

Nash, Steven A., and Jörn Merkert. *Naum Gabo: Sixty Years of Constructivism,* Munich: Prestel-Verlag, 1985.

Olsen, Ruth, and Abraham Chanin. *Gabo, Pevsner.* New York: Museum of Modern Art, 1948.

Piet Mondrian: Centennial Exhibition. New York: The Solomon R. Guggenheim Museum, 1971.

Praz, Mario. *The Romantic Agony.* New York: Meridian Books, 1960.

Rewald, Sabine. *Balthus.* New York: Metropolitan Museum of Art; Harry N. Abrams, 1984.

Rich, Daniel Catton. *The Flow of Art: Essays and Criticisms of Henry McBride.* New York: Atheneum, 1975.

Ruskin, John. *Lectures on Architecture and Painting.* New York: Merrill and Baker, n.d.

Russell, John. *Max Ernst: Life and Work.* New York: Harry N. Abrams, 1967.

Savigneau, Josyane. *Marguerite Yourcenar: Inventing a Life.* Chicago: The University of Chicago Press, 1993.

Schaffner, Ingrid, and Lisa Jacobs, ed. *Julien Levy: Portrait of an Art Gallery.* Cambridge, Mass.: The MIT Press, 1998.

Schouvaloff, Alexander. *The Art of Ballets Russes: The Serge Lifar Collection of Theater Designs, Costumes, and Paintings at the Wadsworth Atheneum, Hartford, Connecticut.* Hartford, Conn.: Wadsworth Atheneum; New Haven, Conn. and London: Yale University Press, 1997.

Schulze, Franz. *Philip Johnson: Life and Work.* New York: Alfred A. Knopf, 1994.

Searing, Helen, ed. *In Search of Modern Architecture: Nineteenth and Twentieth Centuries.* Baltimore: Penguin Books, 1958.

Secrest, Meryle. *Salvador Dalí: A Biography.* New York: E. P. Dutton, 1986.

Sitwell, Sacheverell. *Southern Baroque Art: A Study of Painting, Architecture and Music in Italy and Spain of the 17th & 18th Centuries.* London: Gerald Duckworth & Co., 1951.

Stein, Gertrude. *The Autobiography of Alice B. Toklas.* New York: Harcourt, Brace and Company, [c. 1933].

———. *Four Saints in Three Acts, An Opera to Be Sung.* New York: Random House, 1934.

———. *Lectures in America.* Boston: Beacon Press, 1985.

Stewart, John L. *Ernst Krenek: The Man and His Music.* Berkeley and Los Angeles: University of California Press, 1991.

Sweeney, James Johnson. *Alexander Calder.* New York: Museum of Modern Art, 1943.

Thomson, Virgil. *Virgil Thomson.* New York, Alfred A. Knopf, 1966.

Tomkins, Calvin. *Merchants and Masterpieces: The Story of the Metropolitan Museum of Art.* New York: E. P. Dutton & Co., 1970.

Tommasini, Anthony. *Virgil Thomson: Composer on the Aisle.* New York: W. W. Norton and Company, 1997.

Tuggle, Robert. *Eugene Berman: Drawings for the Stage.* New York: Wheelock Whitney & Company, 1989.

Warburg, Edward M. M. *As I Recall.* Privately published, 1978.

Watson, Steven. *The Harlem Renaissance: Hub of African-American Culture, 1920–1930.* New York: Pantheon Books, 1995.

————. *Prepare for Saints.* New York: Random House, 1998.

————. *Strange Bedfellows: The First American Avant-Garde.* New York: Abbeville Press, 1991.

Weber, Nicholas Fox. *Patron Saints,* New York: Alfred A. Knopf, 1992.

Williams, Egerton R., Jr. *Hill Towns of Italy.* Boston: Houghton Mifflin, 1903.

Wilson, John. *Signs & Wonders upon Pharaoh: A History of American Egyptology.* Chicago: University of Chicago Press, 1964.

Wilson, Richard Guy, Dianne H. Pilgrim, and Dickran Tashjian. *The Machine Age in America: 1918–1941.* New York: Harry N. Abrams, 1986.

Yves Tanguy: A Summary of His Works. New York: Pierre Matisse, 1963.

Zervos, Christian. *Domela: Art and Architecture in the Netherlands.* Amsterdam: J. M. Meulenhoff, 1966.

Page numbers in italics refer to illustrations.

ILLUSTRATION CREDITS

A NOTE ABOUT THE AUTHOR

Eugene R. Gaddis is the William G. DeLana Archivist and Curator of the Austin House at the Wadsworth Atheneum in Hartford, Connecticut. He is the editor and coauthor of *Avery Memorial: The First Modern Museum,* and lectures frequently on American cultural history. A graduate of Amherst College, he holds a Ph.D. in history from the University of Pennsylvania.

A NOTE ON THE TYPE

This book was set in Bodoni, a typeface named after Giambattista Bodoni (1740–1813), the celebrated printer and type designer of Parma. The Bodoni types of today were designated not as faithful reproductions of any one of the Bodoni fonts but rather as composite, modern versions of the Bodoni manner. Bodoni's innovations in type style included a greater degree of contrast in the thick and thin elements of the letters and a sharper and more angular finish of details.

Composed by North Market Street Graphics,
Lancaster, Pennsylvania
Printed and bound by Quebecor Printing,
Fairfield, Pennsylvania
Designed by Virginia Tan